D0857443

ROMANS

Sacra Pagina Series

Volume 6

Romans

Brendan Byrne, S. J.

Daniel J. Harrington, S. J.
Editor

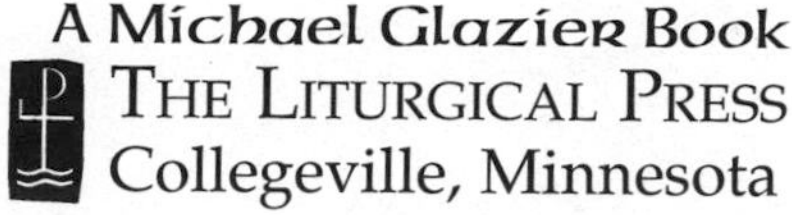
A Michael Glazier Book
THE LITURGICAL PRESS
Collegeville, Minnesota

Cover design by Don Bruno.

A Michael Glazier Book published by The Liturgical Press.

1 2 3 4 5 6 7 8

Library of Congress Cataloging-in-Publication Data

Byrne, Brendan.
Romans / Brendan Byrne ; Daniel J. Harrington, editor.
p. cm. — (Sacra pagina series ; v. 6)
"A Michael Glazier book."
Includes bibliographical references and index.
ISBN 0-8146-5808-3
1. Bible. N.T. Romans—Commentaries. I. Title. II. Series:
Sacra pagina series ; 6.
BS2665.3.B973 1996
227'.1077—dc20 96-10982
CIP

CONTENTS

Translation, Interpretation, Notes

Indexes

EDITOR'S PREFACE

Sacra Pagina is a multi-volume commentary on the books of the New Testament. The expression *Sacra Pagina* ("Sacred Page") originally referred to the text of Scripture. In the Middle Ages it also described the study of Scripture to which the interpreter brought the tools of grammar, rhetoric, dialectic, and philosophy. Thus *Sacra Pagina* encompasses both the text to be studied and the activity of interpretation.

This series presents fresh translations and modern expositions of all the books of the New Testament. Written by an international team of Catholic biblical scholars, it is intended for biblical professionals, graduate students, theologians, clergy, and religious educators. The volumes present basic introductory information and close exposition. They self-consciously adopt specific methodological perspectives, but maintain a focus on the issues raised by the New Testament compositions themselves. The goal of *Sacra Pagina* is to provide sound critical analysis without any loss of sensitivity to religious meaning. This series is therefore catholic in two senses of the word: inclusive in its methods and perspectives, and shaped by the context of the Catholic tradition.

The Second Vatican Council described the study of the "sacred page" as the "very soul of sacred theology" (*Dei Verbum* 24). The volumes in this series illustrate how Catholic scholars contribute to the council's call to provide access to Sacred Scripture for all the Christian faithful. Rather than pretending to say the final word on any text, these volumes seek to open up the riches of the New Testament and to invite as many people as possible to study seriously the "sacred page."

DANIEL J. HARRINGTON, S.J.

PREFACE

Paul's letter to Rome is not only the longest of the New Testament letters, it is also the one that has attracted most comment. Any interpreter of Romans is heir to a vast tradition of interpretation reaching back beyond Augustine to Origen and the earliest Christian writers. At the present time investigation of the letter remains as intense as ever; the flow of commentaries, monographs and particular studies continues unabated. Any fresh commentator must explain what new insight or approach she or he brings, to justify adding to the formidable array of secondary literature on Romans.

Within the overall purpose of the *Sacra Pagina* series of New Testament commentaries, my aim has been to explain the argument of Paul. I provide a running exposition of the text in a way that attempts to elucidate the developing meaning and argument, giving preference to the rhetorical and theological aspects. Because the argument of Romans follows a carefully crafted structure, I have divided the commentary in a fairly schematic way and constantly attempted to relate the various sections to each other. At significant turning points in the letter (1:18; 5:1; 6:1; 9:1; 12:1), a general introduction to the next major section appears before the text of the immediately following subsection. It is in these introductions that the distinctive vision of this commentary unfolds.

For the convenience of the reader, to save the labor of reading two sets of comments on each passage, I have kept the bulk of the commentary in the Interpretation. The Notes serve the purpose of justifying the particular positions adopted in the commentary, while presenting and evaluating alternative points of view. In line with this aim, the "Interpretation" precedes the "Notes" to each section.

I have not, in the manner of an exhaustive commentary, felt obliged to give detailed comment on every word or phrase or allude to every point of controversy. Detailed comment, whether in the Interpretation or in the Notes, primarily serves the establishment of the larger meaning. For the same reason I seldom turn aside from what I consider to be the main argument of Paul to consider questions that have been put to the text in the history of interpretation because of their significance in Christian life and thought but which are not central to the running argument. Such matters find ample coverage in the classic commentaries, including the most recent.

The scope of the commentary has meant severe restriction of the amount of documentation provided. In this I have given preference to primary (ancient) sources over secondary material (modern scholars). This has meant that acknowledgment of debt to previous scholarly work has been considerably curtailed—though I have tried to indicate such debt where something really distinctive is involved. In partial remedy of this lack I would like to acknowledge here my indebtedness to outstanding commentators on Romans in the classic tradition such as O. Kuss, E. Käsemann, C.E.B. Cranfield, U. Wilckens, J.D.G. Dunn and, most recently, J. A. Fitzmyer. The shorter commentaries of D. Zeller and J. Ziesler have been exemplary in communicating a great deal of information in concise format. All Pauline commentators within the Catholic tradition owe an outstanding debt to Stanislas Lyonnet, whose influence has been mediated to me especially through the teaching and inspiration of my first teacher in Paul, the Australian scholar William Dalton. As regards the rhetorical approach to Romans, I have found the writings of N. Elliott and D. A. Campbell particularly enlightening. The "rereading" of Romans proposed by S. K. Stowers provided a stimulating challenge as the commentary approached its final stages.

I am deeply indebted to Michael Glazier for inviting me, an Australian scholar, to contribute to the *Sacra Pagina* series of New Testament commentaries which he inspired and projected and which is becoming a landmark of North American biblical scholarship within the Catholic tradition. Daniel Harrington has been a wise, tolerant, and encouraging editor. On the local scene I am indebted for much helpful advice to my colleagues and friends Antony Campbell, Mark Coleridge, Dorothy Lee, Francis Moloney and John Wilcken. The community of the Pontifical Biblical Institute, Rome, provided companionship and inspiration during my stay there as CBA Visiting Professor in 1993, a time when much of this commentary was written. I am also indebted to Margaret Banson, Pamela Foulkes, Robin Koning, Brian Moore, Rosemary Williams and many members of the community of Jesuit Theological College, Parkville, for help in bringing the manuscript to proper order.

Brendan Byrne, S. J.
Jesuit Theological College,
United Faculty of Theology,
Parkville, Melbourne.

NOTE ON REFERENCES

References to the Old Testament are given according to the New Revised Standard Version. Where the LXX numbering is different and it seems appropriate to call attention to this, the LXX reference is given in brackets (LXX . . .) following the primary reference. When the reference is directly to the LXX, the Hebrew numbering, if different—as usually in the case of the Psalms—is indicated in brackets following the LXX reference.

References to Pseudepigrapha of the Old Testament are given according to the collection edited by J. H. Charlesworth (*The Old Testament Pseudepigrapha.* 2 Vols. Garden City, NY: Doubleday, 1983). References to Qumran material (though not necessarily the translation) follow the edition of F. García Martínez (*The Dead Sea Scrolls Translated.* Leiden: Brill, 1994), save that in the case of the "Thanksgiving Psalms" (1QH), the more traditional column numbering has been retained.

ABBREVIATIONS

Biblical Books and Apocrypha

Gen
Exod
Lev
Num
Deut
Josh
Judg
1-2 Sam
1-2 Kgs
Isa
Jer
Ezek
Hos
Joel
Amos
Obad
Jonah
Mic
Nah
Hab
Zeph
Hag
Zech
Mal
Ps (*pl.*: Pss)
Job
Prov
Ruth
Cant
Eccl (*or* Qoh)
Lam
Esth
Dan
Ezra
Neh
1-2 Chr
1-2-3-4 Kgdms
Add Esth
Bar
Bel
1-2 Esdr
4 Ezra
Jdt
Ep Jer
1-2-3-4 Macc
Pr Azar
Pr Man
Sir
Sus
Tob
Wis
Matt
Mark
Luke
John
Acts
Rom
1-2 Cor
Gal
Eph
Phil
Col
1-2 Thess
1-2 Tim
Titus
Phlm
Heb
Jas
1-2 Pet
1-2-3 John
Jude
Rev

Pseudepigrapha

Adam and Eve Books of Adam and Eve
Apoc. Abr. Apocalypse of Abraham
2-3 Apoc. Bar. Syriac, Greek Apocalypse of Baruch
Apoc. Mos. Apocalypse of Moses
As. Mos. Assumption of Moses
Bib. Ant. Pseudo-Philo, Biblical Antiquities
1-2-3 Enoch Ethiopic, Slavonic, Hebrew Enoch
Ep. Arist. Epistle of Aristeas
4 Ezra Apocalypse of Ezra (= 2 Esdras 3-14)

Jos. Asen.	Joseph and Asenath
Jub.	Jubilees
Odes Sol.	Odes of Solomon
Pss. Sol.	Psalms of Solomon
Sib. Or.	Sibylline Oracles
T. Job	Testament of Job
T. 12 Patr.	Testaments of the Twelve Patriarchs
T. Benj.	Testament of Benjamin
T. Levi	Testament of Levi, etc.

Other Jewish Literature

Josephus	*Ag. Ap.*	*Against Apion*
	Ant.	*Antiquities of the Jews*
	War	*Jewish War*
	Life	*Life*

Philo of Alexandria

References to the works of Philo are given according to the abbreviated Latin titles used in the Loeb edition (cf. vol. 1, pp. xxiii–xxiv)

Dead Sea Scrolls

CD	Damascus Document (from Cairo Genizah and Qumran)
1Q, 2Q, etc.	Numbered caves of Qumran, followed by abbreviation of biblical or non-biblical work
1QapGen	Genesis Apocryphon
1QH	Thanksgiving Psalms
1QpHab	Habakkuk Commentary
1QM	War Scroll
1Q27(1QMys)	Mysteries (Pseudepigraphal Prophecy)
1QS	Community Rule (Manual of Discipline)
1QSa	Rule of the Future Congregation
4QDibHam	Words of the Luminaries (4Q504)
4QFlor	Florilegium (Eschatological Midrashim [4Q174])
4QMMT	Halakhic Letter (4Q394–99)
4QpGen^{a}	Genesis Commentary (Patriarchal Blessings [4Q252])
4QpIsa^{a}	Isaiah Commentary (4Q161)
4QpPs 37	Psalms Commentary (4Q171)
4QpsDan A	(Pseudo-Danielic) Messianic Apocalypse (4Q246)
4QTest	Testimonia (Messianic Anthology [4Q175])
4Q521	Messianic Apocalypse
11QPs	Apocryphal Psalms (11Q5-6)
11QMelch	Melchizedek Scroll (11Q13)

Rabbinic Literature

m. 'Abot	Mishna, Tractate *'Abot*
m. Qidd.	Mishna, Tractate *Qiddušin*
b. Šabb.	Babylonian Talmud, Tractate *Šabbat*
Sipra on Lev	*Sipra* (Commentary) on Leviticus

Periodicals, Reference Works, and Serials

AB	Anchor Bible
ABD	*The Anchor Bible Dictionary.* Ed. D. N. Freedman (1992)
AnBib	Analecta Biblica
AusBR	*Australian Biblical Review*
BBET	Beiträge zur biblischen Exegese und Theologie
BAGD	W. Bauer, W. F. Arndt, F. W. Gingrich, and F. W. Danker. *Greek-English Lexicon of the New Testament and Other Early Christian Literature* (1979)
BDF	F. Blass, A. Debrunner, and R. W. Funk. *A Greek Grammar of the NT and Other Early Christian Literature* (1961)
BETL	Bibliotheca ephemeridum theologicarum lovaniensium
BEvT	Beiträge zur evangelischen Theologie
BJRL	*Bulletin of the John Rylands Library*
BNTC	Black's New Testament Commentary
BTB	*Biblical Theology Bulletin*
BZ	*Biblische Zeitschrift*
BZNW	Beihefte zur *ZNW*
CBQ	*Catholic Biblical Quarterly*
ConBNT	Coniectanea biblica, New Testament
CRINT	Compendia rerum iudaicarum ad Novum Testamentum
DBS	*Dictionnaire de la Bible, Supplément*
DJD	*Discoveries in the Judaean Desert*
DPL	*Dictionary of Paul and His Letters.* Eds. G. F. Hawthorne, R. P. Martin and D. G. Reid (1993)
DS	H. Denzinger and E. Schönmetzer, *Enchiridion Symbolorum* (1973)
EB	Études bibliques
EDNT	*Exegetical Dictionary of the New Testament.* Eds. H. Balz and G. Schneider (1990–93)
EKK	Evangelisch-katholischer Kommentar zum Neuen Testament
EstBib	*Estudios biblicos*
ETL	*Ephemerides theologicae lovanienses*
EvQ	*Evangelical Quarterly*
ExpTim	*Expository Times*
FRLANT	Forschungen zur Religion und Literatur des Alten und Neuen Testaments
FS	Festschrift (Collection in honor of a particular person)
HNTC	Harper's New Testament Commentary

HTKNT	Herders theologischer Kommentar zum Neuen Testament
HTR	*Harvard Theological Review*
ICC	International Critical Commentary
IDBSup	*The Interpreter's Dictionary of the Bible. Supplementary Volume.* Ed. K. Crim (1976)
Int	*Interpretation*
JAC	*Jahrbuch für Antike und Christentum*
JB	Jerusalem Bible
JBL	*Journal of Biblical Literature*
JETS	*Journal of the Evangelical Theological Society*
JSNT	*Journal for the Study of the New Testament*
JSNTSup	*Journal for the Study of the New Testament*—Supplement Series
JSOT	*Journal for the Study of the Old Testament*
JSPseudSup	*Journal for the Study of the Pseudepigrapha*—Supplement Series
JTS	*Journal of Theological Studies*
LD	Lectio Divina
LSJ	H. G. Liddell and R. Scott. *A Greek-English Lexicon.* New ed. by H. S. Jones and R. McKenzie (1925–40; repr. 1966)
LXX	Septuagint
MeyerK	H. A. W. Meyer, Kritisch-exegetischer Kommentar über das Neue Testament
MNTC	Moffatt New Testament Commentary
MScRel	*Mélanges de science religieuse*
MT	Masoretic Text
MTZ	*Münchener theologische Zeitschrift*
NAB	New American Bible
NDIEC	*New Documents Illustrating Early Christianity.* Ed. G.H.R. Horsley, (1981–)
NF	Neue Folge
NJB	New Jerusalem Bible
NJBC	*New Jerome Biblical Commentary* (1990)
NovT	*Novum Testamentum*
NovTSup	*Novum Testamentum,* Supplements
NRSV	New Revised Standard Version
NRT	*La Nouvelle Revue théologique*
NS	New Series
NT	New Testament
NTAbh	Neutestamentliche Abhandlungen
NTS	*New Testament Studies*
OT	Old Testament
PSBSup	*Princeton Seminary Bulletin*—Supplementary Issue
RB	*Revue biblique*
REB	Revised English Bible
RivB	*Revista biblica*
RNT	Regensburger Neues Testament
RSR	*Recherches de science religieuse*
RSV	Revised Standard Version

SB	H. Strack and P. Billerbeck. *Kommentar zum Neuen Testament aus Talmud und Midrasch* (1926–63)
SBLDS	Society of Biblical Literature Dissertation Series
SBLMS	Society of Biblical Literature Monograph Series
SBM	Stuttgarter biblische Monographien
SBT	Studies in Biblical Theology
SE	*Studia Evangelica*
SJLA	Studies in Judaism in Late Antiquity
SJT	*Scottish Journal of Theology*
SNTSMS	Society for New Testament Studies Monograph Series
ST	*Studia Theologica*
SUNT	Studien zur Umwelt des Neuen Testaments
TDNT	*Theological Dictionary of the New Testament.* Eds. G. Kittel and G. Friedrich (1964–76)
TLZ	*Theologische Literaturzeitung*
TP	*Theologie und Philosophie*
TPINTC	Trinity Press International New Testament Commentary
TrinJ	*Trinity Journal*
TynBul	*Tyndale Bulletin*
TZ	*Theologische Zeitschrift*
WBC	Word Biblical Commentary
WMANT	Wissenschaftliche Monographien zum Alten und Neuen Testament
WTJ	*Westminster Theological Journal*
WUNT	Wissenschaftliche Monographien zum Neuen Testament
ZNW	*Zeitschrift für die neutestamentliche Wissenschaft*
ZTK	*Zeitschrift für Theologie und Kirche*

INTRODUCTION

Paul's letter to Rome is unique among his writings in being directed to a Christian community that he had neither founded nor as yet visited. Whereas all his other letters presuppose a relationship between sender and recipients, this one had to establish as well as build upon such a relationship. It had to serve as Paul's self-presentation to the believers in Rome.

The Letter to the Romans has retained this function throughout Christian history. Standing at the head of Paul's writings in the New Testament and containing so large an unfolding of his gospel, it has served to present Paul to generations of readers—from Augustine in the fifth century, through the Reformation era, down to the present day.

While widely acknowledged as the single most influential document in Christian history, it has also been the most controversial. Earlier generations, looking upon Romans primarily as a theological tract, contended over such issues as the meaning of righteousness by faith and the interplay of faith and works in Christian life. At the time of the Reformation the letter became a battleground within Christianity between Protestant and Catholic understandings of the faith. Happily, such strife has now given way to a more ecumenical and collaborative approach to the letter. At the same time, Romans has become central to the issue of the relationship between Christianity and Judaism, as that issue has moved from the periphery to the center of theological enquiry. Likewise, the letter's adoption of an approach to salvation that is truly inclusive has lent it important status in Christian assessment of the position regarding salvation of that vast mass of the human race standing outside the bounds of explicit faith in Jesus Christ.

The interpretation of Paul's letter to Rome has accompanied and stimulated the path of Christian theology down to the present. Romans touches upon virtually all main issues of Christian theology, as well as presenting a rewarding, if demanding, introduction to Paul. The task of the interpreter is to facilitate access to Paul and his gospel through the letter, allowing Christians of today to hear his voice as intelligibly as he hoped it would be heard and acted upon by the Christians of mid-first-century Rome.

A. *RECENT INTERPRETATION OF ROMANS*

1. *History as Paradigm*

For more than two centuries the interpretation of Romans, as indeed of all other New Testament documents, has proceeded along the lines of the historical-critical approach that up till very recently held the field unchallenged in the critical study of the Bible. The prevalence of this approach rested upon the post-Enlightenment conviction that the clue to the meaning of a text lay in fixing as accurately as possible the historical circumstances of its composition. Meaning was taken primarily to be the meaning intended by authors in view of their own situation and the situation of those they addressed. Hence the importance of determining as accurately as possible both the historical context and historical process of composition of any document to be interpreted.

Achieving this in connection with Romans, however, has proved remarkably elusive. The task has been to reconstruct a historical picture of the Roman Christian community from circumstantial evidence provided chiefly by secular historians and then "fit" this into what appears to have been the situation of Paul himself at the time of writing and the various elements making up the great and disparate bulk of the letter. It has proved possible to find a plausible occasion for certain sections of the letter. For example, the famous instruction in Rom 13:1-7 on loyalty to the state and the need to pay taxes fits in well with what we know of historical circumstances in the city of Rome around the middle years of the emperor Nero. But it has not been easy to fasten upon a single occasion and purpose in historical terms that can account for all the parts of Romans taken as a whole: in particular, to explain why so large a theological exposition of the gospel (Rom 1:18–11:36) prefaces a comparatively brief consideration of more practical and particular issues (Romans 12–15).

Many scholars, it is true, now prefer to speak in terms of "reasons" rather than "*a* reason" for Romans: Paul wrote the letter not for a single reason but to achieve several aims at once. But proposing a plurality of reasons is not a particularly satisfying way out of the historical impasse; having a bet so many ways blunts the edge of a single, convincing explanation.

Nor does this solution address a further distinctive feature of Romans: its so-called "double nature" or, more accurately, "double address." From the "frames" of the letter (the Introduction, 1:1-17, and Conclusion,

15:14–16:23), as well as from other indications, it seems clear that the addressees of the letter are Christian converts of Gentile background (1:5-6, 13-15; 11:13, 17-24, 30-31; 15:7-9, 20-22). Yet the opening section of the main body of the letter (1:18–4:25) appears to be addressed to a Jew who has not yet come to faith in Jesus as the Messiah of Israel and who must be persuaded to leave off a quest for righteousness in terms of the law in favor of accepting a righteousness that comes through faith in Christ. This lengthy opening section lends Romans its character as a "dialogue with Jews." Any explanation of the letter in historical terms must explain why it has this "double" and seemingly incompatible "audience"—Gentile Christians and (non-Christian) Jews.

2. *New Approaches to the Interpretation of Romans*

The difficulty of solving these issues in purely historical terms has led interpreters to apply to Romans alternative approaches that have arisen in biblical interpretation in the last two decades. Such approaches, under the influence of similar tendencies in literary theory and philosophy, are all marked by a movement away from history as paradigm and a focus upon authors and their intention, in the direction of concentrating more upon the other two factors in the interpretive situation: the text, viewed apart from its author, and the reader or audience of the text. Inherent in this development is a conviction that the meaning of a text outstrips that intended by the author. Once composed, a text has a life of its own and meanings of its own, meanings to which its various readers also make some contribution. Where historical criticism seeks primarily to go *through* a text to grasp the meaning intended by the author in his or her situation and privileges this meaning above all others, the more recent, audience-oriented approaches seek meanings less controlled by reconstruction of the likely historical circumstances of composition.

Taking a less rigidly historical approach in this way, it becomes possible to make a key distinction between the real author of a text and the persona of the author ("implied author") progressively created by the text in the mind of its audience or readers. The "real author" is Paul the Apostle, who wrote to Rome at a certain stage of his mature apostolic career. The "implied author" is the "Paul" whom the Christians at Rome (and also the modern reader) hear speaking to them as the letter is read.

Correspondingly, one can distinguish between actual readers of a text and the "implied reader" generated by the text in the course of reading. "Actual" or "real readers" are those—ancient and modern—who actually and historically read or hear the letter. The "implied" reader is the reader presupposed and projected by the text as the one sufficiently formed and capable of making all the moves necessary for an understanding of the text. A text will be successful as a piece of communication to the extent to which it brings actual or real readers to identify with the implied reader generated by the reading. A text will *continue* to be influential (and in this sense become a "classic") to the extent to which real readers of subsequent generations continue to make the same identification.

Thus, in the case of Romans, it seems clear that the "implied readers" of the letter overall are Gentile Christians in Rome. However, as noted earlier, the section comprising 1:18–4:25 seems to presuppose a (non-Christian) Jewish audience. There are, then, tensions within the concept of the "implied reader(s)" of Romans, which add to the complexity of the letter's interpretation. Yet the distinction between "actual" and "implied" authors and readers helps pose the problem with greater clarity.

Along with the shift of focus towards the reader in biblical interpretation there has entered a new sense of the text as *instrument of persuasion.* Older approaches tended to view a biblical text such as Romans—particularly Romans, because of its theological density—as primarily a repositum of theology. It was as though Paul were communicating to believers in Rome a systematic account of his theology. But Romans is a document seeking not merely to inform its addressees but also to persuade and move them in various directions. It communicates an experience of the gospel which Paul hopes will not only increase their Christian maturity but also gain for himself a welcome in Rome and support for the enterprises lying before him. It is, in short, a work of Christian rhetoric, aiming to persuade.

Recognition of this has meant the application to Romans in recent years of the insights of rhetorical criticism. The classical world (especially in the works of theorists such as Aristotle, Cicero and Quintilian) handed down a reflective science of rhetoric concerned to stress how the diversity of situation and audience ought influence the mode of speaking to be adopted on particular occasions. This body of rhetorical theory laid down rules for the identification of issues to be addressed and topics pursued, for the arrangement of a speech (order of various arguments); it classified various figures of style (metaphor, irony, pathos, etc.) used to gain maximum effect. It also introduced a classic distinction between three modes of rhetorical address: the judicial (for court of law); the deliberative (for the political assembly); the demonstrative or epideictic (for occasions of celebration). New Testament scholars, building particularly upon the work of classical scholar G. A. Kennedy, have brought these and other insights from ancient rhetoric to the letters of Paul, including Romans.

The application of ancient rhetoric to the New Testament letters is not, however, without its problems. In the first place, while the letters are clearly documents of persuasion, it is not at all certain that canons formulated for the purposes of oral discourse (speech-making) automatically transfer to the genre of the letter. The ancient world had a science of rhetoric and also one of epistolography. There were clearly important links between the two genres but conscious application of rhetorical insights to epistolary theory is rare among ancient theorists and for the most part dates from a time later than the New Testament. One may also question the extent to which even a competent writer such as Paul was schooled in the technical art of rhetoric. Thus the attempts that have been made, particularly in the area of the disposition of speeches, to assign rhetorical categories (*exordium* [introduction]; *narratio* [statement of the case under discussion]; *confirmatio* [proof of the case]; *conclusio* or *peroratio* [conclusion]) to Paul's letters, in whole or in part, have not proved entirely persuasive and will not be employed in this commentary. There is also the consideration that a focus upon Greco-Roman rhetorical models in connection with Paul may involve neglect of the biblical and post-biblical rhetorical tradition in which he, as a Jewish exegete, was undoubtedly steeped. The extensive use of scripture in certain parts of Romans points to the relevance of Semitic techniques of persuasion.

A second point of caution with regard to the use of ancient rhetorical models has to do with their tendency to focus upon the original historical situation. This focus upon history, however, flies in the face of the perception, noted above, that the meaning of a text transcends its original setting in history.

More suitable in this respect is the "New Rhetoric," based particularly upon the foundational and still classic work of Chaim Perelmann. The "New Rhetoric" acknowledges a fundamental debt to ancient rhetorical theory, makes use of its categories and definitions and stands in strict continuity with it. It is, however, less locked into analysis of the historical occasion of discourse and more focussed upon the operation of written rather than spoken discourse. A key concept of modern rhetorical criticism is that of the "rhetorical situation"—the context in which speakers or writers create discourse. More specifically, following L. Bitzer, the rhetorical situation can be defined as "that complex of persons, events, objects, and relations presenting an actual or potential exigence which can be completely or partially removed if discourse, introduced into the situation, can so constrain human decision or action as to bring about the significant modification of the exigence" ("The Rhetorical Situation" [See Bibliography] p. 6).

Understood in this way, rhetorical discourse presupposes three constituent factors: 1. an *"exigence"*—something requiring to be done, some alteration of the situation that is called for, usually with a degree of urgency; 2. the *audience* that is to be constrained to decision and action—persons capable of being influenced by discourse and of being mediators of change (ibid. 8); and 3. the *constraints* which can be brought to bear upon the situation—that is, factors which have the power to constrain decision and action. Sources of constraint can include beliefs, attitudes, authoritative memories or documents, facts, traditions, interests and so forth. Some of these constraints are already existent in the situation; others are conjured up and brought to bear upon it by the speaker or writer in the course of the communication (these would include the speaker's own authority, the proofs brought forward, the style of discourse, etc.).

In a text stemming from a particular historical situation, such as Romans, it is possible to conceive of the rhetorical situation—the situation to be addressed by the writer—as more or less identical with the situation as it can be determined by historical analysis. Modern rhetorical analysis, however, while not neglecting the historical dimension, tends to work in a more "intra-textual" way, seeing the "rhetorical situation" (with its exigents and constraints) as something embedded in the text and projected by the text (cf. D. L. Stamps, "Re-thinking the Rhetorical Situation" [See Bibliography] p. 200). This means that we can distinguish the rhetorical situation *projected by text* of Romans from the *actual* historical situation obtaining in the Roman community in relation to Paul. While knowledge of this actual situation will greatly assist interpretation, it cannot be totally determinative of meaning since the letter projects its own vision of an "exigence" to be addressed. So, for example, an interpretation of Paul's instruction on tolerance in the matter of food and other observances (food, drink, fast days, etc.—Rom 14:1–15:13) cannot be wholly determined by what we may or may not know to have been the historical reality in this area within the Jewish community of Rome. Rhetorical criticism will insist that the text be allowed to make its own presentation of the problem and will seek to evaluate with what success or no, from an argumentative point of view, the problem is addressed.

Along with literary and rhetorical criticism, insights from the *social sciences* have also found a role in contemporary biblical interpretation. We will shortly take note of the contribution sociological analysis can make when considering the pattern of early Christian community life in Rome. On a more theoretical level, however, one may approach biblical texts and the communicative interaction they presuppose from the point of view of the *sociology of knowledge.* Here the concept of a shared "symbolic universe" can be helpful. As a concept within the sociology of knowledge "symbolic universe" refers to the world, not as it is itself, but as it is *known* by persons living within societies. It denotes a comprehensive system of shared knowledge, expressed in language, symbol and myth, serving to define, legitimate and give meaning to institutions and individual identities and to social interactions between them (cf. N. Petersen, *Rediscovering Paul* [See Bibliography] 28–29, 57). (The "Great American Dream," for example, would be an essential element in the "symbolic world" of most citizens of the United States.) It is in accordance with this "knowledge" that human beings are particularly motivated to change or to act. Hence appeal to or modification of the "symbolic universe" will be a key weapon in any strategy of persuasion—from campaigns to sell a particular brand of toothpaste to the highest flights of political or religious discourse.

Where more traditional approaches to biblical exegesis tend to speak in terms of "theology" and to review the different "theologies" to be found across a range of biblical literature, the notion of symbolic universe seems to reflect more accurately the primarily persuasive and argumentative nature of that literature, especially the letters of Paul. Theology can be related to a symbolic universe in the sense that it represents a more detached, systematic reflection upon religious aspects of a shared symbolic world, that is, upon those more transcendent aspects that have to do with ultimate meaning. But human beings are motivated not so much by appeal to what they hold in a strictly systematic sense as by a play upon the key symbols in which belief is implicitly expressed. Thus, when considering the process of persuasion that documents like the letters of Paul purport to initiate, it seems more appropriate to speak of shared symbolic universes rather than shared theologies.

Communication between human beings presupposes a certain sharing or overlap in the symbolic universe proper to each party. In particular, the kind of persuasive communication undertaken by a letter-writer like Paul requires a shared symbolic universe between himself and his readers, along with a certain capacity on his part to play effectively upon the key symbols likely to move his addressees: in rhetorical terms, the factors likely to "constrain" their action. It would seem that rhetorical criticism's notion of the "constraints" of the rhetorical situation dovetails with the sense of "symbolic universe" adduced by the sociology of knowledge. In the study of the persuasive communication represented by Paul's letters, it helps to determine the constraints Paul brings to bear upon his audience in terms of the "world" of effective symbols he shares with them—images from the world of Jewish apocalypticism (that of the last judgment, for example), images of the saving work of Christ (expiation, redemption, reconciliation, etc.), the sense of scripture as authoritative indicator of God's plan for the final age, and so forth. It is also fruitful to ask about the extent to which in the letter as a whole, as well as in individual sections, Paul seeks to modify in some way his audience's key symbolic understandings.

3. *The Approach Taken by This Commentary*

The variety of approaches just surveyed have opened up fresh and liberating possibilities for scriptural interpretation. In particular, as should now be clear, rhetorical criticism's sense of a text as instrument of persuasion is particularly appropriate for a Pauline letter, as a document designed to have a transforming effect upon its hearers. Accordingly, without seeking to apply rigidly a fixed pattern of rhetorical interpretation, the major focus of this commentary will fall upon Romans as an instrument of persuasion. Where ancient rhetorical models and figures can be discerned, I shall draw attention to them. But my primary intent is to elucidate the text as an argumentative exposition of the gospel. Particular attention will be paid to the argumentative structure of each section, as well as to the place of each section within the argument of the letter as a whole. Insights from the alternative approaches outlined above will be used where relevant and, as already indicated, historical-critical analysis will continue to play its indispensable role.

B. *WHY PAUL WROTE TO ROME*

1. *The Historical Circumstances*

Since an appreciation of the historical context remains basic to interpretation, before considering in greater detail Paul's rhetorical task in Romans along the new lines of interpretation just outlined, I shall outline the historical circumstances of the letter, as far as these can be reconstructed with any plausibility. This may best be done under the overall rubric provided by the question, What circumstances led Paul to write in this way to Rome? I propose to consider this issue from the twin poles of Paul's own situation and that of the Christian community he addresses in Rome.

a) *Paul's Own Situation*

It is generally agreed that Paul wrote to Rome during an extended winter stay in Corinth just prior to setting out for Jerusalem with the Collection gathered from the Gentile churches of Macedonia and Achaia (Rom 15:25-26; cf. Acts 20:1-4, 16; 24:17; 1 Cor 16:1-4; 2 Cor 8:1–9:15). Mention of the collection from churches in these two regions suggests that Paul is almost certainly still in Greece and allusions in chapter 16 to Cenchreae (v 1), the western port of Corinth and the indication of a leading figure of the Corinthian community, Gaius, as Paul's host (v 23; cf. 1 Cor 1:14) make Corinth the most likely place of writing. The interpretation of the letter is hardly dependent on a precise fixing of the date in terms of absolute chronology but it may be said that the winter of any year between late 54 C.E. and early 59 C.E. is possible, with the early months of 58 C.E. providing the most likely period (for full discussion and further literature on the question of dating, see Fitzmyer, *Romans* 86–88).

At this juncture Paul stood at a turning point in his apostolic career. The survey of his missionary work given in Rom 15:17-21 shows a sense of having completed his task in the Eastern Empire (Asia Minor and Greece). The immediate goal is to convey to "the saints in Jerusalem" the money collected from the Gentile communities (15:25-27). After that his sights are set upon further missionary work in the West, specifically in Spain (15:24, 28). En route will be the long-desired (1:10-15) but hitherto frustrated visit to Rome (15:23-24, 28-29, 32).

This clear focus upon fresh missionary work ahead would seem to rule out the suggestion (G. Bornkamm) that Paul wrote Romans as a kind of "last will or testament" of an apostle who knew he had reached the final stage of his missionary career. Romans may have become such in fact but the plans Paul himself expresses for the future (Spain, etc.) show that he hardly envisaged the imminent close of his apostolic career.

Likewise, the suggestion (J. Jervell) that Romans represents a preliminary working out in his own mind of the account of the gospel he knows he will be called upon to give in Jerusalem leaves unexplained why he should send this letter to the community in Rome. True, Paul wishes ardently to gain the support of the Roman community for his task in Jerusalem; he earnestly asks for their prayers (15:30-32). But the implied address of the letter to a predominantly Gentile audience is inexplicable in terms of presentation to the Jewish-Christian church of Jerusalem.

More plausible and more widely accepted is the view that Paul wrote the letter basically as a means of self-presentation to the Christians of Rome. Here was a community he had not himself founded or visited (though, as the epithets attached to many of the greetings in chapter 16 show, it did contain quite a few notable persons with whom he had lived and worked). He is by now a highly controversial figure, suspected of playing fast and loose with the Jewish heritage of Christianity (cf. esp. Gal 2:10-15; 5:11; 2 Cor 10:10-11; Rom 3:8). If, as seems likely, the Roman community, despite its predominantly Gentile composition, was known to be one that had remained basically sympathetic to the Jewish heritage in which it had been nurtured, it is very likely that Paul would write "to set the record straight." Before his visit in person, he would be striving to give an authentic and acceptable account of his view of the gospel and its consequences. The hope would be to counter any false and hostile views of himself current in Rome.

It has also been suggested that Paul wrote not merely to ensure a good reception for himself personally in Rome but also to enlist the Roman

Christians in the design he cherished for further missionary work in the West. His future work in Spain, so far from previous bases and sources of support, could hardly succeed without the goodwill and material support of this significant community standing at the threshold of East and West. But, while such a consideration was surely part of Paul's hopes in contemplating his interaction with the Roman community, it is hardly sufficient in itself to account for the letter as a whole.

So much for considerations focusing on Paul himself. What of the situation of the recipient community?

b) *The Christians in Rome*

We do not know precisely how or when belief in Jesus arrived in the imperial capital. Since there are no certain grounds for associating its introduction with a distinctive individual founder (Peter or some such known figure), the origins of Christianity in Rome are most likely to be seen in the multiple contacts, chiefly economic, between Jerusalem and the large Jewish community in the capital (cf., for a somewhat later period, Acts 28:21). Granted the frequency of commerce, it was inevitable that Christian believers in Palestine would make their way to Rome and begin to share their beliefs within the synagogues of the Jewish community (note the listing in Acts 2:10 of "visitors from Rome, both Jews and proselytes" among those who marvelled at the Pentecostal outpouring of the Spirit).

While Christian belief may have spread within the Jewish community through contact of a quite informal nature, synagogue meetings most likely provided the arena for more explicit evangelization and debate. Here the audience would have included, besides native-born Jews, proselytes of pagan origin, along with other non-Jews of varying levels of attachment to Judaism. It is significant that Paul, writing to a community he addresses as Gentiles, presupposes in his audience both an acquaintance with the scriptures of Israel and a readiness to be persuaded by distinctly Jewish techniques of interpretation. Most of his Gentile audience, presumably, had received such instruction during a time when they still frequented the synagogue.

As regards community organization, sociological analysis has shed a good deal of light in recent years upon the Pauline communities in Asia Minor and Greece. In the case of Rome, the task is more complex than it is, for example, with Corinth. Paul clearly addresses the Christian community as a whole in Romans. But he never uses the term *ekklēsia* of the whole body, though he does greet the *ekklēsia* that meets in the house of Prisca and Aquila (16:5) and there are hints of further groupings of this kind (16:7, 10b, 11, 14). This suggests that the Roman community was organized around house churches, with only occasional gatherings of the entire body. While the majority of members were probably drawn from the lower class, perhaps predominantly slaves or freed-persons *(libertini),* some at least were of sufficient means to have houses large enough to accommodate gatherings of the separate *ekklēsiai*. But the numbers of persons of higher social standing was probably very small. Composed largely of persons not born in Rome, the community spoke Greek.

When did the specifically *Christian* identity of this group of believers emerge and what continued to be its relationship with the Jewish synagogues out of which it had grown? It is hard to be precise in these areas. Writing to the Roman Christians in the late 50's, Paul thanks God that their "faith is proclaimed all over the world" (1:8) and protests his own long-cherished (though ever frustrated), desire to come and visit them (1:10-11, 15). In this he clearly presupposes a community that has been in existence for some years—certainly since the early years of the decade, more likely extending back into the mid or late 40's. This agrees with an intriguing statement of the Roman historian Suetonius to the effect that the emperor Claudius (41–54 C.E.) expelled Jews from Rome on the grounds that they were "constantly rioting at the instigation of Chrestus" (*Claudius* 25). The way Suetonius phrases this reference suggests that he understood "Chrestus" to be an agitator personally present in the Jewish community at the time. It is very likely, however, that "Chrestus" refers in fact to Jesus Christ and that the basis of the tradition reflected in Suetonius lay in disturbances between Jews and *Christians* concerning the messianic status of Jesus. Suetonius does not assign the incident to any particular year in Claudius' reign, though a fifth-century Christian author, Orosius, assigns it precisely to 49 C.E. This dating is unreliable in itself but it does agree well with the mention in Acts 18:2 of Paul's meeting in Corinth with the Jewish couple, Prisc(ill)a and Aquila, recently expelled by Claudius from Rome along with other Jews. It is highly likely, then, that around the close of the 40's the pressure created by distinctive messianic claims rendered Christian presence within the synagogues of Rome increasingly intolerable; the Christian movement was compelled to forge its own identity and go its separate way. Certainly, by the time of Nero's brutal pogrom against the Christians in connection with the great fire of Rome in 64 C.E. (recorded in all its gruesome detail by the historian Tacitus [*Annals* 15.44]), the contours of Christian identity were sufficiently sharp for an external party, such as the government, to see in the new movement something quite distinct from Judaism. Paul's letter to Rome, arriving only a few years before this episode, may well have played a role in the fixing of that clear and separate identity.

Many scholars, seeking to pinpoint more precisely the occasion for Paul's letter, link it to consequences arising out of Claudius' expulsion of Jews. If the origins of the Christian community lay in the synagogues, one may reasonably suppose that the *Jewish*-Christian element would have been in the ascendancy in the period prior to the expulsion. When, however, a significant proportion of this leading element was forced to leave Rome under Claudius' edict in 49 C.E., it is likely that leadership passed more to the Gentile element, who may also have set up a less synagogue-oriented style of community organization. With the lapse of Claudius' edict on the occasion of his death in 54 C.E., many Jewish Christians presumably returned to the capital (as we know Paul's friends Prisca and Aquila did). It is likely that these returning Jewish Christians would have sought to regain their previous ascendancy and restore a life-style based on more traditionally Jewish lines. Resultant tensions between the Jewish and Gentile elements would be the immediate cause or occasion of Paul's letter. Paul would be writing to remind the community, on the basis of the gospel, of the true relationship between Jews and Gentiles within the one People of God. More specifically, he would be urging Gentile Christians not to disparage the Jewish heritage but to show tolerance and understanding towards those to whom the promises and the gospel were first addressed.

An explanation of the occasion of the letter along these lines may find support in the specific plea for tolerance addressed to the "Strong" and the "Weak" in 14:1–15:13. The distinction indicated by these epithets can be seen to run along ethnic lines and refer to Gentile and Jewish members respectively. The latter feel compelled to refrain from eating meat (14:2, 21) because either their alienation from the synagogue or the difficulty of finding Jewish butchers after Claudius' expulsion made it impossible for them to procure meat that had been ritually slaughtered *(kosher)*. Gentiles, however, had no such scruples and ate "all things" (14:2). Paul basically shares the viewpoint of the "Strong" (14:14) but, on a wider understanding of the gospel, urges tolerance and "acceptance" of the "Weak brother" (14:1; 15:1).

It is not at all clear, however, that the distinction between "Strong" and "Weak" in this passage runs along ethnic lines. Paul would in any case hardly promote the cause of the Jewish members by referring to them as "the Weak in faith" (14:1). It is possible that in both cases the primary address is to Christians of Gentile origin, with one group—"the Weak"—adopting a more scrupulous attitude to food and drink, possibly through stricter adherence to the legacy of the Jewish ways in which they had been instructed. It must also be noted that Paul's instruction here is couched in reasonably general terms compared to the more pointed parallel response given to the Corinthian community's enquiry in 1 Corinthians 8-10. Paul may not here be writing to correct an actual abuse in Rome of which he had certain knowledge. He may simply be attempting to forestall or prevent the kind of problems that his wide experience taught him to see as prone to break out in recently established communities of believers.

More pointed still, however, is Paul's instruction on submission to civil authorities in 13:1-7. The issue, in the end, appears to come down to the question of payment of taxes and tariffs (cf. esp. vv 6-7). The appearance of this issue fits well with a notice from Tacitus (*Annals* 13) reporting that in 58 C.E. Nero responded to growing complaints about taxes by proposing to abolish all indirect taxes but was in the end persuaded by the senators to abandon the measure and seek instead to curb the rapaciousness of tax-collectors. The report shows that at the likely time of composition of Romans the issue of taxation was "in the air" and highly sensitive. The question of whether or not to pay taxes could well have been a matter of debate within the community.

Again, however, in a context where the issue of how to relate to outsiders has been the subject of the immediately preceding parenesis (12:17-21), it is not surprising that Paul should give instruction concerning Christian obligation to the state. This he may have done as much to show his own adherence to conventional thinking in this regard as to address any current issue in the community of which he has become aware. Part of Paul's rhetorical strategy may have been to assure the Christians of Rome, particularly those who had recently suffered expulsion, that he is not coming among them as one likely to stir up strife with the civil authorities.

Therefore, while a reconstruction of the circumstances of the Christian community in Rome around the late 50's C.E. provides a reasonable background for the occasion of Paul's letter, it is difficult to find a precise "fit" between those circumstances and its specific content. It is not easy to account for the long "kerygmatic" section (1:18–11:36) in terms of a specific need in the community which Paul addresses. In view of the tone and structure of the letter in itself, we have to ask why Paul saw fit to expound at such length the "power" of the gospel (cf. 1:16), while also attaching exhortatory material of both a general and more particular nature (12:1–15:13).

2. *Romans as a Letter and Instrument of Persuasion*

a) *Letter Form*

For all its bulk and systematic nature, Romans is not a theological treatise but a genuine letter written in particular circumstances to a particular audience: the Christian believers in Rome. A great deal of work has been done in recent years on the nature of the New Testament letters precisely as letters within the broader genre of Greco-Roman letter writing and theory. Despite this research, it has proved difficult to place Paul's letter to Rome within any clearly defined category.

The standard structure of the ancient letter consisted of three basic elements:

I. an *Opening*, itself containing three elements: 1. mention of the sender, 2. mention of the addressee(s), 3. a greeting or salutation;
II. the *Body* of the Letter;
III. the *Closing*, normally including a health wish and word of farewell, sometimes greetings to or from particular persons.

As a letter writer, Paul adopts this pattern, though with considerable modification for his own purposes. The letter to Rome represents the Pauline modification of the ancient letter-pattern in its most developed form.

I. In the *Opening*, Paul usually embellishes both the mention of himself as sender (with self-descriptions outlining his apostolic status: "Paul, apostle, . . .") and that of the addressees (attaching various epithets: "saints, etc. . . ."). Such elaboration of the opening address is particularly marked in the case of Romans (1:1, 7). In the greeting that follows, the Hellenistic formula "*Chairein*" becomes the more Christian "*Charis*" ("Grace"), to which Paul adds the Jewish formula "Peace" (Rom 1:7b).

Between the *Opening* and the *Body* of the Pauline letter (except in the case of Galatians and 2 Corinthians) comes the *Thanksgiving*. This distinctive Pauline feature has some precedent in the prayer of supplication to the deity *(proskynēma)*, sometimes associated with an expression of thanks, that occurs in secular letters. Paul's practice is to make the situation of the recipients the basis of the thanksgiving. This enables him to employ it as a device for delicately complimenting his audience on their progress in Christian life, promoting the *ethos* or good feeling towards himself that will serve as the basis for effective communication (1 Cor 1:4-9; Phil 1:3-11; 1 Thess 1:2-10; Phlm 4-7). The Thanksgiving element is particularly serviceable to Paul in the case of Romans (1:8-15[17]), where he faces the formidable task of communicating a sense of his apostolic authority to a community which he has not himself founded.

II. *The Body of the Letter.* This central element, which of course makes up the vast bulk of the letter in the case of Romans, deals with the precise matter or content of the communication. Since it is largely shaped by the problem or issue at hand, it tends to manifest formal elements to a lesser degree than the opening and closing portions. Certain conventional features recur in the opening of the body of the Pauline letter or serve to mark notable points of transition in the argument. In Romans these include the *disclosure formula:* "I do not want you to be ignorant" (Rom 1:13; cf. 2 Cor 1:8; Gal 1:11; Phil 1:12) that indicates the beginning of an important theme; the *formula of request:* "I appeal *(parakalō)* to you" (Rom 12:1; 15:30; 16:17), a fixed epistolary formula found in both private and official

Greek letters, conveying the impression of a friendly appeal rather than an authoritative command; the *confidence formula:* "I myself am satisfied about you, my brothers and sisters" (Rom 15:14; 2 Cor 7:4, 16; Gal 5:10; Phlm 21).

Toward the close of the Body of the Pauline letter there tends to recur a cluster of features all of which serve to communicate a heightened sense of Paul's *apostolic presence* and, most significantly, a statement of his intention to visit the community in the near future, sometimes giving details of his travel plans (Rom 15:14-33; 1 Cor 16:5-9; Phil 2:24; Phlm 22). The sense of apostolic presence tends to culminate in the element of *parenesis* that frequently occurs towards the end of a Pauline letter (Rom 12:1–15:13; Gal 5:1–6:10; 1 Thess 4:1–5:22; cf. Col 3:1–4:6). *Parenesis* is moral exhortation, usually of a fairly general and conventional kind, that relies for its authority upon appeal to the apostolic tradition already accepted by the recipients. It is often accompanied by passages giving eschatological warning, as in Rom 13:11-14 (cf. 1 Thess 5:1-11; Phil 2:12-18; 4:4-7; cf. Eph 5:15-20; 6:10-17).

III. *The Closing*. Here Paul tends to depart most notably from standard conventions. He replaces the customary "health wish" *(errōsthē)* and word of farewell with a formula of grace benediction: Rom 16:20 (cf. 1 Thess 5:28; 1 Cor 16:23; 2 Cor 13:13; Gal 6:18; Phil 4:23; Phlm 25; 2 Thess 3:18). Before this final blessing normally come *greetings,* as most notably in the long list comprising the bulk of Romans 16 (cf. also 1 Cor 16:19-20; Phil 4:21-22; 1 Thess 5:26; Phlm 23-24), usually in association with an injunction for a *"holy kiss"* (Rom 16:16; cf. 1 Cor 16:20; 2 Cor 13:12) and sometimes an *autographed greeting* from Paul or the scribe (Tertius in the case of Romans [16:22]).

Romans, then, broadly follows the epistolary conventions of the ancient world as adapted by Paul. But can we be more specific about the epistolary type to which it most closely conforms? The Greco-Roman world, as well as the Jewish background to a far lesser extent, exhibits a great variety of letter types—ranging from the very occasional to the highly formal and literary. No one mode of classification is agreed upon—though obvious bases for division are provided, on the one hand, by content, on the other by function.

Prominent amongst recent suggestions for Romans has been the type of didactic letter identified by M. L. Stirewalt as the "letter-essay." "Letter-essays" were authentic letters in that they dealt with specific topics and were directed to specific recipients, though others besides the recipients were intended to read them and draw instruction. But "letter-essays" were essentially supplementary to some other writing or instruction of the same author—clarifying, abridging or defending it. This hardly applies in the case of Romans.

A further suggestion concerning the letter type is that Romans falls into the category of an "ambassadorial letter" (R. Jewett) not in a pure sense but in a unique fusion of this type of letter with other types such as the parenetic letter and the philosophical diatribe. It is true that Paul's situation *vis-à-vis* the Roman community does call for considerable diplomacy and that there is a real sense in which Paul is "presenting his credentials" in Romans. Yet credentials would usually be supplied not by the ambassador in person but by the one whom the ambassador represents and would normally be presented on arrival, not sent ahead as in the case of Romans.

Ultimately, then, it may be better not to seek to tie Romans too tightly to any known form of letter from the ancient world but rather to recognize that Paul had at his disposal various models which he could combine and adapt to suit his purpose. While it is important to recognize that Romans remains a letter, exhibiting distinct letter forms and directed to and from specific situations, it also remains true that Romans bears a more generalizing character than any of the remaining authentic letters of Paul. In this respect it marks a step in the direction of the more generalized, but still epistolary deutero-Pauline Letter to the Ephesians and the scarcely epistolary and non-Pauline Letter to the Hebrews.

b) *Instrument of Persuasion*

We noted above the need for a certain reserve in the wholesale application of rhetorical categories to letters stemming from the ancient world. Nonetheless, the basically persuasive character of Paul's letters makes it useful to ask concerning each one which of the three modes of rhetorical address—the judicial, the deliberative and the epideictic—it most closely follows. In the case of Romans there is now widespread agreement that it is this last mode, the epideictic or demonstrative, that particularly comes to mind.

The distinguishing mark of epideictic discourse as determined by the ancient rhetoricians was its celebration of values held in common. This it sought to achieve by praising individuals or institutions notably representing such values or by censuring those that did not. Taking this notion somewhat further, theorists of the New Rhetoric, such as Chaim Perelmann, point out that

> ". . . epidictic *(sic)* discourse sets out to increase the intensity of adherence to certain values, which might not be contested when considered on their own but may nevertheless not prevail against other values that may come into conflict with them. The speaker tries to establish a sense of communion around particular values recognized by the audience and to this end he uses the whole range of means available to the rhetorician for the purposes of amplification and argument" (*The New Rhetoric* 51).

That Paul's letter to Rome sits well within such a mode of discourse is signaled from the start by the bold assertion in the opening thematic statement: "I am not ashamed of the gospel, . . ." (1:16a). The lengthy exposition of the saving power of the gospel that then unfolds (1:16b–11:36), with its recurring theme of "boasting" (5:1-2, 11) and expressions of confidence (5:21; 8:1-2, 18, 31-39), culminating in the evocation of wonder and praise at God's wisdom (11:33-36), sits well with the epideictic sense of celebration of values (commitment to the Christian gospel) which Paul and his already evangelized audience at Rome hold in common. The aim of the letter might very reasonably be characterized in terms of setting out "to increase the intensity of adherence to (these) values."

Significant, too, in this connection is Perelmann's mention of adherence to values in the context of the threat from "other values that may come into conflict with them." Romans is not just an affirmation of the values of the Christian gospel. Its positive assertion of the claims of the Christian gospel stands over against the claims of rival values—notably the attachment to the Jewish law, which Paul sees to be characteristic of that vast bulk of Israel that has not come to faith in Jesus as the Christ (9:30–10:4). Understanding Paul's enterprise as epideictic goes some way towards accounting for the struggle with Jewish claims that runs throughout the letter and lends it the "double character" noted above.

Romans, however, goes beyond celebration. Paul is concerned to confirm his audience's practical as well as notional adherence to the values of the gospel. This can explain why at 12:1 the exposition of the gospel *(kerygma)* gives way to exhortation to live out the consequences of the gospel for Christian life *(parenesis)*, an instruction which continues, first in general (12:1–13:13), then in more specific (14:1–15:13) terms, until the concluding portion of the letter. In fact, however, an exhortatory tone sounds in earlier sections as well (6:12-14, 15-23; 8:12-13; 11:17-24), making a neat division of the letter into exposition of the gospel (chapters 1:16–11:36) and parenesis (12:1–15:13) somewhat misleading. Recognition of the letter's epideictic nature, however, explains the running blend of exposition and parenesis in Romans. It is precisely the celebration of the gospel and its saving power that Paul hopes will evoke the deeper and more willing adherence to the values upon which parenesis depends. By catching up the audience in the splendor and hope of the gospel—highlighted all the more against the threat posed by the alternative destiny to "wrath" which the law is impotent to avert (Rom 4:15; cf. 8:1)—Paul would hope to advance the transformation in ethical terms that the strictly parenetic sections more explicitly aim to achieve.

Overall, then, Romans finds a satisfactory explanation in terms of the epideictic rhetorical mode. This is not to say, however, that individual sections, taken in themselves, may not display features belonging more strictly to other forms of discourse. This is particularly true of the early section making up 1:18–4:25, which taken in itself shows features of what Greco-Roman rhetoric distinguished as a sub-type of the deliberative style: the apotreptic or dissuasive mode. The immediate aim is to win the implied audience (at this point Jews not yet come to faith in Christ) to abandon the quest for righteousness on any other basis ("works of the law") save that of faith in Jesus Christ. Within a broader perspective, however, the section plays its role in Paul's overall epideictic purpose by projecting and rejecting the negative foil against which the positive value of the gospel can be all the more affirmed. It must be admitted, however, as more detailed examination will show, that the opening part of this section (1:18–3:20) is best understood from the Semitic background—as a prophetic declamation within the framework of Jewish apocalypticism.

3. *Why Paul Wrote to Rome: Conclusion*

The consideration of Romans from a rhetorical point of view allows us to be more precise about Paul's purpose in writing to Rome. Early in the letter (1:15), in the "Thanksgiving" section which serves him so well in rhetorical terms, he speaks of his "eagerness" *(to kat' eme prothymon)* to "preach the gospel to you also in Rome" *(kai hymin en Rōmę̄ euangelisasthai)*. Paul normally reserves the Greek verb *euangelizesthai* for preaching aimed at initial conversion to faith in Christ. Since he has just acknowledged his Roman addressees to be believers whose "faith is proclaimed all over the world" (v 7), the use of this term and the aspiration it appears to contain is puzzling. Grammatically, the statement has no time-marker in the Greek, allowing the primary reference to be to a long-standing determination on Paul's part to pursue in Rome his apostolic mission to the Gentiles. He is countering any suggestion that he has been avoiding Rome, insisting that he has always been eager to come but "has been prevented until now" (v 13) by divinely ordained labors elsewhere (cf. 15:18-22). The rise of a community of Gentile believers in Rome has now overtaken his original intention. Nonetheless, the basic "eagerness" to preach in Rome remains. The same divine commission that made Paul "eager" to preach in Rome now makes him equally "eager" ("not ashamed" [v 16a]) to remedy his "absence" by proclaiming the gospel in written form. Thus the letter represents a genuine "preaching of the gospel"—not as an instrument of initial conversion but, in epideictic mode, as a "celebration" of values held in common, to increase adherence to those values and further detachment from rival values that could threaten them.

In the Conclusion of the letter Paul apologizes to the Romans for writing to them "rather boldly" as if they were not already evangelized and able to "correct themselves" (15:14-15). He describes what he has done in the letter as a "reminding" (*hōs epanamimnęskōn*) of them. The "reminding" refers to the gospel. He has not "evangelized" them as if they were not already believers. But, because of the "grace" given him by God to preach the gospel (cf. 1:5, 10), he has felt authorized to "remind them" of the gospel to which they had already given allegiance.

More pointedly, however, Paul's design is not simply to remind the Romans of the gospel held in common. The hope is that his own powerful written evocation of it will bring about in Rome, prior to his visit and his further expedition to the West, a deeper sympathy for and conformity to the specifically Pauline contours of the gospel: most notably the inclusion of the Gentiles as equal citizens in the eschatological people of God (an inclusion which he foresees will stimulate the full inclusion of Israel as well [11:11-26]). It is even conceivably Paul's hope that the effective hearing of his letter will bring the basically Gentile Roman community into the sphere of his own responsibility as "apostle to the Gentiles" (1:5, 13-14; 11:13; 15:16), so that they too will be part of the "offering (consisting) of the Gentiles" which he brings before God in "priestly service" (15:16). Even if they do not now contribute to the Collection "for the saints" (v 25), they may subsequently at least underwrite and support his missionary labors in the West. But Paul's ultimate hope may be that, following the "preaching" or "reminder" of the gospel contained in the letter, the Gentile Christians in Rome will be in the same relationship to himself as the communities he has personally founded.

True to the epideictic pattern, Paul's positive evocation of the "power" of the gospel proceeds over against and at the expense of rival claims. The Jewish law—more precisely, what Paul portrays as a misguided quest on the part of Israel to seek eschatological righteousness on the basis of the law—functions as the "fall guy" in Romans. Paul polemicizes against law-righteousness, not because there is a danger of adherence to the law in Rome but to reinforce Christian identity, an identity in which Gentiles have an equal share, despite the law's apparent exclusion of them from the promises of salvation.

C. *PAUL'S RHETORICAL TASK*

If such be Paul's purpose in writing to Rome, what was the task, in rhetorical terms, that faced him as writer of the letter? Earlier in this Introduction, reviewing new approaches in New Testament interpretation, I mentioned the notion of "symbolic universe" derived from the sociology of knowledge. All communication between human beings presupposes some overlap in the symbolic universes pertaining to each party. Moreover, from a rhetorical point of view, it is more appropriate to speak of shared symbolic universes rather than "theologies" since it is through play upon their universe of symbols that human beings are moved to change and to act. Paul's rhetorical task, then, would be that of crafting his letter to Rome in such a way as to constrain the members of the Roman community to modify the contours of their symbolic universe in the direction of his own.

Hence consideration of Paul's rhetorical task necessarily involves considering also the symbolic universe he shared with the audience he sought to persuade. I propose to outline, first of all, that "knowledge" (symbolic universe) which, as fellow believers within the Christian movement, Paul and the Roman community held in common: elements, that is, which he can simply take for granted without further discussion. This will prepare the way for a review of that "knowledge" which is more characteristically his own: areas of belief and symbol where he would want to modify the "knowledge" of his addressees, in an attempt to "constrain" attitudes and behavior more attuned to his own view of the gospel.

1. *"Knowledge" Paul Has in Common with the Christians of Rome*

a) *The Heritage from Judaism*

A significant portion of the symbolic universe within which Paul can communicate with the Roman community stemmed from the common Christian heritage from Judaism. Writing to a largely Gentile community he has not himself founded, Paul appears able to presuppose a considerable familiarity with this heritage on the part of his audience.

Key aspects of this heritage would include monotheistic belief (cf. 3:29-30); the sense of Israel as a chosen, holy nation, set apart through a distinctive divine election and law (Torah) from the rest of humankind (3:1-2; 9:4-5; cf. Gal 2:15); the authority of scripture (3:10-19; 3:21b; 4:1-25; 9:6–11:36) and scripture's role in indicating the divine plan for the "last days" (15:4); the sense that the scripturally recorded promises made to the patriarchs of Israel—especially Abraham—foretell and contain a hope of entrance into the blessings of the messianic age (4:1-25; 9:6-9; 11:28-29; 15:8-9). Central to these "blessings" is the "inheritance" of that "glory" or "likeness to God" which the late biblical and post-biblical Jewish tradition, on the basis of texts such as Gen 1:26-28 and Ps 8:4-8, saw to be the true destiny of human beings according to the original design of the Creator (cf. Rom 1:23; 2:7, 10; 3:23; 5:2; 8:17, 18-21, 29-30; 9:4, 23; cf. 2 Cor 3:18; 4:4-6, 17; Phil 3:21). Likewise, the sudden introduction of the figure of Adam in Rom 5:12-21 (cf. 1 Cor 15:21-22, 45-49) suggests that Paul presumes knowledge of a Jewish tradition holding the first father of the race to be the one who gave sin entrance into the world, entailing for all his descendants a loss of "glory" and a destiny to death.

Paul also presupposes an adherence on the part of his audience to the *eschatological perspective of Jewish apocalypticism.* Most significant in this perspective was the expectation of a more or less imminent divine judgment of the world in which the issue of "salvation" was to be decided. Paul makes considerable play in Romans upon the emotions of fear and hope evoked by this expectation (cf. 1:32; 2:1-11; 3:19; 5:1, 9, 11; 7:24-25; 8:1, 31-39; 9:22; 13:11-14; 14:10-12). The language of (divine) "wrath," "justification" and "righteousness," so prominent in the early chapters (1:18–4:25), as also the later mention of "condemnation" and "liberation" (8:1-2, 23) has its locus within this framework. The key hope was to be "saved" from the "wrath" (and consequent eternal separation from God) through being found "righteous" (= "being justified") at the final judgment (2:3-16; 5:9-10; 8:2, 31-39). Those "found righteous" would enter into the blessings of salvation, promised to Abraham "and to his seed" (4:13)—that is, to the Israel of the end-time, the eschatological People of God.

Attaching to this "people" are key epithets such as "holy" (= "the saints"), "elect" (8:28) and, above all, the language of divine filiation (8:14-15, 19-21, 23; 9:4, 26). The "children" ("sons and daughters") of God" are those renewed by the Spirit of God in fulfillment of scriptural promises interpreted with reference to the eschatological age (Rom 8:4-13, 14-15, 23-27; cf. Ezek. 36:26; Jer 31:31-33).

Curiously enough, this strong apocalyptic sense of the present pattern of things coming rapidly to an end co-exists with a conservative view, traditional in both the Jewish and wider ancient world, that behind prevailing civil powers and the sanctions they impose lies the authority of the divine Judge. Submission to the civil power is a moral as well as a social necessity (13:1-7).

b) *The Shared* CHRISTIAN *Pattern of Belief*

Paul also communicates to the Christians of Rome out of a shared Christian belief system, centering around faith in what God has done in the person and "career" of Jesus Christ. Pivotal to this central "myth" of Christianity is the belief that Jesus of Nazareth, crucified and raised from the dead, is the Messiah of Israel (9:5), the instrument of God's eschatological saving work, in a unique sense God's "only Son" (1:3-4; 8:3-4, 32), whom believers confess as "Lord" (10:9). Christ died "for our sins" in the sense that, in the shedding of his blood in death, God worked an atonement for human sin that reconciles sinful human beings to God and ushers in the required eschatological justification (3:21-26; 4:25; 5:6-11; 8:3-4; 10:9-11; 14:9; 15:8-9).

The experience of the Spirit, felt in both community life and the hearts of individual believers (8:23-28), is linked to the Christ event in the sense that, through the Spirit, believers experience the power and authority of the unseen risen Lord and are assured of belonging to the eschatological community of the saved (8:9-11, 23, 26-27). In the Spirit, they act out their sense of divine filiation by addressing God as "*Abba*, Father" (8:15; cf. Gal 4:6). Through the Spirit, too, each member has a distinctive "grace," bestowed for the building up of community and the equipment of its members for mission (1:5, 11; 12:4-8).

Paul presumes in his audience at Rome an understanding of what otherwise appears to be a distinctively Pauline sense of Christian existence as an existence "in Christ" (6:1-11; 8:2), that is, as a life lived in the sphere and power of the risen Lord, constituting a kind of corporate person. Shared "knowledge" of this kind may derive from a Jewish sense of the Messiah as somehow "containing" in his own person the wider messianic community. Baptism "into Christ" marks the beginning of this new existence (6:3-4).

In the area of Christian living, Paul presumes instruction in and acceptance of the basic ethical precepts of the Jewish heritage (6:12-13, 17; 13:8-10, 11-14). But the extent to which the Roman community shared his grounding of righteous living in the motif of conformity to the pattern of Christ (6:1-11; cf. 8:17), rather than obedience to the precepts of the Mosaic law, is not clear.

Another point of uncertainty concerns the place of those formerly "Gentile sinners" (cf. Gal 2:15) within the eschatological people of God. Naturally, writing to a community now largely composed of Gentiles, Paul can assume a general acceptance of their place within the body of believers. But a key function of his letter may be to define that place more convincingly and more accurately in relation both to the scriptural promises and the present situation of Israel.

Paul presumes that the addressed community accepts the distinctive role of "apostle" within the Christian movement. Apostles are emissaries of the risen Lord, charged with the founding and nurture of local communities of believers. He introduces himself as such (1:1) and acknowledges a similar status for two members of the Roman community, Andronicus and Junia (16:7).

2. *"Knowledge" More Particularly Distinctive of Paul*

Paul's personal symbolic universe contains a sense of himself not only as "apostle" but as apostle specifically of the Gentiles (11:13), charged with a world-wide responsibility for the Gentile churches (1:5, 13-15; 15:15-21; cf. Gal 1:16). The Collection "for the Saints," raised from the

Gentile churches and being conveyed by Paul to the mother church in Jerusalem, is an important symbol of the acceptance of Gentile believers within the one People of God (15:25-28, 31).

Within a sense of this unity, the symbolic "fatherhood" of Abraham (4:1) consists primarily in his being the "father" of a great company of believers, Jewish and Gentile alike (4:11-12, 16-17). It is, in fact, as the one who "models" the "ungodly" Gentile who comes to faith, rather than the law-obedient, circumcised Jew (4:2-5), that the patriarch received, for himself and "for his seed," the "inheritance of the earth" comprising the full blessings of salvation (4:13).

With respect to the *saving work of Christ,* Paul accepts the common Christian view of it as effecting an expiation of human sin (3:24-25; 5:6-11; 8:3-4, 32). But he more characteristically depicts it in terms of "reconciliation" between God and sinful human beings (5:1, 10-11; cf. 2 Cor 5:18-21) or as an instrument of "justification" for believers (3:24; 4:25; 5:9, 16-19) or as a liberating triumph of grace over the enslaving grip of sin depicted as tyrant "power" (5:17, 21; 6:1-14; 8:1-4).

Paul operates within the *eschatological expectation* of apocalyptic Judaism as outlined above. However, for him the anticipated "program" of the "End" has been significantly modified by God's action in sending Christ. Though full and final "salvation" may still be an object of hope (5:9, 10; 6:5, 8; 8:23; 11:26), for believers the eschatological "now" has already dawned (3:21), the "justification" associated with the great judgment can already be received through Christ (3:24, 26; 4:25; 5:1; 8:30). In a way unforeseen in the traditional eschatology, believers live in a curious time of "overlap" between the old age and the new. *Bodily* they are anchored in the present, passing age, vulnerable to its onslaughts in the shape of temptation, suffering and death, with "resurrection" still an object of hope (8:9-11, 23); in the *Spirit,* however, they here and now enjoy the relationship to God characteristic of the new era (5:5; 8:14-15). The challenge and task of present Christian existence is to live out, in the Spirit, the obedience and righteousness of the new age in the bodily conditions of the old (6:12-13; 8:12-13; 12:1-2).

Within this modification of the traditional eschatology, Paul can present in a new light the *sufferings* which believers undergo at the present time (5:3-4; 8:18, 35-39). Such sufferings in no way threaten the truth that believers are "right with God" (= "justified") and "on the way" to final salvation. The reality lying beneath Christian suffering is conformity to the suffering of Christ; this promises a corresponding conformity also to his "glory" (8:17). Believers can even "boast" in their sufferings (5:3) because of their sure hope that the love of God, shown so powerfully in the death of God's Son for a sinful world, will bring them to the fullness of salvation (5:1-11; 8:14-39).

Paul's treatment of the Jewish *law* (Torah) is the most distinctive and controversial feature of the symbolic universe at stake in Romans. In itself, the law is "holy, just and good" (Rom 7:12). Seen apart from Christ, it is also the criterion of righteousness (2:12-16). But the law has proved incapable of dealing with the root problem of human existence—the proneness of weak human nature ("the flesh") to sin (Rom 8:3). Though sin existed in human life from the beginning (Rom 5:13; 7:9), the advent of the law in the shape of explicit commandment provoked the latent tendency of human nature ("flesh") to rebel against its Creator (7:7-11). Far from restraining sin, the law actually exacerbated the problem: it gave "experience (literally, "knowledge") of sin" (Rom 3:20b), "multiplied transgression" (Rom 5:20a), "provoked sin-producing passions" (7:5) and so "worked wrath" (4:15). The good and holy law thus came to be ranged upon the negative side as accomplice and instrument of sin, leading to (eternal) death.

Paul nonetheless finds an ultimately salvific divine purpose in this negative role played by the law (Rom 7:13b). Through the operation of the law given to Israel, God concentrated sin in a particular way within Israel so that there, by a miracle of grace and on behalf of all humankind, sin might be dealt with once and for all through the sacrificial act of Israel's Messiah, Jesus (7:13; 8:3-4). Where sin "abounded" (in Israel, through the coming of the law), grace was to "abound all the more" (5:20b).

In Paul's eyes the problem with a quest for eschatological righteousness through the law is that such a quest fatally fails to advert to this negative light in which, following the preaching of the gospel, the operation of the law must be seen. The sending of *this* kind of Messiah—that is, one who works God's saving purpose by dying as an expiatory sacrifice for sin (Rom 3:24-25; 8:3-4; cf. 2 Cor 5:21)—points to a prevalence of sin that is universal, including even the covenant people within its scope (Rom 3:9b; 3:23; 5:12d; 11:32). This universal prevalence of sin must mean the abandonment of any quest for eschatological righteousness through the law; the law is, at best, helpless to counter sin and is in fact designed to "increase" it.

For Paul, liberation from law (Rom 7:4, 25; 8:2) is the condition of possibility of the kind of righteous living (6:15; 8:3-11) that leads, in the power of the Spirit, to full salvation (8:9-13). What the law, in itself, justly and rightly required—eschatological righteousness—is now brought about in the lives of believers through the indwelling power of the Spirit (8:4). This is the "law written in the heart by the Spirit" in fulfillment of the prophetic promises for the final age (Jer 31:33; Ezek 36:26-28). Love is now the fulfillment of all the commandments of the law (13:8-10; cf. Gal 5:14).

The law stands at the heart of Paul's "diagnosis" of the "problem" of *Israel* (Romans 9–11) because he sees this Israel as still intent on pursuing a way of righteousness by law ("works of law") long after this has been shown, in Christ, to be both wrongheaded and outdated (10:4). To continue such a quest is to resist the "righteousness of God," the gracious verdict of righteousness made available to all believers in the Christ event (10:3; cf. 3:21-26). It is to act as if Israel is somehow immune from the verdict of universal human sinfulness (3:9, 23; 5:12d) attested by scripture (3:10-20) and addressed by the kind of Messiah actually sent to Israel by God. Israel "stumbled" at the "rock of offense" constituted by the crucified Messiah (9:32-33) because accepting messianic salvation in this form implied that Israel too was cast in a sinful solidarity with the rest of the human race, a solidarity Paul sums up in the symbolic figure of Adam (5:12-21). What Israel failed to see was that this universal solidarity in sin and death was only the obverse of a much more powerful solidarity in grace, righteousness and (eternal) life, a solidarity modeled and facilitated by God's "counter-Adam": Christ (5:15, 17). The law, then—or, rather, the misguided pursuit of righteousness through "works of the law" (that is, through obedience to its prescriptions)—set Israel on a narrow, exclusive path. Following that path means failure to grasp the fully inclusive scope of God's saving design for the human race preannounced to Israel in the scriptures: that the nations of the world, along with Israel, would "glorify God for his mercy" (15:9; cf. vv 10-13).

The failure of the bulk of Israel to respond positively to the gospel constitutes for Paul the gravest threat to its credibility. How can God's saving plan have gone so tragically awry? Paul for a time (9:6–11:10) embarks upon a tortuous attempt to redefine "Israel" in terms of the elective pattern of God's proceeding and the small Jewish-Christian "remnant" that has accepted Jesus as the Christ. Eventually (11:11-32), however, he reverts to the concept of "all Israel" that, on the basis of God's fidelity, will in the end find inclusion, along with Gentiles, in the community of the saved (11:26-27).

From Paul's overall presentation of the gospel in Romans (1:16–11:36) there emerges a view of a God who always acts faithfully and "inclusively." The God who has acted faithfully in Christ to include Gentiles in the community of salvation (1:16–8:39) will not fail, in due course, to include Israel as well (9:1–11:36)—even if that inclusion will involve, in God's mysterious wisdom, a reversal of the expected order (11:26-36).

The *parenesis* (12:1–15:13) runs along more conventional lines. What is perhaps most striking and characteristic is the image with which it all begins: Christian ethical life constitutes a "rational worship," in which a truly renewed "mind" is capable of discerning what is the will of God for the present situation (12:1-2). As regards relations with one's fellow human beings, whether they concern those inside or outside the believing community, the key norm is that of "love": all the obligations previously expressed in the multiple statutes of the Jewish law are summed up and fulfilled in the single command to love one's neighbor as oneself (12:9-21; 13:8-10).

D. *THE STRUCTURE OF THE LETTER*

Paul's letter to Rome follows the conventional letter pattern as adapted by Paul for his own purposes (see above [B, 2, a]). Setting aside the clearly recognizable Introduction (1:1-17) and Conclusion (15:14–16:24), the most distinctive feature of Romans is the long exposition of the gospel and its practical implications that makes up the central Body of the letter. The contribution of each single section to the overall argument I shall discuss in the appropriate places in the commentary proper. Here, before setting out a schematic outline of the letter's structure as a whole, it will help to draw attention to certain features of the broader divisions into which it falls.

If we set aside the clearly separate final parenesis (12:1–15:13), the Body of the letter falls into three main sections. The first, *1:18–4:25,* sets itself apart from the rest of the letter by reason of having an implied Jewish rather than Gentile Christian "audience." To enhance the claims made for the sole saving power of the righteousness based upon Christian faith, Paul conducts a "dialogue" with a Jewish partner not yet won to faith in Christ in order to exclude the possibility of any rival source of righteousness.

In the second main section, *5:1–8:39,* Paul speaks to a Christian audience about the sure hope arising out of the righteousness established through faith. The section is bound together as a whole by similar opening (5:1-11) and closing (8:31-39) sections, forming something of an "inclusion" (like bookends holding together volumes on a shelf). The core of this second main part of the letter is a lengthy sequence (6:1–8:13) furthering the argument for hope in more distinctly "ethical" terms. Paul argues that believers both can and must live out the righteousness required for eternal life because, in a milieu of God's grace, the enslaving grip of sin, aided and abetted by the law, has been replaced by the liberating gift of the Spirit.

The third distinct main section, *9:1–11:36,* stands apart by reason of its focus upon the issue of Israel's current rejection of the gospel. Following his opening statement of grief at this situation (9:1-5), Paul pursues the issue from various angles: first from the elective pattern of God's dealing, pre-announced in key passages of Israel's scripture (9:6-29); then, from the angle of human response, he points to a continuing quest for righteousness on the basis of law as the chief factor inhibiting acceptance of the crucified Messiah (9:30–10:21); finally, and looking more to the future (11:1-32), he insists that Gentile believers retain a respectful hope for the eventual salvation of "all Israel" on the grounds of the irrevocability of the "calling" and "gifts" of God (11:29). The entire section concludes (11:33-36) with a hymn to the divine wisdom that has set in course a fully inclusive scheme of salvation so outstripping human expectation.

OUTLINE OF THE STRUCTURE OF THE LETTER

INTRODUCTION (1:1-17)
- a) Address and Greeting (1:1-7)
- b) Thanksgiving and Theme (1:8-17)

BODY OF LETTER (1:18–15:13)

I. THE INCLUSIVE SAVING POWER OF THE GOSPEL (1:18–11:36)

A. The Inclusion of the Gentiles on the Basis of Righteousness by Faith (1:18–4:25)

i. No Other Righteousness (1:18–3:20)
- a) The Revelation of God's Wrath Against the Gentile World (1:18-32)
- b) Those Who "judge" Are Not Immune from the Wrath (2:1-11)
- c) Possession of the Law Makes No Difference (2:12-29)
  1. The Law and the Gentiles (2:12-16)
  2. The Law and the Jews (2:17-24)
  3. The "Real Jew" (2:25-29)
- d) God's Faithfulness to Israel Stands (3:1-8)
- e) Scripture's Witness to Universal Lack of Righteousness (3:9-20)

ii. The "Righteousness of God" Now Available to All Believers (3:21-26)

iii. Faith, the Sole Basis upon Which the One God Justifies All (3:27-31)

iv. Scripture's Witness to Righteousness by Faith (4:1-25)
- a) Abraham, Justified on the Basis of Faith (4:1-12)
- b) Abraham, Paradigm Receiver of the Promise on the Basis of Faith (4:13-25)

B. The Sure Hope of Salvation Springing from Righteousness by Faith (5:1–8:39)

i. The Hope That Springs from God's Love (5:1-11)

ii. The Legacy of Christ (Righteousness and Life) Outweighs the Legacy of Adam (Sin and Death) (5:12-21)

iii. The Freedom to Live Out the Righteousness of God (6:1–8:13)
- a) Dead to Sin/Alive to God in Christ (6:1-14)
- b) The New Obedience (6:15-23)
- c) Free in Christ from the Law (7:1-6)
- d) The Fatal Encounter with the Law (7:7-13)
- e) Life Under the Law—Ethical "Impossibility" (7:14-25)
- f) Life in the Spirit—Ethical "Possibility" (8:1-13)

iv. Hope of Glory for God's Children (8:14-30)
  a) Children and Heirs of God (8:14-17)
  b) The "Groaning" of Creation (8:18-22)
  c) The "Groaning" of "Ourselves" (8:23-25)
  d) The "Groaning" of the Spirit (8:26-28) and God's Eternal Plan (8:29-30)
v. The Coming Victory of God's Love (8:31-39)

C. The Inclusion of Israel (9:1–11:36)
i. The Bitter Problem of Israel's Present Unbelief (9:1-5)
ii. The Elective Pattern of God's Working (9:6-29)
  a) The Elective Pattern Shown in the Patriarchs (9:6-13)
  b) The Elective Pattern Shown in Moses and Pharaoh (9:14-18)
  c) God's Freedom Defended Against Human Complaint (9:19-21)
  d) The Elective Pattern Shown in the Composition of the Believing Community (9:22-29)
iii. Israel's Present Rejection of the Gospel (9:30–10:21)
  a) "Stumbling" Before the Righteousness of God (9:30–10:4)
  b) Scripture's Witness to Righteousness by Faith (10:5-13)
  c) Israel Has Heard but Not Responded to the Gospel (10:14-21)
iv. Israel's Ultimate Inclusion in the Community of Salvation (11:1-32)
  a) God Has Not Rejected Israel—the "Remnant" (11:1-10)
  b) Israel's "Stumbling" Has a Saving Purpose (11:11-24)
  c) The "Mystery": the Final Salvation of "All Israel" (11:25-32)
v. Hymn to God's Inscrutable Wisdom (11:33-36)

II. SUMMONS TO LIVE ACCORDING TO THE GOSPEL (12:1–15:13)
i. Christian Life as "Rational Worship" (12:1-2)
ii. The Basic Demands of Christian Living (12:3–13:14)
  a) A Due Assessment of One's Personal Gift (12:3-8)
  b) Love in Action Within the Community (12:9-16)
  c) Love in Action Outside the Community (12:17-21)
  d) Duties Towards Civil Authorities (13:1-7)
  e) The Sole Debt of Love (13:8-10)
  f) "Knowing the Time" (13:11-14)
iii. Tolerance in Contentious Areas of Community Life (14:1–15:13)
  a) The Tolerance Incumbent upon All (14:1-12)
  b) The Tolerance Asked Particularly of the "Strong" (14:13-23)
  c) The Example of Christ as Grounds for Tolerance (15:1-6)
  d) Christ's "Acceptance" as Model for Community Acceptance (15:7-13)

CONCLUSION OF THE LETTER (15:14–16:24[27])
i. Paul's Ministry of the Gospel to the Gentiles (15:14-33)
  a) Paul's Apostolic Mission Until Now (15:14-21)
  b) Paul's Plans for the Future and Concluding "Grace" I (15:22-33)
ii. Commendation and Greetings (16:1-27)
  a) Commendation of Phoebe (16:1-2)
  b) Greetings I (16:3-16)
  c) A Warning (16:17-20)
  d) Greetings II and Concluding "Grace" II (16:21-24)
  e) (Inauthentic) Concluding Doxology (16:25-27)

E. *TWO FURTHER ISSUES*

1. *The Integrity of the Letter*

There is some textual evidence for the existence of shorter editions of the Letter to the Romans—one consisting of chapters 1–14, one of chapters 1–15. The second century writer Marcion worked with a fourteen-chapter edition, a situation also reflected in some manuscripts of the Latin Vulgate. More importantly, the very early papyrus P[46] places the doxology comprising 16:25-27 at the close of chapter 15, thus providing some evidence for the existence of a fifteen-chapter edition to which chapter 16 would have been added at a later time. The suggestion on this basis that chapter 16 is additional is bound up with a long-standing hypothesis that the first fifteen chapters of Romans make up an "encyclical letter" intended by Paul to be read in many churches, with chapter 16 representing a series of greetings appended to the copy sent to a particular church—the church at Ephesus being the candidate usually proposed. This view of the textual history of Romans, especially as promoted by the British scholar T. W. Manson, enjoyed wide favor in the years immediately preceding the Second World War.

Despite the support provided by P[46], however, the "Ephesian" hypothesis does not have many adherents today. There are good grounds for seeing chapter 16, especially the long series of greetings, to be thoroughly integral to Paul's rhetorical purpose in writing to Rome, as the detailed exegesis of the chapter will in due course make clear. The thorough investigation of the entire textual history of Romans undertaken by H. Gamble (see Bibliography) has convinced most interpreters that the canonical form of the letter (minus the concluding doxology [16:25-27] and, possibly, the admonition in 16:17-20) represents the original form of the letter Paul sent to Rome.

2. *Paul and Israel*

There is no need to doubt the genuineness of Paul's anguish over the continuing unbelief of Israel (9:1-3; 10:1). Apart from personal disappointment and separation from his "kindred according to the flesh," Israel's failure in this respect was, as already noted, the single most damaging threat to the credibility of his gospel.

Nonetheless, when as readers today we ask about Paul's attitude to Judaism we are prone to put the question in terms that barely fit the situation he had to face. In a post-Holocaust epoch of growing and long-overdue sensitivity to the way in which the use of Christian scripture can reinforce or legitimate hostile attitudes to Jews and Judaism, we ask the question in terms of a confrontation between two religions, related in their origins but long since gone their separate ways. For Paul, though the *present* rejection of the gospel on the part of Israel was clear, the prospect of a continuing and permanent separation was incompatible with his view of the fidelity of God or the fullness of human salvation (11:25-29). Paul speaks, as a Jew, *within* a wider Israel, the vast bulk of which he believes still has to come to terms with the way God has acted in the messianic age. He finds in this Israel a misreading of the scriptures, which for him pointed not to a narrow, nationally defined Israel exclusive of the rest of humankind but to a broad, inclusive Israel, made up of believers from all nations. He speaks of personally "magnifying" his own ministry to the Gentiles in the hope that, on a "jealousy" basis, more of his Jewish kindred might be won for salvation (11:13-14). Thus Paul is in no sense anti-Semitic nor anti-Jewish if by that one means rejection of "Judaism" as a religion definitively separate from Christianity. Such a separation simply did not prevail when he addressed the issue.

There are indeed interpreters of Paul today—notably Lloyd Gaston and, more recently, S. K. Stowers (see Bibliography)—who dispute that Paul saw faith in Jesus Christ as playing the same salvific role for Jews as it does for Gentiles. In this view, Israel's way to salvation remains that of the Jewish law (Torah); Paul's strictures against the law have to do with its imposition upon Gentiles; he faults Jews not for being sinners alongside the Gentiles but for failing to recognize that, through Christ, God is fulfilling a promise made to Abraham to bring Gentiles into the share of salvation marked out for them. In the context particularly of Jewish-Christian dialogue, such an interpretation of Paul has an undeniable appeal. It fails to do justice, however, to Paul's insistence upon the impartiality of God (Rom 2:11) and the inclusion of *all* (Jews and Gentiles) in solidarities of both sin and grace (3:9, 20, 23; 5:12-21; 10:1-13; 11:30-32; Gal 3:22). In particular, apart from difficulties in other contexts (Rom 3:27-28 in the light of 3:20; 4:4-5; 9:30–10:8; 11:6), it clashes with the obvious meaning of Gal 2:15-16, where Paul explains what coming to faith in the crucified Christ meant for Jews such as Peter and himself: it meant owning themselves to be "sinners" just like the Gentiles, needing justification on a basis other than that of the law.

The challenge Paul saw confronting his fellow Jews is the one the gospel (whether in Romans or in any other New Testament document) puts to every human being: "Repent and believe the good news" (cf. Mark 1:14). Confronted with Israel's resistance to the gospel, Paul associated that resistance specifically with the Jewish law on the grounds that a pursuit of righteousness via the law masked the fundamental need for repentance that a hearing of the gospel presupposed. But a reluctance to admit need for conversion can be a failing to which adherents of any religion, Christianity included, are prone; Judaism has no pre-eminence in this respect. By the same token, the kind of progress in religious understanding and life which the conversion demanded by the Christian gospel involves can take place in any genuine religion, Judaism included.

An authentic interpretation of the Pauline writings will not, then, take the religious attitude Paul necessarily portrayed in terms of the Judaism of his day and see it as characteristic of Judaism for all time. Christians today will hear Paul's letter to the (Gentile) Christians of Rome as "gospel" in so far as they hear the call to conversion which it makes, within the vision of God who acts faithfully to include all within the scope of salvation. In no area is that call more urgent or more poignant than in the area of Christian attitude to Jews and Judaism.

GENERAL BIBLIOGRAPHY

Note: Works listed here are subsequently cited by short title only in the NOTES and FOR REFERENCE AND FURTHER STUDY sections following individual sections of the commentary.

There are separate lists for Romans 8 as a whole, Romans 9-11 as a whole, Rom 12:1–15:13 as a whole, standing before the lists for 8:1-13, 9:1-5 and 12:1-2 respectively; works listed there are subsequently cited by short title only. In the case of multi-author collections, the editor's name is added to the short title to facilitate the finding of the initial full reference.

Commentaries on Romans are cited by author's name and page reference only throughout the commentary.

A. *THE SOCIO-RHETORICAL APPROACH*

Aletti, J.-N. *Comment Dieu est-il juste? Clefs pour interpréter l'épître aux Romains.* Paris: Seuil, 1991.

Aune, D. E. *The New Testament against Its Literary Environment.* Philadelphia: Westminster, 1987, 158–225.

Bitzer, L. "The Rhetorical Situation." *Philosophy and Rhetoric* 1 (1968) 1–14.

Campbell, D. A. "Determining the Gospel through Rhetorical Analysis in Paul's Letter to the Roman Christians." *Gospel in Paul: Studies on Corinthians, Galatians and Romans* (FS R. Longenecker). Eds. L. A. Jervis & P. Richardson. JSNTSup 108; Sheffield: *JSOT*, 1994, 315–36.

Consigny, S. "Rhetoric and Its Situations." *Philosophy and Rhetoric* 7 (1974) 175–86.

Doty, W. G. *Letters in Primitive Christianity.* Philadelphia: Fortress, 1973.

Elliott, N. *The Rhetoric of Romans: Argumentative Constraint and Strategy and Paul's Dialogue with Judaism.* JSNTSup 45; Sheffield: *JSOT*, 1990.

Fiorenza, E. Schüssler. "Rhetorical Situation and Historical Reconstruction in 1 Corinthians." *NTS* 33 (1987) 386–403.

Fraikin, D. "The Rhetorical Function of the Jews in Romans." *Anti-Judaism in Early Christianity.* Vol. 1. *Paul and the Gospels.* Eds. P. Richardson & D. Granskou. Waterloo, Ont.: Wilfrid Laurier University, 1986, 91–105.

Hansen, G. W. Art. "Rhetorical Criticism." *Dictionary of Paul and his Letters* (1993) 599–600.

Jewett, R. "Romans as an Ambassadorial Letter." *Int* 36 (1982) 5–20.

Kennedy, G. *New Testament Interpretation through Rhetorical Criticism.* Chapel Hill: University of North Carolina, 1984.

Perelmann, C. and Olbrechts-Tyteca, L. *The New Rhetoric: A Treatise on Argumentation.* Notre Dame: University of Notre Dame, 1969.

Petersen, N. *Rediscovering Paul: Philemon and the Sociology of Paul's Narrative World.* Philadelphia: Fortress, 1985, 27–29, 57–60, 200–06.

Pontifical Biblical Commission. *The Interpretation of the Bible in the Church.* Rome: Libreria Editrice Vaticana, 1993.

Porter, S. E. and Olbricht, T. H. *Rhetoric and the New Testament: Essays from the Heidelberg 1992 Conference.* JSNTSup 90; Sheffield: *JSOT*, 1993.

Porter, S. E. "The Theoretical Justification for Application of Rhetorical Categories to Pauline Epistolary Literature." *Rhetoric and the New Testament* 100–24.

Reed, J. T. "Using Ancient Rhetorical Categories to Interpret Paul's Letters: A Question of Genre." *Rhetoric and the New Testament* 292–324.

Stamps, D. L. "Rethinking the Rhetorical Situation: The Entextualization of the Situation in the New Testament Epistles." *Rhetoric and the New Testament* 193–210.

Stirewalt, J. M., Jr. "The Form and Function of the Greek Letter Essay." *The Romans Debate: Revised and Expanded Edition.* Ed. K. P. Donfried. Peabody, MA: Hendrickson, 1991, 147–71.

Stowers, S. K. *The Diatribe and Paul's Letter to the Romans.* SBLDS 57; Chico, CA: Scholars, 1981.

________. *Letter Writing in Greco-Roman Antiquity.* Philadelphia: Westminster, 1986.

Vorster, J. N. "Strategies of Persuasion in Romans 1.16-17." in *Rhetoric and the New Testament* 152–70.

Wuellner, W. "Paul's Rhetoric of Argumentation in Romans." *Romans Debate* 128–46.

________. "Where is Rhetorical Criticism Taking Us?" *CBQ* 49 (1987) 448–63.

B. *CHRISTIANITY IN ROME*

Brown, R. E. and Meier, J. P. *Antioch and Rome.* New York: Paulist, 1982, 92–127.

Lampe, P. *Die städtrömischen Christen in den ersten beiden Jahrhunderten.* WUNT 2/18; Tübingen: Mohr, 1987, 3–67.

Meeks, W. A. *The First Urban Christians: The Social World of the Apostle Paul.* New Haven: Yale University, 1983.

Penna, R. "Les juifs à Rome au temps de l'Apôtre Paul." *NTS* 28 (1982) 321–47.

Smallwood, E. M. *The Jews under Roman Rule.* SJLA 20; Leiden: Brill, 1976, 120–38, 201–19.

Stern, M. *Greek and Latin Authors on Jews and Judaism.* 3 vols. Jerusalem: Israel Academy of Sciences and Humanities, 1976–84, 2.88-93 (Tacitus); 2.113-17 (Suetonius).

Walters, J. C. *Ethnic Issues in Paul's Letter to the Romans: Changing Self-Definitions in Earliest Roman Christianity.* Valley Forge, PA: Trinity Press International, 1993.

Watson, F. *Paul, Judaism and the Gentiles: A Sociological Approach.* SNTSMS 56; Cambridge: Cambridge University, 1986, 88–105.

Wiefel, W. "The Jewish Community in Ancient Rome and the Origins of Roman Christianity." *Romans Debate* 85–101.

C. *OCCASION AND PURPOSE OF ROMANS*

Bornkamm, G. "The Letter to the Romans as Paul's Last Will and Testament." *Romans Debate* 16–28.

Byrne, B. "Rather Boldly" (Rom 15,15): Paul's Prophetic Bid to Win the Allegiance of the Christians in Rome." *Biblica* 74 (1993) 83–96.

Donfried, K. P. *The Romans Debate: Revised and Expanded Edition.* Peabody: Hendrickson, 1991.

________. "False Presuppositions in the Study of Romans." *Romans Debate* 102–27.

Jervell, J. "The Letter to Jerusalem." *Romans Debate* 53–64.

Karris, R. J. "Romans 14:1–15:13 and the Occasion of Romans." *Romans Debate* 65–84·

Kettunen, M. *Der Abfassungszsweck des Römerbriefes.* Annales Academiae scientarum Fennicae: dissertationes humanarum litterarum 18; Helsinki: Suomalainen Tiedeakatemia, 1979.

Manson, T. W. "St. Paul's Letter to the Romans—and Others." *Romans Debate* 3–15.

Wedderburn, A. J. M. *The Reasons for Romans.* Edinburgh: Clark, 1988.

D. *COMMENTARIES*

Achtemeier, P. J. *Romans.* Interpretation; Atlanta: John Knox, 1985.

Barrett, C. K. *A Commentary on the Epistle to the Romans.* BNTC/HNTC; London: Black; New York: Harper, 1957; 2nd ed. 1991.

Byrne, B. *Reckoning with Romans: A Contemporary Reading of Paul's Gospel.* Good News Series 18; Wilmington: Glazier, 1986.

Cranfield, C.E.B. *A Critical and Exegetical Commentary on the Epistle to the Romans.* ICC; 2 vols.; Edinburgh: Clark, 1975, 1979.

Dodd, C. H. *The Epistle of Paul to the Romans.* MNTC; London: Hodder & Stoughton, 1932; repr. Fontana (Collins): 1959.

Dunn, J.D.G. *Romans.* WBC 38; 2 vols. Dallas: Word Books, 1988.

Fitzmyer, J. A. *Romans.* AB 33; New York: Doubleday, 1993.

Heil, J. P. *Paul's Letter to the Romans: A Reader-Response Commentary.* New York: Paulist, 1987.

Käsemann, E. *Commentary on Romans.* Trans. G. W. Bromiley (HNT 8a; 4th ed.; Tübingen: Mohr, 1980). Grand Rapids: Eerdmans, 1980.

Kuss, O. *Der Römerbrief übersetz und erklärt.* RNT; 3 vols. (chapters 1–11). Regensburg: Pustet, 1957, 1959, 1978.

Lagrange, M.-J. *Saint Paul: Épître aux Romains.* EB; 4th ed. Paris: Gabalda, 1931.

Lietzmann, H. *An die Römer.* HNT 8; 5th ed. Tübingen: Mohr, 1971.
Michel, O. *Der Brief an die Römer.* MeyerK 4; 14th ed. Göttingen: Vandenhoeck & Ruprecht, 1978.
Robinson, J.A.T. *Wrestling with Romans.* London: SCM; Philadelphia: Westminster, 1979.
Sanday, W. and Headlam, A. C. *A Critical and Exegetical Commentary on the Epistle to the Romans.* ICC; 5th ed. Edinburgh: Clark, 1902.
Schlier, H. *Der Römerbrief: Kommentar.* HTKNT 6; Freiburg im Breisgau: Herder, 1977.
Schmithals, W. *Der Römerbrief. Ein Kommentar.* Gütersloh: Mohn, 1988.
Segundo, J. L. *The Humanist Christology of Paul.* Maryknoll, NY: Orbis; London: Sheed & Ward, 1986.
Wilckens, U. *Der Brief an die Römer.* EKK 6; 3 vols. Neukirchen-Vluyn: Neukirchener Verlag, 1978, 1980, 1982.
Zeller, D. *Der Brief an die Römer übersetzt und erklärt.* RNT; Regensburg: Pustet, 1985.
Ziesler, J. *Paul's Letter to the Romans.* TPINTC; London: SCM; Philadelphia: Trinity, 1989.

E. *GENERAL*

Barrett, C. K. *From First Adam to Last: A Study in Pauline Theology.* London: Black; New York: Scribners, 1962.
Beker, J. C. *Paul the Apostle: The Triumph of God in Life and Thought.* Philadelphia: Fortress; London: SCM, 1980.
Bjerkelund, C. J. *PARAKALŌ: Form, Funktion und Sinn der parakalō-Sätze in den paulinischen Briefen.* Oslo: Universitetsforlaget, 1967.
Bornkamm, G. *Early Christian Experience.* New York: Harper & Row; London: SCM, 1969.
________. *Paul.* Trans. D.G.M. Stalker. London: Hodder & Stoughton, 1971.
Bultmann, R. *Theology of the New Testament.* 2 vols. London: SCM, 1952, 1955; New York: Scribners, 1955.
Byrne, B. "Living out the Righteousness of God: The Contribution of Rom 6:1–8:13 to an Understanding of Paul's Ethical Presuppositions." *CBQ* 43 (1981) 557–81.
________. *'Sons of God'—'Seed of Abraham': A Study of the Idea of the Sonship of God of All Christians in Paul against the Jewish Background.* AnBib 83; Rome: Biblical Institute, 1979.
Dahl, N. A. *Studies in Paul: Theology for the Early Christian Mission.* Minneapolis: Augsburg, 1977.
Davies, G. N. *Faith and Obedience in Romans: A Study in Romans 1–4.* JSNTSup 39; Sheffield: *JSOT*, 1990.
Davies, W. D. *Paul and Rabbinic Judaism.* 4th ed.; Philadelphia: Fortress, 1980.
Deidun, T. J. *New Covenant Morality in Paul.* AnBib 89; Rome: Biblical Institute, 1981.
Dülmen, A. van *Die Theologie des Gesetzes bei Paulus.* SBM 5; Stuttgart: Katholisches Bibelwerk, 1968.

Furnish, V. P. *Theology and Ethics in Paul.* Nashville: Abingdon, 1968.

________. *The Moral Teaching of Paul: Selected Issues.* 2nd ed. Nashville: Abingdon, 1985.

Gamble, H., Jr. *The Textual History of the Letter to the Romans.* Studies and Documents 42; Grand Rapids: Eerdmans, 1977.

Gaston, L. *Paul and the Torah.* Vancouver: University of British Columbia, 1987.

Hays, R. B. *Echoes of Scripture in the Letters of Paul.* New Haven and London: Yale University, 1989.

Hofius, O. "Das Gesetz des Mose und das Gesetz Christi." *Paulusstudien.* WUNT 51; Tübingen: Mohr, 1989, 50–74 (orig. 1983).

Hübner, H. *The Law in Paul's Thought.* Edinburgh: Clark, 1984.

Jewett, R. *Paul's Anthropological Terms.* Leiden: Brill, 1971.

Käsemann, E. *Essays on New Testament Themes.* Naperville, IL: Allenson; London: SCM, 1964.

________. *New Testament Questions of Today.* Philadelphia: Fortress; London: SCM, 1969.

________. *Perspectives on Paul.* Philadelphia: Fortress; London: SCM, 1971.

Kertelge, K. *'Rechtfertigung' bei Paulus: Studien zur Struktur und zum Bedeutungsgehalt des paulinischen Rechtfertigungsbegriff.* NTAbh N.F. 3; 2nd ed. Münster: Aschendorff, 1971.

Lyonnet, S. *Études sur l'Epître aux Romains.* AnBib 120; Rome: Pontifical Biblical Institute, 1989.

Martin, B. L. *Christ and the Law in Paul.* NovTSup 62; Leiden: Brill, 1989.

Moo, D.J. "'Law', 'Works of the Law', and Legalism in Paul." *WTJ* 45(1983) 73–100.

________. "Paul and the Law in the Last Ten Years." *SJT* 40 (1987) 287–307.

Moxnes, H. *Theology in Conflict: Studies in Paul's Understanding of God in Romans.* NovTSup 53; Leiden: Brill, 1980.

Munck, J. *Paul and the Salvation of Mankind.* London: SCM, 1959.

Räisänen, H. *Paul and the Law.* Philadelphia: Fortress, 1983.

Rhyne, C. T. *Faith Establishes the Law.* SBLDS 55; Chico, CA: Scholars, 1981.

Sanders, E. P. *Paul and Palestinian Judaism: A Comparison of Patterns of Religion.* Philadelphia: Fortress; London: SCM, 1977.

________. *Paul, the Law and the Jewish People.* Philadelphia: Fortress, 1983.

Scott, J. M. *Adoption as Sons of God: An Exegetical Investigation into the Background of HYIOTHESIA in the Pauline Corpus.* WUNT 2/48; Tübingen: Mohr, 1992.

Scroggs, R. *The Last Adam: A Study in Pauline Anthropology.* Philadelphia: Fortress; Oxford: Blackwell, 1966.

Segal, A. *Paul the Convert: The Apostolate and Apostasy of Saul the Pharisee.* New Haven and London: Yale University, 1990.

Stacey, W. D. *The Pauline View of Man.* London: Macmillan, 1956.

Stendahl, K. *Paul Among Jews and Gentiles.* Philadelphia: Fortress; London: SCM, 1977.

Stowers, S. K. *A Rereading of Romans: Justice, Jews & Gentiles.* New Haven: Yale University, 1994.

Theissen, G. *Psychological Aspects of Pauline Theology.* Philadelphia: Fortress; Edinburgh: Clark, 1987.

Thielmann, F. *From Plight to Solution: A Jewish Framework for Understanding Paul's View of the Law in Galatians and Romans.* NovTSup 61; Leiden: Brill, 1989.

Thüsing, W. *Per Christum in Deum: Studien zum Verhältnis von Christozentrik und Theozentrik in den paulinischen Hauptbriefen* NTAbh NF 1; 2nd ed. Münster: Aschendorff, 1969.

Tomson, P. J. *Paul and the Jewish Law: Halakha in the Letters of the Apostle to the Gentiles* CRINT III. 1. Assen/Maastricht: Van Gorcum; Minneapolis: Fortress, 1990.

Vanhoye, A. (ed.) *L' Apôtre Paul: Personnalité, style et conception du ministère.* BETL 73; Louvain: Leuven University, 1986.

Vollenweider, S. *Freiheit als neue Schöpfung. Eine Untersuchung zur Eleutheria bei Paulus und in seiner Umwelt.* FRLANT 147; Göttingen: Vandenhoeck & Ruprecht, 1989.

Watson, F. *Paul, Judaism and the Gentiles: A Sociological Approach.* SNTSMS 56; Cambridge: Cambridge University, 1986.

Westerholm, S. *Israel's Law and the Church's Faith: Paul and His Recent Interpreters.* Grand Rapids: Eerdmans, 1988.

Winger, M. *By What Law? The Meaning of Nomos in the Letters of Paul.* SBLDS 128; Chico, CA: Scholars, 1992.

Williams, S. K. "The 'Righteousness of God' in Romans." *JBL* 99 (1980) 241–90.

Wright, N. T. *The Climax of the Covenant: Christ and the Law in Pauline Theology.* Edinburgh: Clark, 1991.

Zeller, D. *Juden und Heiden in der Mission des Paulus: Studien zum Römerbrief.* Stuttgart: Katholisches Bibelwerk, 1973.

________. "Zur neueren Diskussion über das Gesetz bei Paulus." *TP* 62 (1987) 481–99.

________. "Der Zusammenhang von Gesetz und Sünde im Römerbrief. Kritischer Nachvollzug der Auslegung von Ulrich Wilckens." *TZ* 38 (1982) 193–212.

Ziesler, J. *Pauline Christianity.* Rev. ed. Oxford and New York: Oxford University, 1990.

TRANSLATION, INTERPRETATION, NOTES

INTRODUCTION (1:1-17)

a) *Address and Greeting* (1:1-7)

1. Paul, a servant of Jesus Christ, called to be an apostle, set apart for the
gospel of God, 2. which he announced beforehand through his prophets
in the holy scriptures, 3. the gospel concerning his Son,
who was descended from David according to the flesh,
4. who was designated Son of God in power according to
the Spirit of holiness by his resurrection from the dead,
Jesus Christ our Lord,
5. through whom we have received the gift of apostleship to bring about
an obedience of faith for the sake of his name among all the Gentiles, 6.
including yourselves who are called to belong to Jesus Christ. 7. To all
God's beloved in Rome, who are called to be saints: Grace to you and
peace from God our Father and the Lord Jesus Christ.

INTERPRETATION

Introduction. Writing to a community which he has not founded but whose goodwill towards himself is crucial for his future plans, Paul faces a significant rhetorical challenge. He must employ the customary literary conventions in such a way as to gain at least a foothold upon the goodwill of the community so that they will give a sympathetic hearing to his presentation of the gospel. The Introduction must create an *ethos* or sense of fellow feeling between the speaker or writer and the audience addressed. Paul has to throw a line to the Roman community across what is possibly a troubled sea of prejudice and misunderstanding as far as he himself and his mission are concerned. He must communicate a sense of his authority as apostle, without alienating the community from the start by appearing highhanded.

The Introduction of Paul's letter to Rome contains the conventional epistolary Address (vv 1-7a) and Greeting (v 7b), the Thanksgiving customary in Pauline letters (vv 8-15) and a solemn statement of Theme (vv 16-17). In Greco-Roman letters of a personal kind, the Introduction is usually a very simple affair (e.g., "Demetrius to Gaius: Greetings"). In Paul's earliest letter, 1 Thessalonians, the same simplicity prevails (cf. 1:1) but subsequent letters show a tendency to add epithets to the naming of both writer and recipients in the Address. It becomes normal for him to introduce himself as "apostle" (1 Cor 1:1; 2 Cor 1:1; Gal 1:1; cf. Col 1:1; Eph 1:1). In Romans, however (cf. already Gal 1:1), the delicacy and complexity of the task leads to a remarkable expansion of the epithets qualifying "apostle" (vv 1-2) and to the attachment of an early Christian creed or summary of the gospel (vv 3-4). This enables Paul to present his apostolic status, its specific direction to the Gentiles and claim upon the (Gentile) community in Rome (vv 5-6) as something grounded in the power of the risen Lord, which the Roman Christians, along with all believers, acknowledge.

Paul: apostle and servant of the gospel (vv 1-2). Paul introduces himself (v 1) first of all as a "servant" (cf. also Phil 1:1) of Christ Jesus. The Greek word *doulos* more normally means "slave" and in this sense could be applied to all believers, who confess Jesus as their "Lord" (*kyrios;* cf. 10:9; 14:4, 7-9) and whose entire existence represents a "service" *(douleuein)* of God (Rom 6:16; 7:6; 12:11; 14:18; 16:18; 1 Cor 7:22; 1 Thess 1:9). But Paul probably uses it more specifically with reference to his own "service" as minister of the gospel (cf. Gal 1:10). The designation aligns Paul with key figures described as God's "servant(s)" in the scriptural tradition—Moses, Joshua, David, prophets in general. Paul sets in train a bold and striking insertion of himself into the scriptural history of salvation that will recur in the course of the letter (vv 5, 14; 11:1-3; 15:15-21).

Similar prophetic allusions underlie the sense of being a "called apostle" *(klētos apostolos)*. In itself the word "apostle" simply means someone "sent" by another (cf. Phil 2:25 [Epaphroditus] and 2 Cor 8:23). But Paul, along with other strains of the early New Testament tradition, uses the phrase "the apostles" in a more technical, distinctively Christian sense to denote a leading group within the wider community of believers (1 Cor 9:6 [in the light of 9:1, 5]; 12:28; 15:3-8; see Note). For Paul, to be an apostle means both to have seen the risen Lord and to have been commissioned by him to preach the gospel and found churches. Paul had to argue for and defend his status as "apostle" (1 Cor 9:1-2; 2 Cor 11:5, 13; 12:11-12). By describing himself here as a "called apostle" he is pointing out that for him personally the vocation to be apostle and the vocation to be follower of Jesus are one and the same thing: the risen Lord who "called" him to faith on the Damascus road also made him, from that moment on, a "sent" herald of the gospel (cf. Gal 1:1; 1:15-16a). The additional sense of being "set apart *(aphōrismenos)* for the gospel of God" evokes the terms in which prophets such as (Second) Isaiah (49:1) and Jeremiah (1:5; cf. *As. Mos.* 1:14) describe their experience of the divine call. Paul sets himself and his mission firmly in continuity with such prophetic antecedents.

The gospel for which Paul has been "set apart" has been "announced beforehand" by his prophets in the holy scriptures" (v 2). This allusion almost certainly signals awareness that "gospel" (Greek *euangelion*) in Christian usage derives from the use of the corresponding Hebrew verbal form *bśr*/*mbśr* in (Second) Isaiah in connection with the announcement to Zion of the "good news" of God's saving intervention (40:9; 41:27; 52:7; 60:6; 61:1; cf. Ps 40:9 [LXX 39:10]; 96:2 [LXX 95:2]; Nah 1:15; see Note). For Paul and other early Christian writers the content of the "good news" was no longer freedom for the exiles in Babylon but a "preannouncement" of the eschatological liberation which God has inaugurated for all peoples in Christ. Paul associates his apostolic role with that of the scriptural prophets since he is the herald who announces the actual realization of the salvation they foretold.

The content of the gospel (vv 3-4). The "gospel of *God*," for which Paul as apostle has been "set apart," is also the gospel "concerning his Son" (v 3). The gospel has this christological focus because God has inaugurated the eschatological liberation which it proclaims by setting up Jesus as messianic agent of the promised liberation. The credal formula which Paul cites to indicate this envisages what might be called the "messianic career" of Jesus in two stages. 1. In terms of his human origins ("according to the flesh"), Jesus fulfills a key requirement for messianic "candidacy" in the understanding of early Christianity and some Jewish circles: birth from the royal house of David. 2. As raised from the dead and entered thereby into the new age marked by the Spirit ("according to the Spirit of holiness"), the messianic "candidate" has been "installed" Messiah in fact ("designated Son of God in power"). The central content of the "good news" ("gospel"), then, is that God has inaugurated the era of messianic liberation by taking the step of setting up the key instrument of that liberation: Jesus Christ as "Son of God" in power (cf. Ps 2:7; 1 Cor 15:23-28).

Along with the biblical background ([Second] Isaiah) noted above, the use of "gospel" in this connection would sound very appropriate to Greek-speaking hearers accustomed to the use of the word *euangelion* (chiefly in the plural form *euangelia*) in connection with royal births, weddings, inauguration of reigns and anniversaries (see Note). The "gospel" tells the "good news" that Jesus is risen and entered into his active reign as risen "Lord" (*kyrios*; cf. Ps 110:1). For believers he is "our Lord" (Rom 1:4) in an intimate sense (cf. 14:7-9). But he also reigns as messianic "Lord," with a divine mandate to bring about the "subjection" of the universe to the glory of God (Phil 2:9-11; cf. 1 Cor 3:21-23; 15:23-28; Phil 3:20-21).

Paul's personal grace: apostle to the Gentiles (vv 5-6). The "definition" of the gospel which Paul has just given is really part of his own self-definition and self-presentation to his audience. The gospel announcement of Jesus' installation as Messiah and Lord provides the background against which to present his own distinctive vocation (v 5). In Paul's understanding, each and every believer has a particular gift *(charis)* bestowed by the Spirit (cf. 12:4-8; 1 Cor 7:7; 12:1–14:40); through the gifts operative in the concrete circumstances of individual human lives, the risen Lord as Spirit carries on his messianic role in the community and the world. Paul's distinctive gift is that of being, not only "apostle," but apostle charged with a unique responsibility for bringing the peoples of the world (Gentiles) into the community of salvation.

Paul's description of this charge—that of bringing about "an obedience of faith (*eis hypakoēn pisteōs;* cf. also 15:18) for the sake of his name"—seems designed to evoke the biblical sense of Israel as "obedient nation." Obedience to God's covenant grace, enacted in observance of the Torah, stood at the center of Israel's self-understanding as God's people. The daily recitation of the *Shemaʿ* ("Hear, O Israel, . . ." [Deut 6:4-6]) served as a constant reminder of special status and responsibility. Now the nations of the world, hitherto characterized by "disobedience" (11:30) and refusal to glorify God (1:19-28), are to be drawn through the gospel into the sphere of the "obedience" that is the mark of the eschatological people of God.

The response sought is an "obedience of faith" in that it proceeds from faith's acknowledgment of and surrender to what God has done through Jesus Christ. As such it is an "obedience" accessible to all human beings, not tied to the religious "system" of any particular nation or culture—notably (though any allusion remains purely implicit at this stage) the religious "system" (Torah) of Israel. It is an "obedience for the sake of his name" in that it draws the nations of the world into the glorification of God's name (cf. 15:7-11). This glorification reverses the original "suppression of the truth about God" (1:18; cf. vv 23, 25, 28) and sets human beings in line to arrive at that fullness of humanity which is the original design of the Creator in their regard (8:28-30; 1 Cor 3:21b-23).

The Addressees (vv 6-7a). Having stated his unique apostolic responsibility for the evangelization of the peoples of the world so solemnly in this way, Paul prepares for the final part of the Address (the naming of the recipients of the letter) by including his audience within that Gentile world (v 6). The inclusion firmly establishes the implied audience of the letter as Gentile Christians in Rome. It may also convey a first suggestion that they too, in so far as they are Gentiles, come within the scope of the responsibility bestowed on him by Christ. Nonetheless, Paul acknowledges their Christian status by applying to them the standard epithets attaching to God's people, inherited by believers from the Jewish tradition. As addressed by the gospel and responsive to it, they are "called" (*klētoi*, cf. 8:30; 9:24-25). They are "saints" (*hagioi*)—not primarily because of the moral quality of their lives but through their membership of a people that is "holy" because of its closeness and dedication to God. By the same token, as God's people, they are "beloved" (*agapēmenoi*; cf. 9:25; 1 Thess 1:4). Paul addresses the Gentile Roman Christians as full citizens of the inclusive eschatological Israel summoned and called into being by the gospel.

The Grace (v 7b). There remains only to complete the Introduction to the letter with the Greeting in the full, christianized form standard in all Paul's mature letters (contrast 1 Thess 1:1). As a whole, the Address and Greeting remain recognizably within the bounds of epistolary convention. Nonetheless, by presenting himself as instrument of the gospel to the Gentiles, backed by the authority of the risen Lord, Paul sets in motion a powerful claim upon the community of Gentile believers in Rome.

NOTES

1. *a servant of Jesus Christ:* For the LXX use of *doulos* to describe key figures of the OT as "servants" (of the Lord, of God), see, with respect to the Patriarchs: LXX Ps 104(105):42; LXX Dan 3:35; 2 Macc 1:2; to Moses: 2 Kgs 18:12; Mal 4:4; Dan 9:11; LXX Ps 104(105):26; Neh 9:14; 10:29(30); to Joshua: Josh 24:29; Judg 2:8; David: LXX Pss 77(78):70; 131(132):10; 143(144):10; Ezek 28:25; 37:24, 25; 1 Macc 4:30; all the prophets generally: 2 Kgs 17:23; 24:2; Amos 3:7; Ezek 38:17; Zech 1:6.

   called to be an apostle: "Apostle" was a somewhat fluid and controversial term in the NT period. The author of Luke-Acts created what came to be the traditional understanding—the "Twelve Apostles"—by identifying "apostles" with "The Twelve" (companions of the earthly Jesus; cf. esp. Acts 1:15-26). But this identification is comparatively late and one Paul himself would contest (2 Cor 5:16). In itself and in general usage "*apostolos*" simply designates someone sent by another; cf. in this sense the description of Epaphras as "apostle" of the Philippian church (Phil 2:25) and the allusion to "apostles of the churches" in 2 Cor 8:23. But Paul, along with other strands of the earlier tradition, uses the phrase "the apostles" in a more technical, distinctively Christian sense, to refer to a specific, significant group within the wider community of believers (1 Cor 9:1-2, 5; 12:28; Acts 14:4, 14 [pre-Lucan tradition, referring to Paul and Barnabas]). The list of resurrection witnesses given in 1 Cor 15:3-8 makes clear that "the apostles" (v 7) were formally distinct from "the Twelve" (v 5)—though there was clearly an overlap in the case of some individuals (notably Cephas; cf. Gal 1:18-19). For Paul, to be an apostle means to have seen the risen Lord, to have been commissioned and sent by him to found churches and to have demonstrated the genuineness of this commissioning through hard labors (cf. 1 Cor 9:1; 15:8-10). The struggle to have his own apostolic status accepted probably had a lot to do with the "lateness" of his vision of the risen Lord (1 Cor 15:8). But he insists on the essential parity of his experience (cf. 1 Cor 9:1) as one commissioned "not through human beings or by human beings, but through Christ Jesus" (Gal 1:1; cf. Rom 1:1; 1 Cor 1:1; 2 Cor 1:1). The key issue for Paul is whether one is truly "sent" by the risen Lord (cf. the concept of "pseudo-apostles" in 2 Cor 11:13-15). Later in Romans (16:7) Paul acknowledges the apostolic status of two persons in Rome, Andronicus and Junia; see Note on 16:7.

the gospel of God: The Greek noun "gospel" *euangelion,* together with the cognate verbal form *euangelizesthai,* appears in Paul's writings more frequently than elsewhere in the NT. Christian use of the motif, however, almost certainly predates Paul, owing something to both the OT-Jewish and the secular Hellenistic backgrounds. In the Hebrew scriptures a noun, *bĕśôrâ* occurs rather rarely (6 times) in the sense of "news" or "reward for bringing good news." Much more frequent is the participial form *mĕbaśśēr* in the sense of "one who brings news" (e.g., 1 Sam 31:9; 1 Kgs 1:42; Jer 20:15). Particularly noteworthy are a cluster of usages in Second (and Third) Isaiah: 40:9; 41:27; 52:7; 60:6; 61:1, with which may be associated usages in Ps 96:2 (LXX 95:2) and Nah 1:15 (LXX 2:1); (cf. also Ps 40:9 [LXX 39:10]). All these have to do with the announcement of a coming salvation and liberation connected with the exercise of the sovereignty and rule of God.

A fragmentary text from Qumran, *11Q Melchizedek* (11Q13), shows a significant development of this tradition in that it associates the key Isaiah *mĕbaśśēr* texts (Isa 52:7 and 61:1) and refers them to a message of eschatological atonement and liberation to be brought about by a high-priestly figure (Melchizedek/Michael); the messenger of this good news (*mĕbaśśēr*) appears to be designated as the "one anointed with the Spirit." Similarly the newly published "Messianic Apocalypse" (4Q521) includes the proclaiming of the good news amongst other activity characteristic of the eschatological (messianic?) era (Frag 2; 2:14; cf. also 1 QH 18:14). These (admittedly fragmentary) texts from Qumran show that, just prior to the rise of Christianity, a Jewish apocalyptic sect consciously associated the Isaiah "*mĕbaśśēr*" texts with the awaited eschatological intervention of God. Like early Christianity and Paul in particular (Rom 1:2), it understood Isaiah's messenger of good news to be referring primarily to the salvation it longed for in its own era (cf. also *Pss. Sol.* 11:1).

Quite lacking, however, in the biblical background (as also in Hellenistic Jewish writers such as Josephus and Philo) is anything corresponding to the Christian use of the singular noun *euangelion* in the sense of "gospel."

In the wider Greek-speaking world the noun *euangelion,* almost always in the plural form *euangelia,* occurs regularly in connection with the announcement of a birth, a marriage or an anniversary (cf. esp. NDIEC 3.10–15, esp. 14–15). A distinctive usage appears in connection with the proclamation of the accession or birthday of rulers, notably the Roman emperor, of which the Priene Inscription (9 B.C.E.) is the best known example: ". . . the birthday of the god (Caesar Augustus) has been for the whole world the beginning of the gospel (*euangelia*); concerning him, therefore, let all reckon a new era beginning from the date of his birth, . . ." A sacral aura, the sense of a new age dawning, attaches to such usages in a manner not dissimilar to the claims made by Christians for the risen Jesus. It is well likely that Christian proclamation of those claims in terms of *euangelion* evoked and were designed to evoke overtones of the more general usage.

As regards the background to the Christian use of "gospel," it is probably necessary, then, to reckon both with influence from the scriptural Isaianic tradition and a certain "inculturation" within the wider Greco-Roman milieu.

The phrase "gospel of God" reflects the earliest sense (cf. Mark 1:14) where the content of the "gospel" is not, as usually in Paul, the messianic status and rule of the once-crucified, now-risen Jesus (cf. esp. 1 Cor 15:3-4) but rather a proclamation of the coming rule of God (cf. Rev 14:6), as in the Qumran texts and, in all likelihood, the preaching of Jesus himself (cf. Matt 11:5 // Luke 7:22 [= "Q"]). It was the early post-resurrection community that drew the announcement of Jesus' death and resurrectional instatement as Messiah (Rom 1:3-4; 1 Cor 15:3-5) into the central content of the "gospel," so that the "gospel of God" became also the "gospel about Jesus Christ" (cf. Rom 1:3).

2. *announced beforehand:* While the Greek verb *proepangellesthai* usually has the sense of "promise beforehand" (e.g., BAGD 705), the more basic sense of "announce beforehand" (cf. LSJ 1478) conveys more effectively Paul's sense of scripture as primarily addressed to the present (eschatological) age (cf. 15:4; 1 Cor 9:10). The prophets (writing) in the "holy scriptures" did not simply "promise" good news at a future date but actually made an anticipatory proclamation of the gospel, which is now being realized (cf. Gal 3:8) and "heard" when they are read.

3–4. Considerations of both form and content suggest that embedded within these verses lies a formulaic summary of the gospel cited from the common Christian tradition. The (Pauline) opening ("concerning his Son") and closing ("Jesus Christ, our Lord") phrases flank a two-stage presentation of the "messianic career" of Jesus, presenting a striking—if not entirely perfect—parallelism of words and phrases (several untypical of Paul; see comments on individual phrases below):

who was descended from David according to the flesh,
who was designated Son of God . . . according to the Spirit of holiness

Paul may have added the somewhat intrusive "in power" phrase after "Son of God" in order to lessen the discrepancy between his own view of the divine sonship of Christ and that of the formula. For a recent defense of Pauline authorship, cf. J. M. Scott, *Adoption as Sons of God* 223–44.

3. *concerning his Son:* This introductory Pauline phrase overwrites the more primitive christology of the credal formula. The latter associates Christ's divine sonship with the moment of his resurrection, whereas in Paul's eyes Jesus is uniquely God's Son (cf. 5:10; 8:3, 29, 32; 1 Cor 1:9; 15:28; 2 Cor 1:19; Gal 1:16; 2:20; 4:4; 1 Thess 1:10), not simply from the time of his resurrection but during his earthly obedience and possibly even as "pre-existent" (cf. the "sending" statements: 8:3; Gal 4:4); see Note on 8:3 and Byrne, *'Sons of God'* 97–211.

   who was descended from David: The Greek verb *ginesthai*, used here in participial form, has more commonly the general sense of "come to be," "become," rather than "be born" (for which the passive form of *gennân* would be usual). The prevalence of the former verb in Pauline christological formulae (Gal 4:4; cf. 3:13; Phil 2:7; Rom 15:8) may hint at a belief that Jesus' human birth was not necessarily the beginning of his personal existence. The present formula embraces the early Christian belief (see esp. Matt 1:1-17, 20; Luke 1:17, 32; 2:4; 3:23-31; Acts 2:29-30; 2 Tim 2:8; Rev 5:5; 22:16) that Jesus was of Davidic descent. The complexity of Jewish messianic belief at the time of Jesus has been increasingly recognized. However, there were undoubtedly circles which interpreted the biblical oracles (2 Sam 7:14-17; 23:1-7; Pss 18:50; 89:35-37, 49; 132:11, 17 [cf. Pss 2:7; 110:1]; Isa 9:6-7; 11:1; Jer 23:5; Ezek 37:24-25; 1 Chr 28:2-8; 2 Chr 6:14-17; 28:4 [cf. also the reference to an "anointed prince" in Dan 9:25]) as foretelling the rise of an anointed prince of David's line who would play a key role in bringing about the restoration of Israel's fortunes in both a political and religious sense. Qumran messianism certainly included expectation of such a Davidic prince, along with priestly and prophetic figures (1QSa 2:14; CD 7:18-20; 4QpGen^{a} 5:1-4; 4QFlor 1:11-13; 4QpIsa^{a} Frags. 8-10 Col. 3:10-18; 4QTest 9-13; cf. also *Pss. Sol.* 17:21-46; 18:5-9). It is not surprising, then, that descent from David should feature in an early Christian credal formula asserting the messianic status of Jesus (cf. esp. 2 Tim 2:8).

   according to the flesh: "Flesh" *(sarx)* here refers simply to the this-worldly, natural origins of Jesus (cf. 9:5; also 4:1), without the pejorative sense it normally has in Paul, especially when paired off with "spirit" *(pneuma)*; see Interpretation and Note on 7:5.

4. *designated Son of God in power:* When used of persons, the Greek verb *horizein* has the sense of "appoint," "install" (cf. esp. Acts 10:42; 17:31). The meaning "declare," which would give a less "adoptionist" tone to the statement of Jesus' divine sonship in the present formula, is not strictly attested in the NT. The "adoptionist" tone is avoided if the phrase "in power," possibly a Pauline addition to the original formula, is taken closely with "Son of God" (rather than with the verb), leaving open the possibility that Jesus was "already" Son of God before his resurrection but in a hidden way where his power was not displayed (cf. 2 Cor 13:4).

   The Hebrew scriptures refer to the Israelite king in terms of divine filiation (Ps 2:7-8 [cf. LXX Ps 109 (110):3]; 2 Sam 7:14; Ps 89:26-27), though the actual title "son of God" never appears in this connection. In later literature it is applied to the individual just Israelite (Wis 2:18; cf. 2:13, 16; 5:5). Thus in the Jewish tradition the title of itself does not imply anything beyond human status. There is as yet no explicit evidence linking "Son of God" with messianic expectation in pre-Christian Jewish literature, though the circumstantial evidence that such was the case is very strong, most notably in the shape of the "pseudo-Danielic" text from Qumran (4QpsDan A[a] [= 4Q246] 2:1), where, in an apocalyptic context, a ruler who serves as God's instrument is hailed as "Son of God" and "Son of the Most High" (see Byrne, *'Sons of God'* 60–62, 223). In the NT the equivalence of "Son of God" and "(Davidic) Messiah" seems to be taken for granted in several contexts: e.g., Matt 26:63; Luke 1:32; Acts 9:20-22. In the present case (Rom 1:4), at the level of the original formula, "Son of God" is probably best taken in the messianic sense—even if as quoted and introduced by Paul it indicates a status going well beyond conventional (merely) messianic expectation (see Byrne, *'Sons of God'* 197–211).

according to the Spirit of holiness: The Greek phrase *kata pneuma hagiôsynēs*, featuring the Semitic adjectival genitive, has a biblical anticipation in the Hebrew of Ps 51:11 (MT 51:13) and Isa 63:10-11 and parallels in Qumran literature (1QS 4:21; 8:16; 9:3; 1QH 7:6-7; 9:32). The Greek phrase occurs in the *Testament of Levi:* ". . . and he (the eschatological Priest) will grant to the saints to eat of the tree of life. The spirit of holiness shall be upon them. And Beliar shall be bound by him and he shall grant to his children the authority to trample on wicked spirits" (18:11-12). This is a significant parallel to the christological statement in Rom 1:4 because it links possession or imparting of the spirit with authority and power to overcome forces hostile to God (cf. 1 Cor 15:25-28). In Rom 1:4 the reference is almost certainly to the Spirit of God. The risen Lord's imparting of the Spirit (1 Cor 15:45; 2 Cor 3:18; cf. John 20:19-23) indicates his own messianic status and the dawn of the new age. "Before" the resurrection, Jesus' messianic qualifications could only be based upon his "fleshly" descent from David; post-resurrection, they are palpable in the shape of the Spirit.

by his resurrection from the dead: The phrase is best taken in a temporal sense (= "since"), as it is from the moment of the resurrection that the "Son" status of Jesus is made known. Paul elsewhere (1 Cor 15:12, 13, 42) uses the phrase *anastasis nekrōn* with reference to the *general* resurrection.

Jesus Christ, our Lord: Closing the formula, Paul sets in apposition to the preceding two christological titles his own preferred one: "Lord" (*kyrios*). The phrase "Jesus is Lord" represents possibly the most primitive Christian confession of faith (1 Cor 12:3; Phil 2:9-11; Rom 10:9, 12-13), the title itself being so venerable as to warrant the preservation of its Aramaic form *(mar)* in the Greek-speaking communities (1 Cor 16:22: *"Maranatha"*). Owning Jesus as "Lord," believers enlist themselves in his service (14:7-9); through their readiness to allow the pattern of his death and resurrection to be reproduced in their own lives they set themselves in line to share also his lordship of the universe (Phil 2:9-11; 1 Cor 3:21b-23; cf. Rom 5:17).

5. *an obedience of faith:* This much-discussed genitive construct (appearing again in the deutero-Pauline doxology at 16:26) is open to three main interpretations in grammatical terms: 1. obedience to the faith (objective genitive:

understanding "faith" as the content of the message, as in Gal 1:23; cf. 2:3, 5); 2. obedience required by faith or which faith works (subjective genitive); 3. obedience which consists in faith (explanatory or qualifying genitive). The last gives the best sense in the present context, where the focus lies upon initial response rather than upon continuing pattern of life. While obedience and faith are closely related concepts in Paul's understanding (cf. 10:16a and 10:16b), it is unhelpful to regard them as virtually interchangeable, thereby rendering the present phrase pleonastic. "Obedience" indicates response in a general kind of way; "faith" defines what precisely that response should be.

among all the Gentiles: Strictly speaking the Greek word *ethnē* refers simply to "nations." Granted Paul's sense of his distinctive apostolic responsibility (cf. 11:13; 15:16, 18; Gal 1:15-16), the technical Jewish sense "Gentiles" (= all who are not Jews) is almost certainly operative here, as elsewhere in the letter.

6. *called to belong to Jesus Christ:* "Calling" refers to the original address of the gospel that creates ("calls into being") the eschatological people of God; see Note on 8:30. Underlying the simple genitive construction here *(klētoi Iēsou Christou)* is Paul's distinctive sense of believers' union, through faith and baptism, with the risen Lord as corporate sphere of salvation (Gal 3:27-28; 1 Cor 12:12-13), conformed to the pattern of his death in the hope of future conformity to that of his resurrection (Rom 6:3-11; cf. 8:9b); see Interpretation of 6:3 and Note on 6:11.

7. *to all . . . in Rome:* Paul addresses the Roman Christians collectively but does not use the word "church" (*ekklēsia;* contrast 1 Cor 1:2; 2 Cor 2:1b; Gal 1:2 ["churches"]; 1 Thess 1:1; cf. 2 Thess 1:1). The arrangement of the greetings given in 16:3-15 suggests that the community may have consisted of several house-churches (cf. Introduction). One significant ms (G) omits the phrase "in Rome" here and in v 15. The omission probably reflects a post-Pauline attempt to bolster the "encyclical" possibilities of the letter (cf. Introduction).

God's beloved: Paul confers upon the Christian community the traditional sense of Israel as "beloved of God," see Deut 32:15 (LXX); 33:26 (LXX); Pss 60:5 (LXX 59:7); 108:6 (LXX 107:7); Isa 43:4; 44:2 (LXX); Hos 3:1; 14:4; Wis 16:26; Bar 3:36 (not ms A); 3 Macc 6:11. Christians are made aware of their status as "beloved of God" through the gift of the Spirit: Rom 5:5; cf. 8:15-16.

called to be saints: The use of *hagioi* in the NT as a standard designation of believers (frequently in Paul [Rom 8:27; 12:13; 15:25; 1 Cor 6:1-2; 14:33; 16:1, 15; 2 Cor 13:12; Phil 4:22; Phlm 5; etc.] and Revelation, more occasionally in Acts, Hebrews and other documents) again shows a Christian sense of inclusion within the privileged status of Israel as God's "holy people."

For Reference and Further Study

Agnew, F. H. "On the Origin of the Term *Apostolos.*" *CBQ* 38 (1976) 49–53.

__________. "The Origin of the NT Apostle-Concept: A Review of Research." *JBL* 105 (1986) 75–96.

Boismard, M.-É. "Constitué fils de Dieu (Rom. 1:4)." *RB* 60 (1953) 5–17.
Brown, R. E. *The Birth of the Messiah.* New York: Doubleday, 1977, 505–12.
Byrne, B. *'Sons of God'* 108–211.
Garlington, D. G. *"The Obedience of Faith": A Pauline Phrase in Historical Context.* WUNT 2/38. Tübingen: Mohr, 1991.
Horsley, R. A. *Bandits, Prophets, and Messiahs.* San Francisco: Harper & Row, 1985.
Hengel, M. *The Son of God.* London: SCM, 1976, 59–66.
Meier, J. P. *A Marginal Jew.* Vol. 1: *The Roots of the Problem and the Person.* New York, etc.: Doubleday, 1991, 216–18.
Poythress, V. S. "Is Romans 1:3-4 a Pauline Confession after All?" *ExpTim* 87 (1975–76) 180–83.
Rengstorf, K. H. Art. *"Apostolos." TDNT* 1. 407–45.
Schlier, H. "Zu Röm 1,3f." *Neues Testament und Geschichte* (FS O. Cullmann). Eds. H. Baltensweiler & B. Reicke. Berlin: Tübingen: Mohr, 1972, 207–18.
Scott, J. M. *Adoption as Sons of God* 223–44.
Strecker, G. Art. *"euangelion." EDNT* 2.70–74.
Stuhlmacher, P. *Das paulinische Evangelium.* Göttingen: Vandenhoeck & Ruprecht, 1968.

b) *Thanksgiving and Theme* (1:8-17)

8. First of all, I give thanks to my God through Jesus Christ concerning all of you, because your faith is proclaimed all over the world. 9. For God is my witness, the God whom I serve with my spirit in the gospel of his Son, as to how unceasingly I make mention of you; 10. always, when I pray, I ask that somehow by God's will I may at long last succeed in coming to you. 11. For I long to see you, in order that I may impart to you some spiritual gift for your strengthening, 12. or, rather, that (when I am) among you we may be mutually encouraged by our common faith, both yours and mine. 13. I do not want you to be unaware, brothers (and sisters), that I have often purposed to come to you—but have until now always been prevented—in order that I may harvest some fruit among you as well as among the rest of the Gentiles. 14. I am under obligation both to Greeks and to non-Greeks, both to the educated and to the uneducated alike: 15. hence my eagerness to preach the gospel to you also in Rome.

16. For I am not ashamed of the gospel: it is the power of God leading to salvation for every one who has faith, to the Jew first and also to the Greek. 17. For in it the righteousness of God is revealed, through faith for faith; as it is written, "The person who is righteous by faith will live."

INTERPRETATION

Introduction. In accordance with his customary modification of the Greco-Roman letter form (see Introduction), Paul changes the conventional thanks to the gods for the well-being of the sender into a thanksgiving for the situation of the recipients. Very soon, however, this becomes a vehicle for clarifying his own situation *vis-à-vis* the Roman community. In particular, Paul uses it to address the delicate issue as to why, granted his responsibility for the Gentiles (v 5), he has delayed so long in coming to visit them.

The handling of this sensitive matter proceeds according to a carefully crafted structure. After the opening statement of thanks for the renowned faith of the community (v 8), there follows a pattern of a threefold protestation on Paul's part concerning his desire (intention) to visit Rome (vv 9-10; 13a; 15), interlocked with a threefold statement of the reason (or grounds) for that intent (vv 11-12; 13b-14; 16-17):

Vv 9-10:	Paul's constant prayer (= *intention*) to visit Rome
Vv 11-12:	REASON (to impart spiritual gift, strengthening)
V 13a:	Paul's long-standing *intention* to visit
Vv 13b-14:	REASON (to reap some harvest among Gentiles)
Vv 15:	Paul's long-standing eagerness *(intention)*
Vv 16-17:	REASON (salvific power of the gospel).

On this pattern, the solemn statement in vv 16-17, usually and rightly recognized as stating the theme of the entire letter, stands as formally part of the Thanksgiving rather than as a separate section in its own right.

The sense of a certain defensiveness on Paul's part emerges from this analysis. As he will make clear in the Conclusion of the letter (15:23-32), he does now plan to visit Rome. But he will do so en route to somewhere else (Spain). When eventually the news of the visit is broken, it will be important not to give the impression that such a visit will be simply a stage in a larger journey. It must appear as the fulfillment of a long cherished desire and plan to include the Roman community in his overall missionary design. If he has not as yet appeared in Rome, this has not been through lack of interest but because he has, up till now, always "been prevented" (v 13).

The less than coherent statement of hopes for what such a visit might achieve (vv 11-12, 13b-14) likewise reflects a certain tension. Paul cannot come as anything other than the "apostle to the Gentiles," responsible to God for the Gentile churches. At the same time, any hint of heavy-handedness on his part may alienate his audience from the start. Paul's task, then, is to raise the issue of a visit to Rome in a way that respects the delicacy of the situation. He will preface the precise announcement of the visit with a celebratory exposition of the gospel (1:16–11:36) and its consequences for Christian life (12:1–15:13). The hope is that the hearing or "reminder" (15:15) of the gospel will work a transformation of the audience, disposing them to receive positively the news of Paul's visit. Then, when at last it takes place, it will be fruitful for all concerned.

Thanksgiving for the faith of the community (v 8). Paul thanks God for the faith of "all" the Christians in Rome. "All" is not simply an expansive gesture but a bid to forge a single audience out of groups accustomed to meeting in separate "house churches" (cf. 16:5, 10, 11, 14, 15), possibly diverse in ethnic origin and point of view (cf. 14:1–15:13). The extravagant suggestion that their faith is "proclaimed all over the world" is to some extent an initial fulsome compliment *(captatio benevolentiae)* designed to win over the audience. Nonetheless, it represents a genuine acknowledgment on Paul's part of the mature Christian status of the Gentile community in Rome. As a widely traveled apostle he can testify that the quality of their faith is a source of admiration in the Christian communities scattered about the Greco-Roman world (cf. 1 Thess 1:8).

Paul's continual prayer (vv 9-10). Quickly, however, Paul moves from thanksgiving and praise to review his own situation *vis-à-vis* the community. He has neither founded nor visited them but this does not mean that they have been far from his mind. As witness to the contrary, he can summon none less than God, since God has been the hearer of his unwearied and constant prayer in their regard. The cultic language in which Paul speaks here of his ministry of the gospel (cf. later 15:16) implies that his ministry amounts to a genuine "worship" *(latreuein)*—though in a spiritual *(en tą̄ pneumati mou)* rather than a physical sense. It has provided the opportunity to have the continual access to God in prayer enjoyed by those who actually minister in the Temple. For many years he has drawn the Roman community and, specifically, his desire to visit them, into this continual prayer to God. In this way he conveys to the community a sense that, though neither founded nor visited by him, they have had a place in his apostolic consciousness from the start. His writing to them is not a bolt from the blue but the expression of a long-standing sense of responsibility and desire to visit.

The fruits of such a visit (1) (vv 11-12). Paul longs to "see" (= visit physically) the community so that he might impart some "spiritual gift *(charisma pneumatikon)* for their strengthening" (v 11). *Charisma* in Paul refers to a concrete instance or effect of God's grace; here it means the sense of God's grace and power individual believers communicate to others through the exercise of the particular gift *(charis)* bestowed upon each one personally by the Spirit. Paul's distinctive "gift" is that of being called to be an apostle (cf. v 5). Hence the *charisma pneumatikon* which he might hope to communicate in Rome would, presumably, flow in some way from his apostolic office. Since the Romans are already believers, the apostolic *charisma* envisaged cannot be that of primary evangelization. It is a matter rather of "strengthening" those who are already Christians.

Sensing that he may already have communicated too one-sided a sense of giftedness, Paul adds (v 12) by way of correction a note of mutuality. From these mature Christians, whose faith is renowned (v 8), he will have something to receive as well as to give. A "mutual encouragement" *(symparaklēthēnai)* will flow from the common sharing of faith.

Paul's long-standing intention (v 13a). With a solemn assertion ("I want you to know, brothers and sisters . . ."), Paul insists that his general longing to visit (v 10) has often been translated into concrete plans but all have been frustrated hitherto. The passive construction ("prevented") hints at a divine hindering (cf. 15:22). Paul deflects responsibility for not visiting away from himself and onto God. His failure to appear in Rome has been part of the mysterious divine plan governing his life and ministry.

The fruits of such a visit (2) (vv 13b-14). Following this explanation, Paul gives a second indication of the aims behind such a visit. His hope has been to harvest "some fruit *(tina karpon)* among you *(en hymin)* as well as among the rest of the Gentiles." The language hints at something beyond the mutual "strengthening" previously mentioned. The phrase "among you" (taken in the sense of "in your milieu") and the following statement of "obligation" suggest the winning of Gentiles to the faith in the wider milieu of Rome. Such ministry would fulfill the deep sense of "obligation" *(opheiletēs eimi)* Paul feels towards the entire Gentile world (v 5). If he now designates that world in four categories "Greeks and barbarians, educated and uneducated alike," it is probably because he wants to suggest—a further *captatio* (cf. v 8)—that, if he has spent time and labor among the "barbarians" and "uneducated" of the East, he is equally obligated to labor amongst the "Greeks" and "educated" such as those in the imperial capital might consider themselves to be. Hence his long-standing "eagerness" *(to kat' eme prothymon)* to proclaim the gospel "to you also in Rome" (v 15).

Paul's eagerness (v 15). At first sight this statement in v 15 seems to express a hope on Paul's part actually to preach the gospel to the Christian community in Rome. As such, however, it would sweep away at one blow the careful diplomacy of the earlier statements of intent (vv 11-12); the Roman Christians would hardly take kindly to any suggestion that evangelizing them is what Paul has in mind. The expression of "eagerness" lacks any time marker in the Greek original. The primary reference seems to be to a long-standing determination on Paul's part to pursue in Rome his apostolic mission to the Gentiles. This intention has since been overtaken by events: a Gentile Christian community now flourishes in the capital. Paul's point, however, is that the same divine commission that led him as apostle to the Gentiles to be "eager" to preach in Rome now gives him authority to proclaim the gospel to them in written form. The Gentile Christians in Rome will in effect be "re-evangelized" through the letter—something which, in the end (15:15), Paul virtually concedes, while overtly using the language of "reminder."

The Theme (vv 16-17). Every element in the long thematic statement that concludes the Introduction to the letter bears great theological and rhetorical weight. Many of the terms and ideas that are to be of central significance in the argument of the letter as a whole appear here for the first time (See Notes for wider elaboration of topics).

Paul's opening (v 16a) insistence that he is "not ashamed of the gospel" represents a standard rhetorical device (litotes) in which an understatement couched as a double negative has the effect of placing even greater stress upon the corresponding positive affirmation. "I am not ashamed of the gospel" really amounts to a forceful "I am mighty proud of the gospel" or, especially in view of the "boasting" motifs to follow (2:17, 23; 3:27; 5:2, 3, 11), "I can boast in the gospel." The clause plays a key role in lending the following exposition of the gospel its epideictic tone of celebration (see Introduction). To the tiny group of believers in Rome, surrounded by a sea of unbelief and competing religious claims, clinging to a divine message rejected by its primary addressees (Israel), Paul communicates a sense of his own confidence in the gospel, along with the implication that this confidence is something which his audience in Rome ought share.

The rest of the thematic statement sets out the grounds for that confidence in the gospel. By calling it the "power of God leading to salvation" (v 16b) Paul invokes a key feature of the symbolic universe he shares with the Roman community and indeed the entire apocalyptic perspective of early Judaism. Basic to that perspective is the sense of the entire world heading towards a more or less imminent divine judgment, in which God's "wrath" would be launched destructively against evildoers, specifically against those forces that prevail in the present (evil) age and oppress the faithful. Negatively, "salvation" *(sōtēria)* denotes rescue from destruction at the time of intensified distress that will precede the wind-up of the present age before the great judgment. More positively, for those who are found faithful ("righteous") at the judgment, salvation implies full entrance into the blessings of the final age (the kingdom of God). Apocalyptic literature often depicts the blessings of the final age in otherworldly, highly imaginative terms. But entrance into salvation does not mean translation into a super-human, heavenly realm. The main line of the tradition sees "salvation" as arrival at that fullness of life and humanity which fulfills the Creator's original design for human beings, created in the image and likeness of God (Gen 1:26-28; cf. Ps 8:3-8).

The Jewish apocalyptic tradition reclaimed this vision of a "saved" humanity as something destined primarily for the faithful in Israel. The Qumran community, for example, promised its members that "all the glory of Adam (or "human nature") would be theirs" (1QH 17:15; 1QS 4:22-23; CD 3:20; 4QpPs 37 3:1-2; cf. also *4 Ezra* 6:54, 59; *Jub.* 22:14; 32:19). "Salvation" in such terms was closely tied to distinctive Jewish prerogatives such as circumcision and law. Paul, however, without specifically excluding such factors at this stage (contrast 3:21), asserts (v 16b) a far more inclusive and universal scope for the saving power of the gospel: it is effective for all human beings, the only condition being the response of faith *(panti tǭ pisteuonti)*.

Nothing is more characteristic of Paul than his insistence upon faith (Gk *pistis*) as the primary response of the human being to God. In line with the OT tradition, Paul understands faith as involving both perception and commitment. At its most basic, faith is that attitude which discerns God acting creatively (that is, as Creator) in the world and in one's own life, urging the surrender of one's life project to that perception in trust and obedience. At a later point, Paul will relate faith more explicitly to Jesus Christ (3:21-26) and to awareness of sin (4:4-8); he will oppose faith to the "boasting" in "works of the law" which in his eyes restricts salvation to the Jews (3:27-30). Here he remains content simply with a positive statement of the universal scope of faith.

Paul does, however, give an important hint of the direction in which his exposition is to go by picking up the "every . . ." (*panti* . . .) in terms of the added phrase, "to the Jew first and also to the Greek" *(Ioudaiǭ te prōton kai Hellēni)*. The phrase acknowledges Israel to be the first addressee of the gospel. Paul never loses sight of this (temporal) priority of Israel. At the same time, he insists from the start upon the inclusive scope of the gospel's saving address: as well as Jews, it invites Gentile (literally, "Greek") believers to take their place among the community of the saved.

The second part of the thematic statement (v 17) explains why (cf. *gar*) the gospel has this saving power: it is because it "reveals" (and makes available) the "righteousness of God" *(dikaiosynē . . . theou)*. Within the framework of the Jewish tradition this is a natural move to make. That tradition sees an intimate connection between "righteousness" and "(eternal) life," to which Ezek 18:5-9 gives classic expression: "If a person is righteous and does what is lawful and right—(there follow fifteen illustrations of what this means)—that person shall surely live, says the Lord" (cf. 33:10-20). To be found righteous in God's eyes leads to life; conversely, to be found unrighteous leads to death. The connection remains axiomatic in the whole sweep of the biblical tradition (cf. Deut 30:6, 15-20; Prov 21:21; Wis 1:15; 5:1-5, 15; 15:3), carrying on into the post-biblical era (for references, see Notes). Paul makes his own distinctive contribution to that tradition. But fundamentally he does not depart from the axiom that life (salvation) flows from righteousness (cf. esp. 8:10c: "the Spirit means life because of righteousness" *[to de pneuma zōē dia dikaiosynēn]*; also Rom 2:6-13; 5:18, 21; 6:20-23; 2 Cor 5:10).

Behind Paul's Greek term *dikaiosynē* lies the biblical and early post-biblical usage of the Hebrew word group *ṣedeq/ṣĕdāqâ* which it overwhelmingly (though by no means exclusively) translates. The notion denoted by the word group is essentially relational and has to do with the assessment of one's action or behavior according to whether it conforms or does not conform to the demands or expectation of some other person with whom one is in relationship. Put in plainer language, the righteous person is the one who "does the right thing" by some other party. Righteousness is the state or status of the person who, in terms of the relationship, is acknowledged by the other to have done the right thing, to be "in the right." The classic biblical illustration is the acknowledgment given by Judah to Tamar at the end of the sordid episode recounted in Gen 38:26: "She is more righteous than I" (for more detailed background to "righteousness," see Note).

In his more specific appeal to the "the righteousness of God" as "revealed" *(apokalyptetai)* in the gospel, Paul stands in continuity with a biblical tradition greatly shaped by the exilic prophet who speaks in Isaiah 40-55. This (Second) Isaiah employed the language of "righteousness" in particular connection with the saving and liberating acts of God on behalf of captive Israel. God's saving acts on behalf of the exiled people are an exercise of righteousness, revealing God to be "righteous" ("faithful") in terms of relationship with Israel.

In Paul's eyes, the gospel "reveals" the "righteousness of God" in that it announces that God has acted faithfully, not only with respect to Israel, but, as Creator, with respect to the entire world. What is at stake is God's own righteousness, which human beings acknowledge in the act of faith (cf., later, 3:26).

At the same time, both the immediate and more remote contexts suggest that the phrase "the righteousness of God" embraces also the human pole of the relationship. At issue in Romans is whether there is a corresponding righteousness on the human side and, in particular, whether Israel's special way to righteousness—that of the Torah—provides the required eschatological righteousness. Paul's response will be that it does not and that, on the human side as a whole (Jewish as well as Gentile) there is no one who is righteous (3:10, 20, 23). In the face of this devastating failure, however, God has acted in Christ graciously to envelop unrighteous human beings in the divine righteousness, thus providing the righteous status required for justification and salvation. So the phrase "righteousness of God" denotes not only the righteousness which God has personally displayed in divine saving acts but also the righteousness (= status of acceptance) which God graciously deigns to find in human beings in virtue of the association with Christ forged through belief in the gospel. It is on this basis that the gospel is the "power of God leading to salvation for everyone who has faith."

In a sentence where every word carries heavy theological freight, Paul ensures that the emphasis falls precisely where he intends. The curious expression "from faith to faith" (Greek: *ek pisteōs eis pistin*), though open to many interpretations (see Note), is best understood in an intensive sense underlying the centrality of faith. The righteousness revealed by the gospel, that which makes it a "power of God leading to salvation," is a righteousness entirely discerned and appropriated through faith. Perhaps we could best paraphrase Paul's phrase and intention by saying, "It is faith through and through, faith from beginning to end." The polemical edge of this assertion will emerge later on through the explicit exclusion of all rival modes of righteousness (notably that which purports to come through "works of the law"; cf. esp. 3:19-20, 27-28). Here Paul wishes to assert positively and as forcefully as possible that it is on the basis of faith that the gospel includes all human beings within the scope of salvation.

As he will do so often throughout the letter, Paul clinches his claim for the centrality of faith through appeal to the witness of scripture. Paul's version of Hab 2:4 omits all pronouns attaching to the original (see Note) in a way that allows the text to speak simply and absolutely of faith. It is through a righteousness flowing from faith (the "righteousness of God") that a person "will live," that is, come to possess the "eternal life" that is the positive aspect of "salvation."

In this way, in "inclusive" fashion, the thematic statement begins and ends upon the note of "salvation." Moreover, the concluding quotation from Habakkuk serves "programmatically" to indicate the track the exposition will follow: first (1:18–4:25), Paul will show that the only righteousness available is that stemming from faith ("The person who is righteous by faith . . ."); secondly (5:1–11:36), he will argue that, upon this basis, all believers find salvation (". . . will live").

NOTES

8. *your faith:* If "faith" refers to initial conversion, Paul could mean that it is a source of pride to other believers that a Christian community is entrenched in the world capital. More likely, the reference is to the quality of the community's faith.

9. *whom I serve with my spirit:* The interpretation of this phrase given in the text proceeds from the fact that Paul sometimes uses "spirit" *(pneuma)* to denote a

presence that is real but not physical; see esp. 1 Cor 5:3-4 (cf. Col 2:5); for other possibilities, see Cranfield 1.76-77. The verb *latreuein* is regularly used in the LXX to denote cultic worship of God.

the gospel of his Son: The genitive in the Greek construction is objective, denoting "the gospel concerning his Son," as "defined" in vv 3-4 above.

10. *always when I pray:* In terms of syntax, this phrase could just as well go with the preceding clause. But this would involve having two adverbs ("unceasingly" and "always") of rather similar meaning in the same clause.

that . . . I may . . . succeed: In view of the subject matter, it is tempting to take the Greek verb (the passive of *euodoun*) in its literal sense and find some hint of a "journey" here. But the more general metaphorical sense "succeed" is standard in the NT; cf. BAGD 323.

11. *spiritual gift:* The classic discussion of "gift" *(charisma)* in Paul is to be found in E. Käsemann's essay, "Ministry and Community in the New Testament" (see Reference). The view adopted in this commentary (finding, in particular, a distinction between *charis* [cf. v 5] and *charisma;* see also Interpretation and Notes on 12:6-8) owes much to the more recent study of N. Baumert (see Reference).

for your strengthening: The same Greek word, *stērizein,* indicates a similar role envisaged for Timothy in 1 Thess 3:2; cf. also Luke 22:32 (Simon Peter); Acts 18:23 (Paul).

12. *or rather:* The Greek expression *touto de estin* (only here in the NT) implies a measure of correction.

(when I am) among you: The translation takes the Greek phrase *en hymin* in a "local" sense: Paul hopes one day to be actually present in Rome.

we may be mutually encouraged: The passive of *symparakalein* could also mean "mutual exhortation," but "encouragement" seems more appropriate in the context.

by our common faith, both yours and mine: Lit. "through the faith which is in each other (i.e., "each one through the faith of the other"), yours and mine"; cf. Cranfield 1.81.

13. *I do not want you to be unaware, brothers (and sisters):* To underline the solemnity or importance of what he is about to say Paul uses an epistolary "disclosure formula" (cf. also 11:25; 1 Cor 10:1; 12:1; 2 Cor 1:8; 1 Thess 4:13 and the similar "I want you to know" in Gal 1:11 and Phil 1:12). Paul establishes a further bond with his audience by addressing them, within the common Christian sense of belonging to the "family" of God (cf. 8:14-17), as "brothers" ("sisters" is lacking in the Greek text).

among you as well: The Greek phrase *kai en hymin* does not imply that Roman *Christians* were to be themselves the object of Paul's missionary endeavor. It means "in your locality" (that is, Rome), which was in fact part of the wider Gentile world for which Paul felt responsible. The occurrence of the simple dative *hymin* in what must be the preferred textual reading in v 15 does not challenge this. The reference there is to a past intention to evangelize in Rome before those who were now Christians (= "you") had in fact been converted.

14. *both to Greeks and to non-Greeks, both to the educated and to the uneducated alike:* Literally: "both to Greeks and barbarians, wise and foolish." The phrase as a whole encompasses the entire non-Jewish world. "Greeks" includes not merely those literally of Hellenic stock but all who thought of themselves by education and social status to be part of or on a par with the Greek culture pervasive throughout the Mediterranean world, including possibly the Roman Christians themselves. "Barbarians" would refer to peoples beyond this range. In the eyes of many of Paul's contemporaries the second contrasting pair, "wise and foolish," might correspond exactly to the former. But Paul may be subtly complimenting the Romans by suggesting that they belonged to the educated "Greek" world, in contrast to the more rustic peoples who had been the object of his evangelizing work in Asia Minor.

15. *my eagerness:* The Greek phrase *kat' eme* adds the sense of "as far as it rests with me" to the general expression of eagerness in the wider expression *to kat' eme prothymon*. Paul is still anxious to attribute his failure to appear in Rome to the (divine) "preventing" (v 13). Since the phrase is not tied to any verb which might fix it in terms of time reference, it ought not be translated as though referring necessarily to the present. A reference to a long-standing eagerness is equally possible. Taken in this way, the determination does not really conflict with the policy enunciated later in the letter (15:20; cf. 2 Cor 10:15-16) of never building on the foundation laid by another.

    to preach the gospel: The Greek verb *euangelizesthai* normally denotes preaching to those who are not yet believers. Paul's usage here, if it has any bearing upon what he still hopes to achieve amongst the Roman Christian community, must intend primarily the "reminder" sense formulated in 15:15.

    to you: The variant reading "among you" *(en hymin)* in some Western mss. (D* b vg) is a secondary assimilation to the same phrase occurring in v 13; the simple dative *(hymin)* is to be preferred.

16. *I am not ashamed of the gospel:* Not being "ashamed" could address the fact that the gospel proclaims as the central vehicle of salvation something that in itself is supremely "shameful"—death upon a cross (cf. 1 Cor 1:23). It could also, paving the way for chapters 9–11, address the blow to the gospel's credibility represented by Israel's rejection. On balance, however, it seems best to interpret the clause as a litotes, as suggested in the Interpretation.

    power of God leading to salvation: As the following verse (v 17) makes clear, the gospel is "the power of God leading to salvation" in that it communicates the "righteousness" ("righteousness of God") that is the precondition for the attainment of salvation at the judgment. "Power" (*dynamis*) comes close here to the sense "capacity"; contrast what is said of the "weakness" (the "incapacity") of the law in 8:3. "Salvation" ("be saved") has a predominantly future reference in Paul: Rom 5:9 (twice); 9:27; 10:9; 11:26; 13:11; 1 Cor 3:15; 5:5; 7:16; Phil 2:12 (cf. 3:20); 1 Thess 5:8-9 (cf. 1:10). In 1 Cor 1:18; 15:2; 2 Cor 2:15 (present participle) the sense is that of being "on the way to salvation." The only usage in the past tense, Rom 8:24, is in fact qualified by hope and has the restricted sense: "(only) in hope do we find ourselves in a situation of salvation."

to the Jew first and also to the Greek: Paul uses "Greek" *(hellēnos)* as a synonym for "Gentile" in general, meaning all who are not Jews. In this highly rhetorical sentence "Greek" provides a better linguistic balance to "Jew." The coupling recurs at 2:9, 10; 3:9; 10:12—with increasing irony, since a prime aspect of Paul's argument is to show that Jews are bound up with Gentiles in a common lack of righteousness. Paul acknowledges the Jewish privileges (3:1-2; 9:4-5) and "priority" with respect to the address of the gospel but by the end of Romans 11 that priority, at least as regards salvation, is shown to have been reversed (cf. 11:11-12, 15, 30-32). From the perspective of the total letter, the sense of the phrase amounts to: "to the Jew first, to be sure, *but also* to the Greek"; the stress falls upon the inclusion of the Gentiles.

17. *the righteousness of God:* 1. **Background.** The *biblical* tradition, with which Paul stands in continuity, applies "righteousness" both to God and human beings (Israel). Yahweh displays "righteousness" through action that conforms to the divine bond with Israel: creating, nourishing and protecting the life of the people (Psalms 47; 67; 93; 95-99 [cf. esp. 96:13; 97:2, 6; 98:1-3]; 111; 145; 147; Isaiah 41; 45-46; 48:12-19; 51:1-16; 54; 61-62). On the human side a corresponding righteousness is required, with respect to both God and fellow human beings. In fact there is a real continuity between the two spheres: prosperity and good social order (*šālôm*) depend on the extent to which key figures (the king, judges, etc.) and indeed all Israelites share and reflect in their lives God's own righteousness (Psalms 1; 18; 72; 82; 101).

Within the human social context, righteousness has reference particularly to the "forensic" or law-court situation where a judge decides whether a person has or has not acted in conformity with community norms. The notion of being acquitted in such a situation, "declared righteous" or "justified," is the root of the whole biblical and theological idea of "justification." In the context of Paul's theology (notably Rom 4:5) it is significant to note that declaring the *un*righteous righteous (to "justify the ungodly") constitutes a classic human *abuse* of justice according to the biblical tradition (Prov 17:15; 24:24; cf. Exod 23:7; Qumran: CD 1:19).

The situation of the Exile in Babylon brought the "saving" aspect of God's righteousness to the fore. In certain Psalms (e.g. 96, 98) and in the exilic ("Second") and post-exilic ("Third") Isaiah (Isaiah 40-55 and 56-66, respectively), *ṣĕdāqâ* characterizes the saving acts God promises to work on behalf of the (captive) people and becomes virtually a technical term expressing "saving faithfulness" (over fifty occurrences). In many cases *ṣĕdāqâ* expresses the *result* of such saving activity, becoming synonymous with "salvation," "deliverance" (Isa 45:8; 46:12-13; 51:5-6, 8; 61:11; 62:1-2), "restoration of national life" (43:16-21), standing in parallel to terms denoting "salvation," "peace," "prosperity," etc.

The Isaianic usage made an indelible imprint upon the "righteousness" tradition. Whether, however, the "saving" sense totally swamps the field, as often maintained, is another matter. There are a few isolated instances where the divine righteousness does seem to refer to punitive action by God, even with respect to Israel (Isa 10:22; cf. 5:16; Lam 1:18; Wis 12:15-16). It seems safer to hold that "righteousness" refers essentially to action in accordance with what is acknowledged to be right. In Israel's view, such action on God's part is almost always salvific. But perhaps one should say that this was so in *fact*, rather than as something belonging essentially to the notion of "righteousness" as such.

In the (exilic) Isaiah and associated Psalm passages, "righteousness" takes on three further aspects particularly important for understanding Paul: 1. the *eschatological:* "righteousness" is the *coming* salvation which in the near future (in "Third" Isaiah, a more distant future) God will bring to the people; 2. the *forensic* (law-court): the prophet portrays God in process with Israel or (more usually) with foreign nations and their gods (41:1, 21; 43:9; 50:7-9); 3. the *universal*—the coming righteousness does not bear only upon the restoration of Israel but implies the sovereignty of Israel's God over all the nations (Isa 45:21-25; 49:6-7; 51:4-5; cf. Ps 96:10-13).

A further significant aspect of the biblical tradition with respect to righteousness is the frequency with which the acknowledgment of God's righteousness accompanies a confession of failure, of *un*righteousness on the human side (e.g., Isa 5:1-16; Pss 51:6-7; 65:1-3; Lam 1:18; Neh 9:33; Dan 9:13-19). God is acknowledged to be in the right and Israel in the wrong; the evils that have ensued are attributed to that lack of righteousness on the human side. Noteworthy in this connection is the tendency on the part of sinful human beings to appeal to God's righteousness as the source of forgiveness, remedy and restoration. Psalm 143 (cited by Paul in Rom 3:20 and Gal 2:16) is the outstanding illustration of this. The psalmist confesses sinfulness and avers that no one is righteous in God's sight (v 2). But the prayer both begins (v 1) and ends (v 11), in "inclusive" fashion, with an appeal for rescue directed precisely to God's righteousness. What is striking here is the confidence of the psalmist that, in the face of infidelity on the human side, God nonetheless remains faithful and so can be expected, in virtue of "righteousness" (standing in parallel with "faithfulness" and "steadfast love" [vv 1, 11-12]) to bring about purification, healing and restoration of the life-giving relationship.

In *post-biblical* Jewish literature the "righteousness" tradition continues, but with a palpable heightening of the eschatological and forensic aspects. Particularly to the fore is the dualistic sharpness characteristic of apocalypticism. There is increasing despair and pessimism about the possibility of any righteousness on the human side—unless it be in the small community of the elect, whose righteousness is more and more seen to consist in faithful practice of the law. Outside the chosen few, all is unrighteousness. The faithful can only wait upon the eschatological intervention of God. This will display the divine righteousness and mean freedom, vindication (= "justification") and salvation for the righteous, but judgment and punishment for all the rest. Axiomatic is the sense that righteousness (being found righteous at the judgment) is the precondition for salvation, for obtaining eternal life: Wis 1:15; 5:1-5, 15; 15:3; *1 Enoch* 1:1-9; 5:6-7 (Greek); 39:4-8; 58:2-3; 62:13-16; 91:12-13; 94-104 passim; *Pss. Sol.* 9:5; 12:6; 14:1-10; 15:6-13; *Bib. Ant.* 51:5; *Sib. Or.* 5:269-70; *T. Naph.* 8:3; *4 Ezra* 8:33-36, 51-62; 9:7-13; *2 Apoc. Bar.* 44:2-15; 51:1-16; 1QpHab 8:1-3; *m. ʾAbot* 6:7.

Within the apocalyptic perspective, some texts from *Qumran* feature a notable development of the biblical tradition of God's righteousness confronting unrighteousness on the human side. In the context of an acute sense of sinfulness, the Qumran psalmist invokes the righteousness of God as an expression of divine grace which here and now will work cleansing, justification and renewal.

> "As for me, my justification is with God. . . . He will wipe out my transgression through his righteousness" (1QS 11:2-3);
>
> "From the source of his righteousness is my justification" (*ibid.* line 5); ". . . If I stagger because of the sin of the flesh, my justification shall be by the righteousness of God, which endures for ever" (*ibid.* line 12; cf. line 14).

In literature such as this we stand at the threshold of Paul's sense of God's righteousness justifying the unrighteous through faith.

Some strands of the post-biblical Jewish tradition tended to drive a wedge between the divine attributes of righteousness and mercy, God's righteousness being seen more in the category of a judicial righteousness rewarding righteous deeds and punishing offenses (*Pss. Sol.* 8:23-26; 9:2). Likewise, translation of the Hebrew word-group *ṣedeq/ṣĕdāqâ* into Greek words of the *dik-* stem brought stricter nuances from Greek philosophic tradition, with the sense of conformity to a norm being understood as obedience to the law of Moses. But the use of *dikaiosynē* in the LXX to translate divine qualities associated with *ṣedeq/ṣĕdāqâ* in the Hebrew tradition, such as *ʾĕmĕt* ("faithfulness" [Gen 24:49; Josh 24:14; Isa 38:19]) and *ḥĕsĕd* ("steadfast love" [e.g., Gen 19:19; 20:13; 21:23]) shows the continuing breadth and influence of the salvific nuance associated with the exilic prophets.

2. **Paul**. Paul's sense of the "righteousness of God" owes much to Isaiah 40-66 but features the dualism and eschatological sharpening characteristic of Apocalypticism. With respect to the problem of sin, Paul stands closest to Qumran. But Qumran knows nothing of Paul's exclusion of "works of the law" as a way to eschatological right-standing with God. A legal text (4QMMT) in facts points to keeping "deeds of the law" (line 113) as a way to "being reckoned righteous in the end" (line 117)—compare and contrast Paul's sense of the "reckoning" of righteousness to Abraham on the basis simply of faith (Rom 4:3, 22-24; Gal 3:6). Likewise absent from Qumran is the idea of a "justification" worked through the atoning death of the Messiah, something which opens up salvation beyond the small elect community to embrace the whole world. For Paul, God displays righteousness through his saving fidelity as Creator to the entire creation, a fidelity exercised finally (that is, eschatologically) and inclusively (that is, including the Gentiles and, ultimately, that part of Israel not yet responsive to the gospel) in the redemptive work of Christ.

References to "God's righteousness," in varying formulations, occur eight times in Romans (1:17; 3:5, 21, 22, 25, 26; 10:3 [twice]), once in 2 Corinthians (5:21), with similar formulations in 1 Cor 1:30 and Phil 3:9. The theory that "righteousness of God" constituted a fixed formula before Paul (so esp. E.

Käsemann) rests on too slight a range of evidence to be convincing (M. L. Soards; see Reference). Likewise, the widely accepted sense of "righteousness of God" as "salvation-creating power" (the Käsemann school) has to reckon with the fact that it is not "righteousness" which is described in terms of "power" in Rom 1:16-17 but the gospel: the gospel is "power leading to salvation" *because* it "reveals" (= makes available) the "righteousness of God." The case for the objective understanding of the phrase in the sense of "genitive of origin" ("righteousness from God") is restated by D. Zeller, *Römer* 45-50, with very full documentation; cf. also Cranfield 1.95(end)-99. But an "either/or" approach to "God's righteousness" in Romans ("subjective" or "objective") is misguided. Neither aspect can be excluded since both God's own righteousness (cf. esp. 3:5, 25-26) and the human situation of (un)righteousness (cf. esp. 1:17d; 2:13; 3:20, 24, 26; 4:2-5, 9-11, 13, 22-25; 5:1, 17, 19, 21; 8:10, 30; 9:30-31; 10:3-4, 5-6, 10) are at issue and an essential part of Paul's strategy is to allow the phrase to cover both the divine and human pole of the relationship. The two aspects come together "christologically": Christ embodies God's righteousness (the saving faithfulness of the Creator to creation) *and* also functions as the sphere ("in Christ") where believers can find a righteous status before God. See also Note on 3:5.

is being revealed: This phrase suggests that Paul intends the total thematic statement contained in vv 16-17 to echo Ps 98:2: "Yahweh has made known his salvation; in the sight of the nations he has revealed (LXX: *apekalypsen*) his righteousness *(tēn dikaiosynēn autou)*"; cf. Fitzmyer 257.

from faith to faith: The Greek phrase *ek pisteōs eis pistin* can be understood in several ways; for a full listing, see Cranfield 1.99–100. Two are worthy of note. 1. Paul here (as also in the Hab 2:4 quotation) exploits the ambiguity latent in the Greek noun *pistis,* which can mean "faithfulness" as well as "faith" (= "trust in . . ."); the first phrase would then refer to God's faithfulness (a suitable parallel to the reference to God's "righteousness" earlier in the verse; cf. 3:3, 5), the second to human faith-response. 2. Both instances of *pistis* refer to human faith; the total expression is a rhetorical device lending intensive force: "through faith from first to last"; cf. 2 Cor 2:16; 3:18; Ps 84:7 (LXX 83:8); Jer 9:3. The second interpretation is more likely on the grounds that, had Paul meant to include a reference to God's faithfulness, he would surely have made the reference clearer. The omission in the following quotation from Hab 2:4 of the personal pronoun ("my" [*mou*]) attaching to *pisteōs* in the best MSS of the LXX text also seems to give a signal in the opposite direction.

as it is written, "The person who is righteous by faith will live": The flow of the Greek sentence as written by Paul (as also in the Hebrew ["The righteous one will live by his faith"] and LXX ["The righteous one will live by my fidelity"] prototypes) suggests that the phrase "by faith" (*ek pisteōs*) attaches to the verb *(zēsetai)* rather than to the subject *(ho dikaios)*; cf. the NRSV: "The one who is righteous will live by faith." The alternative (RSV; margin NRSV) is, however, to be preferred, since the issue for Paul in Romans is not how the righteous person should continue to live (whether through faith or not), but rather, with what righteousness must a person be clad in order to obtain (eternal) life (=

salvation). A number of interpreters find an implied allusion here to Christ's personal faith: Christ is the "righteous one" who lives by faith. But in this initial statement of theme in Romans, Paul appears to have studiously avoided a christological allusion (contrast 3:21-22) and such a concrete personal reference sits oddly with the omission of possessive pronouns in the Pauline formulation (contrast the Hebrew and LXX).

For Reference and Further Study

Baumert, N. "Charisma und Amt bei Paulus." *L'Apôtre Paul* (Ed. A. Vanhoye) 203–28.

Campbell, D. A. "Romans 1:17—A *Crux Interpretum* for the *Pistis Christou* Debate." *JBL* 113 (1994) 265–85.

Cavallin, H.C.C. "'The Righteous Shall Live by Faith': A Decisive Argument for the Traditional Interpretation." *ST* 32 (1978) 33–43.

Dahl, N. A. "The Missionary Theology in the Epistle to the Romans." *Studies in Paul* 70–94.

Käsemann, E. "Ministry and Community in the New Testament." *Essays on New Testament Themes* 63–94.

Kettunen, M. *Der Abfassungszweck des Römerbriefes* 99–126.

Schubert, P. *Form and Function of the Pauline Thanksgivings.* BZNW 20; Berlin: Töpelmann, 1939.

Stowers, S. K. *Rereading of Romans* 198–202.

Stuhlmacher, P. "The Theme of Romans." *Romans Debate* 333–45.

Vorster, J. N. "Strategies of Persuasion in Romans 1.16–17." *Rhetoric and the New Testament* (Eds. S. E. Porter & T. H. Olbricht) 152–70.

Wedderburn, A.J.M. *Reasons for Romans* 25–29, 97–98, 102–23.

On "Righteousness of God."

Brauch, M. T. "Perspectives on 'God's Righteousness' in Recent German Discussion." E. P. Sanders, *Paul and Palestinian Judaism* 523–42.

Bultmann, R. *Theology* 1.270–79.

Garlington, D. B. *Faith, Obedience and Perseverance: Aspects of Paul's Letter to the Romans.* WUNT 79; Tübingen: Mohr, 1994.

Käsemann, E. "The 'Righteousness of God' in Paul." *New Testament Questions of Today* 168–82.

Kertelge, K. Art. "*Dikaiosynē.*" *EDNT* 1.325–330.

Klein, G. Art. "Righteousness in the New Testament." *IDBSupp* 750–52.

Onesti, K. L. and Brauch, M. T. Art. "Righteousness, Righteousness of God." *DPL* (1993) 827–37.

Reumann, J. *Righteousness in the New Testament.* Philadelphia/New York: Fortress/Paulist (1982) 12–22, 41–91, 193–227 (Response by J. A. Fitzmyer).

Soards, M. L. "Käsemann's 'Righteousness' Re-examined." *CBQ* 49 (1987) 264–67.

Wilckens, U. "Exkurs: 'Gerechtigkeit Gottes'." *Römer* 1. 202–33, esp. 202–22.

Zeller, D. "Rechtfertigung, Gerechtigkeit Gottes im AT, im Judentum und bei Paulus." (Excursus) *Römer* 45–50.
Ziesler, J. A. *The Meaning of Righteousness in Paul.* SNTSMS 20; Cambridge: University Press, 1972; also *Romans* 70–71.

BODY OF THE LETTER (1:18–15:13)

I. THE INCLUSIVE SAVING POWER OF THE GOSPEL (1:18–11:36)

A. THE INCLUSION OF THE GENTILES ON THE BASIS OF RIGHTEOUSNESS BY FAITH (1:18–4:25)

The Introduction of the letter (1:1-17) has shown its primary addressees (the implied audience) to be Gentile Christians in Rome. But in the section that now begins, 1:18–4:25, it soon becomes clear that the implied addressee is a Jew as yet to be persuaded of the truth of the gospel. It is this development that creates the problem of the letter's "double address." As argued in the Introduction to this commentary, the problem falls away in the light of Paul's rhetorical strategy in Romans. The overall intent is to convince the Gentile believers in Rome of the power and all-sufficiency of the Christian gospel, specifically in its inclusion of them within the community of the saved. Paul's tactic at this point is to reinforce the claims made for the Christian gospel by allowing them to "overhear" a dialogue with a Jewish partner. This "dialogue," in negative fashion first of all (1:18–3:20), excludes any rival way of finding the right standing with God (righteousness) required for salvation; specifically, it excludes the way of the law. Then (3:21–4:25), over against this negative background, it makes a positive claim for the way of faith, the only viable response to the revelation of God's righteousness in Christ. (The tactic is similar to that deployed in Gal 2:10-21, where Paul rehearses for the benefit of the Galatian Gentile Christians, wavering in their adherence to the gospel [cf. 1:6], the debate he had had with his fellow Jewish-Christian Cephas (Peter) at Antioch.)

A rhetorical glance at individual sections of the letter finds, then, a pattern of roles within roles. Just as Rom 1:18–4:25 plays a distinctive rhetorical role within the wider framework of the letter, so the "prophetic declamation" that makes up 1:18–3:20 plays its own (negative) role within

1:18–4:25. Moreover, the opening section, 1:18-32, which at first sight appears to target the alienation of the Gentile world, has its own rhetorical role to play within the wider block, 1:18–3:20. It catches the Jewish dialogue partner in a rhetorical "trap" (2:1-3; cf. Gal 2:15-16) designed to drive home more effectively the thesis that there is no righteousness to be had on the basis of the law. Recognition of these rhetorical "roles within roles" played by the various sections is vital to interpretation. No single element in the running argument can be taken simply in isolation and given independent value. This caution is particularly important in the case of the first element, 1:18-32.

i. No Other Righteousness (1:18–3:20)

a) *The Revelation of God's Wrath Against the Gentile World* (1:18-32)

18. For God's wrath from heaven is revealed against all ungodliness and wickedness on the part of human beings who in their wickedness suppress the truth.
19. For what can be known about God is plain to them, because God has
shown it to them. 20. Ever since the creation of the world his invisible
nature, namely, his eternal power and deity, has been clearly perceived
in the things that have been made. So they are without excuse.
[I] 21. For although they knew God they did not glorify him as God or
give thanks, but they became futile in their thinking and their senseless
hearts were darkened. 22. Claiming to be wise, they became fools, 23.
and exchanged the glory of the immortal God for images resembling a
mortal human being or birds or animals or reptiles. 24. Therefore *God
gave them up* into the power of the lustful desires of their hearts, to the
uncleanness of the dishonoring of their bodies among themselves.
[II] 25. Inasmuch they exchanged the truth about God for a lie and worshiped and served the creature rather than the Creator, who is blessed
for ever! Amen. 26. For this reason *God gave them up* to dishonorable passions. Their women exchanged natural relations for unnatural, 27. and
the men likewise gave up natural relations with women and were inflamed with passion for one another, men with men committing what is shameless and receiving in their own persons the due penalty for their error.
[III] 28. And since they did not think God worthy of recognition *God gave them up* to a worthless mind that led to improper conduct. 29. They are
filled with all manner of wickedness, evil, covetousness, malice; full of
envy, murder, strife, deceit, craftiness; they are gossips, 30. slanderers,

haters of God, insolent, arrogant, boastful, contrivers of evil, disobedient to parents, 31. senseless, faithless, heartless, ruthless.
32. Though they know God's decree that those who do such things deserve to die, they not only do them but approve those who practice them.

Interpretation

Introduction. The passage shows a highly formal structure (cf. the presentation of the text above). First comes an overarching thematic statement (v 18) of the revelation of God's wrath in the face of human wickedness that "suppresses the truth" (about God). Then, by way of presupposition to what is to come, this suppression is shown to be "inexcusable" (vv 19-20). There follows the main statement in three great "waves" flowing across the text (vv 21-31) each hinging around the striking statement, "God gave them up" (v 24; v 26; v 28). The "waves" do not refer to three separate, sequential instances of rupture in divine-human relations. Each points to the same "original" lapse on the human side and the same corresponding reaction of God. The repetition drives home the all-important correspondence between human failure with respect to God and the lapse into captivity to all manner of viciousness that follows.

Preceding each instance of the phrase, "God gave them up," is a statement describing the fundamental refusal on the part of human beings to acknowledge God as Creator (vv 21-23; v 25; v 28a). Following each instance is an account of consequences in human life and society of that "giving up" on the part of God (v 24b; vv 26b-27; vv 28c-31). The lengthy description of the refusal in the first "wave" (vv 21-23) is balanced by the similarly lengthy description of the effects in human nature in the final, third wave (vv 28c-31), whereas the final, short description of the lapse (v 28a) corresponds to the equally short description of the effects in the first "wave" (v 24b). In this way, a highly artificial structure emerges, all revolving around the constant refrain, "God gave them up." Along with this distinctive overall pattern, the text exhibits many minor rhetorical flourishes, particularly in the catalogue of vices towards the end.

These formal characteristics provide a first indication that the passage is not an *ad hoc* free composition on Paul's part but something based on pre-existing models. Supporting this is the striking parallel between its content and that of tracts against Gentile idolatry to be found in contemporary Jewish literature, most notably in the Wisdom of Solomon (especially chapters 13–14). Both works (Romans and Wisdom) assume that human beings can attain to knowledge of God the Creator through the contemplation of the created world (Wis 13:1-5; Rom 1:20-21). Both find human failure to do so inexcusable (Wis 13:6-9; Rom 1:21d)—though Wisdom's censure is less severe than that of Rom 1:18-32, at least in the case of those who worship God's creatures (heavenly bodies, etc.) rather than idols of their own making. Both see a link between lapse into idolatry and immoral behavior (Wis 14:12-14, 27; Rom 1:24-31); both refer to "unnatural" sexual behavior in this connection (Wis 14:26; Rom 1:26-27). Both feature catalogues of vices (Wis 14:23-27; Rom 1:29-31), seen as liable to divine retribution (Wis 14:30 [cf.12:27]; Rom 1:32). Both mention and condemn complacency in wrongdoing as well as the wrongdoing itself (Wis 14:22; Rom 1:32). Both believe that sin has resulted in a "darkening" of the human mind (Wis 11:15; Rom 1:21). Similar diatribes against the idolatry of the pagan world (likewise seeing idolatry as the fount of all vices) occur in other literature representative of Hellenistic Judaism: *Ep. Arist.* 132-38; *Sib. Or.* 3.8–45; Josephus *Ag. Ap.* 2.236–54; *T. Napth.* 3:3-5; Philo, *Spec.* 1.13–31).

These parallels show that in 1:18-32 Paul argues out of a defined tradition in Hellenistic Judaism. Within the framework of the intra-Jewish dialogue that he is conducting at this point and for his own rhetorical purposes, he is beguiling the implied reader with a conventional polemic against the Gentile world and its idolatry. He is not directly targeting the Gentile world and certainly not the Gentile believers in Rome. He is not even "demonstrating" the sinfulness of the Gentile world; he takes that for granted. As in Gal 2:15 ("We are Jews by birth and not Gentile sinners") and before springing his rhetorical trap (2:1), he induces his Jewish dialogue partner at this point to sit back and say, "Yes, that's the Gentile world we all know."

The revelation of God's wrath against all human suppression of the truth (v 18). The opening statement about the "revelation of God's wrath" is thematic for the entire section down to 3:20. It evokes a key feature of the symbolic universe of apocalyptic Judaism—the sense that the entire world is being ushered to an imminent judgment where God's wrath will blaze out destructively against all human wickedness.

Once this apocalyptic perspective is taken into account, it is not surprising that Paul should speak of the revelation of God's wrath immediately after and to some extent in parallel with the revelation of God's righteousness (1:17a). The two "revelations" are related, even causally (cf. *gar*), in the sense that the revelation of God's wrath means that the final reckoning is under way and human beings are being found wanting in God's sight. The "thesis" to be developed here is that there is "no righteousness" on the human side (3:20). If there is to be any rescue whatsoever, it can only come about through a righteousness stemming totally from God and appropriated by human beings as pure gift through faith. The revelation of God's wrath, then, indicates the circumstances which require that the way of *God's* righteousness, appropriated through faith (1:17), be the sole, necessary and sufficient path for human beings to arrive at salvation (1:16).

Normally in Paul's letters "wrath" has a future reference and, rather than pointing to an emotional reaction of God, denotes in a fairly impersonal, objective way the final eschatological punishment (2:5, 8; 5:9; 1 Thess 1:10; 5:9; cf. also Rom 3:5; 4:15; 9:22). Here, besides speaking of God's wrath as something revealed in the present, the text also suggests a more active, personal involvement of the deity, expressed in the repeated refrain, "God gave them up" (v 24, v 26, v 28). Human beings, turning to idolatry, have abandoned God. God's wrathful reaction has been to "give them up" to captivity to viciousness of all kinds. The vices listed later in the passage are not factors *calling down* the wrath of God. They are *manifestations* of a situation of wrath already present. What provokes the wrath, what initiates the "stand-off" between God and human beings, is something more basic: an "ungodliness" *(asebeia)* and "wickedness" *(adikia)* that consists essentially in the "suppression of the truth."

In the thematic statement (v 18) this phrase is left to stand without further elaboration. But, as the structured sequence will make clear, the "truth" that is suppressed is the "truth" about God precisely as God, the sovereign Creator of the universe. It is the truth which idolatry, virtually by definition, denies. The clear implication is, then, that the "suppression" applies to the Gentile world. The thematic statement, however, speaks of God's wrath being revealed against *"all (pasan)* ungodliness and wickedness on the part of human beings." In the "all" lies a subtle hint of wider inclusiveness, one which the following prophetic accusation (2:1–3:20) will develop, to show that the revelation of God's wrath has an application and scope that is not confined to the Gentile world. All (Jews as well as Gentiles) stand in need of the righteousness of God because all, through "suppression of the truth," stand exposed to the operation of wrath.

Presupposition: Human beings inexcusable (vv 19-20). Before deploying the basic argument in three "waves," the text justifies God's wrathful reaction on the basis that the human suppression of the truth is "inexcusable." The lack of excuse is established by a kind of syllogism in reverse in which a preliminary conclusion ("What can be known about God is plain to them" [v 19a]) is supported by a twofold statement of the revelation of God in the created world (vv 19b-20ab): the "invisible" attributes of God (eternal power and deity) are inwardly (that is, through the mind) made "visible." The reasoning presupposes a "Natural Theology" along lines shared with contemporary Hellenistic Jewish literature of an apologetic kind. The natural theology does not, however, serve an apologetic or missionary purpose (as it does, for example, in Paul's speech before the Areopagus in Acts 17). It stands entirely at the service of the subsequent accusation. In fact, by placing particular stress upon the active role of God, who "has revealed" *(ephanerōsen)* in the created world what can be known of the Creator, the Pauline version brings out all the more forcefully the affront involved in human failure to respond.

The fleeting recognition given in this Pauline text to a revelation of God in the natural world is theologically significant in its own terms. (The First Vatican Council, opposing fideism in its dogmatic constitution "On the Catholic Faith," cited the text in support of its teaching that God can be known by the natural light of human reason apart from positive revelation [DS 3004].) Nonetheless, the judgment to which it leads is inescapably harsh. Modern sensitivity to the very real difficulties attending belief will find it offensive. Paul, however, has no concept of a sincere atheism. He stands within a biblical tradition given classic exposition by the psalmist: "The fool has said in his heart, 'There is no God'" (14:1; 53:2).

"Wave" I: Human refusal to know God and its consequences (vv 21-24). The first of the three descriptions of the lapse begins by describing the *positive* response human beings failed to make (glorifying God as God and giving thanks, v 21a), then elaborates the *negative* decline into which they fell, culminating in the manufacture and worship of idols (vv 21b-23).

"Glorification" and "thanksgiving" represent the appropriate human response to the "knowing" of God established on the basis of the "natural theology" (vv 19-20). In the biblical tradition, human beings cannot see God in God's own being. They "glorify" God by discerning and confessing the divine presence and power in saving events and in the created world (cf. Exod 33:18-19; also 14:19-20, 24). "Giving thanks" adds to "glorify" the sense that it is from God as Creator that one has received all things (cf. 2 Cor 4:15).

Failure to make the appropriate response in these terms has led (v 21b) to a frustration of the very faculty by which human beings "knew" God. Neglecting what ought to be its principal object of contemplation (the divine presence "behind" the created world), the human mind has become "senseless" *(asynetos)*, given to illusion. Human beings delude themselves that they are "wise" (v 22), whereas in fact they have sunk into folly, the very antithesis of the true wisdom that comes from God (cf. 1 Cor 1:18-24). Paul does not attack the power of human reason in itself. It is something for which, in fact, he has great respect (cf. 1 Cor 14:9 and especially Rom 12:2). But in his view reason cannot function properly or remain unaffected by a refusal to admit the truth about God.

There is a subtle irony in the description (v 23) of the ultimate step in this chain of decline, the lapse into idolatry. While the Jewish implied reader would presumably consider idolatry to be something characteristic of the Gentile world, the language here evokes biblical allusions to

Israel's fall into idolatry. "Exchange of glory" echoes the wording of the allusion in Ps 106:20 (LXX 105:20) to the episode of the Golden Calf (Exodus 32)—a lapse which explicitly provoked God's wrath (Exod 32:10-12) and also the language of Jer 2:11, where Israel is condemned for abandoning the Lord to go after other gods (See Note for details). What is "exchanged" in idolatry for the "glory of God" is "likeness" *(homoiōma)* and "image" *(eikōn)* of something merely human or less than human.

Behind the line of argument here would seem to be the biblical tradition, stemming from Gen 1:26-28, where human beings, created in the image (LXX *kat' eikona*) and likeness *(kath' homoiōsin)* of God, are given dominion (cf. *archetōsan* [v 26]; *katakyrieusate* [v 28]) over the rest of creation (fish, birds, animals, reptiles), a motif given more poetic expression in Psalm 8 (esp. vv 5-8). Idolatry represents the summit of "futility" (v 21) in that it has human beings submitting themselves in worship to the creatures over which they were meant to rule. This perverts the whole *raison-d'être* of the non-human created world, subjecting it to "futility" (*mataiotētēs*, 8:20).

Human rupture of relations with God leads inevitably (*dio*, v 24) to consequences in human life that point to the onset of "wrath" (v 18). God manifests wrath, not by inflicting positive punishment but by standing aside, allowing the divine-human relationship to remain frozen. This in effect leaves human beings fearfully exposed. Reason, which according to an ideal widespread in the Greco-Roman world ought to govern human affairs, has lost its primacy because of the misuse to which it has been put and the delusion into which it has sunk (vv 21b-22). With reason dethroned and God standing aside ("letting them stew in their own juice" [J.A.T. Robinson]), human beings are at the mercy of their baser instincts. God "has given them up" to the power of their own "desires" *(en tais epithymiais)*.

This captivity displays itself in "uncleanness" *(akatharsia)*, immediately defined as "the dishonoring *(atimazesthai)* of their bodies among themselves." The sudden introduction of sexual failing goes along with the already-mentioned tendency in contemporary Jewish tracts to see a link between the idolatry and the sexual depravity of the Gentile world. The second "wave" (vv 25-27) will be even more explicit in this respect. Here the "dishonoring" of God on the part of human beings has led to a corresponding "dishonoring" of a key aspect of human existence: life in the body. Paul himself has a high opinion of bodily existence, stemming from his conviction that it is destined to share the risen life of the Lord (1 Cor 6:13; 15:35-39). Later, he will urge his audience to place their bodies at the disposal of righteousness (6:12-13) and present them as "a living sacrifice, holy and acceptable to God" (12:1). The "dishonoring" of the body—the essential instrument of action, union and communication—

represents the lowest point of the captivity resultant upon human refusal to glorify God.

"Wave" II: The baleful "exchange" (vv 25-27). The second "wave" of the sequence repeats the same basic pattern as the first but with less elaboration of the fundamental lapse (v 25) and with far greater elaboration of the consequences in human nature (vv 26-27). Now it is the idea of "exchange" (*metēllaxan*, v 25, v 26; cf. *ēllaxan*, v 23) that serves to bring out the antithesis. Idolatry "exchanges the truth about God" (cf. v 18) for a "lie" (*pseudei*) when it accords to the creature the "worship" and "service" appropriate for the Creator. The very mention of such blasphemy prompts a traditional doxology (v 25c) by way of correction (cf. Rom 9:5b; 11:36b).

What was originally described (v 24) simply as "uncleanness" now receives a striking specification in terms of the "exchange" motif. The "dishonorable passions" (*pathē atimias*; cf. *epithymiai*, v 24) to which God delivers idolatrous human beings involve an "exchange" of "natural" (sexual) intercourse *(tēn physikēn chrēsin)* for that which is "contrary to nature" *(tēn para physin)*, first on the part of females (v 26b), then on the part of males (v 27).

Set against the background of contemporary Jewish tracts against the depravity of the Gentile world (see Note), the otherwise sudden mention of homosexual behavior is not all that remarkable. The subject is not raised because the Christian community in Rome was felt to stand in particular need of moral instruction in this area. Nor does it seem to have been for Paul or any other New Testament writer a pastoral problem of notably pressing concern. It appears here because the text proceeds from a tradition which saw a strong link between the idolatry and sexual depravity of the Gentile world, a depravity which to Jewish eyes was particularly evident in easy acceptance of homosexual behavior.

With respect to both female and male homosexual practice (vv 26b-27), the text points to an "exchange" of the "natural" form of (sexual) relations *(tēn physikēn chrēsin)* for that which is "contrary to nature" *(para physin)*. The language reflects the conventional Stoic sense of "nature" as the established order of things (cf. 11:21, 24). Central to that established order was dominance of male over female as far as gender relationships were concerned. Where ancient writers condemned same-sex relations, what they found offensive was the fact that such relations blurred the all-important distinction of gender role, inducing males to act as females and vice versa. The "reduction" of the male to the female constituted a "shame" contrary to nature. In the Jewish adaptation of such ideas reflected in this text a more theological note may also be present: such behavior is contrary to the design inserted into the natural order by the Creator.

What in fact receives particular stress in the present passage, at least as far as the behavior of males is concerned (v 27), is the strength of the passion involved. Males were "aflame" *(exekauthēsan)* with passion *(orexei)* for one another, and under the force of this passion committed with other males what was utterly shameful *(tēn aschēmosynēn)*. The "due penalty" *(tēn antimisthian hēn edei)* they are said to receive for their "error" *(planē)* is not punishment for this behavior as such (to think in this context of venereal disease, AIDS or even of a fixed homosexual inclination is quite astray) but a permanent incontrollable desire to engage in the activity in question. The "error" *(planē)* is the original failure to recognize God. The essential reasoning of vv 21-23 continues: idolatry has made human beings exchange the dignity that accompanied being created in the image and likeness of God for a captivity in which they are trapped in a most shameful state. The captivity evident in the behavior shows that a state of wrath, a "stand off" in relations between human beings and the Creator, prevails (v 18).

Current debate concerning the ethics of homosexual practice, the treatment of homosexuals both within and without the Christian church, and the emotions and moral dilemmas aroused by the AIDS epidemic have understandably focused attention upon this passage in recent years. Aside from more passing allusions in vice lists in 1 Cor 6:9b-10 and 1 Tim 1:9-10, it provides the only clear reference to homosexual behavior in the New Testament. Interpretation must take into account both the context and specific rhetorical role of this allusion within the wider argument of Romans. In particular, it must reckon with a considerable gap between what is envisaged by this text from the ancient world and the personal situations addressed by contemporary moral and pastoral reflection. What both the ancient literature in general and this text in particular have in mind is homosexual behavior on the part of those who have deliberately chosen to abandon what is considered to be the universal norm—heterosexual relations. The ancient world in general, and early Christian writers such as Paul in particular, made no distinction between being of homosexual disposition as an *abiding* personal psychological orientation, the cause of which remains mysterious to modern science, and free choice on the part of heterosexual persons to engage in homosexual activity. Any modern moral assessment of the issue in which scripture plays a part must clearly take this gap between ancient and modern thinking into consideration. It is also salutary to keep in mind that the allusion to same-sex relations, such as it is in Rom 1:26-27, is not there for its own sake but functions rhetorically as preparation for a "trap" set up precisely to catch those who condemn such behavior and yet, in some way, "do the very same things" (2:1, 3).

"Wave" III: The consequences of a "worthless mind" (vv 28-31). The rhetorical effect in the third "wave" flowing across the passage swings around a word play, difficult to reproduce in translation, upon the Greek

words *edokimasan/adokimon*. Both words cohere around the sense of "try" or "test." The sense conveyed by the former is "they tried God out and, finding the experience unsatisfactory, decided to break off relations," literally, "refused to hold God in knowledge." "Knowledge" *(epignōsis)* here (v 28a) means more than mere awareness of God's existence and chief attributes. It implies the deep personal knowledge (cf. 3:20; 10:2; Phil 1:9; also Col 1:9-10; 3:10) that goes along with due creaturely response to God (cf. v 21a).

Correspondingly, the divine response (v 28b) is to "give them up" to a "worthless *(adokimon)* mind." The human mind, having probed the divine reality and found it wanting, is no longer able to function as an instrument of discrimination in religious and moral affairs (cf. v 21b). This in turn leads to captivity in behavior that is totally "improper" *(poiein ta mē kathēkonta)*, to the pattern of vice illustrated in the lists that follow. It is significant, but not altogether surprising, that the ethical instruction (parenesis) given later in the letter (12:1-2) begins by calling for a "renewal of mind" that will give believers the capacity "to discern *(dokimazein)* what is the will of God—what is good, acceptable and perfect" (v 2).

What constitutes "improper conduct" is detailed (vv 29-31) in a substantial list of vices, arranged according to a distinct rhetorical pattern discernible only in the Greek (see Note). As listed, the vices bear almost exclusively upon the wider societal relating of human beings. The sexual area is notably absent—presumably because it has had a sufficient run already. In any case, the focus upon the area of wider social relationships brings to a fitting conclusion the expanding pattern of captivity discernible across the three "waves": bodily "uncleanness" on an *individual* level (v 24), the distortion of *interpersonal* relations (vv 26-27) and finally vices threatening destruction of the *wider social* fabric. The list begins with "all wickedness" *(adikia)* in a way that forms something of an "inclusion" with "all ungodliness and wickedness *(adikia)* of human beings" in the opening statement (v 18). "Wickedness," the negative correlate to "righteousness" in Romans, first denotes the suppression of the truth about God (v 18) and ends up being portrayed as that which pervades and poisons the totality of human life (v 29). The whole effect, in rhetorical terms, is to reinforce the conventional Jewish reaction of horror and moral indignation at the depravity of the Gentile world. Here indeed the eschatological wrath of God "stands revealed" (v 18).

Conclusion (v 32). The concluding statement of the sequence has long caused difficulty in its suggestion that those who approve the wrong done by others without actually imitating their actions are actually guilty of graver fault. A case can be made out for this proposition (Cranfield). But to fasten upon the issue neglects the main point. Here, as throughout this section (cf. particularly vv 21-23 and 28), the stress is upon the *delusion* (*adokimon noun*, v 28) and foolishness into which human beings have fallen as a result of the basic refusal to acknowledge God as God. The presumption appears to be that, along with the original knowledge of the existence of God (vv 19-20), went a sense also of the divine will for human behavior, the "unwritten law" inscribed in conscience (2:14-15). This sense of moral responsibility before God included an awareness of the sanction (life or death) hanging over human behavior. The divine enactment *(dikaiōma)* to this effect, which the Jews found in their law (cf. esp. Deut 30:15-20), was available through conscience to the rest of humankind. Hence the continuance in wrongdoing on the part of some and the approval given by others shows the foolishness and delusion holding the world in its grip. Humans *know* such behavior leads to death, yet they persist in it and even persuade themselves that it is laudable.

Paul, presumably, is not unaware that the Gentile world contained religious teachers and philosophers (one thinks, for example, of Paul's contemporary, Seneca) who did *not* approve of dissolute behavior and who, in an enlightened and uplifting way, condemned much of the behavior listed. The judgment is hardly meant to be applicable to each and every pagan. Nor would most of the misdemeanors listed in vv 29-31 attract the death penalty in any legal system, no matter how draconian. The verdict Paul wants to elicit, however, is global, a view of the entire Gentile world encompassed in an alienation from God that contains a strong measure of delusion. Ultimately it is the underlying alienation from God, rather than the individual vices, that leads to the penalty of death and the death that is envisaged is not so much physical death (though Paul does see that connected with sin: Rom 5:12-14; 8:10) but death in the eschatological sense of permanent separation from God.

In rhetorical terms, then, Paul would have hoped by the close of this section of his letter, to have created in his readers a *pathos* of horror and revulsion. But the concluding allusion to those who "approve" of the evil-doing has subtly introduced the notion of sitting in judgment upon the actions of others. Those who judge and approve are evidently condemned. But those who judge and *dis*approve—that is his hearers—are also in for a surprise. The "wrath" in which they see the Gentile world to be encased is about to be shown as a threat to them as well.

Notes

18. *God's wrath:* The sense of divine wrath is bound up with the biblical conception of a personal God whose dealings with humankind are attended by an intense moral will. The wrath of God blazes out when that will, and specifi-

cally the love that lies behind it, is thwarted by human pride, rebellion, obstinacy or disloyalty (cf. Zeller 54). In early parts of the OT the destructive force of God's wrath is directed against Israel (see, e.g., Exodus 32). The prophetic literature associated wrath with a coming judgment destined to fall upon either unfaithful Israel or oppressing foreign nations. In the symbolic world of Jewish apocalypticism "wrath" in this sense became a key factor in the scenario of the anticipated eschatological judgment: the righteous could expect deliverance (salvation) from the wrath; its full force, however, would fall upon those who oppress them, whether foreigners or the unfaithful in Israel. In some cases an "epoch of wrath" was seen as a prelude to the final consummation; see further G. A. Herion and S. H. Travis, *ABD* 6.989–98.

from heaven: This phrase attaches to the noun "wrath" (to which it stands closest in the Greek). "Heaven" does not so much indicate the source of revelation as the source of the wrath (cf. *1 Enoch* 91:7-8: "Then a great plague shall take place *from heaven* upon all these: the holy Lord shall emerge with *wrath* and plague in order that he may execute judgment upon the earth"; also *Sib. Or.* 1:165: "And the wrath of the great God will come upon you from heaven"). The phrase underlines the divine-human polarity that is central to the argument at this point.

against all ungodliness and wickedness: Strictly speaking, the first term *(asebeia)* indicates impiety towards God, the second *(adikia)* bad behavior in a more general sense. Here both are probably meant to be taken closely together in the sense that "suppression of the truth" about God underlies all bad behavior. Human *adikia* is opposed to God's righteousness in 3:5; cf. also 6:13.

19. *what can be known about God:* Elsewhere in the NT the Greek word *gnōstos* means "known" (cf. Luke 2:44; John 18:15; Acts 1:19; 4:16; 15:18). Here, as occasionally in the LXX and Classical Greek, the sense is "able to be known."

to them: The Greek phrase *(en autois)* contains the added nuance of "among them," "in their midst," lending the suggestion that knowledge of God should have been a collective possession leading to communal worship.

God has shown it to them: The causal link with the following sentence indicates that the "showing" in question takes place in the created world. A special primeval revelation is not in mind.

20. *Ever since the creation of the world:* The Greek word *ktisis* refers here to the moment and *act* of creation rather than to the (abiding) created world (the meaning of *ktisis* in 8:20-22). The latter understanding would make redundant the subsequent reference to "things that have been made."

his invisible nature . . . has been clearly perceived: The Greek sentence contains an oxymoron *(aorata . . . kathoratai)* that seems designed to bring out the paradox that the visible things made by God enable a spiritual "seeing" ("perception"—cf. the qualifying participial phrase *nooumena)* of the invisible divine attributes. The Pauline text here has a remarkable parallel from the Greek philosophical tradition in Ps.-Arist., *De Mundo* 399b.20: "though by nature invisible to every mortal being, he (God) is seen through his works."

in the things that have been made: What is proposed is not a mystical ascent to the deity above and beyond created things but a reflective discovery of God's presence *in* the created world.

So they are without excuse: The Greek prepositional phrase *eis to einai . . .* is best taken in a consecutive, rather than a final sense (which would imply that the human failure was willed by God).

21. *knew God:* There is at least a surface contradiction between what is presupposed here (that the Gentile world did "know God *[gnontes to theon]*") and the statement in 1 Cor 1:21 to the effect that the world "did not know God" *(ouk egnō . . . ton theon).* But in 1 Cor 1:21 (cf. also 1 Thess 4:5; Gal 4:8) the "knowing" has the fuller Semitic sense that goes beyond intellectual awareness to include the "glorifying" and "thanking" which according to Rom 1:21 is the required follow-up to intellectual awareness of God.

glorify: For "glorify" as the appropriate human response to God as Creator in Paul, see also 4:20 and 15:6, 7, 9; 1 Cor 6:20; 2 Cor 9:13; Gal 1:24. The conclusion of the Christ-hymn in Phil 2:6-11 has the entire universe acknowledging the lordship of Christ "to the glory of God" (v 11). Important also for Paul is the reciprocal sense of human beings participating in and so reflecting in themselves the glory of God (3:23; 9:4; 2 Cor 3:18). "Glory" in this sense, in line with the wider biblical and post-biblical tradition, then becomes a standard way of denoting the eschatological destiny of human beings according to the design of the Creator (cf. Rom 2:7, 10; 5:2; 8:18, 21; 9:23; 1 Cor 2:7; 2 Cor 4:17; Phil 3:21; 1 Thess 2:12). See further Notes on 1:23 and 3:23; also H. Hegermann, *EDNT* 1.344–49, esp. 346–47.

or give thanks: In 2 Cor 4:15 Paul portrays the "overflow" of thanksgiving to God on the part of human beings as the goal of the entire Christian mission.

they became futile in their thinking: The phrase alludes to Ps 94:11 (LXX 93:11): "The Lord knows the thoughts *(dialogismous)* of human beings, that they are futile" *(mataioi),* which is cited explicitly in 1 Cor 3:20. Words of the Greek *matai-* stem are frequently associated with the worship of idols in the LXX (cf., e.g., Lev 17:7; 3 Kgs 16:2, 13, 26; Hos 5:11; Isa 44:9; Jer 8:19; also Wis 13:1). "Thinking" translates the Greek plural *dialogismoi,* which in the NT and frequently also in the LXX has a pejorative sense: an exercise of reason opposed to God and right moral action. For the same idea of culpable descent into illusory knowledge and ignorance, cf. *4 Ezra* 7:21-22.

their senseless hearts were darkened: "Senseless hearts" echoes LXX of Ps 76:5 (LXX 75:6); cf., again, Wis 11:15 (with reference to the idolatry of the Egyptians). "Heart" *(kardia)* in Pauline literature denotes the inward self of human beings as thinking, willing and feeling subjects. The qualifier "senseless" *(asynetos)* suggests that the intellectual aspect is particularly in mind here. A positive correlate to this passage occurs in 2 Cor 4:6, where God's creative act is stated to have overcome the "blindness" of unbelief (cf. v 4) and "shone in our hearts to light up the knowledge of the glory of God on the face of Christ."

22. *Claiming to be wise, they became fools:* There appear to be echoes of the LXX of Isa 19:11 and Jer 10:14 here. The technical ability to make idols is a vain technology, a false "wisdom," because it creates a "nothing."

23. *and exchanged the glory of the immortal God:* The LXX of Ps 106:20 (105:20) runs: "And they changed their glory *(ēllaxanto tēn doxan autōn)* into the likeness *(en homoiōmati)* of a calf that eats grass"; cf. Jer 2:11: "If the nations will change their gods *(ei allaxontai ethnē theous autōn)*, though they are not gods: but my people have changed their glory *(ēllaxato tēn doxan autou)* for that from which they shall not profit"; cf. also Deut 4:15-18. It is not clear whether the "exchange" which takes places affects the object of worship (God, idols) only (as in the exchange implied in Ps 106:20 and Jer 2:11) or whether, as is made explicit in Rom 3:23, there is also an "exchange" on the human side as well—that is, that the exchange involves loss of the reflected glory which the biblical tradition sees attaching to human beings in view of their relationship to God (cf. Ps 8:5-8; 2 Cor 3:18; see Notes on 1:21 and 3:23). In idolatry humans beings give up being "like God" and take on the "likeness" of that which they now worship: a (merely) mortal human being or non-human lower creation (birds, animals and reptiles). Since to have been created in the image of the eternal God is the basis for human destiny to eternal life, the "exchange" also involves losing the destiny to eternal life; cf. esp. Wis 2:23-24: "For God created us (lit. "man") for incorruption and made us (lit. "him") an image of God's own eternal being" (*eikona tēs idias aidiotētos*; cf. the allusion in v 20 to God's "eternal *[aidios]* power and deity").

    for images resembling: This translates the Greek phrase *en homoiōmati eikonos* understood epexegetically: "a likeness which consists of an image."

    a mortal human being or birds or animals or reptiles: The classification of species of idols seems indebted to the prohibition against idolatry in Deut 4:16-18. This, like the creation account in Gen 1:20-30, envisages four classes of animals: beasts "on the earth," birds, reptiles and fish. The Pauline text omits the "fish" category and adds the "human" ("mortal human being").

24. *gave them up:* The implication of the Greek verb *paradidonai* is the handing over of a person into the power of another. The same Greek verb occurs very commonly in the NT with reference to the "handing over" or betrayal of Jesus to captivity and death (cf. Matt 17:22 and parallels; 1 Cor 11:23; Rom 4:25; Gal 2:20 [used reflexively with Christ as subject]); see Note on 4:25. As a counterpart to the present statement, cf. esp. Rom 8:32: "God . . . gave him (the Son) up *(paredōken auton)* for us all."

    into the power of the lustful desires of their hearts to the uncleanness: The translation takes the Greek preposition *en* instrumentally, giving the sense that the "desires" become the means whereby human beings are handed over to the plight represented by "uncleanness." "Desire" *(epithymia)* almost invariably has a negative connotation in the NT; see Note on 7:8. "Uncleanness" (*akatharsia*; cf. also 6:19) normally occurs in a figurative moral sense in the NT, especially in relation to sexual behavior (2 Cor 12:21; Gal 5:19; Eph 4:19).

of the dishonoring of their bodies: The phrase makes the "uncleanness" explicit in both an explanatory and a final sense. On the Pauline sense of "body" *(sōma)*, especially the nuance of "instrument of communication," see Interpretation and Note on 6:6.

among themselves: The contribution of this much discussed phrase (*en autois;* see esp. Kuss 1.49) becomes clearer in the light of the sense of "communication" attaching to "body": the perversion of the sexual faculty redounds ruinously upon social communication amongst human beings themselves. The ruin of the relationship with God affects human interrelating as well.

25. *Inasmuch as they exchanged:* "Inasmuch as" attempts to catch the sense of the opening Greek relative *hoitines,* which suggests continuity with (indeed the repetition of) what has preceded (the first "wave," vv 21-23; cf. esp. *ēllaxan* [v 23] . . . *metēllaxan* [v 25]) and at the same time looks forward to what follows (the new "wave," vv 25-27).

worshiped and served: The first of the two verbs *(esebasthēsan)* refers to religious veneration in general, the second *(elatreusan)* more concretely to cultic practice.

rather than the Creator: The Greek prepositional phrase, *para* with the accusative, has the sense here of "instead of," "in preference to" (cf. Luke 18:14).

26. *dishonorable passions:* The genitive in the Greek phrase *(pathē atimias)* has qualitative force: "passions which bring dishonor." This catches up the earlier reference (v 24) to the "dishonoring of their bodies."

their women . . . their men: Literally, "their females *(thēleiai)* . . . their males *(arsenes)*." The use of the adjectives rather than simply "women . . . men" stresses the sexual, gender difference. Reference to female same-sex relationships is very rare in ancient literature (for a few examples, see Fitzmyer 286). In this respect the Pauline text diverges rather strikingly from the standard pattern, where the focus was almost exclusively on male behavior, specifically in the form of pederasty, prostitution and abuse of slaves. The isolated mention does agree with the Pauline tendency to pair off male and female (Gal 3:28; 1 Cor 7:2-4, 10-11, 12-13, 16, 27-28, 32-34; 11:4-5, 7-10, 11-12, 14b-15) and may also reflect an influence upon the text of the account of the creation of the human couple in Gen 1:27 (cf. v 23). The reference to female homosexual behavior creates difficulties for the thesis (cf. R. Scroggs, *The New Testament and Homosexuality* [See Reference] 116–18, 121–22) that the present text has pederasty—and particularly its exploitative aspect—principally in view.

natural relations: The use of the Greek term *chrēsis* to denote sexual relations was well established; see BAGD 886 (s.v. 3). Taken by itself, the phrase could simply refer to forms of heterosexual intercourse regarded as uncommon. But the corresponding statement about males in v 27 (cf. the introductory *homoiōs te kai*) makes clear the reference to same-sex relations.

for unnatural: The preposition in the Greek phrase *para physin* here has the strong sense of "contrary to . . ."; see BAGD 611 (s.v. III.6). Josephus, *Ag. Ap.* 2. 273, 275, uses precisely the phrase *para physin* in criticism of homosexual union; cf. also Philo *Abr.* 137; *Spec.* 2.50; *T. Napth.* 3:4-5; Ps.-Phocylides 190–91.

Used in this strong sense, the phrase was a commonplace in popular Stoic ethical discussion and features prominently in literature debating the propriety of same-sex love. The Pauline usage reflects a popular appropriation of the Stoic tradition (though, language apart, the differences between the Pauline and Stoic understanding of "nature" are appreciable; see Note on 2:14). For further discussion, see R. B. Hays, "Relations Natural and Unnatural" (see Reference) 192–94, 197–99, who challenges the claim of J. Boswell (*Christianity, Social Tolerance and Homosexuality* [Chicago: University of Chicago Press, 1980] 111–12 and n. 69) that the phrase means simply "beyond nature."

27. *gave up:* The Greek term *aphentes*, corresponding to "exchanged" *(metēllaxan)* on the female side, likewise suggests a deliberate choice. There is no sense of homosexuality as an abiding genetic or nurture-induced condition.

were inflamed with passion: The same idea of "being aflame" with sexual desire appears in 1 Cor 7:9, though with a different verb; cf. also Sir 23:16.

men with men committing what is shameless: The Greek participle *katergazomenoi* is best taken closely with the subject, giving the sense that unnatural "desire" *(orexis)* has passed over into act; cf. Dunn 1.65.

receiving in their own persons the due penalty for their error: The expression in the Greek *(antimisthian . . . apolambanontes)* suggests the reciprocal nature of the transaction; cf. BAGD 75. "In their own persons" *(en heautois)* corresponds to the dishonoring of their bodies in v 24, but the reflexive lends the sense that the penalty is felt not so much in the interrelationship as in each individual's own body. Operative here is very likely the principle, prominent also in Wisdom (cf. 11:16; 12:23, 27; also *T. Gad* 5:1): "By that wherein one sins, by that precisely is one punished." That the "error" *(planē)* is most likely the fundamental error of refusing to "know God" (Rom 1:21-23, 25, 29) is supported by the very close parallel provided by Wis 12:24 ("For they went far astray on the paths of error *[planē]*, accepting as gods those animals that even their enemies despised").

28. *worthless mind:* In its strictly Pauline usage *adokimos* has the strong sense of being tested and found wanting: see 1 Cor 9:27 and especially the usage across 2 Cor 13:5, 6, 7. Elsewhere in the NT (2 Tim 3:8; Tit 1:16; Heb 6:8) the slightly broader sense of "base," "worthless" prevails. On "mind" *(nous)*, see Note on 7:23.

to improper conduct: The expression used here, *ta mē kathēkonta*, occurs in other Hellenistic Jewish literature (2 Macc 6:4; 3 Macc 4:16; cf. Philo, *Cher.* 14) to express inappropriate behavior. A related formula, *to para to kathēkon*, was a commonplace in Stoic philosophy to express action contrary to the moral norms imposed by nature.

29–31. *They are filled with all manner of wickedness . . .:* What may appear in translation to be a fairly arbitrary list of vices actually displays formal aspects of composition in the original. The list contains twenty-three items in all. It opens with two lines, each introduced by an adjectival expression meaning "full": the first is followed by four feminine nouns, all ending in the dative singular of the first declension; the second is followed by five nouns in the genitive. The first line lists more generalized vices; the most specific, *pleonexia* ("covetousness" with overtones of ruthlessness and violence), is widely condemned in all the literature. The vices of the second line relate more specifically to the destruction of the social order. Following the two lines comes a group of twelve nouns, or adjectives standing as nouns, all in the masculine accusative plural and arranged in pairs according to sense ("gossips" and "slanderers"; "arrogant" and "boastful," etc.). The final two pairs consist of four adjectives all beginning with the Greek *a-* privative prefix. The juxtaposition of the first two of these *(asynetou/asynthetou)* creates a clear assonance (shown also in *phthonou/phonou* ["envy" / "murder"] earlier in the list [v 29]). Such lists of vices (and virtues) played an important role in early Christian parenesis and polemic, as also in non-biblical literature. For further references and discussion, see J. T. Fitzgerald, Art. "Virtue/Vice Lists." *ABD* 6.857–59.

32. *God's decree:* The word *dikaiōma* occurs in biblical literature in the following senses: 1. "regulation," "requirement," "commandment," usually with respect to the commandments of the law (so very frequently in the LXX, usually in the plural, as in Rom 2:26; cf., however, Num 31:21 *[to dikaiōma tou nomou]* as in Rom 8:3); 2. "righteous deed" (Bar 2:19; Rev 19:8; cf. Rom 5:18); 3. "righteous judgment" (Rev 15:4); 4. "justification" ([= *dikaiōsis*]—a singular Pauline usage in Rom 5:16, coined to conform with associated words ending in *-ma*); 5. "acknowledgment of (God's) just dealings" (Bar 2:17). The basic sense of *dikaiōma* is that of a requirement or commandment with legal force. In the present context (Rom 1:32) the word probably occurs in the first sense, though the third would also be appropriate.

deserve to die: The Greek word *axios* has here a strictly legal sense: "deserving of death," in the sense that their condemnation would be legally just.

For Reference and Further Study

Bornkamm, G. "The Revelation of God's Wrath (Romans 1–3)." *Early Christian Experience* 47–70.

Dabelstein, R. *Die Beurteilung der "Heiden" bei Paulus.* BBET 14; Frankfurt/Bern: Lang, 1981.

Eckstein, H.-J. "'Denn Gottes Zorn wird vom Himmel her offenbar werden': Exegetische Erwägungen zu Röm 1. 18." *ZNW* 78 (1987) 74–89.

Fitzgerald, J. T. Art. "Virtue/Vice Lists." *ABD* 6.857–59.

Furnish, V. P. *Moral Teaching* 72–82.

Hays, R. B. "Relations Natural and Unnatural: A Response to John Boswell's Exegesis of Romans 1." *Journal of Religious Ethics* 14 (1986) 184–215.

Herion, G. A. Art. "Wrath of God (OT)." *ABD* 6.989–996

Herold, G. *Zorn und Gerechtigkeit bei Paulus: Eine Untersuchung zu Röm 1:16-18.* Frankfurt/Bern: Lang, 1973.

Hooker, M. D. "Adam in Romans i." *NTS* 6 (1959/60) 297–306.

Klostermann, E. "Die adäquate Vergeltung in Rm 1 22-31." *ZNW* 32 (1933) 1–6.

Lyonnet, S. "La connaissance naturelle de Dieu: Rom 1,18-23." *Études* 43–70.
Pohlenz, M. "Paulus und die Stoa." *ZNW* 42 (1949) 69–104.
Popkes, V. "Zum Aufbau und Charakter von Römer 1.18–32." *NTS* 28 (1982) 490–501.
Scroggs, R. *The New Testament and Homosexuality.* Philadelphia: Fortress, 1983.
Stegemann, W. "Paul and the Sexual Mentality of His World." *BTB* 23 (1993) 161–66.
Stowers, S. *Rereading of Romans* 83–104.
Travis, S. H. Art. "Wrath of God (NT)." *ABD* 6.996–98.

b) *Those Who "judge" Are Not Immune from the Wrath* (2:1-11)

1. Wherefore you have no excuse, you whoever you are who sit in judgment. For in judging another you condemn yourself. For you who sit in judgment do the very same things. 2. Now we know that the judgment of God against those who do such things is in accordance with the truth.
3. So do you, who sit in judgment on those who do such things and do the very same, imagine that you will escape God's judgment?
4. Or is not that you despise the riches of his kindness and forbearance and patience, failing to realize that God's kindness is meant to lead you to repentance? 5. In your hardness and impenitence of heart you are storing up wrath for yourself against the day of wrath, when God's righteous judgment will be revealed.
6. Who (God) "will repay each one according to each one's works": 7. To those who through perseverance in good work seek glory and honor and immortality (there will be) eternal life. 8. To those who through ambitious self-seeking disavow the truth and follow wickedness (there will be) wrath and fury. 9. There will be affliction and distress for every human being who does evil—the Jew first, but also the Greek. 10. There will be glory and honor and peace for everyone who does good—the Jew first, but also the Greek. 11. For God has no favorites.

INTERPRETATION

Introduction to 2:1-29 as a whole. In Rom 1:18–3:20, Paul is engaged in a long prophetic accusation designed to exclude the possibility of finding a righteous status before God on any basis other than that offered in the gospel: the righteousness of God made accessible through faith. The overall target of the accusation (the "implied reader" at this point), is the Jewish dialogue partner who rests upon a righteousness derived from practice of the law. Paul's tactic at first has been to lull this audience

(1:18-32) into a complacent, conventional judgment upon the alienation of the Gentile world. Now (2:1) it is time to spring the rhetorical trap. Turning for the first time in the letter to the diatribe style, he addresses the dialogue partner directly: "Each one of you who judges." At the outset the identity of this one "who judges" is not further specified. Only at v 17 is the addressee explicitly identified as "the Jew." But the claims to special consideration, recorded and rejected early on (vv 4-5), are much more understandable coming from Jews rather than Gentiles and the sentiments have clear parallels in contemporary Jewish works such as Wisdom (esp. Wisdom chapters 11–12 and 15; see below). This suggests that the initially generalized nature of the address (v 1, v 3) is for rhetorical purposes only. The principal target from the start is the Jewish audience, seen as sitting in habitual judgment upon the behavior of the surrounding Gentile world.

After the initial springing of the trap (vv 1-3), the tactic is to erode Jewish confidence of being preserved from God's eschatological wrath on the basis of a privileged position with respect to judgment. First of all (vv 4-11), Paul argues that the claim to more favorable treatment on the basis of Israel's special position is illusory (vv 4-5), since the eschatological judgment will be strictly according to a person's works (vv 6-10), with all partiality excluded (v 11). Then, in the light of these twin principles (judgment according to works and divine impartiality), Paul in three stages relativizes and demolishes any sense of advantage stemming from possession of the law: 1. (vv 12-16) possession of the law is no advantage, since performance rather than possession will be the criterion of judgment and Gentiles who do not in fact possess the law (of Moses) are nonetheless in a position to know and practice what the law requires; 2. (vv 17-24) possession of the law does not preserve Jews from factual transgressions of its precepts; 3. (vv 25-29) circumcision is of no avail if not followed by faithful performance of the law.

The "Trap" (vv 1-3). In diatribe mode, Paul suddenly (v 1) turns upon one simply dubbed at this stage "you who judge." The actual logic of the transition from what precedes is not all that clear (see Note). For rhetorical purposes—to gain the maximum force out of his surprising accusation—Paul draws the conclusion ("you are inexcusable") before he has in place all the elements which logically justify it. The crucial premise comes at the end of v 1 and is repeated in v 3: "You do the same." Because the judgers commit the same sins as those they judge, their verdict of condemnation falls equally upon themselves. Like David faced with the accusation of prophet Nathan following upon the death of Uriah (2 Sam 12:1-7), they are themselves trapped in the condemnation they rightly pronounce upon others. Hence, like the Gentile world which they have judged, they too are "without excuse" (cf. v 20).

If, as seems to be the case, Paul already has Jews in mind, the accusation that they "do the same things" creates a problem. Evidence from the ancient world suggests that adherence to the law kept Jews free from idolatry and the excesses, especially in the sexual area, attributed to Gentiles in 1:26-27. Paul may have in mind the vices listed more immediately before in 1:29-31, some of which could apply to Jews as well as pagans. But it is probably wrong to take "the same" too literally at this point. The accusation here is generalized and anticipatory; more specific charges will follow in vv 17-24. The sense is that the "judging" world commits crimes which expose them to the judgment they cast upon others. They too are sinners worthy of God's judgment.

It follows (v 2) that the accurate assessment of the deserts of the Gentile world according to 1:32a ("that those who do such things deserve to die") now, as a result of the accusation in 2:1, applies with equal validity ("according to truth") to the "disapprovers" as well. The sharp rhetorical question in v 3 brings home the conclusion that must then be drawn: if God's judgment is truly upon those who do such things, how can the judging world which also does them hope to escape?

This rhetorical question and the unstated answer it expects—"It cannot!"—provides the "thesis" for the sequence that now unfolds. From here to the end of the accusation (2:29), the argument aims at the erosion of any consideration that might be brought forward against the conclusion just drawn.

No "Special Treatment" (vv 4-5). First (vv 4-5) Paul punctures any hope that a special position as God's favored people will result in favorable treatment at the time of eschatological judgment. Jewish confidence in this respect is, once again, clearly illustrated in the Book of Wisdom. So close, in fact, are the contacts in language and ideas that it is hard to believe that Paul is not writing with Wisdom specifically in mind.

> While chastening us, you scourge our enemies ten thousand times more, so that, when we judge, we may meditate upon your goodness, and when we are judged, we may expect mercy (Wis 12:22).
> But you, our God, are kind *(chrēstos)* and true, patient *(makrothymos)*, and ruling all things in mercy. For even if we sin we are yours, knowing your power; but we will not sin, because we know that you acknowledge us as your own. For to know you is complete righteousness and to know your power is the root of immortality (15:1-3; cf. also 16:9-11).

Paul does not contest that God is kind and patient. He challenges, however, the attitude that falsely takes these attributes to mean that God's judgment of sin will not be severe. Such an attitude, in effect, "despises" them. Whereas the truth of the matter is that God's kindness *(chrēstotēs)*, forbearance (*anochē*; cf. 3:26) and patience (*makrothymia*) are there to provide a space for repentance before the inevitable judgment falls (cf. Wis 11:23). What distinguishes Israel from the rest is not the prospect of milder judgment but the staying of God's hand to provide opportunity for conversion *(metanoia)*. Jews may not be now in the same situation as the Gentiles, in whose pattern of life the wrath is already revealed (1:18). But this does not mean that the wrath will not apply in their case. Quite the contrary. In a kind of ironical reversal of the idea of "storing up" (eternal) life for oneself (see Note), Paul charges (v 5) that "in their hardness and impenitence of heart" (cf. 9:17-18) they are "storing up" *(thēsaurizein)* wrath against the day of wrath and of revelation of God's righteous judgment. The wrath already fallen upon the Gentiles in the shape of the vices to which they are "given up" (1:24, 26, 28) will fall no less severely upon the chosen people unless they repent.

Judgment according to works (vv 6-10). What makes the hope of "special treatment" illusory is the truth that, at the eschatological judgment, the sole criterion will be a person's works, assessed with total impartiality. Paul develops this point in an intricately structured sequence. In v 6 an opening quotation from Ps 62:13 (LXX 61:13; cf. also Prov 24:12) states the basic principle: judgment will be according to works. Corresponding to this in inclusive fashion there comes at the end (v 11) the statement of God's impartiality. In between come two balanced couplets, each asserting, positively and negatively, the principle of recompense according to works. In the first pair, the positive comes first (v 7), the negative (v 8) second; in the second pair (vv 9-10), it is the other way round, so forming a chiasm. In the second pair there is also an internal parallelism created by the appearance at the end of each statement of the refrain, "the Jew first, but also the Greek."

The first, positive formulation of the principle (v 7) speaks of those who "seek" eternal life "through perseverance in doing good." "Seeking" is not the same as "meriting" and to this extent the principle is milder in its formulation than it might otherwise have been (see Interpretation of v 13 below).

In the first negative formulation (v 8) the language seems designed to recall the central thesis of the preceding passage (1:18-32). *Eritheia*, if rightly translated "ambitious self-seeking" (see Note), admirably denotes what appears to be basic human sin in Paul's eyes: the self-regarding revolt of the creature against the Creator, for which in 1:21-23, 25, 28a idolatry forms the basic paradigm. Likewise, "disavowing the truth" *(alētheia)* and following "wickedness" *(adikia)* recapitulate the ideas and phraseology with which the "accusation" began (1:18). Over against the "righteousness" or "truth" of God (1:17; cf. 3:4-5) stands the "wickedness" of human beings, a wickedness which flows from a self-regarding suppression of the "truth" about God. In both cases (1:18; 2:8) the human wickedness is met by a divine response of "wrath" ("wrath and fury"; see Note). The only difference is that, whereas in the case of the Gentile world (1:18) the wrath is already being revealed, in the case of the "judging" (Jewish) world the wrath will confront the wrongdoer at the eschatological judgment. The fact that the same motifs continue throughout the discourse makes clear at last the full extent of the "all" *(pasan)* before the reference to "wickedness" *(adikia)* in 1:18. The "wickedness" in question comprehends the entire world, Jewish as well as Gentile.

The same universalist note emerges explicitly in the second couplet (vv 9-10). The national grouping ("Jew . . . Greek"), unmentioned since the opening thematic statement (1:16), reappears in the parallel statements, on both the negative and positive sides, indicating that the two groups, Jews and Gentiles, are specifically in mind. There is considerable irony in the echoing here of the formula asserted so positively in the great thematic statement of 1:16. The Jewish "priority" ("Jew first, but also the Greek") with respect to the gospel does not imply a special claim upon mercy. The "priority" applies to judgment (condemnation) as much as to reward.

God's impartiality (v 11). An explicit statement of the principle of divine impartiality rounds off the rhetorical figure. This principle, together with the one formulated earlier (v 6) asserting that judgment will be strictly according to deserts, further erodes any sense of special privilege. In the coming eschatological judgment Jews and Gentiles will stand on equal footing in the assessment of their works.

NOTES

1. *Wherefore you have no excuse:* The Greek conjunction *dio* normally draws an inference from what has gone before (cf., in Romans, 4:22; 13:5; 15:7, 22). Here it introduces a new section in the sense that the validity of the condemnation that falls on the "judger" depends on the prior recognition, recorded in 1:32 (repeated in 2:2), that those who do such things are, by God's decree, worthy of death. Across the transition Paul seems to have three classes in mind: 1. those who *practice* the vices listed in the preceding section; 2. those who *approve* of what they do (v 32b); 3. those who *disapprove*, in the sense that they sit in judgment upon the previous two classes (2:1, 3). In the preceding section, it was the first two classes who were "inexcusable" (cf. 1:32), the implication being that those who *disapprove*—that is, those who sit in judgment upon them—would not be "inexcusable," but on the contrary justified. Paul allows this implicit distinction between "approvers" and "disapprovers" to emerge. He then suddenly swings around and brands the disapprovers as "inexcusable" as well and does so as if this were an inference ("Wherefore . . .") from what has gone before—whereas the true inference would seem to go in the opposite direction.

The logic is similar to that of the remonstrance to Cephas (Peter) in the incident at Antioch recorded in Galatians 2, where Paul rehearses (Gal 2:15-17) for Peter's benefit the realization implicit in Jewish conversion to Jesus as the Christ. The statement: "We are Jews by nature and not Gentile sinners" (v 15) could well sum up the complacent judgment expected of a Jewish reader at the end of Romans 1. "But," continues Paul (v 16), "knowing (that is, having realized) that a person is not justified by works of law but through faith in Jesus Christ, we too put our faith in Christ, so that we might be justified by faith in Christ and not from works of law, because 'from works of law shall no human being be justified'" (cf. Rom 3:20). Moreover (v 17), if this mode of justification implies—as it does—that "we too were found to be sinners," that does not mean that Christ is a "minister of sin"—an objection which apparently has to be rebutted. The brief sequence in Gal 2:15-17 reveals the same logic whereby Jewish complacency with respect to righteousness is eroded on the grounds that what God has done through Jesus Christ implies a lack of righteousness on the part of Jews matching that of the Gentile world they judge; Jews along with Gentiles are locked in a common bind of sin. But this is only the negative presupposition for the overwhelming good news of the triumphant common rescue through grace (Rom 3:21-26; Gal 2:16, 21).

you whoever you are who sit in judgment: Here, as throughout 2:1-5, Paul follows a pedagogical strategy familiar from Stoic diatribe sources, where the teacher attacks pretensions, arrogance and conceit of the student with indicting discourse; see further S. Stowers, *Diatribe* 86–88, 111–12.

2. *we know:* Paul frequently uses the Greek expression *oidamen* to express a truth or fact which he believes or hopes is a matter of common ground between himself and those he addresses: cf. 3:19; 7:14; 8:22, 28; 1 Cor 8:1, 4; 2 Cor 5:1.

   in accordance with the truth: The Greek phrase *(kata alētheian)* could simply mean "truly" in the sense of "in accordance with the facts." More likely, it reflects a deeper theological sense where *alētheia* expresses God's fidelity in a way that comes very close to "righteousness" (cf. 3:7 and 15:8; *4 Ezra* 7:34; *2 Apoc. Bar.* 85:9; esp. Qumran: CD 20:29-30; 1QS 4:19-20; 11:14; 1QH 1:26-27; etc.).

3. *you will escape God's judgment:* Cf. *Pss. Sol.* 15:8: "And those who do lawlessness shall not escape *(ouk ekpheuxontai)* the judgment *(krima)* of the Lord." The post-biblical Jewish psalm illustrates precisely the kind of complacent attitude challenged here.

4. *Or is not that you despise:* The alternative, expressed in a rhetorical question, is the more radical one indicating what is actually the case: "or, rather, is it not the case that . . .?". As v 5 will make clear, the "despising" consists in misjudging God's forbearance as leniency.

   the riches of his kindness and forbearance and patience: All three attributes occur in Wis 15:1. Both the language and thought are traditional. The idea of God's "kindness" (*chrēstotēs*; the word occurs no less than three times in Rom 11:22 in contrast to "severity" *[apotomia]*) is common in the Psalms. "Forbearance" (*anochē*; cf. also 3:26) and "patience" (*makrothymia*; cf. also 9:22) both refer to the restraint exercised by God with respect to wrath in the face of human sin (cf. 2 *Apoc. Bar.* 59:6).

failing to realize that God's kindness is meant to lead you to repentance?: "Failing to realize" translates a Greek expression *(agnoōn)* indicating culpable human refusal to acknowledge something about God; cf. 1:21. While the whole idea of conversion is central to Paul's understanding of human response to the Gospel (cf. Gal 2:16), he does not regularly use the language of "repentance" *(metanoia)*, which appears elsewhere only in 2 Cor 7:9-10. Paul is indicting the Jewish audience in the language of its own tradition. The idea that God's forbearance provides opportunity for repentance is characteristic of Wisdom: cf. 11:23; 12:10, 19; cf. also Sir 44:16; 48:15.

5. *In your hardness and impenitence of heart:* Paul turns against his Jewish audience a warning frequently uttered against Israel in the biblical tradition: cf., e. g., Deut 10:16; Jer 4:4. At the end of this indictment (2:29) Paul will appeal precisely to the necessity for "circumcision of the heart." The concept of "hardening" *(sklērynein)* returns at 9:18; cf. 11:25 *(pōrōsis)*.

   you are storing up wrath for yourself: This reverses a current expectation that the righteous individual stores up *(thēsaurizein)* a heavenly credit to be made available on the day of judgment; cf. esp. Tob 4:9-10; *Pss. Sol.* 9:3-5; also *4 Ezra* 6:5; 7:77; 8:33, 36; 2 *Apoc. Bar.* 14:12.

   against the day of wrath when God's righteous judgment will be revealed: The roots of the apocalyptic concept of the judgment as a "day of wrath" lie in the biblical motif of the "day of the Lord" (Amos 5:18; Isa 2:12; 13:6; 24:21; Jer 46:10; Joel 2:1-2; Ezek 7:7; 30:3; Zeph 1:7,15, 18; 2:2-3 [in the last three references the day is specifically a "day of wrath"]; Mal 3:2; 4:1). Paul's usage here (cf. also 2:8, 16; 3:5; 5:9; 9:22; 1 Thess 1:10; 5:9) reflects the appropriation of the idea in later Jewish apocalypticism (cf. *1 Enoch* 45:2-6; *Pss. Sol.* 15:12-13; *4 Ezra* 6:17-24; 7:102). For Paul, however, the "day of the Lord" is also the day of the Lord Jesus (1 Cor 1:8; 5:5; 2 Cor 1:14; Phil 1:6, 10; 2:16; 1 Thess 5:2). "God's righteous judgment" *(dikaiokrisia)* is the negative judgment to be passed upon sinners (cf. *T. Levi* 3:2; 15:2). Paul turns against his audience the conventional expectation that God's righteous judgment would fall upon the persecutor and enemy.

6. *Who (God) "will repay each one according to each one's works":* The quotation corresponds exactly to LXX Ps 61(62):13, save that the direct address to God is altered to the third person singular introduced by the relative pronoun, as in the parallel Prov 24:12 (LXX). For additional biblical formulations of the principle, see Job 34:11 (negative only); Jer 17:10; Hos 12:2 (negative); cf. also Pss 37:37-38; 58:11; Prov 10:16; Isa 3:10-11; 59:18; Lam 3:64. For post-biblical evidence and more general considerations, see K. L. Snodgrass, "Justification by Grace—to the Doers" (see Reference) 77–79, 90, n. 39; also Wilckens, 1.127–31.

7. *through perseverance in good work:* The fact that "perseverance" *(hypomonē)* always denotes a Christian virtue in Paul (cf. also 5:3; 8:25; 15:5; 2 Cor 1:6; 6:4; 12:12; 1 Thess 1:3) lends an entirely positive note to "work" *(ergon)* here.

seek glory and honor and immortality: The virtually synonymous combination "glory" *(doxa)* and "honor" (*timē*; cf. also 2:10; 1 Tim 1:17) denotes the honor and praise one might hope to receive from God at the judgment. "Seeking" such does not imply "works-righteousness" but allowing the pattern of one's life to be shaped by the desire to receive the only commendation that matters—the final commendation from God (cf. 2:29; 1 Cor 4:5; 2 Cor 5:10; 10:18). "Glory" also designates in Paul the eschatological human participation in the life of God which is virtually synonymous with the attainment of salvation and arrival at the state intended by God for human beings from the outset; see Notes on 1:21; 1:23; 3:23. "Immortality" *(aphtharsia)* is a more typically Greek expression of the longed-for salvation: cf. Wis 2:23 and 4 Macc 17:12. In 1 Cor 15:50-54, defending the resurrection of the body, Paul states the necessity for believers to "put on immortality."

eternal life: "Eternal life" *(zōē aiōnios)* is a rather more "Jewish" expression of the gift of salvation (cf. also 5:21; 6:22-23; Gal 6:8 and throughout the NT; cf. also Dan 12:2; 2 Macc 7:9; 4 Macc 15:3).

8. *ambitious self-seeking:* The phrase translates the single Greek word *eritheia*, the meaning of which is disputed because of the almost complete lack of parallels prior to Paul. The meaning "factiousness," based upon a tempting but misleading tendency to see a connection with *eris* ("discord") is almost certainly to be rejected. A use of the term by Aristotle (*Politics* 5.2 [1302b, 4; 1303a, 4]) in the sense of self-seeking pursuit of political office by underhand means points to the sense of "selfish ambition," which also fits well with other occurrences in Paul: 2 Cor 12:20; Gal 5:20; Phil 1:17; 2:3; cf. Jas 3:14; see BAGD 309.

   (there will be) wrath and fury: The verb "to be" has to be supplied in translation to cover the fact that Paul abandons the accusative construction dependent upon "will repay" (v 6) and adopts the nominative. The Greek terms *orgē* ("wrath") and *thymos* ("fury") appear together constantly in the LXX (cf., e.g., Exod 32:12 [cf. vv 10, 11]; Num 12:9; 14:34; 32:14; Deut 29:23, 24, 28) and are virtually synonymous (cf. Rev 14:10; 16:19; 19:15). Here they designate the divine reaction at the final judgment to human wrongdoing.

9. *(There will be) affliction and distress:* The pair "affliction" *(thlipsis)* and "distress" *(stenochōria)* occur again at 8:35 (cf. Deut [LXX] 28:53, 55, 57; Isa 8:22; 30:6), where they refer to the trials affecting believers *before* the judgment—the usual reference of the terms in Paul (*thlipsis*: 5:3; 12:12; 1 Cor 7:28; 2 Cor 1:4, 8; 2:4; 4:17; 6:4; 7:4; 8:2, 13; Phil 1:17; 4:14; 1 Thess 1:6; 3:3, 7; *stenochōria*: 2 Cor 6:4; 12:10). Understood here as effects of the divine wrath, they together indicate the eschatological fate awaiting wrongdoers.

10. *glory and honor and peace:* The list of benefits corresponds to that in v 7, save for the replacement of "immortality" by "peace" *(eirēnē)*. In view of the parallelism, the "peace" is not so much peace with God (as in Rom 5:1) but a peace that is part of the eschatological blessings of salvation (cf. Isa 52:7).

11. *God has no favorites:* Literally: "There is no partiality with God." The Greek word *prosōpolēmpsia* appears to be a Christian (possibly Pauline) coinage from

the LXX phrase *prosōpon lambanein,* used to translate the biblical metaphor of "lifting up the face" in the sense of showing special favor or partiality: cf. Lev 19:15; Ps 82(81):2; Sir 4:22; 35:16 (LXX 35:13). The principle, in various formulations, became axiomatic in the Jewish tradition; see esp. J. Bassler, *Divine Impartiality* (see Reference) 7–119; K. Berger, *EDNT* 2.179–80. Elsewhere in the NT, see Acts 10:34; Eph 6:9; Col 3:25; 1 Pet 1:17; Jas 2:1 (plural); cf. also Jas 2:9.

For Reference and Further Study

Bassler, J. M. *Divine Impartiality: Paul and a Theological Axiom.* SBLMS 59; Chico, CA: Scholars, 1982.

__________. "Divine Impartiality in Paul's Letter to the Romans." *NovT* 26 (1984) 42–58.

Cambier, J.-M. "Le jugement de tous les hommes par Dieu seul, selon la verité, dans Rom 2:1–3:20." *ZNW* 67 (1976) 187–213, esp. 188–96.

Donfried, K. P. "Justification and Last Judgment in Paul." *ZNW* 67 (1976) 90–110.

Sanders, E. P. *Paul, the Law and the Jewish People* 123–35.

Snodgrass, K. L. "Justification by Grace—To the Doers: An Analysis of the Place of Romans 2 in the Theology of Paul." *NTS* 32 (1986) 72–93.

Stowers, S. K. *Diatribe* 79–113.

__________. *Rereading of Romans* 100–09.

Synofzik, E. *Die Gerichts- und Vergeltungsaussagen bei Paulus.* Göttingen: Vandenhoeck & Ruprecht, 1977, 80–83, 140–42.

Watson, F. *Paul, Judaism and the Gentiles* 106–22.

c) *Possession of the Law Makes No Difference* (2:12-29)

1. The Law and the Gentiles (2:12-16)

12. All who have sinned without the law will also perish without the law, and all who have sinned under the law will be judged by the law. 13. For it is not the hearers of the law who are righteous before God, but the doers of the law will be justified—

> 14. When Gentiles, though not having the law, nonetheless do by nature what the law requires, they constitute a law to themselves. 15. They show the work of the law written on their hearts, with their conscience providing confirmation as their conflicting thoughts accuse or perhaps excuse them—

16. on that day when, according to my gospel, God will judge the secrets of human hearts through Christ Jesus.

Interpretation

Introduction. This small pericope, 2:12-16, is awkward from a syntactical point of view in that v 16 does not contain a main statement but rather a time-marking relative clause which attaches far better to the statements in vv 12-13 than to what immediately precedes in vv 14-15. Moreover, apart from the question of syntax, the eschatological reference in v 16 resumes the future statements of vv 12-13, whereas what is said about Gentile possibility with respect to the law in vv 14-15 refers most naturally to the present rather than the future. There are good grounds, then, for regarding vv 14-15 as a parenthesis (the kind of comment modern writers might place in a footnote), explaining how the Gentiles, who do not explicitly possess the law of Moses, have an equivalent access to what the law commands and so can rightly be judged on the principle of performance along with the Jews. Nonetheless, what is said in these verses about Gentile capacity with respect to the law seems integral to Paul's polemic against Jewish confidence in possession of the law and will be treated as such in this commentary.

Possession or non possession of the law irrelevant (v 12). Paul has stated (vv 6-11) the basic principle that judgment will be strictly according to works and will fall equally upon Jew and Gentile. In vv 12-13 he re-asserts the principle in terms of the one factor that might seem to put it in question: Jewish possession of the law. In a strict parallelism that catches up (in reverse order) the "Jew first . . . also the Greek" refrain of vv 9 and 10, he first states the negative possibility: judgment and eternal ruin will fall upon all sinners whether (as Gentiles) they sin "apart from the law" *(anomōs)* or (as Jews) they sin "in the law" *(en nomǭ)*. If sin has been the pattern of life, possession or non-possession of the law makes no fundamental difference (cf. Matt 7:24-27; Jas 1:22-25). The law in fact will function as instrument of judgment (v 12: *dia nomou krithēsontai*).

Following this negative statement in v 12, one might expect a corresponding positive counter statement, to the effect that those who act righteously "within" or "without" the law will be justified. What in fact follows (v 13) does have a positive assertion at the end ("will be justified"). But its initial function is to ground the previous negative statement by making a sharp distinction between "hearers" and "doers" of the law: having the law and so being in a position to "hear" it is of no advantage if—as is the case—performance will be the sole criterion of justification (cf. vv 6-10). The insistence upon "doing" as distinct from merely "hearing" the law is no novelty in a Jewish context (cf. also Matt 7:24-27; Jas 1:22-23, 25). In the present connection, however, where Jews and Gentiles are being played off against each other, its formulation is sharply polemical. The *Shemaᶜ* prayer ("Hear, O Israel", Deut 6:4-5), recited daily, defines Israel as the "hearing/obedient nation" *par excellence.*

Performance the criterion of justification (v 13). Along with the distinction between "hearing" and "doing," a key motif in the symbolic universe of apocalyptic Judaism now makes its first explicit appearance in the letter. "Justification" refers to the verdict of approval and acceptance rendered by God at the last judgment that is decisive for entrance into the blessings of salvation. Contrary to what is often assumed, Paul fully embraces the principle of justification according to one's works. Acceptance of the Christian gospel has indeed led him to be fully convinced that *in fact* no human being will find justification on the basis of works and that, faced with total human unrighteousness, God has graciously effected in Christ an alternative mode of justification for those who believe (3:21-26). But the *principle* of justification (judgment) according to works stands and believers themselves still have to come before the judgment seat of God to be assessed on the way they have preserved and lived out the righteous status graciously granted them through faith (cf. 14:10-12; 2 Cor 5:10; 9:6; 11:15; Gal 6:7). In the present passage, Paul works more directly from within the traditional apocalyptic schema of an eschatological justification to be given by God to those found righteous on the basis of their works. For the purpose of the prophetic accusation and echoing what has already been stated in vv 6-7 and 10, he envisages at least the possibility of a justification on the basis of performance—though very soon (3:19-20, 23) he will deny that this possibility, at least as conventionally understood, could be realized in fact.

Gentiles who perform what the law requires (vv 14-15). In pursuit of this thesis that what will count at the final judgment is performance rather than possession of the law, Paul points to the performance on the part of some Gentiles of deeds corresponding to the dictates of the Mosaic law. In so far as they are human beings they find in their very nature (*physei;* see Note) a moral order corresponding to what the law prescribes. Paul need not have more than a few outstanding individuals in mind (so that what is stated here does not really counter the pessimistic judgment on the Gentile world as a whole formulated earlier on [1:19-32; cf. 3:9, 23]). Nor does he mean that these few "righteous Gentiles" carry out the law in its entirety. The point is that their exceptional pattern of life overthrows any exaggerated claims made for the law as sole moral guide and criterion of judgment.

An appended clause (v 15) explains the inner workings of this access on the part of Gentiles to what the law prescribes. Gentile performance of the "things commanded by the law" shows *(endeiknyntai)* that its impulse or effect (literally "work" *[ergon]*) is written in their hearts. Moreover, besides the evidence of external deeds in this way, there is also the witness of "conscience" (*syneidēsis;* see Note). The fact that Gentiles, reflecting upon their behavior, can suffer pangs of remorse or even feel that what they have done is defensible, is a further testimony to the presence of a "law written in their hearts."

The day of judgment (v 16). What emerges from this reflection (couched in Stoic terms; see Note) upon Gentile moral possibility is a contrast between a law written from without (such as Jews have in the law of Moses) and a law written within human beings directly by God, who alone searches and judges interior things (v 16; cf. vv 28 and 29; 8:27). Paul picks up this sense of God attending primarily to an inner moral core when he returns to round off the earlier allusions to justification and judgment (vv 12-13) with specific allusion to God's "day" of judgment. Odd though it may seem, the idea of judgment is necessarily part of the total complex proclaimed in the gospel. But, according to that same gospel (literally, "my gospel"), the final judgment will not depend upon extrinsic factors such as possession of the law. Instead, God will weigh performance, with particular awareness of and attention to the moral capacity written within the secret depths of human hearts *(ta krypta tōn anthrōpōn)* where God alone has access.

In the end, of course, on Paul's fuller explanation of the gospel (cf. 3:20-30), the eschatological justification can only rest on a "performance" that is entirely the achievement of God's grace (5:17-19; cf. 8:4). In that light, any justification envisaged could apply solely in the case of believers. But Paul refrains from explicit statement in this vein for the present. Within the framework of the conventional schema of justification and last judgment in apocalyptic Judaism, he gives a mere hint of a justification that will look, not to externals, but to the essential inner core of human life. The polemic presses on relentlessly: possession of the law is of little relevance in the context of God's universal judgment.

Reflection: Paul's acknowledgment in this passage of at least the possibility that those beyond the law (the Gentiles) could live righteously and attain justification invites a reflection upon the contemporary situation where Christian believers constitute only a small proportion of the total population of the world. The sense of God's judgment in Christ reaching beyond externals to grasp the moral capacity hidden in the depths of human beings promotes a view of divine grace as something ranging well beyond the bounds of explicit Christian faith. However distant Paul's argument may seem from contemporary concerns, it at least gives a hint that God's work in Christ, as well as initiating a process and a movement of explicit belief, also offers a paradigm of salvation for those who do not explicitly believe.

Notes

12–16. Beyond the syntactical problems mentioned in the Interpretation, there are two ways of viewing this pericope. 1. A more negative understanding takes v 12 as determinative and sees the statements about Gentile performance of the law in vv 14-15 to be addressing the question as to how the Gentiles, lacking the law, can justly be candidates for condemnation, since the law will be the instrument of judgment. This ("pessimistic") interpretation (G. Bornkamm; O. Kuss; E. Käsemann; C. K. Barrett; W. Schmithals; J. Fitzmyer; etc.) has the advantage of agreeing with the verdict later to be given in 3:9, 20: that all without exception stand "under sin" (cf. 1:18-32; 3:23; 11:32). It does less justice to v 13, where Paul, as earlier in v 7 and v 10, states positively and unequivocably that those who do the law will find justification. 2. The alternative approach (adopted in the Interpretation; cf. also U. Wilckens; M. Pohlenz; K. L. Snodgrass; J. Bassler; D. Zeller; F. Watson) stresses v 13 and sees Paul countenancing the possibility that some Gentiles at least "do what the law requires" (cf. the statement about the "[uncircumcised] one who fulfills the law" in v 27 [cf. v 29]). Vv 14-15 then explain how Gentiles can achieve this in their "law-less" state. The tension between this interpretation and the overall "thesis" (1:18–3:20, 23) that all without exception stand "under sin" (3:9) has long suggested to interpreters ancient (St. Augustine) and modern (e.g., Cranfield) that the "Gentiles" Paul has in view in vv 14-15 and v 27 are Gentile *Christians*. It is hard to see, however, how Paul could say of Gentile Christians that, lacking the law of Moses as moral guide, they attain such guidance by the enlightenment of "nature"; for Paul, those "in Christ" find moral guidance and capacity through the Spirit, which creates in them the "mind" or attitude of Christ (cf. 8:1-13; 12:1-2; 13:8-10; cf. 6:17; Phil 2:5). The tension is best resolved when seemingly inconsistent statements across Romans 1–3 are not played off against one another in a systematizing way but seen as individual stages in a total rhetorical construction. Paul's passing endorsement of the possibility that some Gentiles fulfill the law's requirement is designed to highlight the failure on the Jewish side.

12. *without the law:* In most cases the Greek word *nomos* in Paul refers to the law of Moses. But *nomos* also appears in a wider range of meaning: it can refer, in a generic sense, to any system or factor seeking to control behavior; it can indicate what is regularly the case (= "principle" [e.g., Rom 3:27]); it can simply indicate "the Law" (= "the Pentateuch" [e.g., 3:21]) or scripture in general (e.g., 3:19). Paul often exploits this range of meaning (cf. esp. Rom 3:27-28, 31; 7:21-23; 8:2), sometimes, it would appear, with deliberate ambiguity (3:27-31); see further Interpretation of 7:21-23. To allow for such range and ambiguity, this commentary translates (*ho*) *nomos* as "(the) law" rather than "(the) Law" even when the reference is clearly to the law of Moses. In the present case (2:12) the parallel provided in 1 Cor 9:21 shows that for Paul at least the adverb *anomōs* means simply "not under law" in the sense that the law (of Moses) was not applicable. S. Stowers, maintaining that Paul held the Gentiles to be subject to the Mosaic law, translates "in a manner befitting lawlessness" (*Rereading of Romans* 139; cf. 112). But this strains the sense and renders the phrase pleonastic.

will be judged by the law: Parallelism (with v 12a), along with the following context (vv 17-29), suggests that "be judged" (*krithēsontai*) here has the fully negative sense of being condemned. For Jews the law will stand as an instrument of accusation; cf. 3:19.

13. *are righteous before God . . . will be justified:* It is difficult to bring out in translation the cognate nature of the Greek words *(dikaioi . . . dikaiōthēsontai)* underlying both English phrases. The combination brings out well the sense that righteousness does not refer primarily to behavior as such but to the estimation one has in the eyes of God.

14. *When Gentiles:* The relative adverb (lit. "whenever" *[hotan]*) conveys the sense of occasional and isolated performance only; cf. *4 Ezra* 3:36: "You may indeed find individuals who have kept your commandments, but nations you will not find."

do by nature: The translation takes the phrase "by nature" *(physei)* as qualifying the verb rather than the subject ("Gentiles"), from which it is distant. Many interpreters have seen the total statement as an endorsement on Paul's part of the idea of a "law of nature" from which the principles of morality may be derived independently of positive revelation. Popular forms of Stoic philosophy in the ancient world proposed the ideal of living in conformity with one's nature. Truly wise persons know what this conformity entails through the Logos dwelling within them, whereas lesser human beings must rely on positive laws, which, nonetheless, are an expression of the fundamental "law of nature" (cf. Pohlenz, *Die Stoa* [see Reference] 1.131–35). Hellenistic Judaism, most notably in the person of Philo of Alexandria, brought together this Stoic sense of "nature" and the Jewish understanding of God as Creator and Law-giver. Philo and others sought to overcome the particularity and contingency of the law of Moses by identifying it with the law of nature whereby the universe was created and sustained. Philo could also explain on this basis how key figures of Israelite history who lived before the promulgation of the Mosaic law could nonetheless keep its requirements: Abraham fulfilled all the laws and commandments of God "not taught by written words," but through "unwritten nature" (*Abr.* 275; cf. also *2 Apoc. Bar.* 57:2).

What Philo says of Abraham is in fact most instructive for the interpretation of Paul, for whom Abraham represents the archetypal Gentile (cf. Romans 4). By saying that the Gentiles, though not having the law (of Moses), nonetheless perform the requirements of the law *physei*, Paul is asserting for them the possibility Philo envisaged for Abraham. The divine constitution of the world means that it is possible for human beings, apart from positive revelation, to discern and carry out the divine will for human life that is otherwise expressed in the Jewish law. In this sense they "constitute a law for themselves" (*heautois eisin nomos*, v 14b)—a phrase highly reminiscent of Philo's added remark (*Abr.* 276) about Abraham's being "himself a law and unwritten ordinance of God."

Paul's simple assertion in line with the Hellenistic Jewish tradition, while not containing the full theory of "Natural Law" developed in the later Christian tradition does provide some scriptural foundation for it—though Philo himself remained the strongest influence upon the tradition in this respect (cf. H. Köster, *TDNT* 9.266–69). What Paul assumes here with reference to behavior to some extent matches the possibility of "natural theology" assumed earlier in 1:19-20. However, Paul's somewhat colorless use of *physis* elsewhere (cf., esp., 1 Cor 11:14) warns against pressing too much meaning out of this single word. The polemical point is that the moral assistance Jews enjoy through possession of the law is matched by a similar Gentile possibility stemming from human nature as such.

what the law requires: The phrase *(ta tou nomou)* is deliberately vague and wards off any suggestion that Gentiles fulfill the entire law. Paul presumably has in mind the moral kernel of the law such as is contained in the Decalogue (cf. 13:8-10).

they constitute a law to themselves: The sense is not that Gentiles are "a law unto themselves" in the modern sense of complete independence but that they find the kernel of law in their very being as human persons. For a striking parallel to the phrase in Philo, see the Note before last above.

15. *the work of the law.* The Greek phrase *to ergon tou nomou* stands in contrast with the plural form "works *(erga)* of the law," occurring frequently in Paul, always in a negative sense, to denote behavior carried out in a (futile) attempt to establish righteousness through the law: see 3:20, 28; Gal 2:16; 3:2, 5, 10; cf. Rom 4:2, 6; 9:12, 32; 11:6 (cf. Eph 2:9); see Note on 3:20. It is likely that in the present (singular) case the genitive is subjective (so Barrett 52–53), indicating the effect in Gentiles' lives of "the law written in their hearts."

written on their hearts: There is possibly an allusion here to the "new covenant" promise of Jer 31:33, which reads according to the LXX (38:33), "I will surely put my laws into their mind, and write them on their hearts"; cf. 2 Cor 3:3-6. The subsequent references to "letter" in v 27 and v 29, along with the insistence in vv 28-29 upon the superiority of the "inner" over the "outer" reality (cf. 2 Cor 4:16-18), suggest that Paul's focus is upon the *(interior)* "work of the law" written in the heart (by God) in contrast to the *external* written law given to the Jews. *T. Jud.* 20:2-5 provides an interesting parallel to this passage, mentioning not only the "law written in the heart," but also conscience and the idea of God's judging the human heart.

with their conscience providing confirmation: This translation of the complex participial construction in the Greek takes the first participle *(symmartyrousēs)* in the derived, though commonly attested, sense of "confirm," rather than in its primary sense of "witness along with" (cf. H. Strathmann, *TDNT* 4.508–09) and understands the conjunction *kai* before preposition *metaxy* as explicative (cf. Kuss 1.69). On this understanding, to the proof provided by the Gentiles' actions *(ergon)*, there is simply added the confirmation given by their conscience, with a psychological explanation of how the latter proceeds. "Conscience" *(syneidēsis)* here refers to an experience of self-awareness that retrospectively evaluates (condemns or excuses) behavior. This use of *syneidēsis* falls within the popular employment of the term in the Greco-Roman world contemporary with Paul, where it forms the noun equivalent of the verbal expression *heautǭ syneidenai*—"to be conscious of oneself"—and so has the sense of "knowledge shared with oneself" or simply "consciousness." From the first century B.C.E. onwards, the noun occurs in a moral sense already long attested for the verbal form. Predominantly, the consciousness in question is painful, in the sense of having "a bad conscience"; the more positive sense of conscience as moral guide in advance of action is a later development. Paul's usage is indebted to that of Hellenistic Judaism (attested especially in Philo; also Wis 17:11), which had combined the notion of "conscience" that was widespread in popular Greco-Roman culture and was also the object of philosophical reflection in authors of a Stoic bent such as Cicero, Seneca and Plutarch, with the more explicitly theological strain emanating from the Jewish heritage. Conscience is that element of self-awareness that submits one's thoughts and actions to constant evaluation in view of a responsibility that presses in on one from without, independently of one's own being and for which one will ultimately be called to account on the day of judgment (cf. 1 Cor 4:4). Behind the authority of conscience, then, stands the authority of God (cf. also Rom 13:5). In contrast to the prevailing negative tradition ("bad conscience"), Paul can speak more positively, in the sense of having a good conscience (Rom 9:1; 2 Cor 1:12 [cf. 1 Tim 1:5, 19; 3:9; 2 Tim 1:3; Heb 13:18]). Moreover, the prospect that a bad conscience will follow a course of action can make of conscience in Paul not only a retrospective judge of past action but something of a guide to the moral value of intended action (see esp. 1 Cor 10:25-29). See further Kuss 1.76–82 (Exkurs: "Das Gewissen"); Wilckens 1.138–39; Cranfield 1.159–60.

as their conflicting thoughts accuse or perhaps excuse them: This explanatory phrase describes precisely the process of conscience as understood in the sense common to Paul and the ancient world, as outlined in the preceding Note. Many interpreters refer this accusatory witness of conscience to the eschatological judgment—that is, to the "day" referred to in the following clause making up v 16. But this separates, in a temporal sense, the factors—the works and the conscience of Gentiles—which indicate that they constitute "a law to themselves." Admittedly, when the whole of v 15 is referred to the present, the transition to the future statement in v 16 is harsh. But there must be such a transition *somewhere* across vv 14-16; locating it between v 15a and 15b is no less harsh.

16. *on that day when, according to my gospel, God will judge the secrets of human hearts through Christ Jesus:* The harshness of the transition from the previous verse and the fact that the phrase "according to my gospel" occurs elsewhere only in deutero-Pauline texts such as Rom 16:25 (see below) and 2 Tim 2:8 have led many (following R. Bultmann) to consider this verse a gloss. An alternative is to regard vv 14-15 as parenthetical (cf. Sanday and Headlam 62). It should be noted, however, that, setting aside the problem of the time reference (see previous Note), v 16 does relate to vv 14-15 in its insistence that God will judge the "secrets of human hearts": the eschatological judgment will reveal what has up till then remained hidden, namely, the "debate" of conscience (v 15b). The least violent way to overcome the harsh transition to the future in v 16 is to understand some such phrase as "and they will be justified" or "and this will become clear" implied between v 15 and v 16.

For Reference and Further Study

Achtemeier, P. J. "Some Things in them Hard to Understand: Reflections on an Approach to Paul." *Int* 38 (1984) 254–67, esp. 255–59.
Bornkamm, G. "Gesetz und Natur: Röm 2:14-16." *Studien zu Antike und Urchristentum. Gesammelte Aufsätze Band II.* Munich: Kaiser, 1959, 93–118.
Davies, G. N. *Faith and Obedience* 57–67.
Davies, W. D. "Conscience and Its Use in the New Testament." *Jewish and Pauline Studies.* Philadelphia: Fortress, 1984, 243–56.
Eckstein, H.-J. *Der Begriff "Syneidēsis" bei Paulus.* Tübingen: Mohr, 1983, 164–79, 311–12.
Martens, J. W. "Romans 2:14-16: A Stoic Reading." *NTS* 40 (1994) 55–67.
Pierce, C. A. *Conscience in the New Testament,* SBT 15; London: SCM, 1955, 40–53, 84–86.
Pohlenz, M. "Paulus und die Stoa." *ZNW* 42 (1949) 69–104, esp. 75–82.
__________. *Die Stoa: Geschichte einer geistiger Bewegung.* 5th ed. 2 vols. Göttingen: Vandenhoeck & Ruprecht, 1978, 1980.
Räisänen, H. *Paul and the Law* 101–07.
Stowers, S. K. *Rereading of Romans* 109–18, 134–42.
Theissen, G. *Psychological Aspects* 66–74.
Thielmann, F. *From Plight to Solution* 92–96.
Watson, N. M. "Justified by Faith, Judged by Works—An Antimony?" *NTS* 29 (1983) 209–21.

2. The Law and the Jews (2:17-24)

> 17. But if you call yourself a Jew and rely upon the law and boast in God 18. and know the will (of God) and discern what is essential, instructed by the law, 19. and if you are sure you are a guide to the blind, a light for those in darkness, 20. an instructor of the foolish, a teacher of little ones, having the embodiment of knowledge and truth in the law—
> 21. You who teach others, fail to teach yourself; you who preach not to steal, (yourself) steal; 22. you who say not to commit adultery, (yourself) commit adultery; you who abhor idols, (yourself) rob temples; 23. you who boast in the law, dishonor God by breaking the law. 24. Just as it is written, "The name of God is blasphemed among the Gentiles because of you."

Interpretation

Introduction. Close inspection shows this text to have a very formal construction. Each of its three main elements displays a five-member series: in vv 17-18, a five-fold list of Jewish privileges ("Jew"; "relying upon the law"; "boasting in God"; "knowing God's will"; able to "discern what is essential" on the basis of the law); in vv 19-20, a corresponding five-fold list on the public role which the pious Jew might hope to play on the basis of these claims ("guide"; "light"; "instructor"; "teacher"; possessor of the "embodiment of knowledge and truth in the law"); finally, in vv 21-23, a double, but still five-fold list stating the gap that yawns between claim and teaching, on the one hand, and actual behavior, on the other ("teaching"; "preaching not to steal"; forbidding "adultery"; "abhoring idols"; "boasting in the law"). In each of the three sections the final or fifth member makes mention of the law. V 24 rounds off the section as a whole with an appropriate quotation from scripture (Isa 52:5; Ezek 36:20).

Along with the formal structure, the passage reverts to the direct, second-person singular address characteristic of the diatribe. It resumes in this way the attack upon the one described in vv 1-3 as the "one who judges," showing the basic identity between this "judger" and the one "called a Jew" in v 17. Thus the entire sequence (vv 1-29) emerges as a continual diatribal accusation against the Jew who defines himself or herself in terms of possession of the law and (falsely in Paul's eyes) rests confidence therein. By the end of the passage (v 29), Paul will have totally redefined the "true Jew." (Note how the concluding statements in vv 28-29 form an "inclusion" with the opening clause "if you call yourself a Jew" [v 17].)

In the first instance the address is couched in fairly general terms. But as the sequence develops, the identity of the implied addressee emerges more and more as that of a Jewish teacher who seeks to instruct Gentiles in basic moral precepts of the law. The accusation resumed from vv 1-5 can now draw strength from the two principles formulated in the meantime: that judgment will be strictly according to performance, irrespective of possession of the law (vv 6-11; vv 12-13), and will proceed without partiality towards any party, Jews included (v 9b, v 10b, v 11). Moreover, Paul has (somewhat obliquely) aired the possibility that some Gentiles, though they do not possess the law, may find justification on the basis of performance (vv 14-16). Against this backdrop, Paul now points to failure on the part of Jews to perform the works required by the law. This, on the basis of the principle of vv 12-13, implies their liability to failure with respect to justification. What enhances Jewish failure in this respect is the fact that Jews fail in the very matters in which they claim on the basis of possession of the law to be lights, guides and instructors of the Gentiles.

The argument derives much of its force syntactically through the anacolouthon (lack of expected follow-on) set up by the lapsing at the end of v 20 of the conditional sentence begun at v 17. The accumulation of Jewish claims formulated in the long protasis (vv 17-20) leads one to expect a corresponding positive outcome in terms of effect upon the Gentiles. Instead, Paul suddenly breaks out of the conditional and formulates in vv 21-23 the accusations about performance that render the claims hypocritical. A telling gap opens up between high claims made ("boasting") and performance.

All through it is the law which is the crucial factor. The claims are made on the basis of possession of the law (v 17) and the schooling it has provided (v 18, v 20b). What fatally erodes them is failure with respect to what the law commands/forbids (vv 21b-22; v 23). The total effect is to drive home rhetorically the point that possession of the law is of itself no advantage; on the contrary, where performance is lacking, it enhances failure. The possibility formulated in v 12b—that those who sin "in" the law will be condemned "by" the law—has become real.

Basic Jewish privilege (vv 17-18). The opening recital of Jewish status and privilege is one that any Jew could make. "Jew" had become an honorific title. *In itself,* presumably, the title had no negative connotations for Paul. Only in the aspect of *"calling oneself"* a Jew might a note of irony enter in—something to be made patent at the end when Paul redefines the "real Jew" as the one "whose praise comes, not from human beings but from God" (v 29). Similarly, "relying upon the law" is perfectly in order so long as one fulfills the law (the principle formulated in v 13)—a condition which Paul will show to be illusory *in fact* on the basis of scripture's testimony (v 24; 3:10-20; cf. 3:23). "Boasting in God" is actually a Pauline ideal (1 Cor 1:30-31; cf. Rom 5:11; 2 Cor 10:17)—though, again, for Paul it arises solely in virtue of God's act in Christ, something which excludes all boasting in purely human accomplishment. Finally (v 18), possession of the law gives the Jew the unrivaled benefit of being instructed *(katēchoumenos)* by it so as to know God's will *(thelēma)* and be in a position to discern *(dokimazein)* what God regards as essential *(ta diapheronta).* In the moral realm the law provides the clear guidance that leads to justification, a guidance which the Gentile lacks (even if on occasion displaying in action the "work" of the law [vv 14-15]).

Presumed role for others (vv 19-20). Within this Jewish frame of reference, Paul points to the roles that confidence in possession of the law as moral guide leads Jews to adopt *vis-à-vis* others (the Gentiles). The epithets and roles have scriptural antecedents, notably in the role for others foreseen for the "Servant" (Israel) figure in Isaiah 42 and 49. Most can also be paralleled in the literature of contemporary Hellenistic Judaism (See Notes). More singular are the claims in v 20a, though the view of Gentiles as "foolish infants" *(nēpioi aphrones)* appears in Wis 12:24 (cf. also 15:14). The claim to be their "instructor" *(paideutēs)* and "teacher" *(didaskalos)* rests upon consciousness of "having the embodiment *(morphōsis)* of truth and knowledge in the law" (v 20b), a high claim reflecting the identification of the law with the divine wisdom inserted in the universe. On the basis of this identification, the law can claim to hold the key to human life and happiness (cf. Sir 24:23; Bar 3:36–4:1).

The "reality" (vv 21-23). All these lofty claims resting upon possession of the law founder upon the gap between the claims and performance—a gap Paul suddenly proceeds to unmask in an accusatory sequence of considerable severity. The severity of the sustained accusation is striking—especially if, as seems to be the case [see Note], it appears in a series of statements rather than questions. It also conflicts with the reputation for purity in religion and ethical probity that Jews enjoyed in many circles in ancient society, something which drew so many proselytes and "God-fearers" to the religion of Moses. The sharpness of tone falls, however, well within the pattern of the diatribe mode of discourse (cf. especially Epictetus [cf., e.g., *Discourses* 3.1.24; 3.5.14–16])—the context in which, presumably, the audience is meant to take it.

The sequence contains three specific charges—stealing, committing adultery, robbing temples (vv 21b-22)—framed by more general accusations at the beginning (failing to teach oneself, v 21a) and end (dishonoring God by transgression of the law, v 23). The accusation of failure to practice what one teaches or imposes upon others (v 21a) parallels Jesus' severe indictment of the Pharisees in Matthew 23 (cf. Luke 11:39-52). Moreover, there is an impressive similarity between the sequence of specific charges with those leveled against backsliding Israelites in contemporary Jewish literature (cf. esp. *Pss. Sol.* 8:8-13; *T. Levi* 14; Qumran: CD 4:12-17; 8:4-10; Philo *Conf.* 163). This suggests that Paul is employing an established *topos* that may not have been so startling to his original readers. There were undoubtedly Jews who stole and Jews who failed in sexual morality. Less easily understandable in a literal sense is the charge of robbing temples (v 22b; see Note). But Paul is not asserting that all Jews failed in the areas suggested or that the vices were characteristic of the nation as a whole. Within an established rhetorical pattern, he is attempting to drive home the point that possession of the law has not prevented Jews from failing to abide by its key moral precepts as formulated in the Decalogue. What fatally undermines the possibility of "boasting in the law" (v 23)—something which its possession might otherwise seem to afford—is "transgression" *(parabasis)* of its precepts, a phrase summing up the preceding catalogue of specific offenses. The end result is the "dishonoring" of God, the very antithesis of the "boasting in God" that was the original claim (v 17c).

Scripture's witness (v 24). In any case, the grounds for the sustained accusation are not strictly empirical. The scriptural quotation in v 24 provides the real backing, anticipating the extended "proof" from scripture employed later in 3:10-20. God's view, revealed in scripture, clinches the matter for the religious conscience; against this verdict no merely human awareness of contrary evidence can prevail. The use of a text (Isa 52:5) which, as modified by Paul, speaks of the dishonoring of God's name amongst the Gentiles lends a peculiarly sharp and bitter note to the close of the sequence. The Jew who hoped on the basis of the law to promote God's glory among the nations has ended up with precisely the opposite outcome—causing God's named to be blasphemed. Paul could hardly have made his case more sharply or offensively than this (see concluding Reflection).

Notes

17. *a Jew:* The Greek adjective *Ioudaios,* originally used by non-Jews with reference to Jews, came to be adopted by Jews themselves (cf. Philo and Josephus) as an acceptable self-designation, reflecting the privilege of belonging to the people chosen by God. Paul uses the term in a fairly neutral sense to denote members of the Jewish nation. Later in the present passage (vv 28-29) he redefines the term in the sense of the "real (inward) Jew"; see further, W. Gutbrod, *TDNT* 3.369–71, 375–82; Dunn 1.109–10.

rely upon the law: Lit. "rest upon" *(epanapauesthai)*; for the use of the word in this sense, cf. (LXX) Mi 3:11; 1 Macc 8:12.

boast in God: "Boasting" *(kauchēsis; kauchāsthai)* is an important theme in the Pauline corpus, to which it is virtually confined in the NT (cf. only Jas 1:9, 10; 4:16; Heb 3:6). For Paul, one "boasts" in that upon which one relies for security, recognition, justification or salvation. Such boasting is legitimate or illegitimate according to the basis upon which it rests. Boasting has a negative sense when what one relies upon is human achievement that is either illusory, misplaced or somehow unrecognizing of God (cf. 3:27; 4:2; 1 Cor 1:29; 3:21; 4:7; 5:6; 2 Cor 5:12; Gal 6:13). It has a positive sense when it rests upon God or the achievement of God's grace in human agents (cf. Rom 5:2, 11; 15:17; 1 Cor 1:31; 15:31; 2 Cor 1:12; 7:4; 11:16-33 *(passim)*; Gal 6:14; Phil 1:26; 2:16; 3:3; 1 Thess 2:19). Faith, which responds uniquely to God's creative power (cf. Rom 4:17), excludes boasting in the first sense, particularly boasting in "works (of the law)" (3:27). Possession of the law is a flawed basis for boasting, not because keeping the law is in itself wrong (Bultmann) nor because it bolsters nationalistic pride at the expense of acceptance of the Gentiles (J.D.G. Dunn: 1.110, 116–17, 185), but because human beings, unable to fulfill the law's requirements, cannot find justification and salvation apart from God's act in Christ (Rom 7:14–8:4).

18. *know the will (of God):* Lit. "know the will"; cf. 12:2. In accordance with Jewish custom, explicit mention of the Deity is avoided; cf. Michel 86.

discern what is essential: The sense is that of distinguishing what is essential or really significant *(ta diapheronta)* from matters merely optional or indifferent *(ta adiaphora)*; see further the Note on 12:2 where the same verb, *dokimazein,* occurs.

instructed by the law: The law provides the capacity for the two operations just mentioned. For the use of the verb *katēchein* in the sense of religious instruction, see also 1 Cor 14:19; Gal 6:6; Luke 1:4; Acts 18:25.

19. *a guide to the blind, a light for those in darkness:* Cf. Isa 42:6-7 ("light to the nations"; "open eyes that are blind," ". . . who sit in darkness"); 49:6 ("light to the nations, that my salvation may reach to the ends of the earth"); later Jewish literature: Wis 18:4 ("your children . . ., through whom the imperishable light of the law was to be given to the world"); Jos. *Ag. Ap.* 2.279–95; Philo *Abr.* 98; *Sib. Or.* 3.195; *T. Levi* 14:4; cf. *1 Enoch* 105:1; *4 Ezra* 14:20-21. The claims do not necessarily imply a "missionary" role *vis-à-vis* the Gentile world; evidence for such on the part of Jews contemporary with Paul is slender. But some Jews did believe that Gentiles could be saved as "righteous *Gentiles*" provided they observed the key ethical precepts of the law.

20. *the embodiment of knowledge and truth:* The Greek word *morphōsis* has here its Koine sense of "outward expression" or "imparted form," as in the case of an impression made by a seal. The sense is that the lofty aspiration for human life which the ancient world held to be summed up in the terms "knowledge" and "truth" finds concrete (and written) expression in the Jewish law.

21. *you who teach others, fail to teach yourself:* This initial accusation can be read as a question. However, the question form is not so natural in the case of the remaining charges and is virtually excluded for the concluding one by the way in which the supportive scriptural quotation in v 24 is attached. Contrary to the usual interpretation, which softens the charges by reading them as questions, it is more natural to read the entire sequence as straight accusations; cf. Zeller 72. Paul repeats, more explicitly and concretely but with equal rigor, the accusation first leveled in 2:1.

22. *you who abhor idols, (yourself) rob temples:* Strictly speaking, the Greek verb *hierosylein* refers to the pilfering of sacred objects from religious shrines, one of the most serious crimes in the ancient world (cf. G. Schrenk, *TDNT* 3.255–56). The Mosaic legislation in Deut 7:25-26 banned the Israelites from coveting the gold and silver contained in the graven images of the Canaanites, a ruling which Josephus (*Ant.* 4.207) points to as an example of Jewish tolerance. What is likely to be meant in the present context is the sale on the part of Jews of valuable artifacts purloined from pagan shrines on the pretext that since pagan deities have no reality (cf. 1 Cor 8:4) the objects are ownerless and hence may be taken and sold at will. Taking the expression metaphorically (robbing God of due honor; so Cranfield 1.169–70; Fitzmyer 318; D. B. Garlington) disturbs the logical sequence set up by the mention of the previous two crimes (robbery, adultery).

23. *dishonor God by breaking the law:* The Greek term *parabasis* (lit. "transgression") refers to wrongdoing that infringes a specific commandment or prohibition; it thus adds to wrongdoing the connotation of explicit offense against the lawgiver and thus "dishonors God"; elsewhere in Paul, see 4:15; 5:14; Gal 3:19 and cf. the use of *parabatēs* in 2:25, 27; Gal 2:18 and *paraptōma* in Rom 5:20.

24. *Just as it is written, "The name of God is blasphemed among the Gentiles because of you":* In the Greek, the phrase indicating that scripture is being quoted comes—contrary to Paul's usual custom (cf., e.g., 1:17)—almost as an afterthought at the end of the quotation. Literally translated from the Hebrew original, Isa 52:5 reads as follows: ". . . and continually all day long my name is despised." The LXX has no equivalent for "all day long" but features two extra phrases, which Paul was able to exploit: "*On account of you (di' hymas)* my name is continually despised *among the nations (en tois ethnesin)*." According to both the Hebrew original and the LXX it was Israel's *misfortune* that led to the reviling of God's name by the nations. Paul, however, interprets the LXX phrase "on account of you" as "because of your fault," thereby converting what was originally an oracle of compassion towards Israel into one of judgment. For a similar divine complaint against Israel, cf. Ezek 36:20-21.

For Reference and Further Study

Derrett, J.D.M. "'You Abominate False Gods; but Do You Rob Shrines?' (Rom 2.22b)." *NTS* 40 (1994) 558–71.
Garlington, D. B. "*Hierosylein*—and the Idolatry of Israel (Romans 2.22)." *NTS* 36 (1990) 142–51.
McKnight, S. *A Light Among the Gentiles: Jewish Missionary Activity in the Second Temple Period.* Minneapolis: Fortress, 1991, 104–06.
Räisänen, H. *Paul and the Law* 98–101.
Sanders, E. P. *Paul, the Law and the Jewish People* 123–35.
Stowers, S. K. *The Diatribe* 96–98, 112–113.
__________. *Rereading of Romans* 143–53.

3. The "Real Jew" (2:25-29)

25. Circumcision may be of use if you practice the law, but if you are a transgressor of the law, your circumcision has become uncircumcision.
26. If the uncircumcised person keeps the requirements of the law, will not his lack of circumcision be accounted as circumcision? 27. And the one who by upbringing is uncircumcised but nonetheless a keeper of the law will condemn you who despite (possession of) the written code and circumcision are a transgressor of the law.
28. For the real Jew is not the person who is one outwardly, nor is real circumcision that which is outwardly evident in the flesh. 29. But the real Jew is the one who is so in secret, and real circumcision is that of the heart, wrought by the Spirit, not the letter, and the commendation such a person receives comes not from human beings but from God.

INTERPRETATION

Introduction. The topic of circumcision comes rather suddenly upon the modern reader. But, within the Jewish frame of reference presupposed by Paul, so close was the connection between circumcision and being a Jew that the topic of circumcision had to come up in any discussion of the "real Jew," which is what this passage is ultimately all about (vv 28-29; cf. v 17). Just as failure in the area of performance undercuts any advantage stemming from possession of the law, so it equally undercuts any advantage attaching to circumcision. The passage opens with a thematic re-statement, in positive (v 25a) and negative (v 25b) terms, of the continuing principle that all depends upon performance. Then Paul points to the situation of the "righteous" uncircumcised (Gentile) person (vv 26-27), as a preliminary to "defining," first negatively (v 28), then positively (v 29a), the "real Jew," of whom the only valid assessment comes from God (v 29b).

General Principle (v 25). Paul concedes the "usefulness" *(ōphelei)* of circumcision. The "usefulness" in question is eschatological: what is "useful" for salvation in the sense of guaranteeing a favorable verdict at the judgment. The "usefulness," however, is conditional. Circumcision commits the Jew to a life of observance of the law. So tight in fact is the bind between circumcision and law (cf. Gal 5:3) that failure to observe the law annuls the "usefulness" of circumcision. Circumcision does not merely "lapse" in some way; it actually "becomes uncircumcision." In view of the fact that the Greek words for "circumcision" *(peritomē)* and "uncircumcision" *(akrobystia)* describe not merely the physical condition but are used to refer also to the communities of the circumcised (Jews) and uncircumcised (Gentiles) respectively (See Note), this is tantamount to saying that failure to keep the law reduces the Jew to Gentile status. The essential barrier (cf. Gal 2:15) falls away.

The "Righteous Gentile" (vv 26-27). In the positive case of the Gentile—now simply termed "the uncircumcision"—who "keeps" the law (v 26) precisely the reverse obtains: lack of circumcision will now be "reckoned" to be circumcision. The "reckoning" in question is that of God (cf. 4:4-6), the divine assessment set to be given at the great judgment (cf. the future tense and v 29c). Admittedly, on Paul's wider view, to be "reckoned" circumcised in a physical sense will hardly be of much avail, since mere physical circumcision is soon to be discounted in favor of the "circumcision of the heart" wrought eschatologically by the Spirit (v 29). For the present, however, Paul remains content simply to make the polemical point that the usefulness (for salvation) of (physical) circumcision is entirely dependent upon the keeping of the law, a keeping which the previous section (vv 17-24) has just severely contested.

Pressing home the polemic a little further, Paul dwells for a time (v 27) upon the theme of judgment. Common to the eschatological scenario of both apocalyptic Judaism and early Christianity was the expectation that the righteous (Israel or the righteous within Israel) would exercise judgment upon the wicked (chiefly seen as the oppressing Gentile nations; cf. Wis 3:8; 4:16; *Jub.* 24:29; *1 Enoch* 38:5; 95:3; *Apoc. Abr.* 29:19; 1QS 8:6; 1QpHab 5:4-5; Matt 19:28; 1 Cor 6:2; Rev 20:4). Provocatively, Paul turns around this expectation, asserting that the "law-keeping" Gentile will "judge"—that is, "condemn"—the Jew who, despite possession of the "written code" (*gramma*) and circumcision, is nonetheless a transgressor of the law. Paul exploits the dual meaning of the word "circumcision" *(peritomē)*—its capacity to denote both the physical state and the community (the Jews)—precisely to overthrow the tight nexus between physical mark and community identity. Since all rests upon fulfillment of the law, failure to keep the law breaks the nexus, overthrows the value of the purely physical rite and calls for a new definition of Jewish identity.

The "Real Jew" (vv 28-29). The new definition comes in the concluding two verses of the pericope (rounding off the entire section in inclusive fashion: cf. v 17: ". . . call yourself a Jew"). The dual statement—first negative (v 28), then positive (v 29)—rests upon a distinction, prominent also in Stoic literature (cf. also Matt 6:1-6, 16-18 and esp. 2 Cor 4:18), asserting the value of the inward and hidden over the merely external and obvious. In a somewhat confusing though ultimately rich way, Paul elaborates this "inner/outer" distinction alluding to two biblical prophecies that it understandably suggests: the "new covenant" passage in Jer 31:31-34, where God promises to put the law "within" the people and write it on their hearts (v 33), and God's pledge in Ezek 36:26-28 to gather Israel from its scattering among the nations, purify it from its uncleanness and put a new heart and a new spirit "within" it; the replacement of "a heart of stone" with "a heart of flesh" (v 26), will enable the people to follow all God's statutes and ordinances (v 27).

The same pattern of distinction returns at Rom 7:6 and is crucial to Paul's assertion of the superiority of the ministry of the new covenant over that of the old in 2 Cor 3:3-6. The following diagram sets out the pattern schematically:

OUTWARD/EVIDENT		INNER/HIDDEN
[Written in "Stone"—2 Cor 3:3]		[Written in the] "Heart"
"Letter" *(gramma)*		"Spirit" *(pneuma)*
"Flesh"		"Spirit"
Old (Rom 7:6)		New (Rom 7:6)

The distinction, for Paul, is eschatological. "Letter" represents the law in the written, external form belonging to the old, unredeemed dispensation where the prevalence of sin ensures its frustration and perversion (Rom 7:5, 14-25). "Spirit" designates the divine power already at work in the new age inaugurated by Christ's death and resurrection. "Spirit" in this sense brings about the fulfillment of the "righteous requirement of the law" (Rom 8:4; cf. Ezek 36:27) and so opens up the way to eschatological life (Rom 8:10).

Paul sees in the transfer from the field of letter to that of spirit the fulfillment of the biblical pledge to renew Israel and, with more immediate reference to the present context, the eschatological re-definition of the "real Jew" and "true circumcision." The "real Jew" is the "hidden" Jew, that is, not the Jew shown to be such by the external mark of circumcision, accessible to human recognition, but the hidden, secret one, whom God alone ultimately knows and "praises" (v 29c). Correspondingly, "true circumcision" is not the mark evident in the flesh, but that "circumcision of the heart" proclaimed in several biblical texts (Lev 26:41 ["*un*circumcised heart"]; Deut 10:16; 30:6; Jer 4:4; 9:25-26; Ezek 44:7, 9) and widely echoed in the post-biblical Jewish tradition, notably that of Qumran (1QS 5:5; 1QH 2:18; 1QpHab 11:13; cf. also *Jub.* 1:23; *Odes Sol.* 11:1-3; Philo, *Spec.* 1.305; cf. *Mig.* 92).

The parallels from Jewish literature show that in defining the "true Jew" in this way, Paul is not, strictly speaking, going beyond the Jewish frame of reference but simply pointing to the eschatological fulfillment of key prophecies which foresaw God's renewal of the people after a time of infidelity and defilement. *Implicitly*, however, and certainly for the Christian readership in Rome, who "overhear" Paul's indictment of the Jewish dialogue partner at this point, the "spirit" must be the Holy Spirit and the "true Jew" the Christian believer, since the eschatological dispensing of the renewing Spirit that allows true circumcision and fulfillment of the law comes about through God's act in Christ (see esp. 8:1-4). Nonetheless, it is a disservice to Paul's argument to "christianize" it "too early" and fail to appreciate the way in which it operates as an "inner-Jewish" indictment couched in biblical terms.

Reflection. At first sight and taken in isolation the entire sequence across Rom 2:17-29 can appear viciously and dangerously anti-Jewish. Recognizing it for what it originally was—an "inner-Jewish" prophetic accusation in diatribe style—allows a more balanced perspective to emerge. The indictment rests, not on anything specifically "Jewish," but upon failing to live out what one claims to be, a failing which applies to human beings generally and to any religious system in particular. Paul's accusation fastens upon failure with respect to the Jewish law since that was the relevant measure of conduct in the case of Judaism. He found in the prophets—Isaiah, Jeremiah, Ezekiel—both denunciation of Israel's failure to keep the law *and* the promise of a new age when *God* would overcome human incapacity to keep the law through an outpouring of the Spirit. From the perspective of the Christian gospel, Paul saw both aspects of these prophecies—negative and positive—actualized in the situation of his people.

The "re-definition" of the Jew (vv 28-29) does, it is true, appear to annihilate Jewish identity and erect the "righteous Gentile" as the archetypal figure whom God accepts. But Paul has not explicitly identified this "Gentile" with Christian believers and in fact allows the acute problem for Jewish identity to surface in the section immediately following (3:1-2). He will return to deal more thoroughly and extensively with the status of that bulk of Israel that has not recognized Jesus as the Christ in chapters 9–11. There, as his "inclusive" presentation of the gospel reaches its full range, he will ultimately make clear that Jewish identity remains intact and God's promises to Israel unrevoked (11:28-29).

Notes

25. *Circumcision . . . uncircumcision:* "Circumcision" *(peritomē)* can have three meanings: 1. the act of circumcising; 2. the state of being circumcised; 3. the community of the circumcised, that is, the Jews. Paul oscillates between meanings 2 and 3 in the present passage. "Uncircumcision" *(akrobystia)*, likewise, can have three meanings: 1. the foreskin; 2. the state of being uncircumcised; 3. the "community" of the uncircumcised, that is, the Gentile world or the individual Gentile. Cf. Cranfield 1.171–73.

26. *If the uncircumcised person keeps the requirements of the law:* The envisaging here of Gentile capacity to keep the "requirements *(dikaiōmata)* of the law" echoes more concretely the earlier statement concerning Gentile capacity to know and perform the "work of the law written in their hearts" (vv 14-15). No more than in that connection is there any need to hold that Paul has Gentile *Christians* in mind (against Cranfield 1.173); only in vv 28-29 does a hint of Christian fulfillment emerge. For the Greek word *dikaiōma*, used here (in the plural) in the sense of "(just) requirement" or "decree," see Note on 1:32.

27. *by upbringing:* This translates the Greek phrase *ek physeōs*. Since all (males) are *born* in a state of "uncircumcision," *physis* here cannot simply be taken in the sense of "nature" or "birth" in the strict sense (cf. Note on 2:14) but must refer to what one is—or very early comes to be—on the basis of the ethnic or religious group into which one is born; cf. Gal 2:15: "We are Jews by virtue of birth *(physei)* and not Gentile sinners."

    will condemn: The verb has the initial place of emphasis in the Greek thereby forcefully bringing out the turning of the tables upon the "one who judges" of 2:1, 3, now clearly revealed as the Jew. For a similar reversal, cf. Matt 12:41-42 (// Luke 11:31-32).

despite (possession of) the written code and circumcision: The translation understands the Greek phrase introduced by the preposition *dia* as a genitive of "attendant circumstances," parallel to the earlier phrase *ek physeōs* (see above), rather than as instrumental. "Written code" *(gramma)* refers here to the law, anticipating the "spirit"/"letter" contrast to emerge in v 29.

28. *For the real Jew . . .:* Though the overall meaning is clear, the expression in this and the following verse is highly elliptical; subjects and predicates have constantly to be supplied. Cranfield, 1.175, creditably reconstructs a fuller Greek sentence.

29. *wrought by the Spirit, not the letter:* The translation takes the Greek preposition *en* instrumentally, though it could just as well be understood "locally" in the sense of "where the spirit (or "the letter") is the prevailing influence." On the "spirit"/"letter" distinction, see the classic essay of E. Käsemann, "The Spirit and the Letter" (see Reference).

For Reference and Further Study

Käsemann, E. "The Spirit and the Letter." *Perspectives on Paul* 138–66, esp. 138–55.

Lyonnet, S. "Le 'païen' au 'coeur circoncis' ou le 'chrétien anonyme.'" *Études* 70–88 (orig. 1968).

Marcus, J. "The Circumcision and the Uncircumcision in Rome." *NTS* 35 (1989) 67–81.

Snodgrass, K. L. "Justification by Grace—To the Doers: An Analysis of the Place of Romans 2 in the Theology of Paul." *NTS* 32 (1986) 72–93, esp. 79–81.

Stowers, S. K. *Rereading of Romans* 154–58.

Thielmann, F. *From Plight to Solution* 92–96.

d) *God's Faithfulness to Israel Stands* (3:1-8)

I. [Paul] 1. What, then, is the advantage of being a Jew? Or what value has circumcision?

[Partner] 2. Much and in every way. In the first place, they (the Jews) were entrusted with the oracles of God.

II. [Paul] 3. What if some were unfaithful? Their infidelity does not nullify the fidelity of God, does it?

[Partner] 4. Not at all! Let God be true, though every human being be false, as it is written, "That you may be found righteous in all your words and prevail when going to court."
III. [Paul] 5. But if our wickedness proves the righteousness of God, what shall we say? That God is unjust in inflicting the wrath? (I speak in a human way).
[Partner] 6. Not at all! For how else could God judge the world?
IV. [Paul] 7. But if through my falsehood God's truth has abounded to his glory, why am I still being condemned as a sinner?
8. And why not, then, do evil that good may come?—which is just what some slanderously charge us as saying. Their condemnation is just!

INTERPRETATION

Introduction. Paul continues to allow his Gentile audience in Rome to "overhear" a prophetic accusation aimed at a Jewish dialogue partner. So far (1:18–2:29) he has maintained that since all human beings lie exposed to God's impartial judgment and since that judgment will be strictly according to a person's works (2:6-10, 12-13), Jewish possession of the law and circumcision is no guarantee of special favor. On the contrary, infringement of the law (2:17-29) places Jews on an equal footing with the Gentiles with respect to exposure to condemnation at the judgment. This sharp denunciation raises acutely the question as to whether Jews enjoy any benefit whatsoever from being God's covenant people, marked with the sign of circumcision. More seriously still, if they have no advantage whatsoever and if what appeared to be their special vocation has crashed in ruins because of sin, then that redounds not only upon them. It redounds also upon God, who called them to this special vocation in the first place, making high promises in their regard. *God's* faithfulness is put in question alongside that of Israel.

In the dialogic passage that follows (3:1-8) Paul first of all proposes objections that seem to flow from the derogation of Jewish privilege. Very soon, however, a more basic issue emerges. While the passage makes an attempt to address the question of Israel (preliminary to the sustained consideration to be given in chapters 9–11), the real purpose of the dialogue is to bring to the fore once more the issue of God's faithfulness or righteousness, so central to the argument of the letter as a whole (1:17; 3:21; 9:6; 9:30–10:4; 11:29-32). Paul will wring from the Jewish dialogue partner an admission that God *must* be righteous in the face of human sin—though *how* that righteousness can be squared with human sin, specifically Israel's sin, is not explained. For the purpose of the wider argument, Paul is prepared to raise the issue of God's righteousness and leave it for a time hanging in the air, fundamentally unresolved. He does so only so that he can, all the more tellingly, at the right moment (3:21), proclaim that God, in the person of Jesus Christ, has found a way to both be righteous *and* deal effectively with human sin (3:26), thereby opening up to all, including Israel, the salvation contained in the original promises. The passage is not, then, a digression to deal with Jewish objections but an essential element in the rhetoric of Romans.

The passage takes the form of a scholastic dialogue in diatribe mode. It consists basically of four questions or objections (v 1 [double question]; v 3; v 5; v 7) to which is given a corresponding series of responses (v 2; v 4; v 6; v 8). The layout of the text given above (largely, though not entirely, indebted to S. K. Stowers) attempts to reconstruct the pattern of the "dialogue," assigning the individual objections and responses to Paul and the dialogue partner respectively. Adopting the mode of a teacher catechizing a student, Paul flings out objections to which the partner struggles to respond. Syntactically, the leading objections are couched in terms that imply their own refutation (questions expecting the answer "No" introduced by the Greek particle *mē*; see especially v 3b and v 5). Paul, in fact, reserves the "best lines" for himself, suggesting that the objections, rather than reflecting an actual debate with fellow Jews, come from himself and serve—in diatribe manner—to wring responses out of the (hapless) student, so spurring the argument forward (D. R. Hall).

Any Jewish advantage? (vv 1-2). The opening double question (v 1) arises immediately out of the leveling of Jewish privilege implied in the previous section (2:17-29). Paul had there maintained that the "real Jew" is the one God recognizes to be such—not on the basis of physical circumcision but on the basis of a "circumcision of the heart" that entails a true keeping of the law which even a Gentile might attain. This naturally calls into question any advantage of being a Jew in the ordinary (ethnic) sense or of bearing Judaism's special badge: physical circumcision. As in 2:25-29, circumcision and "being a Jew" go together; the "value" *(ōpheleia)* of circumcision is not pursued as a separate issue.

Paul allows (v 2) the "partner" to respond in a rather fulsome way and to become launched on an enumeration of the privileges of Israel similar, one would suppose, to the list appearing later in 9:4-5. But before a fresh objection sweeps in (v 3) there is time for mention of one item only: "the oracles of God." The precise meaning of the unusual expression "oracles" (*ta logia*; elsewhere in the NT only Acts 7:38; Heb 5:12; 1 Pet 4:11) is not clear. If Paul already has in view the "promises" given by God to Abraham, which will be so central to the argument later on (chapter 4), it is strange that the specific term "promise" *(epangelia)* does not occur (cf. 9:5: "promises"). The statement that the Jews "were entrusted" *(episteuthēsan)* with these oracles lends the sense of something committed for safe, faithful keeping—perhaps also the hint that the Jews were to hold them in trust so that *others* (the Gentiles!) might in due course benefit from them as well. Thus, while the oracles contained God's pledge faithfully to bring in salvation, their entrustment also implied a corresponding fidelity on the part of the recipient people as well (cf. Deut 30:15-20).

Objection II: Does Israel's infidelity annul that of God? (vv 3-4). The indictment of the Jews (2:17-29) has, however, set fidelity on the human side totally in question. So the second "objection" (v 3) raises and begins to rebut any suggestion that this human (Jewish) infidelity annuls also the "faithfulness" *(pistis)* of God. The thesis of Jewish infidelity alongside that of the Gentile world cannot be sustained if it brings with it the blasphemous implication that God's promises have proved null and void. Paul will not surrender that thesis but neither will he allow any suggestion that it jeopardizes the faithfulness of God.

The "partner" can only agree (v 4), going on to support the rejection ("Not at all") of the blasphemous suggestion with a theological axiom that simply asserts God's abiding "truthfulness" *(alēthēs)* in the face of total human "falsehood" (*pas . . . anthrōpos pseustēs*—a phrase taken from Ps 116:11 [LXX 115:11]). The assertion that God is "true" reflects the biblical sense of "truth" as fidelity. God will remain faithful to the covenant promises; in contrast to the "falsehood" prevailing on the human side (cf. 1:25), the "oracles" spoken by God were truly meant.

The theological axiom in its turn finds support in a quotation from the great psalm of repentance, Psalm 51 (v 4; LXX 50:6). Whereas in the original Hebrew, the psalm spoke of God's being justified in giving sentence, the Pauline text cites the LXX, which reads "that you may be justified *in your words" (en tois logois sou).* Beyond the assertion that God will be found righteous when condemning human sin, it suggests that, in the face of human sin and falsehood, God will remain true to the saving "words" spoken and entrusted to Israel (cf. *ta logia tou theou* in v 3). The authoritative word of scripture insists that in the long run God will prevail (literally, "conquer" *[nikēseis]*) when going to court against sinful human beings.

Objection III: Is God unjust? (vv 5-6). The upshot is that human (in the context, Jewish) sinfulness, far from annulling God's righteousness, actually serves, by contrast, to highlight it all the more. But this inference and especially the hint of purpose (cf. *hopōs an . . .*) contained in the scriptural quotation, sparks off a fresh line of "objection" (v 5). The idea that human wickedness (*adikia*; cf. 1:18, 29) actually "demonstrates" *(synistēsin)* God's righteousness *(theou dikaiosynēn)* could lead (falsely, as Paul's formulation *[mē . . .]* implies) to the conclusion that God is "unjust" *(adikos)* in "inflicting the wrath." "Wrath" has here the traditional sense of the eschatological punishment falling upon those incurring the divine displeasure at the judgment. Is it fair of God to punish sin when in fact, as Ps 51:4 suggests, human sin only serves to enhance or show up all the more the divine "righteousness" or "glory" (v 7)? Briefly, why should God punish something from which God stands to gain? The objection is trite—as the final comment ("I speak in a human way") appears to concede. But it serves Paul's rhetorical purpose, which is to set in sharper and sharper relief the issue concerning the righteousness of God.

No more profound is the subsequent attempt to rebut this third "objection" (v 6). The dialogue partner can only assert that God *must* be able justly to inflict wrath, on the grounds that this is a necessary corollary of what is axiomatic: that God is the judge of the (entire) world. Once again, the rebuttal consists in a simple reiteration of traditional teaching.

Objection IV: Dangerous implications (vv 7-8). Changing to the first person singular, Paul presses the point (v 8). The objection remains much the same as that formulated in v 5, save that the focus is now not so much upon God and the "injustice" of the divine sentence as upon the dangerous implications for human behavior and moral teaching. If my "falsehood" has only served to show up all the more God's "truthfulness," rendering it abundantly "glorious," it is otiose for God to take me to court (cf. *krinomai*) and regard me as sinner, since the furtherance of the divine glory seems in some sense to "require" my sin—something which would overthrow morality altogether. "My sinfulness" and the furtherance of God's glory cannot be held together in this morally perilous way.

The following and final statement in the sequence (v 8) appears to make explicit the moral consideration underlying the objection just stated (v 7)—the immorality of doing evil in order to procure good. It basically restates that objection and does so in terms which opponents have thrust upon Paul himself. He is, in fact, picking up an accusation which his emphasis upon God's grace has provoked (cf. esp. 5:20; 6:1) and using it to reformulate the same objection.

No rebuttal follows. One has the sense that, for Paul, the very formulation of the objection exposes it for the outrageous slander he holds it to be (*kai mē kathōs blasphēmoumetha . . .*). On this note of indignation, the entire sequence grinds to a halt with a final imprecation upon the detractors: it is *their* libelous criticism that merits condemnation.

The charge that surfaces here is clearly one that dogged the preaching of the Pauline gospel—one which he perhaps anticipated rising in the Roman community as his letter was being read. Paul depicts human sinfulness on such a universal and pervasive scale because he sees it as the presupposition for the "much more" powerful victory of God's superabundant grace (5:15-21). But what for him was a presupposition could easily be caricatured as a means (cf. 6:1). So the charge formulated in v 8 would come readily to the lips of Jews shocked at the implication contained in the Pauline gospel that they were lumped together, along with

"Gentile sinners," in a sinful solidarity alienated from God. (In Gal 2:17 Paul appears to rebut an objection coming from a similar direction. The recognition on the part of Jews such as Cephas and himself that one was a sinner, standing along with "Gentile sinners" in need of justification through faith in Christ [vv 15-17], in no way implied that Christ was "minister of sin.")

Concluding Reflection: The "righteousness of God". In conclusion, we may note the way in which the passage sets in parallel various expressions asserting God's fidelity over against human faithlessness:

V 3b: "the faithfulness of God" *(pistis tou theou)*
V 4a: "let God be true" *(alēthēs)*
V 5a: "God's righteousness" *(theou dikaiosynē)*
V 7a: "the truth of God" *(hē alētheia tou theou).*

The parallelism shows how the key terms—"faithfulness," "truth" and "righteousness"—cohere around the basic sense of "fidelity." This confirms that Paul understands "God's righteousness" in the traditional biblical sense where "righteousness" denotes the status one is acknowledged to have in the eyes of another on the basis of faithfulness shown in action. The quotation from Psalm 51 does not bring in a "forensic" tone alien to the more "saving" presentation of God's righteousness evident elsewhere in Romans. By combining the theological axiom formulated in terms of Ps 116:11 and the scriptural quotation from Ps 51:4, Paul asserts that God is (or will be shown to be) righteous both over against human sin—the condemnation of which is just—*and* in remaining true to the ultimately salvific covenant promise to Israel. This does, it is true, set up a tension between the judging and saving aspects of God's righteousness, a tension which makes the present passage difficult to comprehend if taken in isolation from the wider context. But the eliciting of this tension is all part of Paul's rhetorical strategy. Its resolution will be all the more telling in rhetorical terms when eventually (3:21-26) he proclaims that God has found a way in Jesus Christ both to deal effectively with universal human sin *and* remain faithful to the covenant promise.

Notes

1. *the advantage of being a Jew:* The Greek word *perisson,* formed from the adjective *perissos* ("exceeding the usual amount") lends the sense of "what *more* has the Jew?," rather than the simple sense of "what is the privilege?"

   Or what value has circumcision?: The close link between circumcision and being a Jew means that this question amounts virtually to a repetition of the previous one in the form: "What is the use of being circumcised?," that is, of being one of the "circumcision" (2:26-27; 3:30), being a Jew.

2. *In the first place, . . .:* The Greek phrase *prōton men . . .* which strictly speaking requires a complement, suggests the intention of reciting a whole series of "privileges."

were entrusted with: Paul uses the passive of the same Greek verb *(pisteuein)* to express his own sense of being "entrusted" with the proclamation of the gospel: 1 Cor 9:17; Gal 2:7; 1 Thess 2:4; cf. 1 Tim 1:11; Tit 1:3.

oracles of God: The Greek word *logion,* used here in the plural, refers to a short saying, normally one uttered by a deity or by a prophet in the name of a deity. In the LXX and other Jewish literature "the oracles *(logia)* of God" can denote the whole complex of divine utterance embodied in the Mosaic legisation and/or the prophetic writings; the great bulk of occurrences appear in the Psalms (notably in the lengthy Psalm 119 [LXX 118]); almost always there is a connotation of assurance or salvation (a threatening note occurs only in Isa 28:13; 30:27 [LXX]). This background suggests that *ta logia* here denote various scriptural assurances of salvation resting upon Israel's covenant bonding with God. To think of the entire biblical revelation (so Cranfield; D. R. Hall, "Romans 3.1-8" 185) is too broad. To think solely of the promises to Abraham (so S. K. Williams, "The 'Righteousness of God'" 266–69) leaves unexplained why Paul did not use the term *epangelia* customary in such contexts; cf. 9:5).

3. *What if some were unfaithful?:* There are alternative possibilities of punctuation (see Cranfield 1.179–80) but they hardly affect the overall sense. Paul speaks of "infidelity" *(ēpistēsan)* rather than "sinfulness" (cf. v 9 and v 23b) in order to exploit the variety of meaning attaching to the Greek stem *apist-, (apisteuein; apistia),* which can refer to unfaithfulness in the moral sense, as well as to disbelief (the meaning in 11:20, 23). The present context suggests that what is at stake and provokes the objection is the inclusion of the Jewish world in the sinful mass of humankind (2:21-27; cf. 3:9b, 23). "Some" *(tines)* is an instance of "meiosis": a softening understatement, which does not in fact lessen the universal scope of the accusation.

the fidelity of God: The Greek word *pistis* normally has the sense "faith" in the NT. But the meaning "fidelity," "reliability" is quite common in Greek literature and appears in the NT in passages such as Matt 23:23; Gal 5:22; 2 Thess 1:4; Titus 2:10 (see BAGD 662, s.v. 1.a). *Pistis* is used of God's faithfulness in LXX Ps 32:4 (33:4); Hos 2:20 (22); Lam 3:23 and (of course, most significantly for Paul) Hab 2:4.

4. *Not at all!:* This translates the Greek phrase *mē genoito,* which appears frequently in argumentative contexts in Paul (cf. also 3:6, 31; 6:2, 15; 7:7, 13; 9:14; 11:1, 11; also 1 Cor 6:15; Gal 2:17; 3:21; 6:14). It serves as a strong negation following a rhetorical question which has proposed a false or unacceptable conclusion drawn from the preceding argument; the device then serves, by way of correction, to thrust the argument forward on a new tack.

though every human being be false: The rarity of the Greek word *pseustēs* elsewhere (in the LXX only Sir 15:8; 25:2; Prov 19:22 [in some mss.]) makes a deliberate echo of LXX Ps 115:11 (116:11) very likely.

"That you may be found righteous in all your words and prevail when going to court": Paul's quotation of Ps 51:4 agrees exactly with the LXX (50:6), save for the use of the future "will prevail" (*nikēseis;* taking this as the preferred reading) where the LXX has the aorist subjunctive *(nikēsęs)*. The future lends a more eschatological tone to the citation (but cf. BDF §369 [3]). The Greek infinitive *krinesthai* can be taken as a middle used in an active sense: "contend in a law suit" (cf. LXX Job 9:3; 13:19; Isa 50:8; Jer 2:9; in Paul, 1 Cor 6:1, 6), as in the translation proposed, or else regarded as a true passive: "when you are judged, when you are on trial." Neither in LXX Ps 50:6 nor in Paul's quotation is it clear which sense is present. In the overall context both ideas—that of God's going to court *and* being judged—are included, since "be justified" always involves an assessment in the eyes of another. Since *nikān* is used as a technical term for winning a legal suit (see Sanday and Headlam 72), the sense of "prevail when going to court" seems most appropriate for both the LXX and Paul's quotation.

5. *But if our wickedness proves the righteousness of God:* The clause shows "wickedness" *(adikia)* to be the antithesis to "righteousness" *(dikaiosynē)* in Paul's thought (cf. esp. 1:17-18). The Greek verb *synistēsin* requires the strong translation "prove" (cf. esp. 5:8; Gal 2:18; 2 Cor 7:11; see BAGD 790), rather than simply "illustrate": it is the patent wickedness on the human side that allows God to be shown as righteous and hence win the case. For a striking parallel, cf. *Pss. Sol.* 13:2: ". . . that you might be justified, O God, in your righteousness through our lawless deeds. Because you are a just judge over all the peoples of the earth"; cf. also Wis 12:15-16. Connection with the quotation from Ps 51:4 in the preceding verse lends to the reference to "God's righteousness" here a forensic note that, at first sight, sets it somewhat apart from the "saving" note prevalent elsewhere in Paul. But "righteousness" essentially denotes the assessment one has in the eyes of another (see Interpretation of 1:17). Here God is seen to be in the right in sharp contrast with human failure. In other instances (esp. 3:21-22, 25-26) God will be seen to be in the right because of the divine saving action in faithfulness to the promises. The "saving" note is not intrinsic to "righteousness" but normally attaches to the concept of God's righteousness in the biblical tradition (esp. in Second Isaiah) because God is so often shown to be righteous in virtue of saving activity. The present instance (Rom 3:5) may appear to be an exception but in some ways it illustrates most clearly the core meaning of righteousness in the biblical tradition.

what shall we say?: The Greek phrase *ti (oun) eroumen?* is a regular feature of the cut and thrust of Paul's argument in Romans. It either introduces a false conclusion from the preceding material, which is then rejected, with a new development following (Rom 3:5; 6:1; 7:7; 9:14); or else it introduces a true conclusion from the preceding, which is then developed (8:31; 9:30); the occurrence in 4:1 is somewhat anomalous but it adheres to the first category in that it introduces a false suggestion later corrected (v 2).

That God is unjust in inflicting the wrath?: For Paul's sense of the divine "wrath," see Interpretation and Note on 1:18. The objection is understood in many different ways. For a recent critique of more traditional lines of interpretation, see Watson, *Paul, Judaism and the Gentiles* 124–26.

I speak in a human way: Paul tends to use this or similar expressions when, having taken an example from everyday human life, he feels some need to apologize for applying it to divine matters; cf. 6:19; Gal 3:15; 1 Cor 9:8.

6. *could God judge the world:* The idea of God as judge of the world is axiomatic in the biblical and later Jewish tradition: Pss 7:6-8; 9:8; 96:13; 110:6; Isa 2:4; 13:6-16; 34:8; Dan 7:9-11; Joel 2:1-11; Zeph 1:14–2:3; 3:8; Mal 4:1; *1 Enoch* 90:20-27; *Jub.* 5:10-16; *Pss. Sol.* 2:32-35; 9:2; *Bib. Ant.* 11:2; 11QMelch 2:9,13; cf. Matt 25:31-46; see further Zeller 66–68.

7. *But if:* Adopting the reading *ei de* (א A) rather than the alternative *ei gar* (B D G). The latter involves seeing the conditional sentence in v 7, not as a fresh objection, but as a support for the statement in v 6 rejecting the objection in v 5. However, in that case the protasis clause in v 7 has to be regarded as expressing a condition that is unreal, whereas it very much repeats the protasis of the earlier "objection" in v 5, which cannot be so regarded. The reading *ei de* sets the two "objections" (v 5 and v 7) neatly in parallel.

   through my falsehood God's truth has abounded to his glory, why am I still being condemned as a sinner?: Set over against "truth," "falsehood" (*pseusma* [only here in the NT]) must have the sense "unfaithfulness." It is not clear why Paul places the verb in the protasis in past tense and in the apodosis speaks of "my *still (eti)* being condemned . . ." The past tense may be primarily logical in the sense that, if God has already derived glory from my transgressions, then the case should be closed; it is otiose for God to go on and condemn me as a sinner. This (false) conclusion would then lead to the unacceptable moral principle expressed in the (slanderous) charge quoted in v 8.

8. *And why not, then, do evil that good may come?—which is just what some slanderously charge us as saying:* The translation seeks to bring out the force of Paul's formulation of the sentence, once again, as a question expecting the answer "No" (cf. Kuss 1.104). Paul seems to be attempting to turn the table on the adversaries and show that it is precisely *their* view and not his that leads to such an unacceptable conclusion. The Greek verb *blasphēmein*, as used here in the passive, has the sense not of blasphemy against God, but of slander against human beings; cf. BAGD 142, s.v. 1a.

For Reference and Further Study

Campbell, W. S. "Romans III as a Key to the Structure and Thought of the Letter." *NovT* 23 (1981) 22–40.

Cosgrove, C. H. "What If Some Have Not Believed? The Occasion and Thrust of Romans 3.1–8." *ZNW* 78 (1987) 90–105.

Hall, D. R. "Romans 3.1–8 Reconsidered." *NTS* 29 (1983) 183–97.

Hays, R. B. "Psalm 143 and the Logic of Romans 3." *JBL* 99 (1980) 107–115.

Penna, R. "La funzione strutturale di 3,1-8 nella lettera ai Romani." *Biblica* 69 (1988) 507–42.

Piper, J. "The Righteousness of God in Romans 3,1-8." *TZ* 36 (1980) 3–16.

Stowers, S. K. "Paul's Dialogue with a Fellow Jew in Romans 3:1-9." *JBL* 46 (1984) 707–22.

__________. *Rereading of Romans* 159–75.

Watson, F. *Paul, Judaism and the Gentiles* 127–31.

Williams, S. K. "The 'Righteousness of God.'" 265–70.

e) *Scripture's Witness to Universal Lack of Righteousness* (3:9-20)

9. What then? Do we have an advantage? Hardly!—for we have already charged that Jews and Greeks are all together under sin, 10. as it is written:

> "There is no righteous person, not even one.
> 11. There is no one with understanding. There is no one who seeks God. 12. All have turned aside, together they have become worthless; there is no one who shows kindness, there is not even one."
> 13. "Their throat is an open grave; they use their tongues to deceive." "The venom of vipers is under their lips." 14. "Their mouth is full of cursing and bitterness." 15. "Their feet are hasty to shed blood."
> 16. "Ruin and misery lie in their paths, 17. and the path of peace they have not known." 18. "There is no fear of God before their eyes."

19. Now we know that whatever the law says it addresses to those who are within the law, so that every mouth may be silenced and the whole world stand guilty before God. 20. For through works of the law "shall no human being be made righteous before him." For through the law comes knowledge of sin.

Interpretation

Introduction. In the preceding dialogue (3:1-8) Paul has raised and dismissed objections arising out of the apparent derogation of Jewish privilege in 2:1-29. The overall effect has been to insist that the accusation of Jewish sinfulness does not impugn God's righteousness. In reality, Paul has simply maintained this in an authoritarian way that actually leaves unresolved the issue of God's righteousness in the face of human (especially Israel's) sin. He has in fact heightened the issue in order to make its eventual resolution (3:21-26) all the more effective. But, having warded off the problem for the time being, Paul can bolt home the thesis of universal sinfulness (lack of righteousness) without risk of blasphemy. He does so by recourse to scripture, which—as always—presents God's view of the situation.

No advantage for Jews (v 9). Speaking as a Jew and in the first person, Paul raises again (cf. v 1) the question concerning Jewish privilege: "Do we have an advantage?" (for the translation, see Note). This time, in contrast to the concession in v 2, the privileged position of the Jews is challenged: "Hardly!" The issue is now more specific: it concerns eschatological justification. In *this* area, as Paul has maintained all through, the law does not give the Jews any advantage. God is impartial (2:11). Hence the denial.

Paul supports the challenge, first (v 9b) by reminding his audience that he (literally "we") has "already charged that Jews and Greeks are all together under sin," and then by the scriptural catena that immediately follows (vv 10-18). The "charging" that has already taken place presumably refers to the accusations deployed in 1:18-32 and 2:17-29, though, strictly speaking, nothing has been said there that could justify so sweeping a generalization. It has not been Paul's intent, however, to establish Gentile sinfulness and Jewish sinfulness in a sequential kind of way, with equal stress upon both. Gentile sinfulness is axiomatic (cf. Gal 2:15), requiring no substantiation. The "all" here, as so often in Romans, is inclusive in the sense of "all, that is, *Jews* as well as Gentiles." Jews are included in the sinful mass destined to stand guilty (see Note) before God at the judgment.

Scripture's witness to universal lack of righteousness (vv 10-18). Paul grounds this charge with a catena of scriptural texts quite unparalleled in the New Testament both in its length and in its single-minded focus upon the one theme of universal moral failure. The catena is made up chiefly, though not exclusively, of quotations from the Psalms. With respect to formal principles of composition two features stand out. In the first place, there is the repeated "there is no . . .," appearing four times in vv 10-12 and once (forming an inclusion) at the end in v 18. Secondly, throughout the second half of the catena (vv 13-18), parts of the human body occur as agents of wrongdoing: throat, tongue, lips (v 13); mouth (v 14); feet (v 15). Mention of "feet" leads naturally, within the quotation from Isa 59:7-8, to the talk of "way" or "path" in vv 16-18.

The rather meager element of formality hardly warrants the conclusion that the text existed in some setting prior to the composition of Romans. In the careful crafting of his letter to Rome, Paul has woven various texts together to make a telling conclusion to his prophetic accusation (1:18–3:20). Two passages of scripture are notably prominent: Ps 14:1-3 (= Ps 53:1-3) and Isa 59:7-8. Both offer a dire portrayal of human infidelity but do so in the context of eventual saving intervention by God (cf. Rom 3:21-26, especially in the light of Isa 59:12-19).

The opening words "There is no righteous person, not one" (modeled upon Eccl 7:20) sound the *leit-motif* of the catena. The overall effect is to convey scripture's—and therefore God's—incontestable verdict that no righteousness is to be found on the human side (cf. Gal 3:22: "Scripture imprisoned all things under sin . . .") and to prepare for the concluding verdict given in v 20.

The law's address: "No righteousness" (vv 19-20). While the scope of the accusation is universal, Paul ensures that the focus lies upon the Jews by reminding his audience (v 19) that those whom the law (= scripture) primarily addresses are "those within the law," that is, the Jews. The scriptural ensemble points to Jewish *in*clusion in the total *ex*clusion of any righteousness on the human side. This means that at the final judgment *every* human mouth (that is, including the Jewish) will be silenced. No one will have anything to say by way of defense or excuse. Before God, the whole world will stand guilty and be liable to incur, though Paul does not mention it at this point, the full force of God's wrath.

The final statement of the entire section (v 20) focuses upon the law (of Moses) and its factual impotence to effect justification. Paul cites a clause from the early part of Psalm 143 (LXX 142), in which the psalmist, having called upon God's "truth" (LXX *alētheia*) and God's "righteousness" (LXX *dikaiosynē*), begs that God not enter into judgment (v 1). The basis of the plea is "that no human being (literally, "no flesh") shall be justified in your sight" (v 2b). This assertion of the universal failure to find justification in God's sight rounds off, in "inclusive" fashion, the "thesis" stated at the beginning of the chain: "There is no righteous person, not even one" (v 10). Paul, however, prefaces the quotation from Ps 143:2 (LXX 142:2) with the phrase "from works of law" (*ex ergōn nomou*) in a way that suggests it forms part of the original text, which in fact it does not. What the psalmist meant to be a confession of general human unrighteousness in God's sight, Paul, without losing the universal perspective, transforms into a scriptural exclusion of righteousness through the law, repeating precisely the same ploy with Ps 143:2 made in Gal 2:16. The combined evidence of Gal 2:16 and Rom 3:20 shows beyond doubt that Ps 143:2, "embroidered" in this way, played a key role in Paul's explanation and defense of what it meant for Jews such as himself and Peter (Cephas) to come to faith in Jesus as the Christ.

The phrase "works of the law" (or variations upon it) occurs several times in Romans and Galatians and appears to be a technical phrase of the tradition within which Paul is arguing in these letters (see Note). Clearly Paul cannot mean that *keeping* (that is, fulfilling) the law leads to failure to find justification (the classic Lutheran position), since this would be in stark contradiction to the principle that justification will be according to a person's works, as stated unequivocally in 2:13 and presupposed throughout chapter 2. The desire to fulfill the law is not in itself wrong. What leads to universal lack of justification through "works of the law" is factual failure on a universal scale to fulfill its precepts, a state of affairs Paul finds confirmed in scripture (vv 10-18). This factual failure renders any attempt to find justification through fulfillment of the law something doomed to frustration from the start, as well as being resistant both to God's verdict recorded in scripture and, as Paul will soon proclaim (3:21-26), to God's gracious act of righteousness in Christ (cf. 9:32; 10:3; Gal 2:21). To proceed from "works of law," then, is to carry on as if this divine verdict were not in. It is this resistance to God, rather than any intrinsic wrongfulness of "works" as such, that is the problem.

In a final comment (v 20b) Paul makes clear that, far from leading to justification, what the law brings is "knowledge of sin" *(epignōsis hamartias)*. The "knowledge" in question is not helpful information about what is right and wrong. Rather, for those who possess it—that is, the Jews—the law qualifies wrongdoing as "transgression," as something contrary to the explicit will of God (4:15b; 5:13b, 20a; Gal 3:19b). Through the law one comes to "know" sin as explicit rejection of the Creator. Hence the law reveals to Jews that they, like the Gentiles, stand as sinners before God, liable to condemnation. Possession of the law, which may have been considered to set them apart from the sinful Gentile mass, in fact shows that they are bound up with it.

Reflection. Paul's judgment here is one that few Torah-observant Jews would accept and one that all, with few exceptions, have found and continue to find deeply offensive. Harsh as the verdict may be, however, in applying the accusatory scriptural catena to the Jews, Paul remains true to the original reference of the texts cited, all of which assert or complain about infidelity in Israel. Similar pessimistic verdicts appear in late books of the Old Testament (e.g., Isa 59:12-15; 64:5-12; Ezra 9:6-15; Neh 9:16-38; Dan 9:4-19; Tob 3:1-6) and in the literature of apocalyptic Judaism (e.g., *Jub.* 23:16-21; *4 Ezra* 7:22-24, 46, 62-74, 116-26; 8:35; 1QH 1:25-27; 4:29-31; 6:18-22; 9:14; 12:30-31; 1QS 11:9). Such texts provide some context within which to set Paul's otherwise singular accusation. Speaking as a Jew, from within Israel (cf. the "we" of v 9a), Paul externalizes the self-judgment that had been an essential element of his own conversion (cf. Gal 2:15-16) and which led him to see in a new light the "law-righteousness" in which he had been "blameless" (Phil 3:6).

Both Paul's personal experience and that which he here projects upon his people form an instance of that pattern, found again and again in biblical thought, where God's righteousness confronts and triumphantly overcomes total *un*righteousness on the human side (see Note on 1:17). Psalm 143 gives classic expression to that pattern—which doubtless accounts for Paul's appeal to it in the present context (v 20). In the light of the psalm, the solemn proclamation of God's rescuing righteousness that follows (3:21-26) is not unexpected. Central to the gospel telling of God's inclusion of "all" (Gentiles as well as Jews) under grace is the sense that "all" (Jews as well as Gentiles) are equally locked in a common bind of sin (11:32; Gal 3:22). The long prophetic accusation that now draws to a close has all been designed to prepare the way for and communicate this radical sense of God's inclusive grace.

Notes

9. *What then? Do we have an advantage? Hardly!:* Some interpreters (S. K. Stowers; Fitzmyer 326), noting the way in which this question parallels that of v 1 thereby forming an inclusion, attach this verse to the preceding dialogue. Clearly, it does perform a bridging function. However, the scriptural catena beginning at v 10 also requires some kind of introduction. The verse as a whole bristles with problems of text, punctuation and interpretation; for a comprehensive and fair discussion, see esp. Cranfield 1.189–91. The punctuation adopted takes the opening Greek phrase *(ti oun?)* as a separate question, rather than as the object of the following verb, which is also possible on certain interpretations of the verb.

The Greek verb in question *(proechein)* has the basic sense of "hold before." It is also used intransitively in the sense of "jut out," "be prominent" and hence "to surpass," "have an advantage." In the middle it means "hold before oneself" and so comes to have the metaphorical sense of "put forward as an excuse." Hence the best attested form occurring in the present context, *proechometha*, can be understood in a variety of ways.

1. As a true middle, in the sense "put forward in excuse" (e.g., Dunn 1.144, 146–47), with the opening *ti oun?* phrase understood as its object ("What excuse then can we put forward?"). But this then requires an answering "Nothing," which the following Greek phrase *ou pantōs* hardly supplies. 2. As a true passive, giving the sense, "Are we (Jews) at a disadvantage?" (Stowers; Fitzmyer 330–31). An understanding in this sense, followed by *ou pantōs* taken as a firm denial ("Certainly not"; cf. Epictetus, *Discourses* 4.8.2) leads in well to the following response (v 9b), which states simply an equal subjection of Jews and Gentiles under sin. But nothing in the wider context to this point has suggested an *inferior* situation for Jews. 3. As a middle form with an active sense: "Do we have an advantage?" (most interpreters; RSV; NSRV [main entry]). Instances of *proechein* used in this way are not otherwise attested, though the usage as such is not unparalleled (cf. Lagrange 68–69). The interpretation (cf. Latin Vulgate: *praecellimus*) provides a neat parallel to the opening question in v 1 but has the difficulty of making Paul now give a diametrically opposite response to that question. The problem is eased somewhat if *ou pantōs* is understood in its most natural sense as "not entirely" (cf. 1 Cor 5:10). The translation "Hardly!" seeks to convey the sense of ironical understatement that then seems to be implied.

under sin: The Greek phrase *hyph' hamartian* (cf. 7:14; Gal 3:22) evokes at first sight the distinctive Pauline sense of "sin" as an enslaving power, so prominent in later parts of the letter (chapters 5–8). The context, however, (esp. "We have already charged . . ."; "stand guilty" [v 19]) suggests that the more forensic sense of "guilty" is operative here; cf. Zeller 79–80.

11–12. *"There is no one with understanding. There is no one who seeks God. All have turned aside, together they have become worthless; there is no one who shows kindness, there is not even one.":* Save for minor modifications repeating the "there is no one . . ." refrain, this agrees with LXX Ps 13(14):2b-3, repeated in LXX Ps 52(53):2b-3.

13–14. *"Their throat is an open grave; they use their tongues to deceive":* agrees exactly with LXX Ps 5:10 (9b). *"The venom of vipers is under their lips.":* agrees exactly with LXX Ps 139:4 (140:3). "Their mouth is full of cursing and bitterness.": modeled upon LXX Ps 9:28 (10:7).

15–17. *"Their feet are hasty to shed blood. Ruin and misery lie in their paths, and the path of peace they have not known.":* a somewhat modified and incomplete rendering of LXX Isa 59:7-8a; for the first phrase, cf. also Prov 1:16.

18. *"There is no fear of God before their eyes.":* agrees exactly with LXX Ps 35(36):2.

19. *Now we know:* For Paul's use of this expression *(oidamen)* to express (what he hopes will be) a commonly accepted proposition, see Note on 2:2.

whatever the law says . . . those who are within the law: In the first instance "law" *(nomos)* must have the sense of "scripture as a whole" (cf. 1 Cor 14:21), as illustrated by the combined witness of the catena of texts just set forth. In the second instance, "those within *(en)* the law" (cf. 2:12b) must refer to those who have their pattern of life determined by the law (of Moses)—that is, the Jews. As so often in Romans (cf. 3:27; 7:21-23; 8:2), Paul plays upon the ambiguity in *nomos;* see Note on 7:21.

stand guilty before God: The Greek word *hypodikos,* occurring only here in the NT, has the sense of "already found guilty and awaiting condemnation"; cf. Cranfield 1.197.

20. *works of the law:* This is the first appearance in Romans (cf., however, the singular *to ergon tou nomou* in 2:15) of the phrase *erga nomou* which appears regularly in polemical contexts in Paul (full form: 3:28; Gal 2:16 [three times]; 3:2, 5, 10; shorthand *[ex] ergōn:* Rom 3:27; 4:2, 6; 9:12, 32; 11:6). The phrase designates "deeds demanded by the law" in the sense of works listed in the law as to be carried out by human beings. That Paul is using a technical term of the post-biblical Jewish tradition is suggested by the appearance of Hebrew equivalents in Qumran literature: (4Q Flor 1:7; cf. also 1QS 5:21; 6:18; 1QpHab 7:11 and especially 4Q*Halakhic Letter* (4QMMT) 113 [a context where the "reckoning" of "righteousness" is also mentioned (line 117) in a way highly reminiscent of Paul's use of Gen 15:6 in Romans 4]); cf. also 2 *Apoc. Bar.* 57:2 ("works of the commandments"). In Paul the overtone of "performance" ("doing the works of the law"; Greek *poiein, ergazesthai;* cf. Rom 4:4-5; 10:5; Gal 3:10-12) is implicit in the preposition *ex* governing the genitive plural

ergōn, which is the form in which the phrase regularly appears. The stress upon "performance," however, does not mean that the attempt to perform (perfectly) the requirements of the law is itself sinful (the "strong Lutheran" interpretation). On the other hand, "works of the law" ought not be restricted solely to those particular observances of the law (esp. circumcision, food laws, calendar observance) that served, in a sociological sense, as "identity markers" of Judaism over against the Gentiles (so esp. Dunn, *Romans* 1.153–54 [though later publications show a somewhat broader perspective]; see Reference); see further, Westerholm, *Israel's Law* 116–21; Fitzmyer 337–39.

shall no human being: The Pauline text has *ou . . . pasa sarx*, where the LXX Ps 142:2 translates the Hebrew (143:2) more literally *ou . . . pas zōn* ("living being"). *Sarx* ("flesh") may be a deliberate Pauline alteration; cf., however, the parallel in *1 Enoch* 81:5: ". . . show to all your children that no one of the flesh can be just before the Lord; for they are merely his own creation."

through the law comes knowledge of sin: This is the first of a series of "throw-away" lines Paul offers about the ill effects of the law (see also 4:15b; 5:20a; 6:14; 7:5) before formally sorting out the connection between the law and sin in 7:7-25.

For Reference and Further Study

Bachmann, M. "Rechtfertigung und Gesetzeswerke bei Paulus." *TZ* 49 (1993) 1–33.

Campbell, W. S. "Romans III as a Key to the Structure and Thought of the Letter." *NovT* 23 (1981) 22–40.

Cranfield, C.E.B. "'The Works of the Law' in the Epistle to the Romans." *JSNT* 43 (1991) 89–101.

Davies, G. N. *Faith and Obedience* 80–104.

Dunn, J.D.G. "Works of the Law and the Curse of the Law (Galatians 3.10–14)." *NTS* 31 (1985) 523–42.

__________. "Yet Once More—'The Works of the Law.'" *JSNT* 46 (1992) 99–117.

__________. "Echoes of Intra-Jewish Polemic in Paul's Letter to the Galatians." *JBL* 112 (1993) 459–77, esp. 465–68 ("works of the law").

Feuillet, A. "La situation privilégiée des Juifs d'après Rm 3,9." *NRT* 105 (1983) 33–46.

Gaston, L. "Works of the Law as a Subjective Genitive." *Paul and the Torah* 100–06.

Hays, R. B. "Psalm 143 and the Logic of Romans 3." *JBL* 99 (1980) 107–115.

Keck, L. E. "The Function of Romans 3:10-18: Observations and Suggestions." *God's Christ and His People* (FS N. A. Dahl). Eds. J. Jervell and W. A. Meeks. Oslo: Universitetsforlaget, 1977, 141–57.

Moo, D. J. "'Law,' 'Works of the Law,' and Legalism in Paul." *WTJ* 45 (1983) 73–100, esp. 90–99.

Watson, F. *Paul, Judaism and the Gentiles* 127–31.

Wilckens, U. "Was heißt bei Paulus: 'Aus Werken des Gesetzes wird kein Mensch gerecht'?" *Rechtfertigung als Freiheit: Paulusstudien.* Neukirchen/Vluyn: Neukirchener Verlag, 1974, 77–109, esp. 79–84.

ii. The "Righteousness of God" Now Available to All Believers (3:21-26)

21. But now, apart from law, the righteousness of God stands revealed, although the law and the prophets bear witness to it, 22. the righteousness of God through faith in Jesus Christ for all who believe.

For there is no distinction—23. for all have sinned and lack the glory of God. 24. They are being justified as a gift by his grace through the redemption which has come about in Christ Jesus. 25. God put him forward as a means of expiation, (operative) through faith, in (the shedding of) his blood. This was to display God's righteousness because of the passing over of sins formerly committed 26. in the (time of) God's patience; it was (also) to display God's righteousness at the present time: that God himself is righteous and justifies the one who has faith in Jesus.

Interpretation

Introduction. Within the symbolic universe of apocalyptic Judaism, Paul's argument up to this point has brought his implied audience face to face with the fearful prospect of exposure to God's wrath. What will be required at the eschatological judgment is righteousness. But the long prophetic accusation just deployed (1:18–3:20) has shown the complete lack of righteousness on the human side, even for those (the Jews) who possess the law. The entire world (Jewish as well as Gentile) stands unrighteous before God, a situation which "establishes" rather than derogates from God's own righteousness (3:3-6).

Just at this point, when terror and despair might appear to be the only foreseeable reaction, Paul triumphantly sounds once again the opening thematic assurance concerning the righteousness of God (1:17). "Now," at this "eleventh hour" on the apocalyptic time-scale when all is rushing to destruction and ruin, God has intervened to convert the situation of unrighteousness and "wrath" into one of righteousness and hope. The righteousness required for salvation is now universally available because of what God has graciously brought about in Jesus Christ. Israel's Messiah has, in his death, become a means of righteousness accessible to all humankind. The only requirement on the human side is faith—a faith prepared to own, first of all, that one stands in need of this "gift" of righteousness (because all other source of righteousness, including that of the law, is excluded) and, secondly, prepared to believe that God is so good and so faithful to creation as to make this gesture in the face of human sin.

The announcement comes in what is a complex, overladen statement in the original Greek. The only genuine main statement is the initial one about the revelation of God's righteousness; apart from the aside in vv

22d-23 summing up 1:18–3:20, everything consists of appended participial and infinitive phrases. Nonetheless, a distinct structural pattern can be discerned. Double assertions of the "revelation" (vv 21-22c) or "demonstration" (vv 25b-26) of God's righteousness "frame" a central proclamation of God's justifying the believer in virtue of the death of Jesus Christ, operative as "means of expiation" (vv 24-25a). The rather tortured syntax of the passage and the occurrence of language otherwise not found in Paul (e.g, *hilastērion* ["means of expiation"]; *paresis* ["pardon"]; *endeixis* ["display"]) suggest that in vv 25-26a Paul has taken over a liturgical or credal piece of the early Christian tradition, which he has "embroidered" and expanded for his own purposes.

The revelation of God's righteousness (v 21). Echoing the opening thematic statement (1:16-17), Paul proclaims that God's righteousness "now . . . stands revealed." The "now" is the "now" of the new situation created by God's "eleventh hour" intervention in Christ. This has transformed the prospect of universal condemnation ("wrath") on the grounds of total human unrighteousness (3:9, 19-20, 23) into the hope of salvation on the basis of the "righteousness of God" (cf. 1:17).

In the preceding passage (3:1-8) Paul had juxtaposed human and divine (un)righteousness. Human sinfulness served only to enhance the righteousness and fidelity of God (3:3-6). The implication was that God would display righteousness by executing righteous judgment upon a sinful world. What is now being proclaimed, however, is that God is displaying righteousness in a way that saves rather than condemns and doing so without any injury to the principle that righteousness on the part of human beings is required for the establishment and salvation of the eschatological people of God (see Interpretation of 1:17). The seeds of this saving view of God's righteousness are present already in scriptural texts such as Psalm 143, which is quoted explicitly by Paul in v 20 (cf. Gal 2:16) and largely carries the argument across the transition in 3:21. The psalmist begs God not "to enter into judgment with your servant," owning that "no one living is righteous before you" (v 2). But, at the beginning and end of the plea (v 1, v 11), there is a call precisely upon God's "righteousness" for rescue and salvation. What is at stake here—both in the psalm and in Paul—is a vision of God's righteousness which, along with a sense of God's personal integrity as judge of the world, sees it as involving as well a saving faithfulness to errant creation.

The crucial rhetorical device upon which Paul's argument turns at this point is the ambiguity contained in the phrase "righteousness of God." Following the issue of theodicy thrown up in 3:1-8, especially the allusion to God's righteousness in 3:5, Paul must mean in 3:21-22 a revelation of God's own righteousness (subjective genitive in the Greek), as the concluding statement v 26 also makes clear. At the same time, the whole issue concerning human righteousness (whether through the law or no) aired in the preceding prophetic accusation (2:1–3:20) ensures that "righteousness of God" must refer also to the required eschatological righteousness graciously conferred upon believers by God (cf. v 24 [*dikaioumenoi*] and the end of v 26 *[kai dikaiounta ton ek pisteōs Iēsou]*). As already in the thematic statement in 1:17, both "poles" of righteousness—the divine and the human—are embraced in the one pregnant expression, "righteousness of God." As Paul will soon explain, God has granted unrighteous, sinful human beings access to the righteousness required for salvation by making a share in the divine righteousness available to them in the person of God's Son, Jesus Christ.

In continuity with the previous passage (esp. vv 19-20), Paul insists that this revelation of righteousness is something entirely "apart from law" *(chōris nomou)*. This phrase in fact enjoys the initial position of emphasis in the Greek, suggesting that the exclusion of any possibility of a righteousness based on the law (of Moses) and the proposing of an alternative "righteousness of God" based upon faith is the main purpose of the passage as a whole (cf. the sequel in vv 27-31). Nonetheless, while the new righteousness is "apart from law" in the sense of not being based upon fulfillment of the law's requirements ("works of law," v 20), "law" *(nomos)* functioning in another role, as part of "the law and the prophets" that make up "scripture," bears witness *(martyroumenē)* to the new, alternative righteousness. Paul provides here an anticipatory hint of the scriptural witness to righteousness by faith he will develop at some length around the figure of Abraham in chapter 4. The "law" (the Pentateuch in the shape of Genesis) and "the prophets" (David speaking in the Psalms) will show that Abraham received the promise containing salvation for all on the basis of a righteousness stemming from faith rather than from obedience to law.

A righteousness universally available through faith in Christ (v 22). Law-righteousness excluded, Paul indicates the essential characteristic of the alternative source of eschatological justification, what he has already called the "righteousness of God": it is righteousness operative through faith in Jesus Christ (*dia pisteōs Iēsou Christou* [Note that Greek, unlike English, uses the same stem *(pist-)* for both the noun "faith" and the verb "believe"]). Here for the first time (apart from the isolated allusion in 2:16), the person of Jesus Christ enters the argument of the main body of the letter. Though there are grounds for holding that Paul's phrase refers to Jesus' own faith (subjective genitive—See Note), the divine-human polarity that runs through the passage and the overall thrust of Pauline thought (esp. Gal 2:16) suggest that it is believers' faith *in* Jesus (objective genitive) that Paul has in mind. To be more precise, it is "Christ-qualified" faith in God—faith in God precisely as the One who raised Jesus from the dead (cf. esp. the "definition" of Christian faith given in 10:8-9: "This is the word *[rēma]* of faith which we preach: that if you confess with your mouth that Jesus is Lord and believe in your heart that God raised him from the dead, you will be saved").

What is crucial about faith as the vehicle of human access to righteousness is that, unlike righteousness tied to the Jewish law, it opens up the possibility of righteousness on a universal scale *(eis pantas tous pisteuontas)*. In the preceding section (1:18–3:20) the frequently-recurring "all" (Greek *pantes*) served to indicate the universal bind in sin and alienation from God: all—that is, including the Jews. Now, functioning upon the positive side, it has the sense of "all—that is, including the Gentiles." The common "inclusion" under sin—which so challenged God's righteousness (3:3-8)—is being transformed through God's righteous action into a common "inclusion" in grace, righteousness and eternal life. Hence "there is no distinction" (*diastolē*, v 22d), no distinction, that is, between Jews and Gentiles as far as eschatological justification is concerned. God's impartiality (2:11) works both ways. Whatever may be the Jewish privilege in other respects—which Paul does not deny (3:1-2; 9:4-5)—as regards justification, all human beings are on an equal footing.

The need for such a righteousness (v 23). Paul reinforces this sense of universality in an aside recalling the thesis of universal sinfulness and alienation established in 1:18–3:20. A universal state of "having sinned" *(pantes . . . hēmarton)* connotes a similarly universal lack of the "glory of God" *(hysterountai tēs doxēs tou theou)*. There is an echo here of the language of the Jewish tradition, ultimately founded on Gen 1:26-28 and reflected especially in Ps 8:6, where human beings, created in the image and likeness of God, bear the divine glory. Paul argues within a development of this tradition that closely associated "glory" and "righteousness." Any glory attaching to human beings, is always a share in the divine glory, the effect of the closeness to God which the righteous enjoy (cf. 2 Cor 3:7, 18). While sin involves loss of glory, glory will be particularly the lot of those found worthy to share God's eternal life (cf. 2:7, 10; 5:2; 8:17-18, 21, 30; 9:23; 2 Cor 3:18; 4:17). "To lack the glory of God" is to be unfit, through sinfulness, to share the closeness to God of the final Kingdom.

God's gracious bestowal of righteousness (v 24). But this universally prevailing situation on the negative side is being matched by a divine gift of righteousness of similarly universal scope. God's righteousness stands revealed (vv 21-22) in the gracious offer of justification (righteousness) which the gospel holds out to all believers. As always within the symbolic universe presupposed by Paul (see Interpretation of 2:13), the justification in question is God's verdict of acquittal to be pronounced at the judgment. Moreover, the contrast with the preceding statement about sin (v 23) suggests that "being justified" *(dikaioumenoi)* contains a significant ethical element: believers are being "made righteous," not simply "declared righteous" and this is being achieved, not by a legal fiction—which would in effect be immoral (cf. Isa 5:23; Prov 17:15; Exod 23:7)—but through a distinctive act of God's grace effective in the redemptive work of Christ.

The insistence upon grace appears in two sequential expressions in the Greek: *dōrean* and *en tę̄ autou chariti*. While the former means simply "gratis," the latter is perhaps more concrete, referring to an act of grace—notably, the Christ-event. As the elaboration in the following verses (25-26) will show, God, in an act that is at once both "gracious" and "righteous," makes sinners righteous in virtue of the way Christ's death functions with respect to sin. Both that event (the "giving up" of God's own Son" [cf. 5:5-10; 8:32]) and the justification which it effects are acts of grace.

Paul speaks in this connection of the "redemption *(apolytrōsis)* which has come about in Christ Jesus." The word means simply liberation from some captivity, as in slavery or war (cf. also Rom 8:23; 1 Cor 1:30), without any necessary connotation of a price being paid. God's redemptive act in Christ represents a snatching of human beings away from the captivity to sin and from the prospect of wrathful condemnation at the judgment (cf. 5:9) to which that captivity has exposed them.

The expiatory effect of Christ's death (v 25a). A long appended clause explains more fully the inner working of this "redemption" brought about in Christ Jesus: how it facilitates the eschatological justification of sinful human beings in such a way as to "demonstrate" (vv 25b-26) rather than impugn the divine righteousness (cf. 3:3-7). It does so because in Christ's death—literally, "in (the shedding of) his blood"—God has found a way to deal effectively with sin and with the barrier to divine-human relations (wrath) that it sets up.

Paul expresses this in quasi-cultic language, possibly stemming originally from the common Christian tradition. Although Christ is the focus, the stress is entirely upon the initiative of God, who is said to have "put him forward (*proetheto*—for the 'public' nuance in this, see Note) as a means of expiation" *(hilastērion)*. The interpretation of this last expression has perhaps been the main focus of attention in the passage—though for Paul it serves as an explanation of the way Christ's death functions rather than as the central affirmation. The Greek stem to which the adjective *hilastērion* belongs has the basic sense of "make gracious," usually with respect to appeasing or placating an angry god or fellow human being. From the outset it has to be said that such cannot be the meaning here since, as just noted, God is the subject of the action and it makes no sense to speak of any personage, divine or human, appeasing his or her own wrath. The verb form, chiefly in the composite *exhilasthai*, appears frequently in the LXX as a translation of the Hebrew *kippēr* to express the removal or expiation of human sin on the part of God or God's accredited agent (the priest). *Hilastērion*, whether as an adjective or as an adjective used (in the neuter singular) as a noun, appears with reference to the "mercy seat" or cover (Hebrew *kappōret*) placed over the ark of the covenant in the Holy of Holies of the Temple (Exod 25:17-22). This cover played an important part in the Day of Atonement ritual (Leviticus 16). Upon it, at the culmination of the ritual, the High Priest sprinkled the blood of the goat slain on that day of forgiveness and reconciliation with God. No mere item of furniture, the *kappōret* came to be seen as the focus of the cleansing and renewing presence of God, on the occasion when God "wiped away" the stain of all the accumulated sins of the previous year, inaugurating a fresh epoch of covenant relations between Israel and her God (Lev 16:2-16).

To what extent these ritual associations are present in Rom 3:25 is not clear. Since Christ cannot simply be identified with a piece of Temple furniture (the *kappōret*), *hilastērion* must have at least to some degree a figurative or more than literal meaning. The most secure translation of the indeterminate *hilastērion* occurring in v 25 is simply "a means of expiation." Nonetheless, echoes of the "Day of Atonement" ritual are almost certainly present. Paul, possibly in line with an early Christian tradition (which he presupposes his Roman audience will recognize), sees God as instituting in Christ the culminating exercise of the "Day of Atonement" expiation and renewal. This atonement takes place "publicly" (cf. "put forward"), not in the inner recesses of the Temple, whose atoning function the death of Christ supersedes.

It is this expiatory function that enables the death of Christ to be an instrument of justification. Not, however, in a merely mechanical way. For Paul, faith is an essential component of the total process. Faith is that attitude which discerns God's working in the death of Christ a purely gracious act of expiation and surrenders to it, acknowledging that, because of sin, one stands in need of such divine "redemption." The justification that ensues is entirely the work of God but, on the human side, faith is the vehicle of its operation. Through faith God is able to draw sinful human beings into the scope of the divine righteousness displayed in the obedient death of Christ.

How this displays (reveals) God's righteousness (vv 25b-26). A final clause relates this account of what God was doing in the death of Christ to the issue thrown up in the preceding passage (3:1-8). How is the accusation of Jewish unrighteousness, along with that of the Gentile world, compatible with a sense of God's righteousness or fidelity to the covenant promises to Israel? Whereas in that previous passage Paul had simply *asserted* that God, as Judge of the world, *must* be true, faithful and righteous (vv 3-6), now the Christ event "displays" or "demonstrates" (literally, "provides a proof" *[endeixis]*) of the righteousness of God. Just as year by year, Israel's God, faithful to the covenant, had dealt creatively—through the expiatory rite of the Day of Atonement—with the accumulated sins of the previous year, so now in this final Day of Atonement, God has dealt faithfully and effectively with the all the sins committed by Israel in the time of "God's patience," that is, the time when God held back from inflicting upon Israel the wrath merited by Israel's sin (cf. 2:4-5). The thesis of universal Jewish unrighteousness, along with that of the Gentile world, is not incompatible with the "righteousness of God" (3:3) since God has displayed righteousness precisely by sending a Messiah to deal effectively with that unrighteousness and confer upon Israel, "apart from the law" (v 21), the righteousness required for salvation.

If the first allusion to the "display" of God's righteousness (vv 25b-26a) refers to God's covenant fidelity to Israel, the second (v 26b) probably has a more general reference. Moreover, in contrast to the earlier statement, which had past sinfulness particularly in view, it is a question of what is happening "at the present time" *(en tǭ nyn kairǭ)*. The proclamation of Christ's death through the gospel (cf. Gal 3:1) is making available to the sinful Gentile world the same possibility of expiation and justification that will rescue it as well—at this "eleventh hour"—from the wrath. The preaching of the gospel lifts the saving event of Jesus' death out of its particular time and place so that it can become for all who respond in faith the vehicle of salvation (cf. Gal 3:1-5). In this sense God is "displaying righteousness" not just to Israel but, as Creator, to the entire world.

The final phrase (v 26c) brings together the two "poles" of "God's righteousness"—the divine and the human—that have run through the passage. The conclusion is that in this one single act (the death of the Son) God is both displaying personal righteousness *(eis to einai auton dikaion) and (kai)* conferring righteousness upon (literally "rightwising" *[dikaiounta]*) the human believer *(ton ek pisteōs Iēsou)*. The offer and process of justifying sinful human beings, through their adherence in faith to the person of God's Son, is precisely the mode in which the divine righteousness is shown. In a way unimagined in the earlier sequence (3:1-8), where human sinfulness either impugned or simply served to display by contrast the "righteousness of God," God has displayed righteousness by dealing creatively with human sin. The tension with respect to God's righteousness, set up for rhetorical purposes in the earlier part of chapter 3, has been resolved. The saving exercise of God's righteousness, for which the psalmist made an appeal on an individual basis in Psalm 143, has operated, in Christ, on a universal scale.

It will be noted that on this interpretation of Rom 3:21-26 Paul's intention is not strictly to present Christ's death as a means of ensuring the operation of God's forgiveness in the face of human sin. Varieties of the "Satisfaction" theology of the redemption have long been read in this sense out of the passage. But the issue arising out of the wider argument of Romans (esp. 3:1-20) is not that of how to change an (already adopted) wrathful disposition on the part of God, in order that forgiveness may flow to human beings (propitiation). Rather, it is a question of *God's* removal (through Christ) of the sinfulness on the human side that blocks divine-human relations and threatens the infliction of God's wrath (expiation).

Nor is the issue of God's righteousness for Paul as abstract as later Christian theology has made it. The issue, as we have seen, arises out of the thesis of universal—that is, including Jewish—sinfulness. If human beings are so universally sinful, if there is no righteousness whatsoever on the human side (3:9, 20), then how can God's saving promises to Israel (3:2) be realized? Must not the exercise of God's righteousness be simply punitive and destructive? No, says Paul. While God is not unjust to inflict the wrath in such a situation (3:5-6), wrath is neither God's first nor final word. By putting forth the Son as a "means of expiation" God has found a way to bring the sinful world—or at least those in it who respond in faith—to the eschatological righteousness required for salvation.

Notes

21. *But now:* The emphatic "now" (Greek *nyni*) is primarily logical in the sense that Paul is now considering the situation in the light of the Christian gospel. It is also temporal in the sense that the gospel proclaims the onset of the era of salvation. However, the time of "wrath" is not wholly overhauled (cf. 5:9; 1 Thess 1:10). The "now" is the present time when both the "old age" and the dawning "new age" overlap (see Interpretation of 5:1-11).

    apart from law: Following the phrase "from works of law" *(ex ergōn nomou)* in v 20 and with "apart from works of law" *(chōris ergōn nomou)* to follow in v 28 (cf. *chōris ergōn* in 4:6), the phrase here must be a shorthand form of "apart from works of the law." Paul wants to indicate the revelation of a righteousness that completely bypasses any righteousness based upon doing the works which the law commands.

    stands revealed: The translation attempts to capture the sense of the Greek perfect *(pephanerōtai)*: an action performed in the past (the death of Christ) has an effect that lingers on (in the proclamation of the gospel).

    although the law and the prophets bear witness to it: For "the law and the prophets" as a standard way of referring to the scriptures as a whole: cf. Matt 11:13 // Luke 16:16; Matt 5:17; 7:12; 22:40; Luke 24:44; John 1:45; Acts 13:15;

24:14; 28:23; Sir Prologue (3 times); 4 Macc 18:10. In referring "law" now to a portion of scripture (the Pentateuch), whereas earlier in the sentence it clearly designated a way of life or prescribed code of behavior, Paul is exploiting the ambiguity of the term *nomos*; cf. 3:27; 7:21-23.

22. *through faith in Jesus Christ.* Just as the Greek word *pistis* can mean both "faith" and "faithfulness," so too the genitive in the total phrase is open to either an objective ("faith in Jesus Christ") or subjective ("faith of Jesus Christ") understanding. Formerly a somewhat maverick view, interpretation in the second (subjective) sense has gained ground in recent years, with adherents pointing to the reference to the faith of Abraham *(ek pisteōs Abraam)* in 4:16 as a nearby parallel in an indisputably subjective sense. Syntactically both possibilities are open. Mark 11:22 *(echete pistin theou)* clearly shows the possibility of the purely objective sense. Deciding between the two rests upon the context and an overall sense of Paul's theology. Apart from Rom 3:22, the phrase *pisteōs Christou* (or equivalent) occurs six times elsewhere in Paul: Rom 3:26; Gal 2:16 (twice), 20; 3:22 and Phil 3:9 (setting aside the P[46] reading in Gal 3:26). Some of these occurrences, including that in Rom 3:22, show a certain redundancy if the reference, on the objective understanding, is to believers' faith in Christ. Moreover, the references to Christ's "obedience" in Rom 5:19 and Phil 2:8 show that Christ's subjective disposition in the the face of death played a role in Paul's understanding of the redemption (cf. also 2 Cor 4:13). That Paul considered Christ to have exhibited faith can hardly be doubted. The question is whether an allusion to this faith of Christ coheres well with the overall thrust of his argument in the key issue of faith versus "works of the law." The two occurrences of the phrase in Gal 2:16 argue most strongly for an objective understanding since between them stands the verbal phrase "we too have put our faith in Christ" *(kai hēmeis eis Christon Iēsoun episteusamen)* with its undeniably objective sense. This parallel from Galatians would seem to clinch the matter for Rom 3:22 and 26, since here, as in Galatians the focus is upon God's action and the appropriate human response (faith, as opposed to works) rather than on the personal faith or faithfulness of Christ. For more extended discussion and references, see Fitzmyer 345–46.

For there is no distinction: The identical phrase *(ou gar estin diastolē)* occurs in a more positive context in 10:12a. It could be and perhaps was a slogan or shibboleth of the Pauline missionary movement; cf. W. Schmithals: ". . . in a single succinct phrase Paul denotes the theme of his letter to Rome" (p. 119 [translation mine]).

23. *For all have sinned:* As in 3:9 (cf. 2:12; 3:19-20; 5:12; 10:11-13; 11:32; Gal 3:22), "all" primarily envisages two groups—Jews and Gentiles—rather than all individuals, though the inclusion of all on an individual basis must also be implied.

and lack the glory of God: The connective "and" *(kai)* has a consecutive sense: sin has led to loss of glory. For the motif of loss of the primeval glory in the Jewish apocalyptic tradition the classic passage is *Apoc. Mos.* 20:1 "(Eve speaking) At that very moment my eyes were opened and I knew that I was naked of the righteousness with which I had been clothed. And I wept saying, 'Why have you done this to me, that I have been estranged from my glory with which I was clothed?'"; cf. 21:6 "(Adam reproaching Eve) You have estranged me from the glory of God"; cf. *3 Apoc. Bar.* (Greek) 4:16: ". . . just as Adam through this tree was condemned and stripped of the glory of God, thus those now who insatiably drink the wine deriving from it transgress worse than Adam, and become distant from the glory of God." The close association of "righteousness" and "glory" is apparent in these texts, as it is in Paul. "Glory," like "righteousness," is that which equips human beings to share the eternal life of God, the original intent of the Creator in their regard (cf. already Rom 2:7, 10). Most instructive is the oft-quoted passage from *2 Apoc. Bar.:* "Also, as for the glory of those who proved to be righteous on account of my law, . . ., their splendor will then be glorified by transformations, and the shape of their face will be changed into the light of their beauty, so that they may acquire and receive the undying world which is promised to them" (51:3-4). With the simple substitution of "righteous on account of their faith" for "righteous on account of my law" this passage could well have been written by Paul; cf. esp. 2 Cor 3:18; see also *1 Enoch* 50:1; 62:15-16; *Sib. Or.* 3:282-83; *4 Ezra* 7:95; 8:51-54; 1QS 4:22-23; CD 3:20. See further Byrne, *'Sons of God'* 68–70.

24. *they are being justified as a gift by his grace:* On "justification" see the Interpretation of 2:13 above. For the Greek expression *dōrean* (an adverb derived from the accusative of *dōrea* ["gift"]) used, as here, in the sense of "gratis," "without payment," see LXX Exod 21:11; Matt 10:8; 2 Cor 11:7. In 5:15 the two expressions appearing here in sequence are run together: *hē dōrea en chariti* and in 5:17 Paul speaks of "the gift *(dōrea)* of righteousness." Paul's concept of "grace" stands in continuity with that pervasive in the OT tradition but *charis* in Paul has a dynamic character, functioning later in Romans (5:20-21; 6:14-15) as a personified, liberating divine power set over against the (likewise personified) power of sin *(hamartia).*

through the redemption: "Redemption" *(apolytrōsis)*, a comparatively rare word not attested before the 2nd century B.C.E., appears in secular Greek in connection with the ransoming from slavery of captives and prisoners of war. It also appears in this sense in extra-biblical Jewish literature: *Ep. Arist.* 12, 33; Philo, *Prob.* 114; Josephus, *Ant.* 12.27 and also in Heb 11:35. Elsewhere in the NT (as also in the only LXX occurrence, Dan 4:34) the sense is more generally that of eschatological release from bondage and captivity (Luke 21:28; Eph 1:14; 4:30), often with specific reference to release from the captivity created by sin (Col 1:14 [where it is "defined" as *aphesis hamartiōn*]; Eph 1:7; Heb 9:15). In the three indisputably Pauline occurrences this connotation is clear in Rom 3:24 and 1 Cor 1:30; in Rom 8:23 it is used with reference to the liberation "of our bodies" from the captivity to "corruption" (cf. v 21). Apart from the literal sense evident in Heb 11:35, no connotation of the payment of a price in exchange for release is present in the NT usage, where the stress upon the divine initiative is so clear. "Redemption" can, however, be presented as "costly" in the sense of involving suffering for its central instrument, Jesus Christ (1 Cor

6:20; 7:23). While *apolytrōsis* barely appears in the Greek OT (LXX), the simpler form *lytrōsis* and especially the verb *lytroun* occur in LXX Exodus (6:6; 13:15; 15:13), Deuteronomy (7:8; 9:26; 13:6; 15:15; 21:8; 24:18) and Psalms (77:42 [78:42]; 105:10 [106:10]; 135:24 [136:24]) in connection with the broad biblical motif of Israel's release from Egyptian slavery at the Exodus and the recapitulation of this with respect to the Babylonian captivity in Second Isaiah (41:14; 43:1, 14; 44:23, 24; 51:11; 62:12; 63:9; cf. Jer 15:21; 27:34 [50:34]; 38:11 [31:11]; Mic 4:10; 6:4). This biblical background need not necessarily lie behind the earlier NT usages of *apolytrōsis*, such as those in Paul, but it certainly influenced the broadening out of the concept of "redemption" to become a central motif of Christian theology. See F. Büchsel, *TDNT* 4.351-56; K. Kertelge, *EDNT* 1.138–40; S. Lyonnet, *Sin, Redemption and Sacrifice* 79–103.

in Christ Jesus: This is the first occurrence in Romans of an expression appearing in various forms no less than eighty times in Paul. In the vast majority of cases it expresses the notion of the risen Lord personally constituting a sphere of salvation "in" whom believers live in the interim between justification and full eschatological salvation (see Interpretation of 6:3 and Note on 6:11; cf. also 6:23; 8:1, 2; 12:5). Here, as in a few other instances (2 Cor 5:19; 1 Thess 5:18), the expression appears to have primarily a simply instrumental sense, qualifying God's objective action in the world. But overtones of the more characteristic Pauline usage may also be present in the sense that, while the event of Calvary may be the objective foundation of the "redemption" wrought by God, the application of its benefits in justification comes about for believers in virtue of the union with (the risen) Christ established by faith and baptism.

25. *God put him forward:* The verb *protithenai* in the middle voice in Greek can mean either "propose to oneself," "purpose" or "put forward publicly," "display". While the former sense brings out more strongly the sense of divine initiative and long-standing purpose behind the death of Christ, the alternative is easier from a syntactical point of view and accords well both with the aspect of "revelation" (v 21) and "display" (*endeixis*, vv 25b-26) in the present context. It also brings out, as seems intended, a contrast with the rites performed in the inner recesses of the Temple.

as a means of expiation: For the interpretation of this phrase *(hilastērion)* in terms of the "Day of Atonement" ritual, see esp. the thorough discussion of S. Lyonnet, in *Sin, Redemption, and Sacrifice* 1.159–66; also Wilckens 1.233–43 (Exkurs: Zum Verständnis der Sühne-Vorstellung). The fragmentary "Melchizedek" scroll from Qumran (11QMelch) lends significant support to this interpretation. Associating several "good news" ("gospel") texts from Isaiah (52:7; 61:1-3), it portrays "one anointed with the Spirit" as the "messenger of (the) good news" that "Melchizedek" (= the archangel Michael) will peform the function of High Priest in a culminating Day of Atonement. This will bring about eschatological "release" from sin and captivity to evil spirits; cf. the "redemption" mentioned in Rom 3:24. *Hilastērion* occurs once again in the NT, in Heb 9:5, this time with reference simply to the Temple furnishing ("mercy-seat"), not to Christ. Philo uses *hilastērion* strictly with reference to the "mercy-seat" of the ark (*Cher.* 25; *Mos.* 2.95, 97; *Fug.* 100 ["a symbol of God's beneficent power"]). Apart from usage in a biblical context, the word occurs only six times: as a neuter noun, in the sense of "atoning monument" in two inscriptions from Cos (time of Augustus) and in an inscription quoted by Dio Chrysostom; as an adjective, in a 2nd cent C.E. philosophical fragment on papyrus; in Josephus: "an expiatory monument of fear" (*Ant.* 16. 182); in 4 Macc 17:21-22 (with reference to the Jewish martyrs): ". . ., they having become, as it were, a ransom *(antipsychon)* for the sin of our nation. And through the blood of those devout ones and their atoning death *(tou hilastēriou thanatou autōn)*, divine providence preserved Israel." At first sight this last passage seems to have striking affinity with Rom 3:25. But in fact it reflects the use of *hilastērion* in secular rather than biblical Greek. An allusion to the "Day of Atonement" ritual would not have been lost on Paul's audience in Rome, if, as seems likely, he is quoting early Christian tradition, one which, like that reflected in Mark 15:38 (cf. 14:57-58) saw Jesus' death as taking over the atoning role previously attributed to the Temple; cf. the Qumran community's sense of its "council" performing the atoning function of the defiled Temple in Jerusalem (1QS 8:1-9; 11:7-8).

(operative) through faith, in (the shedding of) his blood: The words in brackets seek to smooth out in translation the syntactical awkwardness of the Greek—generally attributed in large part to Paul's adding the phrase "through faith" *(dia pisteōs)* to the original credal formula. "Faith" is to be taken here in an absolute sense ("faith" as opposed to "works of law"), not with the following phrase in the sense "faith in Christ's blood." "In his blood" is simply a Semitic idiom designating a death brought about through violence; cf. 5:9, where the same phrase stands in parallel to "the death of his Son" in the following verse; also the Pauline/Lucan version of the Eucharistic formula (Luke 22:20; 1 Cor 11:25).

because of the passing over of sins formerly committed: This phrase is sometimes interpreted—in the direction of the "Satisfaction" theory of redemption—in the sense that God *had* to show righteousness (understood in the sense of a judicial or punitive justice) in the Christ event because neglect of sins previously "passed over" (that is, left unpunished) might seem to indicate divine casualness with respect to human sin. But it is not necessary to understand the causal construction in this way. The point is not that God left the sins unpunished but that God left them "undealt with"—in the sense of not having as yet brought about the expiation finally worked in the Christ event. Alternatively, it is possible to take the rare Greek word *paresis* (occurring only here in the Greek Bible) as equivalent to the more common *aphesis* ("forgiveness"; cf. esp. the phrase *aphesis tōn hamartiōn* [Col 1:14; cf. Eph 1:7]) and interpret the prepositional construction (*dia* + accusative) in a prospective or final sense (as in Rom 4:25 [cf. Col 1:5]), suggesting a translation: "with a view to the forgiveness of sins . . ." This, again, avoids the "Satisfaction" sense but it places the syntax under considerable strain.

26. *in the (time of) God's patience:* The traditional verse division curiously separates this phrase from the preceding clause, to which it clearly refers. For the concept of God's "patience" *(anochē)*, see also Note on the earlier (and only other)

occurrence in 2:4. The parallel with *en tǭ nyn kairǭ* (cf. also the use of *makrothymia* in 9:22) suggests that the reference here is temporal: Paul has in view the epoch when God refrained from inflicting (upon the Jews) the eschatological wrath occasioned by human sin.

at the present time: The Greek word *kairos* has the sense of a particularly significant point of time. The phrase *ho nyn kairos* (cf. also 8:18; 11:5; 2 Cor 6:2) denotes the present time in the sense distinctive of Paul's eschatology: the time between the resurrection of Christ and the final consummation (cf. 1 Cor 15:23-28); the new age has dawned and made fundamental claim upon the lives of believers but the old era lingers on in the shape of weakness, suffering and death; believers in this sense live in the time of the "overlap" of the ages (see Interpretation of 5:1-11).

that God himself is righteous and justifies: The interpretation given presupposes that the connective *kai* in the phrase *dikaion kai dikaiounta* associates very closely God's *being* righteous and God's justifying activity, so that the *kai* has virtually intensive force: "righteous precisely in justifying." The alternative is to take the *kai* concessively ("righteous even though justifying . . .") so as to imply the overcoming through Christ's sacrificial death of what might appear to be a discrepancy between God's being righteous and God's justifying sinners. But such an understanding, which implies that Christ died as a propitiatory sacrifice for human sin (as in the "Satisfaction" theory of the redemption), does not really respond to what appears to be Paul's central concern in the passage, which is to integrate Jewish failure with respect to righteousness into an overall sense of the exercise of God's righteousness in Christ.

the one who has faith in Jesus: The sense of the rather cryptic Greek phrase *ton ek pisteōs* appearing here is illuminated by the similar expression *hoi ek pisteōs* occurring in Gal 3:7, 9 as a designation of those whose religious existence rests upon a basis of faith (contrast *hoi ek peritomēs*, Gal 4:12; *hoi ek nomou*, Rom 4:14, 16). In the rather similar construction in Rom 4:16 (*tǭ ek pisteōs Abraam*) the reference is clearly to Abraham's own faith. But, despite the similarity in construction and the reference simply to "Jesus," this cannot confirm a subjective understanding ("faith of Jesus") in the present instance; see the initial Note on v 22 above.

For Reference and Further Study

Blackman, C. "Romans 3:26b: A Question of Translation." *JBL* 87 (1968) 203–04.

Breytenbach, C. *Versöhnung: Eine Studie zur paulinischen Soteriologie.* WMANT 60; Neukirchen-Vluyn: Neukirchener Verlag, 1989, 166–70.

Campbell, D. A. *The Rhetoric of Righteousness in Romans 3, 21-26.* JSNTSup 65; Sheffield: JSOT Press, 1992.

Campbell, W. S. "Romans III as a Key to the Structure and Thought of the Letter." *NovT* 23 (1981) 22–40.

Hays, R. B. *The Faith of Jesus Christ.* SBLDS 56; Chico, CA: Scholars Press, 1983, 170–74.

__________. "Psalm 143 and the Logic of Romans 3." *JBL* 99 (1980) 107–115.

Hooker, M. D. "*PISTIS CHRISTOU*." *NTS* 35 (1989) 321–42.
Howard, G. "On the 'Faith of Christ.'" *HTR* 60 (1967) 459–65.
Johnson, L. T. "Romans 3:21-26 and the Faith of Jesus." *CBQ* 44 (1982) 77–90.
Käsemann, E. "The Saving Significance of the Death of Jesus in Paul." *Perspectives on Paul* 32–59.
Kümmel, W. "*Paresis* and *endeixis*: A Contribution to the Understanding of the Pauline Doctrine of Justification." *Journal for Theology and Church.* Vol. 3. New York: Harper and Row, 1967, 1–13.
Lyonnet, S. "Le sens de *paresis* en Rom 3, 25." *Études* 89–106 (orig. *Biblica* 38 [1957] 40–61).
__________. "The Terminology of Redemption." S. Lyonnet and L. Sabourin. *Sin, Redemption and Sacrifice: A Biblical and Patristic Study.* AnBib 48; 2 vols. Rome: Biblical Institute, 1970, 1.61–184.
Meyer, B. F. "The Pre-Pauline Formula in Rom. 3.25–26a." *NTS* 29 (1983) 198–208.
Piper, J. "The Demonstration of the Righteousness of God in Romans 3:25,26." *JSNT* 7 (1980) 2–32.
Reumann, J. *Righteousness in the New Testament.* Philadelphia: Fortress, 1982, 36–38, 74–77.
Schenke, L. *Die Urgemeinde: Geschichtliche und theologische Entwicklung.* Stuttgart, Berlin; Köln: Kohlhammer, 1992, 138–41.
Stowers, S. K. *Rereading of Romans* 202–26.
Wilckens, U. Exkurs: "Zum Verständnis der Sühne-Vorstellung." *Römer* 1.233–43.
Williams, S. K. "The 'Righteousness of God' in Romans." *JBL* 99 (1980) 270–78.

iii. Faith, the Sole Basis upon Which the One God Justifies All (3:27-31)

27. Where, then, is there a place for boasting? It is excluded. By what law? (A law) of works? No, but through a law of faith. 28. For the basis of our argument is that a person is justified by faith apart from works of the law.

29. Or is God the God of Jews only? Is God not the God also of Gentiles? Yes, of Gentiles also, 30. if indeed, God is one, which means that he will justify the circumcised on the ground of their faith and the uncircumcised through their faith.

31. Do we then overthrow the law by (this principle of) faith? By no means! On the contrary, we uphold the law.

Interpretation

Introduction. In the history of interpretation this small passage has been overshadowed by the interest taken in the immediately preceding passage (3:21-26) with regard to theologies of redemption. In Paul's argument, however, the chief burden of that passage was not so much to treat of the redemptive effect of Christ's death in a "systematic" way but to show, with respect to the righteousness required for salvation, that, while the law was of no avail, God had provided through Christ a new source of righteousness operative through faith. Now (3:27), reverting to the diatribe mode of discourse and still allowing his audience to "overhear" his argument with a Jewish dialogue partner, Paul draws a significant conclusion. If, on the one hand, all hope of a righteousness based upon human effort with respect to the law is illusory (3:10-20) and if, on the other hand, God has provided human beings with a new possibility of righteousness, universal in scope and based upon faith (3:21-26), no grounds whatsoever remain for pursuing the exclusivist path of the law. Faith is the only path to follow and this responds to the very nature of God, whose "oneness" must be reflected in a single design for saving the entire race. Vv 27-28 draw this conclusion in "thesis-like" form; vv 29-30 relate it to the "oneness" of God and v 31 wards off any suggestion that this involves "overthrowing" the Jewish law.

Faith excludes "boasting" (vv 27-28). Paul draws the conclusion (v 27) in terms of the exclusion of "boasting" *(kauchēsis)*, a theme which had been aired briefly in 2:17, 23, as characteristic of the Jewish teacher who, on the basis of possession of the law, seeks to be an instructor of "others" (interested Gentiles) in religious and moral matters. "Boasting," then, refers to a presumption of superiority and privileged position before God based upon possession of the law and faithful fulfillment of its commands. In the prophetic "accusation" deployed by Paul in chapter 2, what undermined that presumption was a painful gap between the claims made and actual performance with respect to the keeping of the law (2:21-24, 27). Now a new factor has entered in to set the seal upon the exclusion of "boasting" in this sense once and for all. God's provision in Christ of a righteousness based upon faith excludes all quest for righteousness on the basis of the law, because faith in God's action involves a judgment that one has failed with respect to the law and indeed with respect to any path to righteousness based upon human moral effort. Faith means accepting the verdict: "all [including oneself] have sinned" (v 23), as the necessary presupposition of the positive thesis that "they are being justified as a gift by his grace through the redemption which has come about in Christ Jesus" (v 24).

So, exploiting the range of meaning that can attach both to the word *nomos* and the qualifying genitive in Greek, Paul proceeds in diatribe mode to ask (v 27b), "On what *nomos* (= 'principle') is 'boasting' excluded?" Dismissing the false suggestion that it might be "(on a law) of works" *([nomos] tōn ergōn)*, he insists that the exclusion must rest upon "a law of faith" *(dia nomou tēs pisteōs)*.

What appears to be operative here are two diametrically opposed ways of regarding (and living) the law of Moses. In the one ("law of works") it is seen as a way of life whereby one people (Israel) pursues righteousness through the faithful performance of the works it commands. The other view ("law of faith") looks at the law from the perspective of faith and sees a totally different picture—not a possibility of righteousness but a verdict of "total failure" upon all human attempts to be righteous in the sight of God (3:19-20). Faith, reading the "law" as scripture rather than as code (3:19, 21), finds there this divine verdict—along with indications of an alternative path to righteousness on a more "inclusive" pattern. It is this view—one which Paul has been maintaining all along (cf. v 28)—that completely excludes any "boasting" in the exclusivist sense explained above.

In pressing this distinction ("law of works"/"law of faith") with respect to the law, Paul does not mean to imply that doing the works commanded by the law is *in principle* wrong (he will later [7:12; 8:4] vindicate the rightness of what the law required). The problem is that continuing to pursue righteousness through the law flies in the face both of God's verdict with regard to keeping of the law (3:10-20) and God's action in providing, in Christ, a new mode of righteousness quite apart from the law (3:21-26; 9:31-32; 10:3).

The following "thesis-type" statement of the principle of justification by faith apart from works of the law (v 28) has been highly significant in the history of interpretation, becoming the watchword of the Reformation movement, which (rightly) understood Paul's simple qualification "by faith" *(pistei)* to have the sense of "by faith *alone*." In the flow of the argument, however, the statement is an aside, something a modern writer would place in a note. It sums up the preceding argument (3:21-26) upon which the present affirmation (the exclusion of "boasting") is based, in much the same way as the aside in v 23 summed up the content of 1:18–3:20. Paul's central concern is to maintain the inference that flows from justification by faith in regard to Jewish attitude to the Gentile world. Faith recognizes that, in the Messiah Jesus, God has acted "inclusively" with respect to the Gentiles, without compromising covenant fidelity (righteousness) toward Israel. In the face of *this* kind of divine intervention, it is impossible for Jews to maintain an "exclusivist," boasting attitude.

One God of Jews and Gentiles (vv 29-30). Paul pursues further validation to this "inclusivist" view of God's action by pointing to its essential agreement with the very core of Jewish belief about God. The God of Israel is God not of the Jews alone but the one Creator and God of the entire world. For all the special position of Israel (which Paul does not deny: 3:1-2; 9:2-4; 11:16, 28-29), God as universal Creator cannot have, as it were, two faces towards the world, granting to one group (the Jews) a principle of justification (righteousness by law) denied to all the rest (cf. the earlier insistence upon the impartiality of God, 2:11). So, in a highly effective ploy in rhetorical terms, proceeding from the heart of Israel's faith in the one God (Deut 6:4-9), Paul "constrains" his Jewish dialogue partner to abandon the "boasting" attitude (cf. Gal 2:15) in favor of a more "inclusive" view of the saving action of God.

The Law "upheld" through faith (v 31). This exaltation of faith at the expense of the law inevitably leads to the suggestion (formulated as an objection in v 31) that faith means "overthrowing" *(katargoumen)* the law. In diatribe mode, Paul allows the objection to rise, only to dismiss it with the brusque but characteristic rejoinder, "God forbid" *(mē genoito)*. He then moves from defensive mode right over to the offensive, making the startling claim to be in fact "upholding" *(histanomen)* the law.

Understanding how this claim is to be understood and pinpointing where in fact it finds support has caused interpreters much pain. Within the one concept of "law" *(nomos)*, however, Paul has already (v 27) made an important distinction—between a "law of works" and "law [read in the light] of faith." Faith certainly does "overthrow" the validity of *nomos* seen as a way of life pursued by a particular people in a quest for righteousness. But faith "hears" in the "*nomos,*" understood predominantly as "scripture," a different message—one that points both to the failure of the "works" way and the offer of a new righteousness created by God in Jesus Christ. In hearing and accepting scripture's witness to human sinfulness and lack of law-righteousness before God (Rom 3:19-20, 23; cf. Gal 2:16), faith acknowledges the validity of the law's verdict upon sin and in this sense "upholds" the law. At the same time, as Paul will eventually show (esp. Rom 8:1-4; cf. 13:8-10; Gal 5:14), those who through faith are "in Christ Jesus" can attain in the Spirit the fulfillment of the righteousness required by the law, the righteousness God promised to supply in the last days (Jer 31:33; Ezek 36:26-27). In both these senses Paul can claim to be "upholding" the law through faith.

Notes

27. *boasting:* On "boasting" in Paul, see Note on 2:17.

it is excluded: As frequently in Paul and biblical literature generally, the passive suggests the action of God—specifically the action described in vv 24-25.

by what law? (A law) of works?. No, but . . .: In 3:19-20 what excluded "boasting" was factual non-performance of the Jewish law: this rendered void the bold claim suggested in 2:17. In this sense "boasting" *was* excluded by "a law of works," which makes the negative that now follows *(ouchi, alla . . .)* somewhat surprising. The sense of the "No, but . . .," may be that a former consideration, valid in itself (3:19-20), has now been surpassed by a far more important one: God's action in Christ requiring the response of faith (3:21-26). Alternatively, Paul may truly be denying that the law (of Moses) in itself excludes boasting, since *in theory* (as will be stated with respect to Abraham in 4:2), if a person fulfills the law, that person can boast (cf. 2:17). What truly excludes boasting is the perspective of faith, which presupposes failure with respect to performance of the law—hence the affirmation that follows the negative. For a discussion of both possibilities, see J. Lambrecht and R. W. Thompson, *Justification by Faith* 24–30.

through a law of faith: Paul's use of *nomos* here in connection with "faith" (cf. the claim in v 31b; also 8:2a; 1 Cor 9:21; Gal 6:2) may suggest some continuing relevance of the law of Moses in the Christian dispensation. More likely the use of *nomos* on the positive side is rhetorical, the meaning now being "principle." Paul exploits the wide range of meaning to which the word is open (see Note on 2:12; cf. esp. 7:21-23; also Wis 2:11-12) to express some measure of continuity between the old and the new dispensation.

28. *For the basis of our argument is . . .:* The translation accepts, along with most commentators, the textual tradition reading the Greek connective *gar*, in preference to the almost equally well-attested alternative, *oun*. The textual uncertainty reflects the difficulty of grasping the precise flow of Paul's argument at this point. The verb (*logizometha*: cf. 6:11; 8:18; 14:11) suggests the formulation of a truth that ought to be taken as established, whereas the polemical context might suggest that this statement, rather than functioning as a support for what has just been said (as the reading *gar* suggests), itself needs establishment. The more prolix parallel in Gal 2:16 suggests that Paul is here formulating (in a kind of footnote) what he believes to be a standard expression of the Jewish-Christian experience of conversion: the full implications of what God has done in Christ (vv 21-22, 24-26) should obviate once and for all any lingering aspiration to find eschatological justification on the basis of the works prescribed by the Jewish law.

that a person is justified by faith: As in v 24, Paul speaks of justification in the present tense, whereas a few lines later (v 30) he will use the future (cf. Gal 5:5). The justification in question is always the eschatological justification but, granted that the believer already stands under the eschatological action of God, the present reference is valid. The oscillation between present and future—and occasionally past (Rom 5:1)—responds to the already-not-yet character of justification in Paul; see Introduction to Interpretation of 5:1.

apart from works of the law: There is no strict clash between what is said here and the *principle* formulated in 2:13 to the effect that "doers of the law will be justified." What is formulated here is not an abstract principle but the factual situation, consequent upon human sin and brought to light by God's action in Christ.

29. *Or is God the God of Jews only?:* Beginning the sentence with the disjunctive particle "or" *(ē)*, Paul argues that, if the statement just formulated (v 28) is not accepted, the following (false) conclusion must be drawn.

Is God not the God also of Gentiles? Yes, of Gentiles also: No Jew would have disputed that God was indeed the God of the entire world but the tendency would have been to view this truth as a matrix for stressing the privileged place of Israel: cf. Deut 26:18-19; 32:8-9; Sir 17:17; 36:1-22; *Jub.* 15:31-32; *4 Ezra* 3:12-19; 5:23-30. For an excellent discussion of the Jewish background to vv 29-30, see esp. N. A. Dahl, "The One God of Jews and Gentiles." *Studies in Paul* 178–91.

30. *if indeed God is one, . . .:* The conjunction *eiper* supports the previous contention by stating an obvious truth or fact necessarily bound up with it (cf. 8:9, 17); cf. BDF §454.

he will justify the circumcised on the ground of their faith and the uncircumcised through their faith: On the reference of justification to the future here, see Note on v 28. The Greek abstract nouns *peritomē* and *akrobystia* are used here to denote the communities of the circumcised (the Jews) and the uncircumcised (Gentiles) respectively (cf. already 2:26; also 15:8; Gal 2:7-8). Why Paul varies the Greek preposition used with respect to the faith of the two communities *(ek, dia)* has never been satisfactorily explained. The distinction is probably stylistic. In any case, it is unlikely that he would wish to introduce a distinction precisely in a context where he has been stressing the commonality of both Jew and Gentile in the one kind of justification. The most one could possibly say is that Paul views the justification of Jews as proceeding from an intensification of a faith in the one true God long held (hence *ek*), while *dia* expresses the sense that the Gentile comes all at once to both faith in God and justification.

31. *Do we then overthrow the law by (this principle of) faith?:* The Greek verb *katargein* can mean both "render ineffective" and "abolish, wipe out" (BAGD 417). The contrast with *histanomen* ("we confirm, establish, make valid") suggests that the former meaning is more applicable here—though, in connection with something authoritative such as *nomos* the two meanings virtually coincide.

By no means! On the contrary, we uphold the law: On Paul's forceful rebuttal *(mē genoito)*, see Note on 3:4. Attempts to grapple with the difficulty presented by Paul's claim here to uphold the law have taken several paths. 1. The use of *nomos* in v 21 in the phrase "the law and the prophets" provides grounds for taking the term here in the sense of "scripture" and seeing both the objection and the response as forming a bridge to the long scriptural proof, centered around the figure of Abraham, that follows in chapter 4 (so esp. C. T. Rhyne). 2. The true validation of the claim to uphold the law does not come in chapter 4 but is postponed till Romans 6–8, where Paul points to a Christian "fulfillment" of the law through the Spirit; cf. esp. Rom 8:3-4; 13:8-10 (J. Lambrecht and R. W. Thompson). 3. Paul sees faith "upholding" the righteous accusatory role of the law (O. Hofius—though in fact finding a reference principally to scripture in the *nomos* of 3:31). 4. Paul distinguishes within the concept of *nomos* the central ethical core of the law, which he upholds, from the ritual prescriptions, which he sets aside (T. R. Schreiner). There is scant evidence, however, that such a distinction, so obvious to modern interpreters, could [consciously at least] have been drawn in Paul's day (cf. Raïsänen, *Paul and the Law* 23–41, 69–72). The interpretation given in this commentary seeks to hold together valid elements in the first three explanations.

For Reference and Further Study

Dahl, N. A. "The One God of Jews and Gentiles." *Studies in Paul* 178–91.

Davies, G. N. *Faith and Obedience* 113–41.

Friedrich, G. "Das Gesetz des Glaubens Röm. 3, 27." *TZ* 10 (1954) 401–17.

Hofius, O. "Das Gesetz des Moses und das Gesetz Christi." *Paulusstudien* (Tübingen: Mohr, 1989) 50–75 (orig. 1983).

Lambrecht, J. and Thompson, R. W. *Justification by Faith: The Implications of Romans 3:27-31.* Wilmington: Glazier, 1989.

Moxnes, H. *Theology in Conflict* 40–41, 78–79, 223–24, 283–84.

Raïsänen, H. "The 'Law' of Faith and the Spirit." *Jesus, Paul and the Torah: Collected Essays.* JSNTSup 43; Sheffield: JSOT Press, 1992, 48–68 (orig. 1979–80).

Rhyne, C. T. *Faith Establishes the Law.* SBLDS 55; Chico, CA: Scholars Press, 1981.

Schreiner, T. R. "The Abolition and Fulfilment of the Law in Paul." *JSNT* 35 (1989) 47–74.

Winger, M. *By What Law? The Meaning of NOMOS in the Letters of Paul.* SBLDS 128; Chico, CA: Scholars, 1992.

iv. Scripture's Witness to Righteousness by Faith (4:1-25)

Introduction to Romans 4: the figure of Abraham. At this point Paul allows his Gentile Christian audience in Rome to "overhear" a scriptural defense of the claims he is making for faith in the interests of a truly inclusive presentation of the gospel. Earlier in the course of the dialogue with the Jewish partner who forms the implied audience of this section of the letter (1:18–4:25) he had maintained that, though God's righteousness is revealed to believers "apart from the law," the "law and the prophets bear witness to it" (3:21-22). The time has now come to make explicit that scriptural witness. It is not so much a matter of "proving" from scripture that righteousness comes through faith (the "therefore" *[oun]* standing at the beginning of chapter 4 in fact suggests deduction rather than proof). Rather, fully confident of the rightness of his contention that justification comes through faith (cf. 3:28), Paul seeks to show that this pattern can be traced also in the scriptures. Scripture *confirms,* rather than grounds, the view of faith (cf. Gal 3:1-9).

Paul's exposition of scripture revolves totally around the figure of Abraham as presented in Genesis 15–17. The force of the argument depends very much on the position occupied by Abraham in the Jewish tradition that forms the framework of discussion. Within this symbolic universe Abraham is not simply one biblical figure chosen among many, nor even a notably suitable example. As in the case of his polemic against the intrusion from the "circumcision" party in Galatia (Gal 3:6-29; 4:21-31), so also here in the letter to Rome, Paul *has* to conduct his argument in terms of Abraham. This is because it was around the figure of Abraham that the key issues of Jewish identity and hopes for the future turned. Abraham is not merely the "ancestor" of the nation. His "ancestral" role continues on in a truly representative way in the sense that the stance he took before God, the choices he made and the promises he received remain determinative for his descendants and for the nation as a whole. One cannot "define" Israel, especially the glorious Israel of the messianic age, without "defining" Abraham and what it means to be his "seed." Hence the necessity for Paul to go in and claim Abraham for faith, to show that it is believing, rather than practicing the law, that makes persons and communities true "seed" of Abraham, heirs of the promise he received.

Abraham in the Jewish tradition. In claiming Abraham for faith in this sense Paul swims against the prevailing current. The post-biblical Jewish tradition, while basically preserving the sense of Abraham as the one who received God's covenant on behalf of Israel, also laid considerable stress upon the patriarch as a figure of obedience and trust. His acceptance of the divine ordinance concerning circumcision was held to be a kind of anticipatory fulfillment of the Torah. His faithfulness under test (Gen 22:1-18) and even his act of faith (Gen 15:6) could be understood as a meritorious act that won blessings for all his descendants. Typical is the statement of Ben Sira:

> Abraham was the great father of a multitude of nations, and no one has been found like him in glory; he kept the law of the Most High and was taken into a covenant with him; he established the covenant in his flesh, and when he was tested he was found faithful. Therefore God assured him by an oath that the nations would be blessed through his posterity; that he would multiply him like the dust of the earth and exalt his posterity like the stars, and cause them to inherit from sea to sea and from the River to the ends of the earth (44:20-21).

This text and others from the literature of the post-biblical tradition (e.g., 1 Macc 2:50, 52; *Jub.* 15:1-10; 16:20-26; 17:17-18; 23:10a; CD 3:1-3; *m. Qidd.* 4:14) illustrate the view of Abraham as model of classic Torah obedience that Paul is contesting in Romans 4.

Paul's presentation of Abraham. To be more specific, Paul has to achieve two things in his scriptural recasting of Abraham. He has to show, first of all, that scripture presents Abraham primarily as a person of faith, as one who became "right with God" on the basis of his faith alone (4:1-12) and, secondly, that it was upon the basis of this right standing with God brought about by faith that he received for himself and for all his descendants the blessings of salvation contained in the promise (4:13-17a). Establishing these two points allows Paul to redefine Abraham's "fatherhood" in terms of being "father" of a great company of believers (Jewish and Gentile) who, believing as he did in the creative power of God (4:17b-25) and forming thereby his true descendants, are being justified and made ready to receive the promise on the basis of faith.

Central to Paul's argument is the sequence of events told in Genesis 15. In response to Abraham's complaint about his childlessness (vv 3-4), God makes a direct promise to Abraham that he will have a son and heir and a progeny as numerous as the stars of heaven (vv 4-5). This may be termed the "son/seed" promise. Abraham responds to this divine promise in terms of faith (v 6a), whereupon the biblical narrator adds the (for Paul) all-important comment: "And it was reckoned to him as righteousness" (v 6b [LXX]). After a lengthy covenant-making sequence (vv 7-20), God promises Abraham that his descendants will inherit the land (Canaan) upon which he presently stands. This promise (given already in 12:7; 13:15 and repeated in 17:8 and 24:7) may be termed the "land" promise. Thus there are two promises made by God to Abraham in Genesis 15, with Abraham's faith coming in between. The "land" promise *follows* upon the righteousness ascribed to Abraham in view of his faith in the original ("son/seed") promise. What is also significant for Paul is the fact that all this takes place well before there is any question of circumcision, mention of which is first made in Gen 17:9-14.

It is finally important to note that Paul's quasi-definition of the "land" promise in v 13 in terms of "inheriting the whole earth" shows that he adhered to a development in the post-biblical Jewish tradition in which this particular promise had undergone a notable broadening. The original reference simply to the land of Canaan now includes the entire world. Beyond this still, in a more eschatological and transcendent sense, the promise can refer to "the age to come", including all the blessings of salvation within its scope (see Note to 4:13).

What is at stake, then, in this discussion concerning Abraham is nothing less than the definition of God's eschatological people. To determine who is and who is not "progeny of Abraham" and thus heir to the promise is to determine who gets a share in the world to come and upon what terms. On the authority of scripture, Paul is establishing a place for non-circumcised Gentile believers within the community of salvation which the "one God" of all (3:29-30) has purposed to create for the entire human family.

a) *Abraham, Justified on the Basis of Faith* (4:1-12)

1. What then shall we say Abraham, our forefather according to the
flesh, found (in God's sight)? 2. For if Abraham was justified by works,
he would have something to boast about—but not before God!
3. For what does the scripture say? "Abraham believed God, and it was
reckoned to him as righteousness." 4. Now to one who works, the wage
is not reckoned as a favor but as something due. 5. Whereas to the one
who does not work but trusts simply in the One who justifies the ungodly, the faith of that person is reckoned as righteousness.
6. So too David pronounces a blessing upon the person to whom God
reckons righteousness apart from works: 7. "Blessed are those whose iniquities are forgiven, and whose sins are covered up; 8. blessed is the person whose sin the Lord will not reckon."
9. Is this blessing pronounced only upon the circumcised, or also upon
the uncircumcised? (Upon the latter surely as well) for we are saying
that faith was reckoned to Abraham as righteousness. 10. How then was
it "reckoned" to him? When he was in a state of circumcision or uncircumcision? It was not when he was in a state of circumcision but when
he was in a state of uncircumcision. 11. And he received the sign that is
circumcision as a seal of the righteousness which he had by faith while
he was still uncircumcised.
The upshot is that he is the "father" of all who in a state of uncircumcision have faith, so that their faith is "reckoned" to them as righteousness
12. and the "father" of a circumcision made up of those who proceed not
from circumcision alone but who also follow the track marked out by the
faith which our father Abraham had when he was still uncircumcised.

Interpretation

Paul's "redefinition" of Abraham in this first part of Romans 4 proceeds according to a clearly recognizable structure. An introduction (vv 1-2) and a conclusion (vv 11b-12) enclose a scriptural proof unfolding in three stages: 1: vv 3-5 (Genesis 15: "the Law"); 2: vv 6-8 (Ps 32: "the Prophets"); 3: vv 9-11a (Genesis 15–17).

The case with respect to Abraham (vv 1-2). The sudden introduction of Abraham (cf. also Gal 3:6-7) suggests that Paul would not expect his audience to be surprised that the argument has taken this turn. There is a shared world of agreement that Abraham is crucial to the debate and must appear at some stage. Likewise, referring to him as "our forefather according to the flesh" *(propatēr hēmōn kata sarka)* forges links within a Jewish framework of discussion—rather ironically, however, in view of the redefining of Abraham's "fatherhood" that it is now Paul's intention to pursue.

Somewhat unusually Paul asks, not what "we" find the case to be with Abraham, but what Abraham himself "found" *(heurēkenai)*. On the one hand, this serves from the start to focus attention on the objective situation rather than the subjective point of view. On the other, behind "found" probably lies the biblical expression "find grace (= be found righteous) in the eyes of the Lord" (used of Abraham in Gen 18:3; cf. also 6:8; 30:27; 32:5 [LXX 32:6]; 33:8, 10; etc.), the implication being that the dialogue partner will respond, according to the conventional view, that Abraham found acceptance on the basis of obedience on which he might "boast."

It is precisely this well-documented view (see above) that Paul sets out (v 2) to challenge. For a moment he entertains the possibility that Abraham found justification on the basis of works and so might provide an example of legitimate "boasting" in the sense of having achievement upon which he really could rely (cf. 3:27). Instantly, however, the possibility is dismissed through an appeal to the all-determining view of God *(ou pros theon)*. The divine view, revealed in the scriptural texts about to be cited, rules out any suggestion that Abraham was justified by works and so excludes the possibility that he had any works to bring before God as a basis for justification. Abraham provides no example of legitimate "boasting" in works.

Scripture proof 1. (vv 3-5). The scriptural proof in support of this recasting of Abraham begins (v 3) with the quotation of the all-important text from Gen 15:6b (LXX), where Abraham's faith (in the "son/seed" promise) is said to be "reckoned" to him "unto righteousness." The goldmine for Paul in this text lay in the simple link it forged between faith and being found righteous in God's sight. Nothing is said in the immediate context—which is all Paul is considering for the present—about any good works or obedience on Abraham's part. He is found righteous simply on the grounds of his believing and, as Paul will later (v 13) insist, receives the second promise, (the "land") on this basis alone.

Paul's commentary upon the text Gen 15:6 (vv 4-5) proceeds by way of an example taken from everyday life—from the acknowledged right of an employee to receive recompense for work done and from the corresponding lack of right to such recompense on the part of one who has not done any work at all. Employees who have worked receive a wage as a right; their hopes for recompense rest on what they have themselves done. But any benefit accruing to an employee who has not worked would have to stem from the pure favor of the employer. Such persons, having no claim whatsoever to recompense, have to look away from themselves and rest all their hopes on the goodness and mercy of the one they were meant to serve.

Typically, Paul's "theological impatience" leads him to pull out of the example before it is quite complete (cf. 6:16). With respect to the employee who "has not worked," he concludes it prematurely (v 5) with the theological statement it was meant to illustrate: faith's trust in the "One who justifies the ungodly" *(ton dikaiounta ton asebē)*. This phrase significantly specifies the Pauline notion of faith. Faith proceeds from an awareness of sin, of failure in terms of the service of God. It involves the perception that God is a God who confers forgiveness and benefit upon those who stand outside the community of the holy and can make no claim upon God. Like the employee who "has not worked," persons of faith rest their hopes for acceptance in the grace and goodness of God alone.

Paul does not explain how he understands Abraham to have been in this situation of "ungodliness." He is probably following a tradition that saw Abraham as the first believer in the one true God, the archetypal convert from paganism (proselyte; see Note). In this sense Abraham approaches God from the Gentile stance that makes him, in Jewish eyes, a "sinner" by very definition (cf. Gal 2:15). In the face of the conventional "model of obedience" picture, Paul boldly aligns Abraham with the Gentile posture before God.

Paul's grounds for depicting Abraham in these terms come from the comment in Gen 15:6b, specifically from the word "reckoned" *(elogisthē)*. The Greek term has a technical usage in the language of bookkeeping ("credit to one's account") which Paul appears to exploit. In the absence of any deserts on the human side (such as would provide grounds for "boasting") God graciously "credits" a status of righteousness to the believer's "account."

Scripture proof 2. (vv 6-8). Paul proceeds to the second stage of his scriptural analysis (vv 6-8) employing an exegetical technique found later in Rabbinic literature (the so-called Second Rule of Hillel). The interpretation of a particular text is confirmed or developed by adducing a further text with which it has a key word in common. Here the common term is the verb "reckon" *(logizesthai)*, found also in Ps 32:2 (LXX 31:2). The psalm as a whole recounts the experience of a person who has been led, through suffering, to acknowledge personal sin; the psalmist describes how this acknowledgment has led to a rewarding sense of acceptance and forgiveness by God. It is this experience which constitutes the "blessing" *(makarismos)* mentioned in the opening verses of the psalm quoted by Paul (vv 7-8). The combination of the two biblical texts allows him to identify the righteousness "reckoned" to the ungodly Abraham on the basis of his faith with this "blessing" in which sin is not "reckoned" to the repentant sinner. Both cases (one involving the positive "crediting" of an an undeserved good, the other the "non-crediting" of a deserved penalty) come together as equally the act of a gracious God. Moreover, by citing a text from "the Law" (that is, the Pentateuch) in the shape of Gen 15:6 and from "the Prophets" in the shape of Ps 32:1-2 (David, the putative author of the Psalms, being reckoned as a prophet) Paul makes good his earlier claim that "the Law and the Prophets bear witness" to the righteousness of God that stands revealed "apart from the law" (3:21b).

Scripture proof 3 (vv 9-11a). Paul has now largely completed his bid to claim Abraham for faith. He has not yet quite arrived at his overall goal, however, because the Jewish dialogue partner, while agreeing with this exegesis of the two texts, could still maintain that, since Abraham and David were circumcised Jews, all that has been demonstrated so far need not break the bounds of Judaism ("the Circumcision") as such. The scriptural proof will be complete only when Paul succeeds in breaking any nexus between the community-defining rite of circumcision and the experience of justification by faith just described. So in the third part of his scriptural proof, retaining the language of "blessing" *(makarismos)* to denote the experience of being found righteous, he reverts to his primary text, Gen 15:6, to break through the barrier of circumcision and bring out the truly universal significance of what "our father" Abraham "found" (v 1).

In so doing, Paul exploits once again (cf. 2:26; 3:30) the fact that the words "circumcision" *(peritomē)* and "uncircumcision" *(akrobystia)*, besides denoting a physical condition, can refer to the respective communities (Jews, Gentiles) as well. This enables him to ask whether the "blessing" Abraham received—not just for himself but, *qua* patriarch, for his whole line—applies to the Circumcision (Jews) or to the Uncircumcision (Gentiles). Contrary to the prevailing Jewish view of Abraham, the response can only be that it applies to the Uncircumcision (Gentiles). Why? Because when the patriarch received that "blessing" in the shape of Gen 15:6a (quoted again in v 9b) he was himself in a state of "uncircumcision" and this set the pattern for all time: the "blessing" of being "reckoned" righteous comes to the "uncircumcised," that is, to those who are in the same situation as Abraham was when reckoned righteous by God.

Circumcision did indeed arrive on the scene. But, as Paul now hastens to explain (v 11a), it came only subsequently (Gen 17:9-14) and its function was to be simply a "sign" *(sēmeion)* or "seal" *(sphragis)* of the righteousness already received through faith. So Paul does find a value for circumcision (cf. 3:1-2), albeit in a limited and subordinate sense. No longer can it be seen as a badge denoting the status enjoyed exclusively by one people (the Jews). Rather, it points beyond itself to a righteousness that is far more universally available and which in fact overthrows that exclusivity. In Paul's eyes physical circumcision is of little value save as an outward expression of a "circumcision of the heart," the moral renewal wrought eschatologically by the Spirit (2:28-29).

The Upshot: Abraham as universal "Father" (vv 11b-12). The argument just deployed from the sequence of events in scripture allows Paul to draw an important conclusion (vv 11b-12), concerning the sense in which Abraham is "father." The fact that Abraham experienced the "blessing" of justification simply on the basis of his faith and did so well before the precept of circumcision entered the scene makes him the "father" of those found to be in a similar situation before God—uncircumcised "Gentile sinners" who, like Abraham, have righteousness "reckoned" to them on the basis of their faith (v 11c). Abraham is "father of the circumcision" (v 12) too—the traditional title—but in a more restricted sense. He is "father" for those who proceed not from circumcision alone but who follow the path of the faith he had when still uncircumcised—in short, Jews who have come to Christian faith (on the interpretative difficulties posed by v 12, see Note).

Thus the "fatherhood" of Abraham, originally (v 1) tied simply to "fleshly" descent from him, that is, to the Jews, has in the course of the argument been radically transformed. It does not merely include Gentiles; it relates essentially to them. Paul has depicted Abraham in such a way as to make the "Gentile" stance before God the norm rather than exception. Scripture's account of the righteousness that Abraham received on the basis of his faith, apart from circumcision or any obedience to law, guarantees a secure place for uncircumcised Gentile believers within the eschatological people of God. By the same token it appears to exclude Jews who have not come to Christian faith. This latter issue Paul leaves for the present, concentrating upon the inclusion of Gentiles. He moves now to complete the picture by pointing to the fresh promise (the "land") Abraham received on the basis of his right-standing with God.

Notes

1. *What then shall we say . . .?:* This opening phrase *(ti oun eroumen)* is a characteristic of the diatribe style. It usually introduces an objection that is to be rejected (cf. 3:5; 6:1; 7:7; 9:14) or, as here, a bold statement of a truth that flows from or corroborates what has just been argued (8:31; 9:30).

   according to the flesh: "Flesh" *(sarx)* is used here in a neutral sense, referring simply to natural, ethnic origins (as also in 1:3; 9:3, 5; 11:14).

   found (in God's sight)?: The odd, absolute use of the Greek verb *heuriskein* appears to have led to alterations in the textual tradition at this point. *Pace* R. B. Hays (see Reference), the generally accepted reading making the infinitive *heurēkenai* dependent upon the verb *eroumen* (א A C*) is to be preferred; cf. the discussion in Cranfield 1.227. The perfect tense of the verb, *heurēkenai,* suggests that what Abraham "found" created a lasting state of affairs—what Paul will later show to be a dispensation of grace.

2. *For if Abraham was justified by works, he would have something to boast about—but not before God!:* The first part of this verse can be understood in grammatical terms as a real condition (cf. esp. the present indicative in the apodosis). But the denial contained in the last phrase makes the conditional unreal. It would make little sense in the context to suggest that, at least in the sight of human beings, Abraham has genuine ground for boasting.

3. *For what does the scripture say? "Abraham believed God, and it was reckoned to him as righteousness":* The quotation agrees exactly with the LXX of Gen 15:6, save for the substitution of *de* for *kai* and the use of the full name "Abraham" instead of the original "Abram."

4. *to one who works:* The simple "employment" image appearing here should in no sense reinforce the (false) judgment that, in contrast with a new (Christian) dispensation of faith and grace, the Judaism of Paul's day was a religion of "works-righteousness"—even if a doctrine of "merits" did develop in some circles at a later stage.

   the wage is not reckoned: "Reckon" *(logizesthai)* appears no less than eleven times in this chapter and so is of pivotal importance to the argument. Any suggestion that it implies a purely extrinsic or forensic "imputation" of righteousness is excluded by the subsequent appeal (vv 6-8) to the deep experience of "conversion" described in Ps 32:1-2.

5. *the One who justifies the ungodly:* To "declare righteous the unrighteous" is strongly deplored as an abuse on the part of human judges in the biblical tradition: Exod 23:7 (LXX: *kai ou dikaiōseis ton asebē*); Prov 17:15; 24:24; Isa 5:23; Sir 42:2; cf. CD 1:19. In the light of this, Paul's characterization of God's action in such terms is, at first sight, highly provocative. But, as the exposition of Ps 32:1-2 in vv 6-8 will show, faith already implies an inward conversion and, while not a "work" in the sense of anticipating God's grace, does imply some measure of human cooperation with the grace offered; cf. Kuss 1.182–83. In the Jewish tradition the Greek term *asebēs* also has the connotation of "conventional sinner," one excluded from the covenant simply by his or her social and ethnic situation, *a fortiori,* therefore, the Gentile. To speak of God's action in regard to Abraham in this respect is less shocking in view of the tradition that looked upon Abraham as the first pagan to come to belief in the true God and hence the archetypal proselyte (cf. *Jub.* 12:1-8, 12-14, 16-20; *Apoc. Abr.* 1-8; Josephus, *Ant.* 1.155; Philo, *Virt.* 219; for rabbinic material, see SB 3.211). In this "ethnic/social" sense Abraham was an *asebēs* when God's address came to him.

6. *So too David pronounces a blessing:* For the simple introduction of a text from Psalms as the "speech" of David, cf. Rom 11:9; cf. also Mark 12:36-37 and parallels; Acts 2:25; 4:25; Heb 4:7.

7–8. *"Blessed are those whose iniquities are forgiven, and whose sins are covered up; blessed is the person whose sin the Lord will not reckon":* Again (cf. Note on v 4), the language of "covering up," "non-imputation" and "not-reckoning" found in the psalm quoted by Paul ought not be allowed to obscure the reality of the forgiveness and acceptance received in justification. By the same token, the emphasis upon sin and forgiveness shows that the religious experience Paul is attributing to Abraham—and to those who follow in his steps—goes beyond that of a turning away from "boasting" in the sense merely of national pride and privilege, expressed in the Jewish ritual "identity markers" (circumcision, food laws, sabbath observance, etc). Boasting is excluded because any sense of superiority, which the "identity markers" might indeed express, is fatally undermined by sinfulness as such (2:17-25; 3:9-20; 3:23 ["all have sinned"]). It is as "sinners" in this comprehensive sense that believers encounter and appropriate the "righteousness of God."

9. *Is this blessing pronounced only upon the circumcised, or also upon the uncircumcised? (Upon the latter surely as well) for we are saying that faith was reckoned to Abraham as righteousness:* The precise flow of argument here is not obvious. The causal conjunction (*gar*) at the start of the second sentence seems to have the sense of, "Keep in mind the scriptural text which has been our primary guide all through: the one that says Abraham's faith was reckoned to him for righteousness." The recall of this fundamental principle prepares the way for the final scriptural proof that follows. The decisive question is, What was Abraham's condition with respect to circumcision at the moment (cf. the aorist *logisthē*) when this comment was made?

10. *How then was it "reckoned" to him?:* Considering the importance of the sequence of events, Paul might well have asked, "When *(pote)* was it reckoned?" He asks, "How *(pōs)* . . .?" not merely because Abraham's condition—whether circumcised *(en peritomę̄)* or not *(en akrobystią)*—is equally crucial but also because the fact that he was in two different states (first uncircumcised, then circumcised) allows him to be "father" for both communities (Gentile and Jewish) respectively.

11a. *the sign that is circumcision:* The translation takes the genitive construction *(sēmeion . . . peritomēs)* in an explanatory sense (= ". . . consisting in circumcision"). The key terms of this verse—"sign," "uncircumcision" and "circumcision"—all appear in the LXX of Gen 17:11-13, where (v 11) circumcision is said to be a "sign of the covenant."

while he was still uncircumcised: This final genitive phrase *(tēs en tę̄ akrobystią)* is best taken as attaching to "righteousness" *(dikaiosynēs)* rather than to "faith" *(pisteōs)*. It is Abraham's righteousness rather than his faith that is directly at issue at this point.

11b-12. *The upshot is that he is the "father" of all who in a state of uncircumcision have faith, so that their faith is "reckoned" to them as righteousness and the "father" of a circumcision made up of those who proceed not from circumcision alone but who also follow the track marked out by the faith which our father Abraham had when he was still uncircumcised:* An articular infinitive construction (*eis to einai auton . . .*) in a consecutive sense governs the entire conclusion, with the two references to Abraham as "father" (*patera,* v 11b and v 12a) standing in parallel and so designating a twin "fatherhood" on his part with respect to two groups: first, Gentile believers (*pantōn tōn pisteuontōn di' akrobystias*); then Jews (*patera peritomēs*). In the second case Paul adds a qualification the wording of which—specifically the second occurrence of the definite article *tois*, before *stoichousin*—suggests a further subdivision into two groups: 1. those who do not proceed from circumcision alone and 2. those who follow in the steps of Abraham. Such a division makes little sense since in v 12 Paul is clearly wanting to characterize one and the same group from first a negative and then a positive point of view. It seems best to regard the troublesome *tois* as a dictational or scribal slip and to understand Paul as presenting, with respect to the "fatherhood" of Abraham, an overall parallelism between two basic groups: Gentile Christians, for whom justification occurs in precisely the same situation as it did for Abraham (hence the recapitulation of Gen 15:6 in v 11c), and Jewish Christians (v 12), consisting of those who are not only Jews (*ou ek peritomēs monon*) but who also follow the track (faith) marked out by Abraham.

For Reference and Further Study

(See end of following section)

b) *Abraham, Paradigm Receiver of the Promise on the Basis of Faith* (4:13-25)

13. For it was not through the law that the promise came to Abraham and to his descendants, that they should inherit the world; no, it came through the righteousness established by faith. 14. If it is those who proceed from the law who are the heirs, then faith is emptied out and the promise abolished. 15. For the law, you see, brings wrath; where there is no law there is no transgression. 16. For this reason the promise depends on faith: in order that it may be a matter of grace and something secure for all his descendants—not to the one who proceeds from the law only, but also to the one who shares the faith of Abraham, who is the father of us all, 17. as it is written, "I have made you the father of many nations"—in the sight of the God in whom he believed, a God who gives life to the dead and calls into being the things that do not exist. 18. Faced with a hopeless situation, with hope nonetheless he (Abraham) believed that he would become the father of many nations, just as he had been told, "So shall your descendants be." 19. He did not weaken in faith when he considered his own body, which was as good as dead because he was about a hundred years old, or when he considered the dead state of Sarah's womb. 20. With respect to God's promise, no distrust made him waver in disbelief, but he grew strong in his faith, giving glory to God, 21. fully convinced that God was able to do what he had promised.

22. That is why his faith was "reckoned to him for righteousness." 23. But the words, "it was reckoned to him," were written not for his sake alone, 24. but for ours also, for whom it will be reckoned—to us, that is, who believe in the One who raised from the dead Jesus our Lord, 25. who was delivered up for our trespasses and raised for our justification.

INTERPRETATION

The Promise tied to faith (v 13). From scripture Paul has redefined Abraham as one who found righteousness in God's sight, not on the basis of obedience to law, but on that of faith, faith specifically in God's first promise in Genesis 15, the "son/seed" promise. This has enabled him to re-draw totally the picture of Abraham's "fatherhood." Abraham is "father" primarily of those who find righteousness on the basis of faith.

Becoming righteous, however, is not the whole story—neither for Abraham nor for his "descendants." The key thing in terms of the argument is what righteousness leads to: namely, full entrance into the blessings of salvation. As explained above, Paul and the Jewish tradition with which he is in dialogue at this point saw these blessings contained in the second promise made by God to Abraham, the "land" promise *(epangelia)*, defined here (v 13) as "the inheritance of the earth" (*to klēronomon auton einai kosmou*; see Note). The same Jewish tradition, with some foundation in texts such as Gen 26:1-5 (cf. 22:15-18), saw Abraham's reception of this promise as following upon his obedience, thereby establishing a pattern linking the promise to faithful observance of the law. To counter this, as an essential second stage in his analysis of scripture, Paul has to cut the nexus between promise and obedience. Accordingly, he insists (v 13) that it was on the basis of being righteous through faith that Abraham received, for himself and his descendants (believers), the all-important promise of the "land."

Righteousness by faith and righteousness by law mutually exclusive (vv 14-15). Paul justifies the severance of promise and law by arguing, in a small parenthesis, the complete mutual exclusiveness of faith and law. If those who attempt to gain righteousness on the basis of law-obedience *(hoi ek nomou)* are genuine heirs—that is, if they are the descendants of Abraham destined to inherit the blessing contained in the promise—faith is "emptied out" *(kekenōtai)* and the promise in fact "abolished" *(katērgētai)*. Why? Because, explains Paul in an enigmatic aside (v 15), the law functions in a totally different way. By making explicit the will of the lawgiver and indicating sanctions, it qualifies wrongdoing in general as explicitly offense against God, as "transgression" *(parabasis)*. That was its basic role and, in theory or original intent, the law was a path to life (cf.

the citation of Lev 18:5 in 10:5 and Gal 3:12 [cf. v 21b]). But the factual prevalence of sin (Rom 1:18–3:20; 3:23) turns the law into an instrument of wrath. It confronts sinful human beings with the brick wall of God's wrath, through which there can be no access to salvation. To seek to proceed by the law, in the delusion that one has escaped sin, "empties out" faith because faith proceeds precisely from an awareness and confession that one is sinful and can only find righteousness through the gift of a gracious God (4:4-5, 7-8; cf. Gal 2:16).

Faith secures the inheritance for all, making Abraham universal "father" (vv 16-17a). The law excluded in this negative way, Paul proclaims the positive reason for the linking of the promise to faith. Only the operation of grace (*kata charin*; cf. vv 4-5)—God's unmerited grace exercised towards sinful human beings—could ensure the fully universal scope of the promise made to Abraham, its being "secure" *(bebaian)* for all his descendants *(panti tǭ spermati)*. Once again, reflecting the "inclusive" sense of God's action in Romans, the stress falls upon the "all." The promise embraces the Jews *(tǭ ek tou nomou)* certainly—and with a certain priority (cf. 1:16)—but the essential and only condition is sharing the faith of Abraham *(tǭ ek pisteōs Abraam)*, who thereby becomes universal father (literally, "the father of us all"; cf. vv 11-12).

In this way Paul sees fulfilled a further text from Genesis. In a repetition of the "son/seed" promise in Gen 17:5-6, God promises Abraham that he will be exceedingly fruitful: that in fact he has been made the "father of many nations" *(patera pollōn ethnōn)*. Since the same term *ethnē* does service for both "nations" and "Gentiles" in biblical Greek, Paul can cite this text as confirmation of what he has been arguing all through. The "fatherhood" of Abraham bears upon his being "father" to all who would adopt his "Gentile-like" stance of faith—not only Jewish believers but a vast progeny drawn from the nations of the world. According to the biblical pattern of "like parent, like child" (cf. Gen 5:3), this multitude of believers constitute "descendants" *(sperma)* of Abraham in so far as they follow the pattern of their "father's" faith (cf. Gal 3:6-9). On the basis of the righteousness established through that faith, they become heirs of the promise made to him "and to his descendants" (v 13). In this sense God promised Abraham that he would become "father" of an eschatological people of God drawn from all nations.

The inner structure of Abraham's faith (vv 17b-21). Paul has firmly redefined Abraham's fatherhood in terms of faith and shown that the inheritance promised to his descendants comes to them also *qua* believers. Now, in order to bring out the true parity in believing between patriarch and descendants, he completes the scriptural discussion by exploring the inner structure of Abraham's original act of faith—his faith in the "son/seed" promise (Gen 15:6a; 17:5-6). Initially (v 17b) the focus is entirely upon God. In what kind of God or, rather, with respect to what particular divine quality, was Abraham's faith exercised? Echoing what appear to have been traditional theological formulations of the Hellenistic Jewish tradition, Paul characterizes God in this context as "One who gives life to the dead *(tou zǭopoiountos tous nekrous)* and calls into being things that do not exist as though they did" *(kai kalountos ta mē onta hōs onta)*—in short, God specifically as Creator.

To explain why faith in God specifically as Creator was at stake, Paul explores (vv 18-19) the circumstances surrounding Abraham's act of faith. He cites the text of the original promise in the language of Gen 15:5: "So shall your descendants *(sperma)* be" (thereby linking Gen 17:5, cited in v 17a, back to the text that has been determinative all through). If Abraham were to accept such a promise he had to "hope against hope" (v 19). He had to confront a situation that was hope*less* as far as human reproductive possibilities were concerned and place all hope in the power of God to bring life out of death. To fulfill the promise God *had* to be operative in such terms because, as Paul points out, a situation of "death" prevailed on both sides of the parental equation. Abraham's advanced years rendered his body as good as "dead" with respect to having children *(to heatou sōma ēdē nenekrōmenon)* and a similar "deadness" *(nekrōsis)* affected the womb of Sarah. If a son and further descendants were to be given him, it would literally have to be a matter of God's "raising the dead"—calling into being something which did not exist. Quite striking here is the realism which Paul (according to the preferred reading; see Note) attributes to Abraham. In his faith Abraham truly confronts (cf. *katenoēsen*) the "deadness" on the human side. He confronts it but does not "weaken" *(mē asthenēsas)* in his belief in the creative power of God.

Where up till this point it had been sufficient to indicate simply the fact of Abraham's believing (cf., in v 3, the Greek aorist *episteusen*), Paul now begins to dwell at some length (vv 20-21) upon the persevering character of his faith with respect to the promise. Pointing to the way in which Abraham overcame any tendency to "waver in disbelief" *(ou diekrithē tę̄ apistią)* and, in fact grew stronger in faith *(enedynamōthē)*, Paul prepares the ground for the next section of the letter (5:1–8:39), where believers will be exhorted to live out in hope and endurance the justification they have received. The focus upon faith that has prevailed up till now begins to shift in the direction of hope—though it might be more correct to say that Paul is now bringing out the essential dimension of hope attaching to his sense of faith.

In this persevering faith, Abraham "gives glory to God (v 20c). This is the very opposite of the human "boasting" *(kauchēma)* on the basis of works that was excluded in Abraham's case at the outset of the exegesis (v 2; cf. 3:27). More significantly still, to give glory to the Creator is exactly the reverse of what humans had refused to do in the lapse into idolatry presented in 1:21-23 as the paradigm of human alienation from God. The faith in God's promise shown by Abraham (cf. vv 17b-19) models the true response of human beings to God, upon which the full realization of their own humanity depends. Faith reverses the primordial lie attaching to all sin from the beginning: that God cannot and will not deliver on promises made (Gen 3:4-5; cf. the "suppression of the truth" in Rom 1:18). Faith is bound up essentially with the hope that God can and will deliver what has been promised (v 21)—even if that involves the "resurrection of the dead."

Abraham's faith, paradigm for subsequent believers (vv 22-25). Paul completes the exploration of Abraham's faith by citing for the third and final time (v 22; cf. v 3, v 9) the determinative text, Gen 15:6b. The "therefore" *(dio)* preceding the citation suggests that not merely Abraham's faith as such but the persevering character of his faith that has just been insisted upon (vv 19-21) played some part in the "reckoning" to him of righteousness. More significantly, though, Paul explicitly recalls the all-important text because he is now (vv 23-24) moving to bring out its truly universal application. What is written in scripture tells not only of the past but discloses God's plans for the "last ages" as well. Scripture's account of the righteousness reckoned to Abraham applies equally to that vast progeny of his who approach God from a similar stance of faith and hope. They too find justification and the promise of salvation to which it leads on the basis of following the path of faith marked out by him (v 12).

What particularly links the faith of Abraham and that of believers is the fact that both involve belief in God as Creator, as One who raises the dead. For Abraham, as we have seen (v 19), belief in the "son/seed" promise meant believing in a God who could bring life out of the "deadness" both of his own generative powers and those of his wife Sarah. Christian faith, says Paul (citing what is almost certainly an early credal formula; see Note) means believing in the "One who raised Jesus our Lord from the dead" (v 24). True, Abraham in his believing looked forward—to the future exercise of God's power in the gift of a son and a long line of descendants, whereas Christian faith looks back—to the past event of God's raising of Jesus. The differing time reference, however, is hardly significant—especially as elsewhere Paul rarely mentions God's raising of Christ without presenting it as an earnest and token of the (future) resurrection of believers (cf. 8:11b: "the One who raised Jesus from the dead will give life *[zōopoiēsei]* to your mortal bodies *[thnēta sōmata]* too through the Spirit dwelling within you"). Paul's stress upon the "persevering" aspect of Abraham's faith (vv 19-21) seems designed to stress that belief ("backwards," so to speak) in what God *has* done for Christ involves continuing belief in the future capacity and faithfulness of God to repeat this for "our mortal bodies" as well.

Paul concludes (v 25) the entire sequence, adding a christological/ soteriological comment almost certainly derived, in whole or part, from the early Christian tradition. The language of "being given up for our transgressions" *(hos paredothē dia ta paraptōmata hēmōn)* echoes unmistakably the thought and language (LXX) of the Fourth Song of the Isaianic Servant (Isa 52:13–53:12; cf. esp. 53:12). It interprets Christ's death and resurrection in terms of the Servant's sufferings that bring about the "justification" of "many" (Isa 53:11; cf. Mark 14:24; Matt 26:28; Rom 5:19). The citation of this formula, in all likelihood known to the Roman community, ties the scriptural retracing of Abraham, which outwardly has proceeded with remarkable absence of christological reference, back to the soteriological statement of 3:21-26. The God in whose creative power the "ungodly" Abraham believed and found justification (4:5) is the God who justifies believing sinners by raising Christ who died upon the cross burdened with the sins of humankind. The resurrection, in first instance, represents God's bodily "justification" of Jesus, the formal divine vindication of the obedience and righteousness of "him who knew no sin" (2 Cor 5:21). At the same time, it brings about the justification of believers, who, though far from sinless, come by God's favor under the scope of the same divine verdict—even if the full pattern of Jesus' justification (bodily resurrection) is yet to run its full course in them (8:23; Phil 3:20-21). To believe in God who calls into being things that do not exist and raises the dead (Rom 4:17b) is really one and the same as to believe in the God who graciously justifies the ungodly (4:5). In both cases it is God as Creator who is the focus of faith.

In this way Paul brings to a close his scriptural "redefinition" of Abraham. By presenting Abraham as righteous through faith and receiver of the promise on that basis, he has redrawn the boundaries of the eschatological people of God, destined to inherit the blessings of salvation. He has done so, moreover, in a way which not merely includes the Gentile world but in fact depicts its way to righteousness as normative. The axiom with which the body of the letter began—"Jew first, but also the Greek" (1:16) has virtually been turned on its head. The "inclusive" presentation of the gospel has truly found a place and an identity for Gentile believers in the people of God but at the cost, it would seem, of its being largely "exclusive" with respect to Israel. For the present Paul leaves this issue hanging in the air. He will return, in chapters 9–11, to address the question as to whether the gospel is ultimately "inclusive" of Israel as well.

Before leaving consideration of this major section of the letter (1:18–4:25), we may note how in the last couple of sentences an important shift has taken place in rhetorical terms. At the beginning of the chapter (v 1) the first person plural address ("Abraham, *our* father according to the flesh") indicated an intra-Jewish debate, a dialogue with persons not yet convinced of the Christian gospel, which Paul allows his Gentile Christian audience in Rome to "overhear." By the end of the chapter, however (cf. esp. vv 24-25), "our" definitely refers to the community of those who accept what God has brought out in Jesus Christ. Subtly though surely, there has been a shift in the implied audience. Paul will now (5:1–8:39) speak directly to a Christian audience of the hope for full salvation that rests upon the justification achieved by faith.

Notes

13. *the promise . . . that they should inherit the world:* For the "land" promise, besides Gen 15:7, 18-21, see Gen 12:7; 13:14-17; 17:8; 24:7; cf. 26:3-5; 28:3, 13; 35:12; 48:4; 50:24; Exod 6:8; 32:13; 33:1; Lev 25:2; Num 15:2; 27:12; 32:11; Neh 9:7-8; Mic 7:20; the idea of possessing the land given to the fathers is pervasive in Deuteronomy (1:8; 6:10; 9:5; 29:13; 30:20), culminating in Moses' eventual vision of it before he dies (34:4). From the start (cf. Gen 15:7) the language of "inheritance" (LXX *klēronomein; klēronomia*) attaches to the "land" promise, becoming, again, pervasive in Deuteronomy. The result is that when in the post-biblical tradition the word "promise" came to be used of God's assurance to Abraham concerning the Land (Josephus, *Ant.* 2.219; *T. Jos.* 20:1), "promise" and "inheritance" came to be virtually interchangeable (cf. 2 Macc 2:17-18; Wis 12:21; 18:6; *Pss. Sol.* 12:6; 4QapGen 21:8-14). Across a broad range of the representative literature, the content of the "promise" or "inheritance" undergoes notable "extension" to include, first, the whole world (cf. Sir 44:21; *Jub.* 19:21; Philo, *Mos.* 1.155; cf. 1 *Enoch* 5:7b) and then, in an eschatological sense, the "world to come," the blessings of salvation (cf. *Pss. Sol.* 12:6; *Bib. Ant.* 32:3; *Sib. Or.* 3:768-69; 4 *Ezra* 6:59; 7:9; *2 Apoc. Bar.* 14:13; 44:13; 51:3; 57:1-3; *m. ʾAbot* 2:7; 5:19; further rabbinic material in SB 3.209). In *Jub.* 22:14; 32:19 the patriarchal blessings specifically apply to Israel the lordship of the world conferred upon human beings (Adam) according to Gen 1:26-28 (cf. Ps 8:6-8)—a hope cherished also at Qumran: 4QpPs 37 3:1-2 (". . . all the inheritance of Adam"); 1QH 17:15; 1QS 4:22-23; CD 3:20; cf. also *4 Ezra* 6:54). Here we see an intersection of what might be called the "Adamic" and the "Abrahamic" trajectories with respect to "promise," "inheritance" and the lordship of the world. Paul's view of the messianic lordship of the risen Jesus (Phil 2:9-11; 1 Cor 15:20-28; Phil 3:20-21) appears to presuppose this intersection (cf. esp. the "messianic" use of Psalm 8 in the latter two passages). Believers come into this "inheritance" through their existence in and conformity to the risen Lord: cf. 1 Cor 3:21b-23; 6:2-3; also Rom 5:17. Paul will resume the "inheritance" motif explicitly in Rom 8:17; cf. also Gal 3:13–4:7.

   and to his descendants: The Greek phrase *kai tō̧ spermati sou* appears in the form of the "land" promise occurring in Gen 13:15; 17:8; cf. 12:7; 15:18; 22:17-18. For the *kai* Paul substitutes *ē*, used in the copulative sense (BDF §446). In Gal 3:16

Paul develops an elaborate case out of this phrase, arguing that the occurrence of *sperma* in the singular implies a reference solely to Christ as the designated heir; believers come into the inheritance only through their baptismal life "in Christ" (cf. 3:26-29). Paul does not develop this christological argument in Romans 4 because he is more concerned to stress that believers are "descendants" *(sperma)* of Abraham by virtue of the parity between their faith and his.

through the righteousness established by faith: The translation (cf. v 11) takes the genitive in the Greek phrase *(dia dikaiosynēs pisteōs)* as qualifying (or a genitive of origin). For the widespread Jewish tradition that righteousness is the precondition for obtaining eternal life (= "the promise"), see Note on 1:17 above; cf. Rom 5:17, 21 and esp. 8:10c.

14. *those who proceed from the law:* The Greek phrase *hoi ek nomou* envisages not merely Jews in an ethnic sense but those who actively seek righteousness on the basis of faithful fulfillment of the law—that is, those who correspond to "one who works" in the image of 4:4; for a similar formula with *ek*, cf. 3:26; 4:12, 16; Gal 2:16.

then faith is emptied out and the promise abolished: For the sake of vividness, Paul composes the apodosis of the conditional sentence as though the condition were fulfilled; logically, however, this is clearly not what he means. For the use of *kenoun* in the strong sense of "render useless, void," see also 1 Cor 1:17; 9:15; 2 Cor 9:3.

15. *For the law, you see, brings wrath:* On Paul's sense of the divine "wrath," see Interpretation and Note on 1:18.

where there is no law there is no transgression: It is not clear why Paul formulates this sentence in the negative. Since he is clearly not interested at this point (contrast 5:13) with a time when there was no law, he might as well—and perhaps better—have said: "because the law makes sin into transgression"; cf. 5:20a; Gal 3:19b. It is probably best to understand this sentence as a comment thrown in to provide logical support for what has proceeded (as in the textual variant reading *gar* in place of the [preferred] *de*) rather than as a continuation.

16. *For this reason:* The introductory *dia touto* could refer either backward (as usually) or forward (as in, e.g., 2 Cor 13:10; Phlm 15; cf. 1 Tim 1:16). The translation favors the second alternative.

the promise depends on faith: The translation supplies "promise" as the continuing subject from v 13 across the parenthesis in vv 14-15.

in order that it may be a matter of grace: The simple phrase *hina kata charin* strongly expresses the divine purpose: ". . . it (conveys) the center of Paul's understanding of God, . . . completely dominated by the Christ event" (Moxnes, *Theology in Conflict* 261); cf. Gal 2:21.

and something secure for all his descendants: Besides its primary consecutive sense, the prepositional phrase *eis to einai bebaian* also expresses here the divine purpose—indicated for Paul in scripture (cf. v 17). *Bebaios* was used in a technical sense to denote legally guaranteed security (cf. Dunn 1.216). Here it stands in opposition to "abolished" (*katērgētai*, v 14; cf. Gal 3:15-18).

not to the one who proceeds from the law only, but also to the one who shares the faith of Abraham: This extended formula raises a problem of reference similar to that in v 12. It clearly envisages two groups. The first group *(tǭ ek tou nomou monon)* could refer to Jews who are not Christians, as contrasted with those who share Abraham's faith *(tǭ ek pisteōs Abraam)*, that is, believers. If the Greek adverb *monon* followed directly after the negative *ou* (as many translations tend to suggest), the text could be read so as to include these (non-Christian) Jews within the scope of the promise—something which the intensive *kai* following the conjunction *alla* would also support. But the actual position of *monon* seems to exclude this group from the promise and in fact sets up a contrast. Moreover, Paul would seriously weaken his case if he were to grant inclusion within the promise to those described simply as *ek tou nomou* without any reference to faith. Logically, then, it seems more likely that, as in vv 11b-12, Christian believers, Jewish and Gentile, are meant in both cases. The concluding relative clause, binding all under a common "fatherhood" of Abraham, also strongly supports this.

who is the father of us all: The contrast between this "inclusive" characterization of Abraham's "fatherhood" and that given in v 1 ("our forefather according to the flesh") shows the extent of the "revision" concerning Abraham now achieved.

17. *as it is written, "I have made you the father of many nations":* The text as quoted agrees exactly with the LXX of Gen 17:5. The rabbinic tradition used this text with reference to Gentiles who as proselytes became converts to Judaism; see SB 3.211.

—in the sight of the God in whom he believed: The Greek preposition *katenanti* can mean both "opposite" and "in the sight of." Here the second sense is operative. The connection of the phrase with what has preceded is not altogether clear. Linking it closely to v 16c ("who is the father of us all") renders the scriptural quotation in v 17a something of a parenthesis. But the quotation, introduced by the solemn formula *kathōs gegraptai*, provides important support for Abraham's common fatherhood (v 16c) and the use of *katenanti* here may be inspired by God's statement to Abraham a few lines earlier on (v 1): "Be well pleasing in my sight" (LXX: *euarestei enantion emou*). The transition is not so abrupt when one keeps in mind that Paul sees Abraham's "fatherhood" as totally bound up with his faith.

a God who gives life to the dead: The designation *(ho zǭopoiōn tous nekrous)* corresponds exactly to the Hebrew of the second of the Eighteen Benedictions, probably already used in Jewish worship at the time of Paul; cf. also LXX Ps 70:20 (71:20); Wis 16:13; Tob 13:2; *Jos. Asen.* 20:7; John 5:21; Rom 8:11; 1 Cor 15: 22, 36, 45; 2 Cor 3:6; Gal 3:21.

and calls into being the things that do not exist: Variations of this formula (*kalountos ta mē onta hōs onta*) occur widely in the Hellenistic Jewish tradition to express the sense of *creatio ex nihilo:* Wis 11:25; 2 Macc 7:28; *Jos. Asen.* 8:9; Philo,

Spec. 4.187; *Op.* 81; *Mig.* 183; *Her.* 36; etc.; cf. also 2 *Apoc. Bar.* 21:4; 48:8. Paul depicts Abraham's faith in terms used by Greek-speaking Jews to commend and defend their belief. He certainly saw conversion and the foundation of communities of the converted as exercises of God's creative power: cf. Rom 8:30; 9:25-26; 1 Cor 1:9, 26, 28; also 2 Cor 5:17; Gal 6:15.

18. *Faced with a hopeless situation, with hope nonetheless he (Abraham) believed:* The translation attempts to bring out the sense of the succinct phrase *par' elpida ep' elpidi*. It seems best to take the preposition *para* in the sense "contrary to" and see *elpida* following it as referring to what could be hoped for in merely human terms. The second phrase (*epi* + dative of attendant circumstances) then describes the true hope in the divine power which accompanied Abraham's act of faith.

that he would become the "father of many nations," just as he had been told, "So shall your descendants be": Grammatically it is more natural to see the articular infinitive phrase, *eis to genesthai auton*, as expressing purpose or consequence rather than the content of Abraham's faith. However, the focus at this point seems to be entirely upon Abraham's attitude rather than the divine purpose or consequences (as in vv 11b-12, 16). The phrase "father of many nations" is repeated from the quotation of Gen 17:5 in v 17a. By quoting immediately as a comment upon this title the last part of the divine promise in Gen 15:5 ("So shall your offspring be") Paul ensures that the text from Genesis 17, which otherwise, with its subsequent circumcision command (vv 10-14, 23-27), could be a dubious asset for his argument, is subsumed under what has been the controlling and determinative scriptural text all through.

19. *He did not weaken in faith when he considered his own body, which was as good as dead because he was about a hundred years old:* The translation rejects the less well attested variant (D G K etc.) placing the negative particle *ou* before "considered" (*katenoēsen*). The reading without the negative has stronger textual support and is clearly the more difficult reading, whereas the variant seems designed to soften the stark realism of what Abraham "considered." "Body" (*sōma*) here, as in 1:24, has an evident sexual tone. The estimate of Abraham's age would seem to come from Gen 17:1, where he is stated to be ninety-nine.

20. *no distrust made him waver in disbelief:* For similar use of *diakrinesthai* with respect to belief, cf. Matt 21:21; Mark 11:23; Jas 1:6.

but he grew strong in his faith: The translation takes "faith" *(pistei)* as a dative of respect, seeing Abraham's faith as the object rather than the instrument of the "strengthening." The form of the verb *enedynamōthē* could be either middle (as translated here) or passive (cf. Eph 6:10; 2 Tim 2:1), the latter implying that it was God who did the strengthening.

giving glory to God: On "glory/glorify God" as the archetypal human response owed to God as Creator, see Note on 1:21 above.

21. *fully convinced that God was able to do what he had promised:* Paul may have in mind the response to Sarah's laughter in Gen 18:14: "Is anything impossible for God?," a text echoed more explicitly in the Lukan annunciation of Jesus' birth to Mary (1:37; cf. v 45).

22. *That is why his faith was "reckoned to him for righteousness":* The translation supplies "his faith" as implied subject of the verb but ignores the adverb *kai* standing before the verb. The omission of *kai* in some manuscripts (B D* F G) suggests that it may be a secondary harmonization of the text with the exact wording of LXX Gen 15:6b.

23–24. *But the words, "it was reckoned to him," were written not for his sake alone but for ours also:* Paul sees a bi-polar purpose in scripture: it was written for Abraham—presumably in the sense that it tells (preserves) his "story"; it was written for "us" (the eschatological people of God) in the sense that it discloses the divine plans in our regard that are now being realized in Christ (cf. 1 Cor 9:8-10; 10:1-11; Gal 4:21-31, esp. v 24). A similar sense of the eschatological meaning of scripture is found in the commentary *(pesher)* literature from Qumran—though not with the same acknowledgment of the original meaning that appears here in Paul.

for whom it will be reckoned: The use of the present tense of the verb *mellein*, with its suggestion of a justification still outstanding, reflects the ambivalent time-reference of believers' justification in Paul. In one sense it is all complete (5:1; cf. 3:24). But final ratification belongs to the endtime judgment (cf. 3:30 *[dikaiōsei]*; 5:18, 19; Gal 5:5). In the meantime believers have to "live out" the justification they have received. As in the case of Abraham, there is an essential note of perseverance and hope in their believing. The next major section (chapters 5–8) will elaborate this.

that is, who believe in the One: Paul uses the comparatively rare construction *pisteuein epi* plus the accusative (cf. 4:5) to bring out the strict parallel between the content of Abraham's faith and that of his believing "descendants." Here, too, God rather than Christ is the object of faith. "Faith" for Paul is fundamentally faith in the God who is active in the Christ event, working justification for "the ungodly." All the classic Pauline formulations of Christian faith (Rom 3:21-26; 4:5, 24; 10:9; Gal 2:16) cohere around this center.

who raised from the dead Jesus our Lord: In designating God in this way Paul is clearly echoing a familiar early Christian formula of faith—one combining (cf. also 1 Cor 6:14; 2 Cor 4:14) what were perhaps the two most primitive creeds of all: "God raised him (Jesus) from the dead" (cf. Acts 3:15; 4:10; 13:30; Rom 8:11; 10:9; Gal 1:1; 1 Thess 1:10; Eph 1:20; Col 2:12; 1 Pet 1:21) and "Jesus is Lord" (Phil 2:11; 1 Cor 12:3; Rom 10:9). On the title "Lord" (*kyrios*), see Note on 1:4 above.

25. *who was delivered up for our trespasses and raised for our justification:* The introductory relative pronoun *hos*, the parallelism of form and content and the use of traditional language (esp. the use of the verb *paradidonai*) point to the citation of a credal or liturgical formula. Use of the language of being "given up" (passive of the Greek verb *paradidonai*) with respect to Christ's death is widespread in the NT, covering both Judas' betrayal and the divine action (cf. later Rom 8:32). With regard to the first clause here *(hos paredothē dia ta paraptōmata)*, cf. LXX Isa 53:12 (Fourth Servant Song): *dia tas hamartias autōn paredothē* (cf. also v 6). The appearance in the present text of "transgressions"

(paraptōmata) in place of "sins" *(hamartias)* may reflect Paul's practice of using *hamartia* in the singular to denote the radical power of sin, retaining *paraptōmata* (or similar expressions) for individual sins (7:5 is exceptional in this respect; 1 Cor 15:3 is a traditional formula). Likewise the reference to "justification" *(dikaiōsis)* in the parallel clause may allude to the reference in Isa 53:11 to the Servant's role of "justifying many" (at least in the Hebrew text; the LXX contains the word *dikaiōsai* but is otherwise rather different).

For Reference and Further Study

Barrett, C. K. *From First Adam to Last.* London: Black, 1962; New York: Scribners, 22–45.

Berger, K. "Abraham in den paulinischen Hauptbriefen." *MTZ* 17 (1966) 47–89, esp. 63–77.

Cranford, M. "Abraham in Romans 4: The Father of All Who Believe." *NTS* 41 (1995) 71–88.

Davies, G. N. *Faith and Obedience* 143–72.

Guerra, A. J. "Romans 4 as Apologetic Theology." *HTR* 81 (1988) 251–70.

Hansen, G. W. *Abraham in Galatians: Epistolary and Rhetorical Contexts.* JSNTSup 29; Sheffield: JSOT Press, 1989, 175–99.

Hays, R. B. "'Have we found Abraham to Be Our Forefather according to the Flesh?' A Reconsideration of Rom 4:1." *NovT* 27 (1985) 76–98.

Käsemann, E. "The Faith of Abraham in Romans 4." *Perspectives on Paul* 79–101.

Lincoln, A. T. "Abraham Goes to Rome: Paul's Treatment of Abraham in Romans 4." *Worship, Theology and Ministry in the Early Church* (FS R. P. Martin). Eds. M. J. Wilkins and T. Paige. JSNTSup 87; Sheffield: JSOT, 1992, 163–79.

Moxnes, H. *Theology in Conflict* 117–69.

Stowers, S. K. *Diatribe* 168–74.

__________. *Rereading of Romans* 227–50.

Van Seters, J. *Prologue to History.* Louisville: Westminster/John Knox, 1992, 248–52 (on the figure of Abraham in the Old Testament).

Watson, F. *Paul, Judaism and the Gentiles* 135–42.

B. THE SURE HOPE OF SALVATION SPRINGING FROM RIGHTEOUSNESS BY FAITH (5:1–8:39)

Introduction to Romans 5-8: The "overlap" of the ages. The beginning of chapter 5 marks a major transition in Romans. Up till this point, Paul's exposition of the gospel has focused upon faith. If Gentiles are to be included as equal citizens within the community of the saved, then faith, not the "works" of the Jewish law, must be the vehicle of the righteousness leading to salvation. Paul has locked home this principle of righteousness by faith by expounding scripture's witness to it in the figure of Abraham, paradigm believer and recipient of the promise on the basis of faith. Now the focus shifts from faith to hope. Abandoning the fictive dialogue with a Jewish dialogue partner yet to be won to faith in Jesus Christ, Paul speaks "within" the community of believers, those whose faith has brought them right standing with God. He expounds and celebrates the hope of salvation that God's gift of righteousness has brought into their lives, the righteousness that makes the gospel "the power of God leading to salvation for every believer—Jew first, but also the Greek" (1:16).

Towards the end of his exposition of Scripture in chapter 4 Paul had prepared the way for this transition to hope by stressing the persevering aspect of Abraham's act of faith (4:18-21). Hope that God would make good the promise (of a son and a long line of descendants) formed an integral part of Abraham's faith. It meant believing that the God who "gives life to the dead and calls into being the things that do not exist" (v 17) would overcome the "deadness" with regard to childbearing constituted by his own advanced age and the barrenness of his wife Sarah. In this respect Abraham's faith is paradigmatic for Christian faith in that believers also have to hope for salvation in the face of the suffering and death characteristic of the present age. The affirmation of hope that forms the main theme of the new section of the letter that now begins (5:1–8:39) confronts what has aptly been called the "overlap" situation of present Christian life. As far as relations with God are concerned, for those justified through faith, the new age has dawned. In their bodily life, however, they remain anchored in the old age, afflicted by weakness, suffering and death. Righteousness has set them on the way but full salvation is grasped only in hope (8:23-25). The challenge is to hear the gospel in such a way that hope stays alive.

Romans 5–8 is bound together by the notable similarity in content between its two "extremities": 5:1-21 (more specifically 5:1-11) and 8:14-39 (more specifically 8:31-39). Like bookends holding upright volumes on a shelf, these form an "inclusion" binding together the material in between. Both sections have "hope" as explicit theme, a hope that rests upon the peace with God brought about by justification (5:9; 8:31-34), attested by the Spirit (5:5; 8:14-15, 23-27). It is a hope, moreover, which confronts and endures the presence of suffering (5:3-4; 8:17-18, 35-39). Above all, the same *a fortiori* logic drives the argument of the two passages: hope rests upon the love of God which, having already found expression in the gift of the Son for us when we were sinners, will all the more ("much more") certainly—now that we are God's friends—see us through to the end (5:6, 8, 9, 10; 8:32).

If the hope of salvation rests upon the new righteousness brought about through faith, the challenge for believers is to preserve or live out that righteousness through to the end (the great Judgment). This explains why, just when one might consider the argument for righteousness through faith to have been won (4:25; cf. 5:1), Paul continues in this new section to skirmish with the law. To state the matter a little more accurately: as a key part of his argument for hope, he plays off the superiority of the power of the Spirit as a source of the necessary righteousness against the impotence ("weakness") of the law in this respect. The hope of salvation is there *because*—not despite—the fact that "the Spirit of life in Christ Jesus has set you free from the law of sin and death" (8:2). This concern to establish the superiority of the Spirit explains the long "ethical" section that enters in between 6:1 and 8:13, before the argument for hope in the face of suffering resumes for the remainder of chapter 8.

i. The Hope That Springs from God's Love (5:1-11)

1. Justified, then, by faith, we have peace with God through our Lord Jesus Christ. 2. Through him we have also obtained access to this grace in which we stand, and we boast in our hope of sharing the glory of God. 3. More than that, we boast even in our sufferings, knowing that suffering produces endurance, 4. and endurance produces character, and character produces hope,

5. and the hope (that we have) will not let us down, because God's love has been poured into our hearts through the Holy Spirit which has been given to us.

6. While we were still weak, at the right time Christ died for the ungodly. 7. Why, one will hardly die for a righteous person—though perhaps for a good person one will dare even to die. 8. What shows God's love for us is that, while we were yet sinners, Christ died for us. 9. Since, therefore, we are now justified by his blood, much more shall we be saved by him from the wrath.

10. For if while we were enemies we were reconciled to God by the death of his Son, much more, now that we are reconciled, shall we be saved by his life.

11. Not only so, but we also boast in God through our Lord Jesus Christ, through whom we have now received the reconciliation.

Interpretation

Introduction. The passage falls into a fairly simple structure. Vv 1-2 form a kind of introductory bridge from what has gone before (justification by faith) to the new theme of hope for the fullness of salvation. Vv 3-4 form a couplet insisting that suffering provides a ground for "boasting." V 5, in a thematic way, states the theological grounds for hope: the love of God made palpable in the Spirit. Vv 6-10, taking up this theme of God's love, stir up and state in two "waves" the "much more" logic that will be the "engine" of the argument from now on. V 11 rounds off the section in an inclusive way, returning to the opening themes of "peace/reconciliation" (cf. vv 1-2) with God and "boasting" (cf. v 2).

Peace with God on the basis of justification (vv 1-2). The section opens with a firm and confident statement of where believers stand in relationship to God. The justification believers have received *(dikaiōthentes . . . ek pisteōs)* has brought about a state of "peace" *(eirēnē)* so that, like ambassadors to the court of a previously hostile but now friendly power, they enjoy (v 2) "access" *(prosagōgē)* to the "favor" *(charis)* in which they stand. Paul will go on to draw out a deeper, more dynamic meaning in the concept of *charis* (esp. 5:15-21). But already, in implicit contrast to the hostility and fear that characterized relations prior to justification, he puts forward a rich sense of Christian living within the scope of God's abiding favor.

The real focus, however, is on what lies ahead. With an irony that is surely intentional, Paul looks to the future (v 2c) in the language of "boasting" *(kauchāsthai)*. Up till this point in the letter, "boasting" has appeared in a highly unfavorable light (2:17; 3:27; 4:2). It implied a confidence in eschatological acceptance by God that rested upon privileged status or human achievement, something which, according to Paul, has been fatally undercut by human sinfulness. But over against this, he can now propose a "boasting" that is truly valid because it rests solely upon the power and operation of God. So believers (literally, "we") not only presently enjoy a privileged access to God's favor but can also "boast" in the hope of (obtaining) the glory of God.

Once again (cf. 1:23; 2:7, 10; 3:23; 8:18-30; 9:4, 23) Paul refers to the hoped-for future in the language of the biblical and post-biblical tradition. According to this tradition, stemming ultimately from Gen 1:26-28 and reflected especially in Ps 8:5-8, "glory" denotes the "likeness to God" based on bearing God's "image"; the process of salvation will be complete when human beings arrive at the fullness of "glory," the Creator's original intent in their regard. What is distinctive for Paul is that the "hope" for this glory rests not upon human achievement but upon God's saving action now being realized in Christ (who already as "Last Adam" both facilitates and "models" this glory [cf. 2 Cor 3:18; 4:4-6; Phil 3:20-21; 1 Cor 15:42-49]). That is why it can be a genuine object of "boast." Over against an illegitimate "boasting," which he has excluded, Paul can proclaim in the ringing tones of epideictic rhetoric a true Christian "boasting" (cf. the similar duality in 1 Cor 1:29-31).

Boasting in present suffering (vv 3-4). Boasting, however, does not look solely to the future. Boldly Paul indicates present suffering as also a grounds for boast (v 3b). With this paradoxical assertion (cf. the personal avowals in similar vein across 2 Cor 11:30–12:10; esp. 12:9-10) Paul confronts a significant aspect of present life of believers. In this time of the "overlap" of the ages, suffering, along with weakness and death, is a form in which the present, passing age impinges upon the bodily existence of those reconciled with God. Paul shares a widespread expectation that the sufferings of the elect would intensify in the time immediately before the final intervention of God (cf. esp. Mark 13:7-8, 19-20). He will confront this prospect more explicitly at the close of this entire section (8:31-39). For the present, he formulates a small, chain-like sequence (vv 3b-4) to provide some basis for the claim that even sufferings can provide an occasion to boast. In rhetorical terms, such sequences ("sorites"; cf. also 8:29-30; 10:14-15) attempt to build up an inexorable logic by making the object of one sentence the subject of the next. So Paul attempts to argue the emergence of hope out of suffering via the middle terms "endurance" *(hypomonē)* and "(tested) character" *(dokimē)*. If suffering can give rise to hope, then one can "boast" in suffering, equally as one "boasts in the hope of (obtaining) the glory of God" (v 2c).

Paul makes the sequence a matter of common agreement ("knowing" *[eidotes]*). Modern readers may well object that it is by no means obvious that the experience of suffering works in this way and that, in fact, what suffering regularly produces is, not hope, but bitterness and despair. Paul, however, presumes acceptance of the idea of "disciplinary" suffering widespread in the Jewish wisdom tradition (see Note). The Stoics also held that character is tested and refined by trial and suffering. Where Paul goes to surprising lengths is in his insistence that the end-product is hope. The ultimate grounds for this are christological, as statements later in the letter (esp. 8:17c) will make clear. Believers are united to Christ through baptism, their existence and destiny conformed inexorably to his (6:3-5). As his sufferings led, through God's power, to his glory, it may be hoped that the same pattern will prevail in those united to him. On this logic, if one "boasts" in that in which one places confidence for salvation, to boast in suffering is tantamount to boasting "in the hope of obtaining the glory of God" (v 2c).

The Love of God poured out through the Spirit (v 5). With this sense of hope emerging even from suffering, Paul begins to develop the major theme of the entire section. In the symbolic universe presupposed by the argument the overarching prospect (reaching a climax in 8:31-39) remains that of the last judgment. Within this perspective, Paul insists that the "hope" that believers cherish will not prove "disappointing" *(ou kataischynei)* in the sense that the Judge might prove hostile at this crucial moment and bar the way to full salvation. The sufferings of the present may indicate the lingering presence of the old age. They certainly do not reflect the hostility of God.

What excludes this is the sense of God's love made palpable in the experience of the Spirit (v 5b). Paul makes a first and rather fleeting allusion here (cf., however, 2:29) to a key aspect of Christian experience that will later (8:1-30) emerge as a central theme. Following upon biblical passages such as Ezekiel 36–37, the apocalyptic tradition saw the Spirit as the eschatological gift *par excellence*—the creative force of the new creation, as it had been of the old (Gen 1:2; 2:7). Through the Spirit the eschatological people of God was to be purified, cleansed and readied for the life of the new age. Since water is the dominant symbol of cleansing and new life, the idea of "pouring" *(ekkechytai)* is a natural association (cf. already Joel 2:28 [Heb 3:1]; cf. Acts 2:17; 1 Cor 12:13). For Paul (and the early Christian tradition generally) the presence of the Spirit is the sure index that, whatever the outward circumstances, as far as relations with God are concerned, the community is already living the life of the new age, enjoying a filial status in which they cry out to God, "*Abba*, Father" (Gal 4:6-7; Rom 8:15). The gift of the Spirit is God's "downpayment" (*arrabōn*, 2 Cor 1:22; 5:5; cf. Eph 1:14), the pledge of the full installment of salvation yet to come.

The hope that springs from God's love (vv 6-10). To ground this theme, Paul sets up (vv 6-10) a kind of *a fortiori* argument centered upon the implications of Christ's death. The argument rolls across the sequence in two "waves" (vv 6[7]-9 and v 10), both displaying a similar logic: if, when we were God's enemies (the much harder or "heavier" case), God loved us to the extent of giving the Son to die for us, how much more (Greek *pollǭ mallon*, v 9, v 10; cf. v 15, v 16), it is certain that, now we are "friends" (the much easier or "lighter" case), God will see us through to final salvation.

In the first part of the first "wave" (vv 6[7]-8), Paul dwells at considerable length upon the past event, the death of Christ as an instance of God's love, before drawing the conclusion with respect to the future (v 9). The key thing is to fix the time *(kata kairon)* when Christ offered his life (note the double "yet" *[eti]* in v 6; also v 8): it was while we were "weak" *(ontōn hēmōn asthenōn)*—that is, without any moral capacity whatsoever—that Christ "died for the ungodly" *(asēbōn)*. This is the language used earlier to designate the wickedness of the unredeemed world against which God's wrath is revealed (1:18; cf. also 4:5). "We" were part of that world alienated from God and it was precisely for us as part of that world that Christ died.

To stress the enormity of the sacrifice involved, Paul invites his audience to consider on what terms human beings might be prepared to sacrifice their life for another (v 7). Even if it is for the sake of a "just" person *(dikaios)*, to give up one's life is a very difficult thing *(molis)*. But it is conceivable that, for a really good *(agathos)* person, one might be prepared to die.

Presuming that his audience will have granted this point—both the difficulty and the possibility of such self-sacrifice—Paul then uses it (v 8) as a foil against which to set the extremity of God's love. In the case of Christ's self-sacrifice it was not a matter of dying for "good" or "just" persons. It was while we were "sinners" *(hamartōlōn ontōn hēmōn)* that Christ died for us—something which demonstrates beyond doubt God's own personal love for us. Christ's self-gift in love is simply an outward, historical expression of the eternal love of God (cf. the sense of divine initiative already in 3:24-26; later, 5:15; 8:31-32, 39).

With this clear evidence of God's love established as regards the past, Paul proceeds (v 9), on the basis of the *a fortiori* "logic," to draw the conclusion for the future. We (believers), who once were sinners *(hamartōloi)*, are now through the shedding of Christ's blood (*en tǭ haimati autou*) "justified" (*dikaiōthentes*; cf. v 1; 3:25), accepted and declared to be in right relationship with God. The argument then is that, if God showed so much love for us while we were sinners (the "heavier" case), how "much more" *(pollǭ mallon)* is it certain that we shall be saved *(sōthēsometha)* through him from the wrath (the "lighter" case). Reference to "wrath" *(orgē)* at this point, when all stress seems to lie upon God's love, is at first sight surprising. But wrath (God's abiding displeasure falling upon the unrighteous) remains a key factor within the apocalyptic perspective of the argument, and "salvation," at least in negative terms, is precisely rescue from the wrath (see Interpretation of 1:16). Paul does not deny the reality of the wrath or refer it simply to the past. But he insists that it is simply non-applicable for those whose relations with God have been transformed by Christ's act appropriated through faith. Like travellers with visas fully stamped ("justified"), believers can confidently expect that God's love will usher them safely through the final barrier.

The second "wave" (v 10) offers a more concise statement of the same basic argument with a change of metaphor. The language of justification ("sinners"/"justified") gives way to that of reconciliation ("enemies"/"reconciled")—a development already foreshadowed in the mention of "peace with God" in v 1. Sin's universal prevalence (3:9-20, 23) had rendered the entire human race "enemies" *(echthroi)* of God. It was into this mass of alienation (the "heavier" case) that God plunged, so to speak, to bring about reconciliation through the death of the Son (Paul writes "his Son" to bring out the personal involvement of God in this costly exercise; cf. 8:3, 32). How "much more" *(pollǭ mallon)* certain it is, now that peace has been established (the "lighter" case), that we shall be saved by his life.

Here once again, as in the earlier statement (v 9), the future hope is expressed in terms of "salvation" *(sōthēsometha)*. Instead, however, of the simple "through him" of v 9b, we have a more specific indication of agency: as the reconciliation has been effected through the death of the Son, salvation will be come about "through his life" (*en tę zōę autou*; cf 4:25). It is probably unwarranted to draw strict conclusions in a systematic way from what may after all be only an attempt at rhetorical balance. Nonetheless, the suggestion is that the risen Lord has an active role to play in the progress of believers to salvation—something confirmed by the close linkage in Paul's thought between the Spirit and the impact of the risen Lord, creating the righteousness that leads to life (cf. 6:22; 8:9-11; 1 Cor 15:45b; 2 Cor 3:18).

Boasting in God (v 11). This reflection upon the love God has already shown (vv 6-9; v 10) has set on a firm base the "thesis" formulated in v 5: that the hope that emerges even out of sufferings will not let us down. Paul brings the section to a triumphant conclusion, reverting to the idea of "boasting." Not only do we have this hope for the future—the prospect of salvation—but right now *(nyn)*, as those who have received reconciliation, we "are boasting *(kauchōmenoi)* in God." This ringing assertion, one of the great celebratory moments of the letter, concludes the whole preoccupation with "boasting" that had begun in 2:17. The Jewish claim to "rest upon the law and boast in God" has been rigorously excluded in the light of God's action in Christ (3:27-28), corroborated by scripture (4:2). Now the wheel has come full circle. Yes, we do "boast in God" (cf. 1 Cor 1:29-31), catching up the ancient privilege of Israel (cf. LXX Deut 10:21; Pss 5:12; 105:47 [106:47]), but the "we" who do so are the eschatological people of God, made up of all those, Jews *and Gentiles,* who through Christ have received reconciliation with God.

Notes

1. *Justified, then, by faith:* The phrase sums up the whole argument of the preceding chapters. The aorist participle *dikaiōthentes,* for the first time in the letter, refers justification firmly to the past (later, 8:30); contrast the present tenses of 3:24, 26, the future tenses of 3:20, 28; cf. 4:24; Gal 5:5. On the Pauline concept of "justification," see Interpretation of 2:13 and 3:24.

   we have peace with God: The translation presupposes the indicative reading *echomen* ("we have") rather than the exhortative (subjunctive) *echōmen* ("let us have"). The latter has stronger textual warrant and some sense can be made of it in the context. But the indicative is far more appropriate: rather than an attitude to be adopted, "peace" indicates a state of affairs upon which an attitude ("hope") is based; cf. also the clearly indicative *kai . . . eschēkamen* that follows in v 2. The subjunctive could easily have arisen through a mishearing on the part of a scribe of the similar vowels "*o*" and "*ō*"; cf. Cranfield 1.257, n. 1.

2. *Through him we have also obtained access to this grace in which we stand:* The perfect tense of both verbs *(eschēkamen, hestēkamen)* brings out the sense that the access and favor won by Christ remains an abiding state of affairs. The word translated "access" *(prosagōgē)* denotes a solemn approach, as on festive occasions or to the throne of a king; cf. LSJ 1500 s.v. II, 1-2. In the case of "grace," it is probably better not to import the full theological meaning *charis* usually has in Paul but, within the image being developed, to see it simply as denoting a sphere or milieu in which one feels welcome on the grounds of enjoying the favor of the person who counts.

hope of sharing the glory of God: On the Jewish tradition of "glory" as the eschatological destiny of human beings according to the original design of God, see Note on 3:23.

3–4. *knowing that suffering produces endurance, and endurance produces character, and character produces hope:* On the motif of God's "disciplinary" chastisement in the wisdom tradition of Israel, see Deut 8:2-5; Prov 3:11-12; Sir 2:1-5; 4:17-18; 18:13-14; 23:1-3; Wis 3:1-6; 11:9-10; 2 Macc 6:12-16; 7:32-33; *Pss. Sol.* 10:1-3; 14:1; elsewhere in the NT, cf. 1 Cor 11:32; Heb 12:5-11; Rev 3:19. The word translated "suffering" *(thlipsis)* literally means "pressure" and then, in a metaphorical sense, the distress brought about through the pressure of adverse external circumstances; it can refer in the NT specifically to the "distress" associated with the "End" (cf. Mark 13:7, 19 [probably going back to LXX Dan 12:1]). "Endurance" *(hypomonē)* is a strong word denoting persevering steadfastness in the face of suffering; it is a favored term of the Greek Stoics and also features prominently in the "martyr" theology of Judaism, reflecting the double sense of fortitude under suffering and trust in God for ultimate deliverance (cf. 4 Macc 1:11; 9:8, 30; 15:30; 17:4, 12, 17, 23); Job was regarded as a particular example of this quality—something reflected already in the LXX translation of the Book of Job (14:19; cf. *T. Job* 1:5; 4:6; 5:1; Jas 5:11). For Paul *hypomonē* is a necessary requirement of Christian life (cf. 2:7; 8:25; 15:4-5; 2 Cor 1:6; 6:4; 12:12; 1 Thess 1:3 *[hypomonē tēs elpidos]*; cf. Col 1:11; 2 Thess 1:4; 3:5. "Character" translates a Greek word, *dokimē*, not attested before Paul; it denotes what results from being tried or put to the test (*dokimazein*: cf. Wis 3:5-6): hence "proven, firm character." For examples of the "chain-like" sequence ("sorites") in other ancient literature, see M. Wolter, *Rechtfertigung und zukunftiges Heil* (see Reference) 145, n. 488.

5. *and the hope (that we have) will not let us down:* Lit. "will not cause shame." This use of the verb *kataischynein* reflects a biblical idiom in which failure is described as "being put to shame" in the sense of being publicly proved impotent or wanting at the critical moment. The translation takes the tense of the verb (*kataischynei*) as a future. It is only the future (the judgment; cf. v 9, v 10) that will show whether or not the present hope has been well grounded.

God's love: The context, with its clear emphasis upon the divine initiative, requires that the Greek phrase *hē agapē tou theou* refer to God's love for us (subjective genitive) rather than our love for God (objective genitive).

6. *While we were still weak:* "Weak" *(asthenēs)* expresses simply the human condition over against the power of God. With this rather mild expression Paul begins a crescendo (cf. later *asebēs, hamartōlos* [v 8]) denoting the state of those for whom Christ died.

at the right time: The Greek word *kairos,* which can have the connotation of the propitious or eschatological moment (cf. 3:26; Gal 4:4), here serves simply to fix the time precisely: "right at that very time," that is, when we were sinners.

Christ died for the ungodly: For *asebēs* see Note on 4:5. Behind the simple prepositional phrase (cf. also *hyper hēmōn* in v 8) lies the whole early interpretation of Christ's death as a death for the benefit of those who, in the face of the coming eschatological judgment, unlike himself, stood in need of reconciliation with God. This interpretation, which found its focus particularly in the eucharistic tradition (Mark 14:24 // Matt 26:28; cf. also Mark 10:45 // Matt 20:28), clearly derives from the motif of the "Servant" figure in Isa 52:13–53:12, whose sufferings justify "many" (53:11). Paul readily assumes and develops this tradition (cf. Gal 1:4; 2:19; Rom 4:25; 14:15; 1 Cor 15:3; 2 Cor 5:14-15, 21; 1 Thess 5:10), linking it with other soteriological images such as that of "reconciliation" (Rom 5:10-11; 2 Cor 5:18-21) and "liberation (from slavery)" (Gal 3:13; Rom 6:1–8:2).

7. *Why, one will hardly die for a righteous person—though perhaps for a good person one will dare even to die:* This verse is often regarded as an aside or correction on Paul's part (sometimes with the second element seen as a replacement for the first) or as an addition to the original text. But it is an integral part of the argument, underscoring the immensity of what God has done. The Greek phrase *hyper agathou* could be taken as a neuter (= "for a good cause"). This would be more consonant with Paul's use of *agathos* elsewhere but the personal reference suits the context much better.

8. *Christ died for us:* See Note on v 6 above.

9. *by his blood:* As in 3:25, *en tą̄ haimati autou* refers to the shedding of Christ's blood in the death upon the cross, the Greek preposition *en* functioning instrumentally and setting the phrase in parallel to "through his death" *(dia tou thanatou . . . autou)* in the following verses.

much more: This phrase *(pollą̄ mallon),* the fulcrum of the *a fortiori* logic, occurs four times in Romans 5 (cf. also v 10, 15, 17) and is implicit in 8:32 (cf. also 2 Cor 3:11; Phil 2:12; Rom 11:12, 24 [*posą̄ mallon* in both cases]). The rabbis referred to the same logical device as *qal wāḥōmer* (lit. "light and heavy"); see SB 3.223–26.

shall we be saved: As usually in Paul, "salvation" refers to the future deliverance; see Interpretation and Note on 1:16.

from the wrath: The explicit designation of the wrath as "God's wrath" on the part of many translations (e.g., RSV; JB) has no warrant in the Greek text, which simply has *apo tēs orgēs*. On the notion of the "wrath," see Interpretation and Note on 1:18.

10. *reconciled to God:* Prior to Paul, there is not much precedent for the use of the idea of "reconciliation" in a religious sense, i.e., as applied to the divine-human relationship (cf., in secular usage, Sophocles, *Ajax* 744; in Hellenistic Judaism: 2 Macc 1:5; 5:20; 7:33; 8:29; Josephus, *Ant.* 6.143; 7:153, 295; Philo, *Praem.* 166; *Frag.* II.670; *Jos. Asen.* 11:18). Paul here, as also in 2 Cor 5:18-21, is more likely to be taking an image from the world of diplomacy (cf. vv 1-2) and applying it to God's work in Christ. For Paul, the reconciliation is made possible through the expiatory function of Christ's death (Rom 3:24-26) but "reconciliation" *as such* need not necessarily include expiatory (let alone sacrificial) connotation; furthermore, the initiative always rests with God. The post-Pauline tradition greatly develops the sense of cosmic reconciliation (inherent already in 2 Cor 5:19): Col 1:20-22; Eph 2:11-19. See esp. C. Breytenbach, *Versöhnung* (see Reference) 40–83, 143–72, 180–83; 193–221.

    by his life: This phrase *(en tą̄ zōę̄ autou)*, rhetorically speaking, balances "through his death" in the preceding clause, which is presumably why Paul speaks in terms of Christ's "life" (i.e., risen life) rather than "resurrection."

11. *Not only so, but we also boast in God:* The first phrase *(ou monon . . .)* alludes elliptically to the preceding main verb *sōthēsometha* (v 10), with a participle *kauchōmenoi* (lit. "boasting") doing service for a finite verb (as often in Paul: 3:24; 7:5; 8:4; etc.; see BDF §468 [1]). The effect is to heighten a distinction between present and future: not only do we have this future expectation (salvation, vv 9-10), but *even now* (in this suffering time—cf. v 3) we are boasting in God.

    through our Lord Jesus Christ, through whom we have now received the reconciliation: The full title given to Christ and the heightened tone suggest that Paul's celebratory conclusion may owe something to an early liturgy.

For Reference and Further Study

Breytenbach, C. *Versöhnung: Ein Studie zur paulinischen Soteriologie.* WMANT 60; Neukirchen: Neukirchener Verlag, 1989.

Dahl, N. A. "A Synopsis of Romans 5:1-11 and 8:1-39." *Studies in Paul* 88–90.

Fitzmyer, J. A. "Reconciliation in Pauline Theology." *To Advance the Gospel.* New York: Crossroad, 1981, 162–85

McDonald, P. M. "Romans 5:1-11 as a Rhetorical Bridge." *JSNT* 40 (1990) 81–96.

Martin, R. P. *Reconciliation: A Study of Paul's Theology.* Atlanta: John Knox, 1980, 135–54.

Nebe, G. *"Hoffnung" bei Paulus: Elpis und ihre Synonyme im Zusammenhang der Eschatologie.* SUNT 16; Göttingen: Vandenhoeck & Ruprecht, 1983, 123–36.

Wolter, M. *Rechtfertigung und zukünftiges Heil: Untersuchungen zu Röm 5:1-11.* BZNW 43; Berlin: de Gruyter, 1978.

ii. The Legacy of Christ (Righteousness and Life) Outweighs the Legacy of Adam (Sin and Death) (5:12-21)

12. Therefore, as sin entered the world through one man and through sin
death, and so death passed to all on this basis, namely, that all sinned—
13. For sin was indeed in the world before the law. Admittedly, sin
is not booked up in the absence of law. 14. Yet death reigned from
Adam until Moses, even over those whose sinning did not follow
the pattern of the transgression of Adam, who is a type of the one
to come.
15. But it is not a case of, "As (was) the trespass, so (is) the gracious gift."
For if through one man's trespass many died, much more have the grace
of God and the gift in the grace of the one man Jesus Christ abounded
for many.
16. And it is not a case of, "As (the effect of) that one man's sin, so the
(effect of the) free gift." For the judgment following that one trespass
brought condemnation, but the free gift following many trespasses
brings justification.
17. For if, through one man's trespass, death reigned through that one
man, much more will those who accept the overflow of grace and the
gift of righteousness reign in life through the one man, Jesus Christ.
18. Well then, as one man's trespass led to condemnation for all, so also
one man's righteous act leads to a justification that brings life for all. 19.
As through the one man's disobedience, many were made sinners, so
through one man's obedience many will be made righteous.
20. The law came in to multiply the trespass. But where sin increased,
grace abounded all the more.
21. So that, as sin reigned in death, grace also might reign through righteousness, leading to eternal life, through Jesus Christ, our Lord.

Interpretation

Introduction. The distinctive feature of this passage is the sustained comparison/contrast between the figures of Adam and Christ which it sets up. In the argument for hope in the preceding section (5:1-11), Paul had again and again stressed the instrumentality of Christ (vv 1, 2, 6, 8, 9, 10 [twice], 11 [twice]). The present section furthers that argument, "unpacking" the instrumentality of Christ with respect to righteousness and (eternal) life, over against the instrumentality of Adam with respect to sin and death.

In other words, Paul wants to say something about Christ and, to do so more effectively, says it over against the negative background provided by Adam. He is not interested in Adam for his own sake nor is he principally concerned to explain how Adam's legacy of sin has been transmitted to subsequent generations. Interpretation of the text down the ages has, it is true, been focused upon this last point, encouraged by the fact that in the opening sentence the statement about the onset of sin and death through Adam is not balanced by a corresponding statement about Christ. Only at v 18 (with some foreshadowing in v 17) does the full, balanced statement of the comparison/contrast truly emerge. It is important, however, to attend to the structure of the passage as a whole and not allow the incomplete sentence making up v 12 to swamp the field.

The reader expects the opening clause about Adam (v 12) to be matched by something like: "so righteousness entered the world through one man and, through righteousness, life, and so life passed to all (?) on the basis of the righteousness they had received" (cf. v 17b). Instead, sensing a difficulty arising out of the absence of the Jewish law in the time between Adam and Moses, Paul breaks off the formulation of the complete comparison to offer a clarificatory note (vv 13-14). Having suggested at the end of this note (v 14c) that Adam is a "type of the one to come" (Christ), he further pauses to build up the sense of the overpowering superiority on the "Christ" side (vv 15-17). Only when this is securely established is the way clear for reiterated full statement (v 18) of the contrast intended from the start (v 18; v 19; cf. v 21). A double statement about the intrusion of the law breaks in just before the end (v 20), preparing the way for the final climactic assertion of the "reign" of grace (v 21). The overall rhetorical effect is to reinforce the argument for hope by highlighting in crescendo, at the expense of Adam, the superiority of Christ and the solidarity in grace that he has founded.

The "Adam" tradition. From the outset (v 12a-c) Paul presupposes in his readers an acceptance of a tradition that saw the first human being (Adam) as responsible for the onset of death in the human race. The existence of this tradition, ultimately derived from God's decree in Gen 3:19, can be verified across a wide range of post-biblical Jewish literature. Classic is the statement of *4 Ezra:* "You (God) laid upon him (Adam) one commandment of yours; but he transgressed it, and immediately you appointed death for him and for his descendants" (3:7; cf. also *2 Apoc. Bar.* 17:2-3; 23:4; 48:42-43; *Bib. Ant.* 13:8; cf. *2 Enoch* 30:16). Some forms of the tradition place the blame firmly upon Eve (Sir 25:24; *Apoc. Mos.* 14) or, upon the devil (Wis 2:23-24).

Far less evident in the Jewish tradition is any sense of the belief (later to appear in the Christian doctrine of "Original Sin") that Adam was responsible not only for the onset of death but also for the prevalence of sin as well. Some passages of *4 Ezra* come close to this—though what is said to be transmitted is a sinful *tendency* (the "evil heart") rather than actual sin:

> For the first Adam, clothing himself with the evil heart, transgressed and was overcome; and likewise also all who were born of him. Thus the infirmity became inveterate; the law indeed was in the heart of the people, but (in conjunction) with the evil germ; so what was good departed and the evil remained (3:21-22; cf. 4:30-32; also [with blame laid upon Eve] *Adam and Eve* 44:2; *Apoc. Mos.* 32:1-2; cf. 14:2).

Interesting in this regard is the insistence of another apocalyptic author:

> For, although Adam first sinned and brought untimely death upon all, yet each of them who has been born from him has prepared for himself or herself the coming torment. And, further, each of them has chosen for himself or herself the coming glory. . . . Adam is, therefore, not the cause except only for himself, but each of us has become our own Adam (*2 Apoc. Bar.* 54:15-19; cf. also *4 Ezra* 7:118-19).

This statement, in a sense, "protests too much" and so bears witness to the existence of a tendency (which it wants to combat) where Adam is made responsible, not only for the onset of death, but also for a hereditary sinfulness as well. The work from which it comes is considerably later than Paul. Nonetheless, together with certain passages in *4 Ezra,* it does provide evidence for the existence of more radical tradition concerning Adam, the sort of thing which Paul's argument in Rom 5:12-21 seems to presuppose.

The Adamic legacy of sin and death (v 12). From the outset, in line with some form of this tradition, Paul boldly presents Adam as instrumental in the onset of sin and death in the human race. In a way that is to become characteristic of this part of the letter (5:12–8:13; cf. already 3:9), he personifies sin *(hamartia)* and death *(thanatos)* as tyrant powers which come, through Adam, to exercise lordship over human beings. He sets up in this way a quasi-drama in which believers are rescued from the tyranny of "Sin" and "Death," so as to come, through Christ, under the sway of "Grace" and "Righteousness," similarly personified. The personification lends a somewhat mythological tone to the entire discussion. But, in personifying sin, Paul in no way wishes to suggest that human beings become helpless tools of a power somehow separate from themselves. Sin for Paul represents a kind of deadly virus in human life, a fundamental revolt against the Creator that places self and the perceived needs of self in the position that should only be occupied by the sovereignty of God. Without denying individual responsibility, Paul's view of sin is "collective" in that it holds the sins of individuals to be manifestations of this force of radical selfishness that holds all human lives within its tyrannical grip. It is also collective in the sense that the prevalence or reign of sin is traced to the instrumentality of the single ancestor, Adam, whose original disobedience to the command of God (Gen 3:1-7) gave sin entrance into the human domain. From this foothold or beachhead it rapidly became the dominating factor in human existence.

Precisely how the legacy of sin was passed on from Adam to his descendants Paul does not explain. (The precision in this area brought by subsequent Christian theological and dogmatic explanations has no real basis in the text.) The picture would seem to be that Adam's act unleashed in the human milieu a force of selfishness that was waiting to burst out and take control. All subsequent human lives enter the "solidarity" of sinfulness thereby created—a solidarity which both precedes each one's moral history and works destructively upon it. As the final phrase *(. . . pantes hēmarton)* makes clear (on this clause, see below), "sin" throughout v 12 refers to responsible, personal sinning, whether on the part of Adam or his descendants. But Adam is more than just a timeless symbol "modeling" all subsequent human sinning. Adam does indeed "model" sin at its fundamental core but Paul's whole appeal to the figure of Adam as a foil to what he wishes to say about Christ would fall if there were not some causal link between the sinning of the patriarch, whom Paul of course believed to have been a real historical person, and that of subsequent human beings. By giving entrance to the tyranny of sin, Adam genuinely facilitated its subsequent dominance in human affairs. No one sins "apart from" Adam, no one sins entirely alone, and no one sins without in some sense adding to the collective sin-burden of the race. Paul conceives, therefore, of a solidarity in sin, over against which he will shortly set a (much more powerful) solidarity in grace.

Paul's principal concern, however, is not with the onset of sin but with what comes in sin's train, namely, death. As in the case of sin, Paul presents death as a tyrant power, whose "reign" over human beings is caused by sin. By "Death" Paul means physical death, simply assuming in this respect the biblical tradition (cf. Gen 3:17-19) that sees death as the punishment for sin. This "theological" view of death is alien to modern sensibility, where death is seen as simply the natural, inevitable term of human life. Paul's view is more "existential"; like the author of Wisdom (1:13-14; 2:23-24), he sees death as something which "ought not be," which is not part of the Creator's original design for human beings. He accepts the reality of physical death—even for believers—but holds that righteousness restores the destiny to eternal life that is the Creator's original intent (Rom 8:10-11; cf. Wis 1:13-15; 15:23). Righteousness draws from death the "sting" placed in it by sin—the sting that renders physical death the eternal "death" of endless separation from God (1 Cor 15:56). It is death in this more basic, final sense that Paul has in mind as the negative counterpart to the "(eternal) life" that is the gift of Christ (v 21; cf. v 17b; 18b).

The final clause of v 12 *(eph' hǭ pantes hēmarton)* presents the chief exegetical difficulty of the passage, a difficulty centering upon the precise interpretation of the connective phrase *eph' hǭ*. It is not within the scope of this commentary to review all the solutions proposed (for guidance to literature on this, see Note). Modern interpreters for the most part explain the phrase in a causal sense ("because all sinned," "inasmuch as all sinned")—though with some misgiving, since, had Paul wished to indicate a standard causal connection, there were simpler ways to say it (with *gar* or *dioti*, for instance). More importantly, the clause, so interpreted, seems to introduce an "overload of causality" in connection with the onset of death: death comes to all human beings as a consequence of Adam's sin (v 12b-c) but also as a consequence of their own responsible sinning (v 12d).

The phrase *eph' hǭ* is in fact best taken as an emphatic causal expression "for this very reason, namely that. . . ." (see Note). Paul employs it because he wants to place particular stress upon the nexus between sin and death, just as on the positive side he will place an equal stress upon the nexus between righteousness and (eternal) life (v 18; cf. 8:10c: *to de pneuma zōē dia dikaiosynēn*). Adam was responsible for the onset of death in the human race because, through his sin, he unleashed a regime of sin or "unrighteousness" in the world, which, becoming pervasive, attracted universally the penalty of death. But all this is said on the negative side simply to highlight the corresponding (and overwhelming) triumph of grace: Christ's righteous act has inaugurated a regime of righteousness in human lives, opening up for believers the prospect of eternal life. On both sides of the argument, negative and positive, the nexus (sin—death, on the one hand; righteousness—life, on the other) is crucial. It is this nexus (at least in its negative expression) which the connective phrase in v 12d serves to underline.

A "double causality" is operative, it is true, in the onset of death. But the two "causes" (Adam's sin and subsequent human sinning) are not separate but intimately connected. Adam's sin influences and pervades subsequent human sinning—just as on the positive side with respect to the gaining of life, Christ's supreme act of grace does not exclude human cooperation (8:1-4, 9-13)—though, once again, a satisfactory explanation of how grace can influence human cooperation without wholly determining it has proved elusive. The major focus in the passage rests upon the agency (causality) of the two figures of universal significance—Adam and Christ. But, on both sides of the equation, in a somewhat tensive way, Paul preserves the sense that the outcomes—death and life—are not simply automatic legacies from the two primary figures but flow from the contrasting "regimes" (sin or righteousness) that each set up in human affairs.

A clarification concerning the law (vv 13-14). The explanation that now interrupts a full formulation of the "Adam-Christ" comparison/contrast addresses a threat to the strict nexus between sin and death just maintained. The threat arises out of the fact that the law was not around during a particular epoch of human history, the time between Adam (considered to have been in a "law" situation in the sense of having received a direct command from God) and Moses, who received the law on behalf of Israel (v 13a). According to a traditional maxim sin is not "booked up (for punishment) in the absence of law" (v 13b). Paul concedes the maxim but insists that the presence or absence of law did not affect the universal "reign" of death as a punishment for sin; death "reigned" even over those whose sinning was not (like that of Adam) "under law" (v 14). So, the essential link between the onset of sin and the universal onset of death remains: death passed to all human beings on the basis of their reproduction of the sin of Adam, even if the pattern of sinning was not precisely the same in the case of those who did not sin "under law."

Once again (cf. especially 2:12), Paul is insisting that the presence or absence of law makes no fundamental difference. Death comes to "all" on the basis of the legacy of sin which all alike "inherit" from Adam. "There is no distinction" (cf. 3:22; 10:12) in this respect between those who have the law (Jews) and those who do not (Gentiles). Later (v 20a) Paul will explain what the role of the law was when eventually it arrived on the scene.

Adam and Christ—alike and unalike (vv 15-17). At the end of v 14, a pointed comment—Adam is a "type of the one to come" *(typos tou mellontos)*—prepares the way for a return to the central schema. Adam is a "type" of Christ in the sense that he is a figure of universal significance for the remainder of the race; his one act breathed an influence affecting the destiny of "many" (= "all"). In this respect—and in this respect alone—can one speak of a similarity between Adam and Christ. In every other respect they are unalike, and unalike in two respects in particular: 1. in *that which flowed from* their behavior (sin/death and righteousness/life, respectively); 2. in the *measure* of the influence they initiated (Christ vastly superior). It is the role of the sentences that follow (vv 15-17) to bring out this "unalikeness" with respect to Adam and Christ. Paul's concern is not to play down too strong a sense of similarity between the figures to which his presentation of Adam as "type" might possibly give rise. His object in this central section of the passage is to stir up the "logic" which will bring out the "superiority" of the Christ side when the time comes to formulate the full "Adam-Christ" comparison/contrast left incomplete at the end of v 12.

The section consists of two parallel "waves" (v 15; vv 16-17), similar in form and content. Each consists of a short, "thesis-like" introduction denying in some respect the similarity between the case of Adam and that of Christ (v 15a; v 16a). There follows in each instance a long conditional sentence, the first clause (protasis) beginning "For if . . ." *(ei gar . . .)* and stating the situation on the "Adam" side, the second (apodosis) beginning with the "much more" *(pollǭ mallon)* phrase that is the "spring" for the assertion of superiority on the "Christ" side. The only thing disturbing this pattern is the explanatory comment appearing in the second half of v 16.

In the first formulation (v 15) Paul simply contrasts Adam's "trespass" *(paraptōma)* with Christ's "gracious gift" *(charisma).* The term *charisma* has the sense here (cf. the *-ma* ending) of a concrete embodiment or effect of grace *(charis).* The act of Christ is a tangible, historical embodiment of God's grace. The following sentence (v 15b) underpins the contrast. The unique element of similarity is noted—the fact that in both cases "one" person's act has an effect upon "many." But, whereas on the "Adam" side there is simply the bald statement that the transgression of the one led to death for many, on the "Christ" side Paul formulates an expansive and extravagant statement of superiority ("much more" *[pollǭ mallon]*). Behind and together with the "gift in grace" (gracious act of self-sacrifice) of Christ comes an "overflow" *(eperisseusen)* of the grace of God. Adam was simply a human being whose one evil act had fatal repercussions for "many." Behind the act of Christ stood the overflowing power and generosity of the Creator.

Whereas the first "wave" (v 15) brought out the contrast in terms of what lay "behind" Christ's act (the grace of God), the second (vv 16-17) seems to focus more upon what it brought as a gift *(dōrēma)*—its effect in human life. The (formally somewhat intrusive) explanation making up v 16b prepares the way for this by presenting the contrast in terms of God's judgment *(krima, katakrima, dikaiōma).* The divine verdict *(krima)* that followed upon Adam's deed opened the way for "condemnation" *(katakrima)* for all. The "gracious gift" *(charisma),* the act of Christ, following upon "many transgressions" leads to an equally wide-ranging "acquittal" *(dikaiōma).* Paul's concise formulation (featuring a wordplay in the Greek upon the *-ma* ending of the four key terms) expresses the sublime paradox of the divine response. One might have expected that, if "one transgression" led to "condemnation," "many transgressions" would have led to condemnation on a universal scale. However, the divine response to the "mass of transgression" was not *katakrima,* but *charisma*—the gift of Christ, who "waded," as it were, into the strong, dark current of human sinfulness and, by giving his life for the "ungodly," (cf. 5:6, 8) converted "condemnation" *(katakrima)* into "justification" *(dikaiōma).*

The way then lies open for Paul to gather these various images together in the magnificent celebratory sentence (v 17) that supports this second and final "wave." Once again there are extravagant expressions of superiority on the positive side, with the contrast now set in terms of death and life. Over against the "reign" of death (cf. v 14b) brought about by "the trangression of the one" (Adam), Paul sets the "reign in life" of "those who receive the overflow of grace and gift of righteousness" that comes in Jesus Christ. Where death simply established its own reign as tyrant power, grace facilitates the reign of others—"those who receive it" *(lambanontes)*. This "reigning in life" is something that lies ahead (cf. the future tense *basileusousin*); the "life" in question is "eternal life" (cf. v 21b). What believers have now is the "overflowing gift" of righteousness (cf. 3:21-26; 5:1), which, on the principle that righteousness leads to life (8:10c), paves the way for full human entrance into the lordship of the universe according to the original design of the Creator (Gen 1:26-28; Ps 8:5-8; cf. Rom 4:13). In an artful ("inclusive") way, Paul ensures that the reference to the "dying" of the "many" at the beginning of the first wave (v 15b) is matched and totally "overwhelmed" by the "much more" certain prospect of the "reigning in life" at the close of the second. Physical death remains, it is true—the abiding legacy of Adam—but the gift of righteousness ensures that physical death is not co-terminous with eternal death; on the contrary, death is "swallowed up" (cf. 1 Cor 15:54-56) by the more powerful forces of life.

Adam and Christ: the comparison resumed (v 18). With the overwhelming superiority of the "Christ" side established (vv 15-17), Paul is now (v 18) in a position (cf. the introductory "Well then" *[ara oun]*) to allow the full expression of the comparison/contrast broken off at the end of v 12 to go ahead. The basis of the similarity remains the fact that in both cases "one" has an influence upon "all." The contrast lies in the differing effects: "condemnation" *(katakrima)* for all in the one instance, "justification leading to life" *(eis dikaiōsin zōēs)* in the other. "Condemnation" here is tantamount to death—so that the first half of v 18 basically recasts the statement of the "Adam" side originally given in v 12. On the "Christ" side, the phrase stating the effect upon "all" encapsulates the standard principle that has been operative throughout: "(eternal) life" (salvation) presupposes and flows from righteousness (1:16-17; 5:1-2; 8:10-11). So this second half of v 18 provides at last the wanting completion (apodosis) for v 12, setting the prospect of justification and life in Christ over against the legacy of sin and death stemming from Adam.

Contrasting effects of disobedience and obedience (v 19). The sentence that follows looks like a simple restatement of v 18 in terms of "obedience/disobedience." In fact, however, picking up the final phrase of v 18, it underpins (cf. *gar*) what has just been said in terms of "justification." Neither death ("condemnation") nor life, in either case, has flowed automatically. Each comes about because the respective figure of universal significance (Adam; Christ) has created either a negative *(hamartōloi katestathēsan)* or positive *(dikaioi katastathēsontai)* situation with respect to the righteousness required at the judgment.

The language of "disobedience/obedience" almost certainly stems from the narrative about Adam in Genesis 3. This does not, however, lessen the significance of Paul's allusion here to Christ's subjective disposition (obedience) in the face of death (cf. Phil 2:8: "obedient unto death, even the death of the cross"). Christ did not die as a passive victim of some higher requirement. He willingly accepted death as the cost of total human fidelity to God in an alienated and sinful world. His obedience consisted not so much in obeying a specific command as in embodying "unto death" the grace (*charisma* [v 15, v 16]) of the Father. His obedience in the face of death is the fine point of focus both of his union with the Father and his self-giving love for the human race (cf. 5:6-8; 14:15; 15:3; 1 Cor 8:11; 2 Cor 5:14; Gal 2:20; Phil 2:6-8). The obedience displayed in one human life gave expression to a divine love capable of overcoming and setting in reverse the whole destructive history of sin and selfishness from the beginning to the end of time.

The place of the law (v 20). At this point, a further statement about the law (v 20) interrupts the balanced formulation of the "Adam/Christ" schema. Mention of the law seems intrusive at first sight. For Paul, however, the law is never fully out of mind. It remains the principal threat to the inclusive, universalist account of the gospel. As earlier in the passage (vv 13-14), he acknowledges the appearance of the law but relativizes its significance, making it a factor of secondary importance in a situation where the really determining agents are those having universal significance, Adam and Christ. The law has a role, it is true. But it is a subordinate role, ranged on the negative side. Its function is to "multiply the transgression," that is, to increase and intensify the evil of human wrongdoing by rendering it an explicit infringement of the Creator's will. Under law, human sinning comes to resemble the sin of Adam, who deliberately disobeyed an explicit command of God (cf. v 14).

What Paul says here about the law has had some foreshadowing in similarly disparaging remarks thrown off earlier in the letter (3:20; 4:15). He is building up an impression of the law's nexus with sin (cf. also 6:14; 7:5) which will shortly (7:7-25) draw from him a more sustained and explicit analysis. In the present connection we may simply note that, following his coming to faith in Jesus as the Christ, Paul apparently came to view the law as given by God to a specific nation (Israel), not to inhibit sin but precisely to "multiply" it, to bring human evil to a point of intense concentration there where it might be effectively dealt with in the person of Israel's Messiah. This (admittedly offensive) view seems necessary to account for the added comment: "where sin increased, grace abounded all the more" (v 20b). "Where" sin increased—through the operation of the law—was Israel. But it was precisely also in Israel, in the person and work of Israel's Messiah, that God's "super-abundant" grace showed its capacity to prevail (cf. vv 15-17). It is only Paul's confidence in the abundance and superiority of God's grace that enables him to hold such a daring (and offensive) view on the negative side as regards the Jewish law.

The triumph of grace (v 21). This extravagant claim for grace clears the way for a triumphant final statement of the balanced schema (set within a purpose clause to underline the intention of God). On the negative side, Adam falls from view—Paul speaks simply of the "reign" of sin shown through the universal factor of death (cf. v 14). Over against this is the "reign" of grace, leading to "eternal life, through Jesus Christ our Lord." The succinct formulation gathers together all the key elements in the process: God's grace operative in Christ has created the righteousness that is the condition for eternal life. The fatal legacy of Adam has been outmatched by the prevailing power of grace. This is why there is hope.

By setting Christ over against Adam in this passage Paul ensures that the argument for hope contained in the gospel proceeds along truly universalist lines. In Adam, as first ancestor, is told the the "sin" story of the entire race—a story that leads to death. In Christ, as "Last Adam," is told the equally wide-ranging "grace" story, one that leads to the fullness of humanity intended by the Creator from the start. Both "stories" run in human lives and human society down to the end of time. Hope that, despite the evidence, life is winning out over death springs from the "much more" of grace, upon which Paul has been so insistent. A long sequence in 8:18-30, embracing also the material world ("creation"), will complete the account of this hope springing from the superiority of grace.

Notes

12. *Therefore:* The opening phrase *(dia touto)* suggests that what follows builds on what has gone before. How this is so is not immediately clear, since the two passages seem to present separate arguments for hope (with *dia touto* in v 12 sitting in parallel to *dikaiōthentes oun ek pisteōs* in 5:1). The causal connection is perhaps justified in the sense that, whereas 5:1-11 drew conclusions from simple references to the Christ-event, Paul now intends to draw out more precisely the implications of that event.

    entered the world: The parallel with (echo of?) the language and thought of Wis 2:23-24 is striking. Wisdom: "For God created human beings (lit. "man") for incorruption *(aphtharsia)* and made them (lit. "him") the image of his own eternal being (*eikona tēs idias aidiotētos;* cf. Rom 1:23), but through the devil's envy death entered into the world" *(thanatos eisēlthen eis ton kosmon;* Paul: *hē hamartia eis ton kosmon eisēlthen).*

through one man: The fact that Paul uses the more generic term *anthrōpos* gives grounds for a more gender-inclusive translation, "through one person." But since Paul clearly regards Adam as a historical individual, the "type" of the (equally historical) Jesus (v 14), it seems best, for the sake of the argument, to retain the more precise reference.

and so: This phrase safeguards the sense that death followed upon sin in subsequent generations exactly as it did in the case of Adam. Had Paul written *houtōs kai* rather than *kai houtōs*, it would be possible to regard v 12 as constituting a complex sentence complete in itself (as some interpreters maintain). But what Paul has actually written—*kai houtōs*—paves the way for the anacolouthon at the end of the verse.

death passed to all on this basis, namely, that all sinned: The translation understands the phrase *eph' hǭ* as a contract form of *epi toutǭ hoti* (the case of the relative pronoun being attracted to that of the unexpressed antecedent), the preposition *epi* with the dative expressing the sense of the grounds upon which a state of being, feeling, action or result is based; see BAGD 287 (II, b, γ). The usage is very similar to that in 2 Cor 5:4, where *eph' hǭ* indicates the grounds for the groaning of believers: they groan because they do not want to be "unclothed" (stripped of the mortal body) but to be "further clothed" (with the heavenly body). Likewise Phil 3:12 can be interpreted in this sense: "I press on to take hold of it (the "prize"—sharing in Christ's risen life; cf. v 11) *on the same basis (eph' hǭ)* as I also was taken hold of by Christ" (the basis being that of suffering [death] leading to life; cf. v 10 *[symmorphizomenos tǭ thanatǭ autou];* Rom 8:17d). The remaining Pauline usage, Phil 4:10, seems to be a case of a simple relative (as also the plural formulation *eph' hois* in Rom 6:21).

For a comprehensive critical review of the numerous alternative explanations given down the ages, see esp. Cranfield, 1.274–81; Fitzmyer 413–16; also *NTS* 39 (1993) 321–339, esp. 323–28. The "consecutive" interpretation of *eph' hǭ* ("with the result that all have sinned"), which Fitzmyer himself now proposes, for all the parallel instances adduced from ancient literature, makes little sense in the context: the nub of Paul's argument is that sin causes death, not vice versa.

In his classic formulation of the doctrine of "Original Sin" Augustine, following the Latin translation *in quo omnes peccaverunt,* found a reference to anticipatory sinning "in Adam" affecting all human beings prior to any personal history of sin. In the Greek, however, the allusion to Adam *(di' henos)* is too far removed to function as an antecedent for *eph' hǭ* understood as a relative. For a thorough historical survey of the theological issues involved, see again Fitzmyer *Romans* 408–10; cf. also Cranfield 1.274–79.

13. *Admittedly, sin is not booked up in the absence of law:* The interpretation takes this clause in a concessive sense. It enunciates a widely accepted principle according to which it is law which qualifies sin for punishment—that is, by indicating wrongdoing as an offense liable to punishment (cf. 4:15; 5:20a). The expression "not booked up" *(ouk ellogeitai)* is taken from the world of commerce, the verb being used in the sense of "charge to someone's account" for subsequent payment (cf. Phlm 18). Behind the usage here would seem to lie

the traditional apocalyptic idea where a person's merits or demerits respectively were entered into the "heavenly books" for subsequent reckoning (*1 Enoch* 104:7; *Jub.* 30:19-23; *T. Benj.* 11:4; 2 *Apoc. Bar.* 24:1).

14. *who is a type of the one to come:* The primary sense of *typos* is that of the impression left by something forcefully applied (e.g., a seal), then the form or outline of that which made the mark—thus "pattern," "model" (cf. 6:17). Here, as in 1 Cor 10:6, the word has the more technical biblical sense of "an event or person from the epoch-shaping beginning time (or the world or of Israel) which provides a pattern for the end time" (Dunn 1.277). "The one to come" must refer to Christ (not Moses, as has been suggested), since Paul needs at least an implicit allusion to Christ in order to introduce effectively the contrast to be promoted in vv 15-17.

15. *"As (was) the trespass . . . if through one man's trespass:* "Trespass" translates the Greek word *paraptōma,* which in itself does not have the same connotation of infringement of a positive command as does *parabasis,* used with respect to Adam's lapse in v 14. Paul's use of *paraptōma* from this point on in the passage (cf. also vv 15b, 16, 17, 18, 20) probably stems from the desire to set up repeated patterns of words ending with the Greek *-ma* suffix, which now becomes a rhetorical feature of the passage *(charisma; dōrēma; krima; katakrima; dikaiōma).* As a result, *paraptōma* in this context probably has much the same sense as *parabasis.*

many died: Paul is not referring simply to the death of those who have lived and died up to this point but to the onset of mortality in the human race as such; cf. 8:10; 1 Cor 15:22.

much more: On this expression *(pollǭ mallon),* see Note 5:9.

the grace of God and the gift in the grace of the one man Jesus Christ: The translation follows the Greek fairly literally to bring out the sense that Christ's "gift in grace" *(dōrea en chariti)* stands in parallel to "the grace of God." The "grace" that grasps believers in the Christ event is always the grace of God. At this point the contrast is not so much between Adam and Christ as between Adam and God active in Christ.

16. *For the judgment following that one trespass brought condemnation:* A wordplay in the Greek distinguishes between *krima* ("judgment" [here meaning the process, though it too can also mean the negative verdict]) and *katakrima* ("condemnation" [verdict]). The phrase is extremely concise and much has to be supplied in translation. The contrast with "following many trespasses" *(ek pollōn paraptōmatōn)* suggests that *ex henos* be taken as a neuter (referring to Adam's act) rather than as masculine (referring to Adam as sinner).

brings justification: Attraction to the *-ma* ending for rhetorical purposes (see Note on previous verse) leads Paul to use *dikaiōma* (which normally [see Note on 1:32] has the sense of "regulation, requirement" [1:32; 2:26; 8:4] or "righteous deed" [as in v 18; cf. Rev 19:8]) for "justification," instead of the more normal *dikaiōsis* (used a few sentences later in v 18; cf. also 4:25).

17. *those who accept:* Paul refrains from a strictly parallel formulation on the positive side in order to allow for the element of free human acceptance of grace contained in the participle *lambanontes*. This balances the sense of responsibility on the negative side contained in the "all sinned" in v 12d; see Lyonnet, *DBS* 7.559.

    the overflow of grace and the gift of righteousness: The order of the two "gift" words—*charis* and *dōrea*—reverses (chiastically) that in v 15. Here the "gift" is not just Christ but what Christ brings to believers—"righteousness" (3:21-26).

    reign in life: Paul may be alluding here to the apocalyptic motif of the "reign" of the just: cf. Dan 7:22, 27; Wis 3:8; 5:15-16; *1 Enoch* 96:1; (possibly) 1QM 12:14-16; cf. the sarcastic appeal to the same motif in 1 Cor 4:8.

18. *Well then, as . . ., so . . .:* The introductory phrase *ara oun* signals that the "superiority" of the "Christ" side is now sufficiently established (in vv 15-17) to allow the resumption of the main argument broken off at 12d (cf. 8:12; 9:16, 18; 14:12, 19). The conjunction *hōs* picks up the *hōsper* of v 12a and *houtōs kai* responds to the *kai houtōs* of 12c.

    as one man's trespass . . . one man's righteous act: The translation in each case sees in the Greek word *henos* a reference to the person (Adam or Christ), rather than to their respective acts; the latter reference is equally possible.

    a justification that brings life: The translation understands the phrase *dikaiōsin zōēs* as a qualitative genitive with a sense of purpose or result (BDF §166). The phrase sums up the fundamental principle that being found righteous at the judgment is the necessary condition for the gaining of life; cf. v 21b; 8:10 and the Interpretation of 1:17.

19. *many were made sinners:* The passive of the verb *kathistanai*, used here with reference both to sin and justification, need not express more than simply "become" (cf. BAGD 390). Nonetheless, Paul's choice of it here suggests that, while respecting the element of human freedom (v 12d, v 17), he does want to emphasize the influence of the "one" in each case.

    many will be made righteous: The future reference shows again Paul's sense of the "already/not yet" aspect of the eschatological justification for believers (cf. 2:13; Gal 5:5; contrast Rom 5:1). Until the judgment is finally given, believers have to live within and "live out" the favorable verdict they have already received so that it may be confirmed at the great eschatological assize (cf. 8:31-39). A sense of restriction in the use of "many" rather than "all" should not be pressed; the variation is probably simply stylistic here as throughout the passage: "all" (v 12); "many" (v 15); "all" (v 18); "many" (v 19). "Many" is probably an intentional echo of Isa 53:11-12 (cf. 4:25).

20. *The law came in:* The verb *pareisēlthon* has the tone of "slip in surreptiously"; cf. its use with respect to the spying of the "false brothers" in Gal 2:4 (the only other use in Paul).

    to multiply the trespass: Since the law was given only to Israel, the "multiplying" can hardly be understood in a spatial (worldwide) or numerical sense.

The "increase" of the law here seems best explained on the basis of a distinction Paul has already made (cf. 4:15; 5:13-14; cf. later 7:7-13) between sin in general and sin as "transgression" against a specific command (of the law); cf. also Gal 3:19. On Paul's sense of the law bringing sin to a point of intense concentration in Israel, see esp. N. T. Wright, *Climax of the Covenant* 38, 196–98, 242.

grace abounded all the more: Paul's extravagant term *hypereperisseusen* caps off the "overflow" language of the passage (cf. v 15, v 17). The "more" *(hyper)* of grace consists in the fact that it suppresses the "more" of sin; cf. 2 Cor 7:4 (Paul "abounding in joy").

21. *so that, as sin reigned in death:* The overall content of vv 12-14 suggests that the phrase "in death" *(en thanatǭ)* be taken in the sense that the (universal) prevalence of death is the visible manifestation and sign of the universal prevalence and power of sin.

grace also might reign through righteousness, leading to eternal life: On the causal link between righteousness (justification) and the destiny to eternal life, see Note on v 18 above. Earlier in the passage (cf. v 17b, v 18b) "life" *zōē* has in fact meant "eternal life." Paul now adds the epithet (cf. 2:7) to bring out the climactic overthrow of death; physical death remains as a lingering effect of sin but "eternal death" has been overthrown by the prospect of "eternal life" (cf. 8:10).

through Jesus Christ, our Lord: The ending has a festal character, suggesting that Paul may be citing or alluding to a liturgical formula (cf. 1:4; 4:25; 5:11).

For Reference and Further Study

Baudry, G.-H. "Le Péché originel dans les pseudépigraphes de l'Ancien Testament." *MScRel* 49 (1992) 163–92.

Brandenburger, E. *Adam und Christus: Exegetisch-religionsgeschichtliche Untersuchungen zu Röm 5:12-21 (1 Kor 15).* WMANT 7; Neukirchen: Neukirchener Verlag, 1962.

Byrne, B. "'. . . The Type of the One to Come' (Rom 5:14): Fate and Responsibility in Romans 5:12-21." *AusBR* 36 (1988) 19–30.

Cambier, J. "Péchés des hommes et péché d'Adam en Rom V.12." *NTS* 11 (1965–66) 217–55.

Davies, W. D. *Paul and Rabbinic Judaism* 31–57.

Dunn, J.D.G. *Christology in the Making.* Philadelphia: Westminster; London: SCM, 1980. Chap. IV: "The Last Adam" (98–128).

Fitzmyer, J. A. "The Consecutive Meaning of EPH' HO in Romans 5.12." *NTS* 39 (1993) 321–39.

Friedrich, G. "*Hamartia . . . ouk ellogeitai,* Rom. 5,13." *TLZ* 77 (1952) 523–28.

Giblin, C. H. "A Qualifying Parenthesis (Rom 5:13-14) and Its Context." *To Touch the Text* (FS J. A. Fitzmyer). Eds. M. P. Horgan and P. J. Kobelski. New York: Crossroad, 1989, 305–15

Hooker, M. D. *A Preface to Paul.* New York: Oxford University, 1979 [= *Pauline Pieces.* London: Epworth], 36–52.

Jüngel, E. "Das Gesetz zwischen Adam und Christus." *ZTK* 60 (1963) 42–74.

Kertelge, K. "Adam und Christus. Die Sünde Adams im Lichte der Erlösungstat Christi nach Röm 5, 12–21." *Anfänge der Christologie* (FS F. Hahn). Eds. C. Breytenbach and H. Paulsen. Göttingen: Vandenhoeck & Ruprecht, 1991, 141–53.

Kirby, J. T. "The Syntax of Romans 5:12: A Rhetorical Approach." *NTS* 33 (1987) 283–86.

Levison, J. R. *Portraits of Adam in Early Judaism.* JSPseudSup 1; Sheffield: JSOT Press, 1988.

Lyonnet, S. "Le Péché originel en Rom 5,12." *Biblica* 41 (1960) 325–55.

__________. Art. "Péché." *DBS* 7 (1966) 524–67.

Moore, G. F. *Judaism in the First Centuries of the Christian Era: The Age of the Tannaim.* 3 vols. Cambridge [Mass.]: Harvard University, 1927–30, 1.474–78.

Scroggs, R. *The Last Adam* 16–20, 32–38, 76–82.

Stone, M. E. *Fourth Ezra.* Hermeneia; Minneapolis: Fortress, 1990, "Excursus on Adam's Sin" (63–67).

Wedderburn, A.J.M. "The Theological Structure of Romans v 12." *NTS* 19 (1972–73) 339–54.

Wright, N. T. *Climax of the Covenant* Chapter 2: "Adam, Israel and the Messiah" (18–40).

iii. The Freedom to Live Out the Righteousness of God (6:1–8:13)

Introduction to 6:1–8:13. At this point in the letter Paul appears to put aside for a time the theme of hope to focus upon how believers ought behave. In many respects the section comprising 6:1–8:13 forms a kind of "ethical excursus." Certainly, it will always have great significance for any study of Paul's moral thinking. It is not really an "excursus," however, and while at times Paul adopts an exhortatory tone, exhortation is not his main purpose. This continues to be the celebration of the hope for salvation contained in the Christian gospel (1:16). Paul's chief endeavor here is to insist upon the freedom that believers have to "live out" the gift of righteousness they have received and so come to eternal life on the basis of that righteousness. Through Christ they have been radically snatched away from the power of sin; it is unthinkable to continue living under its sway (6:1-23). The fact that the law has been replaced as moral guide (by the Spirit) is not a problem. On the contrary, it is the solution! Where the law was impotent in the face of sin and actually became its accomplice (7:1-25), the Spirit creates the freedom that makes it possible to live out the new righteousness (8:1-13). It is this possibility—on the basis of the abiding principle: "life because of righteousness" (8:10c)—that opens up and preserves the prospect of eternal life. So the section as a whole, precisely in its "ethical" content, is part of Paul's wider argument for hope.

Introduction to Chapter 6. Paul establishes the freedom from sin in two more or less parallel sequences making up chapter 6. Each is launched by the rebuttal of a similar false inference (v 1; v 15). In the first, 6:1-14, the argument rests upon the believer's baptismal union with Christ; in the second, 6:15-23, the controlling image is that of a slave's transfer from the service of one master to another. Common to both sequences, is the personification, continuing from chapter 5, of Sin and Death, on the one hand, and Grace and Righteousness, on the other, as the "powers" that determine human existence.

a) *Dead to Sin/Alive to God in Christ* (6:1-14)

1. What shall we say then? Are we to continue in sin that grace may abound? 2. By no means! How can we who have died to sin still live in it?

3. Do you not know that inasmuch as we have been baptized into Christ Jesus we have been baptized into his death? 4. We were buried therefore with him through baptism into death, so that as Christ was raised from the dead by the glory of the Father, we too might walk in newness of life. 5. For if we have been conformed to the pattern of his death, we shall certainly be conformed to that of his resurrection. 6. We know that our old self was crucified with him to take away the body of sin, so that we might no longer be enslaved to sin. 7. For a person who has died is legally free from sin.

8. But if we have died with Christ, we believe that we shall also live with him. 9. For we know that Christ, once raised from the dead, no longer dies; death no longer rules over him. 10. The death he died, he died to sin, once for all, but the life he lives he lives to God. 11. So you also should reckon yourselves to be dead to sin but alive to God in Christ Jesus.

12. Let not sin therefore reign in your mortal body, to make you obey its desires. 13. and do not offer your members to sin as instruments of wickedness, but instead offer yourselves to God as people brought back to life from the dead, and your members to God as instruments of righteousness.

14. For sin will not have dominion over you, for you are not under law but under grace.

Interpretation

Introduction. The passage is not tightly structured. An opening "objection" (v 1) serves to launch the exhortation. V 2 states the overall theme in terms of being "dead" or "alive": having "died" to sin, it is no longer possible to "live" in it. V 11, in an inclusive way, restates this in more positive form ("dead to sin, alive to God"). In between, the body of the passage (vv 3-10) underpins both aspects of this theme with repeated statements of the same basic argument based upon believers' baptismal union with Christ. Vv 12-14 offer a short concluding exhortation, which also serves as a transition to what follows.

Grace does not mean freedom to sin (vv 1-2). Paul, as so often, gives new direction and impulse to his argument with an objection (v 1) followed by a vigorous rebuttal (v 2). The objection arises immediately out of the immense emphasis placed upon the power of God's grace, at the expense of sin, in the previous passage (esp. 5:20-21). The false inference that "we" should sin all the more in order to give God's grace greater scope, might at first sight appear to be the naive conclusion of a libertarian, gleefully anticipating a moral free-for-all. More likely, however, Paul throws up the charge he customarily receives from moral zealots, who claim that this is the kind of outrageous conclusion in ethical terms to which his stress upon grace at the expense of the law leads (cf. the "blasphemous" charge recorded in 3:8).

Paul's thematic response (v 2) is one of startling radicality. We have "died" to sin; we can therefore no longer "live" in it. The idea of having "died to sin" presupposes the continuance (5:12-21) of the idea of sin as a "power" tyrannizing the human race. The "death" we have died—which he is now about to explain—means that we have escaped once and for all from its tyranny; we no longer have to obey its commands, that is, continue to sin. Paul, of course, as a practical pastor, was not blind to the continuance of sin in the lives of believers. Beneath the stark "indicative" of his language, here and throughout the passage, lies an implicit "imperative"—what "ought" not be, what is totally inappropriate. He formulates here, as basic principle, the "fact" from which all Christian living ought to flow.

The baptismal death to sin (vv 3-4). Paul grounds (v 3) the statement that believers have died to sin by pointing to baptism as involving a participation in the death of Christ. For all the significance of this text in the history of sacramental theology, it is not Paul's aim at this point to provide an instruction on baptism. He makes a passing allusion, assuming the Christians of Rome to be as familiar with this rite of Christian initiation as the communities he has himself founded (cf. Gal 3:26-27; 1 Cor 10:2; 12:12-13; cf. 1:13-17).

What may come as a surprise to the Roman community—though this we cannot really tell—would be the particular implications Paul draws out from baptism in terms of the Christian's "death" to sin. Do they not know that being baptized "into" *(eis)* Christ Jesus means being baptized "into his death" *(eis ton thanaton autou)*? As in the parallel references to baptism in Gal 3:27-28 and 1 Cor 12:12-13, behind the expression here lies the characteristic Pauline idea of the risen Lord as personally constituting a sphere of influence or milieu of salvation "into" which believers are drawn through faith and baptism, henceforth to live "in Christ" (cf. v 11). Christ does not lose his individual personal identity but, nonetheless, as risen Lord and "life-giving Spirit" (1 Cor 15:45), he somehow "contains" within his person, in a communal sense, the messianic community destined for salvation. The present allusion to this truth goes beyond earlier presentations (Gal 3:27-28 and 1 Cor 12:12-13) in its suggestion that baptism involves not simply a being joined to Christ in a static "spatial" sense but also a dynamic insertion into what might be called his overall "career"—death, burial and risen life. It is this conformity to the "career" of Christ that lies at the heart of Paul's insistence, negatively, upon Christians' "death" to sin and, positively, their orientation towards a new, righteous life.

The following sentence (v 4) draws a preliminary conclusion. If baptism implies this involvement with Christ in his death, it must mean involvement in the rest of the process as well: his burial and risen life. "Burial" stresses the finality of the "death," the radical cut-off from preceding existence that death implies. It is expressed here in the first of a series of compound verbs with the *syn-* prefix *(synetaphēmen)* which are a feature of the way this passage portrays believers' intimate involvement with Christ's career (cf. v 5, v 6, v 8; also 8:17). But "burial" with Christ is only a stage on the way to arrival at the full term of that career: resurrection. Paul does not speak immediately of the risen glory of believers. Instead, he associates the raising of Christ "through the glory of the Father" with the divine intention (cf. *hina . . .*) that "we should walk *(peripatēsōmen)* in newness of life" *(en kainotēti zōēs)*. Within the biblical tradition "walking" refers to behavior in the sight of God. "Newness" *(kainotētēs)* points to the new creation (cf. 2 Cor 5:17; Gal 6:15; cf. Rom 12:2). There is an eschatological aspect to the "walking"—it flows from the risen life of Jesus and belongs essentially to the new age—but it is something which begins here and now. Though not yet wholly removed from the conditions of the present, passing age (suffering, temptation, death), believers are summoned and empowered to live out the righteousness appropriate for the new. For Paul, it is precisely the hope of one day sharing fully the risen life of the Lord that sheds worth and dignity upon present life in the body (cf. esp. 1 Cor 6:13-14) and motivates the desire to live out God's gift of righteousness.

Conformity to Christ in death and risen life (vv 5-10). What Paul seeks to communicate from this point on (vv 5-10) is part exhortation, part an expression of hope to bolster the appeal of the exhortation. The argument comes in two "waves," each beginning with a conditional sentence (v 5, v 8) expressing the reality of the hope and each supported by appeal to what we "know" to be the case (our radical removal from the "body of sin" [vv 6-7]; Christ's irreversible escape from the the clutches of death [vv 9-10]).

The argument pivots around believers' "conformity" to the pattern of Christ's death, which has brought about release from the tyranny of sin. This has created a whole new possibility. If (v 5) we have really been "conformed to the pattern" of Christ's death, that is, if we have really "died" to sin as he has died to it (cf. v 10), we can hope for a similar "conformity" to his resurrection. The language is striking and fresh but by the same token somewhat elusive (for details, see Notes). The use of "pattern" (*homoiōma;* cf. 1:23; 5:14; 8:3) allows for the fact that believers obviously do not share in Christ's historical, physical death upon the cross. What they "conform to" is the ethical "pattern" expressed in Christ's death to sin (cf. v 6), his self-giving love (Rom 15:3) and obedience (5:19; cf. Phil 2:8). Believers will be "conformed" to Christ's risen life because being "dead to sin" means being empowered to live out the gift of righteousness that is the condition of obtaining it.

The crucifixion of the "old self" (vv 6-7). The statements in vv 6-7 underwrite this hope by stressing the reality of the transformation that has (ought to have) occurred. Paul refers to the former existence as that of "old self" who has been "concrucified" *(synestaurōthē)* with Christ. The phrase "old self" (more literally, "old man" *[palaios . . . anthrōpos]*) points to existence in the old aeon, dominated by the baleful influence of Adam (whose name, of course, in Hebrew simply means "the man"). "Concrucifixion" with Christ (cf. Gal 2:19c) has removed the essential "attachment" to sin, expressed in the phrase "body of sin" *(to sōma tēs hamartias).* Paul does not mean to locate human sinfulness principally in the physical body. "Body" *(sōma)* has here its distinctive Pauline nuance in which, beyond referring to the body in a simply physical sense (as, e.g, in Gal 6:17), it denotes the total person under the aspect of capacity for communication; in this wider sense *sōma* is that by which one is "attached to" or "in touch with" the world of persons and events, both to give and receive impressions. By "body of sin," then, Paul has in mind the whole complex of involvement with that world "under" sin (cf. 3:9), initiated and symbolized by Adam (5:12). For believers, the "concrucifixion" involved in the baptismal union with Christ has radically severed their "attachment" to that world (cf. later 7:4). It has put an end once and for all to their slavery to sin *(tou mēketi douleuein . . . tę̄ hamartią),* the tyrant overlord of the old era. To underline the sense of removal, Paul throws in (v 7) what would appear to be a known axiom enshrining the principle that death releases (literally, "acquits" *[dikaioun]*) a person from the guilt of sin.

The destiny to share Christ's risen life (vv 8-10). The second "wave" (vv 8-10) essentially follows the same pattern, with the opening conditional sentence (v 8) giving again an assurance of hope. Involvement with Christ's death *(apethanomen syn Christǭ)* necessarily implies involvement also with the "end" of his "career": resurrection. Interestingly, Paul speaks of this as a matter of faith: "we believe *(pisteuomen)* that we shall also live with him" *(syzēsomen autǭ)*. On a wider view, this is not altogether unexpected when we consider how he has already insisted on the parity between Christian faith and that of Abraham, who also had to put his faith in a "God who raises the dead" (4:17b). Christian faith looks "back" to the raising of Jesus (4:24) and "forward" to a more general resurrection of which it is the pledge (cf. Rom 8:11; 1 Cor 6:14; 15:12-28; 2 Cor 4:14; 1 Thess 4:14). As in the case of Abraham (Rom 4:18-22), hope is continuous with faith.

In support of this argument for hope, Paul again appeals (vv 9-10) to what Christians "know" (*eidotes*; cf. v 6), concentrating this time more exclusively on the "career" of Christ, before the more general application that comes in v 11. The force of the appeal lies in the "no longer's" *(ouketi* twice) in the first sentence (v 9) and the "once and for all" *(ephapax)* in the second (v 10). Christ's resurrection from the dead signaled the end of what was initiated by Adam (5:12): the lordship of sin and death over the human race. As far as Christ is concerned, death no longer "rules" (*kyreuein*; cf. 14:9); the grip of sin has been shattered by his irrevocable "death to sin" (v 10a). Paul does not mean, of course, that Christ "died to sin" in the sense that all other human beings "die" to it. Sinless as he was (cf. 2 Cor 5:21), Christ never came personally under its sway. He died because he took upon himself the sins of others (4:25; 15:3; cf. Isa 53:11-12) and bore this burden of sin unto death, effecting thereby a more general "death to sin." But, once risen from the dead, any connection with sin, even in this innocent, sin-bearing sense, has come to an end. Instead, his whole existence can now be summed up as a "living to God" *(zę̄ tǭ theǭ)*.

This simple phrase, "living to God," essentially describes the life of the new age, where, set free from all other "lordships" (sin, death, [law; cf. Gal 2:19]), one lives in total openness and surrender to God, acknowledging the sole claim and sovereignty of the Creator. Such an attitude, anticipated already in the obedience and fidelity of Christ's earthly life (5:19; cf. Phil 2:8), continues in his risen existence as well. It is the basis of the lordship of the universe which Christ exercises at the appointment of the Father (cf. esp. Phil 2:11 [". . . Jesus Christ is Lord to the glory of God the Father"]; 1 Cor 15:24, 28; Rom 1:3-4). "Living to God" in this way, the

"Last Adam" (1 Cor 15:45) successfully "models" the true pattern of human existence in relation to God, which the first Adam betrayed. He thereby facilitates human entrance into the "inheritance of the earth" (Rom 4:13), according to the original plan of God (Gen 1:26-28; Ps 8:5-8; cf. 1 Cor 3:21b-23; Rom 5:17).

Dead to sin, living to God (v 11). Rounding off this sequence based upon "death to sin," Paul summons believers to adopt the attitude that responds to this new situation. As Christ is "dead to sin" and now "lives to God," the same mindset must characterize those who share his new existence, those who are "in Christ Jesus" *(en Christǭ Iēsou).* As noted in connection with v 3 above, this phrase represents Paul's most characteristic way of denoting the life of the believers "within" the risen Lord as all-encompassing "sphere" or "milieu" of salvation. Since Christian life is encompassed totally "within" Christ in this way, the "no longer" and the "once and for all" aspect of his personal existence and "career" apply—or ought apply—equally to them. They can no longer live "in" (the power of) sin because they live "in (the sphere and power of) Christ Jesus" (v 11). Though they do not yet enjoy full bodily conformity to the risen life of Christ, though they "await" in this sense "the redemption of their bodies" (8:23), they are to "reckon" *(logizesthe)* themselves as "dead to sin" and "alive to God in Christ Jesus."

There is no element of self-deception or pretense in this "reckoning" (cf. 3:28; 8:18). It is part of the vision of faith—a sober recognition that here and now, through their union with Christ, believers "walk" in the new age (v 4). It is not so much a matter of imitating Christ or even of simply allowing their lives to be "conformed" to the pattern of his (cf. v 5). At base, it is a matter of allowing the attitude or "mind" of Christ, an obedient "living to God" characteristic of both his earthly and risen life, to "well up" within them because of their existence "in Christ" (cf. Phil 2:5). They are called, in short, to allow the risen Lord to live out his continuing obedience to the Father in them as in his own extended person or "body" (*sōma;* cf. 1 Cor 12:12-13). This is the heart of Paul's ethic for the new era of grace.

Exhortation: Making one's body an instrument of righteousness (vv 12-13). There follows a brief conclusion more explicitly exhortatory in tone. It comes in the form of a neatly balanced couplet: two lines of negative warning followed by two lines of positive exhortation. Central to the whole is the continuing sense of human existence as lived under lordship—whether to Sin, as tyrant power, or to God. What believers can place at the disposal of one or other of these allegiances is their present, physical existence, described in the first instance (v 12) as their "mortal body" *(thnēton sōma)* and then (v 13) their "members" *(melē).* "Body," as noted above in connection with v 6, denotes the physical human body under the aspect of vehicle of communication. "Members" adds the nuance of the body's capacity for all kinds of specific action. Taken together, both phrases denote human life in the body in all aspects under which individuals have the capacity to interact, for good or ill, upon the outside world of persons and events.

Negatively, Paul warns (v 12) against allowing sin to establish its "reign" in this sphere. The result will be "obedience" *(hypakouein)* to its "desires" *(epithymiais)*—that is, a life enslaved to the lower passions that were the sign of God's wrath upon the Gentile world (1:24). Nor (v 13a) are believers to place the more specific aspects of their bodily existence (their "members" [*melē*]) at the disposal of the tyrant power, sin, to become "instruments of wickedness" *(hopla adikias)*, furthering its dominance in the world.

Just as life in the body can be instrumental in promoting wickedness, so, insists Paul in the corresponding positive couplet (v 13bc), it can enlisted for the service of God as well. Believers are to "offer" themselves to God "as *(hōsei)* people brought back to life from the dead," that is, as those who have really "died to sin" and now "live (solely) to God" (v 11). Again, there is no measure of pretense in the "as". Fundamentally, believers are people of the resurrection, even if bodily still confined to the present age. Their "living to God" in union with Christ enables their present life in the body to provide "instruments of righteousness for God" *(hopla dikaiosynēs tǭ theǭ)*.

"Righteousness" here has a marked ethical nuance. Yet there is no reason for doubting a firm measure of continuity with the way "righteousness" has functioned in earlier sections of the letter. Just as Christ in his bodily existence has been the supreme instrument of God's saving righteousness in the world (3:21-26), so those who share his risen life through their existence "in" him (v 11) are urged to enlist all aspects of their life in the body in the cause of the same divine righteousness (cf. 2 Cor 5:21 where Paul states that "in Christ" believers "become" the righteousness of God).

The vision of life in the body here is fundamentally positive, even though negative possibilities also remain. Sin has left an irrevocable mark upon the body in terms of its physical destiny to death (5:12; 6:12; cf. 8:10b)—the abiding legacy of Adam. But God's gift of a New Adam has ensured that human life in the body is not simply mortal nor entirely given over to the power of sin. "In Christ" the body is destined for resurrection (6:5, 8), it exists "for the Lord" (1 Cor 6:13) and this destiny and lordship transforms the possibilities of present bodily existence. The bodies of believers, even as the body of their Lord, can and ought be made available as "instruments of (saving) righteousness for God."

Sin no longer rules (v 14). The section as a whole began with the question, "Are we to remain in sin that grace may abound?" (v 1). Paul has developed his definitive "No" to this (v 2) on the basis that "in Christ" sin's reign as tyrant power has been radically broken. Provocatively, however, a concluding comment throws in a fresh reason (cf. *gar*). The reason that sin will not rule *(ou kyrieusei)* is because believers (literally, "you") are not "under law" but "under grace." Originally (v 1), it was being "under grace" that (falsely in Paul's eyes) raised the problem. Now (v 14b), being under grace is the reason that "sin will not rule." What seemed to be the problem has become the solution. A fresh (and for Paul, genuine) source of problem is indicated: the law.

At this point Paul might well have embarked upon the specific treatment of the law that comes later in chapter 7. Instead, he leaves this disparaging comment about the law as a kind of throw-away line and, in a somewhat parallel sequence (vv 15-23), presents a new case for righteous living in an era of grace.

NOTES

1. *What shall we say then?:* On Paul's use of this phrase *(ti oun eroumen),* see Note on 4:1.

   Are we to continue in sin . . .?: The verb *epimenein* has here the figurative sense of "persist in," "remain (stubbornly) in."

2. *we who have died to sin:* Paul uses the complex anticipatory relative, *hoitines . . .*, to lend more stress to what is to constitute the rebuttal: the fact (cf. the aorist *apethanon*) that "we" have died.

3. *Do you not know . . .?:* The question *(ē agnoeite)* could be intended to remind the Roman Christians of what Paul believes they *already* know, or (cf. 7:1) it could signal that he is about to suggest that something with which they are already familiar (baptism) has a deeper or extended meaning: namely, that it involves a "death."

   into Christ Jesus we have been baptized into his death?: The parallels provided by 1 Cor 12:13; Gal 3:27, where there is an implicit sense of Christ as all-embracing corporate person, strongly suggest that Paul intends the Greek preposition *eis* to retain here its basically directional, spatial sense. Note how, after the introductory phrase, the remainder of v 3 forms a chiasm in Greek: *ebaptisthēmen—eis Christon Iēsoun—eis ton thanaton autou—ebaptisthēmen.*

4. *We were buried therefore with him through baptism into death:* The translation takes the final phrase, "into death," with the verb rather than with "through baptism." The chief concern at this point is not to elaborate upon Christian baptism but to show that being a believer involves having "died" (cf. v 1). The allusion to "burial" is almost certainly influenced by the early credal formula cited in 1 Cor 15:3b-5, which mentions that Christ "died. . . . and was

buried," preliminary to being raised and appearing. At the same time, baptism through immersion (the primary meaning of the Greek verb *baptizein* is "to immerse") has an obvious association with burial.

by the glory of the Father: The translation takes the preposition *dia* instrumentally, so that *doxa* is virtually equivalent to the power of God, a sense which it frequently has in the LXX. On the other hand, the way Paul uses "glory" in other contexts (see Note on 3:23) also makes it possible to understand the prepositional phrase as indicating "attendant circumstances": the glory attendant upon Christ's resurrection or, more precisely, the glory or likeness to God, *into* which he rose as Last Adam.

walk in newness of life: For examples of the biblical usage of "walk" (Hebrew: *hālak*) to indicate conduct in God's sight, see Exod 16:4; 18:20; Deut 8:6; 13:5; 2 Kgs 20:3; Prov 8:20; etc.; cf. also Rom 8:4; 13:13; 14:15. For "newness" *(kainotētēs)* with reference to the conditions of the new age, cf. 7:6.

5. *For if we have been conformed to the pattern of his death:* Paul uses the perfect *(gegonamen)* to convey the sense of a sustained growth. The adjective translated "conformed" (*symphytos*, from *symphyein*; cf. Luke 8:7]) means literally "grown together with" or "knit together with" (as skin knits together in the healing of a wound). The translation associates *symphytos* directly with *homoiōmati tou thanatou autou*: believers are associated with the "pattern" of Christ's death. The basic sense of *homoiōma* in biblical literature is that of "likeness." But to do full justice to both the biblical and extrabiblical evidence we have to reckon with two ways in which this is expressed: 1. the copy, image or likeness of something (whether the copy be a perfect reproduction of the original or merely resemble it in some way); 2. the concrete form or pattern in which a reality (sometimes a transcendent reality) manifests itself. The occurrences of *homoiōma* in Rom 1:23 and 5:14 seem to be instances of the first sense, without the suggestion that the resemblance is close. In 6:5, 8:3 and Phil 2:7 the issue is more open. Understanding the *homoiōma* of Christ's death in the second sense in Rom 6:5 has led some to find a reference to baptism here, in the sense that baptism is the sacramental form in which the physical, historical death of Christ upon the cross is reproduced. Allusion to baptism, however, would seem to be ruled out by the implied second reference to *homoiōma* with respect to the resurrection in the second half of the sentence. The interpretation argued for in the text takes the word in a somewhat weak form of the second sense: believers are conformed to the "pattern" or "shape" that Christ's death took—the way in which it was an expression of death to sin, of self-giving love and obedience.

we shall certainly be conformed to that of his resurrection: The genuinely eschatological reference of the future tense here is guaranteed by the parallel provided in v 8, where the hope of resurrection is an object of present belief.

6. *our old self:* The "oldness" is the negative counterpart in the passing evil age to the "newness" *(kainotētēs)* of the new eschatological era (cf. v 4); cf. 1 Cor 5:7-8. Col 3:9 and Eph 4:22 echo Paul's "old self (man)" language here with respect to the former "Adamic" existence under sin.

was crucified with him: This expression *(synestaurōthē),* together with the later references to "living to God" (vv 10-11), forges a strong link between the present passage and Paul's account of his own radical break with the past in Gal 2:19-20.

the body of sin: The genitive is not simply adjectival (= "sinful body") but qualitative in the sense of "body controlled by sin" (= human existence in the ambience totally ruled by sin); cf. 7:24: *sōma tou thanatou.* For the distinctive Pauline sense of "body" *(sōma)* as vehicle of communication, see esp. E. Käsemann, "The Pauline Doctrine of the Last Supper." *Essays on New Testament Themes* 103–35, esp. p. 129; B. Byrne, "Sinning Against One's Own Body" 610–12.

7. *For a person who has died is legally free from sin:* Taken by itself, this statement can be understood in a fully "Pauline" sense, to the effect that a person who has died (with Christ) is justified from (the guilt of) sin. But in the present context the issue is not justification from the *guilt* of sin but liberation from its power and control (cf. vv 1-2). The maxim (contemporary parallels to which are not all that easy to find) uses the verb *dikaioun* in its most basic sense of "acquit" in a way that hardly reflects the normal Pauline usage. The temptation to regard the statement as a gloss must be resisted, since the reference to "died" in v 8 clearly follows on from that in v 7.

8. *we believe that we shall also live with him:* For a similar "definition" of the content of belief in terms of resurrection, cf. 2 Cor 4:13-14: "Since we have the same spirit of faith as the one who wrote, 'I believed, therefore I spoke,' we too believe, and so we speak, knowing that the One who raised the Lord Jesus from the dead will raise us also with Jesus (*syn Iēsou*; cf. *syzēsomen*) and bring us with you into his presence"; cf. 1 Cor 15:16-17.

9. *death no longer rules over him:* "Rules" *(kyrieuei)* is synonymous with the "reign" of death in 5:14, 17. In 1 Cor 15:25-26, in connection with the resurrection of the dead, Paul speaks of the risen Christ "reigning" until all the opposing "powers" have been subdued, the last of which will be death. Instead, then, of being "ruled" by death, the "Last Adam" (v 45) is destroying the rule of death initiated by the first Adam.

10. *lives to God:* The understanding of this phrase given in the Interpretation largely follows that of W. Thüsing, *Per Christum* 67–101.

11. *reckon yourselves:* "Reckoning" for Paul (cf. 3:28; 8:18; 14:14) does not mean merely abstract consideration but a firm judgment with practical consequences.

    in Christ Jesus: To see something truly "local" in Paul's use of this expression need not imply an understanding that is crudely material or "mystical" or "sacramentally-(over) realistic" (cf. the hesitations of Cranfield, 1.315–16). Paul's usage is a metaphor to express a communal living in the sphere of influence of the risen Lord. Virtually synonymous are the expressions "in the Lord," "in the Spirit" (contrast "in the law," "in the flesh"). For an excellent summary, see Ziesler 162–64.

12. *obey its desires:* On the predominantly negative meaning of "desire" *(epithymia)* in Paul, see Note on 7:8. A shorter alternative reading—"obey *it*" (that is, Sin)—has early attestation (P^{46}—also D, G, Irenaeus, Tertullian) but adds little to what is already contained in the sense of sin's "rule."

13. *your members:* The word *melos* basically means "limb" but came to be used more widely with reference to any organ of the body. The sense of its use in the plural here is probably wider still, embracing all the individual acts and services of which the human person, as *body*, is capable; cf. the usage later in 6:19; 7:7, 23 (all with reference to behavior).

    instruments of wickedness. . . . instruments of righteousness: The word *hoplon* (always used in the plural by Paul) could mean simply "instrument," "tool" or else have the more specifically military sense of "weapon." Wider Pauline usage (Rom 13:12; 2 Cor 6:7; 10:4) tells in favor of the latter but the following context (to which this passage is transitional), with its extended image of the service of a slave, argues for the more general sense. As elsewhere in the letter (3:5; cf. also 1:18, 29; 2:8; 9:14) "wickedness" *(adikia)* forms the negative counterpart to "righteousness" *(dikaiosynē)*.

    as people brought back to life from the dead: The expression *hōsei*, not elsewhere used by Paul, has about it more of the sense of "as if," "as though," than the simple *hōs*. But this does not necessarily imply an element of pretense. The expression safeguards the "eschatological reserve"—believers are not yet literally raised from the dead, though they should live as though they were.

14. *For sin will not have dominion over you:* Literally: "will not rule" *(ou kyrieusei)*. With reference to the present life of believers, this may appear overconfident. But the use of the future is not strictly eschatological, on the one hand, nor merely logical or exhortative, on the other. The reference is to the ongoing life of believers here and now in the "overlap" situation: in contrast to the old situation, where they really *had* to submit to sin's rule, now and henceforth they are free ("in Christ") not to do so.

    for you are not under law but under grace: Being "under the law" *(hypo nomon)* characterizes Jewish existence for Paul (1 Cor 9:20; Gal 3:23; 4:4 [of Christ's life as a Jew]). The statement implies—very "offensively" in a Jewish context—that life under the law facilitates the "rule" of sin. Paul will address this issue explicitly in 7:7-25. Already, however, with statements such as this, he is maneuvering "life under the law" into the position where it will function as a negative foil against which to exalt the "life in the Spirit" proclaimed in the gospel.

For Reference and Further Study

Beker, J. C. *Paul the Apostle* 272–78, 287–91.

Byrne, B. "Living out the Righteousness of God: The Contribution of Rom 6:1–8:13 to an Understanding of Paul's Ethical Presuppositions." *CBQ* 43 (1981) 557–81.

du Toit, A.B. "*Dikaiosynē* in Röm 6. Beobachtungen zur ethischen Dimension der paulinischen Gerechtigkeitsauffassung." *ZTK* 76 (1979) 261–291.

Eckert, J. "Die Taufe und das neue Leben. Röm 6,1-11 im Kontext der paulinischen Theologie." *MTZ* 38 (1987) 203–22.

Furnish, V. P. *Theology and Ethics in Paul* 171–77.

Kaye, B. N. *The Thought Structure of Romans with Special Reference to Chapter 6.* Austin: Scholars Press, 1979.

Morgan, F.A. "Romans 6,5a: United to a Death like Christ's." *ETL* 59 (1983) 267–302

Schnackenburg, R. "Die Adam-Christus-Typologie (Röm 5:12-21) als Voraussetzung für das Taufverständnis in Röm 6:1-14." *Battesimo e giustizia in Rom 6 e 8.* Ed. L. De Lorenzi. Rome: Abbayia S. Paolo, 1974, 37–55.

Schweizer, E. "Dying and Rising with Christ." *NTS* 14 (1967–68) 1–14.

Siber, P. *Mit Christus Leben: Eine Studie zur paulinischen Auferstehungshoffnung.* ATANT 61; Zürich: Theologisicher Verlag, 1971, 191–249.

Tannehill, R. C. *Dying and Rising with Christ: A Study of Pauline Theology.* BZNW 32; Berlin: Töpelmann, 1967, 7–43.

Thüsing, W. *Per Christum* 67–101.

Vanni, U. "*Homoiōma* in Paolo (Rom 1,23; 5,14; 6,5; 8,2; Fil 2,7): Un' interpretazione esegetico-teologica alla luce dell' uso dei LXX." *Gregorianum* 58 (1977) 321–45, 431–70, esp. 445–54.

Wedderburn, A.J.M., *Baptism and Resurrection: Studies in Pauline Theology against Its Graeco-Roman Background.* WUNT 44; Tübingen: Mohr, 1987, 37–69

On existence "in Christ" according to Paul.

Best, E. *One Body in Christ.* London: SPCK, 1955.

Moule, C.F.D. *The Origin of Christology.* Cambridge: Cambridge University, 1977, 54–89.

Neugebauer, F. *In Christus: Eine Untersuchung zum paulinischen Glaubensverständnis.* Göttingen: Vandenhoeck & Ruprecht, 1961.

Wedderburn, A.J.M. "Some Observations on Paul's Use of the Phrases 'in Christ' and 'with Christ.'" *JSNT* 25 (1985) 83–97.

Ziesler, J. *Pauline Christianity* 49–52.

b) *The New Obedience* (6:15-23)

15. What then? Shall we continue in sin since we are not under law but under grace? By no means!

16. Do you not know that when you place yourselves in a situation of slavery with its implied obedience, you become slaves of the one to whom you have made yourselves obedient—whether of sin, which leads to death, or of real obedience, which leads to righteousness.

17. Thanks be to God—because you were once slaves to sin, but you have given obedience from the heart to the pattern of teaching to which you were handed over 18. and, set free from sin, you have become slaves of righteousness. 19. I use an example from human life to help you in your human weakness to understand.

For as once you offered your members as slaves to uncleanness and lawlessness, with ever more lawlessness the result, so now offer your members as slaves to righteousness so that holiness may be the result.

20. For when you were slaves of sin you were quite free as far as righteousness was concerned. 21. And what was the fruit you then had from that? Surely, things of which you are now ashamed—for their outcome is death.

22. But now, set free from sin and having become instead slaves of God, the fruit you get leads to holiness and the outcome of that is eternal life. 23. For the wages of sin is death, whereas the gracious gift of God is eternal life in Christ Jesus our Lord.

Interpretation

Introduction. The controlling image throughout this section is that of slavery. More precisely, the argument revolves around the sense of what happens when slaves transfer from one master to another. Paul continues the personification of the key factors at work—"sin" and "righteousness"—but now portrays them not so much as tyrant powers but as slave masters to whom one owes obedience.

Whether asking one's audience to picture themselves in the situation of slaves would have been any more congenial to Paul's original hearers than it is to the modern reader is hard to tell (at one point [v 19a] Paul does seem to acknowledge the difficulty). Certainly, the image would have been very familiar, since perhaps two-thirds of any community of believers consisted either of slaves or "freedmen" (former slaves who had gained their liberty). Slavery was an accepted social institution of the ancient world. While it did not necessarily imply maltreatment and some people sold themselves voluntarily into slavery for economic benefit, it was—understandably—viewed as an inferior and undesirable status; the ideal remained the freedom enjoyed by the full citizen, which is the view Paul assumes elsewhere in his letters when he pictures Christian conversion as a break-through from slavery to freedom (Gal 4:1-11; 4:21–5:1; 5:13; Rom 8:1-2, 15, 21; cf. 2 Cor 3:17). Here, however, he wants to insist that life "under grace" is still a life of "obedience" and, to that end, takes up this image, confident in its power both to evoke a response from the audience and portray the new situation as immeasurably superior to the old.

The section begins in a way parallel to the preceding one—with a false inference followed by a vigorous rebuttal (v 15). The complex sentence making up v 16 formulates the guiding image and principle (all slavery implies an "obedience"). The argument then follows in a series of repeated contrasts between the past (pre-conversion) and present (post-conversion) situation of believers. In the second part of the sequence—after the aside in v 19a—Paul argues more from the perspective of the outcome ("fruit") that follows from the past and present servitude respectively. As in the preceding section (6:1-14), the discourse flows back and forth from "indicative" (past and present state of affairs) to "imperative" (consequences for present living).

Grace does not mean freedom to sin (v 15). The (false) suggestion with which the passage begins is the same as before (v 1): "Shall we continue in sin?" But the reason is different: "we are no longer under law." Without the law to give specific instructions and—perhaps more significantly—to threaten punishment for wrongdoing, can one not do evil and get away with it? Once again, the objection probably does not come from a real dialogue partner of libertarian views. More likely, Paul confronts the fear his law-free presentation of the gospel arouses in those who see in the Jewish law the only safeguard of righteous living. His eventual response (7:1-25) will be *"Au contraire!"*—removal from the law is not the problem but the solution (cf. already v 14b). But for the present he develops the sense that grace equally—and far more effectively—entails an "obedience."

All slavery involves obedience (v 16). The response proper begins with a complex and contracted sentence that introduces both the controlling image (slavery) and the principle which it illustrates: all slavery involves obedience to a master; if one places oneself in a situation of slavery, no matter who the master is, one is simply the slave of that master and must render obedience. Then, as is often his habit (cf., e.g., 4:4-5), in the same breath (v 16b) Paul moves out of the image to address the situation to which it presently applies: one is either in a situation of slavery to sin, which leads to death, or in the service of (true) obedience, which leads to righteousness. There is no other possibility. Though they may delude themselves that they are free (cf. 1:21-23), those who are not obedient to righteousness are in fact slaves obedient to sin—an obedience which will render physical death the death of eternal separation from God.

Past and present contrasted (vv 17-18). An exclamation of gratitude to God (cf. 7:25a) begins the expansion or application of this principle with respect to the past and present of believers, the antithesis which runs throughout the entire sequence from this point on. The image of "obedience under slavery" continues but with the more specific nuance of what happens when a slave loses one master and gains another. Believers must thank God because the transfer in their case has been so fortunate. The

Roman (Gentile) Christians, who were "slaves of sin" *(douloi tēs hamartias)*, have been set free from this slavery to enter upon a new "slavery" to "righteousness" *(edoulōthēte tę̄ dikaiosynę̄)*.

As in vv 12-14, Paul ranges "righteousness" *(dikaiosynē)* as the key player on the positive side." The fact that later, in v 22, he can speak equally of a "slavery to God" shows that "righteousness" and "God" are more or less interchangeable here (cf. v 13). This in turn suggests that "righteousness," although used here in a clearly ethical sense, is still basically the "righteousness of God" first mentioned in the thematic statement of 1:17, reiterated in 3:21-26. For believers, to be "slaves of righteousness" means not only entrusting their hopes for salvation to the righteousness that comes as God's gift in Christ (3:21-26; 5:15-17) but also surrendering their lives to the obedience that that gift entails if it is to be preserved until the day of judgment. Believers must "live out" the righteousness that they have received. More, they must allow God's righteousness, originally "embodied" in Christ (3:21-24; 2 Cor 5:21), to be "embodied" in them also in the concrete situations of their daily lives (6:12-13). This is what the "slavery" to righteousness or the new obedience means.

In connection with this transfer from one service to another Paul uses (v 17b) a somewhat curious and arresting expression: Christians have given obedience "from the heart" to the "pattern of teaching" *(typon didachēs)* to which they "were handed over" *(paredothēte)*. "Obedience from the heart" seems to be set in contrast to the simply servile obedience of the slave. Slaves are forced to render at least external obedience, however much they might internally resent it. The obedience of believers, on the contrary, stems from the free choice of faith (5:17), engaging the whole person within and without. Perhaps it is to bring out the totality of that engagement that Paul speaks, not of believers receiving a "pattern of teaching" but of their being "handed over" to it. The allusion is obscure on more than one account (see Note) but the passive formulation suggests the action of God, who has placed believers in a situation where the risen Lord can place the "stamp" *(typos)* of his own obedience upon their lives. They are not given a "law"—a set of moral instructions—which they ought now attempt to fulfill. Rather, they are "given up" to a new ethical "force" (the obedience of the risen Lord welling up within them; cf. v 11; Phil 2:5). This, taking possession of their lives, ensures that they "live out" the righteousness that is ultimately God's alone (cf. Rom 8:4).

Past and present: the contrasting outcomes (vv 19-23). After a word of excuse (v 19a) for the image he is using (see Note), Paul resumes the contrast between past and present. In three parallel "waves" (v 19b; vv 20-22; v 23), he unfolds the same basic image of a slave's transfer from one master to another, contrasting the outcome in either situation. A slave who has undergone such a transfer might well be asked (by another slave) to weigh the merits of the new situation over against the old. As if placing his audience in this position, Paul asks them to compare the benefits or "fruits" emanating from the "service" in either case, past and present. What emerges is the overwhelming superiority of the new situation. Implied, in fact, is the "much more" *(pollǭ mallon)* "logic" set up in chapter 5 (vv 6-10, 15-17): if you were obedient then (with an obedience that led to shame and death), how *much more* ought you be obedient now (in an obedience leading to freedom, holiness and life).

The first contrast (v 19b) is reminiscent of v 13 in its exhortation to "offer one's members" *(melē)* for service. It introduces, however, the language of "uncleanness" *(akatharsia)* and "lawlessness" *(anomia)* on the negative (past) side and that of "holiness" *(hagiasmos)* on the positive. "Uncleanness" has sexual overtones (see Note) but, combined with "lawlessness," probably has here a more general reference, expressing the conventional Jewish estimation of the moral degeneracy of the Gentile world, lacking God's law and doomed to perpetual "uncleanness" on that account (cf. 1:18-32). Over against this is the "holiness" characteristic of the people of God. In biblical usage generally "holiness" primarily denotes closeness to God in a relational sense; the nuance of moral transformation is secondary (see Note on 1:7). Here, however, set over against "lawlessness" (v 19b) and "things of which you are now ashamed" (v 21), "holiness" denotes the moral transformation to which God's gift of righteousness should lead. Paul unhesitatingly bestows upon Gentile Christians in Rome the epithets that once seemed the prerogative of Israel alone.

The second "wave" of the argument (vv 20-22) draws attention to the outcome emanating from the past and present situations in more precise form. In the old existence, when believers were slaves of sin, they were certainly "free" as far as righteousness was concerned (v 20). They had, in fact, the sort of "freedom" from righteousness envisaged in the original false suggestion (v 15). But, asks Paul (v 21), what kind of freedom was that, really? What, specifically, were its *immediate* results or "fruit" *(karpos)* and in what direction was it *ultimately* leading? Paul supplies the answer to both questions. The immediate "fruit" (v 21b) was "things of which you are now ashamed"—presumably the kind of vices that marked the former existence of Gentile believers (the vice list in 1 Cor 6:9b-11a gives probably the best indication of what Paul has in mind; cf. also Rom 1:29-31). Where it was all ultimately leading was to death—not simply to that physical death, which remains for all the legacy of Adam's sin, but to the abiding separation from God which makes physical death eternal death, the complete ruin of human existence.

Over against this grim picture of the past, Paul sets (v 22) the situation that follows the transfer to a fresh master. In this new situation, believers have been set free *(eleutherōthentes)* as far as sin is concerned; the former master has no claims, no power over them. Instead, they are people who have been "enslaved to God" *(doulōthentes . . . tǭ theǭ)*. As on the negative side, this new situation has both an immediate and an ultimate outcome. The immediate "fruit" is, once again (cf. v 19b), "holiness" (set over against the "things of which you are now ashamed" [v 21b]). The long range prospect (over against "[eternal] death" [v 21c]) is, naturally, "eternal life" *(zōē aiōnios)*. In this way, the argument returns to the "death-life" antithesis that had been so determinative in chapter 5 (cf. esp. v 21).

It was not unusual for slaves in the ancient world to receive some kind of wage or at least a basic allowance (*peculium*—"pocket money"). So, to clinch the matter, in a final supportive comment (v 23) Paul ironically points to death as the "wages" *(opsōnia)* paid by slave master "Sin." On the positive side, there is no talk of "wages" at all. That might suggest some kind of reward for righteous behavior and, while Paul may not have been as nervous about this as many of his later interpreters (cf. 2 Cor 5:5; also 1 Cor 3:14-15), his theological tendency is always to preserve the initiative of God. Hence he reaches for one of his favorite words—*charisma* (cf. already 5:15, 16). The ultimate concrete expression of grace for the faithful "slave" will be the "gracious gift" of "eternal life in Christ Jesus, our Lord."

Paul's contrastive parallel between the "slaveries" of the two eras (past and present) may be set out schematically as follows:

	SLAVERY TO	PRESENT EFFECTS	END RESULT
OLD	Sin »	Uncleanness » Lawlessness	(Eternal) Death
NEW	Righteousness » (God)	Holiness »	Eternal Life

Righteousness and Holiness. It would undoubtedly be wrong to make too rigid a distinction between the concepts of "righteousness" and "holiness" in Paul. The two overlap in the sense that each implies some measure of both relationship (to God) and moral transformation. Nonetheless, recognizing that in the present context Paul has a certain distinction and sequence of outcomes in mind lends clarity and force to the argument. The fundamental principle, derived from the Jewish tradition, is that (eternal) life follows righteousness (8:10c; see Interpretation of 1:17). All Paul has done here is to insert a middle term—"holiness"—

to denote the moral transformation that the gift of righteousness both precedes and brings about. A corresponding sequence (sin—"uncleanness"/"lawlessness"—death) functions on the negative side as well. With the aid of such a scheme, Paul convincingly demonstrates both the necessity and the possibility of obedience in the new era of grace.

Notes

15. *What then? Shall we continue in sin since we are not under law but under grace? By no means!:* The connection with the preceding passage is somewhat strained in that, while the "false inference" flows naturally out of v 14b ("You are not under law but under grace"), it sits rather strangely with v 14a ("For sin will have no dominion over you"), which v 14b supports (cf. *gar*). It is possible that the sequence made up of vv 15-23 had a "pre-history" as a homily or instruction which Paul was wont to give to his Gentile converts; cf. the similarity in language (esp. "holiness"; "uncleanness") to the instruction in 1 Thess 4:3-8.

16. *when you place yourselves in a situation of slavery:* Paul may in fact have in mind here the reasonably common practice of people voluntarily selling themselves into slavery for long-term economic or social benefit. On the institution of slavery in the ancient world, with particular reference to Paul, see S. S. Bartchy, *First-Century Slavery* 37–120 and D. M. Martin, *Slavery as Salvation* 1–49 (for both see Reference).

    whether of sin, which leads to death, or of real obedience, which leads to righteousness: The translation "real obedience" attempts to clear up a rather loose use of terms on Paul's part. In v 16a "obedience" *(hypakoē)* has a neutral value. In the first part of 16b a clearly negative obedience is implied (that rendered by those who are the slaves to sin). But in the final phrase of v 16 "obedience," while used absolutely, has a clearly positive meaning (the obedience of those who are slaves to God). Likewise, in the same final phrase, to balance "(slaves) of sin, which leads to death," we would expect "(slaves) of righteousness (or "of God"), which leads to (eternal) life." A more accurate correspondence of terms emerges as the argument proceeds.

17. *Thanks be to God:* For this exclamation, besides the very close parallel provided in 7:25a (transfer from slavery to freedom), cf. also 1 Cor 15:57; 2 Cor 2:14; 8:16; 9:15.

    because you were once slaves to sin: This clause has to be understood concessively. Otherwise, Paul would be thanking God for his audience's past slavery to sin.

    but you have given obedience from the heart to the pattern of teaching to which you were handed over: Syntactically the phrase is awkward in the context (v 18 follows very smoothly from v 17a if 17b be removed) and contains language ("from the heart"; use of *typos* in sense of "pattern") unusual in Paul. This has led to its being regarded as a gloss; against this, see esp. Wilckens 2.35.

"Pattern of teaching" *(typos didachēs)* probably refers to some kind of catechetical compendium given to new converts; Paul takes his readers' awareness of it for granted.

18. *set free from sin, you have become slaves of righteousness:* In the Greco-Roman world transfer from one master to another could mean upward mobility for a slave and therefore be seen as highly desirable; see Martin, *Slavery as Salvation* 1–49 and (on Rom 6:15-23) 61–62 .

19. *I use an example from human life to help you in your human weakness to understand:* Paul is not necessarily apologizing for using an image taken from slavery but simply explaining that he is using an image; cf. the similar use of the phrase *kata anthrōpon* in Gal 3:15; 1 Cor 9:8 (also Rom 3:5; 1 Cor 3:1). The translation takes the "weakness of your flesh" to refer primarily to intellectual difficulty.

For as once you offered your members as slaves to uncleanness and lawlessness: For Paul's use of "members" *(melē)*, see Note on 6:13 above. "Uncleanness" *(akatharsia)* is predominantly used of immoral, especially sexually immoral behavior in the NT; cf. esp. the use in 1:24 to designate the immoral behavior considered characteristic of the Gentile world. The appearance of "lawlessness" *(anomia)* here is surprising, considering that Paul is responding to problem arising out of the removal of the law (v 15). But the reference is probably to licentious behavior in general rather than to non-conformity to the Jewish law.

with ever more lawlessness the result: What seems to be meant is not a falling into progressively deeper levels of lawlessness but the setting in of a fixed pattern of lawlessness—a relentless necessity to act in this way.

holiness: In usage outside the Bible the primary sense of "the holy" is not ethical goodness but closeness to the deity, consecration, separation from the profane. In the biblical tradition an ethical tone enters in—in the sense that closeness to God necessarily implies moral transformation; but even so the relational sense remains primary. Within the wider concept, the rather rare word *hagiasmos* denotes both the process of making holy ("sanctification") and the resultant state ("holiness"). In the present case, the parallel with *anomia* assures the sense of moral transformation; cf. also the ethical instruction given 1 Thess 4:3-8, where the same terms *(hagiasmos, akatharsia)* occur. On the relationship between "righteousness" and "sanctification" (holiness) in Paul, see Kertelge, *"Rechtfertigung"* 275–84.

20. *you were quite free as far as righteousness was concerned:* In the Judeo-Christian theological tradition one could never really be "free" from the requirement to be righteous. The statement is valid only within the image being used. The translation takes the phrase *tę̄ dikaiosynę̄* as a dative of respect.

21. *Surely, things of which you are now ashamed—for their outcome is death:* An alternative punctuation associating the first phrase more closely with the preceding question is equally possible: "What was the fruit you then had from things of which you are now ashamed?" The sense is not really altered. At first sight, the sense of "shame" referred to would seem to attach to evil behavior in it-

self, with sexual vices particularly in view. But the added explanation suggests that the shame comes from the (post-conversion) recognition that the behavior in fact was leading to (eternal) death; for this "eschatological" sense of "shame," see Note on 5:5 above.

22. *slaves of God:* Paul speaks directly of "God," rather than "righteousness," as master (cf. also v 13)—perhaps to alleviate something of the unpleasantness associated with using the idea of "slavery" with respect to Christian life.

the fruit you get leads to holiness: On the positive side the "fruit" is not simply identified with "holiness"—which might suggest that the latter is something believers can hold and possess. The expression *(karpon . . . eis hagiasmon)* safeguards the sense that all stages of the process remain the gift of God.

eternal life: For the background to this expression of salvation, see Notes on 2:7 and 5:21.

23. *For the wages of sin is death:* On the custom of slaves receiving an allowance or wage, see Bartchy, *First-Century Slavery* 42, 74.

the gracious gift: For the sense of *charisma* in Paul, see Interpretation and Note on 1:11.

in Christ Jesus our Lord: The full christological formula lends a liturgical, hymnic tone to the conclusion (cf. 5:11, 21). It also expresses the theological reality that both the present service and the hope for future life to which it points all come about solely "in Christ," that is, in the sphere of influence of the risen Lord "in" whose person in a corporate sense all Christian existence is contained; see Note on 6:11.

FOR REFERENCE AND FURTHER STUDY

Bartchy, S. S. *First-Century Slavery and The Interpretation of 1 Corinthians 7:21.* SBLDS 11; Missoula: Scholars Press, 1973, 37–120 (Summary 114–20).

Bouttier, M. "La vie du chrétien en tant que service de la justice pour la sainteté: Romains 6:15-23." *Battesimo e guistizia in Rom 6 e 8.* Ed. L. De Lorenzi. Rome: Abbayia S. Paolo, 1974, 127–54.

Bultmann, R. "Glossen im Römerbrief." *TLZ* 72 (1947) 193–98.

Byrne, B. "Living out the Righteousness of God." 557–81, esp. 562–65.

du Toit, A.B. "*Dikaiosynē* in Röm 6. Beobachtungen zur ethischen Dimension der paulinischen Gerechtigkeitsauffassung." *ZTK* 76 (1979) 261–91.

Furnish, V. P. *Theology and Ethics in Paul* 153–57, 194–98.

Kaye, B. N. *The Thought Structure of Romans with Special Reference to Chapter 6.* Fort Worth: Schola, 1979, 113–33.

Kertelge, K. *"Rechtfertigung" bei Paulus* 269–74, 275–85.

Lyall, F. "Roman Law in the Writings of Paul—the Slave and the Freedman." *NTS* 17 (1970–71) 73–79.

Martin, D. M. *Slavery as Salvation: The Metaphor of Slavery in Pauline Christianity.* New Haven: Yale University, 1990, 1–49, 61–62.

Petersen, N. R. *Rediscovering Paul* 240–57.

Thüsing, W. *Per Christum* 93–96.
Westerholm, S. "Letter and Spirit: The Foundation of Pauline Ethics." *NTS* 30 (1984) 229–48.

c) *Free in Christ from the Law* (7:1-6)

1. Surely you must know, brothers (and sisters)—for I speak to people who know the law—that the law has authority over a person only so long as that person is alive.
2. For a married woman is bound by law to her husband as long as he lives. But if the husband dies, she is free from the law that bound her to
the husband. 3. Accordingly, if while her husband is alive, she gives herself to another man, she will be accounted an adulteress. But if the husband has died, she is free from that law and so will not become an adulteress if she gives herself to another man.
4. The conclusion from this, my brothers (and sisters), is that you too have been put to death as far as the law is concerned through the body of Christ, so that you might be joined to another, the One who has been raised from the dead, in order that we might be fruitful for God.
5. For when we were in the flesh sin-producing passions, provoked by the law, were at work in our members, to make us fruitful only for death.
6. But now we have been removed from the law, having died to that which held us bound, so that we render service in a new life under the influence of the Spirit, in place of the old existence controlled by the letter of the law.

INTERPRETATION

Introduction to Romans 7: Paul and the law. Chapter 7 of Romans is dominated by the topic of the law. We might well ask why this is so. Has not Paul, in the interests of his "inclusive" gospel, sufficiently demonstrated the replacement of the law by faith in the first main section of the letter (1:18–4:25)? Why does the law re-emerge as a central issue in the part of the letter devoted to the hope of salvation (chapters 5–8)?

The answer is bound up with the principle that has been central all through: that salvation depends upon righteousness, upon being found righteous in God's sight at the judgment. Paul's argument that the hope of salvation will not prove ineffectual (5:5) has rested upon the fact that all believers (Jewish and Gentile) have been gifted with God's righteousness in Christ in a way which anticipates the final verdict. They have been swept up within a "solidarity in grace" immeasurably more "powerful for salvation" than the solidarity in sin stemming from Adam (5:12-21). The sole task remaining is to "live out" this gift of righteousness in the time that remains, so that the judgment will simply be a ratification of a verdict (justification) already received. In the present section of the letter (6:1–8:13) Paul is establishing both the necessity and the possibility of living out that gift of righteousness upon which the hope of salvation rests. Fundamentally the possibility is there because, for those "in Christ," sin has ceased to be the dominant power (6:1-11); they have been enlisted into a new "service": that of righteousness (6:13-23).

Throughout the long development building up this case for hope, the law has never quite faded from sight. It has hovered around in the background, a dark shadow at which Paul has from time to time thrown wounding shafts, linking it ever more explicitly with the onset of sin: 3:20 ("through the law comes knowledge of sin"); 4:15 ("the law . . . brings wrath"); 5:20 ("the law came in only to multiply the trespass"). The last and most serious has been the reason given in 6:14: "For sin will not have dominion over you, for you are not under law but under grace." Righteous living—and the hope of salvation which it entails—is possible not despite the removal of the law but because of it. For the law, instead of being ranged upon the side of righteousness, has become the tool and accomplice of sin.

The time has now come for Paul to bring out into the open the view of the law lying behind these negative observations, to explain more expressly its mysterious nexus with sin. The Jewish law, the claims made for the righteousness it purports to offer and, in particular, the aspiration to impose it in whole or in part upon Gentiles, constitute the greatest threat or rival to the inclusive vision of the gospel Paul is presenting in Romans. While the case against righteousness through "works of the law" has already been well and truly made in the early part of the letter (1:18–4:25), it will do no harm to drive the bolt home more securely by exalting the moral capacity communicated by the Spirit at the expense of the incapacity obtaining under the law. To use a modern image, Paul in effect makes the law the "fall guy" in the stakes leading to life.

So what Paul offers in Romans 7 is not really a defense of (or "apologia" for) the law, though this is often held to be the case. True, he does disentangle it from simple identification with sin (7:7-12) and he does find a role for it, albeit a negative one, within a wider divine purpose (7:13). But what he really does is present life "under the law" as a negative foil against which to set all the more effectively the freedom and possibility contained in the gospel. In other words, Paul adopts here, no less than in 5:12-21, his favorite rhetorical technique of antithesis. Setting positive over against negative, new situation over against past, he highlights the superiority of the new to reinforce the hope it contains.

First (7:1-6), Paul establishes that believers are factually free from the law (vv 1-4) and that, as far as ethical possibility is concerned, this has brought about a vastly superior situation (vv 5-6). He then sets the negative background, describing how life under the law has led inevitably to sin and, in sin's train, to death (7:1-25). This description is given from two perspectives, the first (7:7-13) telling of the encounter with the law as a narrative, the second (7:14-25) describing it "from the inside" as an experience. Over against this negative background of ethical "impossibility" under the law, Paul then triumphantly proclaims the freedom and "possibility" created by the Spirit (8:1-13). The gift of the Spirit fulfills God's pledge (cf. Ezek 36:26-27; Jer 31:31-33) to defeat the power of sin and place within human hearts a true capacity to live out the righteousness leading to life.

Free from the law: an illustration from marriage (vv 1-3). Paul's first task is to establish that believers are in fact free from the law. He does so with the aid of an illustration based upon the way the law applies in the case of marriage. He begins (v 1) by addressing his audience (for the first time since the Introduction, 1:13) as "brothers (and sisters)" and as those "who know the law." There is a hint here of "in-talk" within a community of experts in the law. One thinks immediately of Jews. More likely, however, Paul continues to address Gentile converts in Rome. Those who "know the law" are those who came to be well acquainted with it and indeed experienced its attraction at a time of adherence to Judaism (as "God-fearers") previous to their coming to faith in Jesus as the Christ. Paul flatters them for their knowledge of the law, but not without a certain irony because it is precisely through "knowledge" of the law that he is going to overthrow any sense that the law has any residual claim upon them.

The basic principle of which those "who know the law" must be aware is that the law can only bind a person so long as that person is alive (v 1b). Death brings about full release from its claims. Paul illustrates (vv 2-3) this freedom by pointing out the way the law applies in the specific case of marriage. The law in question is clearly the Jewish law, which, while allowing a husband to divorce his wife, concedes no corresponding privilege to the woman. A married woman is thus ruled by the law *(dedetai tǭ nomǭ)* binding her to her husband as long as he is alive. If, in these circumstances, she gives herself to another (v 3a), the law will brand her as an adulteress *(moichalis)*. Should the husband die, however, the situation changes completely: the law that bound her to her former husband no longer applies; she can give herself to a new husband without fear of being branded an adulteress. A death (that of the husband) has given her freedom from the law's claim over her in this respect.

The illustration applied to believers (v 4). It is this single point—that a death has brought freedom from the claims of the law—that bears upon the situation of believers (v 4). They "have been put to death as far as the law is concerned through the body of Christ" *(ethanatōthēte tǭ nomǭ dia tou sōmatos tou Christou)*. This "death" has ensured the same freedom from the claims of the law as that enjoyed by the married woman; they, like her, are now free to give themselves to "another," one whom Paul immediately identifies as the risen Lord. Of course, if pressed rigorously or taken as an allegory, the illustration breaks down. In the case of the law regulating marriage, it is the death of the first husband which creates freedom for the woman, who, of course, lives on. Whereas what creates freedom from the law (of Moses) for believers is the fact that *they* have "died" through their union with the dying of Jesus (cf. 6:3-5). The simple point Paul wants to make, however, is that freedom comes about through death and that required "death" is something which believers have already undergone "through the body of Christ."

This last expression can be interpreted in various ways. An obvious sense is to see a reference to the physical body of Christ that died upon the cross (cf. Col 2:22: "in his body of flesh by his death"). But why Paul should feel it necessary at this point to refer to Christ's death in such a physical way is not clear. The wider context (especially 6:12-13) suggests that "body" *(sōma)* here has its distinctively Pauline sense of vehicle of communication and association. Believers have been "put to death to the law" because of their association with the "career" of Christ "into" whom (cf. 6:3) they have been baptized as "into" a personal, yet communal "sphere of salvation" (cf. 6:6: *ho palaios hēmōn anthrōpos synestaurōthē*; Gal 2:19: *Christǭ synestaurōmai*). In this way the principle enunciated in v 1b applies to them: because they are "dead" in this way, the law has no further claim upon or authority over them.

While it is not an allegory, the illustration from the law of marriage does prompt Paul in a certain direction when he begins (v 4b) to point to the outcome intended by God in bringing about a situation of freedom. Free from the law, believers are free, like the woman in the illustration, for a new "union" *(to genesthai hymas heterǭ)*, one with the risen Lord *(tǭ ek nekrōn egerthenti)*, now pictured as new husband. The "marriage" of believers to the risen Lord has been brought about by God to be "fruitful" in the way Paul understands marriages to be normally fruitful: through the begetting of offspring. The "offspring" in the present case, as the following sentences (vv 5-6) make clear, are the good works that flow from believers' union with the risen Lord (cf. the "fruit" *[karpon]* that leads to "sanctification" in 6:22). Such ethical "possibility," such capacity to live out the gift of righteousness, is in no sense their own achievement. It is entirely the influence ("Spirit") emanating from the one to whom they are joined that renders them "fruitful for God" (cf. 6:11; 8:9-11; 1 Cor 15:45; 2 Cor 3:17).

The Past (v 5). To highight and celebrate this new possibility, Paul characteristically plays it off against the negative situation that obtained in the past, a time he characterizes as "when we were in the flesh" *(en tǭ sarki)*. "Flesh" *(sarx)*, which can simply indicate physical human life in the body in a neutral sense (cf. 1:3; 4:1; 9:5), has here for the first time in the letter its more characteristic negative sense, designating human existence as weak, mortal, self-centered, prone to sin, hostile to God. To be "in the flesh" in this sense is to be determined by the sinful conditions of the old era initiated and symbolized by Adam. Paul allows that there was a "fruitfulness" at this time stemming from the union with the law. But it was a fruitfulness only for death *(eis to karpophorēsai tǭ thanatǭ*; cf. 6:21), something which the law brought about by stirring up "sin producing passions in our members" *(ta pathēmata tōn hamartiōn)*. The language is obscure (see Notes). Paul seems to mean that evil, rebellious desires which otherwise would have remained simply latent "in the flesh" were provoked (cf. *energeito*) by the law into concrete external acts (things that happen "in our members" *[melesin]*; cf. esp. 7:23).

The Present (v 6). Over against this grim plight of the past, Paul sets the present *(nyn)* situation of liberation from the law and consequent ethical "possibility." Through the baptismal "death" that they have died with Christ (v 4) believers have died *(apothanontes)* to the law and hence been "removed" (the aorist *katērgēthēmen*) from the hold it once exercised (cf. v 1b). The upshot *(hōste*, v 6b) is that they have been released, not for a freedom of total independence, but for a new service (literally, "slavery" [*douleuein*; cf. the image in 6:16-18]) characterized by "newness of Spirit" *(kainotētēs pneumatos)* replacing the "oldness of letter" *(palaiotētēs grammatos)*. The language of the double antithesis here—"oldness"/"newness" // "letter"/"Spirit"—has had some anticipation in the description given earlier in the letter of the "true Jew" as who has a "circumcision of the heart, in the Spirit and not the letter" (2:29). More completely still, the same double antithesis features in Paul's sustained argument in 2 Cor 3:6-11 for the superiority of the ministry of the "new covenant" over the "old": the old covenant, being one of "letter," involved a ministry of death (cf. Rom 7:5); the new covenant, characterized by the Spirit, gives life (*zǭopoiei*, v 6b). "Letter" refers to the law simply as external code; it "kills" because, as Paul will shortly explain (vv 7-25), it indicates obligation and specifies sanction without giving any capacity to resist the flesh's impulse to rebel; it thus leads, through actual sin, to (eternal) death. "Spirit," on the other hand, is the power of the new age which, released effectively into the human heart, creates the righteousness that leads to life (8:10-11). It is this rich complex of motifs, fundamentally to be seen as the fulfillment of God's promises for the last age (cf. Ezek 36:26-27; Jer 31:31-33), that lies behind the somewhat cryptic allusions in v 6.

Viewing vv 5-6 as a whole, we can see that the two statements in which Paul sets the contrast between past and present anticipate in a programmatic way the descriptions of life "under the law" and life "in the Spirit" that are now to follow. V 5 outlines the sin-provoking encounter with the law that leads to death (vv 7-13; vv 14-25); v 6 anticipates the righteousness-producing effect of the Spirit that leads to life (8:1-13). Paul has shown that believers are factually free from the law (7:1-4) and given a first indication of the way in which that freedom has opened up new ethical "possibility" (vv 5-6). We can set it out diagrammatically as follows:

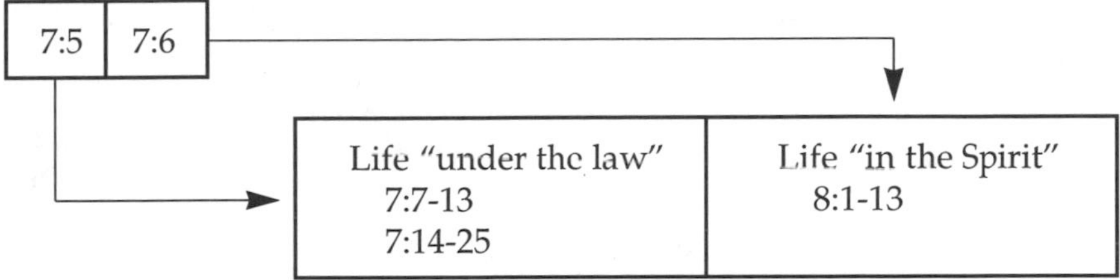

The two passages—the negative (7:7-25, especially 7:14-25) and positive (8:1-13)—function like both panels of a diptych: each illumining the other by way of contrast.

Notes

1. *people who know the law:* The context (cf. esp. v 4 and the illustration from marriage in vv 2-3) makes clear that *nomos* here refers to the Law of Moses.

   the law has authority over a person only so long as that person is alive: The verb *kyrieuein* probably refers here simply to the law's having legal force (in which case the similar statement with respect to sin in 6:7 is not a true parallel). There are later rabbinic parallels to the maxim in this legal sense: e.g., "She (a married woman) acquires her freedom by a bill of divorce or by the death of her husband" (*m. Qidd.* 1:1).

2. *For a married woman is bound by law to her husband as long as he lives . . .:* This reflects the biblical understanding whereby the wife is virtually the possession of the husband (cf. Exod 20:17; Num 30:10-15), is subject to him (the meaning implicit in the word *hypandros* used here to express the married state of the woman; cf. LXX Prov 6:24, 29; Sir 9:9) and where only he can initiate a break-up of the marriage; cf. Deut 24:1. In Roman law of the time the woman could initiate a divorce—as reflected in the Markan form of the divorce logion (Mark 10:11-12). The question of divorce does not arise, however, in Rom 7:1-3.

   the law that bound her to the husband: The translation understands the Greek phrase *apo tou nomou tou andros* to refer to the law of Moses in so far as it binds a wife to remain with her husband. The point of the illustration is whether the law concerning marriage is pressing upon the woman or not. Contrary to my earlier view (see *Reckoning with Romans* 129–30), I do not now think Paul's illustration requires identifying the law with the first husband and the risen Christ with the second—though *eventually* (v 4) Paul does seem to envisage a union between believers and the risen Lord in a marital sense.

3. *gives herself to another man:* The Greek phrase *genesthai andri heterǭ*, which appears twice in this verse and again in v 4, echoes the LXX of the divorce legislation in Deut 24:2; cf. Jer 3:1; Hos 3:3.

   she will be accounted an adulteress: Cf. Exod 20:14; Lev 20:10; Deut 22:22.

4. *The conclusion from this . . .:* The conclusion *(hōste)* as regards believers derives from the principle expressed in v 1b, which the image (vv 2-3) has illustrated.

   you too have been put to death as far as the law is concerned: The translation understands *tǭ nomǭ* here as a dative of (dis)advantage. The law is not abolished (cf. 3:31); it remains as an indication of God's will (cf. 8:4) and as an instrument of condemnation upon human sin (3:20). But believers, having been put to death with Christ, are safely removed from its sphere of application.

   through the body of Christ: The view (proposed in the Interpretation) that finds in this phrase a reference to believers' union with the risen Lord is often described as "ecclesiological" and rejected as introducing into the passage a wider pattern of thought (believers constituting the "body of Christ"; cf. 1 Cor 12:12-13) that is not already there. Calling it "ecclesiological", however, begs the question from the start and it is in fact this terminology that introduces ideas extraneous to the context. It was not the death of Christ considered simply in itself that facilitated believers' "death" to the claim of the law; it was the potentiality of Jesus Christ, precisely as Messiah and "Last Adam," to embrace all within his own person and so associate them with his "career" of death, burial and resurrection. It is this association that "body" expresses. To see a reference to the eucharistic body of Christ would indeed seem to go beyond what is required.

   so that you might be joined to another, the One who has been raised from the dead: The same motif of believers being in a marital relationship with the risen Christ appears in 1 Cor 6:15-18, where, citing the explanation of marriage given in Gen 2:24, Paul uses it to underline the total unacceptability of union with a prostitute. The bodies of believers belong entirely to the Lord and are destined one day to share his risen glory (vv 13b-14); see also 2 Cor 11:2, where Paul claims to have "betrothed" the community to Christ. Behind the idea of believers' "marriage" with Christ may lie the biblical motif presenting the relationship between Yahweh and Israel in terms of a marriage: Isa 54:5-6; 62:1-5; Jer 2:2 (cf. 3:1); Ezek 16:8-14; Hos 2:16-20.

   in order that we might be fruitful for God: The image of "fruitfulness" in the sense of child-bearing is a natural development from that of marriage and features in both v 4 (positively) and v 5 (negatively) and also by implication (positively) in v 6. Paul's view of the ethical life of believers as entirely the product of the "marital" union with the risen Lord parallels the Fourth Gospel's use of the "Vine and Branches" imagery to express the same union (John 15:1-8)—a text appealed to by the Council of Trent in the sixteenth chapter of its decree "On Justification" (DS §1546, p. 377); see further Byrne, "Living Out the Righteousness of God" 579.

5. *in the flesh:* It is virtually impossible to find an accurate translation or paraphrase for Paul's key theological category of "flesh"; it has to be treated as a technical term and translated literally. Paul's usage stands within the general biblical tradition but is particularly close to the use of *bāśār* in the Dead Sea Scrolls: cf., e.g., 1QS 11:6-7, 9, 12; 1QH 4:29-30; 15:16, 21. On the concept in Paul, see further, Bultmann, *Theology* 1.232–46; W. D. Stacey, *Pauline View of Man* 154–80; Ziesler, *Pauline Christianity* 77–80; Jewett, *Paul's Anthropological Terms* 135–60.

   sin-producing passions: The curious Greek phrase *(ta pathēmata tōn hamartiōn)* is difficult both to interpret and translate. The word *pathēma* (always in the plural in the Pauline corpus) occurs chiefly in the sense of "sufferings" (cf., e.g., 8:18); here, as the qualifying phrase makes clear, it has the sense of "emotions," "feelings" in a bad sense and hence means "passions" (cf. Gal 5:24 for a useful parallel in this sense). In the sixty or so occurrences of *hamartia* ("sin") in Paul, all but a handful occur in the singular and usually feature Paul's distinctive sense of sin personified as "power" (see Interpretation of 5:12). In reference to individual sinful acts Paul prefers to use terms such as *paraptōma, parabasis*. In the few places where *hamartia* occurs in the plural it is usually in scriptural quotations (e.g., Rom 4:7; 11:27) or pre-set formulas of faith (1 Cor 15:3b, 17; Gal 1:4). The untypical usage here may indicate that Paul is taking a stock phrase from an early exhortation. The genitive could be one of quality—"sinful passions"—though the plural sits somewhat awkwardly with this. The translation proposed rests upon an objective (or "directional") understanding.

   in our members: For the Pauline sense of "members" *(melē)*, see Note on 6:13.

6. *having died to that which held us bound:* Paul has contracted the expression in the Greek in order to avoid a double mention of the law, which is the implied antecedent of the relative *en hǭ*. The "imprisoning" or at least "restraining" role of the law here matches the presentation of it in Gal 3:23-25, where there is a similar stark contrast between past captivity and present liberation.

   so that we render service: The conjunction *hōste* primarily indicates result. But the result in question is clearly that *intended* by God, who is the implied object of "render service" *(douleuein)*. The latter recalls the sustained "slavery" image in 6:15-23.

   in a new life under the influence of the Spirit, in place of the old existence controlled by the letter of the law: The translation attempts to capture the precise sense Paul's use of the abstract nouns "newness" (*kainotētēs*) and "oldness" (*palaiotētēs*) where one might have expected simple adjectives. Behind the choice of language would appear to lie a concern to express the sense that the long-awaited radical change of epoch has actually come about for believers.

For Reference and Further Study

Earnshaw, J. D. "Reconsidering Paul's Marriage Analogy in Romans 7:1-4." *NTS* 40 (1994) 68–88.
Furnish, V. P. *Theology and Ethics in Paul* 177–78.
Little, J. A. "Paul's Use of Analogy: A Structural Analysis of Romans 7:1-6." *CBQ* 46 (1984) 82–90.
Thüsing, W. *Per Christum* 96–101.
Westerholm, S. *Israel's Law* 209–14.

d) *The Fatal Encounter with the Law* (7:7-13)

7. What, then, shall we say? That the law is sin? God forbid!
But I would not have known sin except through the law.
For I would not have known covetousness, if the law had not said, "You must not covet." 8. But sin, seizing its opportunity, by means of the commandment worked in me all manner of covetousness.
For apart from the law sin is dead. 9. I was alive once, apart from the law. But when the commandment came, sin sprang to life. 10. I died and the commandment, which was meant to lead to life, turned out to be death for me. 11. For sin, seizing its opportunity, by means of the commandment deceived me and through it killed me.
12. So the law is holy and the commandment is holy, just and good.
13. Did what is good, then, prove to be death for me? God forbid! But sin, so that it might reveal itself as sin, through this good thing was working death for me—that is, so that through the commandment sin might become sinful beyond measure.

Interpretation

Introduction. With this text Paul begins the description of life under the law intended to serve as a negative foil against which to highlight life in the Spirit (8:1-13). The description comes in two parts, each adopting its own perspective. Whereas the present passage (7:7-13) tells of the encounter with the law in the form of a narrative relating past experience, the one to follow (7:14-25) explores the same encounter "from the inside," telling it as a gripping account in the present. Formal considerations also suggest a division at the end of v 13: in v 7 a question is put in the first person plural ("What shall we say?") and, after the rebuttal, the passage continues resolutely in the first person singular; in v 14 the first person plural returns briefly ("For we know . . .") and then returns to the singular until the end of the sequence at v 25.

Two issues have dominated modern interpretation of Rom 7:7-25. The first concerns the identity of the "I" who speaks as subject throughout the passage. The second focuses more precisely on vv 14-25 and has to do with the stage of religious existence out of which this "I" speaks: does the anguished dilemma that is described in the present reflect Christian existence or some other stage of religious existence prior to or apart from life in Christ? The two issues are to some extent intertwined but it is more appropriate to postpone consideration of the second to the commentary on 7:14-25.

With regard to the identity of the "I," the most obvious interpretation is to assume that the account is autobiographical; Paul tells of his own experience with the law. The problem with this is that the highly pessimistic account the "I" gives of the encounter with the law is at odds with Paul's (indisputably autobiographical) claim in Phil 3:6b to have been "blameless" with respect to righteousness by the law (cf. also Gal 1:13-14). It is also difficult to see how one born a Jew could say that he "was alive once apart from the law" (v 9). At the extreme edge of this approach are attempts to relate the narrative to difficulties Paul experienced with the law at the time of adolescence (sexual awakening, etc.). But, quite apart from the obvious anachronism this involves, it is hard to see why Paul would want to air such personal matters before the Roman community, one not founded by himself and in all likelihood unsympathetic to him personally.

The difficulties with the approach linking the account with the personal experience of Paul have led to its being understood in a "typical" or "generalizing" sense: the "I" represents the typical experience of "Everyman" or "Everywoman" (strictly, "Every Jew") when confronted with the law. There are parallels for this in Greco-Roman literature, in the Psalms, in the Qumran Thanksgiving Psalms and notably in Paul's own writings (e. g., Gal 2:18-21; 1 Cor 8:13; 10:29b-30; 13:1-3, 11-12). S. K. Stowers has recently argued that such passages, especially Rom 7:7-25, are best understood as examples of the ancient rhetorical technique of "speech-in-character" *(prosōpopoiia)* where "the speaker or writer produces speech that represents not himself or herself but another person or type of character" (*Rereading of Romans* 16–17, 264–79). While to dismiss any measure of autobiography in the sequence would perhaps be too sweeping (on this see Ziesler 181–84), there can be little doubt that the "I" describes an experience meant to be typical of all persons in the situation depicted—"under" the law.

Within this broadly "typical" approach to the "I" in Rom 7:7-25 greater precisions can be made, at least with respect to the first passage

(7:7-13). Unmistakable allusions to the narrative of Genesis 2–3 (cf. esp. v 11) lend the "I" an "Adamic" aura. Adam, it is true, did not live "under the law (of Moses)." But, as Paul has already implied in 5:14, in so far as he received a direct command (prohibition) from God (Gen 2:16-17), he was in a situation similar to those (the Jews) who were later to be "under the law." Nonetheless, as the "I" tells the story, the confrontation with "law" comes in the shape of a commandment from the Decalogue given to Israel at Sinai (vv 7-8; cf. Exod 20:17; Deut 5:21). This suggests that the "I" speaks in the name of Israel, reflecting upon the experience of receiving the law at Sinai.

It seems Paul wants his audience to hear the "I" speaking in tones evocative both of Adam and Israel. The primary emphasis is upon Israel. But Israel's experience of the law is told in terms of the effect God's command had upon Adam. The law when it arrived had the same effect upon Israel as the commandment had upon him (cf. N. T. Wright, *The Climax of the Covenant* 197). The result was to place Jews in the (Adamic) "sin" situation of the rest of humankind. The law, instead of setting Israel apart as a holy nation, has in effect "leveled" Israel down to the common lot, bringing about the situation of "no distinction" (3:22; cf. 3:9). In fact, the law has actually *concentrated* sin in Israel, so that where "sin increased" (in Israel) grace, through the work of Israel's Messiah (Jesus), might "abound all the more" (5:20b). In other words, Paul presents Israel's experience of sin under the law as archetypal of the plight of all humanity, unredeemed yet confronted by moral demand. He makes the "I" tell this painful story as a prelude or foil to the rescue, equally universal in scope, which Israel's Messiah ("the Last Adam" [1 Cor 15:45]) brings as instrument of grace.

The argument is launched in diatribe form with an introductory question and a riposte (v 7a-c), followed by a statement of the essential theme (v 7d). The main exposition then unfolds in two stages: vv 7e-8ab and vv 8c-11 (each begins with a sentence introduced by the causal connective *gar*, followed somewhat later by a clause beginning with the light adversative *de;* each concludes with a similar statement stating how sin "seized its opportunity through the commandment" [v 8ab; v 11]). Stage 1 tells how the law serves to provoke sin in the shape of "covetousness"; Stage 2 develops this further, pointing to sin's replacement of "life" by a destiny to "death." Vv 12-13 offer a conclusion, defending the essential "holiness" of the law, while unmasking sin as the true culprit.

Introduction: Objection, Riposte and Theme (v 7a-d). The suggestion with which the passage begins—that the law is to be identified with sin (v 7ab)—sounds very reasonable after all the negative statements Paul has been making concerning the law (cf. 3:20; 4:15; 5:20; 6:14), culminating with the assertion in v 5 about the law provoking "sin-producing passions," making "us fruitful only for death." Though Paul vigorously dismisses the suggestion (v 7c), he immediately qualifies the dismissal to some extent, introducing the main theme (v 7d): it was through encounter with the law that "I" came to know sin. This "knowledge" of sin (cf. 3:20) is not simply information about right and wrong nor mere consciousness of having done wrong. Paul means "knowledge" in the full Semitic sense that includes experience. Though sin exists apart from the law (cf. 5:13), it was through the law that I came to experience sin as a the grip of tyrant power, alienating me from God and setting me on a path to death.

Encounter with the law I (vv 7e-8b). The narrative first describes the encounter with the law in terms of a confrontation with the prohibition against "coveting" ("desiring"). The text cites the final commandment of the Decalogue in a truncated form ("You must not covet" [LXX *ouk epithymēseis*]), omitting all the objects of the "coveting" specified in the two biblical lists (Exod 20:17; Deut 5:21; cf. also Rom 13:9). In this form the commandment simply prohibits all illicit "desire" *(epithymia)* in absolute terms. That the law should be reduced to this single point is understandable in the light of a widespread tendency in the ancient world, particularly where Stoic influence was strong, to regard "desire" as the root of all evil. Important circles in Hellenistic Judaism (Philo, 4 Maccabees) presented the Jewish law as the only effective antidote against the ravages of "desire" in human life (see Note).

Paul, who has already depicted enslavement to "desire" as something typical of the Gentile world (1:24; cf. 1:26-27), sits broadly within this tradition as regards the evil of "desire." But he strongly contests the specific claim entered in on behalf of the law as antidote to desire. The "I" explains (v 8) that it was the coming of the commandment *(entolē)* forbidding desire that provided sin (still personified as tyrant power; cf. 5:12-21; 6:12-13, 14-23) with the opportunity or foothold (*aphormē*) it needed to arouse desire. How Paul sees the process working in psychological terms is not altogether clear. Appeal to the notion of the allure of "forbidden fruit" is rather trite. What would seem to be in mind is the idea that the prohibition, stemming from God, awoke a latent human propensity to chafe and rebel at creaturely dependence upon the Creator. In this "I" came to know and feel the fundamental "desire" lying behind all concrete acts of wrongdoing: the desire to possess whatever I wish and to do whatever I choose without limit. This, for Paul, is to "know sin" (cf. 3:20).

Encounter with the law II (vv 8c-11). The second phase of the exposition takes the same explanation somewhat further. The outcomes—"life" and "death"—now become key factors, along with law and sin. Paul first envisages a situation "apart from the law"—that is, before the law was given. At this time, sin was "dead" (*nekra*—not non-existent [cf. 5:13] but lying dormant, ineffective) and "I" was alive *(egō . . . ezōn)*. The coming of the commandment *(entolē)* effected a total reversal: sin "sprang to life" and "I died." That is, sin awoke to full virulence and, as a consequence, "I" lost the destiny to eternal life. We may depict the reversal thus:

	Before	[Coming of Commandment]		*After*
"I":	"Alive"	⟶	⟶	"Dead"
"Sin":	"Dead"	⟶	⟶	"Alive"

An added comment (v 10c) brings out the irony involved in this "exchange." The commandment which was "meant" to give (eternal) life *(hē entolē hē eis zōēn)* turned out in fact to be productive only of death.

The subsequent explanation of how this came about (v 11) provides the most explicit allusion to the narrative of Genesis 3. The opportunity (*aphormē*) sin found in the commandment (cf. v 8) involved a "deception" (*exēpatēsen me*) similar to that exercised by the serpent in the Garden of Eden (cf. LXX Gen 3:13: *ēpatēsen me*). Sin played the role of the serpent, exploiting the onset of the commandment as a chance to portray the prohibition, not as life-preserving measure of a benevolent Creator, but as a restriction keeping the creature from discovering and usurping divine "knowledge." What followed, in fact, was not knowledge of divinity but "knowledge of sin" (cf. v 7b; 3:20): the experience of being held in the grip of a tyrant power and locked into an inevitable destiny to death.

Conclusion: the law is good, sin the true villain (vv 12-13). The explanation of sin's use of the commandment enables Paul, by way of conclusion, to distinguish the essential goodness of the law (commandment) from the way in which it has become, willy-nilly, the tool of sin. Far from being identified with sin, as the opening objection (v 7b) suggested, it is both holy in itself and in every one of its precepts (v 12). How then did the "good" and "holy" law become involved in this nexus of sin? To round the matter off and nail the true villain in the piece, Paul allows a further false inference to surface (v 13). Did this "good thing" (the law) in fact bring about "my" death? The objection touches upon the age-old issue of the use of something good in itself to bring about an evil end. The inference is rebutted as vigorously *(mē genoito)* as before (v 7c). But what follows (cf. *alla*) appears to concede that it is in some sense partly true: death did come to me through the law—this "good thing" (*dia tou agathou*, v 13d). But in the process the law was only the helpless tool of the machinations of the real culprit, sin, which is thereby unmasked and forced to display its true colors. By hijacking the law in this way, by using something essentially good—and God-given—to bring death to the human race, sin revealed the magnitude, the "excess" *(kath' hyperbolēn)*, of its own evil.

This statement is wrapped round on either side with what appear to be two statements of divine intention *(hina phanę̄ . . . hina genētai)*. In biblical thought it is an easy step from the fact of a given effect to the idea that this was what God intended. The bold suggestion, then, seems to be that sin's deceptive tactic of harnessing the law to be its instrument in bringing death was in fact encompassed within a wider divine purpose. God gave the law (to Israel) precisely to bring sin to a point of maximum concentration so that right there (Israel) "where sin increased, grace might abound" (5:20b), for the benefit of the entire world, in the person of Israel's Messiah (cf. 8:3-4).

For the present, however, there is only a hint of this wider divine purpose and victory over sin. Paul has disentangled the law from any suggestion that it is identical with sin; he has defended its essential "holiness." Overall, however, he has portrayed human encounter with the law as story of an encounter with death. To reinforce the dramatic effect, he now turns to tell the same story (encounter with the law) from the "inside" (vv 14-25).

Notes

7. *What, then, shall we say?:* On Paul's use of the phrase *ti oun eroumen,* see Note on 4:1.

   God forbid!: On Paul's use of this expression *(mē genoito)*, see Note on 3:4.

   But I would not have known sin except through the law: This sentence, like the one that follows, expresses an unreal (contrary to fact) condition (BDF §360 [1]).

   For I would not have known covetousness, if the law had not said, "You must not covet.": The Catholic tradition "distributes" the prohibition against coveting over two separate commandments—the ninth and tenth; the Protestant tradition, having divided the opening prohibition against idolatry into the first and second commandment, combines the "coveting" prohibition into the one (tenth) commandment. On "covetousness/desire," see the third Note on the following verse.

8. *seizing its opportunity:* The Greek word *aphormē* may retain the original military sense "base of operations," "bridgehead," though the meaning had become more generalized in Hellenistic Greek; cf. also 2 Cor 5:12; 11:12; Gal 5:13; 1 Tim 5:14.

   by means of the commandment worked in me: The use of the Greek noun *entolē* ("commandment") could reflect the LXX of Gen 2:16: *eneteilato kyrios ho theos tǭ Adam.* The translation takes the phrase "by means of the commandment" with the verb, *kateirgasato,* rather than with the participle, *labousa.* This is supported by the addition of the clause "and through it (i.e., the commandment) killed me" in the repetition of the sentence in v 11.

all manner of covetousness: In itself Greek noun *epithymia* ("desire"; translated here as "covetousness" because of the quotation in v 7]) does not have a bad connotation. The latter nuance arises particularly where Stoic influence is strong: cf., for Hellenistic Judaism: Wis 4:12; 4 Macc. 1:3, 31-32; 2:1-6; 3:2, 11-12, 16; Philo *L.A.* 3.115; *Post.* 26. For "desire/covetousness" as the root of all evil, see *Apoc. Mos* 19: 3 ("For covetousness is the origin of every sin"); *Apoc. Abr.* 24:9; Philo *Spec.* 4.84–94; *Decal.* 142, 150, 173; cf. Jas 1:15. 4 Macc 2:4-6 cites the law's prohibition against coveting as an evidence of the power of "reason," schooled by the Jewish law (cf. 1:13-17), to master desire. On the ancient ethical ideal of self-mastery (mastery of "desire") and its possible implications for the interpretation of Paul, see Stowers, *Rereading of Romans* 42–52, 58–74. In Paul, apart from Phil 1:23 and 1 Thess 2:17, *epithymia* has a negative connotation: it is associated with the "flesh" (cf. Gal 5:16, 24; Rom 13:14; cf. 6:12; cf. Eph 2:3), sometimes with the sense of sexual lust (cf. Rom 1:24; 1 Thess 4:5)—though that (*pace* R. H. Gundry—see Reference) is hardly the sense here. Likewise to be rejected is the Bultmannian interpretation of *epithymia* as egotistic desire, not to break the law, but to fulfill it in a way that builds up one's own righteousness over against God. Throughout Rom 7:7-25 the problem is transgressing, not keeping, the law's commands.

For apart from the law sin is dead: For the figurative use of *nekron* in the sense of "ineffective" cf. Jas 2:17, 26. The statement sits in some tension with 5:13-14 where Paul insists that, prior to the coming of the law, sin nonetheless attracted the penalty of death.

9. *I was alive once, apart from the law:* The "death-life" contrast that appears to be operative here suggests that "alive" *(ezōn)* must refer not simply to existence as such but to the fullness of human existence—the life ultimately to be enjoyed as "eternal life." It is tempting to see in this statement an allusion to the state of Adam before imposition of the commandment. But the narrative of Genesis 2 hardly allows for such a stage.

   But when the commandment came, sin sprang to life: The verb *anazān* strictly refers to coming *back* to life (from the dead, through resurrection; cf. Rev 20:5). Paul uses the compound verb here perhaps to avoid the implication that the commandment (law) actually brought sin into being. In any case, the use of a verb implying resurrection is natural after the description (v 8) of sin as "dead" *(nekra)*. The statement can be related to the narrative of Genesis 2–3—though see preceding Note. A reference to the giving of the law at Sinai (so esp. D. J. Moo—see Reference) sits in some tension with the insistence in 5:13-14 that sin remained virulent in the period between Adam and Moses. By the same token, the present statement explains why Paul felt it necessary to deal with the problem in the earlier context.

10. *I died:* The allusion, of course, is not to immediate physical death but to coming under the liability to physical death (mortality) and to the prospect of this becoming eternal death. Like the author of Wisdom (cf. 2:23-24), Paul did not believe that physical death was "natural" for human beings; it came about through sin; see the Interpretation of 5:12; cf. also 8:10.

the commandment, which was meant to lead to life: This is best taken as an allusion to the command received by Adam (Gen 2:16-17), which was, of course, intended as a life-preserving measure—a safeguard against what will result in death—rather than a restriction upon human freedom. If "the commandment" in some sense stands in also for the whole law received by Israel, Paul may have in mind the biblical sense of the law as a path to life: cf. Deut 30:15-20; Lev 18:5 (quoted in Gal 3:12; Rom 10:5); also Sir 17:11; 45:5; Bar 3:9; *4 Ezra* 14:30 ("law of life"); *Pss. Sol.* 14:2; *m. ʾAbot* 2:8. In Gal 3:21b Paul concedes that in principle the law was directed to life but the law that was given proved in practice incapable of achieving this end (because incapable of dealing with sin; cf. Rom 8:3).

11. *For sin, seizing its opportunity, by means of the commandment:* For this, see Note on v 8a, which, like a refrain, it echoes (with change only of conjunction).

deceived me and through it killed me: Despite the use of the longer verb form *(exēpatēsen)* where the LXX of Gen 3:13 has the simple *ēpatēsen,* the allusion to the Genesis 3 narrative is made secure by the explicit allusion in 2 Cor 11:3: ". . . as the serpent deceived *(exēpatēsen)* Eve"; cf. also 1 Tim 2:14. On the sense in which "I" was "killed" see the first Note on v 10.

12. *So the law is holy and the commandment is holy, just and good:* Paul speaks separately of "the law" and "the commandment" perhaps to indicate that not only the law as a whole but also each of its individual commandments is good and holy. Or else "the commandment" may refer specifically to the tenth commandment cited in v 7 as containing the essence of the whole law. Syntactically, the Greek sentence is an anacolouthon: the opening *men* . . ., leads the reader to expect a corresponding sentence beginning with *de* . . .; instead, there follows (v 13) the objection introducing the statement about the extreme wickedness of sin. The construction suggests that the assertion of the "goodness" of the law in v 12 is little more than a stage on the way to the central affirmation about sin.

13. *Did what is good, then, prove to be death for me? God forbid!:* Paul uses the same diatribal technique as in v 7; see Note on 3:4.

But sin, so that it might reveal itself as sin, through this good thing was working death for me—that is, so that through the commandment sin might become sinful beyond measure: Syntactically, this complex sentence lacks a main verb; *egeneto* has to be supplied from the opening sentence of the verse so as to provide a periphrastic sense with the participle *katergazomenē*—"was working." The sense of divine purpose expressed in the two *hina* . . . clauses with respect to the law's unmasking of sin complements the similar remark in 5:20a that the law came in "to multiply the trespass"; cf. also Gal 3: 19 ("The law was given for the sake of transgressions") and Rom 11:32 ("God has imprisoned all in disobedience, in order to have mercy upon all"; cf. Gal 3:22). It is easy to imagine statements such as these provoking the "slanderous" charge against Paul recorded in 3:8 ("Let us do evil that good may come").

For Reference and Further Study

Bornkamm, G. "Sin, Law and Death: An Exegetical Study of Romans 7." *Early Christian Experience* 87–104.

Dülmen, A. van *Theologie des Gesetzes* 106–12.

Gundry, R. H. "The Moral Frustration of Paul before His Conversion: Sexual Lust in Romans 7:7-25." *Pauline Studies* (FS F. F. Bruce). Eds. D. A. Hagner and M. J. Harris; Exeter: Paternoster, 1980, 80–94.

Hofius, O. "Das Gesetz des Mose und das Gesetz Christi" 269–72.

Kümmel, W. G. *Römer 7 und die Bekehrung des Paulus.* Leipzig: Hinrichs, 1929; repr. Münich: Kaiser, 1974, 42–57, 75–89.

Lyonnet, S. "L'histoire de salut selon le chapitre VII de l'épître aux Romains." *Études* 203–30 (orig. *Biblica* 43 [1962] 117–51).

_________. "'Tu ne convoiteras pas' (Rom VII, 7)." *Neotestamentica et Patristica* (FS O. Cullmann). Ed. W. C. van Unnik; NovTSup 6; Leiden: Brill, 1962, 157–65.

Martin, B. L. *Christ and the Law in Paul* 75–78.

Moo, D. J. "Israel and Paul in Romans 7.7–12." *NTS* 32 (1986) 122–35.

Räisänen, H. "Zum Gebrauch von *EPITHYMIA* und *EPITHYMEIN* bei Paulus." *The Torah and Christ: Essays in German and English on the Problem of the Law in Early Christianity.* Helsinki: Finnish Exegetical Society, 1986, 148–67.

Stowers, S. K. *Rereading of Romans* 59–62, 264–69, 278–79.

Theissen, G. *Psychological Aspects* 177–211, 251–60.

Westerholm, S. *Israel's Law* 54–60, 181–86.

Wright, N. T. *Climax of the Covenant* 196–200.

Ziesler, J. "The Role of the Tenth Commandment in Romans 7." *JSNT* 33 (1988) 41–56.

e) *Life Under the Law—Ethical "Impossibility"* (7:14-25)

14. The law, as we know, is spiritual. But I am fleshly, sold into slavery under sin.

15. I am completely at a loss to account for my own behavior. For it is not what I want to do that I do. But I do what I hate. 16. If what I do is contrary to my will, this means that I agree with the law and hold it to be admirable. 17. But the situation is that it is no longer I who do this but sin dwelling within me.

18. For I am aware that in me, that is, in my flesh, there dwells nothing good. For the will to do the proper thing is there, but the power to achieve it is not. 19. For I do not do the good I want to do, but the evil that I do not want, that I do. 20. But if what I do not want, that I do, then it is no longer I who do it, but sin dwelling within me.

21. So this is what I find to be the case with respect to "law": 22. I take delight in the law of God according to my inner self. 23. But I see another

law in my members fighting against the law of my mind and holding me captive to the law of sin, which dwells in my members.
24. Wretched one that I am! Who will deliver me from the body of this death? 25. Thanks be to God, through Jesus Christ, our Lord.

For, left to my own resources, with my mind I serve the law of God, but in the flesh it is the law of sin that I serve.

INTERPRETATION

Introduction. The preceding passage (7:7-13) described the encounter with the law as a quasi-historical narrative about the past. It contrasted life before or apart from the law with what happened when the "commandment" arrived on the scene and sin sprang to life in full virulence, bringing death in its train. Now, changing to the present tense, the "I" describes "from the inside," as it were, the enduring consequences of that fatal encounter: the situation of "ethical impossibility" that results from having been "sold into slavery under sin" (v 14).

The critical question concerning the identity of the "I" continues in this second part of 7:14-25. At one level, the gripping account in the present tense of a personal struggle tends to reinforce the impression that Paul is speaking autobiographically. On the other hand, the desperate struggle to fulfill the law sits at odds with the (undeniably autobiographical) account of life under the law given in Phil 3:5b-6 (". . ., as to the law a Pharisee, as to zeal a persecutor of the church, as to righteousness under the law blameless"). The vital consideration, however, is how the report was meant to come across to the audience in Rome. Paul's aim is not to communicate his own experience but to convey a powerful sense of the "impossibility" under the law, something which his audience could recognize as potentially—and fatally—applicable to themselves. The "I," then, remains the typical "I" who spoke in the preceding section.

Connected with this issue is the question of the time reference of the struggle which the "I" describes. Does the use of the present tense in such a vivid way and certain other factors (especially the "inclusion" of an undeniably "Christian" appeal in v 25a), argue that the "I" speaks out of Christian experience—so that what is said here is meant to be true in certain circumstances of Christian experience? Or do we have an "I" (Paul) who, as a Christian, *looks back* to a stage of religious existence prior to coming to faith in Christ—in which case the struggle portrayed here would not apply to Christian existence?

It is not necessary to repeat at length the many excellent surveys of this question that are available (particularly concise and balanced is that of Ziesler, *Romans* 191–95). Whatever the difficulties stemming from the use of the present tense (a literary convention; see Introduction to Interpretation of 7:7-13 above) and the "Christian" cry in v 25a (see Note), the view that the sequence represents a reflection, from a Christian perspective, upon the experience of life under the law apart from the grace of Christ rests on three considerations that appear unassailable. First, there is the clarity of Paul's earlier insistence (note especially the aorist tenses of verbs and participles) that believers have been "put to death to the law" (7:4; cf. v 6; Gal 2:19), are therefore radically "removed" from it (7:5) and are no longer "under the law" (6:14). Second, there is the notorious "absence" from 7:14-25 of all reference to the Spirit, the determining factor in Christian life for Paul. Finally, only the "pre-Christian" reference of 7:14-25 preserves, across the total passage 7:14–8:13, the contrast Paul has deliberately set up in 7:5-6 between life "in the flesh," where the law is at work, and "service in the newness of the Spirit," the "fruit" of the baptismal union with the risen Lord. The rhetorical effect of the "newness," the breakthrough into freedom in the Spirit proclaimed in 8:1-2, is completely lost on the alternative view which sees Christian life already in 7:14-25; the total sequence 8:1-3 becomes simply a lame anticlimax.

The issue is usually couched in terms of "before" and "after"/"pre-Christian" and "Christian." But purely temporal categories in fact hardly reflect what Paul is about, which is to depict the situation of anyone who finds himself or herself confronted by the demands of external law without the aid of the grace of Christ. Confrontation with the law of Moses is the specific point of departure but the account becomes increasingly more general as it proceeds and so is capable of more universal application. In other words, Paul is taking a standard *topos* of the ancient world—the conflict between knowing what is the right thing to do and being incapable of finding the moral capacity to do it (see Note)—and applying this to the depiction of life "under the law" intended to serve as a negative foil against which to exalt the freedom and capacity brought by the Spirit (8:1-13).

The passage is very repetitive. This is because it aims, not simply to state a truth, but to drive it home to the reader by the repeated descriptions of the plight leading up to the concluding climax. It is in fact carefully structured. Between v 14 and the end of v 23 there are three statements of the dilemma in which the "I" finds itself: vv 14-17; vv 18-20; vv 21-23. Each contains two basic elements: a description of the dilemma (the gulf between willing and [non-]achievement) and an indication of the underlying problem (the grip of sin as indwelling power). The first two statements (vv 14-17 and vv 18-20) stand in close parallel: each begins with a sentence containing the verb to "know" and mentioning the "fleshly" constitution of the "I" (v 14, v 18a); each concludes with precisely the same ten-word phrase attributing responsibility to "indwelling sin" (v 17, v 20b);

in between, each states the moral dilemma in virtually the same words (vv 15b-16a and vv 19-20a). The third statement, vv 21-23, expresses the dilemma in fresh terminology (cf., however, v 21b), revolving around a play upon the Greek word *nomos*. Vv 24-25 offer a climactic conclusion (vv 24-25a) and a retrospective quasi-summary (v 25b).

Introduction: Sold into slavery under sin (v 14). The account begins with a remarkably positive quasi-axiom ("as we know"—*oidamen*) about the law. It is surprising to be reminded that the law is "spiritual" *(pneumatikos)* after it has been aligned with "flesh" and "letter" over against "Spirit" in 7:5-6. In effect, however, the statement goes little beyond the earlier (v 10) characterization of the "commandment" as "meant to lead to life" *(eis zōēn)*. "Spirit" *(pneuma)* in Paul is essentially tied to the communication of eschatological life (8:9, 11; 2 Cor 3:6b, 17-18) and this, at least *in principle,* was what the law claimed to offer (see Note on 7:10).

What has wrecked any life-giving potential of the law is the fact that it has had to confront a human situation which the "I" goes on to dub (v 14b) as "fleshly" *(sarkinos)*. Set over against "Spirit," "flesh" has here its predominantly negative tone in Paul, denoting human existence as weak, self-centered and hostile to God (cf. v 5; 8:5-8; Gal 5:19-21). This sense is intensified by the added comment about being "sold into slavery under sin"—the lingering consequence (cf. the perfect participle *pepramenos*) of the "I"'s "fall" under the dominion of sin described in 7:9-11. Sin, personified as slave master (cf. 6:15-23), has gained firm control of my existence as "flesh," setting this vital aspect over against the essentially "spiritual" law. It is this infestation by sin which sets up the essential conflict within the "I" now to be described in three "waves."

The Dilemma I (vv 15-17). In the first description of the dilemma, the "I" confesses (v 15a) to being totally perplexed *(ou ginōskō)* by its own behavior—that is, what in fact it does, as distinct from what it simply intends. There is a complete split between the "I" that wills and the "I" that eventually acts. The only conclusion to be drawn (the second element in the dilemma) is that "I" have lost control of the moral direction of my life and another force has taken over, a force dubbed again and again as "sin dwelling within me" (*hē oikousa en emoi hamartia;* v 17; v 20; cf. v 23). By speaking of sin as determining power in this way, Paul does not mean to exculpate the "I," as though it had become the helpless puppet of some external power. The language remains metaphorical. Sin is the totality of my own evil acts, making up a constant pattern of wrongdoing from which I cannot break free. In this sense it can be depicted as a slavemaster, to whom I have been sold and whose dictates I am henceforth compelled to obey. In the grip of sin as in-dwelling power, "I" can only helplessly aspire to obey the law but find no capacity to achieve what I desire.

The Dilemma II (vv 18-21). The second statement makes the same two points in terms that are for the most part strictly parallel (see above). The "I" owns *(oida)* the presence of an evil *(ouk . . . agathon)*, controlling force infesting *(oikei)* the "flesh." There is the same tension between what I will and what I manage to achieve—only this time without specific reference to the law, suggesting that a somewhat broader perspective is beginning to enter in. In fact, as is commonly observed with respect to this passage, it presents a Pauline formulation of a *topos* widespread in the literature of the ancient world, to which the Roman poet Ovid gave classic formulation (*Metamorphoses* 7:19-21): *Video meliora proboque; deteriora sequor* ("I see the better way and I approve it; but I follow the worse").

Dilemma III (vv 21-23). The third statement of the dilemma departs from the strict parallel of the earlier two in that it revolves around a complex wordplay upon the term *nomos.* Whatever rhetorical effect he was striving for in this regard, Paul has hardly made his thought clear. *Nomos* appears, in several meanings, no less than five times across the three verses. Behind the individual instances and to some extent holding them together there seems to lie a more general sense of the word where it refers to any system or factor seeking to control behavior. As such it can refer to the law of Moses—the "law of God" (v 22). But *nomos* can also have a negative reference and refer, in a metaphorical sense, to the power which "I" sense to be determining my action—that is, the "law of sin in my members" (v 23). Hence, making use of *nomos* in this broad sense, Paul can say in an introductory way (v 21a), "This is what I find to be the case with respect to 'law'," and then go on to describe the dilemma in terms of this multiple application of the term.

Once again, it is a conflict between what I will and what I find to be possible in effect, namely evil (v 21b). The "I" agrees with the "law of God" (the law of Moses) in the "inner self" *(kata ton esō anthrōpon)*, that is, the inner seat of thinking and willing of the rational being (v 22). But in the sphere of action—for which, again, Paul uses the term "members" (*melē*; cf. 6:13, 19; 7:5)—the "I" detects "another law" at work. The "other law" (*heteron nomon*, v 23) can only be the controlling force (see above) that the "I" finds operative at the level of action. It is virtually the same as what is later called the "law of sin *(tǭ nomǭ tēs hamartias)* which dwells in my members." The language becomes military (cf. 6:12-13): this "other law" is "at war" *(antistrateuomenon)* with the "law of my mind" *(tǭ nomǭ tou noos mou)* and is "holding me captive" *(aichmalōtizonta)*—a use of terms that become all the more significant where one realizes that the usual fate of prisoners of war in ancient times was to be sold into slavery (cf. v 14). The "law of my mind" corresponds to the judgment exercised by the "inner self" *(kata ton esō anthrōpon)*. The external "law of God" has a base—an "antenna," if you like—in the rational, willing center of the

"I." But this "I", for all its sympathy with the law, cannot command what happens on the field of action, where the "other law" is in control.

The situation is, then, that there are basically two forces (two *"nomoi"*) at work and in conflict—the (external) law of God (the law of Moses), which has its representative in the "inner man" in the "law of the mind," and that "other law," the "law of sin," which is at work at the level of action (in the "members"). By "law of sin" Paul does not mean the law of Moses seen as ranged alongside the negative powers of sin and death. He means the controlling force of "sin," metaphorically described in terms of *nomos*, which compels the law of God—in itself always "holy" and "spiritual"—to have disastrous effects when it comes into contact with human nature "sold into slavery under sin" (v 14). Essential to Paul's argument is the distinction between what the law of God is in itself ("holy," etc.) and the effect it has in the prevailing situation in human affairs. The "good" and "holy" law of God, despite its ally within the "inner self," is no match for the "other law" which dominates the sphere of action. Only a more powerful "law"—the Spirit—can break the grip of the "law of sin," as Paul will proclaim in 8:1-4.

Cry for liberation and response (vv 24-25). The threefold statement of the moral plight of the "I" complete, the rhetorical climax comes, when the "I," faced with the total "impossibility" of the situation under the law, can only cry out desperately for rescue—for a savior from some other source, it knows not where: "Who will deliver me . . .?" (V 24). The plight from which deliverance is sought is described as "the body of this death" *(tou sōmatos tou thanatou toutou).* This powerful phrase does not indicate the physical body as the source of captivity—as though physicality as such were the source of the problem. "Body" *(sōma)* retains here its characteristic Pauline sense of sphere of communication and action (see Interpretation of 6:6). The complete phrase refers to the sphere where the captivity to sin is most desperately felt—not the "inner self" (v 22) but the sphere of action where the "I" tries to implement the good intentions of that self. It is a captivity of "this death" in the dual sense of being presently a living death (cf. v 10: "I died . . .") and of leading inevitably to eternal death as a consequence of "condemnation" (cf. 8:1) at the judgment.

In response to this desperate cry, it would seem most appropriate to introduce at this point the proclamation of rescue appearing in 8:1-4. Instead, the text provides two sentences which taken together are hard to fit into the overall sequence. The exclamation of thanks to God through Jesus Christ (v 25a) is understandable as a response to the "I"'s desperate cry for salvation. In a way that anticipates the liberation to be proclaimed in 8:1-2, it allows a "Christian" perspective to finally break through. The problem is, however, that the following statement (v 25b) reverts very much to the preceding "pre-Christian" perspective. It presents the dilemma of the "I" as an experience of feeling the tug of two contrasting "services" (*douleuein*; cf. 6:15-23). In "my mind" (= "my "inner self" [v 22]) I find myself serving "the law of God." But this "service" remains purely internal, intentional only. It does not translate to the area of action—"the flesh"—because in that sphere I serve a more powerful "law," that of sin (cf. v 14b). While the originality of this statement has been questioned (see Notes), it does sum up well the dilemma portrayed throughout the sequence. In particular, its powerful depiction of the plight of the "I" left to its own merely human resources *(autos egō)* prepares the way for the contrasting proclamation of liberation at God's hand that is to follow (8:1-4).

I argued above that the struggle with sin presented throughout the passage does not reflect experience Paul would consider "typical" of ongoing life in Christ. On the contrary, what is described here provides the negative background against which to set all the more effectively the liberation that comes with life "in Christ" (8:1-2). Nonetheless, while not presenting the "Christian" situation as such, the passage presents a significant Christian point of view. It powerfully depicts the bankruptcy of any attempt to correct moral failing simply through the imposition of an external code where the inner root problem of human life (what Paul calls "flesh" infested with sin) is not addressed. In such a situation, law does not help but only exacerbates the problem all the more. Doubtless modern believers, as so many down the ages, will continue to find that the struggle depicted in the passage resonates with their own experience. But, rather than concluding that this is the "normal" situation for the Christian, they should perhaps ask whether in their ethical struggle they are not trying to "go it alone" (*autos egō* [v 25b]) apart from God in a way more redolent of life "before" Christ. The passage can then become a "test of spirits" in the sense of an invitation to turn away from themselves and their own efforts back to the Spirit who alone can create inner healing and the longed-for moral "possibility."

Notes

14. *as we know:* On Paul's use of *oidamen* to express a truth or fact which he believes or hopes is a matter of common ground between himself and those he addresses, see Note on 2:2.

fleshly: The adjective *sarkinos* normally has a neutral meaning (cf. 2 Cor 3:3), whereas the form *sarkikos* (offered here as a variant by some manuscripts) always retains the technical negative sense. But the use of *sarkinos* 1 Cor 3:1, where it also stands in contrast to *pneumatikos*, shows that it can function in the negative sense that is evidently required here.

sold into slavery under sin: The phrase argues strongly against the view that the passage as a whole reflects present Christian experience. The entire argument in 6:15-23 turns around the thesis that believers' former slavery to sin has been replaced by a "slavery" to righteousness.

15. *I am completely at a loss to account for my own behavior:* The translation exploits the wide-ranging sense of "know" in Paul. The sense could be that I do not *understand* my own behavior—that is, the gap between what I want and what I in fact do *(katergazomai)*; alternatively, but less likely, the sense could be that I do not *approve* of my own behavior.

16. *I agree with the law and hold it to be admirable:* The rather vague adjective *kalos* continues Paul's commendation of the law (cf. v 12, v 14). Such statements do not render the passage as a whole an "apology for the law," since each is followed by a strong qualification emphasizing the impotence of the law in the face of sin (cf. 8:3).

17. *sin dwelling within me:* The issue of which "power" (sin or the Spirit) is the indwelling *([en]oikousa, -oun)*, controlling force is a common theme across 7:14–8:13: see 7:17, 18, 20, 23; 8:9, 10, 11 (twice).

18. *in my flesh:* For the Pauline concept of "flesh" *(sarx)*, see Interpretation and Note on 7:5.

19. *For I do not do the good I want to do, but the evil that I do not want, that I do:* As well as the Latin quotation from Ovid, cited in the Interpretation, Paul's expression here (and in similar formulations in vv 15-16, 18, 20a, 21) has a close verbal parallel in Epictetus (*Discourses* 2.26.1–2, 4–5). For the Stoic sage, however, the problem lies not so much in a conflict between will and incapacity for action as in a misperception which confuses the will about what is in its best interest. For Paul's more strictly theological sense of the *topos*, where the incapacity stems from a captivity to sin, Jewish parallels are close at hand, most notably in the profound sense of human weakness and sinfulness over against God described (in the first person singular) in certain of the psalms from Qumran (1QH 1:21-23, 26-27; 11QPs[a] 19:10-16; cf. also the "Two Spirit" instruction in 1QS 3:13–4:26) and also the sense of the human struggle against the "evil heart" or "evil inclination" in *4 Ezra* (3:20-22 [against it the law was powerless; cf. Rom 8:3]; 4:30). For a wider survey of the *topos* in ancient literature, see G. Theissen, *Psychological Aspects* 212–19; S. K. Stowers, *Rereading of Romans* 260–64.

21. *So this is what I find to be the case with respect to "law":* The translation attempts to render the Greek phrase *heuriskō ara ton nomon* in a way that allows for a more abstract usage of *nomos* applicable in several situations, as discussed in the Interpretation (see also Note on 2:12). Cf. A. van Dülmen: "*Nomos* undergoes a broadening from the Mosaic law to an unrestricted extension, which certainly does not exclude the Mosaic law. Anything which can impose a total claim upon the whole person, be it the will of God, be it sin, is called *nomos*"

(*Theologie des Gesetzes* 118 [Translation mine]). The customary translation of *nomos* here as "rule," "principle" or "norm" (in the sense of "what is generally the case") spoils the force of Paul's wordplay across vv 21-23. On the other hand, a strict reference to the Mosaic law renders the sentence unintelligible. Had he meant this, Paul could surely have found an easier way to express it. To see already a reference to the "other law" (= "the law of sin") concretizes the matter "too early" on the negative side. On the use of *heuriskein* for "what I find" or "what turns out to be (for me) the case," cf. 7:10; Gal 2:17.

22. *I take delight in the law of God:* This, rather than the sense of "agreeing with . . .," would appear to be the proper sense of the verb *synēdomai* followed by the dative of a thing; cf. LSJ 1715. The sense of "delight" at the level of intention heightens the contrast with the incapacity experienced at the level of performance.

according to my inner self: This designation of the inner core of the reasoning and willing human being—together with the corresponding reference to "mind" *(nous)* in v 25—stems from the Platonic tradition of Greek philosophy, mediated through Hellenistic Judaism (cf. Philo). Paul uses it here not in the sense of a distinction along Platonic lines between the spiritual core of the person over against the physical body but in the service of the fundamental distinction he is making here between what I can will in my inmost self and what I can manage outwardly to achieve ("in my members"). The fact that the same expression occurs in 2 Cor 4:16 (cf. also Eph 3:16) with clear reference to the life of believers is taken by some to indicate a reference to Christian existence here as well. However, in 2 Cor 4:16 the "Christian" implication stems from the context, not the phrase in itself.

23. *But I see another law in my members . . . holding me captive to the law of sin:* The phraseology suggests a certain distinction between the "other law" and the "law of sin"—the former being the agent that brings about the captivity of the "I" to the latter. This in turn could suggest, particularly in view of v 5, that the "law of sin" be identified with the law of Moses considered in its negative effects. But after the highly positive way in which Paul has been speaking of the law of Moses (v 12, v 14, v 22 ["law of God"]) he could hardly expect his audience to apply such a negative phrase to it without more explicit indication.

law of my mind: "Mind" *(nous)*, which corresponds to "inner self" in v 22 (see Note), describes in Paul the human person as a knowing, reasoning and judging being (cf. 1:28; 12:2; 14:5); it can also designate the *result* of such processes: "will" or "intention" (cf. 1 Cor 2:16; Phil 4:7). Since it almost always includes the idea of "will" or "inclination" as well as the purely rational, it is virtually synonymous with "heart" (*kardia;* cf. 2 Cor 3:14-15; Rom 1:21 and 1:28). Though it refers to a higher aspect of human makeup and can partake of the renewed existence (cf. 12:2; 14:5; 1 Cor 2:16), "mind" is basically neutral in itself and can be subject to human fallenness (1:28) and, for all its good intentions, helpless in the face of sin (7:22, 25). The "law of my mind" would therefore be the law of Moses (or perhaps, more generally, the will of God as I perceive it) internalized and accepted as reasonable within me. In the case of "mind" and "inner self" Paul's language owes more to Hellenistic rather than Semitic anthropology.

24. *Wretched one that I am! Who will deliver me. . . .?:* The formulation is closely matched in Epictetus, *Discourses* 1.3.5: *"ti gar eimi? talaipōrion anthrōparion* (though reflecting a more Platonic sense of conflict within human beings between [godlike] reason and [brute-like] corporeity); cf. also *4 Ezra* 7:62-69, 116-26.

from the body of this death?: The demonstrative *toutou* could equally apply to the first noun so as to give "this body of death." The overall context, insisting that submission to the law has been a way to death rather than life, suggests that the stress falls upon "death" (cf. also 8:2: "law of sin and death").

25. *Thanks be to God, through Jesus Christ, our Lord. For, left to my own resources, with my mind I serve the law of God, but in the flesh it is the law of sin that I serve:* Similar expressions of thanks to God occur in 6:17 and 1 Cor 15:57, where the grounds for thanking God are immediately indicated, which is not the case here, unless one sees 8:1-2 as fulfilling that role. This raises the whole question of making some sense of the flow of statements across 7:24–8:1. Rearrangement of the sentences—notably, placing v 25b before 24—raises the problem of explaining how the present difficult order came about. Many interpreters, following Bultmann, regard v 25b as a gloss. But there is no textual warrant for this, and in many ways the clause provides an apt concluding summary of the "I's" moral dilemma. It is more reasonable to be suspicious of the expression of thanks (v 25a), which appears with some variation in the textual tradition and could represent a pious scribal response to the anguished cry of v 24. In any case, whether Pauline or not, it is an interjection and therefore cannot of itself overthrow the basically "pre-Christian" thrust of the wider argument.

For Reference and Further Study

Bornkamm, G. "Sin, Law and Death: An Exegetical Study of Romans 7." *Early Christian Experience* 87–104.

Dülmen, A. van *Theologie des Gesetzes* 112–19, 138–68.

Dunn, J. D. G. "Rom 7:14-25 in the Theology of Paul." *TZ* 31 (1975) 257–73.

Hahn , F. "Das Gesetzverständnis im Römer- und Galaterbrief." *ZNW* 67 (1976) 29–63.

Heckel, T. K. *Der Innere Mensch: Die paulinische Verarbeitung eines platonischen Motivs.* WUNT 2/53; Tübingen: Mohr, 1993, 148–210.

Kümmel, W. G. *Römer 7 und die Bekehrung des Paulus.* Leipzig: Hinrichs, 1929; repr. Münich: Kaiser, 1974, 58–68, 89–138.

Lambrecht, J. *The Wretched "I" and Its Liberation: Paul in Romans 7 and 8.* Louvain: Peeters/Eerdmans, 1992.

Martin, B. L. *Christ and the Law in Paul* 78–84.

Mitton, C. L. "Romans VII Reconsidered." *ExpTim* 65 (1953–54) 78–81, 99–103, 132–35.
Räisänen, H. *Paul and the Law* 109–13.
Stacey, W. D. *Pauline View of Man* 128–36, 154–73, 181–93, 198–205.
Stowers, S. K. *Rereading of Romans* 16–21, 258–84.
Theissen, G. *Psychological Aspects* 186–90, 211–21.
Vollenweider, S. *Freiheit als neue Schöpfung* 345–74.
Westerholm, S. *Israel's Law* 56–64.

f) *Life in the Spirit—Ethical "Possibility"* (8:1-13)

1. There is therefore now no condemnation for those in Christ Jesus. 2. For the law of the Spirit of life in Christ Jesus has set you free from the law of sin and death. 3. For what the law could not do, in that it was weak because of the flesh, God (has done): sending his Son in the likeness of flesh dominated by sin and as a sin-offering, he condemned sin in the flesh, 4. in order that the righteous requirement of the law might be fulfilled in us, who walk now, not according to the flesh, but according to the Spirit.

5. For those who live according to the flesh have their minds set on the things of the flesh, while those who live according to the Spirit have their minds set on the things of the Spirit.

6. Now the mind-set of the flesh leads to death, whereas the mind-set of the Spirit leads to life and peace. 7. This is because the mind-set of the flesh is hostility to God. For it is not subject to the law of God, nor can it be. 8. Those who really live in the flesh cannot please God.

9. But you are not living in the power of the flesh but in that of the Spirit—that is, if the Spirit of God is indeed dwelling in you. If anyone does not have the Spirit of Christ, that person does not belong to him.

10. But if Christ dwells in you, then, while the body may be mortal because of sin, the Spirit means life because of righteousness. 11. If the Spirit of the One who raised Jesus from the dead dwells in you, then the One who raised Christ from the dead will make alive also your mortal bodies through the power of his Spirit dwelling in you.

12. So then, my brothers (and sisters), we are people under an obligation—not to the flesh, to live according to the flesh. 13. For if you live according to the flesh, you will die. But if, in the Spirit, you put to death the deeds of the body, you will live.

Interpretation

Introduction. There is a palpable change of tone at this point in the letter. Against the dark background of slavery to sin under the regime of the law (7:7-25), Paul invites his audience to rejoice in the new era of freedom and ethical "possibility" brought by the Spirit. The passage brings to a close the long defense of the necessity and possibility of "living out" the gift of righteousness begun at 6:1. On the principle that being found righteous is what paves the way to eternal life (8:10; cf. 1:16-17), the opening up of this possibility now proclaimed will lead to the re-entry of the theme of "hope" at 8:14. More immediately, the passage forms the positive side of the "diptych" begun in 7:7-25. To have its full rhetorical effect, it must be read and heard in close contrast with this negative counterpart—the ethical "possibility" in the Spirit shown up against the "impossibility" under the law.

The two opening verses introduce the main theme: the freedom ("possibility") created by the Spirit. Vv 3-4 trace this freedom back to God's sending of the Son (vv 3-4). Then the body of the passage (vv 5-11) indicates the two responses—living "according to the flesh" or "according to the Spirit"—that are now possible, together with the outcome ("death" or "life") to which each leads. Vv 12-13 round off the passage (and the entire "ethical section" [6:1–8:13]) on a note of admonition.

The liberation brought by the Spirit (vv 1-2). The previous section came to a climax with the desperate plea for release from the slavery to sin (7:24) —a slavery which could lead only to condemnation at the judgment and loss of eternal life. In response Paul triumphantly (cf. 3:21) announces (v 1) a totally new situation for those who, through faith and baptism, are "in Christ Jesus." Those who live in the communal sphere of power and salvation constituted by the risen Lord (the sense of Paul's technical phrase "in Christ"; see Interpretation of 6:3) are radically cut off from the old sin-dominated existence so graphically described and have "now" *(nyn)* entered the life of the new age. It is not that the past situation is destroyed in absolute terms; "outside" of Christ, sin and death still very much prevail and even those "in Christ," as they journey to full salvation, continue to feel the buffet of these powers. But for those made righteous through faith (5:1-2, 19) the grip of the old age has been radically broken, the prospect of "condemnation" (*katakrima*; cf. 2:12, 16; 5:16, 18) removed.

The positive factor excluding condemnation is the "liberation" brought by the Spirit (v 2). On both the positive (v 2a) and negative (v 2b) side, Paul describes this in terms of "law," retaining the broadened sense of "law" introduced in 7:21-23. There Paul had used *nomos* in the generic sense of anything serving to control human behavior, whether for good or ill. Thus the liberating "law of the Spirit of life in Christ Jesus" is not a law in the strict sense of a moral code but the Spirit itself in so far as, in the new age, it constitutes a new norm and possibility of life (cf. Paul's description of himself in 1 Cor 9:21 as *ennomos Christou*). Correspondingly, the "law of sin and death" from which "you" (see Note) are set free is not the law of Moses. Paul has made clear that in itself this law is "holy, just and good" (7:12). Rather, it is the "other law" (7:23), the controlling force of sin in my members that prevented me from fulfilling the law of God. The meaning, then, is that the prospect of condemnation which would arise from lack of righteousness (sin) has been removed because a new moral force (the Spirit), available in Christ Jesus, has brought release from the ethical "impossibility" created by the dominance of sin.

The foundation of the "possibility": God's sending of the Son (vv 3-4). Paul traces this liberating gift of the Spirit right back to its ultimate source: God's sending of "his own Son" to break the fatal grip of sin on human affairs. The context for this divine intervention was the impotence of the law (*to adynaton tou nomou,* v 3a). The law certainly aimed to give life (7:10) and in this sense could even be dubbed "spiritual" (*pneumatikos,* 7:14). But, being purely external and hence unable to confront the problem that was deep-seated *within* human nature ("sin in the flesh"), it proved fatally "weak" *(ēsthenei)*. Impotent to create the righteousness it demanded, it could not open up the way to life (contrast the "power" of the gospel leading to salvation in 1:16-17).

In stark contrast to the situation of "impossibility" under the law came the action of God. The "sending" statement conveys a sense of divine "invasion from outside" into the human realm, while also stressing the depth of divine identification with the human condition. Where the law could only issue external edicts and threats, the Son truly entered the heart of that realm where the battle with sin could be effectively joined and won. Being sent "in the likeness *(en tą̄ homoiōmati)* of sinful flesh" meant full entry into the human situation of "flesh sold into slavery under sin" (7:14). All the weakness, temptation and proneness to sin that the biblical tradition characterizes as "flesh" Christ felt and suffered in his own person, while remaining personally sinless (2 Cor 5:21), "obedient even unto death" (Phil 2:8; cf. Rom 5:19). The language here (cf. also Phil 2:6-7), far from "protecting" or distancing the divine from sin, actually stresses the opposite. In the person of "his own Son" (*ton heatou huion;* cf. 8:32) God truly became vulnerable to the onslaught of sin, lovingly bearing the cost exacted by the conflict (5:6-10).

The culmination of the divine "invasion" came with the death of the Son upon the cross (cf. the progression from "incarnation" to death upon the cross in Phil 2:7-8). The text appears to make allusion to this in a phrase, *kai peri hamartias,* appended to the "sending" clause. The phrase could simply indicate the immediate goal of the sending—the dealing with or removal of sin. More likely (see Note), Paul incorporates here from the early Christian tradition a way of referring to the death of Jesus in cultic terms (cf. the use of *hilastērion* in 3:24). The particular rite in question is that of the "sin-offering" (Lev 9:2; 14:31; Ps 40:6), which in Hebrew is simply referred to as "sin" *(ḥaṭṭāʾt)*, an ambiguity carried over in the LXX translation. Paul seems to exploit this ambiguity in an ironic way. Precisely by "becoming sin" in the sense of both identifying with sinful humanity *and* functioning as an expiatory offering for sin, Christ became the agent of sin's overthrow. The essential comment is provided in 2 Cor 5:21: "God made him who knew no sin into sin *(hamartian)*, so that in him we might become the righteousness of God."

The totality of this "entrance" of the Son into humanity's sinful depth enabled God to succeed where the law had been impotent. God "condemned" *(katekrinen)* sin right there where it was rampant—in the human situation designated as "flesh." The "condemnation" *(katakrima)*, which in the apocalyptic scenario presupposed by Paul hung over human beings because of sin (v 1), falls not upon them—or at least not upon those "in Christ"—but upon sin itself. The true villain in the piece has been nailed. A new possibility and freedom has, through God's action, replaced the "necessity" to sin.

In the purpose clause (v 4) completing the "sending" statement, Paul describes this new possibility as the "fulfillment in us of the righteous requirement of the law" *(hina to dikaiōma tou nomou plērōthę en hēmin)*. At first sight it seems strange that the goal of God's action should be "our" fulfillment of the law—especially if the "law" in question is the law of Moses. As used here, however, the phrase *to dikaiōma tou nomou* does not refer to the law in its entirety nor to any particular commandment but to what the law, in its totality, required of human beings, namely, righteousness, a life lived in faithful conformity to God's will (note how a few sentences later being "subject to the law of God" [v 7] is equated with "pleasing God" [v 8]). The righteousness, which the law required but could not achieve, God has "fulfilled" through the costly "sending" of his Son (cf. Matt 3:15). From this point of view at least, Paul can rightly defend his earlier claim (3:31) to be "upholding" the law (see Note on 3:31).

By speaking of the "fulfillment" in the passive *(eplērōthę)* Paul avoids any sense that the new righteousness is something achieved by believers themselves. It is "our" righteousness in the sense that it is fulfilled "in us" *(en hēmin)* and, as truly communicated to us, it serves to ward off the "condemnation" mentioned in v 1. But it is wholly the creation and gift of God, the "righteousness of God" that depends upon faith (1:17; 3:21-22 [cf. 24-26]; 10:3-4; cf. 1 Cor 1:30; Phil 3:9 ["righteousness from God"]).

Paul speaks in similar terms of the "fulfillment" of the law in Gal 5:14 (where the "whole law" is said to "be fulfilled" *[peplērōtai]* by the love command) and Rom 13:8 (where the one who loves is said to "have fulfilled the rest of the law" *[heteron nomon peplērōken]*). These parallels suggest that the sense of love as the perfect expression of righteousness is not far distant in Rom 8:4 (cf. Gal 5:6b: "faith finding expression in love").

Sin, said Paul in 7:8, worked in human beings "all covetousness" *(epithymia)*, that is, the fundamental tendency to put self at the center of the universe, denying the claim both of the Creator and all other beings. God's "condemnation" of sin in Christ attacks this tendency at its noxious core, creating its very opposite, the possibility of love (1 Cor 13:4-5).

The whole elaborate "sending" statement in vv 3-4 supports the liberating role of the Spirit outlined thematically in v 2. Appropriately, then, at the end of the sentence Paul indicates the Spirit as the more immediate agent at work. Those in whom the righteous requirement of the law finds fulfillment "walk" now "not according to the flesh but according to the Spirit." As in 6:4, "walk" refers to conduct. To "live according to the Spirit" is to allow one's life to be transformed and ruled by the dynamic power of the new age, released by God's act in Christ and, in fact, tantamount for Paul to the influence of the risen Lord (cf. 1 Cor 15:45). Noteworthy here is the fundamentally Trinitarian "shape" of Christian moral life according to Paul. All goes back to *God's* "sending" of the *Son* and the costly victory over sin achieved in his death. This has released in believers a new moral possibility in the shape of the *Spirit*.

The Two Ways: "Flesh and Spirit" (vv 5-11). The body of the passage is basically an elaboration of this new possibility opened up by God's sending of the Son. Paul proceeds in antithetical mode, taking his cue from the concluding phrases of v 4: "not according to the flesh but according to the Spirit." He formulates a kind of "Two Ways" teaching not far removed from that the instruction on the Two Spirits in the Community Rule of Qumran (1QS 3:13–4:26). "Flesh" and "Spirit" do not denote separate elements in the make-up of human individuals ("body" and "soul," for example) but rather two possibilities of human existence—the one self-enclosed, self-regarding and hostile to God, the other open to God and to life.

As the sequence makes clear, living "according to the flesh"—with its fatal consequences—is still a possibility for believers. It is a possibility but not a necessity. This is the crucial difference from the situation portrayed on the negative side of the "diptych" (7:14-25). Under the regime of sin, exacerbated by the law, it was impossible not to sin. In the new era of grace it is possible but not necessary. One has the freedom to say "No" to sin and "Yes" to God. There is, then, a tension in Christian life and choices have constantly to be made. But it is not the fatal tension of the old regime tearing the "I" apart (v 24). It is a constructive tension leading to growth and life.

The detailed argument of the passage runs along the following lines.

1. Vv 5-6 set out the two ways and their respective consequences (death and life) through the idea of the "mind-set" *(phronein/phronēma)* which each entails:
   V 5 explains the "mind-set"; V 6 indicates the destiny in each case.

2. Vv 7-8 elaborate on the grounds for this in terms of the "flesh."
3. Vv 9-11 elaborate on the grounds for this in terms of the "Spirit."
   V 9a: the reality of life in the Spirit;
   V 9b: (by way of contrast) consequences of *not* having the Spirit;
   Vv 10-11: consequences of having the Spirit.

As is so often his way (cf., e.g., 6:20-23), Paul spells out the contrast between the two ways of living in terms of the (eschatological) outcome (death or life) to which each, respectively, leads. As a middle term, however, he introduces (vv 5-6) the idea of the "mind-set" *(phronein/phronēma)* characteristic of each. In Pauline usage *phronēma* goes beyond thought and aspiration to include actual achievement of the object in view—in the present case, death, on the one hand; life, on the other. Those who live according to the flesh have a flesh-centered "mind-set" that will lead to (eternal) death; those taking advantage of the new possibility to live according to the Spirit have a Spirit-centered mind-set leading to the blessings of salvation, here denoted in traditional language as "life and peace" (cf. esp. 2:7, 10).

What makes these two outcomes—death or life, respectively—inevitable is the relationship to God operative within each. In the case of the flesh (vv 7-8), there is nothing but a mind-set of "hostility to God" (v 7a)—a phrase providing what is virtually a definition of "flesh" in the biblical sense presupposed by Paul. Those who live in the flesh cannot relate appropriately to God because they lack both the willingness and the capacity to offer the required obedience—literally, "submit to God's law" (on the sense of "law" here, see Note). Inability to "please God" (v 8) in this sense frustrates the relationship with the Creator upon which the attainment of life depends.

While "living in the flesh" may remain a possibility, it is not the true situation of believers. Reverting (v 9) to the direct (second person) address, Paul reminds his audience that they live "in the Spirit" in the sense of having the Spirit as the determining force of their lives. This creates the possibility of living a life truly pleasing to God (cf. v 8) and so being set towards a destiny of eternal life.

Central to the argument of this section (vv 9-11) is the sense of the Spirit as "indwelling power." In the old era under the law (7:14-25) the root of the problem had been "sin dwelling within me." What makes all the difference in the new situation is the replacement of sin by the Spirit. To make the point Paul ensures that the repeated references to the "indwelling *(enoikein)* of sin" (7:17, 19; cf. v 18, v 23) are matched, on the positive side, by no less than three allusions to the "indwelling" *([en]oikein)* of the Spirit. In the gift of the Spirit, creating new moral "possibility" within believers, God has made good the prophetic promise to put the law within the heart of the people (Jer 31:33) and through the Spirit grant the capacity to fulfill it (Ezek 36:26-27; cf. Rom 2:29; 7:6; *Jub.* 1:23). The community can live "according the the Spirit" (v 4) or "in the Spirit" (v 9) because the Spirit lives "in" them (cf. the thought of the community as "temple" in 1 Cor 3:16; 6:19; 2 Cor 6:16).

A remarkable feature of these sentences is the variety of ways in which Paul refers to the Spirit as indwelling *(oikein)* power. It is the "Spirit of God" (v 9b), the "Spirit of Christ" (v 9c), the "Spirit of the One who raised Jesus from the dead" (v 11a), while at one point we have simply, "If Christ is in you, . . ." (v 10a). All this shows how tenuous for Paul is any distinction between the Spirit and the on-going impact of Jesus as risen Lord. The biblical motif of the Spirit of God as the eschatological gift *par excellence* is firmly tied to the person and "career" of Jesus. To be "in Christ Jesus" (as in vv 1-2) or "in the Lord" or "in the Spirit" or, conversely, to have Christ (v 10) or the Spirit "(dwelling) within you" amounts very much to the same conception of Christian life lived within the influence of the risen Lord who, as "Last Adam," has become "life-giving Spirit" (*pneuma zōopoioun* [1 Cor 15:45]).

The logic of the argument moves from the reality of the indwelling power to the consequences as regards salvation (vv 9b-11). As is so often his way (cf., e.g., 6:17, 19-20; 7:5-6; 8:12, 15), Paul prefaces—and so enhances—the affirmation of the positive with a glance at the negative alternative. If anyone does *not* "have" the Spirit of Christ (v 9b)—that is, if the Spirit of Christ does not dwell within—then that person does not "belong to him" *(ouk estin autou)* in the sense of not being destined to share in the full run of his "career" up to and including resurrection (cf. 6:5, 8). If, on the contrary, Christ really does dwell within (v 10), then, despite physical mortality *(to men sōma nekron)*, there really is a destiny to (eternal) life on the basis of the righteousness created by the Spirit.

The terse clauses of this last statement contain some key planks of Pauline theology. One is the belief that sin has left an abiding mark upon human existence in the shape of the body's destiny to physical death. This is the legacy from Adam no subsequent human being can escape (5:12-14; 7:10-11, 24; 1 Cor 15:21-22). Set over against this is the consideration—essential to the symbolic universe presupposed in the letter and operative throughout its entire argument (see the Interpretation of 1:17)—that righteousness (being found by God to be "in the right" at the final great judgment) is the passport to salvation, the essential condition for entrance into eternal life. So "the Spirit means life because of righteousness" *(to de pneuma zōē dia dikaiosynēn)* because, as indwelling power of the new age, it is creating in believers the righteousness required for eternal life (cf. 1:16-17; 3:21-26; 5:18, 21; 6:22-23). The righteousness that the law rightly required in order to give life but which it in itself could not produce because of sin is being fulfilled in believers through the Spirit (8:3-4). Despite the prospect of physical death, for those who live "in the Spirit" the destiny to eternal life is secure.

A final comment (v 11) places all this in terms of divine fidelity and resurrection. God vindicated the personal righteousness of Jesus—his "obedience unto death" (Phil 2:8; cf. Rom 5:19)—by raising him from the dead. His resurrection was, then, the outward, bodily shape of his "justification" by God. Believers do not have any personal righteousness in this sense; it is as sinners that they are grasped by grace. But "in Christ" the indwelling Spirit fulfills in them the righteousness required for salvation. They can have, then, the confident hope that the God who was faithful to Jesus, raising him from the dead in vindication of his personal righteousness, will raise also "their mortal bodies" because of the righteousness created and preserved in them by the Spirit (cf. 4:25; 2 Cor 4:13-14). God, who has intervened at such cost to create righteousness (8:3-4), will most certainly see the work through to resurrection (8:11).

Concluding Exhortation (vv 12-13). Over against the dark background of captivity under the law (7:7-25), Paul has shown and celebrated the hope of the new era. He rounds off the sequence on a note of fraternal admonition (*Ara oun adelphoi*). This continues the "flesh"/"Spirit" antithesis, resting its force once more on the "outcomes" to which each pattern of life, respectively, leads. Paul plays to some extent on the idea of "life" (*zān*; cf. John 11:25-26). Freed from sin, we are not "obliged" *(opheiletai)* to "live according to the flesh" as in the old era; we can sin but we do not *have* to. To choose to "live" in this (sinful) way (v 13) means in fact a destiny to "death" *(mellete apothnę̄skein)*. Whereas, to opt for "death" in the sense of "putting to death the deeds of the body" opens up the destiny to (eternal) "life" *(zēsesthe)*.

So Paul brings the entire "ethical sequence" (6:1–8:13) to a close, offering his audience a stark choice between "death" and "life" reminiscent of the exhortation of Moses in Deut 30:15, 19. The concluding promise, "you will live," also echoes the text from Habakkuk (2:4) quoted in the opening statement of the letter's theme: "The person who is righteous by faith will live" (1:17d). Over against the dark background of captivity to sin and death under the regime of the law, Paul has affirmed the possibility and necessity of living righteously. On the basis of that righteousness, "lived out" through the Spirit, the God who was faithful to Jesus will faithfully bring risen life to all who have "died to sin" (8:10-11; cf. 6:8-11). All this established, the way now lies open for Paul to resume (8:14) more explicitly the theme of hope that governs this entire part of the letter (5:1–8:39).

Notes

1. *There is therefore now no condemnation:* "Therefore" *(ara)* is somewhat surprising, since this opening statement is not readily understandable as a consequence from 7:25b. This has led to its being regarded, along with the latter, as a gloss. But the new situation upon which the statement in v 1 really rests has already been sufficiently affirmed in 7:6 (cf. *nyni*) and, while not exactly a parenthesis, 7:7-25 has simply provided a negative foil against which it may be more forcefully reasserted.

   in Christ Jesus: For the distinctive Pauline conception of the Christian life lying behind this phrase, see Interpretation of 6:3 and Note on 6:11.

2. *For the law of the Spirit of life in Christ Jesus:* The first genitive ("of the Spirit") is here taken as epexegetic ("the law which consists in the Spirit"; cf. BDF §167); the second ("of life") as qualitative ("leading to [eternal] life"; BDF §165; cf. 5:18). Some (e.g., Dunn, 1.416–17; Wilckens 2.122–23) hold that both instances of *nomos* in this verse refer to the Mosaic law, Paul being able to conceive of it in a two-sided way: either as caught in a nexus of sin and death or (in the new era) as fulfillable in the Spirit. But, in view of such statements as 7:4 and 7:6, it is very hard to see how Paul could conceive of the Mosaic Law, not just as undergoing a transformation in the new era, but as the very *agent* of the liberation. Paul has already broadened the sense of *nomos* in 7:21-23.

   in Christ Jesus: This phrase, understood in the same sense as in the preceding verse to indicate the sphere where the Spirit is active, could be attached to the verb ("set free in Christ Jesus"). It is best taken as a further qualification of the subject ("law . . .").

   has set you free: The variant, "set me free" (A, D), is to be rejected as an assimilation to the sustained use of the first person in 7:7-25. Within the diatribe style Paul "responds" to the anguished "I" of that passage.

   from the law of sin and death: With "law" *(nomos)* understood here in the broader sense of "controlling factor" (cf. 7:21), the first genitive ("of sin") indicates simple belonging or origin ("the law [= control] brought about by sin"; BDF §162); the second ("and death"), likewise referring to *nomos* (cf. *kai*), is qualitative ("leading to death"; BDF §165); cf. the qualification of *sōma* in 7:24.

3. *For what the law could not do . . . God (has done):* The Greek sentence is elliptical in more than one respect. An infinitive ("to do") has to be supplied *to . . . adynaton tou nomou* and this whole expression presupposes some verb of "doing" on God's part. This is not supplied. Paul creates an anacolouthon, moving straight on, after the participial phrase ("sending . . ."), to the idea of God's condemning sin.

   in that it was weak because of the flesh: On the technical Pauline sense of "flesh" *(sarx)*, see Interpretation and Note on 7:5.

   sending his Son: The complete sentence from this point on falls into the form of a "sending of the Son" statement to be found also in Gal 4:4-5 and in the Johannine literature in John 3:16-17; 1 John 4:9. In each case the assertion of the "sending" is followed by a purpose clause indicating the goal of the divine sending in terms of benefits for the human race. The origin of this christological form appears to lie in early Christian ways of seeing the person and role of Christ in terms of the divine saving wisdom (cf. Wis 9:10); see E. Schweizer, *TDNT* 8.375. Of itself the "sending" motif does not necessarily carry the implication that Christ had some form of personal existence ("pre-existence") in the divine sphere "prior" to his human history. The corresponding statement in Gal 4:4-5, however, is more clearly open to such an implication (cf. *genomenon ek gynaikos,* v 4) and it would seem to be demanded by the language in Phil 2:6 and 2 Cor 8:9 (cf. also Gal 2:20; 1 Cor 8:6; 10:4). These parallels suggest that pre-existence is implied also in Rom 8:3; for fuller discussion and references, see Byrne, *'Sons of God'* 180–81, 198–205.

in the likeness of flesh dominated by sin: For the range of possible meaning in the Greek word *homoiōma,* see Note on 6:5. Here, as in Phil 2:7, the meaning most applicable would be that of the concrete form or pattern in which a reality (sometimes a transcendent reality) manifests itself. The all-holy Son of God, who belonged essentially to the divine sphere, manifested himself in the concrete, palpable form proper to human existence. The personal sinlessness of Christ is reconcilable with his identification with the flesh ("flesh of sin") since being "flesh" for Paul implies *existence within* a sphere or realm of human weakness but not necessarily total personal conformity to such a realm.

and as a sin-offering: The phrase *(to) peri (tēs) hamartias* regularly occurs in the LXX as a translation of an explanatory comment indicating the purpose and effect of rituals (slaughter of sacrificial animals and sprinkling of their blood) prescribed for the expiation of sin (cf. esp. Lev 4: 3, 14, 28, 35; 5: 6, 7, 8, 10, 11, 13; Num 6:16; 7:16; 2 Chron 29:23-24; Ezek 42:13; 43:19; cf. Heb 13:11); sometimes it denotes the precise sacrifice known as a "sin-offering" (e.g., Lev 9:2; 14:31; Ps 39:7 [40:6]). Significantly, it also appears in a metaphorical sense in the Fourth "Servant Song" (Isa 53:10), which played a large role in very early attempts to find a meaning in the death of Jesus upon the cross; see Interpretation of 4:25 above. In the present text, the preposition *peri* could be used in a general sense to denote simply the dealing with or removal of sin (see BAGD 644–45 [s.v. 1, g]) but, understood in this way, the phrase becomes pleonastic in the light of the statement about sin's condemnation which follows immediately. The technical usage seems to be so widely prevalent in the LXX as to make the sacrificial allusion self-explanatory, especially if, in a metaphorical sense dependent upon LXX Isa 53:10, it had already been encased in an early Christian explanation of Christ's death.

he condemned sin in the flesh: "Condemnation" here (cf. v 1) must involve more than the simple branding of sin as the evil that it is. It is a passing of judgment upon sin which, while not destroying it absolutely, has radically exposed it for what it is (7:13), reversed its deceptive power (7:11) and broken its *necessary* grip upon human life; for those "in Christ Jesus" sin no longer "reigns" (cf. 5:21).

4. *the righteous requirement of the law:* For the range of meaning in the word *dikaiōma,* see Note on 1:32 above. In the present context, the primary meaning

"commandment," "requirement" would seem to apply. The unusual usage in the singular (elsewhere only LXX Num 31:21) might suggest a specific reference to the Tenth Commandment ("You must not covet") mentioned in 7:7 (so Ziesler 206–07). But, why, if he intended this connection to be made, did Paul not use the same word, *entolē*, in both contexts? Paul most likely uses the singular to avoid any suggestion of a renewed fulfillment of the prescriptions of the Jewish law and to focus attention upon what, reduced to its essential core, the law required: a righteous life before God; see further Byrne, *'Sons of God'* 93–94, n. 53.

might be fulfilled in us: Paul's use of the passive here has ecumenical significance in the context of the Reformation debate over "justification." With respect to the ongoing ethical life of believers, it safeguards the sense of divine initiative so important to the Reformed tradition, while allowing for the Catholic concern to see an intrinsic connection between righteousness and the gaining of eternal life (cf. 8:10); see further S. Lyonnet, "Gratuité de la justification" 175–77 (to which the present interpretation is much indebted); Byrne, "Living Out the Righteousness of God" 569.

who walk now: For the biblical sense of "walk" referring to behavior before God, see Note on 6:4.

5. *For those who live according to the flesh . . . those who live according to the Spirit:* Paul does not have two fixed and separate classes of persons in mind but rather two attitudes or orientations of life which the same person might adopt.

   have their minds set: For similar Pauline use of *phronein* in the sense of "adopt an attitude that determines behavior," see also 11:20; 12:3, 16; 14:6; 15:5; 1 Cor 13:11; Phil 2:5; 3:19.

6. *the mind-set:* As the suffix *(-ma)* indicates, *phronēma* denotes the result or consequence of the process of *phronein*. The modern term "mind-set" usefully captures the sense in a general kind of way. But in the present instance Paul uses *phronēma* to indicate the eschatological consequences ("outcome") of the *phronein* rather than a fixed attitude of mind.

7. *For it is not subject to the law of God:* This observation could seem to imply some continuing validity of the Jewish law in the lives of believers, which would be odd in view of the overall argument. A strict reference to the law of Moses could be maintained on the supposition that Paul sees those who adopt the "flesh" mind-set as reverting in practice to the old era and so being confronted (vainly) by the law prevalent in that era, namely the law of Moses—in which case v 7b would be something of a "flashback" to 7:14-25. But Paul has already broadened the concept of *nomos* (7:23; 8:2) and in v 4 "reduced" the law to the single requirement of righteousness. The essential clue to "law of God" here comes in the following explanation (v 8) where those who are "in the flesh" are stated to be unable "to please God." Paul speaks of "law" for the sake of continuity but does so in the broader sense where *nomos* designates God's will regarding human behavior.

8. *Those who really live in the flesh:* Here, as in 7:5, "in the flesh" *(en sarki)*, which can simply denote present human existence in a neutral sense (cf. Gal 2:20), has the sense of living "according to the flesh"—that is, being determined by it.

   please God: This phrase *theǭ areskein* is virtually a technical expression in Paul denoting the essential goal of Christian behavior in relation to God: see 1 Thess 2:4, 15; 4:1; cf. also cognate forms in Rom 12:1-2; 14:18.

9. *if the Spirit of God is indeed dwelling in you:* The translation takes the conjunction *eiper* beginning this conditional sentence as implying that the condition is in fact a reality and as more or less equivalent to "seeing that"; cf. *eiper* in 3:30; 2 Thess 1:6; possibly Rom 8:17; cf. LSJ 489 (s.v. II). If, as is also possible, *eiper* is taken as leaving open the question of whether the condition is fulfilled (cf. esp. 1 Cor 8:5 and 15:15), then the statement becomes more of a warning or threat.

   that person does not belong to him: The interpretation takes the simple Greek genitive phrase *ouk estin autou* to imply Paul's whole sense of believers' existence as lived out in intimate union with the risen Lord ("in Christ Jesus"; see Note on v 1) and as caught up thereby in the essential pattern of his "career" (death, burial and resurrection); cf. 1 Cor 3:21b-23 where Paul employs this idea *(hymeis . . . Christou)*, expressed in the same genitive construction, to turn the Corinthians' party slogans *(egō . . . Paulou; . . .; egō Christou)* back upon themselves.

10. *Christ dwells in you:* This is the reciprocal expression (cf. also Gal 2:20; 2 Cor 5:17; 13:5) of the reality more usually expressed in terms of believers being "in Christ," etc. (see previous Note).

    then, while the body may be mortal because of sin: The translation takes this remark in a concessive sense, stating the negative antithesis to the following affirmation. That *nekron* refers to physical death and has the sense of "mortal" is confirmed by the reference to *thnēta sōmata* in the following verse. A reference to the baptismal "death to sin" (cf. 6:6 and 8:13 ["put to death the deeds of the body"]) may be implicit, but then Paul would more likely have written "dead to sin" rather than "because of sin" (*dia hamartian*—cf. *dia dikaiosynēn* in the following phrase).

    the Spirit means life: The translation takes *pneuma* here to refer to the Holy Spirit, not to the human spirit—in which case Paul would have written "the spirit is alive," whereas in fact it is the noun *zōē* that he sets in apposition to *pneuma* and the "life" which it denotes must be eschatological ("eternal") life.

    because of righteousness: It is central to Paul's argument that the righteousness in question be the ethical righteousness created in believers through the operation of the Spirit (cf. v 4; 6:12-13, 13). The Protestant interpretative tradition (e.g., Cranfield 1.390, n.4; Dunn 1.432; Ziesler 212) is generally reluctant to accept this on the grounds that it would seem to introduce an "un-Pauline" doctrine of "merits." But Paul has sufficiently allowed for the sense of divine initiative by the passive expression of the notion of "fulfillment" (of due righteousness) in v 4 *(plērōthę̄)*; see Note on v 4.

11. *the One who raised Jesus from the dead:* Behind this phrase almost certainly lies an early formula of faith; cf. 4:24; 10:9; 1 Cor 6:14; 2 Cor 4:14. On the resurrection of Jesus as the outward, bodily expression of God's "justification" of his obedience, see M. D. Hooker, "Interchange and Atonement." *BJRL* 60 (1978) 462–81, esp. 466–71.

    then the One who raised Christ from the dead will make alive also your mortal bodies: The object "mortal bodies" shows that the verb *zōopoiein* must refer to resurrection; cf. 4:17; 1 Cor 15:22, 36, 45; 2 Cor 3:6. In 4:17-23 Paul drew attention to the parity between the faith of Abraham and that of subsequent believers on the basis that in both cases belief in a God who raised the dead was required: Abraham believed that God would overcome the "deadness" of his own reproductive possibilities; Christians believe in "the One who raised Jesus the Lord from the dead" (v 24). The present statement complements this in the sense that believers' faith not only looks "back" to the raising of Jesus but also "forward" to the raising of their own "mortal bodies." Paul now appears to take it for granted that physical death will be the "normal" lot of believers before the coming of the Lord and the final resurrection; contrast 1 Thess 4:15-17; 1 Cor 15:51.

12. *So then, my brothers (and sisters):* The introductory *ara oun,* as frequently in Paul (5:18; 7:3, 25; 9:16, 18; 14:12, 19; Gal 6:10; 1 Thess 5:6), signals an important conclusion. For the fraternal address as marking an important turning point, cf. 1:13; 7:1, 4; 10:1; 11:25; 12:1; 15:14; 16:17.

    we are people under an obligation: The rather rare term *opheiletēs* literally means "debtor," then, in a figurative sense, one obliged to do something for someone; cf. BAGD 598.

    not to the flesh: Logically, one might expect this denial to be followed by a positive assertion of indebtedness to the Spirit. But Paul reverts immediately (v 13) to resting the force of the argument upon the "outcomes" to which each way of life, respectively, leads (cf. vv 5-11).

13. *you will die:* In place of the simple future, Paul uses the verb *mellein* (cf. BAGD 501 [1, c, d]) to bring home the certainty of the consequence—death—which, of course, must mean here eternal death.

    in the Spirit: The simple instrumental dative *pneumati* carries a large burden here, involving the whole sense of the Spirit bringing about for those "in Christ" the fulfillment of the "righteous requirement of the law" (8:4).

    you put to death the deeds of the body: Paul casts the exhortation in the negative probably to make it more forceful. Nonetheless, the reference to "body" *(sōma)* in such a negative context is surprising (cf. 1 Cor 6:13-15); more understandable would be "deeds of the flesh" *(ta erga tou sarkos),* as in Gal 5:19. In any case "body" has to be understood here as more or less equivalent to "flesh."

For Reference and Further Study

Romans 8 as a whole

Balz, H. R. *Heilsvertrauen und Welterfahrung: Strukturen der paulinischen Eschatologie nach Römer 8:18-39.* BEvT 59; Munich: Kaiser, 1971.

Bindemann, W. *Die Hoffnung der Schöpfung: Röm 8:17-27 und die Frage einer Theologie der Befreiung von Mensch und Natur*. Neukirchen: Neukirchener Verlag, 1983.
Byrne, B. "Prophecy Now: The Tug into the Future." *Way* 27 (1987) 106–16.
Osten-Sacken, P. von der *Römer 8 als Beispiel paulinischer Soteriologie*. FRLANT 112; Göttingen: Vandenhoeck & Ruprecht, 1975.
Paulsen, H. *Überlieferung und Auslegung in Römer 8*. WMANT 43; Neukirchen: Neukirchener Verlag, 1974.

Rom 8:1-13
Branick, V. P. "The Sinful Flesh of the Son of God (Rom 8:3): A Key Image of Pauline Theology." *CBQ* 47 (1985) 246–262.
Byrne, B. "Living Out the Righteousness of God." 567–81.
_________. *'Sons of God'* 91–97.
Deidun, T. J. *New Covenant Morality in Paul* 69–78, 194–203.
Gillman, F. Morgan "Another Look at Romans 8:3: 'In the Likeness of Sinful Flesh.'" *CBQ* 49 (1987) 597–604.
Hooker, M. D. "Interchange in Christ." *JTS* NS 22 (1971) 349–61, esp. 354–55.
_________. "Interchange and Atonement." *BJRL* 60 (1978) 462–81, esp. 466–71.
Lyonnet, S. "Gratuité de la justification et gratuité du salut." *Études* 163–77, esp. 175–77.
_________. "St. Paul: Liberty and Law." *The Bridge: A Yearbook of Judaeo-Christian Studies*. Ed. J. M. Oesterreicher. 4 (1962) 229–51. [= "Christian Freedom and the Law of the Spirit according to Paul." *The Christian Lives by the Spirit*. Eds. I. de la Potterie and S. Lyonnet. New York: Alba House, 1971, 145–74].
Martin, B. L. *Christ and the Law in Paul* 28–32.
Osten-Sacken, P. von der *Römer 8* 144–56, 226–44.
Paulsen, H. *Überlieferung und Auslegung* 77–106.
Räisänen, H. *Paul and the Law* 50–53, 62–67.
Schweizer, E. Art. "*huios*." *TDNT* 8.374–76, 382–84.
Thompson, R.W. "How is the Law Fulfilled in Us? An Interpretation of Rom 8:4." *Louvain Studies* 11 (1986) 31–40.
Vollenweider, S. *Freiheit als neue Schöpfung* 372–74.
Wright, N. T. *Climax of the Covenant* 193–225.
Ziesler, J. A. "The Just Requirement of the Law (Romans 8.4)." *AusBR* 35 (1987) 77–82.

iv. Hope of Glory for God's Children (8:14-30)

a) *Children and Heirs of God* (8:14-17)

14. For all whose lives are shaped by the Spirit of God are sons (and daughters) of God. 15. For it is not a spirit of slavery that you have received—(something to drive you) back again to fear. But you have received a Spirit of sonship in which we cry out, "Abba, Father." 16. The

same very Spirit in this way bears witness along with our spirit that we are God's children.
17. And if we are sons (and daughters), then we are heirs as well—heirs of God, co-heirs with Christ—provided we are prepared to suffer with him in order that we might be glorified with him.

INTERPRETATION

Introduction. With this small passage Paul resumes more explicitly the theme governing Romans 5–8 overall: the hope of glory held out for all believers despite the sufferings of the present time. In the long "ethical sequence" making up 6:1–8:13 he has set this hope on a firmer basis: the replacement of the law by the Spirit creates and preserves in human lives a righteousness that opens up the way to salvation and eternal life. Now (8:14-30) the Spirit appears in a slightly different role. In the context of present suffering, Christian experience of the Spirit becomes the supreme pledge of glory. Paul expands upon a theme he had announced succinctly earlier on: "The hope (that we have) will not let us down, because God's love has been poured into our hearts through the Holy Spirit which has been given to us" (5:5).

The small pericope making up 8:14-17 serves as a kind of bridge to this new stage of the argument. It takes up the promise of eternal life *(zēsesthe)* at the close of v 13 and develops it in terms of the motif of "divine filiation" ("sonship"), which from here on will serve Paul as chief vehicle to express the hope engendered by the Spirit. V 14 asserts the fact of the filial status for those led by the Spirit; vv 15-16 ground this reality in believers' experience of the Spirit; v 17 moves on from the motif of "filiation" to that of "inheritance."

Theme: "Sons (and daughters) of God" (v 14). Paul rounded off the short exhortation at the close of the previous passage (vv 12-13) with the promise that "putting to death the deeds of the body" through the power of the Spirit will lead to eternal life *(zēsesthe).* He now (v 14) characterizes those who "are led by the Spirit" (*pneumati theou agontai*; see Note) in this way as "sons (and daughters) of God" *(huioi theou).* The introduction of the language of divine filiation comes rather suddenly upon the modern reader. The fact, however, that Paul simply begins to speak in such terms without explanation suggests he is confident it forms part of the symbolic universe he shares with his audience. The notion of human beings as "children of God" (current also in the wider Greco-Roman world; cf. Acts 17:28) is not simply an apt image plucked out of Paul's imagination at this point. It is part of the technical language in which the Jewish apocalyptic tradition expressed its hopes for the future. Paul presumes it to be familiar and accepted also within the common Christian tradition.

The notion of Israel as God's "child" or "son" is a widespread, if not notably prominent motif in the Old Testament tradition (see, e.g., Exod 4:22-23; Deut 14:1; 32:5-6, 19-22; Isa 1:2-4; 30:9; 63:8; Hos 1:10 [MT and LXX 2:1]; 11:1; Wis 12:7, 21; 16:10, 21, 26; 18:13; 19:6; Sir 36:17). It denotes a privilege reserved to Israel precisely as God's people, redeemed from Egypt, singularly under the divine protection; as God's "son" or "child" Israel enjoys an intimacy and closeness to the divinity shared by no other nation. The motif continues and indeed grows within the post-biblical tradition, where—probably in dependence upon the promise contained in Hos 1:10 (MT 2:1)—it came to be associated particularly with the eschatological Israel, God's people destined to "inherit" the promises of salvation (*1 Enoch* 62:11; *Jub.* 1:24-25; 2:20; *Pss. Sol.* 17:30; *As. Mos.* 10:3; *4 Ezra* 6:58; *2 Apoc. Bar.* 13:9; *Bib. Ant.* 18:6; 32:10; *Sib. Or.* 3:702; 5:202; 4QDibHam 3:4-6; 3 Macc 6:28; etc.).

It is this eschatological thrust that explains why Paul introduces the filial motif at this point. It is appropriate to back up the pledge concerning eternal life at the end of v 13 *(zēsesthe)* with the statement that those led by the Spirit are "sons (and daughters) of God." Within the traditional understanding of the image, this means that they belong to God's eschatological people, destined to inherit the ancient promises. What is implicit here also, though Paul postpones attending to it for a time, is that all believers, without discrimination—Gentile as well as Jews—share equally in this privilege and the hope it contains. This more general application of privileges previously tied strictly to Israel is in fact what lights the fuse sparking off the whole problematic concerning Israel which Paul will address in chapters 9–11.

The Evidence (vv 15-16). The status of being "God's sons (and daughters)" (cf. 2 Cor 6:18) is in itself a hidden thing. In a little parenthesis (vv 15-16) Paul points to the experience of the Spirit as that which guarantees that here and now believers enjoy precisely this status. As is so often his way (cf., e.g., 6:17, 19-20; 7:5-6; 8:9, 12), Paul prefaces what he wants to affirm with a denial of the negative (v 15a): the "spirit" that believers have received is not one of "slavery," reintroducing (cf. *palin*) an attitude of fear. As Paul insists at far greater length in Galatians (4:1–5:1) slavery—and the fear and insecurity that inevitably accompany it—belongs to the past, to the old era of sin and death, from which believers, through God's act in Christ (Rom 8:1-4), have been radically set free.

What believers have received (v 15b) is a Spirit that enables them to be confident that they enjoy filial status (*huiothesia*) in the household of God. In the Greek-speaking world of Paul's day *huiothesia* (not used in the LXX; elsewhere in the NT: Gal 4:6; Rom 9:4; Eph 1:5) was one of a number of terms referring to "adoption"—a widespread socio/legal practice in the Greco-Roman world. Within the strict terms of the language we should translate Paul's phrase as "spirit of adoption." Moreover, since the deity in Judaeo-Christian understanding does not literally beget sons and daughters, "adoption" seems an appropriate way to account for believers' new status and relationship to God.

However, adoption was not a common practice amongst Jews; if Paul is using *huiothesia* in its literal contemporary sense, he is reaching for an image somewhat beyond his own patrimony and the terms of his discourse in Romans up to this point. It is more likely that behind his use of this term stands that broad Jewish tradition of Israel, especially eschatological Israel, as "son/child (sons/children) of God." That Paul is indeed alluding to this tradition is strongly suggested by his listing of *huiothesia* among the privileges of Israel in 9:4. Whether then we choose to translate *pneuma huiothesias* here as "Spirit of adoption" or "Spirit of sonship" or perhaps, by way of compromise, "Spirit of (adoptive) sonship," ("Spirit of divine filiation" seems intolerably clumsy), it should be kept in mind that, as with the remaining language of "filiation" in this and the following chapter, Paul is speaking within the language of the Jewish tradition and claiming it for believers. What believers have received is a Spirit that goes with or attests to the fact that they enjoy the filial privilege pertaining to the eschatological people of God.

The proof that such is the case for believers is the content of the cry which the Spirit causes to well up within them: "*Abba*, Father." Paul draws attention here to a phenomenon he clearly believes to be typical of the religious and possibly liturgical life of any Christian community. He presumes it to be as familiar to the community, which he has not founded, as it is to the Galatian community, which he has (Gal 4:6-7; cf. also Mark 14:36). In this address to God—one of the very few instances where the original Aramaic is preserved—we are obviously encountering something characteristic and distinctive of early Christian life, possibly going back to Jesus' own experience of God (see Note), something, in any case, so precious, venerable and distinctive as to resist the absorption into Greek that was the fate of virtually the entire remainder of the tradition. If we recall the close link in Paul's understanding between the Spirit and the influence of Jesus as risen Lord (cf. vv 9-11; 1 Cor 15:45), it is a small step to recognizing that he—and the early communities—believed that in their Spirit-inspired impulse to address God in this way, the risen Lord continued in them his own characteristic address to the Father (cf. esp. Gal 4:6: "the Spirit of his Son").

Paul's chief point here, however, is that in this cry the divine Spirit is bearing clear witness along with "our spirit" that we here and now enjoy a filial status (expressed now in more gender-inclusive terms as "children [*tekna*] of God" [v 16]). The reference to the human spirit, though not unparalleled in Paul (cf., e.g., Rom 1:9; 1 Cor 2:11; 5:3-5; 7:34; 14:14; 16:18; 1 Thess 5:23), is somewhat curious as it suggests a kind of dual witness in which the divine confirms the human (see Notes). Later (v 26) Paul will speak of the Spirit "coming to our aid in our weakness" and, while the thought is not entirely the same, it does shed light on the witness of the Spirit. The believer's sense that he or she is indeed the child of God can be threatened, perhaps submerged, in the trials besetting Christian life in the present. In the "*Abba*" cry the Spirit brings confirmation and support to the sometimes faltering conviction of the individual believer.

"Heirs" as well (v 17). The filial status, however, is not an end in itself. More significant is the promise it holds for the future as "children" are destined to become "heirs" (*klēronomoi*, v 17a). Within the "filiation" image this is a natural progression to make. But, again, behind the choice of words lies a rich Jewish tradition concerning "inheritance." The motif (especially in the form of the verb, *klēronomein*) occurs very frequently with regard to the promise God made to Abraham regarding possession of the Land; in the later tradition, with the broadening of the "Land" promise to embrace both the present and future world (see Note to 4:13), "inheritance" came eventually to embrace the whole complex of eschatological blessings promised to Israel. In chapter 4 Paul reclaimed this tradition for his "inclusive" gospel, arguing that because Abraham became the "heir of the world" (v 13) on the basis of being right with God through faith rather than "works of the law," the "inheritance" stands open, not only to Jewish believers, but to a multitude of Gentiles as well (vv 16-17a). All this lies behind the simple deduction that, as "children of God," the Roman believers are also "heirs" (v 17a).

Immediately (v 17b), Paul places this sense of "inheritance" upon a firmly christological base. Believers are "heirs of God"—and in this sense Abraham's seed—but they are so as "co-heirs of Christ" (*synklēronomoi Christou*). That is, they have this destiny through their baptismal union with the risen Lord, who as "Firstborn" (8:29) is primary heir.

This union with Christ, however, is not simply a static attachment to his person but a dynamic insertion into what may be termed his total "career"—his passage to resurrection and glory via the obedience of the cross (cf. already 6:3-5, 8). It is by sharing his sufferings *(sympaschomen)* that we are to share also the glory *(syndoxasthōmen)* into which he, as prime "heir of God," has already entered. In this way, stressing the christological basis of being "heirs," Paul brings back the motif of suffering which formed the context for the initial affirmation of "hope" in chapter 5 (cf. esp. vv 3-4). The same mysterious conjunction of suffering and hope of glory returns to become the main theme down to the end of the entire sequence (8:39).

Notes

14. *are shaped by the Spirit of God:* The clear parallel provided by Gal 5:18 *(pneumati agesthe)*, where the ethical demands of life in the Spirit are solely in view, shows that this phrase refers to the Spirit's energizing of Christian behavior as described in vv 12-13.

are sons (and daughters) of God: In the translation of v 14 as a whole, the phrase *huioi theou* is taken as predicative with the demonstrative *houtoi* having inclusive sense. On the motif of "divine filiation" in the biblical and post-biblical Jewish tradition, see the extensive survey in Byrne, *'Sons of God'* 9–78.

15. *For it is not a spirit of slavery that you have received—(something to drive you) back again to fear:* "Spirit of slavery" *(pneuma douleias)* is a rhetorical foil to *pneuma huiothesias.* There is no implication of the existence of some "spirit" in the former condition to be set against the (Holy) Spirit in the new. Likewise, "again" *(palin)* must not be taken with the verb—so as to imply a former reception—but with the final reference to "fear" *(eis phobon).* Needless to say, Paul has moved away completely from his brief employment of the "slave" image on the positive side in 6:16-23.

a Spirit of sonship: The context implies that *pneuma* here refers specifically to the Holy Spirit, rather than to "spirit" in a more general sense. The immediate context—notably, the cry mentioned in the following clause—also suggests that the genitive in the phrase *pneuma huiothesias* is qualitative ("Spirit that goes with . . ." or ". . . indicates *huiothesia*" [cf. 8:23; 2 Cor 1:22; 5:5; cf. Eph 1:14]). On the background to the term *huiothesia* see Byrne, *'Sons of God'* 79–80, 99–100; J. M. Scott, *Adoption as Sons of God* 3–57. In his wider thesis (pp. 61–117) Scott argues that *huiothesia* must be translated strictly as "adoption," that adoption was practiced in Israel and that Paul's metaphorical usage of *huiothesia* with respect to the eschatological status of believers draws upon a Jewish messianic tradition that developed out of the throne promise to David in 2 Sam 7:14, understood as a case of adoption. It is difficult, however, to account for the total range of the Pauline divine filiation motif (including Rom 9:25-26, which Scott neglects) on the basis of 2 Sam 7:14 alone, even granted that Paul read this text in an adoptive sense. It is also unlikely that *huiothesia* in Paul refers solely to the *act* (of adoption) without connotation of the resultant *status* (sonship) as well; cf. the parallel with *douleia* in precisely the verse in question (8:15). For these and other reasons (see my review of Scott, *JTS* NS 44 [1992] 288–94) it makes better sense, with reference to Paul, to translate *huiothesia* as "sonship" or "adoptive sonship."

cry out: The verb *krazein* (also Gal 4:6), which denotes a loud cry, conveys a sense of the confidence with which the cry to God is uttered—in contrast to the "fear" mentioned earlier.

"Abba, Father": This address, also occurring in Gal 4:6 and placed on the lips of Jesus in Mark 14:36, consists of the Aramaic emphatic used as a vocative followed by *ho patēr* as a literal Greek translation. Its usage in Christian circles must certainly go back to the very early Aramaic-speaking community. The

fact that in the Aramaic Targum to Ps 89:27 the (Davidic) King Messiah addresses God as *"Abba"* could suggest that Christian usage of the cry originated in the community's sense of itself as the community of the Messiah now identified with the risen Jesus. The formulation in Gal 4:6 ("the Spirit of his Son . . .") directly attributes the cry to Jesus, an attribution which may have only the risen Lord in view. Nonetheless, the preservation of the address in Aramaic, together with the fact that the both the Synoptic ("Q" and Mark) and the Johannine gospel traditions consistently portray Jesus' relationship to God in "Son-Father" terms, argues strongly for a recollection here of something characteristic of Jesus, expressing a relationship of intimacy with the Father which the post-Easter community later felt itself to share. Earlier scholarly claims (esp. J. Jeremias) for the uniqueness of such an intimate address to God on the lips of Jesus (in the sense of being without precedent in contemporary Judaism) now appear somewhat hazardous. Nonetheless, the significance of the address and its preservation in Aramaic should not be underestimated. See further Fitzmyer 498; Dunn 1.453–54.

16. *bears witness along with our spirit:* The verb *symmartyrein* properly means "witness along with," "confirm." The translation "witness to," favored by some interpreters, strains the linguistic evidence; see further Ziesler 215–16.

God's children: In contrast to the Johannine tradition (which reserves *huios* for Jesus only) Paul uses the more "gender-inclusive" *tekna* interchangeably with *huioi* to express believers' divine filiation.

17. *we are heirs as well—heirs of God:* On "inheritance" in the Jewish tradition, see the extended Note on 4:13. That the sense of believers as "heirs of God" here should be associated with the presentation of Abraham as "heir of the world" in the earlier passage is clear from the more extended development across Gal 3:1–4:7: to be "heirs of God" (Rom 8:17) must be the same as being "heirs according to the promise" (Gal 3:29) since the "inheritance" depends upon God's bequest to Abraham "and to his seed" (Gal 3:15-18). The christological focus is more intense in Galatians (cf. esp. 3:16) than in Romans 4 but it clearly emerges here in Rom 8:17.

co-heirs with Christ: The word *synklēronomos* occurs only in the NT (see also Eph 3:6; Heb 11:9; 1 Pet 3:7). For Paul the risen Christ, as "Last Adam" (1 Cor 15:45), is heir already in possession of the inheritance (Phil 2:9-11); believers are heirs in waiting, and enjoy this status solely in virtue of their union with him (see also Gal 3:16, 26-29). In 1 Cor 3:21b-23 Paul states that "all things" belong to Christians in that they "belong" to Christ; their union with the risen Lord as "Last Adam" sets them in line to come into that lordship of the universe which, in the development of Gen 1:26-28 (cf. also Psalm 8) in the Jewish tradition, represents God's original design for human beings.

provided we are prepared to suffer with him in order that we might be glorified with him: The conjunction *eiper* introducing the conditional sentence adds to the simple condition the sense of fulfillment—either in the sense that sufferings are an evident fact of Christian life (in which case *eiper* means "seeing that" [as in 8:9]) or in the sense that the condition ought readily be conceded as something reasonable (in which case a note of exhortation enters in and *eiper* has the sense of "provided that"). The usage with the first person plural and the following final clause seem to confirm the latter, exhortatory sense here, as does also the transition (cf. *gar*) to v 18.

For Reference and Further Study

Byrne, B. *'Sons of God'* 97–103.

D'Angelo, M. R. "Theology in Mark and Q: *'Abba'* and 'Father' in Context." *HTR* 82 (1992) 149–74.

Fitzmyer, J. A. "*Abba* and Jesus' Relation to God." *À cause de l'Évangile* (FS J. Dupont). Ed. R. Gantoy. LD 123; Paris: Cerf, 1985, 15–38.

Hester, J. D. *Paul's Concept of Inheritance.* Edinburgh: Oliver & Boyd, 1968.

Jeremias, J. "Abba." *The Prayers of Jesus.* SBT 2.6; London: SCM, 1967, 15–67, esp. 57–65.

Obeng, E. A. "Abba Father: The Prayer of the Sons of God." *ExpTim* 99 (1987–88) 363–66.

Osten-Sacken, P. von der *Römer 8* 128–39.

Scott, J. M. *Adoption as Sons of God* 259–66.

b) *The "Groaning" of Creation* (8:18-22)

18. For I reckon that the sufferings of the present time are a small price to pay for the glory that is going to be revealed in us. 19. For creation awaits with eager longing the revelation of the sons (and daughters) of God. 20. For creation was subjected to futility—not of its own volition but on account of the subduer—in the hope 21. that the creation itself would be set free from its slavery to decay in order to share the freedom associated with glory of the children of God.
22. For we know that the entire creation has been groaning together in the pangs of childbirth right up till now.

Interpretation

Introduction to Rom 8:18-30. In this passage, in a striking example of the epideictic mode of oratory, Paul confronts the presence of suffering in the lives of believers. In line with an earlier and briefer argument in 5:3-4, he actually draws the experience of suffering into a wider argument for hope. In so doing he taps richly into the Jewish apocalyptic tradition, relating the great themes of creation and election to the hope of believers, Jewish and Gentile, in the Christian community.

The argument proceeds in four stages, the first three of which all feature in some sense a "groaning" motif, though the subject of the "groaning" is in each case distinct: in vv 19-22 "creation" groans; in vv 23-25 "we" groan; in vv 26-27 "the Spirit intercedes with groans too deep for utterance"; a fourth and final stage in vv 28-30 rounds off the argument for hope, setting the whole process within the broader framework of God's eternal plan. As the argument unfolds, Paul points to each of the "groanings" as an index of hope. The cumulative effect is to convey a firm conviction that the divine plan to bring human beings to "glory" (modeled upon that of the risen Lord) is well under way and proceeding inexorably to its goal.

Background to vv 18-22. This small passage stands as one of the most singular and evocative texts in the whole Pauline corpus. Particularly distinctive is its apparent inclusion of the non-human created world ("creation") within the sweep of salvation. Not only is this unprecedented in Paul; from a contemporary perspective also it offers rich hermeneutic possibilities in view of current concern for the Earth. Appreciation of the argument, however, requires attention to at least three aspects of the thought-background presupposed by Paul.

The first has to do with the meaning of "creation" *(ktisis)*, which, after the introductory thematic statement (v 18), forms the main subject of the text. Since Patristic times, "creation" has been interpreted in a variety of senses: 1. the entire creation, including all human beings; 2. the entire creation, believers alone excepted; 3. the non-human created world; 4. the human world as a whole; 5. the angelic world. Reference to the entire creation (1) is excluded because in v 23 Paul mentions a new subject, "we," clearly distinct from "creation." The same distinction rules out reference to the human world as a whole (4). "*Ktisis*" appears in v 39 with respect to an individual angelic power but there is no evidence of its ever referring to the entire angelic world (5) and angels, moreover, are hardly subject to "corruption" (*phthora*, v 21). The choice, then, lies between 2 and 3. The great advantage of 2—the entire world (human beings included) apart from believers—is that the inclusion of intelligent beings makes much more intelligible the personified presentation of creation as "longing," "hoping" and "groaning"; in favor of this, too, is the reference to "all creation" *(pasa ktisis)* in v 22. But (*pace* some modern interpretations [Käsemann; Schlier; Walter]) the inclusion of human beings would seem to be excluded by the phrase "against its will" *(ouch hekousa)* in v 21, which stands in stark contrast to the presentation of fallen humanity in 1:21, as does also the sense that this same unbelieving human world should long for the revelation of "God's sons (and daughters)" (v 19).

This leaves as possible reference for *ktisis* only the non-human (non-angelic) rest of creation (3). The difficulty concerning the personification of "creation" disappears once we appreciate that a poetic, mythic view, stemming from apocalyptic motifs is involved. In Wis 16:24 and 19:6 "creation" likewise appears in personified form, transforming itself in favor of the "sons ("children") of God" (= the Israelites). "Creation," then, is understood here, as previously in 1:20, to refer to that entire non-human world which the biblical creation stories present as the essential context for human life.

Secondly, along with this understanding of "creation," Paul presupposes a Jewish tradition which saw the non-human created world as intimately bound up with the fate of human beings. "Creation" progresses when the human race progresses; it suffers a fall when human beings fall. Both share, in brief, a "common fate." The tradition goes back ultimately to the biblical creation story, where human beings, bearing the image and likeness of God, are given dominion over the earth (Gen 1:26-28; cf. Ps. 8:5-8). The more immediate source is Gen 3:17-19, where the earth is cursed because of Adam's sin and, as a result, yields its fruits only grudgingly, requiring toil and sweat. A text in *4 Ezra* illustrates the development of the motif in the post-biblical apocalyptic tradition: "For I made the world for their (sc. Israel's) sake, and when Adam transgressed my statutes, what had been made was judged. And so the entrances of this world were made narrow and sorrowful and toilsome" (7:11-12; cf. also 9:19-20). Correspondingly, on the same "common fate" principle but in positive vein, there is the sense that the future salvation of human beings (Israel) will extend to "creation" as well. Creation will both share in and testify to the final restoration, encompassing a cosmic renewal. This motif is prominent in both the prophetic literature of the Bible (e.g., Isa 11:6-9; 43:19-21; 55:12-13; Ezek 34:25-31; Hos 2:18; Zech 8:12) and the later apocalyptic tradition (*1 Enoch* 45:4-5; 51:4-5; cf. 72:1; *4 Ezra* 8:51-54; *2 Apoc. Bar.* 29:1-8; *Sib. Or.* 3:777-95).

A third presupposition, applying still more widely in Romans 8 (cf. esp. vv 35-39) and stemming from Jewish apocalypticism, is the sense that the final vindication and salvation of the elect will be preceded by a time of greatly increased turmoil and suffering, which will likewise have cosmic manifestations. Such an idea lies behind the sense of "creation" groaning "in the pangs of childbirth" (v 22; cf. also the groaning of believers in v 23) as it awaits for the final deliverance (the "birthpangs" of the messianic age; see Note on v 22). It allows Paul to view the sufferings of the present time, not as a threat to salvation, but as a sign that the longed for deliverance is actually close at hand.

As already mentioned, v 18 announces the theme governing the entire section. V 19 points to the "eager longing" of creation. Vv 20-21 function as a kind of parenthesis explaining (on the "common fate" principle) why creation has this hope. V 22 points to the "groaning" of creation as the outward expression its hope.

Overall Theme (v 18). Paul had already reintroduced the note of "suffering" at the close of the previous passage by linking the notion of being Christ's "co-heirs" with sharing his sufferings in order to share also his glory (v 17). The thematic statement in v 18 supports (cf. *gar*) this—and the note of exhortation it contains—by insisting that the sufferings of the present time are a "small price to pay" (see Note) in view of the coming glory (cf. 2 Cor 4:17). Paul does not minimize the sufferings of the present time but seeks to set them within a wider framework that looks beyond the present to the full realization of God's design for human beings and their world.

As elsewhere in the letter (1:23; 2:7, 10; 3:23; 5:2), in line with the biblical and post-biblical tradition, Paul sums up this destiny as "glory" (*doxa*; see Note on 3:23). In essence, "glory" denotes the state of the elect when finally arrived at that likeness to God which was the Creator's original intent in their regard (Gen 1:26-28; Ps 8:5-8), with the concomitant freedom from death and decay (Wis 2:23-24). At present this "glory" is a hidden thing. As the context (cf. esp. v 19, v 23, v 29) suggests, it will be "revealed" when believers, through resurrection, are conformed to the full bodily glory of their risen Lord (cf. Phil 3:21). This is the "glory to be revealed in and through us" *(eis hēmas).*

Creation's "Eager Longing" (v 19). As the first index of hope for the attainment of this glory Paul points out that it is a hope also cherished by "creation." Creation, in fact, is getting very excited (cf. "eager longing"—*apokaradokia*; see Note) at the prospect of its imminent realization. More precisely, what creation looks forward to is the "revelation of God's sons (and daughters)" *(tēn apokalypsin tōn huiōn tou theou).* In the light of the Jewish tradition where divine filiation is the particular prerogative of the eschatological people of God, it is not surprising that the revelation of the "glory" of believers (v 18) and the revelation of "God's sons (and daughters)" should stand in close parallel. As is the case with "glory," the "son (daughter)" status of believers is as yet a hidden reality, attested only by the Spirit (vv 15-16). What creation longs for is the public manifestation of that status. This will come about through resurrection, when human beings share bodily the risen glory of the Lord, himself "designated Son of God in power" at the moment of resurrection (1:4).

The "Common Fate" (vv 20-21). The small parenthesis that follows, in clear allusion to the narrative of the "Fall" in Gen 3:17-19, explains why creation should cherish such an expectation. On the "common fate" principle indicated above, when human beings, in the person of Adam, fell from favor with God, creation also took a "fall": the earth was cursed because of Adam's sin and transformed from being a garden to being an object of hard, unremitting toil (Gen 3:17-19). Creation was in this sense "subjected *(hypotagē)* to futility (*mataiotētēs*; see Note)"—the frustration of its original purpose, which was to be a vehicle of human glorification of God (1:20-21).

The key consideration for the argument, however—and one involving a highly personified, "mythic" view of the non-human created world—is that when creation underwent this subjection, it did so "unwillingly" *(ouch hekousa)*: the lapse was not of its own making or choosing; it came about "because of the subduer" *(dia ton hypotaxanta)*. In the original account of Gen 3:17-19 it is God who curses the earth because of Adam's sin and this has led most interpreters to see God as the "subduer" in the Pauline text as well. But linguistic considerations (see Note) and the presentation of Adam in the wider Jewish tradition as the one to whom the rest of creation was subjected (cf. esp. Ps 8:6) make it more likely that Paul has Adam in mind. On the "common fate" principle, creation was compelled, willy-nilly, to lapse into "futility" because of the lapse of the one who, bearing the divine image, was meant to be its "subduer," meant, that is, to exercise constructive responsibility in its regard as God's viceroy on earth (Gen 1:26-28).

But the very unwillingness attached to this forced compliance of creation in the "subduer's" fall meant that it continued to cherish a hope of reversal. Should the "subduer" be restored to favor with God and once again image the divine glory, then, on the same "common fate" principle (now operative in a positive direction), creation itself (v 21) might be restored. It too would have a share in humanity's restored freedom from the slavery to decay *(douleia tēs phthoras)* and in its own way reflect the "glory" belonging to human beings as "children of God."

The language here seems deliberately designed to echo and set in reverse the account of humanity's lapse into idolatry in 1:18-23. There Paul described how human beings, instead of finding in the non-human created world a vehicle to the praise and glory of the Creator, became "futile in their thinking" *(emataiōthēsan)* and made creatures objects of worship and veneration. This involved "exchanging the glory of God" for the "likeness" of merely mortal *(phthartos)* things (1:23; cf. 3:23), with the consequent enslavement to death and decay that the "exchange" involved. The hope that creation has preserved is that it might be set free from its long, unwilling "subjection to futility" to become once more the vehicle of true human glorification of God. This is the basis of its present "eager longing."

Creation "groaning" (v 22). Paul sees the outward expression of this "eager longing" in the whole of creation's "groaning and being in travail together." He points to this as an object of common knowledge ("we know," *oidamen*), though it is hard to see what reality of the actual physical world he could have in mind to support such a bold assertion. It may in the end be misguided to look for anything concrete of this kind. Clearly, Paul is playing upon the apocalyptic theme of the "messianic woes," confident that his audience will nod their heads and agree. The non-human world, created to be the wider ambience of human relationship with God, is on the verge of giving birth to a new created order which will genuinely embody that role. It shares the sufferings of the present time but these very "woes" are replete with promise of new birth.

Reflection. Clearly, contemporary concern for the environment and well-being of the Earth outstrips the immediate intent of this passage. In itself it simply functions as a stage of Paul's wider argument for hope. Moreover, its personification of non-rational creation and other mythic features lend it imaginative rather than argumentative appeal. Nonetheless, the text does clearly evoke the creation texts of Genesis 1–3, where human beings are set in direct relationship to the rest of the world as a key element of their relationship with God, where they are given responsibility for the rest of creation and where, as a consequence, the "fates" of both parties—humanity and the non-human created world—are inevitably intertwined, for good and for ill. In v 20 we seem to have an allusion to the "story" Paul sees told in Adam, the "sin" story of the human race—a story which redounds ruinously upon the rest of creation as well. It is not fanciful to understand exploitative human pollution of the environment as part of that "sin" story, along with other evils. What is also present (v 21) is a hint of the corresponding "grace" story, told in Christ—the "much more" powerful nature of which Paul insists upon as the fundamental basis for hope (Rom 5:15-17). If creation has suffered and suffers from the ravages of human sin, there is hope that it may also benefit when and where the "grace" story prevails—when a new "subduer," the "Last Adam," faithfully and successfully plays the role that Adam muffed, opening up new possibility for the human race and for creation.

Notes

18. *the sufferings of the present time:* On "the present time" *(en tǭ nyn kairǭ)*, see Note on 3:26 (cf. also 11:5; 2 Cor 6:2). Paul does not necessarily believe his audience in Rome to be undergoing trials more notable than that of other groups of Christians (the more dramatic presentation of Christian sufferings given at the close of the chapter [vv 35-39] has his own apostolic life more in view). He sets the costly aspect attending Christian life in general within the framework of the "woes" expected to herald the onset of the "End."

are a small price to pay: The translation attempts to convey the meaning of the phrase *ouk axia*, understood in a "commercial" sense also to be seen in Prov

3:15 (*pan de timion ouk axion autēs*; cf. 8:11). Something good ("glory") and something painful ("sufferings") are contrasted and the thought is that the good is so desirable that the price paid to obtain it should be accounted as not worth taking into consideration.

the glory that is going to be revealed in us: The "directional" sense conveyed by the final prepositional phrase *eis hēmas*, suggests that believers are the goal or end-point of a process ("glorification") emanating from something outside of themselves (God): cf. the apt phrase of Sanday & Headlam: ". . . to reach out and include us in its radiance" (206). The simple translation "to us" is far too weak.

19. *creation:* For extended surveys of the scholarly discussion concerning the reference of *ktisis* here, see Kuss 2.622–24; O. Christoffersson, *Earnest Expectation of the Creation* (see Reference) 19–21, 33–36.

eager longing: The term *apokaradokia* (confined to Christian literature and appearing first in Paul [cf. also Phil 1:20]) has the sense of eager, confident expectation—without anxiety; cf. D. R. Denton, "*Apokaradokia*." *ZNW* 73 (1982) 138–40.

the revelation of the sons (and daughters) of God: For the distinctive sense of "divine filiation" in the Jewish and early Christian tradition presupposed by Paul, see Interpretation of 8:14. On the distinctively Christian sense of this as something presently hidden to be revealed in the future, see further Byrne, *'Sons of God'* 213–14.

20. *subjected to futility:* The passive verb *hypetagē* suggests a reference to the action of God—presumably the divine cursing of the earth in Gen 3:17-19. The word *mataiotētēs* as used in the Greek Bible means "purposelessness" in the sense of lacking anything to give meaning or usefulness to existence; cf. its abundant use in the LXX of Ecclesiastes to translate the thematic concept of "vanity." It also occurs frequently in connection with polemic against idols. The parallel with "bondage to decay" *(phthora)* in v 21 may imply a sense of mortality here as well; for this cf. LXX Pss 77:33 (78:33); 143:4 (144:4); Job 7:16 (Aquila).

not of its own volition but on account of the subduer: Syntactically, this phrase is something of a parenthesis—wedged between the main verb ("was subjected" *[hypetagē]*) and the following reference to "hope." It is, however, essential for the meaning as explaining why, when subjected, creation retained the "hope." The participial phrase *ouch hekousa* has its more normal sense of "not of its own will"; cf. LSJ 27, 527; BAGD 247, rather than the derived sense "not of its own fault." With respect to the final phrase, *dia ton hypotaxanta*, most interpreters prefer to see God as the "subduer" on the grounds of linkage with the "divine passive" expressed in the preceding *hypetagē*, and because God is the one who in fact does the "subduing" in Gen 3:17-19, as is also the case more generally in the biblical tradition when the "subduing" motif is present. On the other hand, by far the most normal sense of the preposition *dia* followed by the accusative is to indicate the cause or grounds for something—here to indicate whose fault caused the "subjection"; on such an interpretation the subject cannot be God. Moreover, Paul does use the verb *hypotassein* with the risen Christ—the "Last Adam"—as subject (Phil 3:21). Such considerations support the longstanding alternative (Chrysostom; S. Lyonnet; H. Balz). For further discussion, see Wilckens 2.154. In any case, a reference to the sin of Adam is at least implicit, by way of contrast to the "involuntary" fall of creation.

in the hope: This prepositional phrase indicates the circumstances attending the subjection (cf. BAGD 287 [II, 1, b, γ]). The content of the hope is spelled out in the *hoti* clause that follows (see following Note).

21. *that the creation itself:* Reading the conjunction *hoti* rather than the less well attested textual variant *dioti* ("because . . ."). A better sense is provided if v 21 spells out the content of the hope.

from its slavery to decay: The translation takes the genitive as objective. A qualitative understanding ("slavery consisting in decay" or "marked by decay") is equally possible. The "slavery" comes about as a result of the "subjection." "Decay" *(phthora)* occurs with respect to human mortality in 1 Cor 15:42, 50 (cf. Gal 6:8); here it indicates the corresponding impermanence of material creation.

the freedom associated with glory of the children of God: The translation aims to bring out the sense of the first qualifying genitive; a purely adjectival translation ("glorious freedom of the children of God") is far too weak. The negative parallel with "decay" suggests that "freedom" here is specifically freedom from death; cf. 2 Cor 3:17-18. "Glory" *(doxa)* here particularly connotes the sense of immortality: to bear the glory of God, to be "like God" in this sense, means sharing God's own immortal being (cf. Wis 1:14-15; 2:23). On "children *(tekna)* of God," see Note on 8:16.

22. *For we know:* On Paul's use of the phrase *oidamen* as an appeal to what is commonly accepted, see Note on 2:2 (cf. also 3:19; 7:14; 8:22, 28; 1 Cor 8:1, 4; 2 Cor 5:1).

the entire creation has been groaning together in the pangs of childbirth: The adjective "entire" attached to "creation" suggests that the sense of the *syn-* prefix in both compound verbs *(systenazei; synōdinei)* is not "groan . . . *along with*" (sc. "ourselves"; cf. v 23) but "groan . . . *as one.*" Why Paul should wish to indicate the unity of creation at this point is not clear (cf., however, Virgil, *Eclogues* 4:50-52). For the sense that the final consummation will be immediately preceded by a time of greatly increased suffering and distress on a cosmic scale ("messianic woes"): cf. Dan 7:21-22, 25-27; 12:1-3; *4 Ezra* 5:1-13; 6:13-24; 9:1-3; *2 Apoc. Bar.* 25:2-3; 27:1-15; 48:30-41; 70:2-10; *Sib. Or.* 1:162-65; 2:154-73; 3:632-56, 796-806; Rev 6:12-17; for the description of the distress in terms of "birth-pangs" cf. *1 Enoch* 62:4; Matt 24:8 (// Mark 13:8); John 16:21; for the same image cf. 1QH 3:7-18; also *4 Ezra* 10:6-16. Much of this material is later than Paul, reflecting the destruction of Jerusalem. Nonetheless, it best accounts for the mysterious claim made here with respect to creation.

right up till now: The hope which creation has cherished ever since its involuntary "subjection" and which it outwardly expresses through the "groaning" carries right on up till the present. Paul reinforces creation's witness to hope by stressing that its own expectation continues as strong as ever: if creation can endure so long, so ought we! (cf. v 25). If the allusion is to the "messianic woes," then Paul is locating their commencement right back at the time of the original "subjection."

For Reference and Further Study

Balz, H. R. *Heilsvertrauen und Welterfahrung* 36–54.

Bindemann, W. *Die Hoffnung der Schöpfung: Röm 8:17-27 und die Frage einer Theologie der Befreiung von Mensch und Natur.* Neukirchen: Neukirchener Verlag, 1983.

Byrne, B. *Inheriting the Earth.* Homebush (Australia): St. Paul; New York: Alba House, 1990.

__________. *'Sons of God'* 104–08.

Christoffersson, O. *The Earnest Expectation of the Creature.* ConBNT 23; Stockholm: Almqvist, 1990.

Denton, D. R. *"Apokaradokia." ZNW* 73 (1982) 138–140.

Gibbs, J. C. *Creation and Redemption.* NovTSup 26; Leiden: Brill, 1971, 33–47.

Lyonnet, S. "The Redemption of the Universe." *Contemporary New Testament Studies.* Ed. R. Ryan; Collegeville: The Liturgical Press, 1965, 423–36.

Osten-Sacken, P. von der *Römer 8* 78–104, 139–44, 260–66.

Vollenweider, S. *Freiheit als neue Schöpfung* 375–96.

Walter, N. "Gottes Zorn und das Harren der Kreatur. Zur Korrespondenz zwischen Römer 1, 18-32 und 8, 19-22." *Christus Bezeugen* (FS W. Trilling). Eds. K. Kertelge, T. Holtz & C.-P März. Freiburg, Basel, Wien: Herder, 1990, 218–26.

c) *The "Groaning" of "Ourselves"* (8:23-25)

23. And not only creation (with respect to us) but we ourselves, having the firstfruits (of salvation) in the shape of the Spirit, groan with respect to ourselves, awaiting sonship, the redemption of our bodies.
24. Now with this hope we are indeed (already) in a situation of salvation. But a hope that is seen is not really hope at all. For who has to hope for what they already see? 25. But if (as is the case) we keep on hoping for what we do not see, then we await it with endurance.

Interpretation

We too groan (v 23). In addition to the groaning of creation as a ground for hope, Paul points to a parallel groaning of believers themselves.

Creation groans with respect to believers—in the sense that it knows its own freedom to be linked with theirs; believers groan with respect to themselves (*en heautois*; see Note). In this sense Paul sets the longing of believers for salvation within the context of a longing that encompasses the entire universe. But in the case of believers a special factor is operative: behind their "groaning" lies the longing for salvation stimulated by the Spirit.

In this connection, Paul refers to the gift of the Spirit as "firstfruits" *(aparchē)*, the implication being "firstfruits of salvation." The metaphor stems from the harvest ritual of Israel (cf. esp. Deut 26:1-15): the firstfruits of the harvest are brought to the Temple in acknowledgment that the entire yield of the land is the gift of God; the small portion that is offered consecrates the whole. It is this *pars pro toto* sense that the Pauline image means to capture—though the "direction" of the divine-human transaction is reversed: *God* has given the Spirit to believers as a pledge or earnest of the full "harvest" (of salvation) that is to follow (cf. 1 Cor 15:20).

As "firstfruits" in this sense, the Spirit engenders within believers a certain "restlessness" with their lot at the present time when the new age "overlaps" with the old (cf. v 18). Essentially (that is, as far as relations with God are concerned: 5:1-2), "we" are already people of the new era and know this in the Spirit (vv 15-16; 5:5). The keen sense of full salvation lying close at hand makes for a dissatisfaction with and a longing to be free from the attachment to the old, passing age that is felt in the body. Hence the restlessness and the "groaning" to which it gives rise, a groaning which, as in the case of creation (v 22), is not simply a negative reaction to pain but something Paul can point to as a ground for hope.

Appended phrases (v 23b) specify the content of the hope that lies behind the groaning: we await "sonship" *(huiothesia)*, "defined" now as "the redemption of our bodies" *(tēn apolytrōsin tou sōmatōn hymōn)*. This quasi-"definition" of *huiothesia* confirms its essentially future, eschatological reference. Believers, though they are already "sons (and daughters)"/"children of God," have this status in a hidden way, attested only by the Spirit (vv 15-16). They will possess fully the Israelite privilege of divine filiation (cf. 9:4) when their bodies are set free from the conditions of the old era (temptation, weakness and death) in which they are presently enmeshed. They will display *huiothesia* in the full sense when resurrection ensures their full bodily conformity to the conditions of the new age, modeled upon that of Christ (cf. 1 Cor 15:35-49; Phil 3:21). The inward liberty already theirs as "children of God" (v 21) will appear outwardly as well.

Christian Hope (vv 24-25). Paul completes this description of present Christian life with a firm assurance of salvation (v 24a), followed by a short "excursus" on hope (vv 24b-25). The mention of salvation as a reality already present (aorist: *esōthēmen*) is striking, since elsewhere Paul refers "salvation" to the future, eschatological deliverance heralding the arrival of the final age (see Interpretation and Note on 1:16). Here the sense seems to be that the hope we have is so secure that, with (this) hope *(tę̄ elpidi)*, we really are already "in a situation of salvation."

"But," the audience might respond, "where is the evidence that salvation is all but present in this way? How can we put our trust in something we do not see?" The little excursus on "hope" that now intervenes (vv 24b-25) confronts objections of this kind. "Hope" is operative, not when what is hoped for is in view, but precisely when it is not—when all you have to go on is the word and character of the one making the promise. (To take a modern if somewhat banal example: people waiting for a bus or train do not really exercise "hope" if they can already discern, however faintly, its outline in the distance; it is when their repeated glances detect nothing that they can only "hope" for its arrival.) So for believers hope is not an optimism based on encouraging aspects of the present situation. The final consummation is not in sight, nor (cf. v 26) is it something easily imagined. Christian hope, like that of Abraham (4:18-21), involves an unseeing, "enduring" (*di' hypomenēs*, cf. 5:3-4) expectation in the present, suffering situation. It places its trust solely in the faithfulness of God to make good the final installment of salvation already pledged through the Spirit.

Notes

23. *And not only creation (with respect to us) but we ourselves:* There are a large number of textual variants at this point. All include at some stage the phrase *kai autoi*, which shows that Paul means to bring out the parallelism between what has been said of creation and what is about to be said of "ourselves."

having the firstfruits (of salvation) in the shape of the Spirit: Syntactically, it is possible to take this participial phrase in either a concessive ("*though* we have . . .") or causal sense ("*because* we have . . ."). The latter, preferred by most recent interpreters, is supported by the way Paul presents the role of the Spirit in the immediate context (vv 15-17), as well as by the comparable description of the Spirit as "downpayment" *(arrabōn)* in 2 Cor 1:22; 5:5 (cf. Eph 1:14); cf. also Gal 5:5 and 1 Cor 2:9-10, where the Spirit is specifically linked to the hope of the eschatological blessings to come. As in 2 Cor 5:5, the genitive *tou pneumatos* following *aparchēn* is explanatory or exepegetic ("firstfruits consisting in the Spirit" [BDF §167]).

with respect to ourselves: The prepositional phrase *en heautois* could have a "local" sense ("within ourselves" or "among ourselves"). The translation proposed best brings out the parallelism which Paul seems to stress here (cf. *kai autoi*): creation groans with respect to believers; believers groan with respect to themselves.

awaiting sonship: Some important early witnesses (P^{46} D G) omit the word *huiothesian* before the participle *apekdechomenoi*. Along with most recent interpreters (Fitzmyer 510–11 is a notable exception), the longer text is to be preferred. Rather than creating the present overloaded text, a scribe is more likely to have omitted an original *huiothesian* in order to eliminate an apparent conflict between the implication of the long text that "divine filiation" is something we still await and the insistence in vv 16-17 that we are already "children of God." On *huiothesia* and the reason for preferring the translation "sonship" over "adoption," see Interpretation and Note on 8:15.

the redemption of our bodies: The objective understanding of the genitive is confirmed by the reference to the "raising of our mortal bodies" in v 11. Paul does not mean "redemption from the body"—as though, in Platonic/Gnostic sense, bodily existence as such were the problem.

24. *Now with this hope we are indeed (already) in a situation of salvation:* The simple dative *tę̄ . . . elpidi* is open to a variety of interpretations, even when it is understood, as here, in a modal sense. A restrictive sense—"we are saved but only in hope" (so Käsemann 238, in accordance with an "anti-enthusiastic" view of Paul all through)—conflicts with Paul's overall thrust in Romans 5–8, which is to affirm the hope of salvation rather than (as in 1 Corinthians) to dampen down "enthusiasm."

But a hope that is seen: In this instance "hope" *(elpis)* refers not to the (subjective) virtue of hope but, objectively, to hope's content: that is, full salvation. For a similar contrast between what is seen and unseen in an eschatological sense, see 2 Cor 4:18; 5:7; cf. also the classic "definition" of faith given in Heb 11:1.

25. *with endurance:* For Paul's sense of *hypomenē* as a characteristic virtue of Christian life in the present, see Note on 5:3-4.

For Reference and Further Study

Byrne, B. *'Sons of God'* 108–11.

Calle Flores, F. de la "La *'huiothesian'* de Rom 8,23." *EstBíb* 30 (1971) 77–98.

Nebe, G. *"Hoffnung" bei Paulus*. SUNT 16; Göttingen: Vandenhoeck & Ruprecht, 1983 89–94.

Osten-Sacken, P. von der *Römer 8* 266–71.

Scott, J. M. *Adoption as Sons of God* 255–59.

Swetnam, J. "On Romans 8,23 and the Expectation of Sonship." *Biblica* 48 (1967) 102–08.

d) *The "Groaning" of the Spirit* (8:26-28) and *God's Eternal Plan* (8:29-30)

26. In the same way the Spirit comes to our aid in our weakness. For we do not know what it is right to pray for.
But the Spirit himself intercedes for us with groans too deep for utterance. 27. And the Searcher of hearts knows what is the intention of the Spirit: that he intercedes for the saints in accordance with God's will for them. 28. We know that all things work together for the (ultimate) good of those who love God, those called according to his purpose.
29. Because those whom he chose beforehand, he also preordained that they should become sharers in the image of his Son, so that he might become the firstborn among many brothers (and sisters). 30. And those whom he preordained, these he also called, and those whom he called, these he also justified, and those whom he justified, these he has also glorified.

Interpretation

As a third ground for hope Paul points to a mysterious "groaning" on the part of the Spirit (vv 26-27). A more generalized statement in v 28 then functions as a bridge into a consideration of the inexorable unfolding of God's eternal plan for the elect (vv 29-30).

The "Groaning" of the Spirit (vv 26-27). To judge by the expression used at the start *(hōsautōs de kai)*, Paul appears to set the "groaning" of the Spirit in parallel to the other two "groanings" ("creation" [vv 19-22]; "ourselves" [vv 23-25]). Clearly, though, it is of a rather different order. Whereas both "creation" and "we ourselves" groan out of a longing to be set free from present restriction, the activity of the Spirit amounts to a "coming to the aid of our weakness" *(synantilambanetai tę̄ astheneią hēmōn)*. "Our weakness" could refer to a general sense of vulnerability in the conditions of the present age. More likely, however, what Paul has in mind is "weakness" stemming from inability to see or visualize the goal to which we are being led—as outlined in the little excursus on "hope" that has just preceded (vv 24-25). We cannot see, or even imagine, this goal. Hence we do not know what to pray for *(to . . . ti proseuxōmetha*; see Note) and we do not know what is the appropriate prayer to make *(katho dei)*. In the face of "our" incapacity in this respect, the Spirit offers appropriate intercession for us in the shape of "groans too deep for utterance" *(stenagmoi alalētoi)*.

What precisely is being referred to here is not immediately clear. The following explanation (v 27) to the effect that the "Searcher of hearts" knows what is the "intention of the Spirit" suggests that the intercession is something that takes place within human beings. The "groans" would then be *alalētoi* or "inexpressible" because uttered (by the Spirit) at a depth "below" ordinary human consciousness, to which God, as "Searcher of hearts," alone has access. Just a few sentences further on (v 34) Paul refers in very similar terms to the intercessory prayer offered at God's right hand by Christ Jesus as risen Lord. This, together with the fact that Paul makes little distinction between the Spirit and the continuing impact of the risen Christ upon the lives of believers, suggests that the "subconscious" intercessory prayer of the Spirit is not rigidly separate from the prayer of Christ himself. Because believers are "in Christ" (in the technical Pauline sense; see Interpretation of 6:3 above; also 8:1) and have Christ "in" them (v 10) there wells up from within them his continual prayer to God.

Paul explains (v 27) why this groaning intercession, however imperceptible it may be, is a further index for hope. Because the Spirit, unlike "ourselves" (cf. vv 24-25), truly knows what is God's intention for believers, the entreaty he makes is appropriate and therefore efficacious. We can be sure that the "Searcher of hearts" will recognize such prayer and not fail to respond.

Summing Up (v 28). A final comment (v 28) draws together the various phases of the argument for hope. Paul appeals to an axiom of the Jewish tradition expressing the sense that, under God's providence on behalf of the elect (literally, "those who love God"; see Note), "all things" conspire together (for the translation, see Note) to bring about "good" *(agathon)*. "All things" could refer to or at least include the non-human created world ("creation" [vv 19-22]) and the Spirit (vv 26-27). But Paul is more likely to have in mind the sufferings of the present time (v 18) that form the context for hope. Other things being equal, these would normally be considered "evil." But for those whose lives are enveloped in God's love even these things work for "good"—the "good" in this case being salvation, the full realization of God's eternal plan in their regard.

The unfolding of God's plan for the elect (vv 29-30). Those for whom "all things work together for good" are described at the end of the axiom making up v 28 as those "called according to (God's) purpose" *(tois kata prothesin klētois ousin)*. This description moves the argument into its final stage, bringing into explicit consideration the eternal plan of God *(prothesis)*. Those for whom the Spirit prays according to the mind of God are those whose total existence is enveloped and carried forward within an eternal, unfolding design. It is the inexorable unfolding of this plan—already under way—which provides the most fundamental and basic grounds for hope.

Paul presents the unfolding of the *prothesis* in a step-by-step sequence ("sorites"), reminiscent of 5:3-4:

". . . those whom
he **chose beforehand**,
he also **preordained**
that they should becomes sharers in the image of his Son,
so that he might become the firstborn among many brothers (and sisters).
And those whom he **preordained**,
these he also **called**,
and those whom he **called**,
these he also **justified**,
and those whom he **justified**,
these he has also **glorified**."

In this pattern of five verbs in the past tense each refers to a key stage of the divine activity, the second, third, fourth and fifth picking up the one immediately before in such a way as to suggest the inexorable progress of the whole process towards the planned goal. At one point, after the second verb, Paul interrupts the sequence, in order to spell out in christological terms the actual content of the divine "predetermination" in our regard.

The process has begun in the eternity of God with the divine election. "Know beforehand" *(proegnō)* has its biblical sense of "choose beforehand" (cf. Jer 1:5). Paul is applying to all believers the idea of "election" so central to the self-understanding of Israel as People of God. Behind the existence of all who are "in Christ"—Gentiles as well as Jews—stands the eternal "choice" of God.

Behind them also stands the plan or design God has formed *(proōrisen)* in their regard. Breaking into the ordered pattern, Paul "defines" this "predetermination" in christological terms (on the issue of "Predestination," see Note). The language is carefully chosen and must be given its full weight. To be "sharers in the image of his Son" *(symmorphous tēs eikonos autou)* does not mean simply becoming "like" Christ in a general kind of way. *Symmorphos* conveys the sense of "participation in way of being" (see Note) and *eikōn* that of a likeness revealing and making present an inner reality. Thus the total phrase refers to a participation in the way of being that reveals Christ's true identity as "Son of God." In the light of the credal "definition" of the gospel given at the beginning of the letter (1:3-4), this can only be the glorious way of being that is his as risen Lord. In his risen glory Christ "models" the fullness of humanity that was God's eternal design for human beings from the start. The essential commentary is given in 1 Corinthians 15: defending the resurrection of the body, Paul asserts (v 49) that, as we have borne the image *(eikōn)* of the earthly one (Adam), we shall also bear the image of the heavenly one (Christ). We have borne the image of Adam in our existence in the present body, marked down for mortality because of sin (Rom 8:10); we shall bear the image of the heavenly, when our bodies share the glorious way of being proper to him as risen Lord. This will mean full arrival at the goal of God's intent for human beings.

The outcome will be, Paul adds in a final comment (v 29b), that "he (the Son of God) will become the Firstborn among many brothers (and sisters)." The stress falls upon the "many" *(pollois)*. Christ is already "Firstborn" (*prōtotokos*—for the messianic implications, see Note). He will be shown to be "Firstborn among *many* brothers (and sisters)" when others also attain the risen glory presently seen in him alone. The same risen status that has displayed his true identity as "Son of God" (Rom 1:4) will reveal a similar status belonging to believers. This will be the "revelation of the sons (and daughters) of God" longed for by "creation" (v 19), the attainment in the full public sense of the privilege of divine filiation *(huiothesia)* pertaining to God's eschatological people (v 23; cf. 9:4).

With the content of the divine design for human beings now clear, Paul resumes (v 30) the "chain" sequence outlining its inexorable realization. The first step setting the whole process in motion has been God's "calling" *(ekalesen)*. The Jewish tradition presupposed by Paul closely associated "calling" with God's creation ("calling into being") of a people for himself (cf., e.g., Hos 11:1). In the light of this, the "call" that has gone out as the first stage in the realization of God's plan refers to the summons contained in the gospel. By means of the gospel God has "called" into being a People of God, made up of Jews and Gentiles (cf. 9:24; 1 Cor 1:26), destined to display God's original design for human beings.

This new people of God has already been "justified" *(edikaiōsen)*. In the Jewish apocalyptic tradition justification refers more strictly to the verdict of acceptance to be awarded by God at the final judgment (see Interpretation of 2:13). While retaining this eschatological thrust, Paul has made clear in the early part of the letter (chapters 1–4; esp. 5:1-2; cf. 1 Cor 6:11) that believers have, by God's grace mediated through the Christ event (3:21-26), already received eschatological justification. In Christ, God has reached out into the morass of human sinfulness that had frustrated the original design of the Creator, to create out of Jews and Gentiles a just and sanctified people, destined to inherit the ancient promises. In this sense "justification," like "calling," can be spoken of as something already in process.

More suprising, however, is the setting in the past of the final term of the process: "glorification" *(edoxasen)*. "Glory" normally designates the eschatological destiny of the just—their final arrival at the state of "likeness to God" intended by the Creator from the start (see Note on 3:23).

Here, however, in view of the close association of "glorification" with "justification" (cf. esp. 3:23-24), Paul can write "has glorified" on the basis of a hidden glorification already under way. Such a process appears to be in view in 2 Cor 3:18, where he writes of believers being "transformed" by the Spirit into the same "image" (*eikōn* = the risen glory of Christ) "from one degree of glory to another." What Paul would have in mind, then, is a process that has already begun, but which, like the status of being "children of God" (v 16), is still a hidden thing, to be publicly revealed (cf. v 18) when believers share, in resurrection, the glory already shown in Christ.

Summing up, we may note how the christological note upon which this entire section (8:18-30) draws to a close catches up the "christological proviso" appearing in v 17. It is as those who have "suffered with" Christ that believers will be glorified with him and so enter fully into his inheritance. Paul has deployed his argument for hope by setting the sufferings necessarily attached to existence in the present "overlap" time within the context of the unfolding design of God for human beings—the term of which has already been glimpsed in the glory of the risen Lord. The resurrection is not, then, an "exception" or an "irruption" into the normal course of human affairs. It is the symbol and pledge of a humanity reaching its proper goal, where the "sin" story of human life told in Adam is overtaken and consumed by the "grace" story told in Christ.

Notes

26. *In the same way:* By stressing the similarity of the "groaning" attributed to the Spirit, this phrase confirms the positive nature of the earlier "groanings" (v 22; v 23).

the Spirit comes to our aid in our weakness: The sense of the double compound verb *synantilambanesthai* is that of lifting another's burden by sharing responsibility for the task in hand; cf. Luke 10:40 (of Martha's request that her sister be made to help her).

For we do not know what it is right to pray for: The formulation in Greek *(to . . . ti proseuxōmetha)* shows that the problem is not *how* to pray (in which case Paul would have written *pōs*) but what *(ti)* to pray for. The translation also takes phrase *katho dei* in parallel with the *kata theon* of the following verse, rather than with the verb *ouk oidamen,* which would introduce a sense of blame foreign to the context. For the general idea, cf. 1 Cor 2:6-12, where, with reference to eschatological destiny ("what God has prepared for those who love him"), the Spirit imparts knowledge of "what no eye has seen, nor ear heard, nor the human heart conceived."

the Spirit himself intercedes for us: Behind this idea would seem to lie a widespread Jewish tradition in which angels or notable human figures of the past (patriarchs, prophets, etc.) make intercession for the people before the throne of God; cf. Job 33:23-26; Tob 12:15; *1 Enoch* 9:3; 15:2; 99:3; 104.1: *T. Levi* 3:5-6; 5:6; *T. Dan* 6:2; on this see the studies of E. A. Obeng cited in Reference. Early Christian attribution of this role to the Spirit probably flows from the close association of the Spirit and the risen Christ, whom Paul pictures exercising a similar function in v 34.

with groans too deep for utterance: Some consider Paul to be alluding here to charismatic prayer within the community—specifically prayer involving the gift of tongues (so esp. Käsemann). This interpretation has the advantage of having Paul point to a readily observable phenomenon of Christian life. But the gift of tongues involves praise rather than intercessory prayer, as here. Moreover, the "groans" involved in tongues are audibly expressed, albeit in strange language, and are to that extent unintelligible, whereas the adjective Paul uses, *alalētos,* refers not so much to something unintelligible as inexpressible.

27. *the Searcher of hearts:* The phrase encapsulates a characteristic attribute of God in the biblical and post-biblical tradition: 1 Sam 16:7; 1 Kgs 8:39; Pss 7:9; 17:3; 26:2; 44:21; 139:1-2, 23; frequently in Proverbs and Jeremiah; Wis 1:6; Sir 42:18; *Bib. Ant.* 50:4.

knows what is the intention of the Spirit: On "intention" *(phronēma),* see Interpretation and Notes on 8:5-6.

that he intercedes: The translation takes the opening *hoti* in a declarative, rather than a causal sense ("because he intercedes"); the declarative sense accords best with the *ti* before *phronēma.*

for the saints: On "the saints" as a standard designation for the members of God's (eschatological) people in the biblical tradition, see Note on 1:7.

in accordance with God's will for them: For the use of the phrase *kata theon* in a similar sense, see also 2 Cor 7:9-11.

28. *We know that all things work together for the (ultimate) good . . .:* On the use of *oidamen* to express what Paul believes to be an accepted truth, see Note on 2:2. The full Greek sentence allows for at least three possibilities as regards its subject: "God"; "the Spirit"; "all things" (as in the translation above). 1. The first possibility, taking "God" as subject, is supported by an impressive textual tradition (P^{46} A B), which actually includes *ho theos* after the verb *synergei*—though the extra phrase almost certainly represents an early attempt to clear up the confusion of subject. With God as subject (with or without *ho theos*), the verb *synergei* can be understood intransitively ("God cooperates in every way"—taking *ta panta* adverbially) or transitively ("God works all things together . . ."—though such a transitive usage of the verb is unattested elsewhere). Taking God as subject, in either of these ways, sits a little awkwardly after the reference to God in the phrase "those who love God." It accords well, however, with the following context, where God is clearly the agent in the whole sequence. 2. By the same token, taking the Spirit as implicit subject means a smooth flow from the preceding context but makes for a rather stark change of subject (to God) in the following sentence—though, again, this is

perhaps already implicit in the word *prothesis* introduced in the final phrase. 3. The third possibility, taking the neuter plural "all things" as subject (as in the Latin Vulgate), gives by far the smoothest rendering of the Greek. It does rather suddenly introduce a thought new to the immediate context but this is less problematic on the basis that it is a summarizing and bridging statement.

those who love God: This description of the beneficiaries of the process should not be understood in the sense that human love directed to God somehow conditions the workings of divine grace. The phrase is simply a conventional way of referring to the members of God's people in the biblical and post-biblical tradition, cf. Deut 7:9; Ps 145:20 (LXX 144:20); Tob 13:12 (BA), 14; Sir 1:10; 2:15, 16; *Pss. Sol.* 4:25; 10:3; 14:1; 4QpPs 37 3:4-5.

those called: See Note on v 30 below.

according to his purpose: For Paul's use of *prothesis* to designate God's eternal purpose, see also 9:11; this sense is picked up in Eph 1:11; 3:11; 2 Tim 1:9; cf. also Philo, *Mos.* 2.61.

29. *he chose beforehand:* Literally, "knew beforehand." The verb *progignōskein* here, as in 11:2 (possibly also 1 Pet 1:20), reflects a biblical idiom where "foreknowledge" connotes "choice" and "election" as well; cf. Gen 18:19; Jer 1:5; Hos 13:5 (Hebrew); Amos 3:2; also 1QH 9:29-30.

he also preordained: The verb *proorizein* is not simply a synonym for *progignōskein* but adds the sense that God has formed a plan in respect of those who have been chosen; cf. 1 Cor 2:7 and the development of this Pauline usage in Eph 1:5, 11. The language of "election" and "preordination" here does not imply a doctrine of predestination in the classical sense of a divine fixing of individual human lives in a set direction towards salvation or damnation. Paul does not have individuals principally in mind but is applying the biblical privilege of election communally to the Christian community made up of Jews and Gentiles. The perspective is positive and inclusive, rather than exclusive, indicating God's will to bring all to the fullness of humanity. Whether or not some individuals fail to be included is not at issue.

sharers in the image of his Son: The sense of the Greek adjective *symmorphos* as indicating participation in way of being is enhanced by its use in the present passage with the genitive *(eikonos)*, which gives the adjective virtually substantival force; cf. also the use of *symmorphos* in Phil 3:21 with reference to Christ's power to make the "body of our lowliness" (that is, our present mortal body) conform to the way of being belonging to the "body of his glory." If the complete phrase is not to become tautologous, the second genitive *(tou huiou autou)* must be epexegetic, giving the sense "the image which his Son is." In 2 Cor 4:4 Paul speaks of the risen Christ as the "image *(eikōn)* of God" and a few lines earlier of believers being "transformed into that same image" (3:18). These parallels strongly support the suggestion that implicit in the present description of God's plan for human beings is the sense of Christ, as risen Lord and "Last Adam" (1 Cor 15:45), displaying and "modeling" for the new humanity the original design of the Creator according to which human beings "image" God before the rest of creation (Gen 1:26-28;

Ps 8:5-8)—the role in which the "First" Adam failed. Some interpreters (see esp. Käsemann) find in the *symmorphous* phrase a strong note of conformity to Christ in his sufferings. Conformity to the total "career" of Christ—suffering as well as glory—is certainly implicit in the overall Pauline view (cf. esp. v 17c). But Paul is spelling out here the *goal* of the divine *prothesis*—the end God has in view for us (cf. *eis agathon* in v 28), rather than the stages on the way.

firstborn: Prōtotokos probably has a messianic sense derived from its use as an epithet for the Davidic king in LXX Ps 88:28 (89:27); cf. Heb 1:6; Rev 1:5 (where there is clear allusion to Ps 89:27).

30. *called:* For the sense of God's "calling" as an act of "creation" in Paul, see esp. Rom 4:17 (where the God in whom Abraham believed is described as a God "who gives life to the dead and calls into being the things that do not exist"); 9:25-26; 1 Cor 1:26-28 (where it is also a question of "calling into being" a new Christian community). Philo's terminology in *Spec.* 4.187 comes remarkably close to Paul's in this respect. For the frequent association of "calling" and "divine filiation" in the biblical and Jewish tradition, cf. Hos 1:10 (MT, LXX 2:1); Sir 36:17; *Jub.* 1:25; *Bib. Ant.* 18:6; *4 Ezra* 6:58; 4QDibHam 3:4-5; see further Byrne, *'Sons of God'* 120.

justified: On "justification" in Paul, see Interpretation of 2:13 and 3:24.

has also glorified: The only previous usage of the verb *doxazein* in the letter has been in connection to the refusal of human beings to "glorify" God as Creator in 1:21. Here, in ironic reversal, God accords to human beings the glorification they had refused their Creator (cf. Dunn, 1.485).

For Reference and Further Study

Bindemann, W. *Hoffnung der Schöpfung* 76–81.

Black, M. "The Interpretation of Rom 8:28." *Neotestamentica et Patristica* (FS O. Cullmann). NovTSup 6; Leiden: Brill, 1962, 166–72.

Byrne, B. *'Sons of God'* 111–27.

Grayston, K. "The Doctrine of Election in Rom 8:28-30." *SE* 2 (1964) 574–83.

Käsemann, E. "The Cry for Liberty in the Worship of the Church." *Perspectives on Paul* 122–37.

Leaney, A. R. C. "'Conformed to the Image of His Son' (Rom. viii. 29)." *NTS* 10 (1963–64) 470–79.

MacRae, G.W. "A Note on Romans 8:26-27." *HTR* 73 (1980) 227–30.

Niederwimmer, K. "Das Gebet des Geistes, Röm 8:26f." *TZ* 20 (1964) 252–65.

Obeng, E.A. "The Origins of the Spirit Intercession Motif in Romans 8.26." *NTS* 32 (1986) 621–32.

__________. "The Reconciliation of Rom 8.26f. to New Testament Writings and Themes." *SJT* 39 (1986) 165–74.

__________. "The Spirit Intercession Motif in Paul." *ExpTim* 95 (1984) 360–64.

Osten-Sacken, P. von der *Römer 8* 63–78, 271–87.

Scott, J. M. *Adoption as Sons of God* 245–55.

Scroggs, R. *The Last Adam* 59–112.
Vallauri, E. "I gemiti dello Spirito Santo (Rom 8,26s.)." *RivB* 27 (1979) 95–113.

v. The Coming Victory of God's Love (8:31-39)

31. What shall we say to all this?
If God is for us, who can be against us? 32. God who did not spare his
own Son, but gave him up for us all, how could it be that he will fail to
give us all things with him?
33. Who will dare to bring accusation against those God has chosen?
(Seeing that) it is God who acquits. 34. Who will condemn? (Seeing that)
Christ Jesus, the one who died, or rather is raised, (is the one) who
stands at the right hand of God and makes intercession for us.
35. Who (or what) shall separate us from the love of Christ?
Shall affliction or distress, or persecution
or hunger or nakedness or danger or the sword?
36. As it is written, "For your sake we are being done to death the whole
day long. We are reckoned as sheep ready for the slaughter." 37. But in
all these things we are more than conquerors through the one who has
loved us. 38. For I am convinced that neither death nor life, nor angels
nor rulers, neither things present nor things to come, nor powers, 39. nor
height nor depth nor any other created thing, will be able to separate us
from the love of God that comes to us in Christ Jesus, our Lord.

Interpretation

Introduction. Paul began his broader argument for hope (Romans 5–8) with the bold assertion that we "boast even in our sufferings" (5:3)—that is, the "sufferings of the present time" (8:18). Now he brings that argument to a close, returning explicitly to the theme of the prevailing power of God's love (so forming an "inclusion" with 5:1-11). In a passage justly celebrated and cherished for its rhetorical power, he evokes all the agencies and factors that might seem capable of thwarting God's plan for the elect and defiantly dismisses any threat they might pose.

For all its rhetorical effectiveness, the passage moves between the earthly and the heavenly, between present and future, in a way that puzzles the modern reader. Above all, the concluding list of spiritual powers seems to introduce an alien and mythic conception hard to relate to present reality. We are asked to enter a symbolic universe that attributes suffering to the machinations of angelic powers (cf. 2 Cor 12:7), which, while not necessarily evil, are basically unfriendly and all too ready to become prosecutors and agents of the divine wrath against sinful human beings. Fundamentally, however, it is a question—modern as well as ancient—of how to reckon with suffering within the framework of religious belief.

Within the apocalyptic perspective just outlined, Paul vigorously contests that present or future suffering implies any threat to relations with God already established or to the hope of final salvation. Specifically evoking the scene of the final Judgment (vv 33-34), he insists that the hostile powers have not and will not gain the upper hand. For those "in Christ Jesus" there is "no condemnation" (v 1). In the context of God's favor (v 31) the sufferings of the present time are simply absorbed into the overwhelming victory (v 37) of God's love.

Following the introductory question in v 31a, the passage unfolds in two main parts (vv 31b-34; vv 35-39), each introduced by thematic questions (v 31b; v 35) and each divisible into two further sub-sections. This provides a regular structural pattern, which can be set out as follows:

Introductory Question: v 31a ("What shall we say . . .?")
Part I: Theme: God is for us, Who can be against us? (vv 31b-34)
Ia: God is for us (vv 31b-32)
Ib: Who can be against us? (vv 33-34).
Part II: No separation from God's (Christ's) love (vv 35-39)
IIa: Earthly Trials (vv 35-37)
IIb: Spiritual Powers behind the Earthly Trials (vv 38-39).

God is for us (vv 31b-32). The introductory question, "What shall we say to all this?" (v 31a) ensures that this final part of Paul's argument for hope builds upon the unfolding of God's eternal plan for the "good" (v 28) of the elect. From the total range of that plan and its implementation up to this point, one can only conclude that "God is for us"—a phrase that could well stand as a summary of the gospel contained in the letter as a whole.

Paul reinforces the sense that God is "for us" by formulating once more (v 32; cf. 5:8-11) an assertion of the love and favor of God shown in the Christ-event. The formulation echoes the language of Gen 22:16, where Abraham is praised by the angel for being prepared "not to spare" (LXX: *ouk epheisō*; cf. Rom 8:32: *ouk epheisato*) his own beloved son (Isaac). The suggestion seems to be that what God did *not* in the end require of Abraham, he *did* for love of us require of himself: the "giving up" (*paredōken*; cf. 4:25) to death of his "own Son" *(tou idiou huiou)*. Nowhere else (cf., however, v 3) does Paul state the "vulnerability" to which God exposed himself so poignantly as here. Significantly, too, in the context of what seems to be an allusion to Abraham, Paul notes that God gave up his Son "for us all" *(pantōn)*—a subtle reminder of the "inclusive" outreach of

God's love (to Jew and Gentile alike), in fulfillment of the universalist promise to Abraham (4:16).

The rest of the sentence draws the conclusion from this on the kind of *a fortiori (pollą̄ mallon)* logic familiar from chapter 5 (vv 9-10; vv 15-17): if God has *already*—and in such conditions (when we were "sinners," "enemies" [5:10])—shown such extremity of good will towards us, how could it be that he will hold back from graciously bestowing *(charisetai)* all (the rest) *(ta panta)*? Read in view of the lists to follow (vv 35-39) and especially in the light of 1 Cor 3:21-23, where Paul assures the community that "all things *(panta)* are yours" [v 21b]), "all the rest" must refer to the "inheritance of the earth" (cf 4:15) that belongs to the elect as "heirs of God, co-heirs of Christ" (v 17). The point is that God, having already done so much, will certainly see that no hitch arises at the judgment to get in the way of this goal.

Who Can Be Against Us? (vv 33-34). The evocation of the final judgment becomes explicit as Paul takes up (v 33) the sub-theme, "Who can be against us?" (cf. v 31b). The formulation appears to owe a good deal to a passage towards the end of the Third Isaianic Servant Song (Isa 50:8-9a):

> He who vindicates me *(ho dikaiōsas me)* is near.
> Who will contend with me? Let us stand up together.
> Who is my adversary? Let him come near to me.
> Behold, the Lord God helps me; who will declare me guilty?

Paul transfers this conception to the final eschatological tribunal, where, in line with the Jewish apocalyptic tradition, angelic powers were thought of as destined to act as accusers of human beings before the throne of God (see above). The two rhetorical questions, "Who will . . . bring accusation?" (v 33a), "Who will condemn?" (v 34a) are interwoven with terse statements about God (v 33b) and Christ (v 34b-e). These exclude anything but a clear "No" to the questions in both cases. What angelic power would dare to bring an accusation when the presiding Judge is himself "acquitting" *(dikaiōn)* the elect? Through their response in faith to the proclamation of the gospel, believers have already had pronounced over them the eschatological acquittal (3:24; 4:25; 5:1; 8:30); what will happen at the judgment will be simply the public ratification of that divine verdict. It is something no power, heavenly or earthly, can possibly challenge.

To the picture of the divine Judge as totally "for us" Paul adds (v 34) that of Christ. Far from acting as "prosecutor" *(ho katakrinōn)*, Christ crowns his saving "career" (his dying and rising) with continual "intercession" on our behalf (cf. what has been said of the intercession of the Spirit in vv 26-27). In response to his obedient death upon the cross, God raised him and placed him in full messianic dignity at his own right hand (cf. esp. Phil 2:8-9). What other agent could dare to condemn the elect when the one whom they can own as "Brother" (cf. v 29) stands in such privileged closeness to God, offering entreaty on their behalf?

No separation from God's love (vv 35-39). With the possibility of condemnation at the final judgment excluded, Paul moves to draw the implications with respect to the "sufferings of the present time" (vv 35-39; cf. v 18). These cannot be interpreted—as a conventional Jewish apocalpytic theology might be tempted to interpret them (see above)—as evidence that some spiritual power is now successfully prosecuting believers before the throne of God.

The trials and agencies that come into question in this regard appear in two lists (v 35b and vv 38-39a) that could be seen to stand more or less in parallel—the first cataloguing earthly trials, the second heavenly opponents. But the logic of the passage seems better served if, in accordance with the worldview outlined above, the physical trials listed in v 35b are taken to be the manifestation of the hostility of super-human forces listed later on. Behind even such mundane things as hunger and nakedness, as well as the more overtly hostile pressure of religious persecution and threat of punishment from the civil authorities, stand the machinations of "spiritual" forces whose control still lingers in the present, passing world. They are "spiritual" forces in the sense of being supra-human and being linked with angels in the Jewish apocalyptic tradition. But they not "spiritual" in the sense of operating apart from or above ordinary human life. Their impact, their control, their oppression is felt in all the social and physical pressures brought to bear upon individuals and small vulnerable communities.

Paul acknowledges that such trials are or can be the experience of believers in the present age. The list is cumulative in effect: all the trials are life-threatening, building up to the climactic "the sword" that necessarily implies death. Hence the quotation (v 36) from Ps 44:22 (LXX 43:23) gives an accurate account of Christian existence at the present time. As believers, as those who belong to Christ and God (hence the relevance of the opening "because of you"), Christians run the daily risk of death and appear to all as "sheep marked out for slaughter" (cf. Isa 53:7; Zech 11:4, 7). By the same token, the fact that such an existence finds so accurate a depiction in scripture is a sign also that it has been foreseen by God and gathered into a wider salvific purpose.

The crucial turning point in the passage comes (v 37) with the great "But" following the quotation. The trials as listed may be the present reality but this does not mean that the forces behind the trials, including the threat of death, are getting the upper hand and successfully prosecuting the elect before the throne of God. Precisely "in these things"—that is, in the sufferings—*we* and not they are conquerors. We are in fact "super-conquerors" *(hypernikōmen)* through the one who has loved us *(dia tou agapēsantos hēmas)*. This last phrase refers particularly to the love of Christ as concretely shown (cf. *charisma*, 5:15) in his giving himself up to death on our behalf (cf. 5:6, 8 and esp. Gal 2:20: ". . . the Son of God, who loved me *[tou agapēsantos me]* and gave himself up for me"). To all external appearance that death looked like his overthrow by the forces that rule the present age. But in this they were totally deceived: by crucifying in ignorance the "Lord of glory" they in fact ensured the triumph of God's salvific plan (1 Cor 2:7-9). In this supreme victory of Christ's love the radical, definitive blow has been struck against the powers still holding sway in the present, passing world. Believers share in that victory through their union with the risen Lord.

A triumphant concluding sentence (vv 38-39) grounds and drives home this sense of victory. Speaking out of his own personal conviction *(pepeismai)*, Pauls lists as comprehensively as possible all the forces that could conceivably lie behind the trials previously mentioned and denies them any power to separate believers from God's favor and love. The list is somewhat mixed in the sense that some of the members ("death"/"life; "things present"/"things to come") seem to refer to circumstances (temporal, spatial), whereas others ("angels," "rulers," "powers," "any other created thing") refer more directly to the controlling spiritual forces (on "height" and "depth," see Notes). The overall effect is to suggest that in whatever situation believers find themselves—whether dead or alive, whether in the present or in the days to come—no spiritual force or power from the full extent of the universe will be able to separate them from God's favor.

Behind Paul's confidence here is his belief in Christ's ongoing messianic "subjection" of the universe (1 Cor 15:23-28; Phil 2:9-11; cf. Col 2:15; Eph 1:20-23). In 1 Cor 3:21b-23 Paul depicts the sharing in that lordship on the part of believers in terms very reminiscent of the present context. Rebuking the Corinthians for seeking to be "owned" by their teachers and so dividing into factions around them, Paul turns (1 Cor 3:21b-23) their slogans around to conjure up a vision of present sharing in the universal lordship of Christ:

> "For all things are yours:
> whether Paul or Apollos or Cephas, or the world or life or death,
> whether things present or things to come:
> all belong to you and you belong to Christ and Christ belongs to God."

In Romans 8 there is more of a sense of the struggling continuing. But, as in 1 Corinthians 3, the decisive battle has been won. None of the forces listed, despite their lingering power, can separate believers from Christ or hinder them from ultimately sharing in that lordship of the universe which he has won on their behalf.

The concluding phrase—"the love of God that comes to us in Christ Jesus, our Lord"—brings the entire sequence to a close on a hymnic note. In its own way, it sums up the entire argument for hope across Romans 5–8, which has so consistently depicted the complete unity and continuity between the love of Christ and the love of God. The love of Christ, shown in the Christ-event is the embodiment, the concretization (cf. *charisma*, 5:15) of the eternal love of God. "In Christ" (cf. 8:1, 9-11) believers are grasped within the love of God and drawn irrevocably into the fulfillment of the Creator's design for human beings already manifested in the glory of the risen Lord.

Notes

31. *What shall we say to all this?:* On Paul's use of the phrase *ti oun eroumen*, see Note on 4:1 above.

    If God is for us, who can be against us?: For a similar idea and expression, see Pss 23:4; 56:9; 118:6-7.

32. *God who did not spare his own Son:* LXX Gen 22:16 has "you did not spare your beloved *(agapētou)* Son" but the difference between "own son" and "beloved son" is not great, especially in view of the underlying Hebrew *(yāḥîd)*, which can go in both directions.

    but gave him up for us all: On the "giving up" motif in the early Christian tradition, see Notes on 4:25. The active "giving up" of the Son as an exercise of God's saving love notably contrasts with the triple description of the "giving up" of sinful humanity as a manifestation of divine wrath in 1:24, 26, 28.

33–34. *Who will dare to bring accusation against those God has chosen? (Seeing that) it is God who acquits. Who will condemn? (Seeing that) Christ Jesus, the one who died, or rather is raised, (is the one) who stands at the right hand of God and makes intercession for us?:* The translation attempts to make some running sense out of Paul's highly concise expression across these verses. Along with the majority of recent interpreters, it follows the punctuation of Nestle-Aland in placing a question mark only after the first and third phrases. Making all the others questions (as NEB) sets both God and Christ amongst the potential accusers. Even if in both cases the suggestion is instantly dismissed, it is hardly likely to be one that Paul would for an instant entertain. The accepted punctuation places in neat parallel both the questions and the interposed references to God and Christ.

    With respect to the activity of God (v 33b), the language of "justification" appears in its strictest sense, denoting the declaration of aquittal in forensic setting. But this is not a departure from statements about "justification" earlier in the letter; all have had reference to the final, eschatological "justification"; see Interpretation of 2:13.

Behind the four references to the "career" of Christ lie traditional credal (cf. 1 Cor 15:3-5) and/or hymnic formulae. In particular, the motif of Christ's sitting at God's right hand stems from early christological use of the royal Psalm 110:1b, the most cited scriptural text in the NT. On the role of heavenly intercessor attributed to the risen Lord, see Note on v 26.

35. *affliction or distress, or persecution or hunger or nakedness or danger or the sword?:* The seven-fold list of trials parallels to some extent similar lists provided by Paul in connection with the perils and hardships of his own life as apostle (1 Cor 4:10-13; 2 Cor 4:7-12; 6:4-10; 11:23-27; 12:10). Such lists in Paul reflect a widespread topos, appearing not only in Stoic and Jewish apocalyptic literature but also in writers such as Josephus and Plutarch, as well as Mishnaic and Gnostic writings; cf. R. Hodgson, "Paul the Apostle and First Century Tribulation Lists." *ZNW* 74 (1983) 59–80. The first two terms, *thlipsis* and *stenochōria* occur also as a pair in Rom 2:9 (see Note), though there they designate punishment following the eschatological judgment, whereas here they refer to the earthly trials of the elect in the period leading up to it. For NT parallels to the remaining terms, see Cranfield 1.440.

36. *As it is written, "For your sake we are being done to death the whole day long. We are reckoned as sheep ready for the slaughter":* The quotation agrees exactly with LXX Ps 43:23 (44:22), a psalm later rabbinic literature applied to the Maccabean martyrs. "The whole day long" is a Semitic way of indicating the unrelenting nature of the trials.

37. *we are more than conquerors:* The verb *hypernikān* (only here in the NT) represents one of the intensive *hyper* constructions to which Paul is very attached; for a full list, see Dunn 1.506.

38–39. *neither death nor life, nor angels nor rulers, neither things present nor things to come, nor powers, nor height nor depth nor any other created thing:* The list offers a regular pattern of four corresponding pairs—death/life; angels/rulers; things present/things to come; height/depth—interrupted by the somewhat intrusive "powers" and concluded by the singular "any other created thing." "Death" can be a personified power in Paul (as notably in Rom 5:12-21; cf. also the presentation of it in 1 Cor 15:26 as the "last enemy") but its pairing here with "life" suggests that physical death is meant; the combined sense of "neither death nor life" is "whether we live or die." The pair "things present" *(enestōta)* and "things to come" *(mellonta)* appears also in 1 Cor 3:22 similarly linked with "death" and "life." The terms "angels," "rulers" and "powers" refer, as in similar lists in the NT (cf. 1 Cor 15:24 *[archē, exousia, dynamis]*; Col 1:16 *[thronoi, kyriotētes, archai, exousiai]*; 2:15 *[archai, exousiai]*; Eph 1:21 *[kyriotētēs, archē, exousia, dynamis]*; 6:12 *[archē, exousia]*) to the controlling spiritual forces of the old era, seen as hostile to God's salvific design for human beings and thus as conquered or being conquered by Christ. The inclusion of "angels" in the list is not all that surprising since Paul uses *"angelos"* simply to refer to heavenly beings (cf. 1 Cor 4:9; 13:1) and almost always the reference is negative (cf. 1 Cor 6:3; 11:10; 2 Cor 12:7; Gal 3:19). On the basis of later astrological references, "height" *(hypsōma)* and "depth" *(bathos)* have been taken to refer to spirits ruling the upper and lower heavens. But it seems more secure to see here simply a spatial reference taken from ancient astromony, where *hypsōma* is the highest point reached by a star as it rises, *bathos* the lowest point to which it sinks when it dips beneath the horizon. Taken together, the terms embrace the worlds above and below the earth respectively and designate, by metonymy, the ruling spirits of both regions; cf. Phil 2:10c. For the worldview presupposed in the use of the whole range of these "ruler" terms in the NT, see esp. W. Wink, *Naming the Powers* (See Reference), to which the interpretation given here is much indebted (on Rom 8:38-39, see pp. 47–50).

For Reference and Further Study

Balz, H. R. *Heilsvertrauen und Welterfahrung* 116–23.

Beker, J. C. *Paul the Apostle* 362–67.

Caird, G. B. *Principalities and Powers: A Study in Pauline Theology.* Oxford: Clarendon, 1956.

Carr, W. *Angels and Principalities.* SNTSMS 42; Cambridge: Cambridge University, 1981, 112–14.

Hodgson, R. "Paul the Apostle and First Century Tribulation Lists." *ZNW* 74 (1983) 59–80.

Loader, W. R. G. "Christ at the right hand—Ps xc 1 in the New Testament." *NTS* 24 (1978) 199–217.

Osten-Sacken, P. von der *Römer 8* 14–60, 309–19.

Paulsen, H. *Überlieferung und Auslegung* 137–77.

Snyman, A. H. "Style and the Rhetorical Situation of Romans 8.31–39." *NTS* 34 (1988) 218–31.

Thüsing, W. *Per Christum* 219–22.

Wink, W. *Naming the Powers.* Philadelphia: Fortress, 1984.

C. THE INCLUSION OF ISRAEL (9:1–11:36)

Introduction to Romans 9–11. It is no secret that in recent years the question of the relationship of the Christian Church to the Jewish people has moved from the periphery to the center of theological concern. This has meant that Romans 9–11—the most sustained consideration of Israel and the gospel in the New Testament—has received unprecedented attention. From being something of a "Cinderella" section of the letter, it has become the focus of considerable enquiry and discussion.

These three chapters clearly do form a unit within the letter. So distinct is the unity that at times the section has been regarded as more or less detachable from the remainder of the letter—a separate "treatise" on the fate of Israel. Such a judgment has now given way to the almost universal recognition that chapters 9–11 form an integral and necessary element of Paul's total project in Romans.

In the body of the letter to this point Paul has presented and pursued a truly "inclusive" account of the gospel. The negative presupposition has been that all humankind—Jews and Gentiles—are locked together in a common bind of sin and alienation from God; in this respect, there is "no distinction" (3:22) between Jews and Gentiles. The positive affirmation is that the common bind under sin has been victoriously addressed by God, who through Israel's Messiah, Jesus, has brought about a "much more" powerful solidarity in grace, leading to eternal life for all who respond in faith. The outcome has been the establishment of a community, made up of Jews and Gentiles, set in line to inherit the promises God made to Abraham. All the ancient privileges of Israel—election, calling, divine filiation, inheritance, glory—have been mentioned (esp. in 8:14-39), without discrimination, in reference to this community inclusive of Gentile believers.

The extension of Israel's privileges to Gentile believers and the inclusion of those Gentiles within the eschatological people of God constitutes a problem in its own right. What vastly exacerbates the problem and presses insistently for consideration is the all too notorious fact that, not only have a great many Gentiles come in, but the vast bulk of Israel, by not responding positively to the gospel, appear to have been excluded. The gospel presented by Paul so "inclusively" with respect to the Gentiles has proved to be overwhelmingly "exclusive" with respect to Israel. Has God "included" the Gentiles at the terrible cost of "excluding" the People to whom the promises were originally entrusted?

The issue, then, that clamors for consideration at this point in the letter is not so much—as often presented—the single issue of Israel's "unbelief" but the double issue of the gospel's apparent failure with respect to Israel *and* its paradoxical "success" with respect to the Gentiles. The credibility of Paul's presentation of the gospel hangs upon a satisfactory resolution of this issue.

The issue is *theological* in the sense that it raises the question of God's appearing to have acted in a way contrary to the original promises. Paul had allowed this aspect to surface and offered a provisional response earlier in the letter (3:1-8), in connection with Israel's inclusion in the common sinful mass of humankind. Now, following the inclusion of the Gentiles in the positive promise of the gospel (4:1–8:39), the issue of theodicy has become still more pressing.

At the same time, the issue is *personal* in the sense that so inclusive a presentation of the gospel with respect to the Gentiles risks appearing careless concerning the fate of the Jews. Is Paul indifferent to the salvation of his people? His eventual appearance in Rome will be divisive and counterproductive for his wider aims (Jerusalem; Spain) unless he can show both his gospel and his personal attitude to be equally "inclusive" with respect to the Jews.

Romans 9–11, then, is no less part of the "inclusive" presentation of the gospel than what has gone before. In chapters 1–8 Paul has shown that God has acted "inclusively" in Christ to bring Gentiles into the community of salvation. The gospel of a God who always acts "inclusively" will be complete only when Paul has shown that the God who has acted inclusively with respect to Gentiles acts equally inclusively with respect to the Jews—an "inclusive" pattern that ought be reflected in ongoing Christian community life (chapters 12–15). Schematically, Paul's enterprise in Romans can be set out in the following way:

Paul's Inclusive Gospel in Romans

Romans 1–8	Romans 9–11	Romans 12–15
Inclusion of *Gentiles* ("Rejection" of Israel)	Inclusion of *Israel*	Parenesis: "Live 'inclusively'"

That Gentiles would have a share, at least to some degree, in Israel's salvation had long been part of Jewish expectation; Paul's sense of "inclusion" in this respect was nothing new. What was truly novel was the reversal of order: not, Israel first, Gentiles second; but, Gentiles first and Israel second—and only following a sustained period of rejection.

Paul's immediate task, then, is to establish this pattern as the one truly intended and presently being accomplished by God. This explains why so much of Romans 9–11 consists of scriptural exposition. Since it is in scripture that God has announced the plans for the "last days," it is on the field of scripture that the contest to justify this vision of the gospel must be joined. Just as Paul had had recourse to scripture to account for the inclusion of the Gentiles (chapter 4), so now he has recourse to scripture to explain the (temporary) rejection and eventual inclusion of Israel (chapters 9–11).

Paul pursues this task in a rather roundabout way. The opening avowal (9:1-5) sets up the problematic of the entire section. The issue is then addressed in three great blocks. 1. From a strictly "theological" perspective and in a "theodicy" mode, Paul presents (9:6-29) a long scriptural argument to make clear God's sovereign freedom to bring into existence an eschatological people totally according to his will as Creator, without any tie to ethnic identity or human deserts. 2. Paul then (9:30–10:21) examines the dual issue of Israel's rejection and Gentile inclusion from the aspect of human response: if Israel has not been set on the way to salvation, that is because she has resisted God's righteousness and clung to her own (9:30–10:4); her failure cannot be ascribed to any inadequacy on the part of the gospel (10:5-21). 3. Having "exculpated" in this way both God's word and the gospel, Paul finally (11:1-32) confronts directly the fact of Israel's unbelief and in a remarkable *tour de force* holds out to the Gentile believers in Rome a vision of Israel's eventual inclusion within the community of salvation. A hymn to God's unsearchable wisdom (11:33-36) offers an appropriate conclusion to the entire exposition of the gospel (Rom 1:16–11:32).

In pursuit of the ultimate inclusion of Israel Paul draws a very long bow indeed. As the above analysis of the structure of chapters 9–11 will have shown, for a long time what is uppermost in the argument is Israel's rejection rather than her eventual acceptance. Modern readers who look to this section of Romans to find some positive reflection upon the fate of the Jewish people have to wait a long time before receiving satisfaction and even then the relevant passage (11:25-32) is not altogether without ambiguities of its own. Only in the context of the whole does Paul's basically "eirenic" vision emerge; on the way to this complete vision several passages, taken by themselves, appear to cast Jews in a far from favorable light. It is important, when considering individual elements, always to keep in mind the broader, ultimately "inclusive" vision pursued by Paul.

i. The Bitter Problem of Israel's Present Unbelief (9:1-5)

1. I speak the truth in Christ, I do not lie, with my conscience bearing me witness in the Holy Spirit, 2. that I have great sorrow and unceasing anguish in my heart. 3. For I could pray that I myself were accursed and cut off from Christ for the sake of my brothers (and sisters), my kinsfolk by race.

4. They are Israelites, and to them belong
the divine filiation, the glory, the covenants,
the giving of the law, the worship, and the promises;
5. to them belong the patriarchs, and of their race, according to the flesh, is the Christ.
God who is over all be blessed for ever. Amen.

Interpretation

Paul's Protestation (vv 1-3). The new section of the letter opens with a vehement personal affirmation on Paul's part that the protestation he is about to make is indeed true. He solemnly protests the reality and depth of his grief before making explicitly clear what precisely it is that he is grieved about. He simply presumes that, following his attribution of the historic privileges of Israel to the Christian community made up of Jews and Gentiles, the failure of the bulk of Israel to come to faith in the gospel and so be set in line to inherit the promises will be something burning in the forefront of his readers' consciousness at this point.

Paul's opening avowal is in fact reminiscent of the beginning of the letter where he appears to be defending himself against a charge of indifference to the Roman community, shown by his failure to visit them up till now (1:9-15). It is likely that the personal vehemence of the present passage stems largely from a sense of having to defend himself against a similar charge of being indifferent to the fate of his own people: that he simply takes the privileges of Israel and ascribes them to Gentiles, without a care for the serious issues this raises with respect to the faithfulness of God.

Only so, it would seem, can one explain the hyperbole contained in the extraordinary wish or prayer in v 3. It is hard to conceive of anything more devasting for Paul than being formally separated *(anathema)* from Christ and the salvation contained "in" him (cf., e.g., Phil 1:21). Yet, were it in any sense permissible for him to do so and if it could really benefit them, he would pray to exchange his own hope of salvation for that of his "kinsfolk according to the flesh." The condition is unreal. But it underlines the strength of feeling persisting throughout the entire section of the letter devoted to this issue (cf. 10:1; 11:1).

The Privileges of Israel (vv 4-5). To give concrete expression to his concern and to place the entire issue on the level of God's fidelity, Paul acknowledges the privileges accruing to Israel as chosen People of God. First of all, they are "Israelites," bearers of the ancient, honorific title which God bestowed upon the patriarch Jacob (Gen 28:38-39). Heading then what appears to be a formal, six-member list (possibly taken over by Paul from the Hellenistic Jewish community; see Notes) is the motif of "divine filiation" *(huiothesia)*. This has been the key focus of the argument for hope deployed in chapter 8. The fact that it also forms the starting point for the whole discussion about to begin (vv 7-8) suggests that here we have the central privilege as far as Paul is concerned. What has so sharply focused the issue concerning Israel has been the attribution to the mixed community (Gentile as well as Jewish) of the *huiothesia* hitherto seen as reserved for Israelites alone (see Interpretation of 8:14).

The remaining privileges of the formal list go with the salvation history of Israel as recounted in the Bible: God's manifestation to Israel and abiding presence ("glory"); the covenant originally made at Sinai and repeatedly renewed; the giving of the law; the Temple cultus and the privilege of "serving" God that went with it; the promise originally made to Abraham and constantly renewed. To this list Paul adds, first of all, "the fathers," that is, the patriarchs, whose scriptural "story" he will shortly reinterpret (vv 7-14); the sense of God's irrevocable loyalty to "the fathers" will play an important role in the later argument for the inclusion of Israel in the community of salvation (11:28; cf. 15:8). The crowning privilege—one which only a Christian could see as already actuated—is that of being the people from whom the world's Savior, Jesus Christ, took his natural origins.

There is great poignancy and irony in this final member (on the status of the concluding doxology, see Note), since it is precisely Israel's failure to recognize the Messiah to whom she gave birth that puts in question all the other privileges and gives rise to this entire discussion. By bringing the recitation of the privileges to a climax in this way, Paul sharply focuses the central theological issue: where does Israel's failure with respect to the gospel leave the validity of God's original word? The whole effort from here on will be to show that the privileges (especially divine filiation) are not removed from Israel but that her way to them is roundabout and wholly dependent upon an eschatological exercise of God's creative power and mercy.

Notes

1. *with my conscience bearing me witness in the Holy Spirit:* The expression is almost a conflation of 2:15 (conscience bearing witness) and 8:16 (Spirit bearing witness). Here the fact that the witness is "internal" (as in 2:15; contrast the Spirit's "cry" in 8:15) suggests that *symmartyrein* has the sense "witness to" rather than "witness along with." On "conscience" in Paul, see Note on 2:15.

2. *great sorrow and unceasing anguish:* The two "grief" words (*lypē* and *odynē*) occur together in the LXX in an oracular doublet appearing in Isa 35:10 and 51:11.

3. *For I could pray:* The translation takes the imperfect tense of the verb as equivalent to an imperfect with *an*, giving the sense of an unreal condition. The simple verbal form *euchomēn* can also have the sense of "I could wish." The English expression "Would to God . . .!" captures both ideas nicely; cf. Dunn 2.524.

   that I myself were accursed and cut off from Christ: The translation attempts to render the sense of *anathema*, which originally refers simply to something set up as an offering in a shrine. The chief sense in the LXX and subsequently in Paul is that of something or someone delivered over to God as objects of divine wrath, destined to destruction—hence excluded from the salvation community and from salvation itself (cf. Gal 1:8-9; 1 Cor 16:22).

for the sake of my brothers (and sisters), my kinsfolk by race: The preposition *hyper,* as in soteriological formulae with Christ as subject (cf. Rom 5:6-8; Gal 1:4), means "for their salvation." Because "brothers (and sisters)" would normally indicate fellow *Christians* (cf. 1:13; 7:1, 4; 8:12; 10:1; 12:1; 15:14) Paul specifies that he means his kinsfolk by race—"flesh" *(sarx)* simply indicating here natural descent (cf. 1:3; 4:1).

4. *They are Israelites:* In the post-biblical period "Israel/Israelite" was the preferred self-designation in Jewish circles—"Jew/Jews" being used by outsiders. In Romans 9–11, in contrast to the more distanced tone of 2:17-29; 3:9, Paul consistently refers to "Israel."

to them belong the divine filiation, the glory, the covenants, the giving of the law, the worship, and the promises: In the Greek original this sequence forms a three-member doublet, the initial term in each line *(huiothesia/nomothesia)* having the *-esia* ending, the second *(doxa/latreia)* having the feminine singular of the first declension, the third *(diathēkai/epangeliai)* having the feminine plural. *Huiothesia* in secular Greek regularly means "adoption"; the grounds for translating it as "sonship" in Pauline usage (see also 8:15, 23; Eph 1:5) and relating it to Israel's sense of divine filiation stemming from a whole range of biblical texts and culminating in a distinctive eschatological interpretation in the post-biblical period, are set out in the Note on 8:15. On "glory" *(doxa)* in general, see Note on 3:23; the reference here is probably more strictly to the manifestation and presence of God, beginning with the events of the exodus (Exod 16:10; 24:16; 40:34-35; Isa 6:3; Heb 9:5). The plural form "covenants" *(diathēkai;* cf. Sir 44:12, 18; Wis 18:22; 2 Macc 8:15; *4 Ezra* 3:32; 5:29) presumably indicates subsequent renewals of the original Sinai compact. *Nomothesia,* as in 2 Macc 6:23; 4 Macc 5:35; 17:16 and frequently in Philo, may refer to the result of the law-giving—"code of law" (= Pentateuch), rather than to the actual bestowal at Sinai. "Worship" *(latreia)* refers in the first instance to the Temple cultus (cf. LXX Josh 22:27). Paul spiritualizes and broadens this sense of worship to make it include the service of God in everyday life (cf. 12:1; also Phil 3:3) but it is not clear that such a broadening is already intended here. The central "promise" *(epangelia)* for Paul is the "land" promise to Abraham, which in the post-biblical apocalyptic tradition focused upon the inheritance of the eschatological blessings; see Note on 4:13. The plural form, if not simply stylistic, would make allowance for subsequent renewals of the original promise; cf. 15:8: "the promises to the fathers."

5. *to them belong the patriarchs:* Literally, "fathers" *(pateres).* In the Jewish tradition the reference is in the first instance to the patriarchs, with whose election and calling God initiated the history of Israel, but embracing also the exodus generation and indeed all outstanding figures of the past (cf. the "Praise of the Fathers" in Sirach 44–50). Paul probably has the patriarchs, especially Abraham, particularly in mind.

and of their race, according to the flesh, is the Christ: While *Christos* here must have its basic sense of "the Christ, the Messiah," the very formulation—"of their race" (lit. "from whom")—already suggests a Messiah who will have a role extending beyond the confines of Israel.

God who is over all be blessed for ever. Amen: The translation, along with most interpreters, sees here a doxology piously added after the long list of all God's gifts to Israel, rather than a qualification attributing to Christ as Messiah a divine status unparalleled in the New Testament before John 1:1, 18; 20:28 (cf. also Titus 2:13) and somewhat at odds with other christological statements in Paul, who accords Christ divine status but always in subordination to God the Father (cf. Phil 2:11; 1 Cor 8:6). See further Cranfield 2.464–70; Ziesler 238–39 (concise summary).

For Reference and Further Study

Romans 9–11 as a whole:

Aageson, J. W. "Scripture and Structure in the Development of the Argument in Romans 9–11." *CBQ* 48 (1986) 265–89.

Aletti, J.-N. *Comment Dieu est-il juste?* 137–203.

Beker, J. C. *Paul the Apostle* 328–47.

__________. "Romans 9–11 in the Context of the Early Church." *The Church and Israel: Romans 9–11. PSBSup* 1 (1990) 40–55.

Bell, R. H. *Provoked to Jealousy: The Origin and Purpose of the Jealousy Motif in Romans 9–11.* WUNT 2/63; Tübingen: Mohr, 1994.

Dahl, N. A. "The Future of Israel." *Studies in Paul* 137–58.

Getty, M. A. "Paul and the Salvation of Israel: A Perspective on Romans 9–11." *CBQ* 50 (1988) 456–69.

Guerra, A. J. "Romans: Paul's Purpose and Audience with Special Attention to Romans 9–11." *RB* 97 (1990) 219–37.

Harrington, D. J. *Paul on the Mystery of Israel.* Zaccheus Studies; Collegeville: The Liturgical Press, 1992.

Hofius, O. "'All Israel Will Be Saved': Divine Salvation and Israel's Deliverance in Romans 9–11." *The Church and Israel* 19–39.

Hübner, H. *Gottes Ich und Israel: Zum Schriftgebrauch des Paulus in Römer 9-11.* FRLANT 136; Göttingen: Vandenhoeck & Ruprecht, 1984.

Johnson, E. E. *The Function of Apocalyptic and Wisdom Traditions in Romans 9–11.* SBLDS 109; Atlanta: Scholars, 1989.

Käsemann, E. "Paul and Israel." *New Testament Questions of Today* 183–87.

Lambrecht, J. "Israel's Future According to Romans 9–11: An Exegetical and Hermeneutical Approach." *Pauline Studies: Collected Essays.* BETL 115; Leuven: Leuven University/Peeters, 1994, 33–54.

Lorenzi, L. de (ed.) *Die Israelfrage nach Röm 9-11.* Benedictina, Biblisch-ökumenische Abt. 3; Rome: Abbazia di San Paolo fuori le mura, 1977.

Munck, J. *Christ and Israel: An Interpretation of Romans 9–11.* Philadelphia: Fortress, 1967.

Räisänen, H. "Paul, God, and Israel: Romans 9–11 in Recent Research." *The Social World of Formative Christianity and Judaism* (FS H. C. Kee). Eds. J. Neusner et al. Philadelphia: Fortress, 1988, 178–206.

Segal, A. F. "Paul's Experience and Romans 9–11." *The Church and Israel* 56–70.
Siegert, F. *Argumentation bei Paulus: Gezeigt an Röm 9-11*. WUNT 34; Tübingen: Mohr, 1985.

Rom 9:1-5:
Bartsch, H. W. "Rom 9,5 und 1. Clem 32,4: Eine notwendige Konjektur im Römerbrief." *TZ* 21 (1965) 401–09.
Byrne, B. *'Sons of God'* 79–84.
Epp, E. J. "Jewish-Gentile Continuity in Paul: Torah and/or Faith? (Romans 9:1-5)." *HTR* 79 (1986) 80–90.
Kuss, O. "Zu Römer 9,5." *Rechtfertigung* (FS E. Käsemann). Eds. J. Friedrich et al. Tübingen: Mohr, 1976, 291–303.
Luz, U. *Das Geschichtsverständnis des Paulus*. BEvT 49; Munich: Kaiser, 1968, 26–28, 269–74.
Metzger, B. M. "The Punctuation of Rom 9:5." *Christ and Spirit in the New Testament* (FS C.F.D. Moule). Eds. B. Lindars and S. S. Smalley. London: Cambridge University, 1973, 95–112.
Rese, M. "Die Vorzüge Israels in Röm 9:4f. und Eph 2:12." *TZ* 31 (1975) 211–22.

ii. The Elective Pattern of God's Working (9:6-29)

Introduction to Rom 9:6-29. This first stage of Paul's consideration of Israel's failure with respect to the gospel amounts to a theodicy. Can the present situation according to Paul's gospel—the inclusion of the Gentiles and apparent exclusion of Israel from the community of salvation—be squared with God's ancient assurances to Israel? Does not it imply that God has not been faithful to his "word." Paul's task is to explore God's "word," as recorded in scripture, in such a way as to show that the present—"mixed"—composition of the eschatological people of God responds to the way God has acted all along and manifests the sovereign freedom that must always attend the action of the Creator. In dealings with key figures of Israel's past, along with further statements and explanations recorded in scripture, God gave sufficient indication of the way things would go in the final age. The present composition of the People of God does not mean that God's "word" to Israel has "fallen through" (v 6a).

The structure of the long scriptural argument is best discerned by working "backwards," so to speak. Vv 22-29 declare *what* God has done: calling into being an eschatological people of God, made up of Gentiles and the Jewish-Christian "remnant." Vv 6b-21 prepare the way for this by tracing in scripture God's declared intention to proceed in this "elective" way, exercising the sovereign freedom of the Creator. The opening thematic question in v 6a, "Has God's word (to Israel) fallen through?," thus receives a resounding negative response—though one that is, in fact, left unstated because of the anacolouthon occurring at the end of v 23.

Within the first main section, vv 6b-21, Paul pursues the elective pattern of God's operation towards Israel in four stages, the first three (vv 6b-9; vv 10-13; vv 15-18) centering in turn upon a key phase of biblical history, the fourth (vv 19-21) employing a stock biblical image (potter and clay) designed to counter any possible human objection to God's freedom of action; v 14 serves to give fresh impetus to the argument with an objection about God's "fairness."

The second main section, vv 22-29, falls into two parts. In vv 22-23 Paul begins to apply what has been established concerning the freedom of God's action in the past to the present situation. In vv 24-29 he cites texts from Hosea and Isaiah to show how the present make up of the believing community is in accordance both with what God had promised and the exercise of freedom.

We can set it all out as follows:

Introductory Thematic Question: v 6a: "Has God's word fallen through?"

I. The "Elective/Promise" pattern of God's action in the *past*: vv 6b-21.
    1. God's free mode of forming a People shown in Isaac: vv 6b-9.
    2. God's free mode of forming a People shown in Jacob and Esau: vv 10-13.
  Objection: Can we charge God with unfairness?: v 14.
    3. God's freedom shown in Exodus figures (Moses and Pharaoh): vv 15-18.
    4. God's freedom defended against human complaint: vv 19-21.

II. Application to what God has done in the *present:* vv 22-29.
    1. God's right to act in this way: vv 23-23.
    2. The "calling" of the mixed community "pre-announced" in scripture: vv 24-29:
      General statement of the call: v 24:
        a) Gentiles: vv 25-26.
        b) Jewish-Christian "remnant": vv 27-29.

The section as a whole displays an "inclusive" structure in that both at its beginning (vv 7b-8a) and end (vv 24-29) the issue is that of who constitutes the "people" ("Israel") "called" in the eschatological era by God to enjoy the privilege of "divine sonship" (cf. the first two privileges named in the list of vv 4-5).

a) *The Elective Pattern Shown in the Patriarchs* (9:6-13)

6. But it is not as if the word of God has fallen through.
For not all those who belong to Israel by descent are "Israel,"
7. nor because they are descendants of Abraham are all children (of God). But (the principle runs) "in the line of Isaac shall descendants be called into being for you."
8. This means that it is not the children of the flesh who are children of God but the children of the promise are reckoned as descendants. 9. For the word of the promise runs as follows: "At the right time I shall come and Sarah will have a son."
10. And the same principle can be seen also in the case of Rebecca, when she was with child as a result of one single act of intercourse with Isaac, our father. 11. While the boys were as yet unborn and had had no chance to do anything good or bad, in order that the elective purpose of God might stand 12. and rest not on human achievement but solely on God's call, she was told, "The elder will serve the younger," 13. as it is written, "Jacob I have loved, but Esau I have hated."

INTERPRETATION

God's mode of forming a people shown in Isaac (vv 6-9). As a first stage in his defense of God's faithfulness, Paul makes (v 6b) a key distinction, casting it in terms of the first two of the privileges listed in vv 4-5—"Israelites" and "divine filiation." With respect to the privilege of belonging to the "people" of God as "Israelites," those who bear this title are not simply coextensive with Israel nationally defined nor (v 7a) are all "descendants of Abraham" (*sperma Abraam*, here understood in a neutral "ethnic" sense) "children (of God)" (*tekna*; see Note). With respect to the eschatological realization of these privileges, as far as God is concerned, some other criterion—other, that is, than ethnic descent—is operative.

What this criterion is Paul finds in the scriptural account of the circumstances surrounding the birth of Abraham's son Isaac. This set a pattern indicative and determinative for the future. Abraham originally had not been able to have a child by Sarah, though he had a child, Ishmael, by her Egyptian maid, Hagar (Genesis 16). The mysterious visitors who come to the tent in Mamre (Gen 18:1-15) assure him that he will have a son by Sarah (v 10, quoted in Rom 9:9). Later, when Isaac is born in fulfillment of this promise (Genesis 21), Abraham is prevailed upon by God (and Sarah) to cast out Hagar and the older boy. God assures Abraham: "It is through the line of Isaac that your descendants *(sperma)* shall be called *(klēthēsetai)*" (v 12). Paul finds (v 7b) in this restriction of the "descendants" to Isaac a justification for making the distinction just formulated between wider (ethnically defined) "descendants" of Abraham ("children of the flesh") and a special line of descent, running through Isaac and "called" into being in response to a divine promise. In this sense scripture provides an indication of God's intention to "call" into being non-ethnically defined "descendants of Abraham," who will enjoy the privilege of divine filiation in the last days (*kata ton kairon*; cf. the quotation of Hos 1:10 [LXX 2:1] in v 26).

It is important to note that Paul has not at this point identified the "true" (Isaac-line) "descendants of Abraham" with any particular community—Christian or otherwise. He has not defined a "(true) Israel within Israel," from which Jews who have not come to faith in the gospel would be excluded. The focus remains upon God and the indications given in scripture that "promise" and "calling," rather than ethnic belonging, mark the pattern of divine action.

God's mode of forming a people shown in Jacob and Esau (vv 10-13). The second stage of Paul's analysis of scripture moves to the next patriarchal generation. Here God has given an even stronger indication that his eschatological design runs solely by free choice and the exercise of creative power. The indication comes in the divine attitude taken towards Rebecca's twin sons, Esau and Jacob. Before the twins were born and therefore before either had a chance to do good or evil and so merit one way or the other (vv 10-11a), God reversed the natural order by telling their mother that the "elder" was to serve the "younger" (v 12b, quoting Gen 25:23). This, comments Paul, (vv 11b-12a), safeguards the principle that God's "purpose" (*prothesis*; cf. 8:28) proceeds upon a wholly "elective" *(kat' eklogēn)* basis. It was not to depend in any sense upon human "works" *(ex ergōn)* but solely upon the "calling" *(kalountos)* of God. A later scriptural passage, Mal 1:2-3, is cited (v 13) to clinch the matter with its bald statement of divine preference (lit. "love) for Jacob as against "hatred" for Esau (on the Semitic idiom involved, see Note).

What this highly dense stage of the argument particularly brings out is the sovereign freedom of God to pursue a creative purpose quite independently of any contribution from the human side. Human behavior ("works") in no sense determines the path God chooses to pursue. The language of "works" immediately calls to mind the polemic against "works of the law" in the earlier part of the letter. Paul briefly recycles this polemic in order to prepare the ground for his subsequent (9:30-33) explanation of why it is that Israel, despite her pursuit of righteousness, has failed to attain the long-sought goal. The truth is that no amount of "works righteousness" on the part of Israel can condition the operation of God's eschatological purpose or limit its scope to one people alone. God's free, creative mode of operation leaves open the possibility of including within the final "Israel" those (believers—Jewish and Gentile) who have no "works" to show whatsoever.

NOTES

6. *But it is not as if the word of God has fallen through:* By "word of God" here Paul means the whole complex of God's address to Israel, recorded in the scriptures and grounding the privileges just listed; cf. 3:2. The idea of God's (or a prophet's) word "not falling" reflects a common idiom of the biblical and post-biblical tradition (cf. Josh 21:45; 23:14; Ruth 3:18; 1 Sam 3:19; 2 Kgs 10:10; Tob 14:1 [S]).

   For not all those who belong to Israel by descent are "Israel": Distinguishing a "true Israel" within the wider mass of the people is not totally unparalleled in the Jewish tradition: cf., for example, at Qumran: CD 4:2-12; 4QFlor 1:14-19; also (presuming that "the wicked" includes unfaithful Jews) *1 Enoch* 1:8-9. Cranfield's neat phrase, "an Israel within Israel" (2.474) is not quite accurate, since it restricts the "Israel" which comes about as a result of God's elective purpose simply to Jews. Paul has not yet defined this "Israel"; it is better to see him as stating simply that the two "Israel's" are not coextensive. This leaves open the possibility that the "(true, called) Israel" can include Gentile believers—a possibility which Paul depicts as a reality in vv 24-29. L. Gaston ("Israel's Enemies" 94) argues that what Paul is asserting here is the inclusion of Gentiles within the true Israel, rather than the exclusion of certain Jews: not all who belong to the (true) Israel are Israel (= Jews). But it is far more natural to refer the first "Israel" phrase (*hoi ex Israēl*) to those of Jewish descent, rather than the second; cf. the telling critique of E. E. Johnson, *Functions of Apocalyptic* 139n, 194.

7. *nor because they are descendants of Abraham are all children (of God):* "Descendants (seed) of Abraham" (*sperma Abraam*) occurs elsewhere in Paul (Rom 11:1; 2 Cor 11:22) and the wider Jewish and Christian tradition (cf. *Pss. Sol.* 9:17; 18:4; John 8:33, 37) as an honorific title for Israelites, with the specific connotation, in virtue of the promises to the patriarchs, of destiny to "inherit" the blessings of salvation (cf. esp. Gal 3:29). Here Paul seems to use the phrase in a neutral, "secular" sense, simply indicating natural descent. Some preserve the honorific sense by understanding the phrase here as predicative: "Nor is it as though all his children are Abraham's seed" (Dunn 2.540). But this destroys the parallelism with the preceding statement concerning "Israel." The true predicative phrase "children" (*tekna*) is normally taken to mean "children (of Abraham)," as though Paul were distinguishing (mere) "descendants" of Abraham from his "children." But v 8, which gives an explanation of the scriptural text cited in v 7b and which stands in parallel with v 7a, speaks in terms of divine filiation: "children of God" (*tekna tou theou*). This argues strongly that the simple *tekna* in 7a should be understood in the same way. Paul is then taking up the first two of the privileges in the list of vv 4-5: the "people" ("Israel") privilege and the "divine filiation" privilege; the recurrence of the same two at the end of the sequence, in vv 25-26, forms a typical Pauline "inclusion."

   But (the principle runs) "in the line of Isaac shall descendants be called into being for you": The quotation agrees exactly with the LXX of Gen 21:12. Paul understands it in a restrictive sense ("only in Isaac") and takes the verb *klēthēsetai* very emphatically ("will be [that is, in the eschatological age] called into being").

8. *This means that it is not the children of the flesh who are children of God:* Paul does not mean to exclude the possibility of "children of flesh" (that is, the Jews) being "children of God" but simply denies that being the one *necessarily* means being the other. On the privilege of divine filiation expressed in the phrase, "children of God," see Interpretation of 8:14-15.

   are reckoned as descendants: "Reckoned" *(logizetai)* recalls Paul's sustained use of Gen 15:6 (God's "reckoning" of righteousness to Abraham) in chapter 4 to argue that righteousness is not brought about by human works but through God's gracious, creative action on behalf of believers. The use of the term here implies that the privilege of divine filiation accrues to the "children of the promise" not on the basis of natural descent but solely on that of God's creative "reckoning" of them to be "descendants of Abraham." Cutting the tie with natural (ethnic) descent allows for Gentile believers to be "reckoned" among the "descendants of Abraham"—*sperma* here apparently having the honorific sense. In Gal 4:28 Paul dubs the Gentile Galatians "children of the promise."

9. *For the word of the promise runs as follows: "At the right time I shall come and Sarah will have a son":* The quotation is basically from Gen 18:14 (LXX) with some influence from Gen 18:10 *(kata ton kairon)*, with the reference to "in the spring" omitted and with "I shall come" *(eleusomai)* instead of "I shall return." The modifications make the text convey a sense of the divine intent for the eschatological era; cf. the use of *kairos* with respect to God's saving eschatological intervention in 5:6.

10. *And the same principle can be seen:* The translation draws from the opening phrase *(ou monon de, alla kai)* the main verb otherwise lacking in the very imperfect sentence making up v 10.

    when she was with child as a result of one single act of intercourse with Isaac, our father: The Greek word *koitē* literally means "bed" but has extended, euphemistic meanings in the sense of "marriage bed," "sexual intercourse" and even "seminal emission" (cf. BAGD 440). Paul probably wants to underline the equality between the twins, Esau and Jacob, by stressing not simply that Rebecca had intercourse with one man (*ex henos* = Isaac; the reference is to Gen 25:21) but that they were conceived from one and the same sexual act.

11. *While the boys were as yet unborn and had had no chance to do anything good or bad:* This clause appears as a genitive absolute, lacking a subject and beginning a long rambling sentence making up vv 11-13. Paul introduces the steps of his argument in an order that is virtually the opposite of the logical. In particular, the introduction of the idea of human merit is unprepared for—unless Paul is confident that it remains a continuing issue.

    the elective purpose of God: Paul's use of *prothesis* to express the divine purpose in regard to the eschatological salvation and glorification of human beings emerges very clearly in 8:28. *Kat' eklogēn* means "operating by selection"; cf. also 11:5.

12. *and rest not on human achievement:* The phrase *ouk ex ergōn* expresses in a form appropriate for the epoch before the giving of the law the principle more regularly stated as "not from works of the law" *(ouk ex ergōn nomou)*; on this see Note on 3:20.

God's call: On the distinctive Pauline sense of God's "calling," see Note on 8:30.

she was told, "The elder will serve the younger": The quotation agrees exactly with LXX Gen 25:23.

13. *as it is written, "Jacob I have loved, but Esau I have hated.":* The quotation of this text, Mal 1:2-3 (LXX, with slight word-order variation), means that, as in 3:21 and 4:3-8, the scriptural testimony comes from both the "Law" and the "Prophets." Malachi assured Israel ("Jacob") of God's persevering love by pointing to God's equally constant repression of Israel's adversary, Edom ("Esau"). Paul simply takes the oracle as a confirmation of the preference for Jacob expressed in Gen 25:23. "Hating" in this context simply reflects a Semitic way of expressing a choice made for one party over another. There are no grounds for erecting a theory of "double predestination" on the slender scriptural base provided by Paul's quotation of this text. He is simply pointing to this text as an indication of the divine intent to proceed in a sovereignly free, "elective" way, which human qualities or claims cannot touch or determine; nothing is said about the ultimate fate of Esau.

For Reference and Further Study

(See list following commentary on 9:22-29)

b) *The Elective Pattern Shown in Moses and Pharaoh* (9:14-18)

14. What shall we say then? Is there injustice on God's part?
By no means!
15. For he says to Moses, "I will have mercy on whomsoever I have mercy, and I will show pity to whomsoever I show pity."
16. So then it is not a matter of human willing or achieving, but of God exercising mercy.
17. For the scripture says to Pharaoh, "For this very purpose I have raised you up: to display through you my power in you, so that my name may be proclaimed in all the earth."
18. So then he has mercy upon whomsoever he wills, and he hardens the heart of whomsoever he wills.

c) *God's Freedom Defended Against Human Complaint* (9:19-21)

> 19. You will say to me then, "Why does he still find fault?
> For who resists his will?" 20. But (I say) who are you, mere human being, to answer back to God? Does something that has been made say to its maker, "Why have you made me thus?"
> 21. Has the potter no right over the clay, to make out of the same lump one vessel for beauty and another for menial use?

INTERPRETATION

The elective pattern shown in Moses (9:14-16). The strong emphasis Paul has placed upon the purely elective mode of God's working—that God "loves" and "hates" completely independently of any human conditioning—understandably raises the objection (v 14) that this projects upon God a way of proceeding that is unfair. Rather than representing a difficulty posed by a real dialogue partner, the objection, in diatribe mode, serves to spur the argument on to its next stage, where Paul continues his scriptural justification of God's total freedom of action. Moving on to the generation of the Exodus (vv 15-18), he sets the two key figures in the drama, Moses and Pharaoh, in contrastive parallel illustrating two opposite poles of God's free operation. Both were addressed by God, and in each case—positively in the one, negatively in the other—that address constituted an unequivocal divine assertion of freedom to act without any regard to human deserts.

In the case of Moses (v 15), it is a matter of mercy: Paul cites the final part of Exod 33:19 as a statement of the divine intent to exercise mercy in an entirely free way—the force of which comes out in the repeated "whomsoever . . . whomsoever." From this a first conclusion emerges (v 16)—similar to that derived from the divine choice of Jacob over Esau (vv 10-13): the exercise of God's mercy is not dependent upon any amount of "willing" *(thelontos)* or "achieving" *(trechontos)* on the human side; it depends totally upon God, as one who exercises mercy *(tou eleōntos theou)*. It is ironical (and perhaps not unintentionally so on Paul's part) to portray Moses—the one who might reasonably be considered representative *par excellence* of righteousness through works of law—as the symbol of God's design to exercise mercy independently of all human achievement.

The elective pattern shown in Pharaoh (9:17-18). Pharaoh represents a similar exercise of divine freedom but one that goes in a completely different direction. Paul cites (v 17) the divine message to Pharaoh (Exod 9:16) in a form that suggests that the entire purpose of the Egyptian king's appearance on the stage of history was simply to serve to display God's power and to make known his name throughout the earth. Implicit is the motif of God's "hardening" *(sklērynein)* of Pharaoh's heart (Exod 4:21; 7:3; 9:12; 14:4, 8, 17), which corresponds, negatively, to the exercise of mercy with respect to Moses (cf. v 18). Pharaoh's heart is not hardened because of antecedent evil dispositions on his part—to posit such would destroy the point Paul is making. The "hardened" Pharaoh became an instrument of a wider purpose—the achievement of worldwide "glory" for God's name through the miracle of the Exodus liberation.

Later (11:7, 25) Paul will speak of a "hardening" *(pōrōsis, epōrōthēsan)* in connection with that part of Israel that has not come to faith in Jesus as the Christ. It would be premature to see in the "hardened" Pharaoh of the present context an explicit symbol of this unbelieving Israel. Nonetheless, Paul is preparing the ground for the solution he will finally give, when the principle of divine freedom has been sufficiently established. In Pharaoh, scripture has shown God's sovereign freedom to "harden," as well as to exercise mercy (v 18). But it has also shown that a "hardening" brought about by God can serve a wider, salvific purpose. This leaves open the possibility for interpreting the present failure of Israel with respect to the gospel as a similar instance of divine action—the implication being that it too might also contain the seeds of an ultimately salvific, positive purpose, the proclamation of God's name in all the earth, that is, throughout the Gentile world (cf. 11:11-15, 30-32).

God's freedom defended against human complaint (vv 19-21). The scriptural argument centered upon Moses and Pharaoh (vv 15-18) has hardly met the earlier charge that God is unfair (v 14); Paul has simply driven more deeply into the assertion of God's freedom. He now (v 19) restates the objection in a somewhat more specific form (more precisely, he places it himself upon the lips of his reader: "You will say . . ."). The divine mode of acting illustrated in the two cases just cited—especially the "hardening" of Pharaoh—so appears to eliminate human freedom and responsibility that it is unreasonable for God to find fault with human beings for their obstinacy.

Taking up the objection in this form, Paul does not, as in the three earlier sections, turn to a specific biblical episode or divine announcement. Instead, in diatribe style, he first of all sharply reminds (v 20a) the objector of creaturely status ("mere human being") over against God and then introduces (vv 20b-21) a stock biblical image designed to exclude the very thought of human protest against the Creator's sovereign freedom. The image derived from the potter's freedom to shape vessels to any use at will creates difficulty for the modern reader but would hardly come as a surprise to an audience steeped in the biblical tradition (see Note). The force of the image as Paul employs it (cf. also Jer 18:1-11; Sir 33:13) stems from the fact that the potter has to make vessels for a wide variety of uses, some noble (the banquet cup), some homely (the chamber pot); he will turn the same lump of clay in either direction as he sees fit. Like the potter, the Creator has a perfect right to turn the creature in whatsoever direction he chooses; like the clay, the human creature has no right to complain about being made for one use (an ignoble one) and not another ("Why have you made me thus?," v 20b).

Again, it has to be said that this hardly answers the difficulty posed, which concerned God's "blaming" in a context where human responsibility had been suppressed. Moreover, human beings are not simply lifeless, passive clay. To this Paul would probably respond that he has not in fact been speaking of God's blaming at all. The objection in a sense sidetracks the main issue and Paul more or less brushes it aside. The image is brought forward simply to illustrate and evoke a basic biblical dogma—one emerging above all from the Book of Job—that, in the end, the Creator as Creator has the right to proceed in a way totally unaccountable to human beings. This is the sole point being made. It is quite misguided to press out of the homely image more wide ranging theological conclusions (as in the long-standing debate over "Predestination"; see Note on 9:18). We have here neither Paul's first nor his last word on the nature and operation of God.

Notes

14. *What shall we say then?:* On Paul's use of the phrase *ti oun eroumen,* see Note on 4:1 above.

    Is there injustice on God's part?: While it can have a more general usage, the word *adikia* in Romans is especially used as the negative correlative of *dikaiosynē* ("righteousness"); see esp. 3:5; 6:13; cf. also 1:18. As in 3:5 *(adikos),* the objection seems to suggest that God is acting contrary to what is right or just in an absolute sense.

15. *For he says to Moses, "I will have mercy on whomsoever I have mercy, and I will show pity to whomsoever I show pity.":* The quotation agrees exactly with LXX Exod 33:19.

16. *So then it is not a matter of human willing or achieving but of God exercising mercy:* The highly contracted formulation in the Greek requires that an introductory phrase, "it is not a matter of," be supplied. It is surprising that the word *anthrōpou* ("human beings") does not occur after the first two participles *(thelontos . . . trechontos)* since Paul clearly intends a contrast between human willing and achievement, on the one hand, and God's willing and having mercy *(eleōntos),* on the other (cf. the use of *thelein* with respect to God in v 18 and v 22). The Greek word translated "achieving" *(trechontos)* literally means "running"—a more intense expression of the biblical idea of "walking" used

with respect to human behavior in God's sight; see Note on 6:4. Later, Paul will point to the divine mercy as the principle upon which God's salvation will *universally* operate (11:30-32; 15:9; cf. also 9:23).

17. *For the scripture says to Pharaoh:* Strictly speaking according to the account of Exodus 9, the text (Exodus 9:16) introduced by this phrase represents the divine message given to Moses to pass on to Pharaoh. Paul knows that God did not speak directly to Pharaoh, so he presents Pharaoh as addressed by scripture, which for Paul always represents a statement of the divine intent.

    "For this very purpose . . .": This opening phrase of Exod 9:16 as quoted by Paul *(eis auto touto exēgeira se)* stands much closer to the original Hebrew rather than to the LXX *(heneken toutou dietērēthēs)*; the effect is to place greater stress upon the precise intention of God.

18. *So then he has mercy upon whomsoever he wills, and he hardens the heart of whomsoever he wills:* This statement, together with other elements of the surrounding context—notably the "Jacob-Esau" contrast in vv 10-13, the "Pot" illustration in vv 20b-21 and the phrase "vessels of wrath, ripe for destruction" in v 22—have been the chief scriptural source for the Augustinian doctrine of "Double Predestination," taken up at the time of the Reformation especially by John Calvin (see esp. the Excursus on the topic in Kuss 2.828–95). Without going into the matter at length, the following points may be made: 1. The doctrine in question wrongly applies the verse to the eternal (eschatological) salvation/damnation of individuals, whereas Paul is positing God's historical dealing with two figures, Moses and Pharaoh as an illustration of the sovereignly free operation of God's plan in history, not with respect to individuals, but to communities (Jews, Gentiles). 2. If Pharaoh's "hardening" in some sense anticipates the *pōrōsis* that in Paul's eyes has come upon Israel and Paul regards the latter condition as temporary (11:25-26), this suggests that neither is Pharaoh's *sklērynein* permanent. 3. A total theological system cannot be erected on the basis of Rom 9:10-23, since this is only a stage in Paul's total argument, one where theological statements are provisional, one-sided and incomplete. The objection in v 19 represents essentially an admission on Paul's part that he is, for the sake of his present argument, neglecting the element of human freedom and responsibility, upon which he can elsewhere (cf. 6:1–8:13; 2 Cor 5:5) be so insistent.

19. *You will say to me then, "Why does he still find fault?":* Paul's use of the diatribe style is prominent here; cf. Jas 4:12; Epictetus *Discourses* 1.18.9–10. The objection is similar in form to that in 3:7, though the grounds are somewhat different.

    For who resists his will?": The point is that no one in fact resists God's will and hence the complaint in the first question is justified. The formulation is reminiscent of Job 9:19 (LXX: *tis oun krimati autou antistēsetai*), which is repeated in Wis 12:12.

20. *But (I say) who are you, mere human being, to answer back to God?:* The question is strongly reminiscent of God's response to the anguished questioning of Job: cf. 38:2-3; 40:1-2.

Does something that has been made say to its maker, "Why have you made me thus?": The introduction to the question agrees exactly with the central part of LXX Isa 29:16; the question itself appears to be (more loosely) based upon the parallel text in Isa 45:9; cf. also Wis 12:12.

21. *Has the potter no right over the clay, to make out of the same lump one vessel for beauty and another for menial use?:* For the "potter/clay" image in the biblical tradition, cf. Ps 2:9; Job 10:8-9; Isa 29:16; 41:25; 45:9; 64:8; Jer 18:1-12; Sir 33:13. The description of the potter's work in Wis 15:7 offers a remarkably close parallel to Paul's use of the image here: along with similarity of language (*kerameus, plassein, skeuos*), both feature the motif of the potter producing from the same clay (Wisdom: *ek tou autou pēlou*; Paul: *tou pēlou ek tou autou phyramatos*) pots for both noble and less noble ends according to his will. The use made of the image is very different, however, Wisdom relating it to the pagan manufacture of idols. The sense of a human being as something moulded by God out of "clay" is pervasive in the psalm literature from Qumran to express both the sense of creaturely "distance" from the Creator and the wonder of the divine grace and condescension: 1QS 11:22; 1QH 1:21; 3:20-21, 23-24; 4:29; 11:3; 12:26, 32; 18:12.

For Reference and Further Study

(See list following commentary on 9:22-29)

d) *The Elective Pattern Shown in the Composition of the Believing Community* (9:22-29)

22. What if God, desiring to show his wrath and to make known his
power, endured with much patience vessels of wrath ripe for destruction, 23. and in order to make known the riches of his glory for the vessels of mercy, which he has prepared beforehand for glory, . . . (Well, is
not that his right?). 24.—us, that is, whom he has called, not from the
Jews only but also from the Gentiles?
25. As indeed he says in Hosea,
"Those who were not my people I will call 'my people,'
and her who was not beloved I will call 'my beloved.'"
26. "And in the very place where it was said to them, 'You are not my
people,' they will be called 'sons (and daughters) of the living God.'"
27. And Isaiah cries out concerning Israel:
"Though the number of the sons of Israel be as the sand of the sea, only
a remnant of them will be saved; 28. for it is by completing and curtailing that the Lord will carry out his word upon the earth."

29. And as Isaiah predicted, "If the Lord of hosts had not left us descendants, we would have become as Sodom and been made like Gomorrah."

Interpretation

Introduction. The argument up to this point has shown how God gave sufficient indication in scripture that the divine way of proceeding would be sovereignly free, completely unconditioned by human response or deserts. It is now time to see how the present situation with respect to the constitution of the eschatological people of God—Gentiles included; Jews (save for a "remnant") excluded—responds to that view of the divine way of proceeding. If there is indeed a correspondence, then it cannot be said that "God's word has fallen through" (v 6a).

Paul, it must be said, could have gone about showing this correspondence rather more clearly. Vv 22-23 make up the protasis of a long conditional sentence for which the apodosis is lacking. In place of the apodosis, Paul begins, in v 24, a relative clause which describes God's "calling" into being of the eschatological people of God, made up of Gentiles and the Jewish-Christian remnant, as foretold in the scriptures (vv 25-29). The opening conditional clause (vv 22-23) states what God has done, the apodosis that the reader has to supply is a rhetorical question, expecting an affirmative answer ("Well, is not that his [God's] right?"), arising out of the preceding establishment from scripture of God's total freedom of action (vv 10-21). The logical transition between v 23 and v 24 only really makes sense when such a question is supplied. Vv 24-29 then explain that, in creating a "mixed" eschatological people, God has done what he had a total right to do and had in fact announced (through scripture) that this is what he would do. So the creation of such a community, heir to the privileges of Israel (vv 4-5), does not mean that God has been untrue to his "word" (v 6a).

"Vessels of wrath" (v 22). Paul, in fact, "homes in" on the present situation very gradually, like an aircraft pilot beginning a descent upon a small landing strip still a long way off. The "descent" comes in the long conditional sentence in vv 22-23, which is all concerned with the intention of God (cf. *thelōn* . . ., v 22; *kai hina* . . ., v 23). In the long scriptural proof (vv 14-21) Paul had defended God's right to deal positively and negatively with human beings as he saw fit. So now he frames the divine intention which has given rise to the present situation in terms of the same duality and uses language which consciously recalls the key scriptural examples (Moses [v 15], Pharaoh [v 17]) and the "potter/vessel" image (vv 20b-21). Paul speaks of God's (negative) intentions with respect to *"vessels (skeuē)* of wrath," on the one hand (v 22), and (positive) intentions with respect to *"vessels* of mercy," on the other (v 23).

Paul does not immediately identify who he has in mind in speaking of "vessels of wrath" and it is important to consider the phrase in the context in which he has placed it before hastening to such identification. "Wrath" does not refer precisely to an emotion in God but denotes the situation created by human defiance of the divine will; it is normally to be equated with eternal punishment, though, as in Rom 1:18-32 there can be "anticipations" of it before the final reckoning (see Interpretation and Note on 1:18). "Vessels of wrath," therefore, would designate those who are actually subject to the punishment stemming from God's disfavor or at least set in line to incur it. The fact that Paul qualifies "vessels of wrath" here with the phrase "ripe for destruction" *(katērtismena eis apōleian)* suggests that here the latter is the case: the "vessels" are "ripe" or "ready" for eternal destruction and loss but have not yet been given over to it.

If they are still preserved, it is because God has borne *(ēnegken)* with them in much patience *(makrothymia)* and this for a double reason: to display his wrath and to make known his power. It is tempting to understand God's patient "bearing" with the "vessels of wrath," "ripe for" but not yet given over to destruction, as intended to create time for repentance (cf. 2:4). But there is no hint of repentance in the context and the fact that the language sits closely to that of the divine utterance to Pharaoh in v 17 suggests that the situation of Pharaoh functions in some way as a paradigm for that of the "vessels of wrath." God did not destroy Pharaoh at the first sign of his resistance but kept him alive, "enduring" his continual frustration of the Israelites' hopes to depart. But all this was only so that the Exodus, when eventually it took place, would constitute a far more stupendous display of God's power, a display which included the destruction of Pharaoh and his entire army. God's "patience," then, served to enhance the display of his wrath when the climax came. Paul seems to understand the "vessels of wrath" to be in a "Pharaoh" situation in an eschatological sense. Though "ripe for destruction," they have not been immediately destroyed. God bears with them in order that the manifestation of his wrath may be all the more striking and more widely known.

Few statements of Paul would be as alien to modern religious sensibility as this picture of the divine mode of operation sketched by Paul in v 22. He never explicitly identifies who the "vessels of wrath" are. But, when the corresponding "vessels of mercy" are identified, in v 24, with the believing community "called into being" out of the Gentiles and the Jewish-Christian "remnant," it becomes inescapably clear that the "vessels of wrath, ripe for destruction" are in fact that large part of Israel that has not responded positively to the Christian gospel. The Jewish apocalyptic tradition had used the concept of God's "patience" preceding a final display of wrath with respect to the continued existence of the sinful (Gentile) world oppressing the faithful (Nah 1:2-3; 2 Macc 6:12-16; *4 Ezra* 7:74). Paul has dared to turn this negative conception of the divine "patience" against a portion of Israel itself, who for the time being he simply leaves "hanging there," as it were, facing but not consigned to eternal destruction. This is not, of course, Paul's final word on this "Israel"; the "space" provided by the divine patience will receive a far more positive and more hopeful interpretation in chapter 11. Here he is simply looking at the phenomenon of Israel's unbelief from a biblical perspective which reasons from the fact that something is the case to the inference that God intended it to be so and actually brought it about. On the basis of scriptural precedents and "pre-announcements" Paul defends the divine right so to act, in order that the negative side of the present situation cannot give grounds for leveling a charge of infidelity against God (v 6a).

"Vessels of mercy" (v 23). As is clear from the following sentence (v 24), the "vessels of mercy" named on the corresponding positive side must refer to the Christian community made up of Gentiles and the Jewish-Christian "remnant." It is precisely the inclusive aspect of this community that displays the "richness" of God's glory—the worldwide reach of the divine presence and power. It consists of "vessels of mercy" in the sense of owing its existence solely to the free exercise of the divine mercy (*eleos*; cf. v 15) upon those who of themselves have done nothing to deserve or merit the favor in which they now stand.

This community has, however, been "prepared beforehand for glory" *(proētoimasen eis doxan)*. This phrase takes the reader back to the content of the divine "purpose" *(prothesis)*, the "unfolding" of which Paul pointed to as the ultimate basis for Christian hope in 8:28-30 (cf. 9:11: *hē kat' eklogēn prothesis*). The Christian community, made up of Jews and Gentiles, is the realization in history of God's eternal design that human beings share in the reflection of the divine glory already manifest in the risen Lord (8:29; on "glory" as the fulfillment of the Creator's intent for human beings, see Note on 3:23). The existence of the mixed believing community does not represent a failure or an aberration from the divine purpose but the fulfillment of an original design conceived in eternity and now being worked out.

The composite community (Jews and Gentiles) "called" into being (vv 24-29). As we noted above, Paul leaves his audience to supply the rhetorical question, "Well is not that his (God's) right?" and the required affirmative response. He also leaves aside any further consideration for the time being of the "vessels of wrath ripe for destruction" and turns (v 24) to identify the "vessels of mercy" with the Christian community ("us"), made up "not only from Jews but also from Gentiles," whom God has "called" (*ekalesen*; cf. v 7) into being through the preaching of the gospel.

In sentences (vv 25-29) made up almost entirely of quotations from scripture (Hosea and Isaiah), he shows that the "calling into being" of the mixed community was exactly what God had intended and preannounced all along.

A: Gentile believers (vv 25-26). Paul first takes up God's calling of the Gentiles, applying Hosea's warning to the wayward Northern Kingdom of Israel to the calling of those who did not originally belong to the People of God. Paul constructs the oracle by combining a somewhat altered form of Hos 2:23 (MT and LXX 2:25) with part of Hos 1:10 (MT and LXX 2:1). In the quotation of Hos 2:23, the order is changed so that the reference to "people"/"not my people" comes first, "not pitied" becomes "not loved"/"loved" and, most significantly, "I will call" *(kalesō)* replaces "I will say" *(erō).* The second text, Hos 1:10, quoted exactly according to the LXX (2:1), contains one of the classic Old Testament statements of the divine filiation privilege of Israel ("sons of the living God"), explicitly linked with the motifs of being/not being God's "people" and associated with God's "calling." Thus "calling" appears in both elements of the oracle as reconstructed by Paul. Each proclaims a transfer from the status of being "not my people" to being "my people," and the whole comes to a climax with the triumphant prophecy of divine filiation. Rearranging and combining the texts in this way, Paul has "found" in Hosea a clear divine announcement of intent to "call" into membership of the people of God and into the privilege of divine filiation those who were originally "not my people"—that is, the Gentiles. The key privileges of being "Israel" and God's "children" were not something pertaining to Israel from the start. They have come into being "eschatologically," through an exercise of God's creative power calling into being an "inclusive" people made up of Jews and Gentiles.

B. The Jewish "remnant" (vv 27-29). So Paul has accounted for the presence of Gentiles in the nascent eschatological people of God, the inheritor of the privileges ascribed to Israel. There remains the task of accounting, not for the presence of Jewish members—that is no issue—but for their presence in such comparatively small numbers. Here Paul turns to two texts of the prophet Isaiah which both speak of the reduced numbers of Israel. The first of these, Isa 10:22-23, distributed across vv 27b-28, contrasts the former "number" of Israel "as the sands of the sea" with the mere "remnant" *(hypoleimma)* that is to be saved and speaks (in the latter part of the quotation occurring as v 28) of God's "whittling down" activity (see Note). In this sense Paul finds in Isaiah's "crying out" *(krazei)* concerning Israel a preannouncement that God would drastically reduce the numbers of those to be saved.

An oracle from Isaiah 1:9 completes (v 29) Paul's scriptural proof. The oracle relates originally to the near destruction of Judah following the

Assyrian invasion of 701 B.C.E., the destruction of Sodom and Gomorrah having become a byword in the biblical tradition for the total obliteration of human communities. The text is linked with the preceding one both in its sense of a drastic reduction of Israel and also in God's sparing of at least a "remnant." In line with the LXX, the reference to the remnant comes in terms of "seed" *(sperma)*. This may be intended to convey a small glimmer of light: if the small Jewish element of the composite Christian community represents a "remnant" in biblical terms, it is also a "seed" which can contain a hope relating to Israel as a whole (cf. 11:5).

Summing up, we can say, then, that Paul has defended the fidelity of God (v 6a) on the basis that the present composition of the community of salvation—Gentile believers and the Jewish-Christian "remnant"—responds to a preannounced divine intention and mode of procedure. He has done so, however, at the price of leaving that bulk of Israel that has not come to belief in the gospel hanging in the air, "vessels of wrath ripe for destruction" (v 22). These, though belonging to Israel by descent (lit. "from Israel," v 6b) no longer seem to belong to the "Israel" that constitutes the community of salvation. A great ambiguity has been opened up concerning "Israel," which will only be resolved when the essentially *provisional* view that has been provided here is completed in accordance with Paul's fully *inclusive* ultimate vision in chapter 11.

Notes

22. *What if God, desiring to show his wrath:* The translation and interpretation takes the opening participial phrase *(thelōn)* in a causal or modal sense, that is, as expressing God's intention in "enduring with much patience. . . ." The causal sense is supported by the parallel with the statement of God's intention in v 17, by the further parallel provided by the following *hina* clause and seems to be implied already in the meaning of *thelōn* itself. The alternative concessive understanding ("though he desired. . . ."), favored by some interpreters, demands the subordination of the purpose *(hina)* clause in v 23 to the main verb *ēnegken* of v 22, which is difficult to reconcile with the *kai* occurring before *hina* (the textual variant removing *kai* is clearly secondary). On God's "wrath," see Interpretation and Note on 1:18.

    with much patience: On God's "patience" *(makrothymia)*, see Note on 2:4.

    vessels of wrath: The sense is that of "vessels" in whom the wrath of God is displayed (cf. *endeixasthai tēn orgēn*). Although "wrath" is normally associated with the future eschatological punishment in Paul (2:5, 8; 5:9; 1 Thess 1:10; 5:9), here, as in 1:18-32 (cf. 1 Thess 2:16), a present, proleptic revelation of God's eschatological wrath seems to be meant.

    ripe for destruction: Though the phrase *(katērtismena eis apōleian)* stands in parallel with the clause "which he has prepared beforehand for glory" in the next verse, it is not appropriate to find in it a sense of negative predestination; see Note on v 18. *Apōleia* does certainly mean "eternal destruction" (cf. Phil 3:19)—the negative counterpart to *doxa* ("glory')—but Paul has chosen his language (the perfect participle) carefully in order to convey the sense that, though the "vessels of wrath" stand on the brink of eternal loss and serve presently to display God's wrath (see preceding Note), their ultimate consignment to it is by no means assured.

23. *vessels of mercy:* While in the present context this phrase can refer only to believers (cf. v 24), later (11:30-32) Paul envisages a more universal operation of God's mercy.

which he has prepared beforehand for glory: On the motif of "glory prepared for the elect," see also 1 Cor 2:7-9 (cf. Eph 1:11). Paul's use of the verb "prepare beforehand" *(proētoimazein)* in the present context has a fine parallel in Wis 9:8, where Solomon speaks of the Temple he has built in Jerusalem as "a copy of the holy tent, which you have prepared *(proētoimasas)* from the beginning."

24. *us, that is, whom he has called:* The translation follows the punctuation given in the Nestle-Aland edition; for other possibilities, see Cranfield 2.497–98.

not from the Jews only but also from the Gentiles: For this duality (sometimes with "Gentile[s]" replaced with "Greek[s]"), see also 1:16; 2:9, 10; 3:9; 10:12.

25. *I will call 'my people':* On the "creative" sense of God's "calling" in Paul, see Note 8:30.

26. *". . . they will be called 'sons (and daughters) of the living God.'":* This text from Hos 1:10 (MT and LXX 2:1) became an important "carrier" of the "divine filiation" privilege accruing to Israel in the Jewish tradition: cf. *Jub.* 1:25; *Jos. Asen.* 19:8; see further Byrne, *'Sons of God'* 15–16, 53, 120, 137, 194, 216.

27. *"Though the number of the sons of Israel:* This part of the text is taken not from Isa 10:22 but from the very similar expression occurring in Hos 1:10 (LXX 2:1), that is, from the first part of the text Paul has just quoted in v 26 with reference to the Gentiles. In this way Paul subtly exploits an inner link between the two prophecies (Hosea and Isaiah) suggestive of the unity of the divine purpose that has issued forth in the "calling" into being of a composite people of God (cf. v 24).

only a remnant of them will be saved: Paul uses *hypoleimma* where the LXX has *kataleimma* (cf. 11:5: *leimma kat' eklogēn charitos*). On the biblical motif of the "remnant," see Note on 11:5. In the present context, though there is no actual word of condemnation, Paul appears to remain faithful to the original, negative sense of Isa 1:9, the stress falling upon the idea of diminishment, rather than upon that of new life growing from the "remnant" (contrast 11:2-6).

28. *for it is by completing and curtailing that the Lord will carry out his word upon the earth.":* This latter part of the quotation of Isa 10:22-23 represents a considerable variation on the LXX, which itself is a very free rendering of the difficult original Hebrew. Paul appears to have adapted the text to his own meaning, which was to express the idea that God fulfills his "word" (*logon*; cf. v 6a) by diminishing Israel in a quantitative sense (cf. esp. *syntemnōn*).

29. *And as Isaiah predicted, "If the Lord of hosts had not left us descendants":* Paul understands the oracle of Isaiah to be a foretelling *(proeirēken)* of what has occurred in the constitution of a believing community containing such a comparatively small number of Jews. The quotation agrees exactly with LXX Isa 1:9, including the translation of the Hebrew idea of a "few survivors" by the Greek word *(sperma),* which thus retains both the sense of "remnant" (cf. *hypoleimma,* v 27) and "descendants" (for the association of the two ideas cf. Isa 6:13; 37:30-32; CD 2:11-12; *1 Enoch* 83:8 with 84:6).

For Reference and Further Study

Aletti, J.-N. "L'argumentation paulinienne en Rm 9." *Biblica* 68 (1987) 41–56.
__________. *Comment Dieu est-il juste?* 157–78.
Berger, K. "Abraham in den paulinischen Hauptbriefen." *MTZ* 17 (1966) 47–89, esp. 77–83.
Byrne, B. *'Sons of God'* 130–40.
Gaston, L, "Israel's Enemies in Pauline Theology." *Paul and the Torah* 80–99.
Hays, R. B. *Echoes of Scripture* 63–68.
Hübner, H. *Gottes Ich und Israel* 15–59.
Johnson, E. E. *Function of Apocalyptic* 131–33, 147–50, 193–98, 217–19.
Munck, J. *Christ and Israel* 34–75.
Piper, J. *The Justification of God: An Exegetical and Theological Study of Romans 9:1-23.* Grand Rapids: Baker, 1983.
Rese, M. "Israel und Kirche in Römer 9." *NTS* 34 (1988) 208–17.
Siegert, F. *Argumentation bei Paulus* 123–40.
Stegner, W. R. "Romans 9.6–29—A Midrash." *JSNT* 22 (1984) 37–52.
Zeller, D. *Juden und Heiden* 113–22, 203–08.

iii. Israel's Present Rejection of the Gospel (9:30–10:21)

Introduction to 9:30–10:21. This section forms the second main part of Paul's response to the double phenomenon most threatening to the credibility of the gospel: the fact that a great number of Gentiles appear set in line to inherit the historic privileges of Israel, while the great bulk of Israel, by failing to come to faith in Jesus as the Christ, appear to be letting slip their hold upon these privileges. If the divine "word" spoken to Israel appears to have been so ineffective (9:6a), where does this leave God's faithfulness? In 9:6b-29 Paul considered the issue from the point of view of God's declared intention and characteristic pattern of action. A long analysis of scripture showed that the admission of Gentiles to the eschatological people of God and restriction of Israel to a "remnant" was in accord with God's preannounced plan and elective mode of proceeding.

Now, in 9:30–10:21, Paul considers the issue from the point of view of human response: if the bulk of Israel does not appear set on the way to salvation, that failure (9:30–10:4) cannot be ascribed to inadequacy on the part of the gospel (10:5-21).

While the positive aspect of the present situation—the inclusion of the Gentiles—remains in view, the chief focus lies upon the failure of Israel. The aim is not to blame Israel—to establish Israel's "guilt" or anything of the kind—but to analyze why the failure occurred and to do so as a preparation for the incorporation of that (temporary) failure within a wider vision of God's saving purpose (11:11-32). The operation of God's "mercy" will ensure that "failure" is not the last word.

The passage breaks down into three sections. 1. The opening section, 9:30–10:4, states the present situation in its twin aspect (9:30-31) and then explores Israel's failure, attributing it to a wrong-headed pursuit of righteousness by way of the law, to the neglect of the righteousness offered by God in Christ (10:1-4). 2. The central section, 10:5-13, establishes from scripture the eschatological validity of the latter kind of righteousness over the former in the sense that only righteousness by faith allows for a truly "inclusive" community of salvation. 3. The final section, 10:14-21, reverting once more to Israel's response, shows that it cannot be attributed to a divine failure to reach her effectively with the word; scripture accurately pointed to a worldwide and effective presentation of the gospel; the failure is Israel's alone.

a) *"Stumbling" Before the Righteousness of God* (9:30–10:4)

9:30. What then shall we say? (The situation is) that Gentiles, who did
not pursue righteousness, have got hold of it, a righteousness, that is,
that stems from faith, 31. while Israel, which did pursue a law of righteousness, did not manage to arrive at that law.
32. Why was this the case? Because they did so not from faith but as if it
were to be attained from works. They stumbled at the stone of stumbling,
33. as it is written, "Behold, I am setting in Zion a stone of stumbling and
a rock of offense, and the one who puts faith in it shall not be put to
shame."
10:1. Brothers (and sisters), the goodwill of my heart and my prayer is
before God on their behalf that they may attain salvation. 2. For I testify
that they do indeed have a zeal for God, but not one that is according to
knowledge. 3. For disregarding the righteousness of God and seeking to
establish their own, they have not submitted to God's righteousness. 4.

For Christ is the (true) goal of the law, in a way that leads to righteousness for everyone who has faith.

Interpretation

The present situation with regard to Israel and the Gentiles (9:30-31). Paul describes the present situation in a way designed to bring out the paradox as sharply as possible. What one party (Gentiles) were not seeking (righteousness), it obtained; what the other party (Israel) was most zealously seeking ("a law of righteousness"), it has not. This is the situation that appears to have made a mockery of God's "word" to Israel (9:6a).

Within the symbolic world of apocalyptic Judaism presupposed by Paul, "righteousness" is not strictly synonymous with "salvation" but refers to that eschatological verdict of right-standing in God's sight, which is the essential condition for obtaining it (see Interpretation of 1:17). Thus, by speaking here in terms of obtaining or not obtaining righteousness, Paul is not foreclosing the issue of salvation. Israel may not have obtained righteousness but that is not tantamount to missing out, finally, on salvation; Gentile believers may have obtained righteousness but that is not an automatic guarantee of salvation (cf. 11:17-24). The situation, though paradoxical, is still open, which is why it is so important to discern how and why Israel has presently gone wrong.

It is not that a different kind of righteousness is involved in either case. What is crucial for Paul is the differing attitude taken by both parties towards the same righteous status in God's eyes. He explains the difference in terms of a favorite image—that of athletes running in a race (cf. esp. Phil 3:12-16; 1 Cor 9:24-27). If the "prize" is righteousness, the Gentiles were not really entered in the race at all: the righteous status conferred upon Gentile believers came to them as a pure gift of God's grace, a "prize" thrust upon them as "ungodly" sinners without any seeking or merit on their part (cf. 4:5); all that was asked of them was to believe that God was so good and so gracious as truly to be offering acceptance on such generous terms. Israel, on the other hand, was really "pursuing" *(diōkōn)* that righteous status and pursuing it through the law. Paul, in fact, sees Israel's pursuit of righteousness to be so closely tied up with the law that, instead of describing what Israel pursued as a "righteousness through the law," he actually writes a "law of righteousness" *(nomon dikaiosynēs)* and describes Israel's failure with respect to righteousness in terms of a "not arriving at the law" *(eis nomon ouk ephthasen)*. The implication, which will become clearer a few sentences further on (10:4), is that pursuing righteousness in this way Israel completely misread the purpose of the law. It was never intended to communicate the kind of righteousness required for salvation. As earlier sections of the letter have made clear (3:20; 4:15; 5:20; 7:13; cf. Gal 3:19), the law's role was the negative one of preparing the way for faith by convicting Israel of sin.

Israel's "stumbling" in the race (vv 32-33). The following sentences explore more deeply how a misreading of the law led Israel to fail with respect to righteousness. It was because of a pursuit of righteousness "as though" *(hōs)* it were to be obtained "through works" *(ex ergōn)* and not "from faith" *(ek pisteōs)*. Beneath these concise formulae lies a wealth of meaning that Paul would hope to have clarified in the earlier part of the letter. The problem is not that "works" (living in accordance with the commandments) are in themselves wrong; Paul never contests that God requires an obedient life of human beings (cf. 6:1-23; 8:12-13). The problem with pursuing righteousness the "works" way is that it flies in the face of God's verdict given in scripture that "all have sinned and stand deprived of the glory of God" (3:23; cf. 3:10-20; 5:12d). To seek righteousness on the basis of fulfilling the "works of the law" is to refuse to admit that one is part of the sinful mass of humanity addressed by God's grace. It is to make of the law a fence around a "holy nation" set over against the unholy rest of humankind—whereas the path to salvation opened up by God in Christ requires Israel's owning that she is bound up with the rest of humanity in a solidarity in sin now matched by a "much more" powerful solidarity in grace (5:12-21).

Within the continuing image of the "race," Paul describes Israel's failure as a "stumbling at a stone of offense" *(prosekopsan tą̄ lithą̄ tou proskommatos)*. He takes up what is evidently an early Christian combination, for apologetic purposes, of two well-known texts from Isaiah (Isa 8:14 and 28:16), which had been applied to God's action in Christ and the response of human beings to it. As comparison with 1 Cor 1:23 makes clear ("We proclaim a crucified Christ, a stumbling block to Jews, . . ."), the "stone of stumbling" and "rock of offense" that God "places" in Israel (lit. "Sion") is the crucified Messiah, Jesus. The Messiah that God sent to Israel was not a triumphant leader who carried all before him but one "put forward" as a *hilastērion* for sin (3:25)—the sins of Israel and of the entire world. This was the Creator's response, in a "display" of divine righteousness (3:21, 25-26), to the total lack of righteousness on the human side, Israel included. Israel "stumbled" at this Messiah because accepting such a Messiah meant accepting the need for such a Messiah and such redemptive action on God's part. It meant accepting the verdict, contained in Paul's sustained "accusation" in 2:1–3:20, that Jews had not been and would never be a "righteous nation" on the basis of the law (cf. Gal 2:16). Israel, clinging to a pursuit of righteousness through "works of the law," resisted this verdict, acceptance of which is a key element in coming to faith, and "stumbled" in this way at the "stone" which is

Christ. Israel thereby placed salvation in jeopardy, whereas—in the words of the second part of the quotation—those who *do* "put faith in it *(ho pisteuōn ep' autǭ)* will not be put to shame" *(ou gar kataischynthēsetai)*. That is, putting their faith in such a Messiah will set them on the path to salvation (cf. Rom 1:16).

Israel's misplaced zeal (10:1-3). Following a brief interruption (10:1) to restate (cf. 9:1-3) his good will and continual prayer for "their" salvation, Paul resumes (vv 2-4) his analysis of Israel's "stumbling" with respect to the gospel. In line with the personal avowal just made, he concedes that Israel has a genuine "zeal for God"—the kind of single-minded, unswerving loyalty to the God of the covenant exemplified in figures such as Elijah (1 Kgs 19:10; cf. Sir 48:2) and Phinehas (Num 25:6-13). This zeal, however, is a "zeal . . . not according to knowledge" (*ou kat' epignōsin*; cf. 3:20) in the sense that it is masking the bitter truth that is the negative presupposition of the gospel—that Israel, equally along with the Gentiles, is a sinful nation and stands in need of the kind of redemption from sin that the gospel of the crucified Messiah proclaims. Nothing can be more inhibiting of the creative operation of God's grace than a religious zeal that masks real need for God's mercy.

Paul probes more deeply this lack of "knowledge" on Israel's part in a neat chiastic statement (v 3) "framed" by the motif of "God's righteousness" *(hē dikaiosynē tou theou)*:

Israel did not acknowledge God's righteousness – A
Israel sought to establish her own righteousness – B
Israel did not submit to God's righteousness – A'

As the earlier part of the letter has made abundantly clear (1:17; 3:21-26; 5:17), "God's righteousness" is something both displayed and offered in the Christ event, as proclaimed in the gospel: it is, at one and the same time, God's own righteousness—revealed in saving activity on behalf of an errant creation—*and* the righteous status which God graciously acknowledges in believers in virtue of their union with Christ (3:26; see Note). Israel's failure to "acknowledge" *(agnountes)* God's righteousness implies not simply a lack of recognition in an intellectual sense but a failure to offer due creaturely "submission" (cf. *ouch hypetagēsan*) to the manifestation of God (cf. 1:21-23). Christ crucified, proclaimed in the gospel, represents the revelation of the righteousness of God (3:21-22). To "stumble" (9:32-33) at this "stone" is to fail to submit to God's righteousness, which alone is the path to salvation (1:16-17).

At the center of the statement (v 3b) Paul pinpoints, once more, the root problem underlying this failure. It was an attempt to establish—through the law, as the sequence in v 4 makes clear—"their own *(idian)* (righteousness)." The essential contrast lies between God's offer of salvation and human beings' trying to achieve something out of their own resources apart from the Creator (see Note). Though outwardly "zealous for God" (v 2), Israel's continued attempt to pursue righteousness through "works of the law" represents in fact a resistance to God—a refusal to acknowledge God's verdict that, despite possession of the law, Israel is bound up with the unrighteous rest of the human race, equally in need of the gracious offer of salvation that comes to all in Christ.

The true goal of the law—Christ (v 4). To clinch the matter Paul throws in a comment (v 4), designed, apparently, to explain why Israel's continued attempt to establish her own righteousness through the law represents a failure to submit to God's righteousness. It represents such a failure because it fundamentally misreads the role of the law according to the mind of God. What precisely Paul means by asserting that the *telos* of the law is Christ is controversial since *telos* can mean "end" in the sense of simple termination as well as (more usually) "goal" or "purpose" (see Note). If, as seems likely, the "athletic" imagery—with its sense of "pursuit" of a goal—continues, it seems more probable that Paul sees Christ as "goal" of the law in the sense that the law, from the outset, was designed, not to erect a system of righteousness on its own terms, but to lead solely to the means of righteousness constituted by Christ. The cumulative effect of the predominantly negative statements made earlier in the letter concerning the effect of the law (3:20; 4:15; 5:20a; 6:15; 7:5, 13; cf. also Gal 3:23-24) suggests that the law was given to Israel, not to constitute a means of righteousness—though it did "require" righteousness—but "to multiply transgression," to concentrate sin in Israel, in the most overt form of human rebellion against God ("transgression"), so that it could be dealt with effectively by God in the person of Israel's Messiah, Jesus (8:3-4). In this sense, "where sin increased (in Israel), grace abounded all the more" (5:20b), bringing righteousness and life to the whole world beyond Israel, in accordance with the ancient, universalist promises (4:13). The goal of the law, then, is Christ, in the sense that the law served essentially to prepare the way—by "multiplying" sin—for the kind of redemption God actually worked in Christ, "putting him forward as a means of expiation" (*hilastērion,* 3:25) leading to the justification of all (Jews and Gentiles) who respond in faith. To seek righteousness by means of the law is to completely misread its role in regard to justification.

Reflection. If this interpretation presents a Paul highly unsympathetic to the Jewish pursuit of the Torah, which of course continues today, we must keep in mind that for Paul all theology moves out from the center constituted by faith in God's action in the crucified Messiah, Jesus. Paul's vision is wide but everything is viewed from this single, all-determining focus. Paul attributed Israel's failure at the Cross to misguided zeal for the law. That is primarily a theological rather than a historical judgment. It is also the obverse of a wider, more positive perspective—the centrality of Christ. A modern hermeneutic may and must question whether faith in Christ necessarily implies such a judgment even in theological terms. While it is true that nothing masks human need for the *gift* of salvation so successfully as misguided religious zeal, that failure is not tied to any particular religion nor is the faith that overcomes it tied to any particular religious system—Christianity or any other. Both attitudes are possible within theistic systems and both are equally possible within Judaism and Christianity.

Notes

9:30. *What then shall we say?:* This stock phrase (see Note on 4:1) here, as in 8:31, introduces a bold statement of a truth flowing from or corroborating what has just been argued.

righteousness: The "righteousness" in question is the righteousness at issue throughout Romans within the apocalyptic framework which the argument presupposes: the righteousness required (at the judgment) for the attainment of eschatological salvation; see Interpretation of 1:17. A vaguer understanding of "righteousness" in the sense of "life as God's covenant people" (so Ziesler 250, 252; cf. E. P. Sanders, *Paul and Palestinian Judaism* 491–95) is excluded by the consideration that those who already had the sense of belonging to God's people would hardly "pursue" righteousness in this sense.

31. *a law of righteousness:* The genitive phrase *nomon dikaiosynēs* can be taken in a variety of ways: "law requiring righteousness"; "law promising righteousness"; "law leading to righteousness." The last seems to be the most appropriate in the present context; cf. the phrase *eis dikaiōsin zōēs*—"a justification that brings life"—in 5:18.

32. *Because they did so not from faith but as if it were to be attained from works:* A main verb is lacking in the Greek original. It seems necessary to supply the idea of "pursuing" from the preceding sentences. What is implied is the "pursuit" of righteousness (cf. v 30), not the pursuit of the law, as the immediate transition from v 31 might suggest. Basic to the entire section and carried over into 10:5-6, is the sustained contrast (cf. esp. 3:27-28) between two ways in which righteousness might be considered to be gained: through "works of the law" or through faith. For the technical Pauline understanding of "works (of the law)," see Note on 3:20. The phraseology here "as if . . . from works. . . ." *(hōs ex ergōn)* has been understood as implying that ethical striving in itself is something wrong, in that it necessarily involves a self-seeking attempt to establish one's status over against God (so esp. Bultmann; cf. *Theology* 1.315–16). As Paul has made clear in Rom 1:18–3:20 (cf. also 7:14-23), it is not works as such but human failure to perform the works required by the law that has excluded the possibility of gaining righteousness through the law.

33. *Behold, I am setting in Zion a stone of stumbling and a rock of offense, and the one who puts faith in it:* In the quotation of LXX Isa 28:16 Paul has replaced an original "stone" phrase with two "stone" phrases from Isa 8:14—"stone of stumbling" *(lithon proskommatos)* and "rock of offense" *(petran skandalou)*. This lends a more negative tone to the passage: what was originally (in the Hebrew) "a stone, a tested stone, a precious cornerstone," has become a "rock of offense." The fact that the same two texts from Isaiah also appear together in 1 Pet 2:6-8 suggests that Paul is drawing upon an early Christian apologetic tradition that had already associated these texts on the basis of their common allusion to "stone," the "stone" being understood messianically with respect to Jesus (cf. the use of Ps 118:22 in Matt 21:42 and parallels; Acts 4:11). Reinforcing the association in Paul's eyes may have been the fact that in the LXX form of both texts the idea of "trusting (believing) in him (it)" occurs.

shall not be put to shame: The phrase—both in the original and as quoted by Paul—reflects the biblical idiom of being "put to shame" in the sense of being publicly proved impotent or wanting at the critical moment, in this case (cf. the future tense) the eschatological judgment determinative of salvation; see Note on 5:5.

10:1. *Brothers (and sisters), the goodwill of my heart and my prayer is before God on their behalf that they may attain salvation:* Behind the solemn reference to prayer to God "on their behalf" may lie the OT motif of the prophet as intercessor for the people; see, e.g., Exod 32:9-14; Deut 9:18-20; 1 Sam 7:5-11; Ps 106:23; Jer 15:1; 18:20.

2. *a zeal for God:* Paul is, of course, ascribing to Israel an attitude of which he had personally been an outstanding example before coming to faith in Jesus as the Christ (cf. Gal 1:14; Phil 3:6; cf. Acts 22:3).

3. *the righteousness of God:* On the "bi-polar" nature of "the righteousness of God" in Paul, see the Interpretation of 1:17. The contrast with "(righteousness) from works" (9:32) suggests that in the present context the human "pole" is primary.

and seeking to establish their own: This phrase has been taken to imply that Paul faulted Israel for seeking, through perfectionistic fulfillment of the law, to amass merit and so have a claim upon God. But, set over against "the righteousness of *God*," "*their own* righteousness" *(tēn idian dikaiosynēn)* is more likely to refer to a quest for righteousness that proceeds from purely human effort, a quest that is not marked by perfection in keeping the law but by factual transgression—the sort of hopeless effort depicted in 7:14-25. Such "righteousness" would also be "their own" in the sense of being a righteousness confined to Israel as people of the law and unattainable to the rest of humankind. But the "God/human being" dichotomy seems primary.

they have not submitted to God's righteousness: The aorist *hypetagēsan* probably refers to what is for Paul now a clearly established fact: setting aside the Jewish-Christian "remnant," Israel as a whole has not responded positively to the gospel. A useful commentary upon the verse as a whole is provided by Phil 3:9: ". . . that I may be found in him (Christ), not having a righteousness of my own *(tēn emēn dikaiosynēn)*, based on law, but that which is through faith in Christ, the righteousness from God that depends on faith" *(tēn ek theou dikaiosynēn epi tę̄ pistei)*. Paul, who once shared the "zeal" for God and the law which he freely attributes to Israel (v 2; cf. Phil 3:6 *[kata zēlos]*), faults Israel for not having undergone the experience of coming to faith which has been his. This experience involves "submitting" to the "righteousness of God" in the sense that it means acknowledging that one's own quest for righteousness is futile (cf. esp. Gal 2:16), that one is not set apart from Gentiles in this sense (Rom 3:9, 23) and has to throw oneself entirely upon the gift of righteousness offered in Christ (5:17).

4. *For Christ is the (true) goal of the law:* The translation attempts to bring out the sense that the law had no other purpose than to lead to Christ and the righteousness of God available to believers in him; cf. esp. Gal 3:23-24. Disregarding two specific references to taxes (Rom 13:7) and usage in adverbial phrases, three principal meanings arise for *telos*. 1. "end" in the sense of simple termination (cf. Luke 1:33; Heb 6:11; 1 Pet 4:7)—possibly 2 Cor 3:13. 2. "final part" (as of a drama)—1 Cor 10:11; 15:24. 3. "goal"—"purpose"—Rom 6:21-22; Phil 3:19; 2 Cor 11:15 (cf. 1 Tim 1:5; 1 Pet 1:9). Setting aside Rom 10:4, it can be said, then, that *telos* never unambiguously has the meaning of simple termination in Paul. If, as argued here, the *telos* of the law is Christ in the sense that the law's purpose has been to "concentrate" sin to the point where God can deal with it in Christ (on this, see further Note on 7:13), then, of course, the sense of "termination" is implicit. The "purpose" in question is a thoroughly negative one. A positive purpose, especially, one involving some real continuity of the law in the new era, would seem to be excluded by Paul's insistence in earlier chapters upon believers' radical cut-off from the law (cf. esp. 6:15; 7:1-4, 6). Paul's claim in 3:31 to "uphold the law" is highly ambiguous (see Note on 3:31) and cannot of itself require a positive understanding of the purpose of the law in 10:4. For further discussion, see esp. R. Badenas, *Christ the End of the Law* (see Reference); B. L. Martin, *Christ and the Law* 129–54.

in a way that leads to righteousness for everyone who has faith: The translation sees the phrase *eis dikaiosynēn* as attached to the entire preceding phrase, rather than to *nomos*. Apart from being grammatically smoother, the consecutive sense thereby obtained opens up the universalist perspective, which will shortly come to the fore (v 12): the intervention of Christ makes righteousness available universally (cf. 3:23-24, 26, 29-30; Gal 3:23-29). The Greek word *panti* lying behind "everyone" has, as so often in Romans, the sense of "Gentile as well as Jew."

For Reference and Further Study

Badenas, R. *Christ the End of the Law: Romans 10:4 in Pauline Perspective.* JSNTSup 10; Sheffield: JSOT, 1985.

Barrett, C. K. "Rom 9:30–10:21: Fall and Responsibility of Israel." *Essays on Paul.* London: SPCK, 1982, 132–53.

Bechtler, S. R. "Christ, the *Telos* of the Law: The Goal of Romans 10:4." *CBQ* 56 (1994) 288–308.

Campbell, W. S. "Christ the End of the Law: Romans 10:4." *Studia Biblica 1978.* Vol 3. Ed. E. A. Livingstone. JSNTSup 3; Sheffield: JSOT, 1979, 73–81.

Hays, R. B. *Echoes of Scripture* 73–83.

Howard, G. E. "Christ the End of the Law: The Meaning of Romans 10:4ff." *JBL* 88 (1969) 331–37.

Johnson, E. E. *Function of Apocalyptic* 151–59.

Lindars, B. *New Testment Apologetic*. London: SCM, 1961, 175–79.

Martin, B. L. *Christ and the Law* 129–44.

Meyer, P. W. "Romans 10:4 and the End of the Law." *The Divine Helmsman* (FS L. H. Silbermann). Ed. J. L. Crenshaw and S. Sandmel. New York: Ktav, 1980, 59–78.

Munck, J. *Christ and Israel* 75–84.

Rhyne, C. T. *Faith Establishes the Law* 95–116.

———. "*Nomos dikaiosynēs* and the Meaning of Romans 10:4." *CBQ* 47 (1985) 486–99.

Sanders, E. P. *Paul, the Law and the Jewish People* 36–43.

Stowers, S. K. *Rereading of Romans* 302–08.

Westerholm, S. *Israel's Law* 126–30.

b) *Scripture's Witness to Righteousness by Faith* (10:5-13)

5. For Moses writes concerning the righteousness which is based on the
law that the person who has performed its commandments shall live by
them.
6. But the righteousness based on faith says, "Do not say in your heart,
'Who will ascend into heaven?'" (that is, to bring Christ down) 7. "or
'Who will descend into the abyss?'" (that is, to bring Christ up from the
dead). 8. But what does it say? "The word is near you, in your mouth
and in your heart" (that is, the word of faith which we preach);
9. because, if you confess with your mouth that Jesus is Lord and believe
in your heart that God raised him from the dead, you will be saved. 10.
For it is by believing in the heart that one gains righteousness and it is
by confessing with the mouth that one gains salvation. 11. For scripture
says, "Everyone who believes in him will not be put to shame." 12. For
there is no distinction between Jew and Greek; the same Lord is Lord of
all and bestows his riches upon all who call upon him. 13. For, "every
one who calls upon the name of the Lord will be saved."

INTERPRETATION

Introduction. The preceding passage ascribed Israel's "stumbling" with respect to the gospel to a failure to recognize and submit to the new righteousness that God was offering to all human beings in Christ. More specifically, it pinpointed the nub of the problem as consisting in a wrongheaded persistence in a quest for righteousness by way of the law, when in fact what God has done in Christ, in the interests of a more universal salvation, ought to have ruled out such a quest (v 4). The present passage does not so much open up a new stage in the argument as bring scriptural confirmation to what has just been asserted. It presses further the rigorous distinction between the two ways of righteousness—that by law and that by faith—and asserts the exclusive eschatological validity of the latter, in accordance with God's design to make salvation universally available in Christ.

The argument falls basically into three main sections. 1. V 5 cites Lev 18:5 to give scripture's witness to righteousness by law. 2. Vv 6-8 expound several texts from Deuteronomy to give scripture's witness to righteousness by faith, while vv 9-10 relate this to present Christian practice. 3. Vv 11-13, again with reference to scripture, point out how the preference for righteousness by faith serves the universal scope of salvation.

Scripture's witness to righteousness by law (v 5). Citing Lev 18:5, a text, already used for the same purpose in Gal 3:12, Paul lets "Moses" speak for the principle of righteousness by the law. The text clearly establishes that it is a "doing" righteousness: it promises (eternal) life *(zēsetai)* to the one who performs *(poiēsas)* the prescriptions of the law. The corollary is that one who has not performed these prescriptions will not attain righteousness or life in this way. According to Paul's gospel, as 1:18–3:20 (cf. 3:23) has already made clear, this condition has not in fact been met. The implication is that the attaining of righteousness by this means is not possible. This "doing" righteousness has proved to be beyond human capacity.

Scripture's witness to righteousness by faith (vv 6-8). Over against this "doing" righteousness, based upon the law, Paul finds in scripture the announcement of an alternative righteousness, based upon faith. In the original setting of Deuteronomy (30:11-14), it is equally Moses who speaks here, but Paul, true to his general tendency to range Moses upon the passing, "law" side of things (cf. esp. 2 Cor 3:7-18), suppresses any mention of the great law-giver and lets "faith-righteousness" speak for itself. Likewise, where the original had presented the idea of the fulfillment of the Torah as not involving tasks of superhuman difficulty (journeys to the heavens or across the seas), Paul, suppressing any mention of the commandments, co-opts this motif (with "descending into the abyss" substituted for crossing the sea) entirely for righteousness by faith. To modern sensibility the exegetical procedure is forced; in particular, it appears to pit scripture against itself in a way that has no foundation in the original. But Paul is not so much "proving" anything from scripture as "finding" validation in scripture for the superiority of the new dispensation God has brought about through Jesus Christ.

The essential point Paul takes from Deuteronomy is the ease of what God requires of human beings—more literally, its "nearness" *(engys)*. For Paul (if not for the original thrust of Deut 30:11-14, which maintains precisely the opposite), whereas the way of law-righteousness (v 5) required a "doing" and an effort on the part of human beings—an effort doomed to frustration—the way of righteousness by faith requires simply a submission to and acknowledgment of what *God* has already done. The essential contrast is, again, as in 9:30-32 and 10:3 (cf. also 9:15: "not of human achieving *[trechontos]*"), between human striving on the one hand and acceptance of the divine gift (righteousness) on the other. Paul turns Deut 30:12-13 into a formal prohibition by prefacing it with a phrase, "Do not say in your heart . . .," derived from an earlier part of Deuteronomy (8:17 or 9:4). This provides a scriptural exclusion of any contemplation of the kind of human effort the rival mode of righteousness would involve. To ask (v 6b), "Who will ascend to the heavens?" is tantamount to denying what God has done in Christ. Seeking to "bring Christ down" (v 6c) implies that God has not already "sent" (from heaven) "his own Son" (cf. 8:3-4) on a saving mission. Correspondingly, to ask (v 7a), "Who will descend into the abyss?" is tantamount to denying that Christ died for our sins. Seeking to "bring Christ back from the dead" (v 7b; on the sense of the verb *anagagein*, see Note) amounts to a denial that he really died for us and was raised by God "for our justification" (4:25; cf. 1 Cor 15:17). The whole complex of these saving acts—the sending, death and resurrection of Jesus—amounts to the "revelation" of God's righteousness, as proclaimed in the gospel (3:21). To persist in the way of law-righteousness is to refuse to acknowledge and submit to the "righteousness of God" (10:3); it constitutes a rebuff of the grace of God, that renders Christ's death "for us" in vain (Gal 2:21).

Continuing (v 8) the exposition of Deuteronomy 30 (v 14) but now in positive vein, Paul "hears" righteousness by faith announce that what it involves is simply a "word" *(rēma)*, so "near" as to be "in your mouth" and "in your heart." This "word" Paul identifies (v 9c) as "the word of faith" *(to rēma tēs pisteōs)*, which is the subject of the Christian proclamation *(kēryssomen)*. In place of the moral striving demanded by righteousness by law, righteousness by faith involves simply an announcement of what God has done and a corresponding human response in heart and tongue.

Confessing and believing the "word of faith" (vv 9-10). Preserving the "heart" and "mouth" language of Deut 30:14, Paul goes on to indicate more explicitly this response and its saving effects. What righteousness by faith requires is simply confession and internal acknowledgment of the essential truths of the Christian gospel: that Jesus is Lord and that God has raised him from the dead. The essential point is to acknowledge the divine action (raising Jesus from the dead) and submit to its implications (the lordship of the risen Savior). This is what leads to the salvation (cf. *sōthēsę*) or "life" which the way of the law could not procure.

The emphasis here upon faith and simple confession might seem at first sight to represent a playing down, in a "quietistic" kind of way, of the importance of human behavior in relationship to God and life in the world. Paul has, however, already confronted this issue in 6:1–8:13 and insisted that the new era of grace involved an "obedience" no less demanding—though more realistic—than that of the old dispensation. If for the moment (cf. already 9:11, 16) Paul moves away from a stress upon action, this is simply to pinpoint and establish what is most basic in the response God requires of human beings. Prior to any good works, the response of faith entails admitting that one has no "works" to offer to God, no righteousness of one's own, that as a human being and a sinful one at that, one can only "submit to" (v 3) and humbly receive the "gift" of righteousness offered in overflowing abundance by God (cf. 5:17). This response, while in essence "near" and "easy," is perhaps more difficult to wring from human beings than any commitment to a program of action no matter how arduous (cf. John 6:28-29). It is one which Israel, on Paul's analysis, failed to confront (cf. 9:32-33).

Scripture's witness to the universal scope of salvation (vv 11-13). Paul has established the fundamental difference between the two kinds of righteousness and pointed to scripture's indication of the superiority of that of faith. There remains to draw the conclusion which the final part of the statement in v 4 had already forestalled: that all this has been in the interests of making justification (and salvation) available to believers on a universal scale.

To reintroduce the universalist note, Paul returns to the "stone" text, Isa 28:16, which he has been reading (cf. 9:33) as a statement of the divine intent and action in the eschatological age. The final part of this text promises that the one who puts faith in "it" (literally, the "stone"; in reality, Christ) would not "be ashamed"—that is, would find salvation on the day of the great judgment (see Note). In the fresh quotation of Isa 28:16 appearing in v 11 there appears an "everyone" *(pas)* which does not stand in the original, though it is at least implied. Modified in this way, the text provides a restatement in more universalist terms of the link between believing and attaining salvation formulated in the preceding sentences.

This inclusive note is developed in the following sentences (vv 12-13) when Paul introduces once more the "no distinction" *(ou . . . diastolē)* cry familiar from the earlier part of the letter (3:22; cf. 2:9-11; 3:9b). There it had served to signify the truth that Jews, though possessing the law, were united with the Gentiles in a common bind under sin, both groups lacking the required eschatological righteousness. Now, in the opposite, positive direction, it signifies the solidarity of all believers, Jewish and Gentile, on the path to salvation.

Just as he had previously appealed to the oneness of God to establish a common basis for justification (3:29-30), so Paul now rests the exclusion of separate paths to salvation upon the fact that all believers call upon one and the "same Lord," Jesus Christ, who "enriches" *(ploutōn)* both communities. All alike, Jew and Gentile, were "impoverished" in the sense of having no claim whatsoever upon salvation. Christ, "who was rich" (by reason of his divine origins; cf. Phil 2:6) made himself "poor" ("unto death" [Phil 2:7-8]) for the sake of human beings, that they "might become rich" (that is, attain the blessings of salvation) through his "poverty" (2 Cor 8:9). The common bind in the "poverty" of sin has been replaced by a community graced with the "riches" of salvation. This fulfills in a universalist sense the prophecy of Joel 2:32 ([LXX 3:5] quoted in v 13) to the effect that "Everyone (*pas*—Jew and Gentile) who calls upon the name of the Lord (vv 9-10) will be saved." Alongside Isaiah, the prophet Joel declares God's intent to open up through faith a truly inclusive possibility of salvation.

Notes

5. *For Moses writes concerning the righteousness which is based on the law that the person who has performed its commandments shall live by them:* The translation follows the reading adopted in the 26th edition of Nestle-Aland (following P[46]; also B [less *tou*]), as against that which reads the conjunction *hoti* immediately after "writes" (*graphei*) and makes "righteousness" the object of "performed" (*poiēsas*). On this reading, as also in Gal 3:12, the Pauline quotation agrees with LXX Lev 18:5 exactly. In Gal 3:11-12 the contrast between the two modes of righteousness is brought out by setting Lev 18:5 with Hab 2:4, a text which has already appeared in Romans as the conclusion of the great thematic statement in 1:16-17. Both in Gal 3:11-12 and here in Rom 10:5-8 Paul is prepared to allow one piece of scripture (Hab 2:4 and Deut 30:12-14) to overrule the same text from Leviticus (18:5). The aorist form of the participle *poiēsas* is significant: what is required for obtaining "life" is *having* performed the commandments; what constitutes the barrier to eternal life is not (legalistic) "performance" (so Bultmann; see Note on 9:32) but *not* having performed.

6–8. *But the righteousness based on faith says:* The translation (as also the Interpretation) understands the introductory *de* here in an adversative sense: that is, as introducing a contrasting righteousness (that of faith) to the righteousness from the law which was the subject of the previous sentence. This contrast has run throughout the letter (cf. esp. 3:20-22, 27-28; 4:16; cf. also Gal 2:16; 3:21-22) and has come to the fore again a few sentences earlier (9:30, 32).

"Do not say in your heart, 'Who will ascend into heaven?'" (that is, to bring Christ down) "or 'Who will descend into the abyss?'" (that is, to bring Christ up from the dead). But what does it say? "The word is near you, in your mouth and in your heart": This passage from Deut 30:11-14 inspired widespread reflection in post-biblical Judaism. In Bar 3:29–4:1 it is linked with the quest for wisdom, subsequently identified with the law. Philo explicitly uses it no less than four times (*Post.* 84–85; *Mut.* 236–37; *Virt.* 183; *Praem.* 80), along with other allusions. A version in the Targum Neofiti is interesting in that it coheres with Paul in interpreting the crossing of the sea as a descent into the abyss (Dunn, 2.604, sets out the various traditions in a helpful comparative way). The parallels show that the liberties Paul takes with the original text were not at all unusual in contemporary interpretive practice. Some (e.g., Zeller 186; Dunn 2.605–06) wish to relate the "ascending" and "descending" to the death and resurrection of Christ understood strictly in terms of descent into the underworld and subsequent exaltation (the reverse order in the text being determined by the order in Deut 30:12-13). But since Paul clearly sees the salvific action of God as beginning with the "sending" of the Son (cf. esp. 8:3; Gal 4:4), there is no good reason against seeing in the "ascent to heaven" a reference to acting as though God had not already sent the Messiah "from heaven." Likewise, "bringing Christ back" is not necessarily a reference to actual resurrection but to acting in a way which would deny that Christ died and rose again; it would "bring him back from the dead" in the sense of pretending he has never died but has remained alive all along; this would imply that the kerygma proclaiming his death and resurrection is erroneous. Paul quotes the final part of LXX Deut 30:14 in a way that links "word" *(rēma)* very closely with "mouth" and "heart"; there is no sign of the subsequent reference in the text to the word's being also "in your hands to do it."

the word of faith: "Faith" here can be understood either as the human disposition *(fides qua)* which the word calls forth or the content of message *(fides quae)*. Paul may well have intended the phrase to be open to both meanings—though the context seems to tilt the balance towards the latter.

9. *if you confess with your mouth that Jesus is Lord and believe in your heart that God raised him from the dead:* The order is not strictly logical in the sense that internal acknowledgment should precede outward confession and God's raising Jesus from the dead is the basis for the Christian acclamation of him as "Lord." But Paul is following for the time being the order provided by the text of Deut 30:14. Both clauses echo eariy Christian credal formulas. For "Jesus is Lord," see esp. the acclamation in 1 Cor 12:3 (cf. the Aramaic acclamation *Maranatha* preserved in 1 Cor 16:21) and the confession (wrung from the entire universe) at the end of the Christ-hymn in Phil 2:6-11. The second credal formula, referring to God's raising Jesus from the dead (cf. already Rom 4:25; 8:11; also 1 Cor 6:14; 15:15; 2 Cor 4:14), is closely associated with the first in

the sense that recognition of Jesus' "lordship" flows from belief in his being raised and exalted to God's right hand (Ps 110:1 playing a crucial role); see further W. Kramer, *Christ, Lord, Son of God* (see Reference) 19–26, 65–71; Cranfield 2.527–30.

10. *For it is by believing in the heart that one gains righteousness and it is by confessing with the mouth that one gains salvation:* The translation takes the twin phrases *eis dikaiosynēn* and *eis sōtērian* in the consecutive sense: literally, "unto the gaining of righteousness, . . . salvation." Here, in the interests of preserving the duality provided by the scriptural text, "righteousness" and "salvation" come close to being identified—something which confirms the essentially eschatological sense of "righteousness" in Paul. On the relationship between the two concepts in Paul (righteousness as the presupposition for salvation), see Interpretation of 1:17; also 8:10c.

11. *will not be put to shame:* The eschatological reference of *kataischynthēsetai* (cf. also 5:5) is confirmed here by parallels in two directions: with *sōtērian* at the end of the preceding verse and *sōthēsetai* at the end of v 13.

12. *For there is no distinction between Jew and Greek:* As in the thematic statement in 1:16 (cf. also 2:10; 3:9), of which there are notable echoes in the present context, "Greek" here stands in for "Gentile"—presumably to give a more balanced phrase.

    the same Lord is Lord of all and bestows his riches upon all who call upon him: The context requires that "Lord" *(kyrios)* refers to the risen Jesus, rather than to God, in line with the early Christian tendency to transfer epithets and functions reserved for God in the OT to the risen Jesus understood as exercising, in God's name, the "lordship" of the universe (cf. Phil 2:9; see Note on v 9 above).

13. *For, "every one who calls upon the name of the Lord will be saved":* 1 Cor 1:2 would seem to indicate that the phrase "those who call upon the name of the Lord" represents a technical self-designation of the early Christian community (cf. also the quotation of Joel 2:32 [MT and LXX 3:5] in Acts 2:21, 39). Paul's chief point of interest in the present context would lie upon the opening universalist assertion: "Everyone *(pas)* . . ." and he would understand the "calling upon the name of the Lord" as simply another way of expressing faith's confessing of Jesus as "Lord" (v 9).

For Reference and Further Study

Badenas, R. *Christ the End of the Law: Romans 10:4 in Pauline Perspective.* JSNTSup 10; Sheffield: JSOT, 1985, 118–35.

Black, M. "The Christological Use of the Old Testament in the New Testament." *NTS* 18 (1971–72) 1–14.

Hays, R. B. *Echoes of Scripture* 73–83.

Johnson, E. E. *Function of Apocalyptic* 133–37, 155–59.

Kramer, W. *Christ, Lord, Son of God.* SBT 50; London: SCM, 1966, 19–26, 65–71.

Munck, J. *Christ and Israel* 84–89.
Seifrid, M. A. "Paul's Approach to the Old Testament in Rom 10:6-8." *TrinJ* 6 (1985) 3–37.
Stowers, S. K. *Rereading of Romans* 308–12.
Suggs, M. J. "The Word Is Near You: Rom 10:6-10 within the Purpose of the Letter." *Christian History and the Gospels* (FS J. Knox). Ed. W. R. Farmer et al. Cambridge: Cambridge University, 1967, 289–312.

c) *Israel Has Heard but Not Responded to the Gospel* (10:14-21)

14. How then are people to call upon him in whom they have not believed? And how are they to believe in him of whom they have not heard? And how are they to hear in the absence of a preacher? 15. And how are they to preach unless they are sent out? As it is written, "How beautiful are the feet of those who preach good news!"

16. But not all have responded to the gospel; for Isaiah says, "Lord, who has believed our report?" 17. So you see that faith comes from hearing, a hearing, that is, that comes about through the preaching of Christ.

18. But I say, can it be that they have not heard? Of course they have; for "Their voice has gone out to all the earth, and their words to the limits of the inhabited world."

19. But I say, could it be that Israel did not know?

First Moses says, "I will provoke you to jealousy by those who are not a nation; with a foolish nation I will make you angry."

20. Then again Isaiah makes bold to say, "I have been found by those who did not seek me; I have shown myself to those who did not ask for me." 21. But of Israel he says, "All day long I have held out my hands to a faithless and contrary people."

Interpretation

Introduction. Paul has demonstrated from scripture God's declared intent to make salvation universally available on the basis simply of faith. He now explores more deeply the failure of Israel to place itself in the line of salvation by joining those who "call upon the name of the Lord" (v 13). How to account for this failure? Where has the breakdown occurred and which of the parties chiefly involved—God, the preachers of the gospel or Israel—bears responsibility for it? The prime focus lies upon Israel but, as is the case throughout Romans 9–11, Paul never considers Israel's failure with respect to the gospel apart from the paradoxical accompanying phenomenon of the gospel's success in the Gentile world (cf. 9:30-31). In fact, he now begins to posit a causal, interactive relationship between the two.

Paul proceeds by outlining the total process lying behind "calling upon the name of the Lord" that leads to salvation (vv 14-15a). God has set the process in motion (preachers of the message have been sent and they have preached; v 15b). But there has been a breakdown at the level of response (vv 16-17). This breakdown cannot be attributed to a failure at the level of "hearing" (v 18). It must then have occurred at the level of "knowing" (vv 19-21). At this level Israel is responsible because scripture had announced both the inclusion of the Gentiles and that Israel would have difficulty with it. Israel therefore knew but chose not to respond appropriately.

The "process" behind the "calling" already set in motion (vv 14-15). Following upon the statement in v 13 linking the attainment of salvation with "calling upon the name of the Lord," Paul formulates a chain-like pattern ("sorites"; cf. 5:3-4; 8:29-30 and see Note on 5:3-4) setting out all the stages preliminary to and required for the possibility of this "calling." The "process" works backwards—calling (upon the name of the Lord) presupposes believing, believing presupposes hearing, hearing presupposes preaching, preaching presupposes a sending out of those who are to preach. Each stage is presented as a question—"How can . . . if . . . not (unless) . . .?" This lends to the argument the sense that all the possible excuses that can be mounted to account for Israel's failure are being dismissed one by one. The process falls into two main parts: 1. the acts of propagation of the message which are basically God's responsibility, even if human agents are at work (sending, preaching) and 2. those which belong to the side of human response (hearing, believing, calling). The quotation (v 15b) from Isa 52:7 (echoed in Nah 1:15 [MT and LXX 2:1]) serves to indicate that those acts—sending and preaching—for which God is responsible have indeed been carried out. (Second) Isaiah's joyful message concerning the return of the exiles Paul applies, in an eschatological sense, to ministers of the Christian gospel.

The failure (vv 16-17). In the area of response, however, the unfolding process has not met with success on all fronts: "Not all have responded *(hypēkousan)* to the good news" that has been announced—a failure which Paul presents as both foreseen and formulated once again in the opening of the Fourth Servant Song of (Second) Isaiah (53:1). Included amongst the "not all who have not believed" would obviously be Gentiles, since Paul is perfectly aware that not all the Gentile world has responded (cf. 2 Cor 2:15). But the phrase (cf. the "some" of 3:3) would seem to have Israel principally in view.

Significantly, Paul does not in this connection say "not all have believed"—even though "believed" *(episteusan)* is the term appearing in the quotation from Isa 53:1. To indicate the lack of response he uses a word of broader and more ambiguous meaning—*hypakouein*—ranging across "listen to," "believe," "obey." He does so presumably because he wants to raise the possibility, by way of "excuse" for Israel, that there has been a problem on the level of "hearing"—a desire which seems to lie behind the otherwise rather difficult comment added as v 17 (see Note). This comment draws a conclusion (*ara*—"So you see . . .") from the Isa 53:1 quotation, highlighting the importance of "hearing": between the "preaching" (lit. the "word *[rēma]* about Christ") and the response of faith *(pistis)* comes the all-important condition of "hearing" *(akoē)*.

Excuse I: Israel has not "heard" the gospel (v 18). Paul has therefore prepared the way to bring in the first of the two "excuses" he intends to present. Perhaps it is the case that those who have not "responded" have not "heard" *(ouk ēkousan)* the message. This "excuse" is mentioned, however, only to be instantly swept aside in a dismissal ("Of course they have") supported by a quotation from Ps 19:4 (LXX 18:5). The psalm originally proclaimed the glory of the Lord "told" in the span of the heavens. Paul applies this to the worldwide proclamation of the gospel by Christian missionaries, beginning from Jerusalem (cf. 15:19). The conclusion is inescapable: if a worldwide proclamation has gone out from the midst of Israel, then Israel, of all nations, can hardly claim not to have heard.

Excuse II: Israel has not "known" (vv 19-21). The first "excuse" dismissed, Paul brings in the second: perhaps Israel has not "known" (*ouk egnō*, v 19a). It is not easy to pinpoint precisely what it is that Israel failed to "know" (the argument is highly elliptical at this point). Whatever the "knowledge" in question is, however, it must be something which the texts appearing in the following quotations (vv 19b-21) make inescapable for Israel; Paul cites them to show that Israel must have known—so that lack of "knowledge" in this respect cannot be entered as an excusing factor.

In the first of the three texts (v 19b), taken from LXX Deut 32:21, Moses utters in the name of God a complaint about the idolatry of Israel: Israel has provoked God to jealousy with what is a "not god" (that is, an idol); God will provoke Israel to jealousy with what is a "not nation," with what is a "non-understanding *(asynetos)* nation." Paul clearly finds in the "not nation" a reference to the Gentiles. For him the text announces a divine intention to make Israel "jealous" of the Gentiles—a motif to be developed in connection with the ultimate fate of Israel at a later stage of the exposition (11:11, 13-14).

The second (v 20) and third (v 21) quotations come from the first and second verses of Isaiah 65 and describe in turn the situation between God and the Gentiles, on the one hand, and God and Israel on the other. The

Gentiles have "found" and had revealed to them a God they did not "seek" (Isa 65:1). Israel, "a faithless and contrary people," constantly resists the divine appeal (65:2; cf. 9:30-31).

Paul's point is that the sum total of these texts (taken from the "law" [Moses] and the "prophets" [Isaiah]; cf. 3:21; 4:3-8) should have provided Israel with an inescapable indication both that God intended to include the Gentiles in the community of salvation and that this would create difficulty for Israel (provoke her to jealousy). The conclusion must be (the answer to the question in v 19a) that Israel cannot plead lack of "knowledge"—knowledge, that is, of how things were to run at the time of God's eschatological intervention. If Israel has balked at the gospel, which to a large extent it has, this cannot be due to a failure either to "hear" or to "understand." The failure lies, rather, in the area of response—a refusal to submit in faith to the righteousness of God (10:2-3).

Paul thus brings to a close his analysis of the present situation (acceptance of the gospel on the part of the Gentiles; rejection on the part of most of Israel) from the point of view of human response. The failure is Israel's alone. At the same time the exposition of scripture has shown that, within the mysterious interplay between the working out of the divine will and free human response, the present, paradoxical situation was foreseen and in a sense intended by God all along. It is precisely this incorporation of Israel's failure within a wider purpose that contains the seeds of the ultimately salvific vision of Israel's future that Paul will eventually unfold (11:11-32).

Notes

15. *As it is written, "How beautiful are the feet of those who preach good news!":* The quotation of Isa 52:7 in general agrees with the Hebrew rather than the LXX. To allow for the fact that the Christian gospel is preached by a group of apostles, "evangelization" is attributed to a plurality of agents *(euangelizomenōn)*, rather than to a single herald, as in the original. Rather than the derived sense of "beautiful" (as in the Hebrew original), Paul may have meant the Greek adjective *hōraioi* to be understood in its more basic meaning of "timely," suggesting eschatological fulfillment of the two conditions (sending and preaching) for which God is responsible; cf. Dunn, 2.621–22.

16. *But not all have responded:* "Not all" *(ou pantes)*, like "some" *(tines)* in 3:3, represents a rhetorical figure (meiosis) providing a diplomatic softening of the sharp reality of the situation: "not all" = (comparatively speaking, with respect to the Jews) "hardly any"!

    for Isaiah says, "Lord, who has believed our report?": The quotation agrees exactly with LXX Isa 53:1. The Greek word *akoē*, which is open to the sense both of "hearing" (the act of hearing) and "report" (what is heard), must clearly have the latter sense here.

17. *So you see that faith comes from hearing, a hearing, that is, that comes about through the preaching of Christ:* The function of this verse has never been satisfactorily explained. The problem is that the opening *ara* should introduce a conclusion, whereas what seems to be called for is an explanation. Rather than seeing the two elements of the verse as making up a small "chain" sequence, as in vv 14-15a, the translation sees the second element as something of an explanation of the former, with the word *akoē*, in both its occurrences in the verse, now having the sense of "hearing"—otherwise the second phrase in the verse becomes virtually tautologous, since *rēma* here must refer to the content of the gospel. The suggestion is that the "hearing" upon which faith depends is brought about (cf. the instrumental *dia*) through the preaching—and brought about *effectively* since behind the proclamation of the gospel stands the efficacy and power of the risen Lord. Paul is preparing the way for dismissing the possibility that Israel has not heard.

18. *"Their voice has gone out to all the earth, and their words to the limits of the inhabited world":* The quotation agrees exactly with LXX Ps 18:5 (19:4). A link with the context is provided through the occurrence (in the plural) of the key word *rēma* (v 8; v 17 *dia rēmatos Christou*). Clearly, any literal application of the text to the extent of the gospel's proclamation in Paul's day involves an immense exaggeration. He thinks in terms of the worldwide eschatological fulfillment of what Christian preachers have already begun; besides Rom 15:18-19, cf. also Acts 19:10; Col 1:23; 1 Tim 3:16b.

19. *could it be that Israel did not know?:* For the view that the Jews who rejected Jesus as Messiah acted in ignorance, see esp. Acts 3:17; 13:27.

    First Moses says, "I will provoke you to jealousy by those who are not a nation; with a foolish nation I will make you angry.": Paul's quotation of LXX Deut 32:21 makes it a direct address to Israel—"you" instead of "them." "First" *(prōtos)* attaching to Moses lends the sense that the indication given to Israel goes right back to its very origins and key foundational figure.

20. *Then again Isaiah makes bold to say:* The "boldness" stated in the verb *apotolmān* probably refers to the utterance itself. It is particularly "bold" in the Pauline interpretation, which takes what was originally a protestation of divine availability to Israel and applies its more positive element (v 20) to the Gentiles and its more negative element (v 21) to Israel.

    "I have been found by those who did not seek me; I have shown myself to those who did not ask for me": The quotation agrees with LXX Isa 65:1a, with some transposition of phrases.

21. *But of Israel he says, "All day long I have held out my hands to a faithless and contrary people":* The text agrees with LXX Isa 65:2, save that the phrase "all day long" appears in the initial position of stress. The double quotation from Isa 65:1-2 may be designed to suggest an interrelationship between the (successful) divine appeal to the Gentiles and God's continuing faithfulness to Israel; cf. Dunn 2.627.

FOR REFERENCE AND FURTHER STUDY

Bell, R. H. *Provoked to Jealousy* 81–106.
Johnson, E. E. *Function of Apocalyptic* 158–59.
Kramer, W. *Christ, Lord, Son of God*. SBT 50; London: SCM, 1966, 19–26, 65–71.
Munck, J. *Christ and Israel* 89–104.
Siegert, F. *Argumentation bei Paulus* 152–56.

iv. Israel's Ultimate Inclusion in the Community of Salvation (11:1-32)

Introduction to Romans 11. Behind Romans 9–11 as a whole lies the paradox that Israel, the original recipient of the promises of salvation, seems set to miss out on obtaining them, while Gentiles, who previously appeared to have no part in them, now seem to have salvation firmly within their grasp (9:30-31). This twin fact has raised acutely the *theo*logical issue concerning the faithfulness and reliability of God (9:6a). On the human side, it poses the question about the present status and ultimate fate of Israel with respect to salvation.

By the end of chapter 10 Paul might claim to have largely vindicated the faithfulness of God. He has shown from scripture that it was God's declared intent to act with sovereign freedom in fulfilling the promises, calling into being a composite community of salvation made up of Gentiles as well as Jews (9:6b-29). He has also shown (9:30–10:21), again from scripture, that responsibility for Israel's "stumbling" (9:32-33) cannot be attributed to the gospel or to the preaching but to Israel's refusal to surrender a view of the way to salvation at odds with the eschatological action of God. In the end we have been left with the picture of a God stretching out hands to an unresponsive people (10:21).

Paul has, therefore, essentially vindicated the faithfulness of God and the efficacy of the gospel. But he appears to have done so at the price of simply cutting out from salvation the Israel that has not come to faith in the gospel. Has the attempt to be "inclusive" with respect to the Gentiles proved "exclusive" with respect to Israel? What is the status of this people? They appear to have rejected God's offer of salvation in Christ. Does this mean that God has rejected them?

Paul's response falls basically into three parts. 1. For a while (vv 1-6) he continues to treat this as an essentially *theo*logical issue—defending God's faithfulness to Israel by pointing to the existence of the Jewish-Christian "remnant" whom God has clearly not rejected. This still leaves the question of the remainder, whom God has "hardened" (vv 7-10). By the end of v 10, far from being resolved, the issue seems sharper than ever. 2. Gradually, however, the argument begins to turn a corner with respect to this "hardening" (vv 11-16): the "hardening" of Israel has a role to play in the gospel's proclamation to the Gentiles and, in turn, the success of that proclamation holds out hope that "some of them" may be saved (v 14). The salvation of Israel and the salvation of the Gentiles are inextricably bound up one with the other. Hence Paul sees it appropriate at this point (v 17) to issue a warning to Gentile Christians, by means of the extended "Olive-tree" allegory (vv 17-24), that they not vaunt themselves at the expense of the original "stock," as though their own salvation was now unshakably secure and Israel's had fallen away. 3. As a climax to the entire section, Paul expounds the "mystery" that holds out hope for the salvation of "all Israel" (v 26) on the basis of an all-embracing, "inclusive" operation of God's mercy (vv 25-32). This leads in to a sustained doxology (vv 33-36) that brings to a close the entire presentation of the gospel in Rom 1:16–11:32.

a) *God Has Not Rejected Israel—the "Remnant"* (11:1-10)

1. I ask, then, has God rejected his people? By no means!
I myself am an Israelite, a descendant of Abraham, a member of the tribe of Benjamin.
2. "God has not rejected his people" whom he foreknew.
Do you not know what the scripture says of Elijah, how he pleads with
God against Israel? 3. "Lord, they have killed your prophets, they have
demolished your altars, and I alone am left, and they seek my life." 4.
But what is (God's) oracular response? "I have kept for myself seven thousand men who have not bowed the knee to Baal."
5. So too at the present time there is a remnant, chosen by grace. 6. But if it is by grace, it is no longer on the basis of works; otherwise grace would no longer be grace.
7. What then? What Israel sought, this it failed to obtain.
The elect obtained it, but the rest were hardened, 8. as it is written, "God gave them a spirit of stupor, eyes that they should not see and ears that they should not hear, down to this very day."
9. And David says, "Let their table become a snare and a net, and a trap
and a retribution for them; 10. let their eyes be darkened so that they cannot see, and bend their backs continually."

Interpretation

Following the initial raising of the issue (v 1), the rebuttal of the suggestion that God has rejected Israel falls loosely into two parts according as the focus is first upon the Jewish-Christian "remnant" (vv 2-6), then upon the "rest" of Israel which has been "hardened" (vv 7-10).

God has not rejected Israel (v 1). Paul raises and then dismisses in characteristic fashion ("By no means!" [*mē genoito*]) the suggestion that seems to flow naturally from what has preceded. Conscious perhaps that some in the Roman community may have given credence to the charge that he is indifferent to the fate of his people, he rebuts any such implication by insisting once more (cf. 9:1-2; 10:1) upon his own peerless Jewish credentials: "Israelite," "from seed of Abraham," "of the tribe of Benjamin" (cf. 2 Cor 11:22; Phil 3:4-6). To one who is *still* (cf. the present tense) fully proud to call himself by these titles the suggestion that God has rejected Israel is unthinkable.

The Jewish-Christian "remnant" (vv 2-6). As a more solid basis, however, for rebutting the suggestion, Paul turns to the scriptural example of Elijah. After his successful contest with the prophets of Baal, Elijah had fled to the wilderness (1 Kgs 19:1-8) and, being asked by God what he was doing there (v 9), replied in the words represented by Paul (Rom 11:3) as his "entreaty" (*entygchanei*) or complaint against Israel. The Israelites have slain God's prophets, overthrown his sanctuaries; he alone is left and his life is threatened (1 Kgs 19:10, 14). In other words, faithful Israel exists only in him and he is likely to be done away with and so there will be nothing left of faithful Israel at all. But, says Paul (v 4), this complaint of Elijah is not allowed to stand. God rebuts it immediately with a solemn response (*chrēmatismos*): Elijah is *not* the only faithful remnant of Israel. God has "left for himself seven thousand who have not bent the knee to Baal" (19:18). Israel is not about to be extinguished even if the prophet himself should die.

Paul sees (v 5) in this divine "correction" of Elijah's lamentation a type or pledge (cf. *houtōs oun kai*) of what is happening now in the eschatological era (*en tǭ nyn kairǭ*; cf. 3:26; 9:9). Whereas he (Paul) might be tempted to make the complaint of Elijah his own and feel that he alone remains of Israel (cf. 1b), God is indicating the existence of a new "seven thousand," a "remnant" (*leimma*), whose existence belies any suggestion that God has rejected his people. As in 9:27-28, Paul has recourse to the biblical idea of "remnant" in connection with the overall issue under consideration. But, whereas in the earlier passage, the existence of the "remnant" (*hypoleimma*, v 27) served simply to indicate the numerical diminishment of Israel according to the flesh, here the motif stands in its more developed and positive biblical sense as a sign and pledge of the continuing fidelity of God.

This note is brought out by the qualification which Paul attaches to the notion of the Jewish members of the believing community as constituting a "remnant" in this biblical sense. The "remnant" is one that has "come about on the basis of an election proceeding from grace" *(leimma kat' eklogēn charitos)*. It is not a "faithful remnant" if by "faithful" some human quality is in view. The "faithfulness" attaching to this remnant is the faithfulness of the God of grace. This insistence upon election and grace, contains an implication highly significant in the present context: if God's grace has worked effectively for the "remnant" in such independence of human behavior—in fact, in the face of human failure and sin (acknowledged by Jewish-Christians when they came to faith; cf. esp. 3:21-26; 4:5; Gal 2:16)—there remains the hope that grace may ultimately triumph in the face of Israel's current failure with respect to Christ. In this sense the existence of the "remnant chosen by grace" stands as a sign that God has not rejected his people.

An added comment (v 6) upon the significance of this "remnant" recalls and restates a key thesis from the earlier part of the letter (chapters 1–4). The fact that the Jewish-Christian "remnant" owes its existence entirely to grace excludes any sense that it pursues righteousness through practice of the Jewish law ("not from works of the law" *[ouk ex ergōn]*). The principle of works is incompatible with grace (cf. esp. 3:27-28; 4:13-16) and it is as a God of grace that God has been revealed (3:21, 24; 5:17). Paul has pointed to a "pursuit" of righteousness by law as the chief factor inhibiting Israel's "submission" to the saving righteousness of God (9:31–10:3). If the Jewish-Christian minority has attained righteousness (cf. v 7), it is because, unlike their compatriots, they have abandoned a quest for righteousness by law and, along with Gentile believers, flung themselves entirely upon the God of grace (cf. 10:4; cf. Gal 2:16). The continuing polemic against "works of the law" seems otiose at this stage of the letter. For Paul, however, it is important to stress that Israel's identity carries on (in the "remnant"), an identity not based upon keeping the law but solely upon divine election and grace.

The Situation: the "remnant" and the "rest" (vv 7-10). Having pointed to the existence of this (Jewish-Christian) "remnant," Paul pauses (v 7: *ti oun*) to review the present situation with respect to the two groups he has now discerned. The assessment is similar to that of 9:30-32, except that, while there it was a case of Israel (= "the Jews") and "Gentiles," here the distinction is within Israel: between the Jewish-Christian "remnant" that has come to faith in Christ and "Israel" in the sense of "the rest" *(hoi loipoi)*, who have not. The situation is the same paradoxical one as before: what this "Israel" was seeking—the eschatological righteousness which would lead to salvation (cf. 9:30-31)—this it has failed to obtain; whereas the "elect" (*eklogē*, = the Jewish-Christian remnant) did obtain precisely this status, not on the basis of being a "faithful remnant" in conventional Jewish terms of keeping the law but in the unconventional mode of acknowledging, in faith, that it had no righteousness on that basis and stood along with "Gentile sinners" in need of the righteousness of God (Rom 1:18–3:20; cf. Gal 2:15-16).

As for the other party ("the rest" = the great bulk of Israel), these, says Paul (v 7c) "were hardened" *(epōrōthēsan)*. The thought here, if not the language, recalls what had been said earlier (9:17-18) concerning God's "hardening" *(sklērynein)* of the heart of Pharaoh in the service of a wider divine purpose. The "hardening" is not a punishment following upon unbelief. Rather, it denotes a spiritual insensitivity which precedes unbelief, inhibiting appropriate response to the action of God. While the passive form points to the action of God (cf. 9:17-18), the element of human choice is not necessarily excluded; the analysis of Israel's responsibility carried out in 9:30–10:21 may still stand. As so often in the Bible, what we are faced with here is a reflection upon human failure which, in order to encompass such failure within a wider divine purpose, attributes it to the action of God.

This wider purpose Paul will indicate in due course. For the present (vv 8-10) he is content to remain simply with the fact of the *pōrōsis* and to indicate scriptural foreshadowings that such a hardening would be part of God's eschatological plan for Israel. In pursuit of this, Paul turns, first of all (v 8) to Moses' admonition to Israel in Deut 29:4 (LXX 29:3), rearranged to some extent and with the phrase "heart to know" replaced by the much more severe "spirit of stupor" imported from Isa 29:10. The original sense of the text from Deuteronomy is that, whereas "until this day" the exodus community of Israel had not been able to appreciate the full meaning of all that God had done for them—since the Lord had not given them "eyes to see and ears to hear"—now at last they were in a position to understand and respond accordingly. Paul transforms the negative so as to lend the sense that God *has* (already) given them a spirit of stupor, eyes *so that* they may *not* see, ears *so that* they may *not* hear "down to this very day." This modification, enhancing the note of judgment, transforms Moses' admonition into a statement of deliberate "hardening" on God's part. Israel's remaining in unbelief right down to the time ("this day") when Paul is writing becomes the outcome of a deliberate divine action announced beforehand in scripure.

To this scriptural testimony from the "Law" (Pentateuch) in the shape of Deuteronomy, Paul adds (vv 9-10) one from the "Prophets" in the shape of David, author of the Psalms: Ps 69:22-23 (LXX 68:23-24). The two texts are linked, in accordance with a standard exegetical technique (see Note), by a common phrase: "eyes that they may not see" (v 8; v 10). Psalm 69 (LXX 68) is a psalm of lament from one undergoing severe persecution. It is quoted frequently in the NT, especially in connection with the sufferings and death of Jesus (Matt 27:34 and parallels; 27:48 and parallels.; John 2:17; 15:25; 19:28; Rom 15:3; Heb 11:26). Paul cites the beginning of a passage (vv 22-28) where the psalmist begins to call down various curses upon those who afflict him. At first sight, then, the citation of this text implies a judgment upon Israel that is very severe. It is unlikely, however, that the reader is meant to pay heed to all the details mentioned as part of the curse and apply them literally to unbelieving Israel. The chief point in the citation of this part of the psalm is the allusion to the "darkening" of the eyes "that they may not see." This, as noted above, is the common motif linking the Psalm text to the one from Deuteronomy cited just before (v 8). It provides the scriptural warrant and "pre-announcement" for the divine "hardening" *(epōrōthēsan)* that has come upon contemporary Israel (v 7b).

Granted that Paul does not necessarily intend his audience to apply all the details of the curse in the citation from Ps 69:22-23 to Israel, it must still be conceded that the passage ends on a very pessimistic and severe note. The confident dismissal of the suggestion that God has rejected his people (v 1) now seems very far away. Paul's grappling with this issue is tension-ridden and takes many dramatic turns and twists before arriving at its final goal (11:32).

Notes

1. *I ask, then, has God rejected his people?:* The form of the question (*legō . . . mē . . .*; cf. also 10:18, 19; 11:11) presupposes a negative answer. The biblical texts upon which the question is based, 1 Sam 12:22 and Ps 94:14 (LXX 93:14), both contain the firm assertion that the Lord will not reject his people.

   By no means!: On Paul's use of this exclamation *(mē genoito)*, see Note on 3:4.

   an Israelite, a descendant of Abraham, a member of the tribe of Benjamin: On the first of these honorific titles see Note on 9:4 above; on the second, see Note on 9:7; the third appears in the corresponding list in Phil 3:5. Some think that Paul's purpose in inserting this self-description is to point to himself—an Israelite of such impeccable credentials—as a living refutation of the idea that God has rejected his people (cf. Cranfield 2.544; Wilckens 2.236–37). This involves Paul's attributing to himself a singularly high status and significance—something not impossible in view of claims he makes elsewhere (cf., e. g., 15:16). But one wonders, then, how he thought a claim to such exalted status would have gone down in Rome. The argument seems better served when the "refutation" rests totally upon the scriptural proof from the story of Elijah and the "remnant."

2. *whom he foreknew:* On the biblical use of this idea of "foreknowing" in the sense of "election," see Note on 8:29.

   what the scripture says of Elijah: Lit. "in Elijah, what scripture says." Paul uses a familiar way of alluding to a scriptural sequence concerning a particular character; cf. Mark 12:26.

how he pleads with God against Israel?: The sense is probably not so much that Elijah entreats God to do something *against* Israel (in the sense of punishment) but that he *complains* to God about his own lot in view of the false behavior with which Israel can be charged (hence *kata . . .*); for use of the verb *entygchanein* in a similar sense, cf. 1 Macc 8:32; 10:61, 63; 11:25.

3. *"Lord, they have killed your prophets, they have demolished your altars, and I alone am left, and they seek my life":* Paul cites the text appearing in both v 10 and v 14 of 1 Kings 19, transposing it somewhat so that the phrase about the killing of the prophets appears first—perhaps to reinforce the sense of Elijah as the sole prophet left alive. Elijah hardly serves as a type for Paul *vis-à-vis* the Israel of his own day; Paul cites the Elijah episode to introduce the motif of the "remnant," which is the principal support at this point for the principle that God has not rejected his people (vv 1a; 2a); cf. Wilckens 2.237.

4. *But what is (God's) oracular response?:* Paul uses the term *chrēmatismos,* rare in biblical Greek (cf. 2 Macc 2:4), to highlight the sense of an authoritative divine rebuttal of the complaint of Elijah.

   "I have kept for myself seven thousand men who have not bowed the knee to Baal": The quotation is based upon 1 Kgs 19:18 but in fact bears little resemblance to the expression of the LXX. Paul's version has the utterance in the first person singular (as also in the Hebrew), adds the phrase "for myself" *(emautǭ)* and transposes the tense into the aorist—all of which serves to emphasize the sense of the divine intent and initiative.

5. *at the present time:* For the sense of this phrase *(en tǭ nyn kairǭ),* see Note on 3:26.

   a remnant, chosen by grace: The Greek phrase *leimma kat' eklogēn charitos* means literally "a remnant according to the selection of grace" (cf. Fitzmyer 605); cf. the similar expression of divine choice *(hē kat' eklogēn prothesis)* in 9:11. The biblical motif of the "remnant" arose as an expression of the grim fate (reduction to a small residue) awaiting Israel, particularly in the context of the crises surrounding the threats from Assyria and Babylon: e. g., 2 Kgs 21:14; Amos 5:15; Isa 1:8-9; 6:13; 7:3-4. It later became a fixed *topos,* designating, in a more positive sense, the remainder of the people that could hope for salvation: cf. Isa 4:3; 10:20-22; 11:11, 16; 14:22, 30; 28:5; 37:31-32; Jer 50:20; Mic 5:7-8; 7:18; Zeph 2:9; 3:12-13; Zech 13:8-9; 2 Kgs 19:30-31; Ezra 9:8, 15; Sir 44:17; 47:22; 1 Macc 3:35. Paul's appeal to the motif here reflects the more positive, salvific sense in which it had come to be used in the later prophetic and post-biblical tradition; cf. esp. the sense in which the Qumran community, with similar appeal to the divine initiative, saw themselves as a "faithful remnant" of Israel (CD 1:4-5; 1QM 13:8; 14:8-9; 1QH 6:8; cf. also *4 Ezra* 9:7-8). On the entire background to Paul's use of "remnant" here, see the article of R. E. Clements cited in Reference.

6. *But if it is by grace, it is no longer on the basis of works:* Since Paul has already indicated misguided zeal for the law as the chief factor causing the bulk of Israel to fail to submit to God's righteousness (9:31–10:3), the phrase *ex ergōn* probably stands in here for the longer formulation "from works of the law"

(on which see Note on 3:20). In itself, however, the shorter form *ex ergōn* need not always have specific reference to the law of Moses, as shown by occurrences where the law is not in question: e. g., 4:2 (Abraham); 9:12 (Jacob and Esau); it can simply refer to human behavior, whether the law is present to prescribe it or not. The fundamental Pauline antithesis, of which this passage is one expression, lies between *God's* grace and (failed) *human* works, whether carried out in accordance with the law or not. The use here of the expression "no longer" *(ouketi)* in connection with this antithesis is logical rather than temporal.

7. *What then?:* The phrase *ti oun,* is short for the more usual *ti oun eroumen* (see Note on 4:1), which introduces the similar statement of the present situation given in 9:30-32.

What Israel sought, this it failed to obtain: What was "sought" was "righteousness" in the sense, pervasive in Romans, of the eschatological right-standing with God which is the basis of final salvation as God's people; see Interpretation of 1:17.

The elect obtained it: The word *eklogē,* which in v 5 and earlier in 9:11 in the phrase *kat' eklogēn* had the sense of (God's) "election" (that is, the process), must here refer to what has come about as the result of that election: "the elect." While Gentile believers are clearly part of God's "elect" in a broader sense (cf. 8:28-29; 9:24-25) and while the parallel provided by 9:30-31 might seem to suggest that the same "Gentiles/Israel" antithesis is operative here, the fact that Paul is making a contrast within Israel (cf. "the rest" in the following phrase) argues that *eklogē* here denotes the *Jewish*-Christian "remnant."

the rest were hardened: The verb *pōroun* has the basic sense of "petrify" and was used in connection with medical conditions involving calcification or the formation of stones in the bladder. Paul's metaphorical usage of "hardening" (9:18; 11:7, 25; 2 Cor 3:14) reflects a comparatively widespread motif in the NT: cf. Mark 3:5 *[pōrōsis]*; 6:52; 8:17; John 12:40; Eph 4:18 *[pōrōsis]*. Behind all these instances may lie Isa 6:9-10, explicitly cited in John 12:40; cf. also Mark 4:11-12 [explanation of Jesus' use of parables] and Acts 28:26-27.

8. *a spirit of stupor:* The rare word *katanyxis* (elsewhere in the LXX only Ps 59:5 [60:3]) means "stupefaction" or "torpor."

down to this very day: Behind the Greek lies a common biblical expression indicating the permanence of a name or resulting state of affairs. Paul probably sees in the phrase something to account for Israel's abiding resistance to the gospel, despite over two decades of Christian preaching. A notable parallel, with several linguistic echoes, occurs in the sustained comparison of the two "ministries"—that of the old covenant and that of the new—in 2 Cor 3:12–4:4, where, in a midrash upon Exod 34:33-35, Paul sees in the veil that shielded from the Israelites the (waning) glory (of the old covenant) upon the face of Moses a forerunner of the "hardening" of contemporary Israel that causes a "veil" to lie upon their hearts, preventing them from seeing "to this day" (*achri . . . tēs sēmeron hēmeras,* v 14; *heōs sēmeron,* v 15).

9–10. *And David says, "Let their table become a snare and a net, a trap and a retribution for them; let their eyes be darkened so that they cannot see, and bend their backs continually":* The combining of texts from "the law" and "the prophets" reflects an exegetical technique found later in Rabbinic literature (the so-called Second Rule of Hillel). The interpretation of a particular text is confirmed or developed by adducing a further text with which it has a key word in common; cf. 4:3-8. The quotation agrees with LXX Ps 68:23-24 (69:22-23), with inversion of the final two phrases of v 23 and the insertion of the phrase "and for a net" (*eis thēran*) in place of "before them," possibly for the sake of balance. It is tempting to relate "table" (*trapeza*) to Jewish table fellowship, with its sense of exclusion of all that is regarded as unclean. However, as noted in the Interpretation, it is not at all clear that Paul means all details in the quotation to be pressed in this way. Along the same lines, the final imperative to "bend (*sygkampson*) their backs," rather than implying condemnation to perpetual slavery, may be connected with the central motif of "not seeing"—in the sense that those who are bent over cannot see ahead. In any case, the temporal phrase *dia pantos* means "continually" and refers to the persistence of Israel in unbelief "down to this very day" (v 8); it does not necessarily imply that this persistence will endure for ever.

For Reference and Further Study

Clements, R. E. "'A Remnant Chosen by Grace' (Romans 11:5)." *Pauline Studies* (FS F. F. Bruce). Eds. D. A. Hagner & M. J. Harris. Exeter: Paternoster, 1980, 106–21.

Hanson, A. T. "The Oracle in Romans xi.4." *NTS* 19 (1972–73) 300–02.

Hays, R. B. *Echoes of Scripture* 68–70.

Johnson, D. G. "The Structure and Meaning of Romans 11." *CBQ* 46 (1984) 91–103.

Johnson, E. E. *Function of Apocalyptic* 160–63.

Munck, J. *Christ and Israel* 104–16.

b) *Israel's "Stumbling" Has a Saving Purpose* (11:11-24)

11. So I ask, have they stumbled so as to fall? By no means! But through their trespass salvation has come to the Gentiles, so as to make them jealous.
12. Now if their trespass means riches for the world, and if their failure means riches for the Gentiles, how much more will their fullness mean!
13. Now I am speaking to you Gentiles. Inasmuch as I am an apostle to
the Gentiles, I magnify my ministry 14. in the hope of making my fellow
Jews jealous, and thus of saving some of them.

15. For if their rejection has meant reconciliation for the world, what will
their acceptance mean but life from the dead?
16. If the dough offered as firstfruits is holy, so is the whole lump; and if
the root is holy, so are the branches.
17. But if some of the branches were broken off, and you, a wild olive,
have been grafted in among them and become sharers in the richness
stemming from the root of the olive tree, 18. do not boast over the
branches. If you do boast, remember that it is not you that support the
root, but the root that supports you.
19. You may well say, "Branches were broken off so that I might be
grafted in." 20. True enough. They were broken off because of their lack
of faith, but you stand fast only through faith. So do not harbor proud
thoughts, but fear. 21. For if God did not spare the natural branches, neither will he spare you.
22. Note then the kindness and the severity of God: severity toward
those who have fallen, but God's kindness towards you, provided you
continue in his kindness; otherwise you too will be cut off.
23. And even the others, if they do not persist in their unbelief, will be
grafted in, for God has the power to graft them in again. 24. For if you
whose natural belonging was to a wild olive tree have been cut off from
that and grafted, contrary to nature, onto a cultivated olive tree, how
much more will those who belong to it naturally be grafted back into
their own olive stock.

INTERPRETATION

Introduction. The argument of the passage falls into two parts: vv 11-16 and vv 17-24, the latter dominated by the "Olive-Grafting" allegory. In the first part, the key issue (whether Israel's rejection is final) is recalled in v 11a, with the remainder of the verse indicating, in a thematic way, the main lines of the response. Vv 12-15 develop the "thesis" enunciated in 11b, with vv 13-14 offering a short parenthesis in which Paul explains his own apostolic strategy in view of the "jealousy" motif enunciated in v 11c. V 16 introduces fresh images to confirm the preceding argument and acts as a bridge to the extended allegory developed in vv 17-24. In this second half of the passage, vv 17-18 introduce the allegory, stating the warning to the Gentiles that is its basic role. In vv 19-20 Paul thrusts aside an objection, before resuming in vv 21-22 the warning to the Gentiles ("You too can be cut out."). The allegory concludes on a positive note in vv 23-24, stating the hope that Israel can just as easily be grafted in.

God's design in Israel's stumbling (vv 11-12). Despite the vigorous rejection earlier on (v 1) of the suggestion that God has abandoned his people, the argument has in fact made little advance as far as the bulk of Israel is concerned. The existence of the Jewish-Christian "remnant" has shown that, God has not *entirely* abandoned his people. But the "hardening" of "the rest" (v 7) has been depicted in very negative terms (vv 8-10). Addressing himself more precisely to the fate of this group, Paul reformulates (v 11) the issue, responding with a similar rebuttal ("By no means!"). The formulation of the question appears to hark back to the "stumbling" motif from Isa 28:16 quoted in 9:33. Paul distinguishes between a "stumbling" *(heptaisan)* from which one can recover to rise again and a stumbling leading to a fall that is permanent and irreversible *(pesōsin)*. The latter is not the situation of Israel. Israel's stumbling occurs within the compass of a wider divine purpose embracing both the salvation of the Gentiles and a renewed hope for Israel itself.

Within this divine purpose, the "trespass" *(paraptōma)* of Israel—her rejection of the gospel—has led, in the first place, to the salvation of the Gentiles. Paul gives a theological and indeed causal explanation of what has been in fact the historical reality: the rejection of the gospel on the part of most Jews and its acceptance on the part of an ever-increasing number of Gentiles. This last development is not, however, an end in itself. Within the same divine purpose, it is designed to redound positively upon Israel. God's declared intention (Deut 32:21, cited in 10:19) to "provoke them (Israel) to jealousy with a 'not-nation,'" is now interpreted positively: awareness of what the Gentiles have attained will bring about a change of heart in Israel, reverse the initial rejection and set them at last on the way to salvation. Previously, Paul had set the twin phenomena—the failure of Israel and the Gentile attainment of justification—simply in contrastive parallel (9:30-33; cf. 10:19-21; 11:7). Now, within the framework of the overall divine purpose, he finds a causal/instrumental interconnection between the two.

To reinforce this suggestion, Paul employs (v 12; cf. v 15) the *a fortiori (pollǭ [posǭ] mallon)* argument familiar especially from chapter 5 (vv 9-10, 15, 17; cf. 8:32). Israel's failure has led to the salvation of the Gentiles (v 11b). If so great a "wealth" *(ploutos)* of salvation has flowed in the negative case (the failure and diminution *[hēttēma]* of Israel), how much more "richness" is not to be expected in the positive case—that is, when the full complement of Israel (*plērōma*) is finally restored?

Paul's tactic in view of this (vv 13-14). What this overwhelming "richness" might consist of Paul will suggest shortly (v 15). For a moment, addressing his hearers specifically as "Gentiles," he breaks into the natural flow of the sequence to offer a parenthetical reflection upon his own ministry in view of the "provocation to jealousy" motif. As they well know, his own unique charism is that of being "apostle to the Gentiles" (1:5, 13-14; cf. 15:15-19; Gal 1:16). Precisely as such, he sees himself as having a salvific role *vis-à-vis* his Jewish brothers and sisters as well. He is not indifferent to the situation of his co-religionists (cf. 9:1-3; 10:1; 11:1). By making sure that they are kept aware of the success of his ministry to the Gentiles (literally, by "magnifying his ministry"), he promotes the operation of the "jealousy" principle just enunciated, in the hope of saving "some" (v 14). In short, his very mission to the Gentiles is ultimately a mission to Jews as well.

It is not immediately clear how Paul saw the "jealousy" principle operating in practice. The collection contributed by the Gentile churches which Paul is conveying to Jerusalem (cf. esp. 15:25-27, 31) was surely a tangible sign of the effectiveness of his ministry among the Gentiles. It was destined for the "Saints"—that is, the members of the Jewish-Christian "remnant" resident in Jerusalem—but presumably other Jews would not long remain unaware of the large sum they had received and would doubtless be impressed. If this is what Paul means by "magnifying his ministry," the allusion is somewhat oblique. Perhaps, on a less material level, he has in mind the gift of the Spirit—the "downpayment" of the full gift of salvation (2 Cor 1:22)—which Gentile communities have received in full measure, as a sign of the dawning of the new age and their inclusion within the community of salvation. Paul's "glorification" of his ministry might then consist in pointing to the pouring out of the Spirit in the new communities (cf. Rom 15:19a; 1 Cor 2:4) and the gifts of love, joy and peace flowing from it. Struck by this phenomenon, Jews who have previously resisted the gospel might be led to think again and allow themselves to be drawn into the path of salvation. Paul is hardly thinking of conversions *en masse.* He indicates a tactic on his own part which ensures that his preaching directed to the inclusion of the Gentiles is also to some degree at least inclusive of his own people as well.

The underlying hope (vv 15-16). Following this brief parenthesis, Paul resumes (v 15) his earlier line of thought (v 12), though now the focus is more upon the action of God than upon human response. God's "rejection" (*apobolē*) of the Jews has meant the "reconciliation of the world"—that is, it has provided the opportunity and the impulse for the gospel to be effectively proclaimed in the wider Gentile world. On the same "much more" logic, Paul can therefore argue that, if so great a benefit has flowed in the negative case, what immeasurably greater benefit can we not expect in the positive case, when those who have been rejected are now "accepted" *(proslēmpsis)*? Earlier (v 12) Paul had left this expectation hanging in the air. Now he specifies it as "resurrection from the dead" *(zōē ek nekrōn).* Within the apocalyptic framework presupposed by the argument, this can only be an allusion to one of the key events preliminary to the final consummation: the general resurrection of the dead. Traditionally, "resurrection" had to do with ensuring that the faithful in Israel who had died before the final victory would also be participants in the final Kingdom of God (cf. esp. Dan 12:1-3). Paul envisages that God's "acceptance" of Israel will be the immediate prelude to the revivification of the faithful departed. With hitherto unbelieving Israel "received" and the faithful dead raised, the stage will be set for the constitution of the final eschatological Israel, "inclusively" made up of Jews and Gentiles, heirs to the promised blessings of salvation.

Paul thus sees the inclusion of that part of Israel as yet unresponsive to the gospel to be an indispensable element in the events of the End. Through the "jealousy" motif he has even offered some kind of explanation of how, in human terms, this inclusion will come about. He has not yet explained, however, the fundamental *theological* grounds upon which the hope is based. This he now (v 16) begins to do through two images, the second of which is then developed at considerable length in the following sequence.

The first image (v 16a) probably alludes to the requirement of offering a cake containing a portion of the dough as set out in Num 15:17-21; the first portion of the dough was offered to God as a token acknowledgment on Israel's part that the whole produce of the land into which they were entering was the gift of God. The original rite did not imply that the dedication of the firstfruits worked the sanctification of the entire lump. But Paul appears to derive from the rite this *pars pro toto* sense (cf. his reference in Rom 8:23 to the Spirit as "firstfruits" *[aparchē]*, that is, as first "installment" of the full measure of salvation; also 1 Cor 15:20). If a quality of holiness pertains to the "firstfruits" of Israel—namely, the patriarchs (see Note for alternative suggestions)—the same holiness endures in the Israel descended from them.

In parallel fashion, the same basic argument recurs in the second part of the verse (v 16b), but with the image now changed to that of a plant: if a holiness pertains to the "root"—again the patriarchs—the same holiness may also pertain to the "branches"—Israel (believing and unbelieving)—that draw life and nourishment from the root. It is this holiness, enduring still in the Israel that has not come to faith in Jesus as the Christ, that forms the basis for the hope that Israel's present "stumbling" is not irretrievable.

The "olive-grafting" allegory (vv 17-24): Warning to the Gentiles (vv 17-18). At this point (v 17) Paul develops the "root and branches" image he has just introduced into an extended allegory based upon the traditional motif of Israel as an "Olive Tree" (cf. Jer 11:16; Hos 14:6). Somewhat surprisingly, considering that the failure of Israel remains the central issue, this allegory becomes for a time the vehicle of a stern warning to Gentile believers: they are not to "boast" (v 18) over their inclusion in the people of God at the expense of the Israel that has not responded to the gospel. The warning to the Gentiles, however, is not the entire purpose of the allegory, since at the end (vv 23-24) what is once more in view is the hope for Israel stemming from the capacity of God to "graft back in" the "branches" of the original tree that had been earlier cut out. The admonition is of a piece with similar moments of parenesis occurring earlier in the letter (6:12-14; 8:12-13). In more strictly rhetorical terms, it may also serve the tactical purpose of countering any sense that Paul is callous or indifferent to the fate of his people: he tolerates no such attitude in Gentile converts.

The long sentence introducing the allegory (vv 17-18a) develops the "root and branches" motif of v 16 into the more specific image of the olive tree to whose branches a grafting procedure is applied. Central to the new image is a distinction between cultivated and uncultivated ("wild") olives. The current situation is that "some" of the original branches of the cultivated olive have been "broken off" and others, from a "wild olive," have been grafted in. Gentile believers now find themselves part of the cultivated olive (the people of God). They enjoy the "rich sap"—the benefits of salvation—flowing from the "root," the patriarchs of Israel. But let them keep in mind (to sharpen the warning Paul, in diatribe mode, employs the second person singular address, "You") that they are there among the remaining original branches as "wild ones," as strangers. In this situation it is totally inappropriate that they should vaunt themselves at the expense of the original branches, whether those that have been cut out or those (the Jewish-Christian "remnant") that remain. If (v 18b) they should vaunt themselves in this misguided way, they are then showing themselves forgetful of the basic fact that it is not they (the grafted-in branches) that bring nourishment and support to the root but precisely the other way round.

In making this point Paul appears to draw upon the Jewish motif of the election and merits of the fathers being a sustaining channel of grace for subsequent generations (cf., more explicitly, v 28). At first sight, this seems to stand notably at odds with his earlier (cf. esp. 9:24-29) insistence that the eschatological Israel is entirely the free creation of God, independent of human deserts or ethnic allegiance. Paul does not, however, speak of "merits" in connection with the fathers. In his understanding it is through *God's* fidelity that the eschatological community has come to promises spoken to the "fathers" and cherished by them in faith (cf. esp. 15:8). It is as recipients of the promises of salvation that the fathers "carry" the "branches" consisting in the eschatological people of God.

An objection and response (vv 19-20). To sharpen the warning, Paul allows the (Gentile Christian) dialogue partner to make an obvious objection. If, as Paul has earlier suggested (v 11), the original branches were broken off precisely so that "I" (the Gentiles) might be grafted in (the passive and the purpose clause suggests the design and action of God), have I not, then, the right to see myself in their place? The objection neatly expresses the theory that Jews have been "displaced" from the people of God in favor of Christians—a view which has been a controlling element of Christian attitude to Judaism down the ages.

The tragic consequences of such a belief might have been avoided had Christians taken more note of Paul's response (v 20). The Apostle concedes the element of truth that lies in the objection *(kalōs)*. But the fact that the process of "breaking off" and "cutting in" has all revolved around faith or the lack of it should essentially determine the attitude the Gentile believer ought now adopt. If the original "branches" have been cut out because of their lack of faith *(apistią)*, Gentiles (literally, "You") "stand" *(hestēkas)* in their present attachment to the olive tree on the basis of faith *(pistei)*. As Paul has made abundantly clear in the earlier part of the letter (cf. esp. 4:17-25), faith is precisely an attitude that turns away from any resting upon one's own achievement or privileged position, to rely entirely upon the grace and power of God as Creator. Christian "standing," then, in a situation of attachment to the olive tree, in place of the cut-off branches, is something resting entirely upon God's power and favor. In this situation it is totally inappropriate to harbor proud thoughts *(hypsēla phronein)*. On the contrary, what is fitting is an attitude of humble and salutary fear.

Gentiles can be cut out again (vv 21-22). In the second half of the allegory (vv 21-24), Paul bolsters the warning just given by drawing attention to the implications of what God has already done—"breaking off" unbelieving Israel, "grafting in" the Gentiles—as a reminder of what it is possible for him still to do. What now becomes central in the image is the fact that the grafting has involved the removal and attachment of branches contrary to their "natural" *(kata physin)* belonging to the tree. So the "logic" runs (v 21), on familiar *a fortiori* lines (cf. v 12): if God has not spared but broken off from the olive stock (Israel) "branches" that "naturally" belonged to it (the Israel that has not come to faith), how much easier it would be to break off (literally, "not to spare") the branches from the grafted wild olive (Gentile believers) that did not "naturally" belong to it.

This telling argument is reinforced (v 22) by an appeal reminiscent of the "accusation" employed against Jewish presumption early in the letter (2:3-4). There Paul had attacked the complacency of the Jewish person who is confident that God's "kindness" *(chrēstotēs)* would grant Israel favored treatment at the judgment, meaning that Jews would escape the severe verdict due to fall upon the Gentile world. In the face of such complacency Paul had insisted upon the "impartiality" of God's judgment to all, Jew and Gentile alike (2:10-11). Now, in a way that to some extent restores a balance, he insists (v 22a) that the Gentile likewise must consider two aspects of God—that God is not only a God of "kindness" but also a God of "severity" *(apotomia)*. For the present, God's severity is manifest in Israel (literally, "the fallen" *[tous pesontas]*, v 22b; cf. 9:22). God's "kindness," on the other hand, is what the Gentile has experienced—being brought to faith and so "grafted on" to the stock of Israel (v 22c). The point is, however (v 22d), to "remain" *(epimenein)* in that "kindness" precisely as God's kindness—something graciously bestowed upon no basis of pre-existing merit. Gentile boasting in a status that has been brought about solely through such divine kindness carries with it the possibility that they too could be "cut out" *(ekkopēsę̄)* and so placed outside the life-giving stock; there they would revert to the situation that was once theirs as "Gentile sinners" (cf. Gal 2:15) before they experienced the kindness of God.

Israel can be cut in again (vv 23-24). The warning to Gentile believers concluded, the allegory ends on a positive note that returns to the major theme of the passage: the hope of salvation for all Israel. What has brought about Israel's present undoing is lack of faith *(apistia)*—her "stumbling" at the gospel of the crucified Messiah (9:31-33). In the sight and plan of God, however, what ultimately matters is not original lack of faith but *persistence* in it. If "they" *(kakeinoi)* do not "remain" (*epimenousin*; cf. v 22d) in their unbelief, they will be "grafted in" *(egkentristhēsontai)* again. At this point the argument goes well beyond the limits of the allegory strictly conceived, since the normal thing is that branches broken off are left to wither and die; it would be highly unusual—and humanly impossible—to graft them back on after any period of time. For Paul, however, it is all a matter of the capacity of God. The God, whom he has already characterized, with respect to Christian believing, as the One who "gives life to the dead and calls into being things (not existing) as though they were" (4:17b), is the God who is perfectly "capable" (*dynatos*; cf. 4:21) of grafting them in again—even if this should involve revivifying branches that had been cast off, apparently to die.

In support of this Paul adds (v 24) a final consideration based on the continuing "much more" (here *posǭ mallon*) logic. The fact that God has already achieved the harder case: grafting in, "contrary to nature" *(para physin)*, branches that belonged "by nature" *(kata physin)* to the wild olive, holds out good hope of success in the easier case: the grafting in of branches that did belong "by nature" to the original stock and so can be grafted in to "their own proper olive" *(tę̄ idią elaią)*.

In this way, Paul presents the inclusion of the Gentiles as both the hope-giving precedent and the paradigm for the "re-inclusion" of Israel. Just as he himself and fellow Jewish-Christians found justification by accepting in faith that they stood in a "Gentile-like" state of sinfulness and need before God (Rom 3:10–4:25; cf. Gal 2:15-16), so once more the final salvation of Israel rests upon God's dealing with her on the pattern already established for the Gentiles. To this extent the "priority" of Israel (cf. 1:16; 2:9-10) has been reversed. At the same time, however, Paul makes abundantly clear the abiding "holiness" that attaches to Israel even in her "stumbling" because of her "natural" linkage with the sanctified "root" (the "fathers"). While the mode of inclusion of Gentile believers—by grace and "kindness"—may be paradigmatic for all, they will always constitute a "wild stock" *added* to Israel. Their salvation is part of a total salvation embracing the entire "tree." Far from any "replacement" view of Christianity with respect to Judaism, Paul cannot think of the salvation of believers apart from the restoration of the original stock. Salvation is always the salvation of "all Israel" (v 26).

NOTES

11. *have they stumbled so as to fall?:* The two verbs *ptaiein* and *piptein* overlap in the sense of "fall" but the formulation of the question clearly implies a distinction between them at this point, with the second referring to a "falling" that is irreversible (contrast v 22 where the same verb in the participial form *pesontas* obviously does not designate those who have fallen irrevocably). Likewise, behind the conjunction *hina* must lie the sense of divine intention. The question then means: when God allowed them—or, perhaps more accurately, "made" them—to stumble, was it the divine intention to bring them to everlasting ruin?

    By no means!: On Paul's use of *mē genoito*, see Note on 3:4.

    through their trespass: The dative *paraptōmati* is instrumental. The literal, etymological meaning of *paraptōma* is that of "false step" or "trip" and, in the light of the description of Israel's failure as a "stumbling" in 9:32-33, it is natural to read the literal meaning here. Elsewhere, however, Paul always uses *paraptōma* in a metaphorical sense to indicate concrete transgression (cf. 4:25; 5:15-18, 20; 2 Cor 5:19; Gal 6:1). The derived, ethical nuance can hardly be excluded here. The translation "trespass" attempts to hold both aspects together.

    salvation has come to the Gentiles: The Greek lacks any verb which might give a time reference to *sōtēria*. Normally Paul refers "salvation" to the final eschatological deliverance but occasionally it can designate present anticipations of this, such as the gift of the Spirit (cf. esp. 8:23). Here, since Gentiles have already been set on the path to salvation, the broad sweep of both present anticipation and final consummation is likely to be in view. Hence the translation "has come."

    so as to make them jealous: The prepositional infinitive construction clearly indicates the divine intention and hence the fulfillment of the declaration of Deut 32:21 cited in 10:19.

12. *Now if their trespass means riches for the world:* For the description of "salvation" in terms of "richness," cf. esp. 2 Cor 8:9 where, on an "interchange" pattern, Christ, who was "rich" in his divine life with God (cf. Phil 2:6), became "poor"

for our sakes, so that we might become "rich" through his "poverty"; cf. also Rom 9:23; 10:12; Phil 4:19. "World" *(kosmos)* here, as in 3:6, means the human population of the world apart from Israel, as the parallel with "Gentiles" *(ethnōn)* shows.

their failure: The word *hēttēma* has the sense of "defeat" in its two other occurrences in biblical Greek (LXX Isa 31:8; 1 Cor 6:7). Here the contrast with *plērōma* suggests that the idea of "diminution" is also in view; cf. 9:27-29.

much more: On Paul's use of the "much more" logic, see Note on 5:9.

their fullness: The word *plērōma* is open to a wide range of meaning: 1. (actively) "that which fills or makes complete," "the final part"; 2. (passively) "that which is filled or completed" or "the sum total" or "state of being full"; 3. (the process) "the fulfilling." The context (cf. *pas Israel,* v 26) suggests that numerical completeness is principally in view here.

13. *Now I am speaking to you Gentiles:* From the outset of this section of the letter (9:1), Paul has consistently referred to the Jews in the third person ("they"). At this point he again makes explicit the fact that his address is principally to Gentile believers; cf. 1:5, 13. The sense is: "I am speaking to you precisely as Gentiles."

Inasmuch as I am an apostle to the Gentiles: The opening phrase *(eph' hoson men oun)* lends the sense of, "Contrary to what you might think *(men oun),* it is precisely as *(eph' hoson)* apostle to the Gentiles that I (have a concern for the Jews and hence) magnify. . . ." On Paul's sense of his specific apostolic charism, see Interpretation of 1:1 and 1:5.

I magnify my ministry: The verb *doxazein,* elsewhere used more theologically of human praise of God (cf. 1:21; 15:9), would here seem to reflect the more basic sense of the Greek word *doxa*—the opinion or repute one has in the eyes of another. Paul means, then, that he actively promotes amongst Jews knowledge of the success of his ministry among the Gentiles—as part of the "provocation to jealousy" motif. *Diakonia* here has its usual sense in Paul: the apostolic "service" of the gospel; see Note on 12:7. On the collection for the "saints," see Interpretation of 15:25.

14. *my fellow Jews:* Literally, according to Hebrew idiom, "my flesh." Paul now sees himself as an instrument of the divine intent (cf. 10:19; 11:11) to make Israel jealous.

saving some of them: As in the case of "salvation" in v 11, "save" here includes not only final salvation but also the process of conversion paving the way for it. Paul's mission is not the conversion of "all Israel" (cf. vv 25-32) but of some individual Israelites as a preliminary to that.

15. *For if their rejection has meant reconciliation for the world, what will their acceptance mean:* The reference to "reconciliation" *(katallagē)* here (cf. esp. 5:10-11; 2 Cor 5:18-21) ensures that the focus lies upon the action of God, rather than on the response of Israel (as in v 12). Hence "rejection" *(apobolē)* refers to God's (temporary) hardening of unbelieving Israel and "acceptance" *(proslēmpsis)* to God's final acceptance of them when that period has come to an end.

life from the dead: This phrase *(zōē ek nekrōn)* is sometimes understood figuratively. But the fact that the "life" follows upon rather than precedes the "acceptance" of Israel suggests an eschatological reference—the general resurrection as a prelude to the final consummation.

16. *If the dough offered as first fruits is holy, so is the whole lump; and if the root is holy, so are the branches:* The echoes in the Greek of the phrase *aparchēn phyramatos* appearing twice in LXX Num 15:20-21 ensures that the first part of this double statement alludes to the rite described in that passage; cf. also Philo, *Sac.* 107–08; *Spec.* 1.132; Josephus, *Ant.* 4.71. "First fruits" *(aparchē)* here is often taken as a reference to the Jewish-Christian "remnant." But the parallel with "root" *(riza)* in the following phrase, which all agree must refer to the patriarchs, suggests that the latter are in mind in the first case as well (cf. also v 28; *1 Enoch* 93:8). On the Jewish background to the images ("dough," "plant," "olive") Paul uses here, see the study of K. H. Rengstorf cited in Reference.

17. *you, a wild olive, have been grafted in:* Paul uses the technical term *(engkentrizein)* for grafting. The practice of grafting shoots from a wild olive onto a cultivated olive in order to rejuvenate the latter is attested in the ancient horticultural writer Columella, a contemporary of Paul (*De re rustica* 5.9.16–17; 5.11.1–15). This means that the long-standing charge against Paul that he (as a city-dweller) displays ignorance of horticultural procedure should at last be laid to rest; see esp. the study of A. G. Baxter and J. A. Ziesler cited in Reference. The same scholars also see Paul's image as containing the idea that the inclusion of the Gentiles will lead to the rejuvenation of Israel. But this would undermine the later contention (v 18) that "it is not you that support the root, but the root that supports you."

among them: That is, among the branches remaining—the Jewish-Christian "remnant."

sharers in the richness stemming from the root of the olive tree: The translation attempts to convey what is suggested by Paul's overladen genitive construction: *sygkoinos tēs rizēs tēs piotētos tēs elaias.* The first genitive *(rizēs)* follows after *sygkoinos* (cf. 1 Cor 9:23; Phil 1:7); the second is open to either a qualitative ("fat root") or appositional ("in the root, that is, in its fatness") sense; the translation adopts the latter. Within the image, the "root" would signify the patriarchs (see Note on v 16). The "fatness" ("richness") flowing from them would then be the blessings of salvation promised to them "and to their descendants."

18. *do not boast over the branches:* The prefix *kata* in the verb *katakauchāsthai* (elsewhere in the NT only Jas 2:13; 3:14) adds to the basic idea of "boasting" (which, of course, has featured extensively in the earlier part of the letter: see esp. 2:17-24; 3:27; 4:2) the sense of "competitive superiority" (Dunn 2.661–62). It is not clear whether "branches" refers to Jews who have not accepted the gospel (that is, branches broken off) or the Jewish-Christian believing remnant or both. The "some" in v 17 suggests the more inclusive reference.

If you do boast, remember that it is not you that support the root: The translation tries to bring out the sense of Paul's eliptical conditional sentence: logically it runs, "If you do boast (which you should not), you must remember that . . . (and so abandon your unfounded boast)"; cf. 1 Cor 11:16 and see BDF §483.

19. *You may well say:* This phrase *(ereis oun)* is a diatribal way of allowing an objection; cf. 9:19.

Branches were broken off so that I might be grafted in: The Greek word order, placing the stress on the aspect of "breaking off," conveys the sense that the breaking off is irreversible. This is precisely what Paul is going to contest.

20. *True enough:* The diatribe-style expression *kalōs* admits the element of factual truth in the objection. But Paul goes on to expose it as a dangerous, self-centered half-truth. It looks at the breaking-off only from the aspect of the branches grafted in, failing to consider that God may have a further plan in regard to the broken-off branches.

They were broken off because of their lack of faith, but you stand fast only through faith: The translation takes the first dative *(apistią)* as causal, the second *(pistei)* as instrumental. The perfect tense of the second verb *hestēkas* lends the sense of a continuing state ("standing") brought about by an initial act ("believing"). For this sense of "standing" in the faith in Paul, cf. also 1 Cor 15:1-2; 2 Cor 1:24.

So do not harbor proud thoughts, but fear: Having proud thoughts over against other human beings (cf. v 18) implies also arrogance before God. The opposite of this is appropriate "fear" of God, something which Paul, for all his stress upon the sure hope of salvation (cf. esp. 5:1-11; 8:18-39), still sees as part of Christian life: see esp. Phil 2:12: ("work out your salvation with fear and trembling"); 2 Cor 5:9-11; also 7:1.

21. *if God did not spare:* The continuing image lends to "not spare" here the concrete sense of "break off."

the natural branches: The phrase *kata physin,* here translated "natural," was used widely to denote the Stoic sense of life, development or action in accordance with the innate or established order of things; see further the Notes on 1:26 and 2:14. Here, as also in its two occurrences in v 24, it refers to the branches' relatedness to the tree stock from which they have been cut, not to the grafting process (though the latter *is* the reference in the case of *para physin* in the central phrase of v 24).

neither will he spare you: The translation omits a textual variant (P^{46} א) reading *mē pōs* ("perhaps") before this clause; it probably represents an addition, softening the severity of Paul's categorical threat.

22. *the kindness and the severity of God:* On "kindness" *(chrēstotēs),* see Note on 2:4. "Severity" *(apotomia)* occurs only here in the NT. Only the correlative adjectival and adverbial forms appear in the LXX, all in Wisdom (5:20, 22; 6:5; 11:10; 12:9; 18:15). The basic sense is that of unflinching adherence to norms or judgments.

those who have fallen: Appearing here in opposition to "stand" in v 20, the verb *piptein (pesontas)* does not have the final, irrevocable sense that it has in v 11. The reference is, of course, specifically to Jews who have "fallen" in the sense of not believing in the gospel (9:31-33); Paul is not formulating a principle according to which God would be habitually "severe" towards the "fallen" in general.

24. *contrary to nature:* As noted above with respect to v 21, the phrase *kata physin* occurring twice in this verse refers to the branches' mode of belonging to the tree, whereas the phrase *para physin* ("contrary to nature") occurring between them refers to the "unnaturalness" of the process. With respect to the latter, cf. the apt comment of Baxter and Ziesler: "Paul calls it *para physin,* not because it does not and cannot happen, but because it is interfering with nature" ("Paul and Arboriculture" 29).

For Reference and Further Study

Baxter, A. G. and Ziesler, J. A. "Paul and Arboriculture: Romans 11:17-24." *JSNT* 24 (1985) 25–32.

Bell, R. H. *Provoked to Jealousy* 108–25.

Davies, W. D. "Paul and the Gentiles: A Suggestion Concerning Romans 11:13-24." *Jewish and Pauline Studies*. Philadelphia: Fortress, 1984, 153–63.

Munck, J. *Christ and Israel* 116–31.

Rengstorf, K. H. "Das Ölbaum-Gleichnis in Röm 11:16ff." *Donum Gentilicium* (FS D. Daube). Ed. E. Bammel et al. Oxford: Clarendon, 1978, 127–64.

Riggans, W. "Romans 11:17-21." *ExpTim* 98 (1986–87) 205–06.

Wright, N. T. *Climax of the Covenant* 246–49.

Zeller, D. *Juden und Heiden* 215–18, 238–44.

c) *The "Mystery": the Final Salvation of "All Israel"* (11:25-32)

25. For I do not want you to be ignorant, brothers (and sisters), concerning this mystery, lest you be wise in your own judgments,
the mystery, namely, that a hardening has come upon part of Israel, until
the full number of the Gentiles has come in, 26. and so all Israel will
be saved; as it is written, "The deliverer will come from Zion, he will
banish ungodliness from Jacob 27. and this will be my covenant with
them when I take away their sins."
28. As regards the gospel they are enemies, for your sake; but as regards
election they are beloved, because of the fathers. 29. For the gifts and the
call of God are irrevocable.
30. For just as you were once disobedient to God
but now have received mercy because of their disobedience,
31. so they have now been disobedient, in the interests of mercy for you,
in order that they also may in time receive mercy.
32. For God has imprisoned all in disobedience, in order to have mercy
upon all.

Interpretation

Introduction. The passage falls clearly into two main sections. 1. After the opening invocation, vv 25-27 consist of a basic exposition of the "mystery" concerning the ultimate salvation of Israel (vv 25-26a), followed by scriptural support (vv 26bc-27). 2. Vv 28-32, in a series of epigrammatic sentences, reflect upon the paradoxical operation of God's mercy that has reversed previous expectations concerning the priority of Israel *vis-à-vis* the Gentiles yet ultimately brings salvation to all: v 28 sets out the current situation of Israel in an antithetical couplet; v 29 offers a grounding for this in the faithfulness of God; vv 30-31 repeat the basic thesis in a tightly rhetorical compound sentence; v 32 offers a further grounding in terms of the "inclusive" operation of God's mercy.

The "Mystery" (vv 25-26a). Paul now brings his reflection upon the fate of Israel to a climax. Still directing his address to Gentile Christians (cf. v 13), he underlines the solemnity of his conclusion by the invocation, "I do not want you to be ignorant, brothers (and sisters)," last used in the Introduction to the letter (1:13). What he is now about to proclaim does not really break new ground upon his earlier reflections, which have clearly suggested the ultimate salvation of Israel (11:11-12, 15, 23-24). Rather, it gathers what has already been expressed under the over-arching rubric of what is termed "this mystery" *(mystērion touto).*

"Mystery" conveys the sense that the vision of Israel's future Paul is about to project forms part of privileged revelation concerning the events of the End. It is not something accessible to or derivable from mere human reflection upon what might be the case. This is why the audience must be warned against being "wise in (their) own judgments"; human thinking by itself is totally inadequate to grasp what God has in store (cf. esp. 1 Cor 1:18-25; 2:6-16) and may well lead to the misguided conclusion that God has in fact written off Israel. At the same time, Paul's appeal to "mystery" does not necessarily imply that he has knowledge of the fate of Israel through direct personal inspiration of an esoteric kind. The argument derives from scripture and a conviction concerning the faithfulness of God.

The "content" (cf. *hoti*) of the "mystery" has to do with "when" and "how" Israel will find salvation. More precisely, the mystery concerns the circumstances or conditions that must run their course before the climactic event occurs: a substantial portion of Israel (*apo merous*; see Note) will undergo a period of "hardening" *(pōrōsis)*; this period will endure until *(achris hou)* the full number of the Gentiles "enters in" *(eiselthę̄)*; then, and only then, will "all Israel" *(pas Israēl)* be saved. What has to be appreciated here is the reversal this implies for traditional Jewish expectation. The reference to the "entering in" of the full number of the Gentiles probably alludes to the traditional motif of the eschatological pilgrimage of the nations to Zion (Isa 2:2-3; 56:6-7; 60:3-14; Mic 4:1-2; Zech 14:16-17; Tob 13:11 (B); 14:6-7 (B); *Pss. Sol.* 17:31, 34; 2 *Apoc. Bar.* 68:5; *Test. Benj.* 9:2; *Sib. Or.* 3:772). In the conventional understanding Gentiles come very much as secondary participants in privileges belonging with clear priority, to Israel. As Paul presents the operation of the "mystery," this priority is radically reversed. Those members of Israel who have been "hardened" must wait "outside," as it were, watching the Gentiles "enter in" (cf. Matt 21:31b), entering in themselves only when the full number *(plērōma)* of the latter is complete. Paul unhesitatingly affirms (v 26a) that "all Israel" *(pas Israēl)* will find salvation *(sōthēsetai)*, meaning by "all Israel" ethnic Israel constituted once again in its totality when the unbelieving majority is joined once again to the presently believing (Jewish-Christian) "remnant" (see Note). But the main point of the mystery is to assert that it will be "thus" *(houtōs)*: that is, with this paradoxical reversal of priority with respect to the bulk of Israel and only after a time of "hardening."

Scripture's testimony to the operation of the "Mystery" (vv 26b-27). This "mystery" Paul finds foretold in scripture. To be more exact, he finds in a composite text made up of Isa 59:20-21a (vv 26bc-27a) and part of Isa 27:9 (v 27b) not only a pledge of Israel's salvation but an indication of how (cf. *kai houtōs*, v 26a) it will be achieved. The two texts are combined on the basis that both feature the motif of the removal of sin from Israel (Jacob), a removal to be accomplished by a "deliverer" *(ho rhyomenos)* who "will come from Zion" *(hēxei ek Sion)*. In the original text of Isa 59:20-21 "the deliverer" is God. Paul, however, almost certainly intends a reference to Christ (cf. 1 Thess 1:10: *Iēsoun ton rhyomenon*): Isaiah foresaw that one to come "from Zion" (Israel's Davidic Messiah; 1:3; 9:5; 15:8) would "deliver" Israel by acting as God's agent for the removal of "ungodliness" *(asebeia)* from Jacob.

The third and fourth lines of the composite quotation (v 27) present this removal of sin as God's fulfillment of the divine "covenant" *(diathēkē)* with Israel. That is, scripture foresaw and announced that the discharging of the divine covenant obligation to Israel will consist principally in the removal of sin, the necessary and sufficient process for Israel's attainment of final salvation. Earlier in the letter (2:1–3:20) Paul had charged that Israel was locked in a common bind of sinfulness with the Gentile world and so stood equally in need of the gift of righteousness offered by God in the crucified Messiah. Clinging to a pursuit of their own righteousness (through "works of law"), the bulk of Israel "stumbled" at that offer (9:31-33; 10:3) and underwent the "hardening" that has opened up salvation to the Gentiles. Paul adduces the Isaiah quotation as a divine pledge that the hardening will not be final. God's covenant fidelity will ensure that Israel herself will arrive at the salvation that has already gone out from her ("from Zion") to the Gentiles. At the same time, however, the text makes clear that Israel's salvation will come about on the same basis as has applied in the case of Gentile believers and the Jewish-Christian "remnant." Israel must own the truth, against which she has up till now been resistant ("hardened"): that she is part of the common sinful mass of humankind (2:1–3:20; 3:23) and can find salvation through faith in the God who "justifies the ungodly" (4:5-8) in the expiatory death of Christ (3:24-26; cf. Gal 2:16). (For the alternative, "*theo*logical" interpretation of the process of Israel's salvation, see Note on v 26.)

The irrevocable character of God's gifts (vv 28-29). In conclusion (vv 28-32), Paul offers a series of reflections upon the mysterious and paradoxical operation of God's mercy that has so drastically reversed previous expectations of the priority of Israel *vis-à-vis* the Gentiles. Each element displays a balanced rhetorical structure, couched in the antithetical pattern of which Paul is so fond.

First (v 28) comes a couplet stating two contrasting things about the bulk of Israel. With respect to the requirements of the preaching of the gospel *(kata . . . to euangelion)* and for the benefit of "you" (Gentiles), "they" are "enemies" *(echthroi).* But, on the basis of God's election *(kat' eklogēn)* and with respect to "the fathers" (the patriarchs), they remain "beloved" *(agapētoi).* As far as purely formal considerations go, there is a very strict correspondence between each element of the antithetical couplet. But the formal correspondence, designed for rhetorical effect, does not mean that each formally similar phrase bears equal weight. Israel's present "enmity" is not part of the content of the gospel. God has fixed (cf. *pōrōsis,* v 25) Israel in this state of alienation to bring the Gentiles *(di' hymas)* within the scope of the salvation proclaimed in the gospel. But before, beyond and ultimately overriding this present hostility is Israel's election by God. This election was first manifested to and received by "the fathers." But the grace that came personally to them represented in effect an election of the entire people, abiding beyond their own personal history and resting not on their response but solely upon divine grace. Thus, whatever her present behavior, on the basis of this election Israel remains "beloved because of the fathers."

What is said here concerning ethnic Israel stands, at first sight, in considerable tension with 9:6-8, where Paul appears to drive a wedge between Israel ethnically considered ("according to the flesh") and the eschatological people God intended to call into being as "children of the promise." The tension is resolved, however, when one notes that in both cases the stress is upon God's freedom of choice set over against merely human considerations. Ethnic Israel has no claim on God based simply on physical descent from Abraham or human behavior (9:12, 16). But ethnic Israel remains "beloved" of God because of *God's* original choice and *God's* fidelity. In this sense, Paul can boldly assert, in the following supportive sentence (v 29), that God's "gifts of grace" *(charismata)* to Israel (presumably, the privileges listed in 9:4-5) and "calling" (the creative summons to be eternally the people of God) are "irrevocable." Paul is quite prepared to concede an abiding special status to Israel, providing the "specialness" rests entirely upon God.

The inclusive operation of God's mercy (vv 30-32). A hope, then, attaches uniquely to Israel. But its coming into operation will follow the pattern of grace and mercy that has already been operative in the case of the Gentiles. As Paul has long since made clear (3:29-30), the one God of Jews and Gentiles does not operate in two different modes with respect to Israel and the rest of humankind. Always and in every particular, God remains the God of grace, grace which "superabounds" precisely where sin has "abounded" (5:20b). This "parity" in the experience of grace and mercy Paul now (vv 30-31) expounds, in a highly symmetrical composite sentence, which memorably contains and brings out all the factors involved. It will help to set it out in a way that shows the formality of the construction in the Greek original:

Protasis ("You" [Gentiles]): For just as you were ONCE *disobedient* to God
but NOW have *received mercy*
because of their *disobedience,*
Apodosis ("They" [Israel]): so they have NOW been *disobedient,*
in the interests of *mercy* for you,
in order that they also may IN TIME *receive mercy.*

Protasis "You" (Gentiles)
[A] once disobedient
[B] now mercy . . . their disobedience
Apodosis "They" (Israel)
[B′] now disobedient . . . mercy for you
[A′] in time mercy

It will be seen that, without being strictly a conditional sentence, the total sentence has the protasis-apodosis structure that builds up the case for the similarity and interconnection between the experience of Gentiles and Israel, while indicating the reversal as regards temporal priority. The protasis (v 30) basically concerns the Gentiles, though it mentions at the end "their (= Israel's) disobedience"; the apodosis (v 31) basically concerns Israel, though, correspondingly, mentions at the end "your (= Gentiles') mercy." The addition of these phrases in the two central elements, along with the arrangement of the time indicators ("once," "now," etc.), lends a chiastic structure that cuts across and complements the basically sequential flow from protasis to apodosis. The last element (v 31b) draws attention to itself by cutting across the established pattern in that it consists of a purpose clause *(hina . . .)* stating the divine intention with respect to Israel.

If Paul himself is responsible for the construction of a literary figure of such rhetorical complexity, it can only be because of the extent and depth of his reflections upon the issue which is its subject: the similarity, interconnection and mysterious time-reversal of what the two parties—Israel and the Gentiles—had experienced (were to experience) according to his understanding of the gospel. Before their conversion, Gentile believers were ("once") in a state of radical "disobedience" to God (cf. 1:18-32; cf. Gal 2:15). They have "now" received mercy (cf. 3:21-26) following upon and in the circumstances of Jewish "disobedience" with respect to the gospel (*tę̄ toutōn apeitheią*; cf. esp. 9:31-33). The situation "now" is that "they" (the Jews) are disobedient, while the Gentiles are experiencing mercy. But all this is so that ultimately ("in time"; see Note) they too may share the experience of God's mercy, which has already come upon the Gentiles.

All is then summed up in a concluding explanatory sentence (v 32) giving perfect expression to Paul's "inclusive" vision of the gospel. God, wishing to relate to the human world as a God of grace and mercy (cf. 4:5; 9:16; 11:6), "imprisoned" *(synekleisen)* "all" within a common bind of disobedience (3:9, 23). The "all" *(tous pantas)* that appears twice in this sentence resumes the universalistic note that has run throughout the letter (1:16, 18; 2:9-11; 3:9, 19-20, 22-23; 4:11, 16; 5:12-21; 9:24-26; 10:11-12). As in the case of these other references, Paul does not have primarily in view all human beings taken in an individual sense; the sense is communal: "all—that is, Jews as well as Gentiles." Previously (chapters 1–8), the universalistic note served chiefly to underline the "inclusion" of the Gentiles; now (chapters 9–11) it sounds again with particular respect to Israel. The God who has exercised "inclusive" mercy upon the disobedient Gentiles will equally draw disobedient Israel within the same scope of "inclusive" mercy. The wheel that began turning at 1:18 has now come full circle. God's "word" to Israel (9:6a) has not "fallen through" (9:6b). The gospel remains the "power of God leading to salvation for *all* believers" because it reveals and makes available to all the saving righteousness of God (1:16-17).

Notes

25. *For I do not want you to be ignorant, brothers (and sisters):* On this emphatic invocation, see Note on 1:13.

this mystery: Whereas in Greek literature the term *mystērion* appears in connection with the secret teaching of the mystery cults, Paul's usage reflects that of late-biblical (Dan 2:18-30, 47) and post-biblical Jewish apocalyptic literature (*1 Enoch* 16:3; 41:1; 46:2; 103:2; 104:10, 12-13; 106:19; *2 Enoch* 24:3; *4 Ezra* 10:38; 12:36-39; *2 Apoc. Bar*. 48:3; 81:4; 1QS 3:23; 4:18; 9:18; 11:3-5, 19; 1QH 2:13; 4:27-28; 7:27; 11:10; 12:13; 1QpHab 7:1-5, 8-14; 1Q27[1QMyst] 1:3-4), where "mystery" has reference to God's eternally conceived but hidden design for the final consummation; access to the divine "mystery" in this sense is given, by various means (revelations, heavenly transports, etc.), to privileged persons (seer, prophets), who receive them on behalf of the faithful community for its comfort and assurance in the trials preceding the end. See further Paul's instruction concerning the final transformation in 1 Cor 15:51; cf. also 1 Cor 2:7; 4:1; 13:2; 14:2; 2 Thess 2:7. In (the deutero-Pauline) Colossians and Ephesians the Pauline usage has developed into virtually a technical term to express what God has accomplished in Jesus Christ; cf. also 1 Tim 3:9, 16; Rom 16:25 (deutero-Pauline).

a hardening has come upon part of Israel: For the background to Paul's concept of "hardening," see Note on v 7 *(epōrōthēsan)*. The translation sees the Greek phrase *apo merous* ("partly") as modifying the verb *gegonen* in a quantitative sense, so as to indicate that not all Israel was subject to hardening; cf. vv 5, 7, 17. One could relate it to *pōrōsis*, so as to give "a partial hardening." But this introduces something which is not in the context, whereas the notion of quantitative limitation certainly is.

until the full number of the Gentiles has come in: On the term *plērōma* see Note on v 12. Here the sense is that which, being added, makes that to which it has been added complete. When all the Gentiles yet to be won for the gospel are added to the number who presently believe, then "the full number" of the Gentiles will be complete. Paul is thinking globally; he does not necessarily mean every individual Gentile.

26a. *and so:* The phrase "and so" *(kai houtōs)* bears the stress and has both a temporal ("when") and a modal ("how") sense: "Israel *will* be saved, but at *this* time (after the "full entrance" of the Gentiles) and in *this* way (from out of and subsequent to a situation of "hardening").

all Israel: A widespread early (i.e., Patristic) interpretation of this phrase referred it to the totality of believers, Jewish and Christian. But this flies in the face of the clear meaning of "Israel" in v 25 and is generally rejected today in favor of a reference to the whole of ethnic Israel; cf. the corresponding mention of the "fullness of the Gentiles" (v 25). The reference, however, is communal. Paul is not necessarily asserting that each and every individual Israelite will find salvation.

will be saved: As generally in Paul, "saved" has the eschatological sense of rescue from condemnation at the final judgment and entrance into eternal life (see Interpretation of 1:16). In recent years, especially in the context of Jewish-Christian dialogue, the absence of any reference to Christ in the context (not since 10:13) has led to a "theological"—as distinct from a "christological"—interpretation of this text in the sense that the "salvation" of the Jewish majority who have not accepted the gospel will come about simply through the power of God without their being required to come to faith in Jesus Christ. Despite its obvious advantages in terms of Jewish-Christian relations, the positing of this "special way" (German: *Sonderweg*) for Israel has to be rejected as a viable understanding of Paul. The following scriptural quotation, in its centering upon the removal of sin, makes clear that Israel will find salvation through a conversion involving the kind of repentance that present believers (Gentile and Jewish-Christian) have already undergone in their coming to faith in Christ (3:21–4:25; Gal 2:15-16). It is also evident from v 23 of the present chapter that it is Israel's persistence in "unbelief" *(apistia)* that prevents her being "regrafted" back into the basic stock; the implication is that she will come to salvation when she finds *pistis*. But this *pistis* must be specifically faith in Christ (or in the God who acts in Christ) since Paul has already conceded that Israel has faith (literally, "zeal") in God (10:2) but such (simply "theological") faith is not leading to salvation. To imply that Paul has two concepts of justifying "faith" and thus two ways to salvation stands at odds with his insistence upon the unitary dealings of the "one" God with the human race in 3:29-30. For scholarly literature representative of either side of the debate, see Reference.

26b–27. *"The deliverer will come from Zion, he will banish ungodliness from Jacob and this will be my covenant with them when I take away their sins":* The first three elements of the quotation agree exactly with LXX Isa 59:20-21, save for *ek* before "Zion" (in place of *heneken*) and the omission of a conjunction *(kai)* before the second verb. The final element comes from part of Isa 27:9, with "his sin" in the original made plural: "their sins." Granted that the "deliverer" is Christ, many interpreters relate the future reference in the prophecy ("will come") to the moment of his eschatological return (*parousia;* cf. 1 Thess 1:10): that is, when the Gentiles have "entered in," as a prelude to the final consummation, Christ will "work" a final reconciliation of Israel. The problem then is how to relate this future function of the glorious Christ to his original expiatory work upon the cross, which is the proper object of believers' faith (Rom 3:21-26), the same faith which, it seems (see previous Note), Israel must eventually come to share. It is much simpler to see Paul understanding the prophecy as speaking out of its proper time reference, pointing to a "coming" (of a "deliverer") which for Isaiah lies in the future but which for Paul has already been realized in the original appearance and saving work of Christ. Paul cites the prophecy as a pledge that, some time before the End (cf. 11:15), Israel will eventually find salvation. But his presentation of the "mystery" does not further specify that this will be by some mass reconciliation at the parousia quite other than the way the rest of the world comes to faith.

28. *As regards the gospel they are enemies, for your sake; but as regards election they are beloved, because of the fathers:* Rather than implying that the "enmity" of Israel is part of the gospel, the preposition *kata* in the opening phrase (*kata to euangelion*) can be taken in the looser sense of "as regards what has been required for the spread of the gospel (to the Gentiles)." Likewise, the two prepositional (*dia* + accusative) phrases concluding each line, while both basically causal, do not have precisely the same meaning: the first has a forward-looking

causal sense ("for your advantage"); the second looks backward ("because of the promises God made to the fathers"). As regards "enemies" (*echthroi*), the parallelism with the clearly passive "beloved" in the second half of the verse might suggest a corresponding passive sense: "regarded as hostile" (by God; cf. esp. 9:13, 18). However, elsewhere in Paul the motif of "enmity" has an active sense: 5:10; 8:7; 12:20; 1 Cor 15:25-26; Gal 4:16; 5:20; Phil 3:18; cf. also 1 Thess 2:15-16 (though how far this reference to the hostility of the Jews of Judea ought be generalized is a matter for discussion).

29. *For the gifts and the call of God are irrevocable:* The adjective *ametamelēta* has the initial position of stress in the Greek and literally means "unregretted"; cf. esp. 2 Cor 7:10 (the only other occurrence in biblical Greek). For the Pauline sense of *charisma* as a concrete instance of grace, see Interpretation and Note on 1:11. The noun *klēsis* occurs only here in Romans but is clearly connected with the sense of God's "calling" expressed in verbal forms: 4:17; 8:28, 30; 9:7, 12, 24-26. For Paul, "calling" relates to the coming into being of God's people and to membership of that people (cf. esp. 1 Cor 1:26; 7:17-24); see Note on 8:30.

30. *because of their disobedience:* The translation takes the phrase (*tę̄ toutōn apeitheią*) as a dative of cause (BDF §196); cf. 11:11.

31. *in the interests of mercy for you:* Some interpreters understand this phrase in a causal sense and include it, at least as far as meaning is concerned, within the following purpose clause: "so that they too may now be shown mercy as a result of the mercy shown to you" (Fitzmyer 627–28; cf. Cranfield 2:583-85). But this distorts the carefully crafted formal structure of the sentence and is not required by the sense, provided that the phrase in question (*tǭ hymeterǭ eleei*) be understood as a dative of advantage, rather than as a causal dative, as *is* the case with the corresponding phrase in v 30.

   in time: The sense seems to require some such translation of the Greek adverb *nyn* (lit. "now"), which is, in fact, wanting in several major text witnesses (P^{46} A D, etc.). The difficulty of relating an original *nyn*, understood strictly as "now," to the future showing of mercy to Israel could have worked for its omission from the textual tradition.

32. *For God has imprisoned all in disobedience, in order to have mercy upon all:* The sentence has a striking parallel in Gal 3:22: "But scripture imprisoned all (*ta panta*) under sin (*hypo hamartian*; cf. Rom 3:9) in order that the promise might be given through faith in Christ to all believers."

For Reference and Further Study

Aletti, J.-N. *Comment Dieu est-il juste?* 179–99.

Aus, R. D. "Paul's Travel Plans to Spain and the 'Full Number of the Gentiles' of Rom. XI 25." *NovT* 21 (1979) 232–62.

Bell, R. H. *Provoked to Jealousy* 126–53.

Brown, R. E. *The Semitic Background of the Term "Mystery" in the New Testament.* Facet Books, Biblical Series. Philadelphia: Fortress, 1968.

Getty, M. A. "Paul and the Salvation of Israel: A Perspective on Romans 9–11." *CBQ* 50 (1988) 456–69.

Harrington, D. J. *Paul on the Mystery of Israel.* Zaccheus Studies; Collegeville: The Liturgical Press, 1992.

Hofius, O. "All Israel Will Be Saved": Divine Salvation and Israel's Deliverance in Romans 9–11." *The Church and Israel. PSBSup* 1 (1990) 19–39.

Lohfink, N. *The Covenant Never Revoked: Biblical Reflections on Jewish-Christian Dialogue.* New York: Paulist, 1991, 58–82.

Munck, J. *Christ and Israel* 131–41.

Refoulé, F. *". . . Et ainsi tout Israël sera sauvé": Romains 11,25-32.* LD 117; Paris: Cerf, 1984.

Rese, M. "Die Rettung der Juden nach Römer 11." *L'Apôtre Paul* (Ed. A. Vanhoye) 422–30.

Stanley, C. D. "'The Redeemer Will Come *ek Siōn*': Romans 11:26-27 Revisited." *Paul and the Scriptures of Israel.* Eds. C. A. Evans & J. A. Sanders. JSNTSup 83; Sheffield: JSOT, 1993, 118–42.

Stowers, S. K. *Rereading of Romans* 312–16.

Zeller, D. *Juden und Heiden* 129–37, 245–67.

The Interpretation of 11:25-26

["Theological"]

Gager, J. *The Origins of Anti-Semitism: Attitudes Towards Judaism in Pagan and Christian Antiquity.* Oxford and New York: Oxford University, 1983, 252, 261–65.

Gaston, L. "Israel's Misstep in the Eyes of Paul." *Paul and the Torah* 135–50, esp. 147–48.

Mussner, H. "'Ganz Israel wird gerettet werden,' (Röm 11:26) Versuch einer Auslegung." *Kairos* 18 (1976) 241–55.

__________. *Tractate on the Jews: The Significance of Judaism for Christian Faith.* London: SPCK; Philadelphia: Fortress, 1984.

Stendahl, K. *Paul among Jews and Gentiles* 3–4.

["Christological"]

Davies, W. D. "Paul and the People of Israel." *Jewish and Pauline Studies.* Philadelphia: Fortress, 1984, 123–52, esp. 140–43.

Hahn, F. "Zum Verständnis von Römer 11:26a: '. . . und so wird ganz Israel gerettet werden.'" *Paul and Paulinism* (FS C. K. Barrett). Eds. M. D. Hooker & S. G. Wilson. London: SPCK, 1982, 221–36.

Holtz, T. "The Judgment on the Jews and the Salvation of All Israel: 1 Thes 2,15-16 and Rom 11,25-26." *The Thessalonian Correspondence.* Ed. R. Collins; BETL 87; Leuven: Leuven University, 1990, 284–94.

Hvalvik, R. "A 'Sonderweg' for Israel: A Critical Examination of a Current Interpretation of Romans 11.25–27." *JSNT* 38 (1990) 87–107.

Sanders, E. P. *Paul, the Law and the Jewish People* 192–98, esp. 194–95, 205, n. 88.

v. Hymn to God's Inscrutable Wisdom (11:33-36)

33. O the depth of the riches and wisdom and knowledge of God!
How unsearchable are his judgments, and how inscrutable his ways!
34. "For who has known the mind of the Lord,
or who has been his counselor?"
35. "Or who has given a gift to him in the hope of being repaid?"
36. For from him and through him and to him are all things.
To him be glory for ever. Amen.

Interpretation

Introduction. This short hymnic section forms a conclusion not merely to the handling of the problem of Israel in chapters 9–11 but to the entire presentation of the gospel up till this point. Paul began by carefully according a "priority" to Jews: the gospel is the "power of God leading to salvation for everyone who has faith—the Jew first but also the Greek" (1:16-17). But in the course of the exposition that priority had been radically reversed, at least as far as the "program" of salvation goes. God is "including" all (Jews and Gentiles) within salvation but doing so in a way that reverses and confounds conventional human (especially Jewish) expectation. Hence this concluding hymn to divine wisdom. Paul seeks to catch up his audience in an overwhelming sentiment of awe and praise, designed to absorb any lingering doubts concerning the validity of his inclusive gospel.

The passage shows its hymnic character from the start, not merely by its content, but particularly in the highly formal structure, in which a triadic pattern appears again and again. In the first place, the hymn divides into three basic units: 1. the opening exclamation (v 33); 2. the scriptural rhetorical questions (vv 34-35); 3. the concluding doxology (v 36). The first unit lauds the "depth" of three divine attributes (v 33a); the second unit asks three rhetorical questions, each of which, in reverse order, appears to address those three attributes; in the third unit, before the concluding doxology, three prepositional phrases are applied to "all things" (v 36a). The only elements standing outside this triadic pattern are the double exclamation making up the second part of v 33 and the concluding doxology (v 36b).

Within a basic "wisdom" pattern principally indebted to the Book of Job, the hymn weaves together a remarkable combination of motifs stemming from the biblical, apocalyptic and Hellenistic Jewish traditions. While the traditional nature and formal structure suggest the use of preformed material, there are no compelling grounds for denying Pauline authorship. Paul's competence in composing pieces of a highly rhetorical character is well-attested (cf. vv 30-31; 1 Cor 1:18-25; 13:1-13; etc.).

The unsearchable "depth" of God's Wisdom (v 33). The central motif of the hymn is the notion that God's "ways" are beyond the grasp of human understanding. Following a pattern reminiscent of the Book of Job (Job 28), the opening exclamation (v 33) expresses awe at the "depth" *(bathos)* of God's operation. First of all, human beings cannot plumb the depths of God's "riches" *(ploutos)*—presumably the "riches" of God's saving power (cf. 9:23; 10:12; 11:12), which through the "superabounding" of grace (5:20b) has proved capable of reversing the universal human bind in "disobedience" and sin. Secondly, there is the depth of God's "wisdom" *(sophia)*, here not so much the wisdom displayed in creation but the saving wisdom manifest in the paradoxical reversal of the "program" of salvation. The final divine attribute—God's "knowledge" *(gnōsis)*—is linked with wisdom but in Romans is also closely associated with "election" (8:29; 11:2; cf. Gal 4:9). Paul may be exclaiming at the mysterious way in which God's election of Israel has worked itself out so as to gather up the hitherto apparently "non-elect" Gentiles (cf. 9:25-26) within its scope.

The second line of this first unit (v 33b) expresses wonder at the ways in which God's wisdom has in fact worked itself out. In biblical usage, God's "judgments" *(krimata)* and "ways" *(hodoi)* frequently refer to the enactment of divine decisions. What God has done—notably the "hardening" of Israel (v 7, v 25) and inclusion of the Gentiles—will not yield to human attempts to understand. God's ways elude human probing. Otherwise, God would not be God.

Who can be God's counsellor (vv 34-35). The central unit of the hymn continues the same theme with three rhetorical questions taken from scripture—the first two (v 34) from Isa 40:13, the last (v 35) from a form of Job 41:11 (MT and LXX 41:3a) most closely corresponding to the Hebrew. The three questions respond, in reverse order, to the three divine "qualities" mentioned in the preceding unit (v 33a). Since God's "knowledge" is so deep, no one can know God's mind. No mere human can offer counsel *(symboulos . . . egeneto)* to one whose "wisdom" is so profound. Finally, to one so "rich" (in saving grace) there is no question of giving something in such a way as to place God under debt—an echo, surely, of Paul's sustained earlier insistence that justification is by grace (God) and faith alone (3:21-28; 11:6). In relation to God, human beings are always receivers; the very capacity to respond is itself a gift (cf. esp. 8:4).

Doxology (v 36). The concluding doxology flows naturally from this sense of God as "Giver" (cf. *hoti*). The three prepositional phrases bring together the sense of God's acting in creation ("from him"), redemption ("through him") and final salvation ("to him"). "All things" (*ta panta;* cf.

8:28, 32; 1 Cor 3:21b-23), that is, both the entire creation in a static sense and the dynamic sweep of events, are gathered into the one supreme purpose—the "glory of God" (v 36b). The only thing that human beings may appropriately "give" God is "glory" (cf. 4:20c). The entire kerygmatic portion of the letter (1:16–11:36) thus ends with an invitation to give to God the recognition ("glory") which it is the essence of sin to refuse (1:21-23). God's dramatic intervention in Christ (3:21-26) has overcome the blockage thrown up by human sin, creating out of all nations—Jews and Gentiles—a people united in the common glorification of God, the supreme goal of human existence (15:8-12).

Notes

33. *O the depth of the riches and wisdom and knowledge of God!:* It is best to take all three nouns in the genitive as dependent on "depth" *(bathos)*. For the metaphorical use of "depth" in a "wisdom" context, cf. 1 Cor 2:10 (the Spirit plumbing the "depths" of God); Eccl 7:24; *1 Enoch* 63:3. This is the only reference to "wisdom" in Romans; contrast 1 Corinthians, where the community's preoccupation with wisdom causes Paul to refer to it seventeen times.

    How unsearchable are his judgments, and how inscrutable his ways!: Long adjectives beginning with the *alpha* privative are a feature of Greek speculation about the nature of divinity. The first one here, "unsearchable" *(anexeraunētos)*, occurs nowhere else in the Greek Bible. The second in its basic etymological sense literally means "untrackable" (cf. Job 28:13) and occurs in the LXX of Job 5:9; 9:10; 34:24; cf. Eph 3:8. God's "judgment" *(krima)* is here used in one of the biblical senses attaching to the Hebrew *mišpāṭ* indicating "execution of judgment" (cf. Isa 26:8-9) that is, the implementation of a divine decision. For "way" in the biblical sense of "way of acting," cf. Gen 18:19; Exod 33:13; Deut 26:17; Pss 81:13; 103:7; Prov 8:22; Ezek 18:25-29.

34. *"For who has known the mind of the Lord, or who has been his counselor?":* The quotation corresponds to the first two thirds of LXX Isa 40:13 with only minor replacements and an inversion. Paul quotes the same text in 1 Cor 2:16 (with the final third added and the second [quoted here] omitted) with reference to the Spirit's capacity to plumb depths of God impervious to merely human powers of knowing.

35. *"Or who has given a gift to him in the hope of being repaid?":* The citation is not found in the LXX. It reflects to some degree the Hebrew of Job 41:3a, though in fact Paul's version comes closest to that of the Targum on Job. The verb *antapodidonai* is used here, in the passive, in a positive sense (cf. Luke 14:14; 1 Thess 3:9), in contrast to the more frequent sense of "pay back in punishment or revenge" (as in Rom 12:19). For parallels to the three rhetorical questions concerning the Godhead, see *2 Apoc. Bar.* 14:8-10; 54:12; 75:1-5; *1 Enoch* 93:11-14; 1QH 7:28.

36. *For from him and through him and to him:* This element of the formula most particularly reflects Stoic assertions about the deity, though these undoubtedly came to Paul via Hellenistic Judaism. The parallel formula cited in 1 Cor 8:6 attributes the "instrumental" functions ("through him . . .") to Christ. The lack of christological reference here is of a piece with the general pattern of chapter 11 and, more generally, reflects Paul's tendency always to "order" Christ and his work to the ultimate glory of God: cf. esp. Phil 2:11; 1 Cor 15:24-28.

    To him be glory for ever. Amen: For similar doxologies elsewhere in Paul, see 1:25; 9:5; Gal 1:15; Phil 4:20; cf. Rom 16:27. Note also the hope expressed in doxological terms in the prayer later in Romans (15:6) that "together and with one voice you (Jews and Gentiles) may glorify the God and Father of our Lord, Jesus Christ."

For Reference and Further Study

Bornkamm, G. "The Praise of God." *Early Christian Experience* 105–11.
Deichgräber, R. *Gotteshymnus und Christus-hymnus in der frühen Christenheit.* SUNT 5; Göttingen: Vandenhoeck and Ruprecht, 1967, 60–64.
Johnson, E. E. *Function of Apocalyptic* 164–74.
Zeller, D. *Juden und Heiden* 267–69.

II. SUMMONS TO LIVE ACCORDING TO THE GOSPEL (12:1–15:13)

Paul has concluded his more or less systematic account of the gospel of which "he is not ashamed" (1:16). In accordance with a pattern set in earlier letters (Gal 5:13–6:10; 1 Thess 4:1–5:22; cf. later, Col 3:1–4:6; Eph 4:1–6:20), he now (12:1) begins the exhortation *(parenesis)* that makes up the remainder of the body of the letter. True to the epideictic rhetorical mode in which it is cast (see Introduction), the exposition of the gospel has already included passages of an exhortatory nature (6:12-14; 8:5-13; 11:17-24); in this sense it is not appropriate to make a rigid distinction between exposition *(kerygma)* and exhortation *(parenesis)*. However, from now on, in a more sustained way, Paul summons his implied audience—Gentile believers in Rome—to live out as a community the consequences of the "inclusive" gospel by which they have been grasped.

The parenesis falls into two main sections in that, after a brief introductory summons (12:1-2), a fairly generalized series of instructions (12:3–13:14) gives way to a more specific plea for tolerance in the matter of food (14:1–15:13). It is not easy, however, to discern a formal principle of organization and some elements of the parenesis can be more closely applied to conceivable historical circumstances in Rome than others (see Introduction). In the earlier part (12:1–13:14), following the thematic opening (12:1-2), Paul appears to focus upon relationships *within* the community, (12:3-16) and then move to consider how believers should relate to those *outside*—first outsiders in a general sense (12:17-21) and then specifically the ruling authorities (13:1-7)—with the Christian "debt" of love functioning as governing principle. The choice and arrangement of topics seems derived largely from experience as missionary and pastor to Gentile communities. That is, rather than responding closely to circumstances in the Roman community of which he was aware, Paul composes an exhortation raising and addressing the kind of issues he knows to be significant in the life of Gentile Christian communities trying to live out the gospel in the wider Mediterranean world.

i. Christian Life as "Rational Worship" (12:1-2)

1. I appeal to you therefore, brothers (and sisters), by the mercies of God, to present your bodies as a living sacrifice, holy and acceptable to God, the worship you owe as rational beings.
2. Do not be conformed to this world but be transformed by the renewal of your mind, that you may discern what is the will of God: what is good and acceptable and perfect.

Interpretation

Life in the body as "rational worship" (v 1). In these two sentences, appealing to the communal (Jewish and Gentile) experience of God's mercy just outlined (11:30-32), Paul solemnly summons (cf. *parakalō*) the community to a pattern of life responsive to the hearing of the gospel. This summons, which provides a thematic base for the entire parenesis down to 15:13, has had a brief foreshadowing in 6:12-14 where Paul urged the community to "offer *(parastēsate)* . . . (their) members *(melē)* to God as instruments of righteousness" (v 13). Now, once again, he makes his ethical appeal in terms of the bodily existence of Christians (v 1). Believers are to "offer" *(parastēsai)* their bodies as "a living sacrifice" *(thysian zōsan)* to God. "Body" *(sōma)* for Paul refers to the physical, material body but connotes also the sense of communication. It is as "body" that human beings are "in touch" with the world of persons, events and things beyond the self to give and receive impressions. Hence "bodily life" embraces the entire existence of believers, with particular emphasis upon interrelatedness within the community and interaction with the surrounding external world.

As part of his opening prophetic accusation (1:18–3:20) Paul had depicted the "fallen" existence of the Gentile world as something stemming from a "suppression of the truth about God." Human beings could use their minds to pass from perception of the created world to knowledge of God as Creator (vv 18-20). The appropriate response was to give God glory and thanks. Instead, they "became futile in their thinking" (v 21) and, in idolatry, "worshiped and served the creature rather than the Creator" (v 23; v 28)—a fundamental lapse ruinous in its effects upon their bodily life (vv 24, 26-27). The present appeal (12:1-2), with its stress upon "renewal of mind" (v 2) and "bodily worship," seems designed to respond to that earlier picture. Faith, which for Paul is always faith in God as Creator (cf. 4:17b), finds expression in a bodily obedience that is the "rational worship" owed by human beings to God.

Paul describes the offering of believers' bodies as a "living sacrifice" presumably in contrast to the animals and inanimate produce offered in sacrifice in the Jerusalem Temple or in the pagan shrines which Gentile Christians may have frequented before their conversion. The great prophets of Israel, especially Hosea, Isaiah and Jeremiah, frequently pointed out the meaninglessness of sacrifices unaccompanied by true inner conversion and commitment to social justice (e.g., 1 Sam 15:22; Isa 1:10-20; Jer 6:20; Hos 8:11-13; Amos 5:21-27; cf. Pss 50:8-15; 51:16-17). They laid down criteria for what is and what is not sacrifice "pleasing to God" *(euareston tǭ theǭ)*. Paul stands within the broad flow of this tradition when he extends to life in the body the notion of a "sacrifice" which God is truly pleased to receive from creatures.

This "lived sacrifice" Paul finally describes as "the worship you owe as rational beings" *(tēn logikēn latreian hymōn)*. Precisely because life in the body is at stake it would be wrong to see in this phrase a polemic against material sacrifice as such. That is not Paul's concern. For him the "worship" constituted by Christian life in the body is "spiritual" *(logikē)*, not in the sense of being opposed to the physical, but in the sense, familiar from Hellenistic-Stoic usage, of proceeding from that which is distinctive of human beings as rational, reflective creatures whose highest powers are engaged in the homage they bring to their Creator (just as sin correspondingly involved the misuse of such powers: 1:21-23). Paul may or may not be suggesting that a fully integrated Christian life obviates the need for the kind of sacrificial ritual still practiced by Jews in the Temple at the time of writing. But he certainly implies that obedience of life, rather than specific ritual gestures, constitute for believers the true essence of worship.

Discerning God's will (v 2). Paul completes the picture of Christian life as lived sacrificial consecration to God by indicating how believers are to know what it requires in practice (v 2). Negatively (v 2a), it means not being conformed to the pattern of this world. Presupposed here, as throughout Romans, is the apocalyptic, eschatological schema according to which present Christian life is lived in the "overlap" of the ages (see Interpretation of 5:1-11). The new age inaugurated by the resurrection of Christ has become palpable in the experience of the Spirit, attesting a new relationship with God (cf. 5:5; 8:23). But the conditions of the sin-laden old era endure for the time being and will continue to do so till Christ's victory is complete (cf. 1 Cor 15:23-28). In their bodies believers feel and suffer the onslaughts of the old era. They have to live out the values of the new—especially in relation to God and fellow human beings—in the conditions of the old. Hence, on the negative side, their "worship" involves a constant resistance to the "pull" of the passing age upon their bodily existence.

More positively (v 2b), they must allow their "minds" to undergo the renewal of existence that life in the new era involves. "Mind" *(nous)* for Paul denotes the thinking, discerning aspect of the human person (see Note on 7:23). As such, it is morally neutral: it can sink to the level of the fallen age (cf. 1:21, 28) or, as Paul here requires, it can partake of the new. What is striking is the way Paul insists that the new moral life is something that proceeds from this renewed inner faculty of discernment. In no sense does it involve simple conformity to a blueprint provided by external law or sanction. It is something that is to proceed from the inner moral core of the person, now capable of discerning *(dokimazein)* the "will of God." (The casting of the appeal in the second person plural suggests that communal rather than individual discernment is principally in view.)

Significantly, then, Paul's fundamental principle of moral discernment, laid down here prior to any concrete norms or maxims, is that Christian obedience involves a constant quest for God's will in the confusing and difficult circumstances of the present, "overlap" time. He displays a remarkable confidence in the capacity of the "renewed mind" to determine God's will and so arrive at behavior which, in conventional terms, is "good, pleasing (to God) and perfect." The principle set out here stands in sharp contrast—in all likehood intentional—to what he had written earlier on, lampooning the claim of the Jewish teacher to "know the will (of God) and discern *(dokimazein)* what is essential, instructed by the law" (2:18). Believers have no need to be instructed by such a law, just as they have no need to go to a temple to offer sacrifice to God. Their "renewed mind" creates in them the capacity to discern what is required to live according to God's will. The bodily obedience flowing from that discernment makes their lives a continual "sacrifice" pleasing to God.

Reflection. These two sentences contain a spirituality and a theory of ethical discernment that is both suggestive and open-ended. Granted the vast cultural and historical gap between the ancient world and our own, scripture provides little concrete guidance for the ethical dilemmas of modern life. The abiding values of the gospel have to be discerned and lived out in totally different circumstances, with science and technology, in particular, throwing up ethical challenges unimaginable in the biblical world. In these circumstances, Paul's stress upon the capacity of the "renewed mind" to discern, his sense of the need to test (allowing for some measure of trial and error), his readiness to speak in the language of the surrounding secular world ("good and acceptable and perfect") offer contemporary moral theology an important biblical charter as it confronts the issues of our time.

Notes

1. *I appeal to you therefore, brothers (and sisters):* Paul uses a conventional epistolary formula *(parakalō)* to stress the solemnity and authority of the appeal he is now making (cf. 15:30; 1 Cor 1:10; 4:16; 2 Cor 2:8; 10:1; Phil 4:2; Phlm 10). The fraternal address *(adelphoi)* lends a more familial note of Christian fellow-feeling; cf. 1:13; 7:4; 11:25.

   by the mercies of God: The plural form ("mercies") suggests biblical (Hebrew) overtones, with the prepositional construction (*dia* + genitive) having instrumental force: "my appeal comes to you with the authority emanating from our communal (Jewish and Gentile) experience of God's mercy" (cf. 11:32).

   to present: The verb *paristanai* reflects technical language of sacrifice found in Greek literature and inscriptions.

   your bodies: On the distinctive Pauline sense of "body" *(sōma)* as instrument of communication, see Interpretation of 6:6.

   as a living sacrifice, holy and acceptable to God: The language of "sacrifice" *(thysia)*, along with the accompanying epithets, connotes the sense that the believer's entire existence is now wholly given over to God (cf. the sense of "living to God": 6:10-11; also 15:3) and has irrevocably entered into the "sphere of holiness" constituted by God's presence, as is the case with something consecrated and sacrificed to God in Temple worship.

   the worship you owe as rational beings: The phrase stands in apposition to the entire preceding statement: that is, from "present your bodies . . ." onwards. The Greek word *latreia* denotes the action of worshiping and hence implies the sense of a continual offering of believers' entire selves. As regards the adjective *logikos*, two possible meanings emerge from the rich background provided by Greco-Roman literature and philosophy: 1. "spiritual" in the sense of "inward" as opposed to the external, physical and material: so that Paul would be mounting a contrast with the material sacrifices of ordinary cult (Jewish or pagan) or else drawing attention to the sense of proper interior disposition that alone validates cultic action; 2. "rational" in the sense of that which is distinctive of humans as rational, reflective beings (as particularly stressed by the Stoics: cf. esp. Epictetus, *Discourses* 1.16.20–21; 2.9.2; also Philo *Spec.* 1.277). The former meaning ("spiritual") does not agree with Paul's insistence upon the bodily aspect of the new Christian worship. The second accords well with the stress upon the renewal of mind and rational discernment in the following sentence and is to be preferred.

2. *Do not be conformed to this world but be transformed:* Both compound verbs (*syschēmatizesthai* and *metamorphousthai*) connote, in the present context, a sense of profound conformity and transformation (cf. the use of *metaschēmatizein* in Phil 3:21). The *syn-* element in the first verb lends the sense of attachment to and control by something both foreign and external (here the present age). The second verb appears in connection with believers' "transformation *(metamorphoumetha)* into the "same image" (the glory of the risen Lord) in 2 Cor 3:18; see further Note on 8:29.

the renewal of your mind: The word *anakainōsis* (Paul's usage is the first in Greek literature) suggests the "newness" of the "new creation" inaugurated by the resurrection of Christ; believers are appropriated to it by their living "in" him; cf. 6:4 ("walk in newness of life"); 2 Cor 5:17; Gal 6:15. The "renewal of mind" must therefore imply the liberation of the mind from its captivity to the old, sinful age (1:21, 28; 7:23, 25) and its transformation, through the Spirit, into an apt instrument for the discernment of God's will.

that you may discern: The verb *dokimazein* (cf. also 1:28; 2:18; 14:22; 1 Cor 11:28; 2 Cor 13:5; Gal 6:4; Phil 1:10; 1 Thess 2:4; 5:21) can mean either 1. "prove" or "test"; or 2. "approve" (as a result of testing). Here the former meaning is more appropriate, with the more specific sense of arriving at a decision as a result of a process of discernment beween various possible courses of behavior; cf. the use of the verb with respect to *ta diapheronta* in 2:18 and Phil 1:10. The sense comes close to the verb *diakrinein* ("discern"), especially as the latter is used with respect to the discernment of prophecy in 1 Cor 14:29 (cf. 12:10; 11:29; also 1 John 4:1).

what is the will of God: what is good and acceptable and perfect: The translation takes the last three epithets as standing in apposition to the phrase "what is the will of God." The sense of the second is "acceptable to *God*," as in all other instances of the *euarest-* stem in the NT (Titus 2:9 being a sole exception).

For Reference and Further Study

On Rom 12:1–15:13 as a whole.

Furnish, V. P. *The Love Command in the New Testament,* Nashville: Abingdon, 1972; London: SCM, 1973, 102–18.

Piper, J. *"Love Your Enemies": Jesus' Love Command in the Synoptic Gospels and the Early Christian Paraenesis.* SNTSMS 38: Cambridge: Cambridge University, 1979.

Spicq, C. *Agapè dans le Nouveau Testament.* 3 vols; EB; Paris: Gabalda, 1958–59.

Thompson, M. *Clothed with Christ: The Example and Teaching of Jesus in Romans 12:1–15:13.* JSNTSup 59; Sheffield: JSOT, 1991.

Wilson, W. T. *Love without Pretense: Romans 12.9-21 and Hellenistic-Jewish Wisdom Literature.* WUNT 2/46; Tübingen: Mohr, 1991.

On Rom 12:1-2.

Betz, H. D. "The Foundations of Christian Ethics according to Romans 12:1-2." *Witness and Existence* (FS S. M. Ogden). Eds. P.E. Devenish & G. L. Goodwin. Chicago/London: University of Chicago, 1989, 55–72.

Bjerkelund, C. J. *PARAKALŌ* 161–73.

Evans, C. F. "Rom 12:1-2: The True Worship." *Dimensions de la vie chrétienne.* Ed. L. de Lorenzi; Rome: Abbaye de S. Paul, 1979, 7–33.

Piper, J. *"Love Your Enemies"* 102–06.

Schunack, G. Art. *"Dokimazō." EDNT* 1.341–43.

Thompson, M. *Clothed with Christ* 78–86.

Wilson, W. T. *Love without Pretense* 136–39.

ii. The Basic Demands of Christian Living (12:3–13:14)

a) *A Due Assessment of One's Personal Gift* (12:3-8)

3. For by the grace given to me I bid every one among you not to think of yourself more highly than is appropriate but instead to adopt a sober attitude of mind, each according to the measure which God has assigned at the moment of coming to faith.
4. For just as each of us has in one body many members and all the members do not have the same function, 5. so all of us, many as we are, form one body in Christ, and are individually members one of another,
6. with gifts that differ according to the grace given to us:
whether (the gift be) prophecy—manifested according to its capacity to build up faith; 7. or (the gift of) service—shown in the exercise of serving or one might be a teacher—shown in one's teaching; 8. or (one might give) exhortation—showing it in (the quality of) the exhortation; the one who gives alms, will display it in sincerity of motive; the one who provides resources, in ready concern; the one who does acts of mercy, in the cheerfulness with which they are carried out.

Interpretation

Introduction. Paul has communicated his basic vision through the image of Christian life in the body as a continual "sacrifice" to God (v 1). He has summoned (v 2) the community to activate the capacity they have as believers to discern how that vision is to be implemented in everyday life. He now begins to fill out that picture with a more detailed account of how relationships within the Christian community ought to proceed. Taking up the appeal he has just made for a "rational" worship and "renewal of mind," he calls (v 3) for the adoption of a sober attitude of mind as the key factor in the establishment of the right relationships that underpin successful community life. The basis for this attitude of mind is found in a right assessment of the distinctive gift *(charis)* that God has given to each and the due exercise of that gift. The sentences that follow (vv 4-8), setting out the image of the community as "body" and listing the various gifts, are primarily descriptive in character and do not constitute separate exhortations relating to the exercise of the separate gifts. Any prescriptive force attaching to them is designed to undergird the opening thematic appeal to adopt a sober, accurate attitude towards oneself.

Adopt a right attitude of mind (v 3). Paul makes his appeal in virtue of the "gift" *(charis)* given him. Tactfully he holds back at this point from being explicit concerning this gift but clearly the allusion is to his God-given charge to be the apostle responsible for establishing and pastoring the Gentile churches (cf. esp. 1:5; 11:13; later, 15:15). In virtue of this gift Paul can make the present appeal in strongly personal and authoritative terms. With a wordplay upon the Greek stem *phron-* that is difficult to convey in translation, Paul characteristically formulates the appeal first in negative (v 3b) and then positive (v 3c) terms: each one is to refrain from adopting an attitude "higher" than appropriate *(hyperphronein)* but rather to "think" *(phronein)* in a way that leads to a sober understanding *(sōphronein)*.

The attitude of mind commended here is not in itself distinctively Christian. It corresponds to the virtue of moderation *(sōphrosynē)* widely esteemed in popular Greek philosophy of the day. The Christian aspect arises in connection with the basis for this attitude which Paul indicates (v 3d). The sober self-assessment of believers rests upon the way in which they perceive themselves to have been gifted by God at the moment of coming to faith (on the difficult phrase *metron pisteōs*, see Note). Presupposed is Paul's distinctive view that each person, on coming to Christian faith, is addressed by God in a way that constitutes their "calling" *(klēsis)* and bestows upon them the distinctive "gift" *(charis)* which they then contribute to Christian community life. The assessment of oneself as a Christian rests upon a due perception of one's own gift—not hankering after or pretending to have the gift of others—and then upon the way in which one exercises the gift within the community. Community life flourishes in good relationships when each one discerns his or her own gift and exercises it effectively for the common good.

The Christian community as "body" (vv 4-5). Paul illustrates this vision of a community endowed with different gifts by appealing to the image of a "body." The image was employed widely in the ancient world—as also today—to illustrate the interrelatedness and working of a human group, such as a city or a state. Paul had already employed this common image with reference to community experience of the gifts of the Spirit in 1 Cor 12:12-27. In that earlier letter, written to a church which he himself had founded and which was therefore familiar with his distinctive theology, he offers a more developed presentation of the conventional image: believers are not only *like* a body but actually constitute the "body of Christ"—that is, they are somehow contained within the sphere of salvation constituted by the risen Lord in such a way as to be united with him and with each other as members of his "body" (cf. esp. 1 Cor 12:12, 27). Such a conception presumably *underlies* the "body" image here. But, writing to a community not familiar with this tenet of his own theology, Paul restricts himself to the simple illustration which the Roman audience would instantly recognize and accept.

The image serves to illustrate the diversity of gifts operative within the overall oneness of a community. Each human person lives within a body that is recognizably a unity. Yet this one body has many members or limbs *(melē)*, each one exercising a different function *(praxin)* for the common good. So it is, says Paul (v 5), with respect to the Christian community. Within the overall unity constituted by being "in Christ"—that is living "in" the sphere and power of his presence as risen Lord (see Interpretation of 6:3)—"many" believers make up one "body," each representing a limb that functions with respect to other limbs *(to de kath' heis allēlōn melē)*.

Illustrative list of the various gifts and their functions (vv 6-8). Developing (vv 6-8) this basic description of Christian community life, Paul points to a number of the functions exercised by the "limbs" within the one body. In an introductory clause (v 6a) he dubs these functions *charismata*: there are a range of *charismata* (literally, "different *charismata*") according to the "grace" *(charis)* given to each. The formulation suggests some distinction between *charis* and *charisma*. *Charis*, while it can refer generally to the grace of God (cf. esp. 5:12-21), refers here to the distinctive favor or "gift" that individual believers receive from God at the moment of coming to faith (in Paul's case [cf. v 3], the grace of being apostle for the Gentiles). *Charisma* refers to the way in which the gift *(charis)* impacts upon others: more precisely, *charisma* denotes the sense of God's graciousness that the gifted person communicates to others through the exercise of his or her own particular *charis*. This is why, in the illustrative list that follows (vv 6b-8), Paul not only indicates seven gifts but adds after each an indication of each one's function or effect; the first term in each case refers to the *charis*, the second indicates the *charisma*.

Heading the list (v 6b) is the gift of "prophecy" *(prophēteia)*. As shown throughout the discussion of gifts in 1 Corinthians 12-14, this is a gift Paul values very highly (cf. esp. 14:1, 5). In the early Christian context "prophecy" denotes a capacity—under inspiration but with full possession of one's "mind" and in fully intelligible terms (cf. 14:13-19)—to discern and declare God's working in various events and God's will for the community. The qualifying phrase *(kata tēn analogian tēs pisteōs)* is highly ambiguous (see Note). Though quite different in form from the phrases qualifying the remaining gifts (indicating the way they are exercised), it is best understood in similar terms: that is, as a reference to the way the gift of prophecy is exercised. The value of prophecy precisely as *charisma* (see above) stands in proportion *(kata tēn analogian)* to its capacity to evoke or enhance faith *(tēs pisteōs)*—other believers' faith and the faith of the community as a whole.

Likewise the remaining gifts (vv 7-8). The gift of "service" *(diakonia)*—here a range of services provided to the community by specially designated individuals would appear to be in mind (see Note)—manifests its *charisma* precisely in the service provided. The one who "teaches" *(ho didaskōn)*—that is, one concerned with the consolidation of the faith following initial conversion—shows it in the quality of the teaching provided. The person (v 8a) who "exhorts" *(ho parakalōn)* displays *charisma* by promoting implementation of the ethical teaching of the gospel in everyday life (for alternative understandings, see Note).

The remaining three "gifts" (v 8bcd) all seem to be concerned in some way with the exercise of charity. In each case Paul explicitly calls attention to the quality with which the gift has to be exercised in order that the sense of *charisma* be communicated. One—presumably a reasonably well-off person is in mind—who provides relief from his or her own resources must do so with sincerity of motive *(en haplotēti)*, that is, without any touch of self-seeking. One—again, presumably, someone of influence or position—who acts as a patron *(ho proistamenos)* must do so in a way that indicates eager dedication *(spoudē)*. Finally, the one who brings relief to the the unfortunate (literally, exercises mercy, *ho eleōn*)—must do so with the cheerfulness that indicates that performing the service is a privilege and not a burden.

It may well be that in the case of these last three "gifts" a more exhortatory note enters in, preparing the way for the clearly "prescriptive" list that follows. However, all seven gifts and their respective exercise are cited for the same overriding reason. Within the vision of the Christian community here described, the way each member exercises his or her own distinctive "grace" for the benefit of the rest of the community provides the basis for the right assessment *(sōphronein)* of each one's worth (v 3). Paul summons (cf. *legō*, v 3) individual members of the community to look solely to their own gifts and to review their exercise of those gifts as a way of acquiring and preserving the right measure of self-judgment upon which overall harmony depends.

NOTES

3. *not to think of yourself more highly than is appropriate:* The Greek verb *hyperphronein* has in the present context the sense of "overrating" oneself and one's sphere of operation—an attitude leading to the kind of interference in the spheres of others which, in Paul's experience, leads inevitably to resentment and quarreling.

each according to the measure which God has assigned at the moment of coming to faith: The translation attempts to render a very cryptic clause, in particular the phrase *metron pisteōs,* which is open to a variety of interpretation. The Greek word *metron* has two basic meanings, each extended in various ways: 1. that by which something is measured—an instrument of measurement, then (metaphorically) a criterion or standard; 2. that which results from measurement—a quantity or portion, then due measure, due proportion. Likewise "faith" *(pistis)* is open to a range of meaning: "faithfulness," "faith" (= the subjective disposition [*fides qua*]) common to all believers), "faith" (= a special strength of faith, possessed by some as a particular gift [miracle-working; cf. 1 Cor 13:2]), "the faith" (the body of truth which is the object of Christian believing [*fides quae*]). It is possible to take *metron* in the first sense ("criterion") and "faith" in the subjective sense and understand the phrase to mean "according to the standard which a person's own depth of faith ought to establish" (cf. Cranfield 2.615; Wilckens 3.11). This does not make for a particularly smooth transition to what follows (the "body" image and presentation of various gifts). Alternatively, with *metron* understood as "measure" and recognizing the possibility of differing levels of faith existing within the community (cf. 14:1), Paul can be understood to be saying that an individual's self-assessment should depend on the level of faith which he or she possesses in comparison with others ("according to the measure of faith [different in each person] which each one has"; cf. Dunn 2.721–22). But this would hardly serve Paul's purpose in a context where he is discouraging comparisons of this kind. It is preferable, on the basis esp. of 1 Cor 7:17 *(ei mē hekastǭ hōs emerisen ho kyrios),* to see an allusion here to Paul's conviction that God gives a particular gift (lit. "allots a measure" [*emerisen metron*]) to each person who comes to faith at the moment of their coming to faith (cf. esp. Zeller 208). This gift—and, notably, the effectiveness or not, with which the person exercises the gift—is the true basis for self-judgment; cf. also 2 Cor 10:13-15. On this understanding, the second member of the phrase, *pisteōs*, has to be understood (as a qualifying genitive) as an allusion to the moment of coming to faith—or to "the faith."

4. *each of us has in one body many members and all the members do not have the same function:* Paul's presentation of the community in terms of the human body with its many limbs all serving the common good, particularly in the allegorical form developed in 1 Cor 12:12-27, has notable parallels in ancient literature, especially in connection with ethical reflection upon the responsibility of the city-state to care for weaker members: e.g., Plato, *Republic* 462c–d; also Livy, *History* 2.32 (fable of Menenius Agrippa); Epictetus, *Discourses* 2.10.4–5.

5. *all of us, many as we are, form one body in Christ:* On the background and origin of Paul's distinctive use of the "body" image with respect to the Christian community, see the comprehensive survey of Dunn 2.722–24. On the extent to which Paul identified the community with the "body" of the risen Lord (community = "Body of Christ"), see the very balanced discussion of C.F.D. Moule, *Origin of Christology* (see Reference) 69–83. For the related Pauline idea of Christian life as life "in Christ," see Interpretation of 6:3.

   individually members one of another: The more natural force of the "body" image would be to suggest that individuals (cf. *to de kath' heis* [BDF §305]) are "members" (limbs) in relation to the body as a whole. But it serves Paul's purpose to stress interrelatedness (cf. *allēlōn melē*) rather than overall unity at this point.

6. *with gifts that differ according to the grace given to us:* Underlying the translation is a participial phrase (*echontes de charismata* . . . [lit. "having gifts . . .]), not followed by any main verb. Many interpreters (and translations, e.g., RSV), as a prelude to finding a prescriptive sense in the account of the various gifts (vv 6-8), begin a new sentence here, supplying a main verb in the imperative ("Having gifts . . ., let us use them . . ."). There is no real necessity or justification for this. The participial phrase relates the "body" image (v 4) to the Christian community (vv 5-8): the existence of different gifts within the community corresponds to the way in which different limbs, with separate functions, all serve the good of the one body. The interpretation given here owes much to the study of *charisma* in Paul provided by N. Baumert (see Reference). See also Note on 1:11.

   whether (the gift be) prophecy—manifested according to its capacity to build up faith: The phrase qualifying "prophecy" attempts to translate a further cryptic phrase in Greek: *kata tēn analogian tēs pisteōs*; cf. *metron pisteōs* in v 3d. The two phrases are generally closely associated in interpretation. Hence, following the two main interpretations of *metron pisteōs* (see Note on v 3), come two corresponding interpretations of the present phrase: 1. "according to the standard or norm constituted by faith" (*fides qua* [Cranfield 2.621] or *fides quae* [Wilckens 3.14]); 2. "in proportion to (= "according to the measure of") faith" (= the prophet's personal reliance upon God [cf. Dunn 2.728]). While "*metron*" and "*analogia*" can overlap in meaning in the sense of "due measure" or "proportion," it is not necessarily helpful to regard them as equivalents. In the present instance the immediately preceding (v 6a) *kata* . . . phrase provides a more obvious parallel. Also, the fact that in the following sequence the mention of each gift precedes a reference to its exercise, suggests that here too the reference is to the (fruitful) *exercise* (cf. *praxin*, 4b) of the grace. *Analogia* expresses (mathematical) proportion, analogy, relationship, likeness; and then right relationship, due proportion. Hence, the suggested interpretation and translation, with the genitive *pisteōs* taken in a qualitative sense: prophecy shows its value in direct proportion (*kata tēn analogian*) to its capacity to build up faith (or extend understanding of "the faith"), which is the chief task of the prophet (cf. 1 Cor 14:3-4, 22).

7. *or (the gift of) service—shown in the exercise of serving:* In the strict sense *diakonia* refers to the function or service performed by a *diakonos* that is, one commissioned to perform a designated task on behalf of another or others—an authorized emissary, a go-between; cf. J. N. Collins, *Diakonia* (see Reference) 194. The NT usage is fairly wide-ranging. At the highest level, *diakonos* designates one solemnly charged by God for the "delivery" of the gospel; *diakonoi* can also be the representatives of churches sent on various tasks. In the present context, *diakonia* seems to refer to service performed within the community by certain persons set apart and commissioned by the church as a whole to see to various tasks and concerns (cf. the setting aside of the Seven in Acts 6:1-6). Beyond this, it is difficult to be more precise about the nature of the service performed. That it had specifically to do with the relief of poorer and more disadvantaged members, as is often thought, is offset by the fact that such relief seems to be catered for in the last three "gifts" mentioned (v 8bcd)—unless the latter refer to the private initiatives of individuals, whereas the *diakonia* is performed specifically in the name of the church by designated officials.

teacher: The teacher differs from the prophet in the sense that the instruction imparted stems not from immediate inspiration but from knowledge of and reflection upon the scriptures, the tradition about Jesus, early creeds and other more or less fixed formulas of faith (cf. 6:17).

8. *give exhortation:* Rather than being concerned with the more practical (ethical) aspects of instruction (as suggested in the Interpretation), the role of the *parakalōn* may have been to give comfort and assurance; cf. the Johannine view of the Spirit as "Paraclete" (John 14:16, 26; 15:26; 16:7; 1 John 2:1).

the one who gives alms, will display it in sincerity of motive: The qualification provided by the attached prepositional phrase—*en haplotēti* (lit. "in simplicity [of spirit]")—suggests that giving of alms from one's own resources, rather than those of the community, is in view; this is also the more proper sense of the verb *metadidonai*.

the one who provides resources, in ready concern: The Greek participle, *ho proistamenos*, could refer to "the one who presides" (that is, someone in authority; cf. 1 Thess 5:12; 1 Tim 3:4-5, 12; 5:17). Or else Paul could mean one who provides resources, in the sense of a well-off person who acts as a *patronus* for the less-advantaged. The fact that in the present context this gift occurs between two others denoting "social service" suggests that the latter is what Paul has in mind. The Greek word *spoudē* occurring in the added phrase, basically connotes "eagerness," "diligence," "zeal"; Dunn (2:731) helpfully suggests "zest."

the one who does acts of mercy, in the cheerfulness with which they are carried out: Here Paul seems to move away from the more "official" acts of social concern to those for which no special qualifications or resources are necessary save a tender and generous disposition. It is likely that care of the sick or disadvantaged is particularly in view.

For Reference and Further Study

Aune, D. E. *Prophecy in Early Christianity and the Ancient Mediterranean World.* Grand Rapids: Eerdmans, 1983, 198–217.

Baumert, N. "Charisma und Amt bei Paulus." *L'Apôtre Paul* (Ed. A. Vanhoye) 203–28.

Best, E. *One Body in Christ.* London: SPCK, 1955.

Collins J. N. *Diakonia. Re-interpreting the Ancient Sources.* New York and Oxford: Oxford University, 1990, 232–34.

Fee, G. D. Art. "Gifts of the Spirit." *DPL* 339–47.

Käsemann, E. "Ministry and Community in the New Testament." *Essays on New Testament Themes* 63–94.

__________. "The Theological Problem Presented by the Motif of the Body of Christ." *Perspectives on Paul* 102–21.

Moule, C.F.D. *The Origin of Christology.* Cambridge: Cambridge University, 1977, 69–89.

Wilson, W. T. *Love without Pretense* 139–42.

Zeller, D. Art. "*sōphrosynē*." *EDNT* 3.320–30.

b) *Love in Action Within the Community* (12:9-16)

9. Let love be genuine;
hate what is evil, cleave to what is good;
10. with the love of brothers and sisters, show each other family affection; anticipate one another in showing respect;
11. cast off all slackness in your eagerness,
be aglow with the Spirit,
in service make the most of the time remaining,
12. rejoice in your hope,
be steadfast in affliction, persevere in prayer.
13. contribute to the needs of the saints,
seek out opportunity to show hospitality.

14. Bless those who persecute (you);
bless and do not curse them.
15. Rejoice with those who rejoice,
weep with those who weep.
16. Aim at having a common mind amongst yourselves;
do not adopt a haughty frame of mind, but associate with the lowly; be not wise in your own thoughts.

INTERPRETATION

Introduction. Allowing a more prescriptive tone to return, Paul lists a series of qualities that ought attend the interplay of gifts in Christian community life. These qualities function as "oil" ensuring a smooth and fruitful interaction. Just as in 1 Corinthians an instruction concerning the interplay of spiritual gifts (*charismata,* 1 Cor 12:1-31) had been followed by an exposition on "love" (1 Cor 13:1-13), so now "love" *(agapē)* heads and governs the entire sequence (cf. Rom 13:8-10). The series of injunctions comes chiefly in the form of participial phrases in the Greek. This may reflect Semitic prototypes. But the content suggests that the passage taps a considerable variety of source material: the prophetic and wisdom traditions of the Old Testament, the "Jesus" tradition preserved in the early communities, ethical reflection and maxims of popular Greco-Roman philosophy. In any case, the close parallels with similar sequences in 1 Thess 5:12-22 and 1 Pet 3:8-12 suggest that the immediate source of the present sequence is the early Christian parenetical tradition, which had already associated and absorbed more remote material.

The sequence does not show a tight flow of thought, though the clustering of associated motifs and catchwords suggests a certain pattern. After the heading provided by the injunction concerning "love" in v 9a, there follows down to the end of v 13 a sequence of six couplets, mostly participial in form (vv 9b, 9c; 10a, 10b; 11a, 11b; 11c, 12a; 12b, 12c; 13a, 13b); the couplet in v 14 features a more regular imperative, while that in v 15 has an infinitive imperative. The reappearance of the *phronein* motif in v 16 forms an "inclusion" with v 3a and seems to mark the end of the sub-section.

Genuine love as the rule of community life (vv 9-13). Up till this point in the letter *agapē* has referred to God's love, most notably in 5:1-11 (esp. vv 5-8) and 8:31-39. Now (v 9a) Paul indicates "genuine love" *(agapē anypokritos)* as the quality distinctive of believers. With reference to the divine *agapē,* he had stressed the way in which God's saving action in Christ represented a totally unmerited act of pure love and reconciliation offered to those who were "enemies," alienated because of sin (cf. esp. 5:6-10; 8:32). The *agapē* asked of believers represents the outflow in their own lives of this same divine love. When Paul requires not simply "love" but "sincere *(anypokritos)* love" he is demanding a love that, like the love that inspired God's action in Christ, goes beyond mere words and protestations to embrace the alien and the enemy (v 14; v 17; v 20), that seeks to "overcome evil with good" (v 21). The opening phrase—"genuine love"—sets the tone for the entire sequence.

The initial couplet (v 9bc) seems to commend something fairly obvious. But the strength of the language ("hating" what is evil, "cleaving" to what is good) suggests that the "program" of life required by "genuine love" proceeds from a stark initial choice (cf. the similar dualistic demands required in Qumran literature: 1QS 1:3-4; 3:13–4:26).

Proceeding from this radical option for the "good" *(agathon)*, love's first field of play lies in relationships within the community. In line with a Christian tradition going back to Jesus (cf. Mark 3:31-35; Matt 12:46-50; Luke 8:12-21), Paul applies (v 10a) to Christian living terms normally employed to express the closeness of intra-family relationships (see Note). A family—or at least the traditional Mediterranean family which Paul had in mind—works as a unit, each member defending the honor of the other. So Paul insists (v 10b) that love in action will also mean the lack of a competitive spirit. Each one will actively go out of his or her way (cf. *proēgoumenoi*) to show respect to someone else (cf. 1 Cor 13:4-6; Phil 2:3-4).

The following couplet (v 11ab) pursues this vigorous sense of love's action. Love is not a passive waiting for occasion to arise; it actively seeks opportunity to go into operation (*tę̄ spoudę̄ mē oknēroi*, v 11a)—an eagerness, which the parallel line (v 11b) suggests to be an effect and sign of the Spirit's working. So persons whose love has been fanned into flame, as it were, by the Spirit (cf. 8:4; Gal 5:5-6) can be said to be "aglow *(zeontes)* with the Spirit," as metal glows with the blast from a forge.

Mention of the Spirit, the "firstfruits" (8:23) or "downpayment" (2 Cor 1:22; 5:5) of the full "inheritance" to come, introduces an eschatological tone that dominates the following two couplets (vv 11c-12a; 12bc). Textual uncertainty renders the sense of the first line (v 11c) somewhat obscure (see Note). However, within the overall eschatological perspective now introduced and with the sense of vigorous action continuing from before, Paul seems to be urging his audience to seize the present time (reading *tǭ kairǭ*; see Note), ambiguous and provisional as it is, and find in it an opportunity for "service" *(douleuontes)*. The present age is ambiguous because it involves living in the time of the "overlap" of the ages. In the resurrection of Jesus and the experience of the Spirit, the new age has radically "dawned" (cf. 5:1-2; 6:1-11; 8:1-4). Yet in their bodily existence believers continue to feel the onslaught of the lingering, sin-laden old era (see Interpretation of 5:1-11). Thus, echoing in more exhortatory tone the thought of 5:3-4, Paul summons the community to a paradoxical combination of joy (prompted by "hope") and steadfastness in adversity (*hypomonē*; cf. esp. the sequence in 5:2-4; also 8:25). The "adversity" in mind is hardly the kind of savage persecution, such as was to break out in Rome some years later (64 C.E.), but the day-to-day difficulties encountered by a small, vulnerable community surrounded by a non-comprehending and suspicious world. The final recommendation (v 12c) —perseverance in prayer—is something commended throughout the New Testament in contexts of eschatological expectation (cf. Mark 13:33; 14:38; Matt 24:36–25:13; 26:41; Luke 21:36; 22:40, 46; Acts 1:14; 2:42; 6:4; Eph 6:18; Col 4:2).

From this "vertical" (God-directed) and eschatological perspective, Paul returns in the final couplet (v 13) to a more "horizontal" expression of love. Now a charity towards fellow believers that ranges beyond the local community is in view. The injunction to be ready to contribute "to the needs of the saints" may contain an allusion by way of anticipation to the collection for Jerusalem that Paul will specifically mention later on (15:26-27, 31). More likely, since all believers are "saints" (cf. 1:7), it reflects a general sense that comparatively well-off local churches ought contribute to the support of those in a weaker position. A more specific regular service to fellow local churches is that of hospitality (v 13b). In a situation where many believers were constantly on the move, either for business or on mission, or perhaps as a result of persecution and expulsion, the high premium placed upon this service in the New Testament is well understandable. The ready provision (cf. *diōkontes*) of hospitality *(philoxenia)* was one of the signs attending the proclamation of the kingdom and missionaries were enjoined to entrust themselves to it (Mark 6:10-11; Matt 10:11-15; Luke 9:4-5; 10:5-12).

Blessing persecutors (v 14). The injunction to bless and not curse persecutors cuts somewhat intrusively into the sequence that otherwise appears to be taken up primarily with the exercise of *agapē* between Christians. Since the "persecutors" *(diōkontas)* are hardly fellow believers, the perspective here must turn for a time to the outside world (cf. vv 17-21). The injunction adheres closely to the teaching of Jesus in Matthew's Sermon on the Mount (5:44; cf. Luke 6:27-28); Paul draws upon authentic teaching of Jesus at an earlier stage of its preservation in the early Christian tradition. The repetition (v 14b) of the command to bless persecutors, with the added prohibition against cursing them, reflects a sense of the difficulty of what is being asked—an extreme statement of the love Jesus wished to be characteristic of his followers. It is at this point (cf. later vv 17-21) that the *agapē* required of believers most closely matches that which they have received from God in Christ, who, while "we were still enemies," died to work our reconciliation (5:10).

Sympathy in all circumstances (v 15). The somewhat isolated command to adopt a sympathetic stance towards the rejoicing and the weeping reflects the Jewish wisdom tradition (cf. esp. Sir 7:34). Most likely, sympathy towards fellow believers is again in view—though relations with outsiders are not necessarily to be excluded. In any case, such sympathy—harder perhaps in the case of rejoicing in another's joy than feeling sorry for his or her misfortune—requires a going beyond oneself and one's own immediate concern that is the basis of true *agapē* in action.

Basic principle (again): a sober reckoning of oneself (v 16). A final appeal for unity brings to an end a section principally concerned with the exercise of love. Each member of the three-line unit in Greek features the "mind" *(phron-)* stem which had dominated the beginning of the sequence in v 3. The "inclusion" so formed (v 3–v 16) reflects the Pauline sense that "mind-set" (*phronēma*; cf. "renewal of mind," v 2; 8:6-7) determines action. Paul does not mean, of course, that everyone is to think exactly alike—something undesirable and impossible in any case—but that all legitimate diversity of view be encompassed within a wider aspiration (*phronēma*) of unity. As he had insisted at the start (*mē hyperphronein,* v 3), the key to this is that people do not "think haughty thoughts" (*mē ta hypsēla phronountes*; cf. also 11:20: *me hypsēla phronei*), that is, assess themselves more highly than the reality warrants. The antidote for this divisive tendency (v 16c) is to associate with the lowly *(tois tapeinois synapagomenoi)*, that is, with the poor and disadvantaged, who in worldly terms are of no value but who, according to the gospel, have supreme value in the sight of God (cf. 1 Cor 1:26-29; Luke 6:22; 16:9). The final warning (v 16d) comes from the Book of Proverbs (3:7): the community is to take care not to become "wise in their own thoughts" (*phronimoi par' heautois*; cf. 11:25), something which inevitably makes people resistant to perceiving and accepting the plans of God, which constantly surpass, confound and overthrow human wisdom (cf. 11:33-36; 1 Cor 1:18-25; 2:14; 4:10).

Notes

9. *Let love be genuine:* For the same expression *(agapē anypokritos)* see 2 Cor 6:6; cf. also 1 Pet 1:22. The adjective stems originally from the theatre in the sense that it denotes the antithesis of the *hypokritēs* ("hypocrite") who, like an actor playing a role, speaks not his or her own thoughts but those of the character being played.

   hate what is evil, cleave to what is good: The expression of commands in the form of participles—from here down to the end of v 13—in all probability points to an underlying Semitic tradition; cf. the studies of D. Daube and P. Kanjuparambil cited in Reference.

10. *with the love of brothers and sisters, show each other family affection:* The translation seeks to bring out the force of the two key words in the phrase. *Philadelphia* in its strict sense refers to love between siblings. The noun *philostorgia*, used only here in the NT, likewise expresses the warmth of family love, especially that of parents for their children.

 anticipate one another in showing respect: The phrase might also be translated "outdo one another in showing respect" (cf. RSV; NRSV) or, rather differently, "in honor prefer one another." But "anticipate," "go before" best reflects the basic meaning of the verb *proēgeisthai*.

11. *be aglow with the Spirit:* In Acts 18:25 the same expression used with respect to Apollos probably indicates simple eagerness of (human) spirit. Apollos, having received only the baptism of John, had not yet received the Holy Spirit. Paul's sense of the Spirit as the anticipatory force of the dawning new age suggests that *pneumati* here refers to the Holy Spirit: the Spirit is the driving force of Christian "eagerness" (*spoudē*, v 11a).

 in service make the most of the time remaining: The translation adopts the "Western" (D* F G, etc.) reading *tǭ kairǭ* over against that of the remaining tradition (P[46] ℵ A B, etc.) *tǭ kyriǭ*, which is usually preferred. The latter gives a very bland sense ("serving the Lord") that adds little in the context. In favor of the Western reading is the consideration that it would be highly improbable, especially granted the reference to the "Spirit" close by, that a christological reference in connection with "serving" would have been transformed into a non-christological one giving such a difficult idea; cf. C. Spicq, *Agapè* 2.142, n. 2. The reading *kairǭ* is generally rejected on the grounds that "serving the time" had the same negative overtones in ancient literature that attach to the sense of "time-serving" today. This may well have been the case but it is not unthinkable that Paul's fondness for strength and vigor of expression would lead him to express in a rather daring way the sense of "grasp the occasion," "exploit to the full" the opportunity for service that remains in this present time. The deutero-Pauline (Col 4:5; Eph 5:16) expression "redeeming the time" *(exagorazomenoi ton kairon)* may represent a "taming" of this bold expression. So understood, the phrase fits in well with the eschatological tone that dominates the following three lines.

12. *rejoice in your hope:* The dative phrase *en elpidi* is open to both a local and an instrumental sense: the hope can be either the object of the rejoicing or its cause (cf. 5:2; 8:24-25).

 be steadfast in affliction: For the sense of the Greek terms *hypomonē* and *thlipsis* as used by Paul, see Note on 5:3.

13. *contribute to the needs:* The translation, along with most interpreters, accepts the reading *chreiais* ("needs") over against the Western reading *mneiais* (giving the sense of "joining in the remembrance of [= prayers for] the saints").

 the saints: When mentioned in connection with monetary relief elsewhere in Paul (cf. 15:25-26; 1 Cor 16:1; 2 Cor 8:4), "the saints" refers to the Christian community in Jerusalem. A general reference is more likely here: that is, Christian communities in places other than Rome, including, of course, Jerusalem; see Note on 1:7.

seek out opportunity to show hospitality: The translation aims to express the sense of vigorous effort implied in the verb *diōkein.*

14. *Bless those who persecute (you):* The Greek verb *diōkein* just used with reference to hospitality now expresses the idea of "persecution." This verbal link probably accounts for the introduction, somewhat intrusive at this point, of a command dealing with outsiders. The textual variant (P^{46} B) omitting "you" *(hymas)* probably represents the most original form of the text, the pronoun being added later to supply the implied object.

16. *a common mind amongst yourselves:* Paul frequently expresses his hope for community unity in terms of the phrase *to auto phronein;* cf. 15:5; 2 Cor 13:11; Phil 2:2; 4:2.

associate with the lowly: The translation of the final phrase takes the Greek adjective *tapeinois* ("lowly," "humble") as a reference to "lowly" persons. The adjective could, however, be neuter (giving the sense "but adopt humble thoughts"), which would give a tighter correspondence with the neuter plural *hypsēla* in the previous phrase. But *tapeinos* normally has a personal reference in biblical Greek.

For Reference and Further Study

Daube, D. "Participle and Imperative in 1 Pet." *The New Testament and Rabbinic Judaism.* London: Athlone, 1956, 90–97, 102–03.

Furnish, V. P. *Love Command* 103–06.

Kanjuparambil, P. "Imperatival Participles in Rom 12:9-21." *JBL* 102 (1983) 285–88.

Spicq, C. *Agapè* 2.141–52.

Talbert, C. H. "Tradition and Redaction in Romans 12:9-21." *NTS* 16 (1969–70) 83–94.

Thompson, M. *Clothed with Christ* 90–107.

Wilson, W. T. *Love without Pretense* 142–86.

c) *Love in Action Outside the Community* (12:17-21)

17. Repay no one evil for evil, but in the sight of all take thought for what
is honorable. 18. If possible, so far as it depends upon you, live peaceably with all.
19. Beloved, never avenge yourselves, but make allowance for wrath; for
it is written, "Vengeance is mine, I will repay, says the Lord." 20. No, "if

your enemy is hungry, feed him; if he is thirsty, give him drink; for by so doing you will heap burning coals upon his head."
21. Do not be overcome by evil, but overcome evil with good.

INTERPRETATION

Introduction. As the previous two sections of the parenesis had been "enclosed" as a unit by the wordplay upon the *phron-* stem in v 3 and v 16, so this part, dealing with the obligations of *agapē* towards those outside the believing community, is similarly "enclosed" by the double reference to "evil" *(kakon)* at the beginning (v 17a) and end (v 21). In contrast to the swift movement from one theme to another in the previous sections, all is now centered, more or less, upon the single theme of non-retaliation, stated in the opening verse and restated in a more positive and hopeful sense at the end. Again, Paul appears to be drawing upon both the Wisdom tradition of Israel and the teaching of Jesus refracted through the common Christian tradition (cf. 1 Pet 3:9). In contrast, however, to the preceding section, he cites scripture explicitly (vv 19b-20) to reinforce the high demands of his appeal.

Peace with all rather than retaliation (vv 17-18). The sequence opens (v 17) with a blunt statement of its theme in negative terms: in the context of hostility coming from the surrounding world, Christians are not to repay evil for evil (v 17a). This contradiction of the *lex talionis*, represents a Pauline form (cf. the very similar formulation in 1 Thess 5:15 [also 1 Pet 3:9]) of the teaching of Jesus recorded in Matt 5:38-42 and Luke 6:27-36. As a positive counterpart, Paul adds a recommendation taken from the Book of Proverbs (3:4): "in the sight of all," believers are to "give thought to what is honorable" *(kala)*. We meet here Paul's sense of Christian life as a drama played out upon a worldstage before a basically hostile, non-comprehending audience (cf. esp. 1 Cor 4:9; 2 Cor 2:14-15), which is nonetheless a field for conversion (cf. Phil 2:15-16). In such a situation the temptation is always to give in to dark, resentful sentiments. Instead, Paul urges (v 17b) the cultivation (cf. *pronooumenoi*) of thoughts that are "noble" (*kala*—a term summing up all the surrounding Hellenistic world found admirable and worthy of aspiration). Such a positive attitude will lead to the desire to live peaceably with all (v 18). Paul realizes that this may not always be possible, since peace requires the cooperation of both parties involved. Hence a double qualification brings a note of realism into the high ideal: "If possible, so far as it depends upon you. . . ."

Leave vengeance to God (vv 19-20). The following sentences repeat the opening appeal, now specified as not taking vengeance for injury received *(mē heautous ekdikountes)*. Instead, the community ought "give place to wrath" *(orgē)*. Though unspecified (cf. also 5:9), "wrath" means here the wrath of God, which in the symbolic universe presumed by Paul refers to the eschatological punishment destined to fall upon the unrighteous at the final judgment (cf. 2:5, 8). The meaning is not that believers should refrain from seeking to inflict punishment upon the adversaries in the hope that this will mean all the more severe punishment for them later on at the hands of God. Rather, the appeal comes out of a longstanding biblical and post-biblical prohibition against human beings taking vengeance into their own hands. Vengeance is entirely a prerogative of God. In line with this tradition, given classic statement in Deut 32:35 (quoted v 19b), what is required of human beings is a trust and confidence that God will see to the restoration of the order of justice that has been disturbed.

But beyond simple abstention from taking vengeance in the face of injury, Christian *agapē* in action is to "go over to the offensive," as it were, in the positive sense (v 20). Once again the Book of Proverbs gives the cue with its injunction (25:21) to revive with food and drink the hungry and thirsty enemy. Had Paul ended his quotation at this point (v 20a) he would have saved interpreters much labor. Instead he goes on (v 20b) to cite also the following sentence in Proverbs (25:22a) which purports to explain the effect that such charitable action will have upon the adversary. The meaning of "pouring burning coals upon (one's adversary's) head" is obscure in Proverbs as well as subsequently in Paul. "Fiery coals" suggests punishment and a long-standing opinion (see Note) has interpreted Paul to mean that the generous deeds presently performed by Christians will intensify the eschatological punishment the enemy is eventually to incur.

That love should have such motivation has long appeared bizarre, however, and totally at odds with the thrust of the passage as a whole. On such an understanding, vengeance is not abandoned; it is simply postponed, albeit left in the hands of God. More consonant with the overall flow of the argument—reaching right back to the heading (v 9a) in terms of "genuine love"—and most notably with the concluding maxim that follows in v 21 is the equally long-standing interpretation (see Note again) that sees in the "burning coals" a reference to conversion. Where vengeance simply intensifies and encases hostility, answering enmity and injury by kindness can melt the heart and effect lasting reconciliation.

Overcoming evil with good (v 21). The final injunction sums up the positive advance now reached. In the face of a world that is frequently hostile and bent upon inflicting evil, believers could well allow that evil to triumph radically by allowing evil to emerge from their own hearts in the shape of revenge. Instead, adopting the active stance just mentioned, they can allow goodness to triumph over evil (cf. 8:37). In this way the *agapē* asked of Christians becomes a true reflection and extension of the divine *agapē*, which met the evil and hostility of the world with love and, in the shape of Christ's resurrection, triumphed over that evil. What Paul requires of believers, as an outworking of their "renewed mind" (v 2; cf. v 3, v 16), is that they allow their present bodily existence to become the vehicle of the divine *agapē* that works the reconciliation of the human race to God (2 Cor 5:14-19, 20-21).

NOTES

17. *but in the sight of all take thought for what is honorable:* It is difficult to determine the precise force of the phrase "in the sight of all" *(enōpion pantōn anthrōpōn)*. Paul hardly desires believers to aim at what the world *holds* to be honorable—since elsewhere he makes clear that Christian morality has to go well beyond and frequently oppose what the world holds to be good (12:2). Nor can the Greek prepositional phrase with *enōpion* be made equivalent to a simple dative, rendering the sense, "plan (to do) what is honorable with respect to all". The clear model provided by LXX Prov 3:4 *(kai pronoou kala enōpion kyriou kai anthrōpōn)* and the parallel with 2 Cor 8:21 suggest that what Paul has in mind is aiming for what is good in the sight of (that is, before the arena) of the world.

19. *Beloved:* The address "beloved" is added at this point doubtless to strengthen the force of the appeal in this difficult area.

    wrath: On "wrath," see Interpretation and Note on 1:18.

    "for it is written, "Vengeance is mine, I will repay, says the Lord": Paul quotes Deut 32:35 in a form closer to the Hebrew than the LXX (cf. also Heb 10:30). The final phrase, "says the Lord," does not occur in the text. Paul adds it—somewhat redundantly after the opening "it is written"—perhaps to give the statement prophetic force. The idea that vengeance is to be left to God and not undertaken by human beings is a standard *topos* in the OT (cf., e.g., Lev 19:18; Prov 20:22; 24:29; Sir 28:1) and later Jewish tradition (*T. Gad* 6:7; Qumran: 1QS 10:17-19; CD 9:2-5).

20. *"if your enemy is hungry, feed him; if he is thirsty, give him drink; for by so doing you will heap burning coals upon his head":* Paul's quotation corresponds to the LXX of Prov 25:21-22a (save for the use of *psōmize* in place of LXX *trephe* [as also in LXX MS B]); omitted is the final clause (v 22b): "And God will repay you with good." Regarding the original text in Proverbs, it is hard to avoid the sense that one's own good acts serve to highlight the wickedness of the enemy, so rendering him liable to a greater measure of punishment at God's hands; "glowing coals" in Pss 120:4 and 140:10 clearly refer to punishment and the phrase "upon (one's) head" occurs in the sense of ill deeds being requited upon one's head in Joel 3:4, 7 (LXX 4:4, 7) and Obad 15; cf. also 1QM 11:13-14.

    But what is Paul's understanding? 1. Chrysostom and other Greek Fathers understood Paul in the "punitive" sense that seems to attach to the phrase in

Proverbs: by doing good to one's enemies one makes them liable to receive (eschatologically) even more severe punishment from God; for a modified modern version of this, see the studies of K. Stendahl, C. Spicq and J. Piper cited in Reference. The interpretation flies in the face of the overall thrust of the passage and, specifically, hardly responds to the *alla* (here translated "No"), which seems to introduce the quotation from Proverbs as a corrective. 2. Origen, Augustine, Pelagius and Jerome and others understood Paul in a more positive sense: "heaping coals of fire" refers to bringing one's enemy to the sense of shame and remorse that will lead to a change of heart. Evidence for "coals of fire" signifying remorse is not elsewhere attested, though the translation of Prov 25:22b provided by the Targum already seems to presuppose some measure of conversion. Many recent interpreters have felt able to embrace the more positive understanding on the basis of support coming from evidence of an Egyptian ritual in which a pannier of blazing coals was carried upon the head as a sign of repentance; see the studies of S. Morenz and W. Klassen cited in Reference—though the connection between this Egyptian ritual and Paul is tenuous.

For Reference and Further Study

Furnish, V. P. *Love Command* 106–08.

Klassen, W. "Coals of Fire: Sign of Repentance or Revenge?" *NTS* 9 (1962–63) 337–50.

Morenz, S. "Feurige Kohlen auf dem Haupt." *TLZ* 78 (1953) 187–92.

Piper, J. *"Love Your Enemies"* 111–19.

Ramaroson, L. "'Charbons ardents': 'sur la tête' ou 'pour le feu' (Prov 25,22a–Rm 12,20b)." *Biblica* 51 (1970) 230–34.

Spicq, C. *Agapè* 2.152–57.

Stendahl, K. "Hate, Non-Retaliation, and Love: 1 QS x, 17-20 and Rom. 12:19-21." *HTR* 55 (1962) 343–55.

Talbert, C. H. "Tradition and Redaction in Romans 12:9-21." *NTS* 16 (1969–70) 83–94.

Wilson, W. T. *Love without Pretense* 186–99.

d) *Duties Towards Civil Authorities* (13:1-7)

1. Let everyone be subject to the governing authorities.
For there is no authority except that which is given by God and the powers currently ruling have been established by God. 2. This means that anyone who resists them has resisted the ordinance of God. Moreover, those who resist will incur judgment. 3. For rulers are not a

terror to good conduct but to bad. Do you want not to have to fear the authority? Well then, do good and you will have commendation from him. 4. For he is God's servant to you for good. But, if you do wrong, then be afraid. For he does not wear the sword to no purpose and he is God's servant charged with the execution of wrath upon the wrongdoer.
5. Therefore, it is necessary to be subject, not only in consideration of the wrath, but also on account of conscience.
6. For the same reason you also pay tribute. For they are God's ministers charged to engage themselves in this very matter.
7. Render to everyone their dues: the tribute to whom the tribute is due, the tax to whom tax is due, fear to whom fear is due, respect to whom respect is due.

Interpretation

Introduction. At this point the reader is confronted by perhaps the strangest and most controversial passage in the entire letter. Abruptly Paul enjoins his audience to "be subject to the powers placed over us" (v 1) and, in support, embarks upon a line of reasoning uncharacteristic of his thought elsewhere. There is no appeal to christology nor indeed is there anything distinctly Christian about the *theo*logical argument deployed, with its very conventional stress upon rewards and punishment. More remarkable still, the command to be subject to the governing structures of the present age displays not a trace of the Pauline sense that the whole framework of the present era is passing away (cf. esp. 1 Cor 7:29-31), that the true "citizenship" *(politeuma)* of believers is in heaven (Phil 3:20), that every rule and authority and power is being done away with in preparation for Christ's handing over the kingdom to the God and Father (1 Cor 15:24). The absence of this eschatological sense is all the more striking in the present context in that only a few lines later (vv 11-14) Paul appeals strongly and explicitly to the nearness of the end as a concluding reinforcement of the general parenesis. Moreover, the suggestion (vv 3-4) that only evildoers have anything to fear from the governing powers hardly accords with Paul's earlier acknowledgment that believers "are being done to death the whole day long" (8:36).

These considerations have led several recent interpreters to regard the passage as an addition to the original text of Romans—an insertion by a later hand, anxious to invest with "Pauline" authority a message of submission to state authority. Where better to place it than in the letter to the community living in the imperial capital? These considerations are weighty and it must be added that the removal of 13:1-7 from the text of Romans leaves a smooth flow across 12:9-21–13:8-10, governed by the overall theme of love, with the "eschatological" ending (13:11-14) reinforcing the ethical appeal. But 13:1-7 is more closely linked to its context than appears at first sight. Relations with the governing powers fits neatly into the overall tendency of the parenesis from 12:3 onwards to "work outwards" from responsibilities and the demands of love within the Christian community (12:3-16), to those affecting relations with outsiders (12:17-21); in effect, it naturally extends and specifies the command to "live peaceably with all" (12:18). There are, moreover, verbal links with both the preceding (*orgē*: 12:19; 13:4, 5; *apodidonai*: 12:17; 13:7; *ekdikountes* 12:19; *ekdikos* 13:4; *proskarterountes* 12:12; 13:6) and following (*tas opheilas* 13:7; *mēden opheilete* 13:8) sections; in particular, a theme of "good" *(agathon)*/"bad" *(kakon)* runs through the entire context (12:2, 9, 17, 21; 13:3a, 3c, 4a, 4b, 4d; 13:10).

A skillful interpolator could perhaps have contrived this conformity to the language of the wider context. But, the "interpolation" theory, while it may go a long way to save the reputation of Paul as a consistent theologian, does not, in the end, solve many problems. Rom 13:1-7 is part of the letter as it has come down to us and part also of its interpretive history. There is no textual warrant for regarding it as secondary and no persuasive case for setting it aside so long as some explanation can be found for the inclusion of such an instruction in Paul's letter to Rome.

As noted already in the Introduction, a plausible historical setting for the present instruction can be found in the civil unrest among the populace of Rome that came to a head in the late 50's centering upon abuses in the collection of taxes. Things came to such a pitch in 58 C.E. that Nero seriously considered abolishing indirect taxes altogether but was persuaded by advisers to institute reforms designed to curb abuses. Aware of such a climate of civic disturbance in Rome and suspecting or knowing the Christian community to be divided on the matter (whether taxes ought to be paid or not), Paul may have been anxious lest the highly vulnerable Christian churches adopt imprudent policies sure to bring them into conflict at least with minor government officials. In such a context it is well conceivable that he might have adapted for his own purposes an instruction concerning obedience to earthly rulers, framed in traditional, conventional terms and circulating in Hellenistic-Jewish diaspora communities. Much of the language in the text in fact reflects standard Hellenistic ways of describing duties towards civic authorities. And the closely parallel, but independent instruction appearing in 1 Pet 2:13-17 (cf. also 1 Tim 2:1-3; Tit 3:1-3) shows that we are dealing here with an attitude, possibly even a set pattern of instruction, shared across a range of early Christian communities.

From a more strictly rhetorical point of view the passage can also be seen to play a significant role in Paul's self-presentation to the Roman community. The inclusion of the passage serves as a corrective to any impression that the gospel proclamation of the onset of the new age implied freedom from any obligation to rule and authority belonging to the present, passing era. The community need not fear that they are to receive a visit from an apostle bent on stirring up trouble with authorities, rendering their civic position more precarious than ever. In this sense the instruction, for all its oddity—and for all the hermeneutical issues it has raised and continues to raise (see below)—is nonetheless part of Paul's overall sense of present Christian life as involving a delicate balance between the realities of the present age and the demands of the new (see Interpretation of 5:1-11).

The argumentative structure of the passage is clear. A blunt opening sentence (v 1a) states the basic instruction—"Be subject. . . ." Vv 1b-2a then provide a first theological underpinning for this command (behind earthly rulers lies the authority of God). V 2b states the theme of a second supportive argument, which is then developed in vv 3-4 (through subjection to authorities one avoids the punishment they have power to inflict as instruments of God). As a first conclusion, v 5 restates the initial instruction, introducing as well the notion of "conscience." Vv 6-7 commend the payment of taxes, in all likelihood the climax to which all else has been driving. The last two lines (v 7bc) offer a neatly balanced couplet in the Greek, with a tight correspondence of very similar, twice-repeated terms:

A *(phoron . . . phoron)* + B *(telos . . . telos)*
A′ *(phobon . . . phobon)* + B′ *(timēn . . . timēn).*

"Be subject" (v 1a). The basic command, stated at the outset in quasi legal form, calls for "subjection" *(hypotassesthō).* This is by no means the same thing as the "obedience" *(hypakoē, hypakouein, peithesthai)* Paul calls for elsewhere (cf. 6:15-23). "Be subject" means primarily to recognize that one is in a subordinate position to those (the governing authorities, *exousiais*) who are "placed over" *(hyperechousais)* and to be ready to act in accordance with this recognition.

The ruler enjoys divine sanction (vv 1b-2a). The theological rationale for adopting such an attitude stems from the belief, pervasive in the ancient world, including the Jewish world, that rulers and kings owe their authority to divine disposition. The authorities presently in power *(hai . . . ousai)* wield a God-given authority. (Paul may have in mind local magistrates, whose authority would bear more immediately upon his audience than the supreme authority of the Emperor.) To resist this, then, is tantamount to resisting God (2a).

Seeking commendation, not punishment (vv 2b-4). The text reinforces this (to modern ears, chilling) logic by a consideration of what resistance to this divine disposition (the establishment of worldly authorities) will entail:

"condemnation" *(krima)*. In the ultimate sense, the "condemnation" in question is divine and eschatological. But the suggestion seems to be that worldly punishment which civil authorities inflict upon wrongdoers anticipates in some sense the final eschatological sanction of God, "the wrath" (*orgē*, v 4c). This is because, as the text twice asserts (v 4a, 4d), in bestowing "praise" *(epainos)* for good behavior and inflicting punishment in respect of bad, the civil ruler acts as God's commissioned agent *(theou . . . diakonos)*. An ambiguity, undoubtedly intentional, hovers throughout the argument: the sanction is both divine and human, the fear *(phobos)* which it inspires is fear both of human rulers and of the deity who stands behind the authority they wield. Likewise, the "sword" which the ruler wears as a sign of power to inflict penalty is no mere decoration (*ou gar eikę̄*, v 4c), neither in the human sphere nor in the divine. It is a symbol of power (to inflict punishment) ultimately received from God.

Be subject for conscience's sake (v 5). By way of a preliminary conclusion (*dio*), the text arrives securely at the principle formulated at the start (v 1a): it is "necessary" *(anagkē)* to be subject *(hypotassesthai)*. To this bald formulation it adds a rider (v 5b): the "necessity" to be subject stems not merely from fear of punishment *(dia tēn orgēn)*; "conscience" *(syneidēsis)* also enters in. This appeal to conscience, which very likely represents a Pauline addition to what is otherwise largely a traditional formulation, is of a piece with the summons to a "rational worship" that stands, thematically, at the head of the entire parenesis (12:1). For Paul "conscience" refers to that self-awareness which submits one's thoughts and actions to constant evaluation in view of a responsibility pressing in on one from without (see Note on 2:15); ultimately, for Paul, it is a responsibility before God, the supreme moral arbiter, before whom one will be called to account on the day of judgment (cf. 1 Cor 4:4; 2 Cor 5:10). So when Paul urges the Roman community to be subject also "for conscience's sake," he is suggesting that for believers a mere outward conformity through fear of temporal penalty is insufficient and unworthy. In the context of faith, their "conscience" makes them aware of the divine will standing behind the civic requirement (vv 2a, vv 3-4). "Subjection" to state authority becomes part of that obedience encompassing every aspect of the life of the believer as an embodied rational being.

Taxes and tariffs (vv 6-7). As already indicated, it is likely that the entire argument to this point has served to provide a general framework for the more specific injunction to pay taxes and tariffs that now (v 6) emerges. The motive for conforming to this specific requirement is the same (cf. *dia touto*) as before: the officials charged with the collection of taxes are, in their own way, "God's ministers" *(leitourgoi . . . theou)*. Hence this obligation comes under the scope of "conscience," in the sense outlined above.

By way of conclusion (v 7) to the entire piece Paul formulates a general ethical principle—"render to everyone their dues" *(opheilas)*—reminiscent of Jesus' response to the test question about payment of taxes (Mark 12:17 // Matt 22:21 // Luke 20:25). This serves to set the final, symmetrical couplet (see above) stating the "dues" (direct and indirect taxes; see Note) owed to tax-gathering officials within the framework of the wider "dues" owed to "all" *(pasin)*. The taxes are owed to the relevant lower officials but more fundamental "dues"—"fear" *(phobos)* and "respect" *(timē)*—are owed to the supreme authorities. The matter is not entirely clear (see Note) but it is very likely, on the basis of comparison with 1 Pet 2:17b ("Fear God, honor the king"), that the authority to whom "fear" is due is God, while the one to whom "respect" is due is the Emperor, from whom the authority of all lesser officials in the human scale descends. The final line, then, neatly catches up both the distinction and the continuity between divine and human authority that has run through the entire passage.

Reflection. The unqualified injunction to be submissive to worldly authority, along with the rationale accompanying it, has been one of the most influential passages of Romans down the ages. Theologies of Church-State relations have been erected upon it, and autocratic governments or those who have supported them have demanded civil obedience in its name. Believers who have found it necessary to resist or seek to overthrow civic power in certain of its historical manifestations have found the passage at best an embarrassment, at worst something to be rejected in the name of the broader claims of the gospel. For some it represents the "most hateful" passage in scripture.

To modern sensibility the extraordinary measure of divine guarantee attributed here to earthly rulers is naive and simplistic in the extreme. No allowance is made for abuse of power on the part of the human authority; nor is there any thought that on occasion it is the good who feel the brunt of penal sanction through either mistake or overt miscarriage of justice. In such situations, where the conditions of just government which it presupposes, do not obtain, the text loses all relevance.

Even in more positive conditions, the text scarcely applies in regard to the modern democratic state where authority derives immediately from the people, regularly exercising their democratic right to choose a government. In such a situation the theological assertion that all authority, including civic authority, ultimately derives from God, requires a great deal of nuance. Certainly, the narrow focus of the text ought to rule out any attempt to build upon it a systematic "theology" of civil authority or relations between church and state.

The text does, however, preserve the valid reminder that no government is a law entirely unto itself. At least in the perspective of the believer, all rule, all exercise of authority, is accountable to the supreme authority, God. From the side of the citizen, what also remains is the sense that civic responsibility does form part of the "worship owed by rational beings" (12:1). In the present situation, before the *parousia* of the Lord, the believer cannot simply withdraw from civic responsibility and participation simply on the plea that his or her true *politeuma* is in heaven (Phil 3:20). All is drawn before the bar of conscience and behind conscience lies accountability to God.

Notes

1. *the governing authorities: "Exousia"* in the Pauline writings normally designates the capacity, right or warrant to do something or the power exercised by those in authority. The word appears here in the sense of one who is the subject of "authority"; cf. also Luke 12:11; BAGD 278. The participial epithet *(hyperechousais)* does not refer to the supreme authority—that is, the Emperor—but simply to those "placed over" the mass of citizens, that is, the major officials of the state. The suggestion (current in the immediate post-Second World War period and especially connected with O. Cullmann) that "*exousiai*" here refers both to human rulers and to angelic powers standing behind and acting through them is now almost universally rejected. It is scarcely conceivable that Paul would call for believers to submit themselves to angelic beings, whose authority he elsewhere insists has been or is being done away with by Christ (cf. esp. Rom 8:38-39; Phil 2:9-11; 1 Cor 15:22-28; also Col 2:14-15); see further Cranfield 2.656–59.

   For there is no authority except that which is given by God: The belief, pervasive in the ancient world, that human rulers wielded divine authority comes to expression in a variety of contexts in biblical and other Jewish literature: in the "Wisdom" tradition either to exalt wisdom (Prov 8:15-16) or to stress the supreme authority of God as ruler of the universe (Sir 10:4; 17:17) or to counsel respect for rulers (Prov 24:21) or to remind rulers of their responsibility (Wis 6:1-8; in this sense see also *Ep. Arist.* 15–16, 219, 224; 4 Macc 12:11); the prophets portrayed rulers as instruments of God (Isa 10:5-6; 41:2-4, 25; 45:1; Jer 27:5-7) and the apocalyptic writers comforted Israel with the thought that earthly rulers, especially oppressive ones, ruled only at divine disposition, which could—and in due course would—be withdrawn (Dan 2:21, 37-38; 4:17, 25; 5:18-21; also *1 Enoch* 46:5; *2 Apoc. Bar.* 82:9); the Jewish historian Josephus also saw God as the one who presided over the exercise of worldly power: *War* 2.140, 390.

2. *will incur judgment:* The phrase follows Semitic idiom: a negative "judgment" (= "condemnation") is meant.

3. *For rulers are not a terror to good conduct but to bad:* "Terror" translates the Greek word *phobos*, which normally refers to the emotion of fear (cf. v 7c) but here to that which arouses fear. Presupposed seems to be the idea that such "fear" of authority is salutary since it restrains wrongdoers in society. The text com-

pletely ignores the possibility that authority can also be a "terror" to good citizens—as believers in Rome were to experience only a few years later at the time of Nero's pogrom against Christians (64 C.E.). The totally different attitude towards the state adopted by the Book of Revelation reflects this latter experience; cf. also the corrective provided by Acts 5:29: "We must obey God rather than human beings."

Do you want not to have to fear the authority?: The text here adopts the diatribe mode, using second person singular address. The question is then equivalent, logically, to the protasis of a conditional sentence, to which the following command supplies the apodosis.

commendation: The aspiration for "commendation" *(epainos)* from those in authority reflects values typical of the Greek city-state and the Hellenistic world generally.

4. *God's servant:* On the basic sense of *diakonos* as "commissioned agent," see Note on 12:7.

for good: The negative parallel to this phrase provided by *eis orgēn* towards the end of the verse means that "good" here must stand in contrast to "punishment." It does, therefore, have the ethical sense of "to help us lead good lives" but refers to well-being in the widest sense, ranging from well-being as a citizen here and now to the well-being of eternal salvation.

For he does not wear the sword to no purpose: The significance of the reference to the sword is much discussed, especially as in Paul's day the Latin phrase *ius gladii* referred to the exercise of disciplinary power in the military field only. The allusion would, however, add little to the context if the idea of power to inflict the death penalty—rather than just general policing and punishing powers—were not specifically in view. What lesser form of penalty could a sword signify?

the execution of wrath: Normally in Paul "wrath" stands simply as a designation for the eternal, eschatological punishment (2:5, 8; 5:9; 1 Thess 1:10) understood in a fairly objective way somewhat "detached" from God (though cf. 1:18-32); see Interpretation of 1:18. Here (and in v 5) it simply means "punishment"—but in a broad sense, so that the more proper reference to eschatological punishment "flows back," so to speak, to embrace the punishment inflicted by human authorities as well.

6. *For the same reason you also pay tribute:* The full causal phrase *dia touto* (contrast the simple *dio* in v 5) argues that in the matter of the payment of taxes the passage reaches its intended climax. The alternative interpretation, understanding vv 6-7 as bringing further supportive illustration or argument, lapses on the grounds that the statement in v 6 hardly brings sufficiently self-evident support to what has gone before. In itself v 6a can be taken either as a statement or as a command, according as the main verb *teleite* is understood as indicative or imperative. In strictly syntactical terms the following supportive sentence beginning with *gar* requires the indicative. However, the overall sense requires at least an implied imperative: "For this reason you pay taxes—you are right to do so and should continue to do so!"

For they are God's ministers charged to engage themselves in this very matter: The use of a different Greek word *(leitourgoi)* for the state officials reflects the change to a more particular issue—taxation; officials charged with the collection of taxes and tolls are now in view. The word group *leitourg-* is commonly used in secular sense with respect to public service and does not of itself carry religious overtones. Hence the tax officials are not invested with a cultic aura—though the total statement does claim for them the same divine authorization applied earlier to higher officials (*diakonoi*; cf. v 4). The phrase "in this very matter" *(eis auto touto)* is best taken as referring precisely to the collection of taxes.

7. *Render to everyone their dues:* The Greek verb *apodidonai* has the sense of giving back something owed as a debt. The same verb, in precisely the same form *(apodote)*, features in the Synoptic logion concerning the payment of tax (Mark 12:17 // Matt 22:21 // Luke 20:25). In Luke's version the introductory question refers to the tax as *phoros*, as in Rom 13:4, 5. Moreover, the sequence in Romans from the "tax" issue of 13:6-7 to the passage about the primacy of the "debt" of love (13:8-10) has an interesting parallel in Mark's gospel in that the "tax" question (12:13-17) is followed very closely by the question about the "first commandment *(entolē)* of all" and Jesus' response in the terms of the primacy of love (12:28-34). In the light of these considerations, some connection with the Synoptic tradition is hard to exclude.

the tribute to whom the tribute is due, the tax to whom tax is due: The distinction between *phoros* ("tribute") and *telos* ("tax") is that between direct and indirect taxes. Roman citizens were exempt from paying the former (Latin: *tributum*) in Rome; the latter involved mainly taxes on commercial transactions, revenues from rents, etc. (Latin: *vectigalia*).

fear to whom fear is due, respect to whom respect is due: The chief reason arguing that God rather than earthly rulers should be seen as the object of the "fear" is that "fear" very rarely, if at all, has earthly rulers as object in the NT, whereas references to "fearing God" are regular. Moreover, if v 7c contains an injunction to render fear to earthly rulers, such a positive commendation of "fear" would clash with the way in which "fear" of earthly rulers is presented in vv 3-4: as something negative, applicable only to wrongdoers. The chief difficulty faced by the "theological" interpretation is that it appears to pair off the deity with merely human rulers in a list of those to whom honor is due. However, formal considerations of constructing the epigrammatic couplet might have overriden theological sensitivities at this one point.

For Reference and Further Study

Bammel, E. "Romans 13." *Jesus and the Politics of His Day.* Eds. E. Bammel & C. F. D. Moule. Cambridge: Cambridge University, 1984, 365–83.

Barrett, C. K. "The New Testament Doctrine of Church and State." *New Testament Essays*. London: SPCK, 1972, 1–19.

Borg, M. "A New Context for Romans 13." *NTS* 19 (1972–73) 205–18.

Bornkamm, G. *Paul* 210–16.
Bruce, F.F. "Paul and 'The Powers That Be.'" *BJRL* 66 (1984) 78–96.
Cullmann, O. *The State in the New Testament*. New York: Scribners, 1956, 55–70, 93–114.
Friedrich, J., Pöhlmann, W. and Stuhlmacher, P. "Zur historischen Situation und Intention von Röm 13,1-7." *ZTK* 73 (1976) 131–166.
Furnish, V. *Moral Teaching* 115–41.
Käsemann, E. "Principles of the Interpretation of Romans 13." *New Testament Questions of Today* 196–216.
Kallas, J. "Romans 13:1-7: An Interpolation?" *NTS* 11 (1964–65) 365–74.
McDonald, J. I. "Romans 13.1–7: a Test Case for New Testament Interpretation." *NTS* 35 (1989) 540–49.
Moxnes, H. "Honor, Shame, and the Outside World: Paul's Letter to the Romans." *The Social World of Formative Christianity and Judaism* (FS H. C. Kee). Ed. J. Neusner et al. Philadelphia: Fortress, 1988, 207–18.
Stein, R. H. "The Argument of Romans xiii 1–7." *NovT* 31 (1989) 325–43.
Winter, B. W. "The Public Honouring of Christian Benefactors. Romans 13.3–4 and 1 Peter 2.14–15." *JSNT* 34 (1988) 87–103.

e) *The Sole Debt of Love* (13:8-10)

8. Be indebted in no way to anyone, save in respect to loving one another. For the person who loves has fulfilled the other part of the law.
9. The commandments, "You shall not commit adultery, You shall not kill, You shall not steal, You shall not covet," and any other commandment, are summed up in this sentence, "You shall love your neighbor as yourself." 10. Love does no wrong to a neighbor.
Love, therefore, is the fulfillment of the law.

Interpretation

Introduction. This attractive little sequence with its focus upon "love" resumes and completes the exhortation begun in 12:9 with the words, "Let love be genuine." Thus the theme of "love" brackets the entire central section of the parenesis, 12:9–13:10, including the otherwise intrusive passage on obedience to civil authorities. Paul hardly means to suggest the payment of taxes ought be inspired by love. But the "bracketing" does enfold all obligations, from the sublime to the most mundane, within the one central response of love. No domain of Christian life stands apart from this core requirement.

The passage itself shows a neatly "inclusive" structure. The dominant theme of love as the "fulfillment of the law" occurs at the beginning (v 8b) and end (v 10b), "framing" the intervening scriptural argument in v 9, which supports it.

The sole "debt": Love (v 8a). Paul skillfully ties the section to what has gone before by picking up the note of "payment of debt" upon which the preceding section had ended. Debts should be paid to those to whom they are due (v 7), and Christians are not exempt from this fundamental human reponsibility. In one area, however, they will never be able completely to discharge the debt they have contracted. Love *(agapē)* is an inexhaustible debt because it is one created directly by the infinite love which believers have themselves received from God in Christ. This costly love (8:32), which grasped them as "enemies" (5:10), has created a corresponding (inexhaustible) "debt" of love owed to fellow human beings, deserving or undeserving as the case may be. To all—even the most difficult and unlovable—believers owe a debt of love flowing from the love with which God loved them as unreconciled and "enemies."

Love fulfills the law (vv 8b-10). Somewhat surprisingly at first sight Paul supports the commendation of love by speaking of it as the "fulfillment" of the law (cf. v 10b). Though there is undoubtedly a polemical edge to this statement, the primary concern is not to drive yet another nail into the coffin of law-righteousness. What is said about the law stands at the service of the commendation of love. To readers who have been led to see in the ethical requirements of the Jewish law the sole and irreplaceable guide to righteous living Paul insists that love provides a sufficient and more fundamental basis.

A parallel passage in Gal 5:14 insists that "the whole law" is fulfilled in the command to love one's neighbor as oneself (Lev 19:18). Here (Rom 13:8b) Paul speaks of the fulfillment of "the other (part of the) law" *(ton heteron nomon)*. The fact that he goes on (v 9) to list four commandments specifically relating to conduct towards the neighbor—prohibitions against adultery, homicide, stealing and coveting—suggests that "the other part of the law" refers to the "Second Table" of the law, that is, to the final five commandments of the Decalogue specifically concerned with duties towards one's fellow human beings in distinction to the earlier ones concerned with duties towards God (for an alternative way of understanding *ton heteron*, see Note). All these and—Paul adds in a catch-all aside reinforcing the polemical tone—"any other commandment there might be" are "summed up" in the single injunction taken from the Book of Leviticus (19:18), "You shall love your neighbor as yourself". Paul does not necessarily mean that all commandments are reduced to love but that love—expressed in this way—goes to the essence of the matter. The one who truly loves in the way described will be found to have fulfilled all the commandments of the law bearing upon duties to the neighbor.

The following statement (v 10a) about love doing no wrong to a neighbor seems negative and inadequate at first sight. Surely love is about a lot more than not harming (literally, doing no evil to) one's neighbor? But the negative is exactly Paul's point. The commandments cited are prohibitions; they all proscribe things that would harm the neighbor. Together they suggest that this is the law's way: negatively to restrain harmful action (cf. 7:7). Whereas love, picking up the essence of the law as defined in Lev 19:18, is a positive thing that catches up and goes beyond the prohibition. It invites one to place *oneself* precisely in the position of the neighbor and allow one's action to flow from the question, "What would I desire in this situation?" rather than, "What ought I do or refrain from doing with regard to this person?" This is why love is "the fulfillment *(plērōma)* of the law" (v 10b). It fulfills all the law requires, and actively goes beyond it (cf. Matt 5:43-48).

In the light of the central thesis earlier in the letter (3:21–4:25; 7:1–8:4) that believers are essentially removed from the law, one might well ask why there remains at this point any suggestion at all that the law is something to be "fulfilled." Paul clearly believed that the central ethical values of the law, as distinct from the more ritual prescriptions (circumcision, food laws, sabbath and feasts), remained in force for believers. Nowhere, however, does he explicitly make such a distinction within the law and, in fact, it does not appear to have been one made in Judaism as a whole. Rather than a distinction "within" the content of the law, what is more likely to be implicit here is a distinction between what the law prescribes *as law* and the values which it enshrines as an expression of God's will for human beings in an ethical sense. For believers these do not impose themselves as law, as something from without. Rather, they are "fulfilled" within believers through the indwelling gift of the Spirit (Rom 8:4. 9-11), in realization of the promises for the eschatological age contained in Jer 31:33 and Ezek 36:26. The "fulfillment" of the law by love is, in terms of law, a metaphorical fulfillment only. It is Paul's way of communicating to Christian converts who may have a lingering sense of the law as the perfect expression of God's will that love is a more than adequate way to carry out all that the law, in the old dispensation, required.

Notes

8. *to loving one another:* "One another" *(allēlous)* probably refers in the first instance to members of the community but there is no reason, especially in view of 12:17-21, to exclude a wider reference.

For the person who loves has fulfilled the other part of the law: The translation and interpretation given involves attaching the phrase *ton heteron* to *nomon* as part of the object of the verb *peplērōken* rather than seeing it as supplying the object for the participle *agapōn,* so as to give the sense "the person who loves another." The latter is usually preferred on the grounds that the absolute use of *ho agapōn* is unprecedented in Paul and that he never distinguishes two "laws" in the way that such a use of *heteros* would suggest. But the way is prepared for the absolute use here by the thematic expression *hē agapē anypokritos* in 12:9. Secondly, there is no question of two "laws" but of an allusion to what was known as the "Second Table" of the Decalogue, the commandments dealing with duties to the neighbor (cf. Philo, *Decal.* 121). Moreover, had Paul intended *ho agapōn* to have an object ("neighbor"), instead of the adjective *heteros* (used as a noun), he would more likely have written *ton plēsion* ("neighbor"), the formulation in Lev 19:18, which he is about to quote.

9. *The commandments, "You shall not commit adultery, You shall not kill, You shall not steal, You shall not covet":* Paul quotes the seventh, sixth, eighth and tenth commandments (in the traditional Catholic numbering: the sixth, fifth, seventh and a combination of the ninth and tenth). The order of the first two differs from that of the Hebrew in Exod 20:13-17 and Deut 5:17-21; it is that reflected in LXX Ms B and certain other witnesses.

are summed up in this sentence, "You shall love your neighbor as yourself": The verb *anakephalaiousthai* was used of the summary or recapitulation of the main points made by a speaker towards the end of an oration (cf. BAGD 55–56; H. Schlier, *TDNT* 3:681-82). The sense is therefore that of drawing all things together under a single statement which can stand for all. Paul's citation of Lev 19:18 in this way almost certainly reflects some dependence upon the Jesus tradition, manifest in the Synoptic logion of the "Great Commandment" (Matt 22:34-40; Mark 12:28-34; Luke 10:25-28), though Paul here (as also in Gal 5:14) omits any mention of the prior requirement to love God and makes no explicit appeal to the authority of Jesus. The idea of the law being summed up under a single head is neither distinctively Christian nor unprecedented in Judaism, though instances cited for Judaism do not certainly antedate the rise of Christianity (e.g., R. Akiba's [early 2nd century C.E.] pointing to Lev 19:18 as the greatest comprehensive principle of the entire Torah [*Sipra* on Lev 19:18; SB 1.357], as also R. Hillel's oft-cited negative statement of the "Golden Rule": "What is hateful to you, do not do to your neighbor: that is the whole Torah, while the rest is commentary on it. Go and learn" [*b. Šabb.* 31a; SB 1.357–58]).

10. *Love does no wrong to a neighbor:* The negative formulation is matched by the predominantly negative formulation of the "descriptions" of love in action (eight out of eleven) given in 1 Cor 13:4-6.

the fulfillment of the law: The Greek word *plērōma* is open to a wide range of meaning; see Note on 11:12. The parallel with the verbal form in the perfect, *peplērōken* in v 8, suggests that "fulfillment" is the best translation here in the sense of the effect resulting from the process of fulfilling having been completed; this is also the most literal sense communicated by the *-ma* ending. Some interpreters (e.g., Cranfield 2.678; Wilckens 3.71; cf. also Dunn 2.780–81) see here the more active sense "fulfilling" but this places far too much emphasis upon the law and brings with it the whole problem of how and to what extent believers are considered by Paul to (actively) fulfill the law. Paul customarily uses *plērōma* in the passive sense: cf. 11:12, 25; 15:29; Gal 4:4; 1 Cor 10:26.

For Reference and Further Study

Dülmen, A. van, *Theologie des Gesetzes* 225–30.
Furnish, V. P. *Love Command* 108–11.
Hübner, H. *Law in Paul's Thought* 83–86.
Lyonnet, S. "La charité plénitude de la loi: (Rom 13, 8-10)." *Études* 310–28.
Räisänen, H. *Paul and the Law* 26–27, 33–36, 64–66.
Sanders, E. P. *Paul, the Law and the Jewish People* 93–122.
Schreiner, T. R. "The Abolition and Fulfilment of the Law in Paul." *JSNT* 35 (1989) 47–74.
Spicq, C. *Agapè* 1.259–66.
Thompson, M. *Clothed with Christ* 121–40.
Wischmeyer, O. "Das Gebot der Nächstenliebe bei Paulus. Eine traditionsgeschichtliche Untersuchung." *BZ* 30 (1986) 161–187.

f) *"Knowing the Time"* (13:11-14)

11. In all this recognize the time, that it is already the hour for you to wake from sleep. For our salvation is nearer now than when we first believed; 12. the night is far spent, the day is at hand. Let us then cast off the works of darkness and put on the armor of light; 13. let us conduct ourselves decently as in the day, not in reveling and drunkenness, not in sexual licence and debauchery, not in quarreling and envy. 14. But put on the Lord Jesus Christ, and do not carry out the intent of the flesh to gratify its desires.

Interpretation

Introduction. Paul began his general exhortation (parenesis) in 12:1-2 on an eschatological note, summoning his audience not to be "conformed to this world" but to "be transformed by the renewal of (their) mind" (v 2). Now, in "inclusive" fashion, he rounds off the parenesis on the same eschatological note. An appeal to eschatology to strengthen exhortation is comparatively widespread in the NT (cf. Phil 4:4-7; Col 4:5; Eph 5:16; Heb 10:25; 1 Pet 4:7; Jas 5:7-11; Matt 24:37-51; 25:1-30; Mark 13:33-37; Luke 12:35-46). In particular, the present passage has a notable foreshadowing in a passage in Paul's earliest letter: 1 Thess 5:1-11.

The exhortation is built upon a swift flow of associated metaphors, all proceeding from the basic image of people awakening from sleep at the onset of morning. The core of the text appears to consist in a set-piece baptismal instruction or hymn, which Paul has elaborated to make it serve his more immediate parenetic purpose. The original can probably be reconstructed from elements of vv 11-12 as follows (cf. Wilckens 3.75):

> It is already the hour for you to wake from sleep;
> the night is far spent, the day is at hand.
> Let us then cast off the works of darkness
> and put on the armor of light.

As reconstructed in this way the "hymn" may be compared to similar lines in Eph 5:14:

> "Awake, O sleeper,
> and arise from the dead,
> and Christ will shine his light upon you."

Pauline elaborations would consist of the introductory v 11a and the explanatory v 11c, then the more specific exposition of the "works of darkness" in v 13 and the exposition of "the armor of light" in terms of "putting on" Christ (v 14).

Recognize the time (v 11). Paul reinforces the parenesis by calling attention to "the time" *(kairos)* in which believers now stand. The Greek term *kairos* has the sense of a particularly significant time (cf. 3:26; 5:6; 8:18; 9:9; 11:5 and see Note on 3:26). What believers must recognize is the precise significance of the present time, which, according to the distinctive early Christian eschatology, is the time of the "overlap" of the "ages": outwardly the old age still prevails—in the persistence of suffering and death and the continuing allure of the "flesh" (v 14b; cf. 8:5-8); inwardly, however, the eye of faith discerns in the resurrection of Jesus and the gift of the Spirit the true dawning of the new age, which brings a total transformation of relationships—with God and fellow human beings. "Recognizing the time" means penetrating the outer shell of the old passing world (cf. 1 Cor 7:31b) to discern the new reality that is taking shape within (Rom 8:22). It means allowing that new reality and the sense that it will soon outwardly and finally prevail (cf. 1 Cor 15:24-28) to shape the pattern of one's life.

Paul develops (v 11b) the call to this discernment of the time by introducing the controlling image of the entire passage: that of a person waking from sleep at the onset of dawn. The ethical intensification comes from the sense of "it's time" *(hōra)* to get up: time to slough off the "sleep" of attachment to the old age, to wake up and adjust to the reality of the "new day" (new age) about to dawn.

An explanatory comment (v 11c) underlines the urgency: the further we are from the time of our first believing *(episteusamen)* the closer we are to our full salvation *(sōtēria)*. As normally in Paul, "salvation" refers, negatively, to the final rescue of believers from the "wrath" (= eschatological punishment) due to fall upon the world at the time of the great judgment (2:5; 5:9; 1 Thess 1:10); positively, it means full entrance into blessings in store for the eschatological people of God. The present life of believers is situated "between" justification (in which the final relationship with God has been established through faith) and salvation in this future sense. Paul's reasoning, then, is that the further we are from our initial act of believing, the further we are along the road to salvation. Hence the demands of the "time" press more insistently rather than less. The fact that the "gap" between justification and salvation has, for subsequent readers down to the present, stretched immeasurably wider than Paul envisaged does not really undercut his argument, since in no sense is it anchored upon a particular calculation of time. It rests simply upon the discernment that a new world is being born and that Christian existence belongs radically to that new world rather than to the old.

Clothing for the day (v 12). The text resumes the hymn stating the reason for the summons just given to awake: the night is far spent *(proekopsen)*, the dawn (literally, "the day") is close at hand *(ēngiken)*. The time envisaged would seem to be that final half-hour or so of darkness before the onset of the light of dawn. In the ancient world (as also in present-day societies where electricity is not available) the prudent rose at this time in order to take maximum advantage of the light of day. The image of waking from sleep can shift naturally, then, to that of changing clothes (v 12bc). As a person getting up casts off night wear and puts on clothes in preparation for the work of the day, so "we" are exhorted to "cast off *(apothōmetha)*" the "works of darkness *(ta erga tou skotous)*" and "put on *(endysametha)*" the "armor of light *(ta hopla tou phōtos)*."

With these phrases, the imagery of "night" and "day" subtly changes into that of "darkness" and "light" widespread in biblical and extrabiblical literature. In the phrase "works *(erga)* of darkness" it is hard for one who has followed the entire letter not to hear some overtones of the earlier polemic against reliance upon "works of the law," which represents adherence to the doomed structures of the old, passing age. The mention on the positive side, not of "works" but of "armor" (*hopla*;

cf. 6:13) lends the sense (cf. already 1 Thess 5:8 [developed in Eph 6:10-17]) of equipping oneself for battle with the (demonic) forces ruling the present age, which will not give in without a struggle. Only as "armed" in this way will the believer be able to survive and operate in the present time. The nearness of the end, when the forces of evil will make a last devastating onslaught before being overcome (cf. Mark 13:7-8, 19-20, 24) makes it all the more urgent to gird oneself effectively for battle.

Conduct becoming of the day (v 13). The quotation of the hymn ended, Paul resumes and develops the "night"/"day" imagery. The force of the exhortation derives from the common perception that conduct characteristic of the night differs from that characteristic of the day. In the day, when all can observe, human beings tend to act "decently" *(euskēmonōs)*; the darkness of the night, however, provides a cloak for all kinds of evil deeds, which would bring only shame if exposed in the light of day (cf. John 3:19-21). Paul does not elaborate on what, for believers, "walking decently" in the light of day might mean; in a sense, that has already been the burden of the entire exhortation from 12:3 onward. On the negative side, however, in three parallel couplets, he does enlarge upon (v 13b) what, specifically, the "works of darkness" (v 12b) might consist in: drunken revelry, unbridled sexual indulgence and the kind of quarreling and rancor that easily breaks into violence. The description tallies well with indications from ancient authors of what went on in the taverns of Rome at night. Paul hardly means to suggest that his Christian audience at Rome stood in urgent need of warning against participation in such vice. The list on the negative side is designed to lend force, by way of antithesis, to the positive injunction to live "decently as in the day," that is, to adopt the pattern of life appropriate for those who recognize that they live in the dawn of the new day ushered in by Christ.

Put on Christ (v 14). Resuming the "clothing" image, Paul summons his audience, on the positive side, to "put on *(endysasthe)* the Lord Jesus Christ." Apart from the image of getting dressed stemming from the context, the motif of "putting on Christ" had an independent currency particularly in connection with baptism (cf. esp. Gal 3:27: ". . . inasmuch as you have been baptized into Christ, you have put on Christ"; cf. Rom 6:3). Behind the image may lie the background of the Greek drama where the garment "put on" by actors portraying a particular character was customarily so all-enveloping that they could rightly be said to have abandoned their individual identity to "put on" completely that of the character portrayed. To "put on" Christ is to "put on" the renewed humanity of the new age, which he models and facilitates as "Last Adam" and risen Lord (1 Cor 15:45, 49; Rom 8:29-30; 2 Cor 3:18; Phil 3:21). As later in Col 3:9-10 and Eph 4:24, the "indicative" associated with baptism appears here as an imperative "put on" *(endysasthe)*. The conformity to the risen Lord radically established in baptism is the beginning of a lifelong task to allow that conformity to find expression in one's subsequent pattern of life (cf. esp. Rom 6:3-5). Thus Paul draws the wider motif of "putting on Christ" into the imagery of the present passage centered upon rising from sleep to clothe and arm oneself for the challenges and opportunities of the day.

"Putting on the Lord Jesus Christ" means taking firm action against the "flesh" (*sarx*, v 14b). The list describing behavior characteristic of the night given in v 13b corresponds very closely to the list of "works of the flesh" given in Gal 5:19-21. They are all manifestations of "flesh" understood as human nature weak, vulnerable to sin, hostile to God, oriented towards death rather than life. So long as believers remain in the "overlap" of the ages, their bodies not yet sharing the risen life of their Lord, they necessarily remain "in the flesh" and feel the pull of its orientation towards sin (cf. Rom 8:5-8). The difference, however, between the present situation (dominated by the Spirit: Rom 7:6; 8:1-13) and the former (dominated by sin: Rom 7:5, 14-25) is that, though "*in* the flesh" *(en sarki)*, they do not have to live "*according* to the flesh" *(kata sarka)*. The struggle is not unequal (see Interpretation of 8:5-11). The Spirit gives the capacity to restrain the impulse of the flesh, so that they do not *have* to give in to "its (evil) desires" *(eis epithymias)* but can truly live the life of the new era (cf. 6:4).

Notes

11. *In all this recognize the time:* The Greek phrase *kai touto* is an idiom serving to introduce additional circumstances enhancing the force of what has just been said (cf. 1 Cor 6:6, 8). "Recognize" translates the participle *eidotes*, which, like the participles in 12:9-21, has imperative force.

that it is already the hour: Again, the phrase represents a Greek idiom—*hōra* followed by an infinitive—to express the sense of "It's time to do something"; *ēdē* ("already") contributes an additional note of urgency. The sense of God's appointed eschatological "hour" is close to that of LXX Dan 8:17, 19; 11:35, in each of which passages *hōra* and *kairos* appear together; cf. also *2 Apoc. Bar.* 82:2.

to wake from sleep: The image of "sleep" to denote a negative state from which one ought to "wake" was familiar in ancient literature; see H. Balz, *TDNT* 8.545–56. In the NT, as in biblical and post-biblical Jewish literature, the reference is primarily ethical and eschatological; cf. Prov 6:9; *4 Ezra* 7:31-32; Matt 24:42-44 (para. Luke 12:39-40); Matt 25:1-13; 1 Cor 15:34; 1 Thess 5:6-7; Eph 6:18; Rev 3:2-3; 16:15.

our salvation is nearer now: The translation takes the possessive pronoun *hēmōn* as attached to the noun *sōtēria* rather than as qualifying *engyteron* to give the sense "salvation is nearer to us." Apart from being more natural, the former agrees with Paul's tendency to personalize "salvation" (cf. 2 Cor 1:6; Phil 1:28; 2:12).

when we first believed: The aorist tense *(episteusamen)* points to the moment of initial faith—the beginning of Christian life (ingressive aorist; cf. BDF §331); cf. Gal 2:16.

12. *the night is far spent:* The verb *prokoptein* has the sense of "go forward," "advance" (BAGD 707–08); the translation attempts to catch the sense of the aorist.

the day is at hand: The text uses the same Greek verb, *engizein,* that is used in the Synoptic tradition for the near approach—but not yet arrival—of the Kingdom (Rule) of God (Mark 1:15; Matt 3:2; 4:17; 10:7; Luke 10:9).

Let us then cast off the works of darkness and put on the armor of light: For the first verb *apothōmetha* a variant textual tradition (P^{46} D* F G) has the more vigorous *apobalōmetha* ("let us throw off"). Either way the sense is scarcely affected. The context so clearly suggests the image of changing from night apparel to day apparel that the hesitations of some interpreters (e.g., Cranfield 2.685) on the basis that it seems not to have been the custom in the first century to wear special garments at night seem overdrawn. The image of "light"/"darkness" is widespread in the Bible (e.g., Pss 43:3; 44:19; Isa 9:2; 42:6-7; 60:1-3; Matt 4:16; Luke 16:8; John 1:4-5; 3:2, 19-21; 8:12; 9:1-41; 11:9-10; Acts 26:18; 2 Cor 6:14; Eph 5:8; Col 1:12-13; 1 Thess 5:4-5) and forms one of the notable points of comparison between the NT and the literature of Qumran: 1QS 2:7; 3:20-26; 1QM 1:1, 3, 7-10; 3:6, 9; 13:5, 10-12, 15-16; 15:9. For Paul's use of "works" *(erga)* in connection with the law, see Note on 3:20. For the use of "armor" (lit. "weapons" *[hopla]*) in an ethical context, see Note on 6:13.

13. *let us conduct ourselves decently as in the day:* It is possible to see in "day" a reference to the dawning new age giving the sense "as if the Day were already here." But it seems best to stay within the terms of the image: we are to behave as people do during the day, that is, "decently" *(euschēmenōs).* Staying within the image also obviates a problem that arises for some in the sense that with the latter adverb Paul seems to be commending "bourgeois" rather than notably Christian virtue. Believers are not being asked simply to live "decently." What the image contributes is the thought that, *just as* people tend to adjust their behavior in daytime, so believers ought to live (Christian) virtues appropriate for "the Day" which they believe to be dawning.

not in reveling and drunkenness, not in sexual licence and debauchery, not in quarreling and envy: Each pair within the three-line block amounts, more or less, to a single composite idea (hendiadys): so "drunken reveling," "sexual debauchery," "thrusting quarrelsomeness," with the plural forms of the first two pairs suggesting repeated practice. Four of the six items *(kōmai, methē, aselgeiai, zēlos)* appear also in the list of "works of the flesh" in Gal 5:19-21, suggesting that Paul is working from a reasonably standardized list, though the list in Romans is far more intentionally arranged in line with the careful structuring of the passage as a whole.

14. *put on the Lord Jesus Christ:* The possibility of a theatrical background to this Pauline expression is reinforced by the fact that an earlier Greek author, Dionysius of Halicarnassus, also uses the verb occurring here *(endyesthai)* with respect to an actor playing a role: "to play the role of *(endyesthai)* Tarquin"; cf. A. Oepke, *TDNT* 2.319; Dunn, 2.790.

do not carry out the intent of the flesh to gratify its desires: The sentence is normally translated with the words *pronoian . . . poieisthai* interpreted as a fixed phrase attested in Greek literature with the meaning "make provision for something" or "be concerned about something," thus rendering the total statement "and make no provision for the flesh to satisfy its desires" (cf. BAGD 708–09). But this seems very weak considering Paul's strongly negative sense of "flesh," particularly as illustrated by the behavior catalogued in v 13b. The fact that the phrase does not occur elsewhere in the NT offers some grounds for taking *pronoian* separately here and understanding the genitive *(sarkos)* subjectively, as in the translation given in the text; cf. Käsemann 363. The sense then comes very close to Gal 5:16: *kai epithymian sarkos ou mē telesēte*. "Desire" (*epithymia*) has here the bad sense customary in Paul: cf. esp. 1:24; 7:7-8 and the Note on 7:8.

For Reference and Further Study

Lövestam, E. *Spiritual Wakefulness in the New Testament.* Lund: Gleerup, 1963, 25–45.

Thompson, M. *Clothed with Christ* 141–60.

Vögtle, A. "Röm 13,11-14 und die 'Nah'-Erwartung." *Rechtfertigung* (FS E. Käsemann). Ed. J. Friedrich et al. Tübingen: Mohr, 1976, 557–73.

__________. "Paraklese und Eschatologie nach Röm 13:11-14." *Dimensions de la vie chrétienne.* Ed. L. de Lorenzi; Rome: Abbaye de S. Paul, 1979, 179–94.

iii. Tolerance in Contentious Areas of Community Life (14:1–15:13)

Introduction to 14:1–15:13. Up to this point, save for the instruction concerning civil authorities (13:1-7), Paul's exhortation (parenesis) has been general in nature. Now (14:1) it addresses what appears to be a far more specific issue concerned with eating and drinking and the reckoning of holy days.

But the passage does not provide a clear picture of the precise issue at stake and, as a result, many interpretative questions arise. Paul initially (14:1-2) refers to "the person weak in faith" and towards the end summons "the strong" (with whom he identifies himself) to "bear with the weaknesses of the weak" (15:1). These allusions have led interpreters to distinguish two parties or groups addressed—the "strong" and the "weak" (cf. similar references to the person of "weak conscience" in 1 Cor 8:7 [cf. vv 9, 10, 11, 12])—and to seek to determine the "profile" of each on the basis of behavior or attitudes described. The "strong" have sufficient faith to be confident that they can eat "all things" (14:1-2), including meat (v 21), and drink wine (v 20); they also reckon no particular day to be more significant than any other (v 5). The lesser faith of the "weak," on the contrary, leads them to eat only vegetables (v 2); they refrain from meat and, it would appear, also from wine (v 21), and they do reckon some days to be more significant than others. The "strong" tend to "belittle" the "weak" (vv 3a, 10b), who in turn "pass judgment upon" (= condemn) the "strong" (vv 3b, 10a).

From a historical and sociological perspective, it is by no means easy to assign persons having such "profiles" to identifiable groups likely to be represented in the Christian community in Rome. Nonetheless, the centrality of the distinction between Jews and Gentiles in the letter has led many to see in the "weak" representatives of a particularly Jewish concern for the prescriptions of the law in matters of food and the observance of days (sabbaths, festivals, fasts), while the "strong" would represent those who had decidedly moved away from or never shared such concerns. Such a division would not simply run: "weak" = believers of Jewish origin; "strong" = believers of Gentile origin. Some Gentiles might remain deeply attached to principles and practices they had learned to adopt as "God-fearers" or proselytes, while some Jews—like Paul himself (cf. 15:1)—might equally range themselves among the "strong."

The problem is that, while the Jewish Torah did of course provide strict laws concerning food and the observance of days, it did not prescribe abstention from meat nor forbid the consumption of wine. What is alluded to in Romans 14 goes well beyond normal Jewish practice. This has led certain scholars to look in other directions for the scruples of the weak in faith: to the wider pagan background, in particular the ascetic and vegetarian tendencies represented by neo-Pythagorean groups. Others think of influence stemming from the kind of syncretistic Jewish tendencies (possibly tinged with a species of proto-Gnosticism) rejected in the letter to the Colossians (cf. esp. the reference to "food and drink . . . festival, new moon, sabbath" in 2:16).

One important factor is the use of the technical Jewish legal term "unclean" *(koinos)* in 14:14. It is hard to explain this allusion on any basis other than Jewish religious sensitivities. Moreover, there is evidence of strict Jews abstaining from certain dishes in circumstances (pagan environments) where correct implementation of what the food laws required could not be guaranteed: cf. Dan 1:8, 12, 16; Tob 1:11; *Add. Esther* 14:17; 2 Macc 5:27; Josephus *Life* 14 (a reference to Jewish priests held captive in Rome, who lived on figs and nuts, probably for fear of eating food tainted with idolatry).

In the light of such allusions—admittedly somewhat scattered and remote—it could be that the weak in faith abstained from eating meat because, in a pagan environment, they could not be sure that it had been slaughtered in accordance with the law's requirements (the blood properly drained: Lev 3:17; 7:26-27; 17:10-14; cf. Acts 15:20, 29). Another source of scruple would be the possibility that meat sold in the open market may have come from animals used in pagan sacrifice—the issue that agitated Paul's converts in Corinth, eliciting from him a parallel but by no means identical response (1 Corinthians 8–10). The scruples of the weak in faith would then have stemmed from a more general Jewish (and Christian) abhorrence of idolatry and/or a sense that blood contained the divine principle of life, whereas a "stronger" faith has found its way to a surer sense of the boundaries between the divinity and the created world. (Abstention from wine—if such really was an issue [see below]—could be similarly explained on the basis that at some stage prior to its being sold it might have been associated with the libations customary in pagan worship.)

As regards food, specifically meat, the evidence of the Apostolic Decree formulated in Acts 15:28-29 is important because it includes amongst the "essential things" from which it does not exempt Gentile believers "what has been sacrificed to idols," "what is strangled" and "blood" (v 29; cf. v 20; also Acts 21:25). The combination here of both "idol-meat" *(eidolothyta)* and "blood" (the textual status of "what is strangled" is uncertain) argues against coming down on one side or other of the suggestions made. Paul has chosen to speak simply of eating meat in Romans, avoiding specific mention of "idol meat," as constantly in 1 Corinthians 8–10. The Apostolic Decree in fact reflects the position of the "weak in faith" and testifies to its later prevalence in important circles of the community. What Paul may be seeking to project in Romans is the kind of tolerance that would find room for the range of concerns reflected later in the Decree.

As just noted, Paul identifies himself with the "strong" (15:1) and it is to them that the parenesis is principally addressed. The language used —the epithets "strong" and "weak"—in any case must reflect the "in-talk" of the "strong." It is hard to see how the "weak in faith," if such a "party" existed, would find the epithet attached to them anything but offensive. Did Paul expect a party addressed in such terms to respond positively to the appeals to refrain from judging which he appears to launch early in the sequence in their direction (14:3-4, 10)? It could be that the instances where, in diatribe form, both "parties" are addressed in a formally balanced way amount to nothing more than a rhetorical ploy on

Paul's part—to make the "strong" feel that they are not the sole offenders or single target of his challenge.

On these lines, the way lies open to identify the implied audience of the parenesis with Gentile believers whose "strong" faith tempts them to be impatient with the hesitations of brothers and sisters (Jewish or Gentile) who adhere more closely to the kind of Jewish religious sensitivity reflected in the Apostolic Decree. Paul may not necessarily be attempting to smooth out disputes in the Roman community that have already come to his attention; to what extent, if at all, he directs the instruction to an actual situation in Rome we simply cannot know. What the sequence projects is a sense of Paul attempting to curb the intolerance of those who share his own point of view, within the framework of a more general appeal for tolerance in Christian community life. Pastoral experience may have led him to believe that problems over food regularly constituted a source of friction in the mixed communities of the Mediterranean world and that Rome was likely to be no exception in this regard. But it is also possible that the instruction concerning food—along with the vaguer allusions to "counting days" and drinking wine—may simply be designed, amongst other things, to communicate a less alarming image of himself. The announcement of a visit from Paul, when finally stated (15:24), will be more generally acceptable if preceded by an exhortation to tolerance directed to those in Rome who particularly share his point of view.

Paul does not compromise that point of view in this instruction. But he does show how a religious community may creatively handle dissent on non-essentials when such disagreement is placed within the wider and more essential context of the "inclusive mercy" all alike have received from God (cf. 11:30-32; 15:9).

Structure. The sequence as a whole is bound together by an "inclusion" formed by the theme of "acceptance": the opening summons (14:1) to accept the person weak in faith (because God has accepted that person, v 4) is matched by the culminating appeal (15:7) to "accept one another, just as Christ has accepted you." This final appeal continues down to the end of the parenesis at v 13.

Within this overall framework, the sequence unfolds in four parts: 14:1-12; 14:13-23; 15:1-6; 15:7-13. The block making up 14:1-12 consists of an appeal for tolerance that is, formally at least, addressed to two groups. V 13 functions as a bridge to a new section, 14:13-23, where the appeal is far more exclusively directed to the "strong in faith," the central argument (reiterated three times: v 13b, v 15, vv 20-21) being that of not putting a stumbling block in the way of the brother or sister for whom Christ died, so causing his or her ruin. This appeal to the "strong" is renewed in a reflection, 15:1-6, upon the example of Christ foreshadowed in the scriptures (vv 3-4), capped off by an extended prayer-wish (vv 5-6). Though this last item would provide an appropriate conclusion to the entire instruction, the "inclusion" formed by the section commending mutual acceptance, 15:7-13 (cf. 14:1) suggests that it too ought be seen as the true conclusion of the overall instruction (note the further prayer-wish in v 13).

a) *The Tolerance Incumbent upon All* (14:1-12)

1. As for the person who is weak in faith, accept that person,
but not with a view to settling matters over which there is dispute. 2.
One believes anything may be eaten, while the person weak (in faith)
eats only vegetables.
3. Let not the one who eats belittle the one who abstains,
and let not the one who abstains pass judgment on the one who eats; for
God has accepted that person.
4. Who are you to pass judgment on the slave of another? It is in relation
to their own master that slaves stand or fall. And they shall stand, for the
master is able to make them stand.
5. One person judges one day as more significant than another, while another judges all days alike. Let each one be fully convinced in their own
mind.
6. The one who takes account of the day, does so to the Lord. And the
person also who eats, does so to the Lord—for indeed that one gives
thanks to God; while the one who abstains, abstains to the Lord and likewise gives thanks to God.
7. None of us lives for ourself alone, and none of us dies to ourself alone.
8. If we live, we live to the Lord, and if we die, we die to the Lord; so
then, whether we live or whether we die, we belong to the Lord. 9. For
to this end Christ died and lived again, that he might be Lord both of the
dead and of the living.
10. Who are you to pass judgment on a fellow believer?
Or who are you to belittle your fellow believer?
For we shall all stand before the judgment seat of God;
11. for it is written, "As I live, says the Lord, every knee shall bow to me,
and every tongue shall give praise to God." 12. So each of us will have
to give account of ourself before God.

[*Note:* In the interests of gender-inclusiveness, the above translation departs somewhat from the literal sense of the Greek original, which, apart from a few instances of the first person plural, uses the masculine singular throughout. In v 10 "fellow believer" translates *adelphos* (lit. "brother") occurring in the original.]

Interpretation

Introduction. The argument for tolerance that makes up this section consists chiefly in the twin appeals—not to belittle and not to pass judgment—that appear, in chiastic arrangement, in v 3ab and v 10ab respectively. The central argument flows from the image of a slave's having no right to criticize the behavior of a fellow slave, since it is only to his or her master that a slave is accountable. Within the overall framework provided by this image (including the idea of final judgment in vv 10c-12) other motifs enter in on a supportive basis: notably, that of giving thanks to the Lord (v 6) and that of the universal lordship of Christ (vv 7-8).

Accept the one weak in faith (v 1). The opening, thematic summons to "accept the person weak in faith," is obviously directed to those who by contrast are "strong" in faith, though this identification is not explicitly made for some time (15:1). The language presupposes differing degrees of "strength" within the fundamental conviction of faith to which all believers adhere. Faith, for Paul, is always faith in God as Creator, an ability to discern God acting creatively (specifically in the Christ-event) and to surrender one's life wholly to that perception (see Interpretation of 1:16). Some (the "strong" in faith) pursue the implications of that perception into associated areas of life more confidently than others. The latter (the "weak in faith") do not lack sufficient measure of faith for Christian existence but they have not as yet allowed it to permeate all areas of life. Paul's call is for tolerance. Within the *basic* act of faith characteristic of all, Christian community living can tolerate gradations in the working out of faith's implications. It is not necessary to settle all matters once and for all at the cost of community peace.

Eating and not eating (vv 2-3). The basic principle established, Paul indicates (v 2) the first area of difference: eating and not eating (meat; cf. v 21). He summons (v 3) each in turn to refrain from taking the attitude to the other to which they are, respectively, tempted. Those who eat are tempted to "belittle" *(exouthenein)* the hesitation of those who do not, doubtless dismissing their hesitations as a relic of a pre-Christian attitude that they ought long since to have abandoned. The "weak," on the other hand, unwilling to be pushed in this way, are prone to retaliate by "passing judgment upon" *(krinein)*—condemning as immoral—the free practice of the "strong." Both attitudes and tendencies are characteristic of religious movements where values are deeply held. It is not a matter of mere trivia, since in the area of religion even the simplest rites and practices can enshrine fundamental values and beliefs. Paul will later (v 14) make his own position perfectly clear. But meanwhile he calls for mutual tolerance, indicating (v 3c) as fundamental grounds for this the essential principle enunciated in the gospel. If God has accepted one's fellow believers precisely as they are (cf. esp. 3:21-26; 5:6-11), one cannot do otherwise as a Christian than to allow that "acceptance" to determine one's own attitude and behavior (cf. 15:7).

Accountability to one Lord alone (v 4). In support of this appeal for nonjudgmental "acceptance" Paul introduces the controlling image of the passage: that of domestic service (or slavery)—though the actual reality of believers as servants accountable to Christ as "Lord" soon takes over the main argument (vv 6-12). A domestic servant *(oiketēs)* in the service of one master is in no position to pass judgment upon the performance of a fellow servant. Each is accountable to the master and stands or falls by his verdict alone. Hence Christians ought not to proceed as if responsibility for the uprightness of fellow believers depended solely upon them. In an added comment (4b), which is perhaps already beginning to move out of the image, Paul assures those inclined to judge, that the "standing" or "falling" of their fellow believer is the Lord's responsibility, not theirs. The same Lord is more than capable of seeing to it that the brother or sister they see to be in error will in fact "stand"—that is, find approval and ultimate salvation at the judgment. The upshot is, "Leave the matter to the Lord."

Judging one "day" more significant than others (vv 5-6). A second area where differences of view can arise concerns accounting some days more significant than others. The allusion here—presumably along the same pattern of alignments as in the case of food—would seem to be to differences over the continuing validity of Jewish celebration of the sabbath and other festivals. This particular issue is not developed further and seems to be of secondary importance to the main question concerning food. Paul simply counsels (v 5c) that each "be fully convinced in his (or her) own mind," introducing a principle that is to be fundamental from this point on: in these areas of living it is not so much the objective action which determines rightness or wrongness from a moral point of view but a person's interior disposition: whether he or she is acting out of peaceful conviction or in doubtful and wavering mind proceeding from a bad conscience (though, in contrast to 1 Corinthians 8–10, Paul never explicitly mentions "conscience" in this passage).

In the light of this principle, those who take account of a particular day as holy, as also those who eat or do not eat, do so (or ought to do so) "to the Lord" (v 6). The sense is that their peace of mind and conviction in the matter allows for free cognizance of the presence and claim of the Lord. What shows this (v 6c) is the fact that the "eating" (meat) or "not eating" (meat) is accompanied by grace, literally, "giving thanks to God" *(eucharistei tǭ theǭ)*. The implication is that, so long as each one is convinced in their own mind that what they are doing is right, all is encompassed within the overall pattern of Christian life as a "living to God" (cf. 6:10-11); the differences in actual behavior do not disturb the fundamental service of the Lord to which all in common are bound.

Living and dying to the Lord (vv 7-9). Paul underlines this sense of common accountability with a more generalized description of Christian existence, centered upon the "lordship" of Christ. The total statement has a symmetrical structure (six lines consisting of three pairs of corresponding couplets) and a hymnic ring about it, suggesting the quotation of an early Christian hymn or statement of faith. That no one lives or ought to live for himself or herself alone was a commonplace of conventional wisdom. The distinctively Christian note (if it has not already been suggested by the phrase "none of us") comes with the parallel addition concerning death. The reason that believers no longer live or die "to themselves" is that they no longer truly "belong" to themselves. Through his obedient death and ensuing resurrection Christ gained a "lordship" over life and death (v 9; cf. Phil 2:6-11); this was the very purpose *(eis touto)* of his entire mission. Believers have acknowledged that lordship in faith (10:9) and in baptism "died" to all other allegiances (6:1-11; 2 Cor 5:14-15). Their abandonment of living "to oneself" (cf. Gal 2:19-20) and their belonging henceforth totally to the Lord means that all facets of existence, not excluding (physical) death itself, are encompassed within the transcendent relationship to the Lord (1 Thess 5:10), in virtue of which believers are set in line to share Christ's risen life (6:4-5, 8; 1 Cor 6:13-14) and messianic rule over the cosmos (1 Cor 3:21b-23; Rom 5:17).

Accountability to God alone (vv 10-12). What is central for Paul in the present context, however, is not this ultimate goal but the present truth which guarantees it: namely, that believers "belong" totally to the Lord in the sense that slaves "belong" to their master (Rom 6:16-23). The all-important "vertical" relationship to the Lord and the accountability that goes with it eclipses "horizontal" accountability to fellow believers in the areas under discussion. It eliminates the right to pass judgment upon the conduct of one's "brother" or "sister" (within the continuing image: one's fellow slave). Hence, addressing both groups in diatribe mode ("Who are you . . .?"), Paul rules out (v 10) the same attitudes of passing judgment and belittling that he had excluded before. The all-determining relationship to the Lord means that, as "slaves," we are accountable to him and to him alone; it is before his judgment seat and that alone that we shall have to stand (v 10c; cf. 1 Cor 4:3-5; 2 Cor 5:10). The image of the slave having to render an account to the master has finally given away to the general Christian belief that all will be accountable to God at the final judgment.

This last observation (v 10c) adds an eschatological note to what has been stated up till now primarily in christological terms. Paul reinforces it (v 11) with a quotation from Isa 45:23. The text triumphantly proclaims the coming submission of all creation to the rule of Israel's God. It appears, with a more explicitly christological reference, in the final stanza of the hymn in Phil 2:6-11. The effect of the quotation, as previously that of the christological statements in vv 7-9, is to gather the whole of Christian existence into the all-embracing framework of God's eschatological lordship over the cosmos now being realized in Christ (1 Cor 15:25-28). Nothing less than this is the setting for the account which, as servant (cf. v 4), each and every believer will have to render to the Lord (v 12). In the face of this awesome responsibility it is ludicrous to look "sideways," as it were, and seek to call a fellow Christian to account in matters such as food and the reckoning of days.

Notes

1. *the person who is weak in faith:* Paul is distinguishing various levels of "faith" within basic Christian faith. There is no need, however, to distinguish sharply the faith in question here from the basic Christian faith. The similarity in language between what is said of faith in this passage (cf. *ho asthenōn,* v 2; *plērophoreisthō*, v 5; *diakrinomenos*, v 23) and what is said of Abraham's paradigmatic faith in 4:19-21 (cf. *mē asthenēsas,* v 19; *ou diekrithē tę̄ apistią,* v 20; *plērophorētheis*, v 21) points to an element of continuity; the distinction is not one of quality but of degree. In the parallel sequence in 1 Corinthians 8 the "weakness" is associated with "conscience" (*syneidēsis*: cf. esp. 8:7, 10) rather than with faith. It is not clear why Paul avoids referring to "conscience" in Romans 14, especially since whether or not one acts in conformity with what one inwardly believes to be the truth becomes a crucial factor in the discussion (cf. 14:5, 20, 22-23) and that is the same as acting according to one's conscience (cf. esp. 2:15; 13:5).

   not with a view to settling matters over which there is dispute: The underlying Greek phrase *(mē eis diakriseis dialogismōn)* is open to a variety of interpretations. The second noun *dialogismos* can be taken in the more negative sense of "scruple" to give the meaning "not in order to pass judgment on scruples" (so Cranfield 2.701) or "not to come to disputes about (mere) scruples" (Wilckens 3.80–81). This presents Paul as dismissive, perhaps even contemptuous, of the views of the weak in a way that seems at odds with the overall tenor of the passage. It is better to take *dialogismos* in the sense of "doubtful matter" and translate "not with a view to settling (once and for all) disputes about doubtful matters" (cf. Dunn 2.798–99). Paul's point is that there is no need to come to oneness of view on *everything*.

2. *the person weak (in faith) eats only vegetables:* For a discussion of the identity of those who adopt this dietary stance, see Introduction to 14:1–15:13.

3. *belittle:* The Greek verb *exouthenein* can have a strong sense of contemptuous rejection: cf. Luke 23:11 (of Herod's treatment of the captive Jesus).

pass judgment: The Greek verb *krinein* here (in contrast to v 13b) has the sense "judge negatively" (= "condemn")—a human condemnation connoting the expectation that God will condemn as well.

4. *Who are you to pass judgment on the slave of another?:* Though the verb used here, *krinein,* previously referred to the action of the weak, the diatribe address—*sy* . . .—is probably meant to include both points of view (cf. v 10, which addresses both parties). The *oiketēs* is the domestic slave, whose relationship with the master would be more immediate than that of one involved in work or business outside the house. The attached adjective *allotrion* does not mean that the object of the "judgment" is the slave of another master. The point is that the fellow slave is exempt from judgment because he or she, like the one tempted to judge, is the possession of "another" person (the master), whose sole prerogative it is to assess performance.

   It is in relation to their own masters that slaves stand or fall: The phrase (rendered in the plural for the sake of gender inclusiveness) is perfectly understandable within the terms of the image: what is determining for the well-being of a slave is the assessment of the master, not that of a fellow slave. But the fact that Paul uses the word *kyrios* ("lord") rather than *despotēs,* which would suit the image better, suggests that the flow of thought is already moving out of the image to state the reality of Christian life, where the *kyrios* is the risen Christ. The implied accountability would then be that due at the final judgment (cf. v 10c; 1 Cor 3:12-15; 2 Cor 5:10) and the "rising" and "falling" would refer to the verdict to be received at that moment. In either case—image or reality to which the image refers—the dative, *tǭ kyriǭ,* is best taken as one of respect.

   And they shall stand, for the master is able to make them stand: The translation (again made plural) takes the first verb, *stathēsetai,* as a middle ("shall stand"), rather than a passive ("will be made to stand"), which would render the final phrase tautologous.

5. *One person judges one day as more significant than another, while another judges all days alike:* The key term "judge" *(krinein)* must now bear the implication "prefer" (one day to another). As background to this "judging" or "reckoning" (v 6) of days, some have suggested the pagan reckoning, possibly based on astrology, of particular days as propitious or unpropitious. Something like this seems to lie behind the allusion in Gal 4:9b-10 to the pagan past which Paul's Gentile converts have left behind. But precisely in view of this slighting reference in Galatians it seems unlikely that Paul would now adopt a tolerant attitude to a reckoning of days in this sense. More likely observance of Jewish Sabbath and other festivals is in view.

   Let each one be fully convinced in their own mind: The same Greek verb (*plērophorein,* used in the passive) appears with respect to the "conviction" involved in Abraham's faith according to 4:21. Reference to "mind" *(nous)* recalls the "renewal of mind" called for in the opening summons of the entire parenesis, 12:1-2. Faith, while it may tolerate different points of view, never acts on a doubtful conscience; the point is reiterated still more strongly in vv 22-23.

6. *to the Lord:* This (repeated) phrase, *kyriǭ*, is normally taken as a dative of advantage but the sense is more that of being directed to the Lord in free and open acknowledgment of his lordship and presence; cf. "living to God" (6:10-11).

   gives thanks to God: The context of "eating/not eating" suggests that *eucharistein* here has specific reference to the grace accompanying meals, though a more general and fundamental sense of "giving thanks to God" can hardly be excluded (cf. 2 Cor 4:15).

   while the one who abstains, abstains to the Lord and likewise gives thanks to God: It could be that Paul added this (otherwise somewhat unnecessary) phrase (v 6c) because he sensed that he had perhaps given the "strong" an advantage over the "weak" in that only in regard to them (and not in the case of the "reckoning of days" on the part of the "weak," v 6a) had he mentioned "giving thanks to God" (cf. Cranfield 2.706–07). But v 6b is not so much paired with v 6a ("reckoning of days," which is not the main issue) but with v 6c. The couplet is central to Paul's argument in the sense that he can point to the saying of grace on the part of both as indication that both "eating" and "non-eating" (the central issue) are equally performed in God's sight and for God's glory.

7. *None of us lives for ourself alone:* For parallels to this in Greek and Latin literature, see Cranfield, 2.707, n. 3, who also rightly insists that the Pauline statement rests upon the Christian conviction of subordination to the Lord; Paul is not formulating a general principle along "No man is an island" lines, however true such a principle may be in itself.

   and none of us dies to ourself alone: The allusion to Christ's lordship over both "the dead and the living" in v 9 argues that the "dying" in question here refers primarily to physical death, rather than to "dying to oneself" in an ethical sense; cf. W. Thüsing, *Per Christum* 32.

8. *we belong to the Lord:* This phrase *(tou kyriou esmen)* gives the sense in which "living to the Lord"/"dying to the Lord" should be understood—not precisely as datives of advantage but as expressing the sense that the whole of Christian existence, including death, takes place within the sphere of Christ's lordship and under his authority; see Note on v 6 above.

9. *that he might be Lord both of the dead and of the living:* The purpose clause *(hina)* expresses the divine intent behind the total "career" of Christ (cf. the "sending of the Son" formulae in Rom 8:3-4 and Gal 4:4-5). Becoming "Lord" in the exaltation that followed upon his obedient death (Phil 2:6-11), Christ radically broke the grip of sin and death ("the last enemy," 1 Cor 15:26) upon human beings, so that the original design of God in their regard might go ahead (Gen 1:26-28; Rom 8:29-30; 1 Cor 3:21b-23) and the entire cosmos return to the sovereign rule and design of God (1 Cor 15:28). Dunn (2.808) rightly draws attention to the Adamic christology latent here.

10. *pass judgment on . . . belittle your fellow believer?:* The Greek reads literally "your brother" *(ton adelphon sou)*. The "logic" of the "slave" image continues

(see v 4) even though the customary designation of fellow believers as "brothers" ("sisters")—last used in 12:1—takes over from that of being fellow "slaves."

For we shall all stand before the judgment seat of God: Though already "justified" (cf. *dikaiōthentes,* 5:1) and in this sense already in possession of a verdict of acquittal, there is still an "already-not yet" aspect to justification for Paul. Believers, in their continuing bodily life, have to "live out" the justification they have received, so that it may be "ratified" at the final judgment. In this sense Paul can occasionally speak of justification as something still in the future (cf. 5:19; Gal 5:5). In the parallel statement of this future moment of accountability in 2 Cor 5:10, it is the judgment seat of *Christ,* rather than that of God before whom believers will have to stand. Paul can readily interchange the christological and theological perspective because of his sense of the complete ordination of the work of Christ to that of God; on this see esp. Thüsing, *Per Christum* 35–38.

11. *for it is written, "As I live, says the Lord, every knee shall bow to me, and every tongue shall give praise to God":* The quotation is composite. The introductory formula, "As I live, . . .," appears in a number of places (Num 14:28; Jer 22:24; Ezek 5:11), though Paul probably has the instance in Isa 49:18b in mind. The bulk of the quotation repeats LXX Isa 45:23b with only a slight transposition (*pasa glōssa* appearing before *exomologēsetai,* as also in Phil 2:11). In Phil 2:11 the allusion is to the submission of the entire cosmos to God through acknowledgment of the lordship of Christ. Here the accountability of individual believers is placed within the same framework; cf. also 15:9.

12. *So each of us will have to give an account of ourself to God:* Virtually every word of this conclusion must be stressed—especially "each" *(hekastos)* and the reflexive pronoun *(heautou).* The final phrase, "to God," omitted by several important witnesses (B D*), may represent a later addition under the influence of v 11.

For Reference and Further Study

(See list following commentary on 14:13-23)

b) *The Tolerance Asked Particularly of the "Strong"* (14:13-23)

13. Then let us no more pass judgment on one another, but rather determine not to put a stumbling block or hindrance in the way of a fellow believer.

14. I know and am fully convinced in the Lord Jesus that nothing is unclean in itself; but it is unclean for any one who thinks it unclean. 15. If your fellow believer is being injured on account of what you eat, you are no longer proceeding according to love. Do not let what you eat destroy that one for whom Christ died.

16. So do not let the good you enjoy be criticized as evil. 17. For the kingdom of God is not food and drink but righteousness and peace and joy in the Holy Spirit; 18. the one who serves Christ in this way is well pleasing to God and finds human approval. 19. Let us then pursue what makes for peace and for building one another up personally.

20. Do not, for the sake of what you eat, destroy the work of God. Everything is indeed clean, but (eating becomes) evil in the case of the one who eats as a result of being made to stumble 21. (whereas) it is an admirable thing not to eat meat or drink wine or do anything else likely to make your fellow believer stumble. 22. The faith that you have, keep between yourself and God; happy are those who have no reason to condemn themselves for what they approve. 23. But those who have doubts are condemned if they eat, in that their eating does not proceed from faith; for whatever does not proceed from faith is sin.

[*Note:* In the interests of gender-inclusiveness, "fellow believer" translates the Greek word *adelphos* (lit. "brother") occurring in vv 13, 15 and 21 of the above text. Likewise, in vv 22b-23a the original expression in the masculine singular has been rendered in the plural.]

INTERPRETATION

First conclusion and transition (v 13). What has emerged from the first major section of Paul's plea for tolerance in the matter of food (vv 1-12) is a sharp challenge, in diatribe mode, designed to exclude the very thought of sitting in judgment upon fellow believers. In conclusion (v 13a), Paul exhorts the entire body of believers to refrain from such judging *(krinein).* Then, by way of transition, he exploits (v 13b) the ambiguity inherent in the Greek verb *krinein* to open up a new line of argument aimed more explicitly at the "strong" (in faith). Instead of "judging" *(krinein),* they are to "come to a determination" *(krinate)* about one particular thing: not to place a stumbling block or hindrance in the way of a fellow believer (literally, "brother"). This consideration, which forms the central plank in the argument from this point on, is developed in two main "waves" (vv 14-15 and vv 20-23), interspersed with a more general exhortation to pursue what makes for peace (vv 16-19).

No stumbling block 1. (vv 14-15). The necessity to avoid providing a stumbling block for the "weak in faith" (cf. also v 15, v 20, v 21) reflects a more common New Testament belief (cf. Mark 9:42 // Matt 18:6-7 // Luke

17:1-2) that the more powerful and authoritative members in a community can have an influence for ill as well as for good upon the fate of the "little ones" and hence bear a graver responsibility. Taking up this idea, Paul requires from one group (the "strong") a particular form of action—in fact, a refraining from action—which is not required of the other party (the "weak"). He does so on the grounds that the latter are vulnerable in a way that the former are not, vulnerable in what concerns their very salvation. The appeal rests upon promoting in the "strong" a powerful sense of the responsibility they bear and a readiness to exercise it despite the sacrifice of freedom which it entails.

Paul does in fact fully identify (v 14) with the view of those to whom he appeals. As a Christian (literally, "in the Lord Jesus") he is as fully convinced as they are that nothing is "unclean" *(koinon)* in itself. The conclusion of mature belief in the overall sovereignty of God and the divine declaration of all creatures as "good" (Gen 1:1–2:4) can only be that no taint of idolatry or divinization adheres to created things in themselves. But, in the context of human use of the created world, a qualification must be entered in. What determines the ethical quality of human action is not simply the objective order but the disposition and attitude of the subject as well. Hence, when a person, albeit erroneously, thinks that something is "unclean"—in the technical sense of religious taboo—that thing really is unclean for that person. Usage or non-usage of it raises the essentials of relationship to God, not omitting the question of eternal salvation.

In the light of this qualification Paul issues (v 15) a somber warning to the "strong." Their action in eating (meat) can really "injure" a fellow believer. The "injury" *(lypeitai)* is not mere emotional distress but a real wounding of conscience in a way that may jeopardize salvation. How this fatal "wounding" operates in fact Paul does not explain. What he has in mind emerges more clearly when the same argument reappears in a second "wave" in vv 20-23. Social pressure created by the example of the "strong" may induce the weak in faith to eat in bad conscience. That is what puts their eternal salvation at risk.

To create a "stumbling block" in this way is to cease to "proceed according to love" (v 15b) and in fact to "destroy that one for whom Christ died" (v 15c). The reasoning rests upon Paul's conviction that a believer can never look upon a fellow Christian in any way other than as one whom Christ "loved" and for whom he "delivered himself up" (cf. Gal 2:20). This truth confers upon the brother or sister a preciousness that simply overwhelms all selfish considerations (2 Cor 5:14-17). The exercise of Christian *agapē* is a continuation of the fundamental *agapē* of Christ in giving himself up to death for us all when we were "weak" (Rom 5:6, 8, 10). Paul appeals to the "strong" to be ready to display towards their fellow believers "weak in faith" (14:1) the same kind of self-sacrificing love which they, themselves once "weak" (5:6), received from Christ.

Pursuit of peace and the building up of one another personally (vv 16-19). At this point Paul pauses to draw a preliminary conclusion (v 16), followed and supported by a general reflection on community harmony (vv 17-19). The "strong" are not to let the "good" which they enjoy become an occasion for misrepresentation as evil (literally, "be slanderously reviled" [*mē blasphēmeisthō*]; cf. 3:8). By "the good" *(to agathon)* Paul most likely has in mind the freedom to eat that stems from the accurate perception of their "strong" faith (for alternative understandings, see Note). The exercise of this freedom in contexts where "weak" faith is also present runs the risk of being misinterpreted and so leading to something genuinely evil.

In support of this conclusion there follows (vv 17-19) a brief reflection on the way in which the "peace" of the kingdom of God should characterize community relationships. In its comparatively rare occurrences in Paul the "kingdom of God" usually refers to the future blessings of salvation which human beings are destined to "inherit" or "not inherit," as the case may be (1 Cor 6:9, 10; 15:50; Gal 5:21; cf. Eph 5:5; Col 4:11). Here, by contrast (cf. also 1 Cor 4:20), Paul speaks of the "kingdom" in more "realized" terms, as something actually present and palpable in the effects it produces in Christian community life: "righteousness, peace and joy in the Holy Spirit" (v 17b; cf. 1 Cor 4:20). All three qualities are the fruit of the Spirit (cf. *en pneumati hagiǭ*), which for Paul constitutes the foretaste—"firstfruits" (8:23) or "downpayment" (2 Cor 1:22; 5:5)—of full salvation. In comparison with these blessings attaching to and attesting the presence of the kingdom, such matters as the freedom to eat and to drink (*brōsis kai posis*) pale into insignificance; in no way do they belong to the essence of the kingdom.

Hence to "serve Christ" by acting in this way *(en toutǭ)*—preserving peace by refraining from the exercise of one's freedom in the matter of food—is to do something which will merit approval from every angle, divine and human (v 18). Those who so act can look for a favorable verdict from God at the time when they stand before the ultimate tribunal. Equally, their conduct is worthy of respect in human terms as well. It is not always for the best that freedom should find outward expression. To allow it to remain inward for the sake of a higher good is perfectly honorable and at times even better.

By way of conclusion to this brief sequence, Paul exhorts the "strong" to "pursue" what makes for "peace" and "building one another up personally" (v 19). The thought of a Christian community as something in process of being "built" comes naturally to him (cf. esp. 1 Cor 3:9-17). All have an obligation to see that the work continues. A key factor in the process is the preservation of "peace."

No stumbling block 2. (vv 20-23). The exhortation to pursue peace and so contribute to the "building" prepares the way for a return to the central argument (v 20). If the "building" can be constructed and preserved, it can also be destroyed (cf. also 1 Cor 3:17) and in the present context what can threaten such destruction is disputation over food. Hence Paul's renewed appeal not to "wreck *(mē . . . katalye)* the work of God" (= the community understood as "building") for the sake of exercising the right to eat whatever one likes. The language is weighty. Paul is, once again, seeking to relativize the position of the "strong" by placing it in the context of the magnificent picture of what God has done and is doing in Christian community life. It is unthinkable—and in fact fearsome—to contemplate the destruction of God's edifice (the community) by insisting upon the exercise of a non-essential right, even one stemming from the insight of faith.

Once more (v 20b; cf. v 14a) Paul concedes the fundamental rightness of the insight that goes with "strong" faith: "all things are clean" *(kathara)*—and therefore in principle all kinds of food are available for eating. But, in the community context, the same qualification as before (v 14b) enters in. What is a "good" in the case of the "strong" (the freedom to eat any kind of food; cf. *agathon*, v 16) becomes an "evil" *(kakon)* when a person (the fellow believer weak in faith) eats in bad conscience under the pressure of the "stumbling block" provided by the "strong" (for an alternative understanding, see Note). The upshot is (v 21) that it is in fact a "fine thing" (*kalon*; the sense is virtually, that of "a better thing") not to eat meat or wine or take any other action that may cause a fellow Christian to stumble *(proskoptei)*. In matters that are not truly obligatory and where my *exercise* of freedom may cause a brother or sister to fall, freedom must yield to the overriding demands of love. The "strong faith" which has led to this freedom need not and ought not in this circumstance find outward expression. Without any injury to its own essential quality it can and ought be kept as something between oneself and God alone (v 22a).

A concluding couplet (vv 22b-23) at last sheds light on how Paul sees the inner process working. He reminds his audience of the basic principle of human moral action, looking first at the positive, then the negative case. The person who acts with firm conviction (literally, without any trace of self-condemnation [*mē krinōn heauton*, v 22b]), following upon a moral discernment *(en hǭ dokimazei)*, is "blessed" *(makarios)*, that is, assured of receiving approval by God. Sadly, this is not the case (v 23a) with the one who eats with "wavering conviction" *(ho diakrinomenos)*. Such persons not only "condemn" themselves but render themselves liable to a more fundamental condemnation, that of God. They place themselves in such a position because what they do flows not from a genuine perception of faith *(hoti ouk ek pisteōs)* but from the pressure arising out of the "stumbling block" constituted by the action of the "strong."

The sweeping statement (v 23b) that clinches the matter has caused controversy down the ages. Taken in the widest sense, it is patently untrue that "whatever does not proceed from faith is sin." Human beings, believers included, perform many actions that do not proceed from faith and yet are not sin; one does not brush one's teeth in faith! The statement must be seen in close connection with the frame of reference of the letter as a whole. Faith refers essentially to a person's perception of relationship to God. Righteous action is action in accordance with that perception; unrighteous action—sin—occurs when a person acts out of accord with that perception. The faith of the "weak" who do not eat may be imperfect ("weak") but at least they act—or refrain from acting—in accordance with the perception flowing from their faith. Whereas the "weak" who succumb to pressure and eat in poor conscience act against their basic vision of faith, and so they sin. Their action may accord with the faith vision of the "strong." But it is not *their* faith vision and that is the essential point.

Summary. Paul communicates here his acute sense that human action is only truly human, truly moral, when it engages the entire person and proceeds from free insight and firm will. External expression, outward conformity or non-conformity is nothing without inner integrity and a sense that one is acting in right relationship to God. What Paul requires here accords with the respect he constantly displays for human conscience—both his own (1 Cor 4:3-4; 10:28-29) and that of those to whom, as apostle, he proclaims the gospel (2 Cor 4:2). The "strong" are summoned to realize that these are the issues at stake for the "weak in faith"—whereas, for themselves, "eating" or "not eating" does not raise a crucial dilemma. That is why, in the context of love, a sacrifice can be required of the "strong," that is not, correspondingly, asked of the "weak." This is precisely the principle Paul goes on to formulate in 15:1.

Notes

13. *not to put a stumbling block or hindrance in the way:* The warning here in terms of "stumbling block" *(proskomma)* and "hindrance" *(skandalon)* echoes closely 1 Cor 8:9, 13; for *proskomma*, cf. also the use of Isa 28:16 in 9:33.

14. *I know and am fully convinced in the Lord Jesus:* For similar appeals, see Gal 5:10; Phil 2:24. Underlying the expression is Paul's characteristic sense of believers' "belonging" to the risen Lord as to a communal sphere of salvation; see Interpretation of 6:3 and Note on 6:11.

unclean in itself: "Unclean" translates the adjective *koinos*, used among Greek-speaking Jews as a technical term for what is ritually unclean (1 Macc 1:47, 62;

cf. Josephus, *Ant.* 11:346; 12.112; 13:4; also Mark 7:2, 5; Acts 10:14; 11:8). V 20 expresses the same principle in terms of the positive counterpart *katharos* ("clean"); cf. Titus 1:15; Mark 7:19; Acts 10:15.

it is unclean for any one who thinks it unclean: For Paul the criterion of "cleanliness" stems from the attitude of the human subject. This diverges somewhat from the teaching attributed to Jesus in Mark 7:14-23, where the criterion is whether something comes from "within" or "without" a person.

15. *is being injured:* That the Greek verb *lypein* can indicate something more than mere emotional distress is shown by the sequence in 2 Cor 2:1-11. Paul warns against continuing punitive measures against an offending brother lest the "grief" caused him become excessive (*perissotera*, v 7) and render both him —and the community—a prey to the wiles of Satan (v 11). In the parallel passage in 1 Cor 10:27-28 a more specific context is envisaged, one where believers of divergent attitude in the question of "idol-meat" are both guests of a pagan host. If nothing is said about the provenance of the meat, they may freely eat it. But if it is in fact declared to be "idol meat," then for the believer weak in faith a "context of idolatry" is established which makes the eating of it a denial of basic belief. For such a one to go ahead and eat, under social pressure would be to act in bad conscience. It is, admittedly, hard to square this sense of yielding to social pressure with the "judgmental" attitude attributed to the weak in the previous section (v 3, v 10). But it is difficult to understand how the "injury" comes about otherwise.

on account of what you eat: The translation to some extent paraphrases the Greek, which reads, literally, "on account of (your) eating" *(dia brōma).*

proceeding according to love: Lit. "walking" *(peripatein)* according to love; on this biblical idiom, see Note on 6:4. That love ought be the controlling factor of Christian life has already been made clear in the general parenesis (12:1–13:14) preceding this more particular one (cf. 12:9; 13:8-10).

Do not let what you eat destroy that one for whom Christ died: "Destroy" *(apollye)* here (as also in 1 Cor 8:11a) must refer to final, eschatological ruin; cf. esp. v 20, v 23. The contrast between the banal "what you eat" *(brōmati sou)* and the strong term "destroy" makes the point very forcefully: how unthinkable that insistence upon the exercise of personal freedom in so trivial a matter as food should endanger someone else's eternal salvation.

16. *So do not let the good you enjoy be criticized as evil:* The translation attempts to convey the sense of the verb *blasphēmein* used in the passive (cf. also 3:8). The statement, as a whole, is open to a range of meanings in several respects; for exhaustive discussion, see Cranfield 2.715–17. Some interpreters, looking to what seems to be a wider perspective in v 18, hold that the "criticizing" in question would come from outsiders (Zeller 227; Dunn 2.821–22). But this seems intrusive in the present context. If, as is more likely, inner-community tensions are in view, then those who misinterpret would be the "weak in faith" (the same verb *blasphēmein* is used with respect to the attitude taken by the "weak" in 1 Cor 10:30), and—remaining within the strict terms of the passage—the "good" would be the liberty enjoyed by the "strong" (Wilckens

3.93; Ziesler 333). Paul fully recognizes the "goodness" of such liberty but he cautions against exercising it at the expense of harm to another.

17. *righteousness and peace and joy in the Holy Spirit:* Though the three qualities listed are undoubtedly the fruit of the divine action and in this sense related to God, the context requires that the primary reference here be "horizontal": "righteousness" displayed in right conduct towards one's fellow believers, from which flows "peace" in the community—the central concept (cf. v 19)—and from this in turn a sense of "joy." "Joy," along with "love" and "peace," is listed as a "fruit" of the Spirit in Gal 5:22.

18. *serves Christ in this way:* "In this way" translates the Greek expression *en toutǭ* the precise reference of which is very open. It is best seen as a reference to the kind of behavior (not insisting upon the exercise of freedom to eat all things) which will promote the qualities just listed.

    is well pleasing to God and finds human approval: The discernment and performance of what "pleases God" is the core ethical consideration for Paul; cf. esp.12:2; also 8:8. Only here does Paul refer the Greek adjective *dokimos* to human approval, an allusion clearly intended as a positive counterpart to the human *dis*approval mentioned in v 16.

19. *Let us then pursue what makes for peace:* The phrase "pursue . . . peace" may be an echo of a similar phrase from Ps 34:15 (LXX 33:15). Despite the very strong textual support for the indicative variant *diōkomen* ("we pursue") as against the subjunctive *(diōkōmen)*, the overall parenetic tone of the passage (cf. v 16, v 19) argues in favor of the latter.

    and for building one another up personally: While Paul sometimes applies the "building up" motif to the individual (e.g., 1 Cor 8:10; 14:7), here the primary reference would seem to be to the community as a whole.

20. *Do not, for the sake of what you eat, destroy the work of God:* For the sake of emphasis Paul returns to the second person singular address; cf. v 4, v 10. The verb translated "destroy" *(katalyein)* is the negative counterpart to "building"; cf. Matt 26:61; 27:40; 2 Cor 5:1; Gal 2:18. On the community as "the work *(ergon)* of God," cf. esp. 1 Cor 3:9-15, where the community which human ministers help God build is constantly referred to as *to ergon* (vv 13-15).

    Everything is indeed clean: This statement may represent something of a slogan or catchcry of the "strong" in faith (so Cranfield, 2.723). *Katharos*, while used as the positive counterpart of *koinos* (see Note on v 14), has a broader ethical meaning, less strictly tied to the technical sense of ritual cleanliness. It is thus natural for Paul to proceed, in the following corrective statement, to speak in terms of "evil" *(kakon)*.

    but (eating becomes) evil: Sense requires the supplying of a reference to "eating" (Greek: *to esthiein*) as an implied subject for "evil" *(kakon)*.

    in the case of the one who eats as a result of being made to stumble: The translation understands the subject of the phrase to be the person "weak in faith," who eats as a *result* of being overcome by the "stumbling block" afforded by the "strong" (*dia proskommatos—dia* with the genitive indicating "attendant circumstances"). Alternatively, the subject could be the person "strong in faith," who eats with the *effect* of providing a stumbling block to another (the "attendant circumstances" now indicating effect rather than cause), in which case the translation would run, "in the case of the one who eats with the effect of causing another to stumble." The matter is very open and either way the overall flow of the argument is not greatly affected.

21. *(whereas) it is an admirable thing not to eat meat or drink wine:* For the first time, Paul indicates that it is the eating of meat that is the issue; presumably, he has been confident all along that the audience will have taken his references to eating in this specific sense. More surprising is the reference to wine—although "drinking" was mentioned alongside "eating" in v 17 in connection with what was not central to the kingdom of God. Most likely, "not to drink wine" does not indicate a parallel issue but prepares the way, rhetorically, for the more generalized clause that follows (v 21b; cf. the similar passing allusion to "drinking" in 1 Cor 10:21); see further Cranfield 2.725. With reference to "eating" and "drinking" Paul uses the Greek aorist infinitive, suggesting that he is recommending abstention not by way of a permanent ban but as something applicable when the danger of providing a "stumbling block" is present.

22. *The faith that you have:* "Faith" here is not simply confidence in a general sense but the conviction, stemming from one's basic belief in God as Creator, that all foods are "clean"; see Note on v 1.

    happy are those who have no reason to condemn themselves for what they approve: Most interpreters see here a "blessing" upon persons "strong in faith" (balancing a corresponding reference in v 23a to the "weak") who are not subject to condemnation, either in the sense of having exercised freedom at the expense of the "weak" or of being exposed to divine condemnation for the same cause. But, rather than applying the statement closely to the "strong," it is preferable to see Paul formulating a general principle (completed by a negative counterpart in v 23a) about the necessity ("happiness"/"non-happiness") of always acting with a convinced conscience ("faith"): a person who acts with clear conscience (literally, "not condemning himself or herself") is "happy."

23. *But those who have doubts are condemned if they eat:* Though applicable to the "weak in faith" in the present instance, the sentence states a more general principle (the negative counterpart to the "blessing" indicated in v 22b): the one who acts with doubtful conscience (lit. "doubting faith" *[diakrinomenos]*) is liable to (divine) condemnation *(katakekritai)*. The conditional clause, "if they eat," is significant in that it shows that the "stumbling block" operates, not just by "distressing" the "weak" emotionally but by actually causing them to go ahead and eat against their conscience.

    in that their eating does not proceed from faith; for whatever does not proceed from faith is sin: "Faith" *(pistis)* here means the "conviction stemming from faith." "Sin" *(hamartia)* does not have here the distinctive Pauline sense of enslaving "power" (as esp. in Rom 5:12–8:4) but simply means wrong-doing offensive to God.

For Reference and Further Study

Cambier, J.-M. "La liberté chrétienne est et personelle et communautaire (Rom 14:1–15:13)." *Freedom and Love: The Guide for Christian Life (1 Cor 8-10)*. Ed. L. de Lorenzi; Rome: St. Paul's Abbey, 1982, 57–84.

Donfried, K. P. "False Presuppositions in the Study of Romans." *Romans Debate* 102–25.

Furnish , V. P. *Love Command* 115–18.

Karris, R. J. "Romans 14:1–15:13 and the Occasion of Romans." *Romans Debate* 65–84.

________. "The Occasion of Romans: A Response to Professor Donfried." *Romans Debate* 125–27.

Meeks, W. A. "Judgment and the Brother: Romans 14:1–15:13." *Tradition and Interpretation in the New Testament* (FS E. E. Ellis). Eds. G. F. Hawthorne & O. Betz. Grand Rapids: Eerdmans; Tübingen: Mohr, 1987, 290–300.

Minear, P. S. *The Obedience of Faith*. London: SCM, 1971, 6–35.

Rauer, M. *Die "Schwachen" in Korinth und Rom nach den Paulusbriefen*. Freiburg: Herder, 1923.

Thompson, M. *Clothed with Christ* 161–207.

Thüsing, W. *Per Christum* 30–39.

Watson, F. *Paul, Judaism and the Gentiles* 94–98.

Wedderburn, A.J.M. *Reasons for Romans* 30–35, 59–62, 84–87.

c) *The Example of Christ as Grounds for Tolerance* (15:1-6)

1. We who are strong ought to support the weaknesses of the weak, and not be content simply to please ourselves; 2. let each of us please the neighbor with a view to what is good and builds up the community.
3. For Christ did not please himself; but, as it is written, "The reproaches of those who reproached you fell on me." 4. For whatever was written beforehand was written for our instruction, so that, in situations where endurance is called for, we might have hope through the encouragement provided by the scriptures.
5. May the God of endurance and encouragement grant you to live in such harmony with one another, according to Christ Jesus, 6. that together and with one voice you may glorify the God and Father of our Lord Jesus Christ.

Interpretation

This short section largely carries forward the preceding exhortation (note especially the terminology—"strong," "weak" in vv 1-2). At the same time, it forms a self-contained unit presenting its own (christological) grounding for tolerance (v 3). A general reflection upon the role of scripture (v 4) underpins the appeal to Christ's example and the passage concludes with a prayer-wish calling for a common glorification of God (vv 5-6).

Bearing the burdens of others in love rather than pleasing oneself (vv 1-2). At this point the "strong"/"weak" duality which has run through the entire exhortation emerges explicitly and becomes something of an image in its own right. "Strong" persons are those who, besides carrying their own burdens, have strength left over to shoulder those of others too. Paul, making explicit at last his own identification with the "strong," indicates the obligation *(opheilomen)* which flows from being "strong." It is the obligation to help the "weak" carry the burdens which their own "weaknesses" create for them.

Carrying out this "obligation" will entail "not pleasing oneself." This negative phrase recalls the sustained description of what "love" *(agapē)* does "not" do or require as described in the hymn appearing in 1 Corinthians 13 (cf. esp. v 5). The "obligation," then, stems from love, which, as Paul has already made clear (13:8), is the only "obligation" ("debt") to which believers ought consider themselves bound. "Not pleasing oneself" means turning away from the desire to assert self and the claims and wants of self that are for Paul the nub of sin (cf. esp. 7:7) and which are destructive of all relationship, both with respect to God and to fellow human beings.

"Pleasing one's neighbor" (v 2), on the other hand, does not mean simply a facile attempt to make the neighbor happy at all costs. As the qualifying phrases show, it means placing one's life project at the service of "the (common) good" *(eis to agathon)*, in a way that makes for the "building up" *(oikodomē)* of the community as a whole. What Paul asks of the "strong" is that they turn away from self in this radical sense, that they refrain from the exercise of a perfectly legimitate freedom in the interests of the deeper freedom of love. Individual freedom, revealing itself in love, grows within the framework of the entire body.

The example of Christ (v 3). Paul justifies the radical call that lies behind the simple negative phrase, "not to please oneself," by appealing to the pattern set by Christ. The statement that "Christ did not please himself" does not refer to some isolated act but to the whole dynamic of his saving "career" on our behalf, culminating in the obedience of the cross. The Christ who "did not please himself" is the one who did not rest in the "likeness to God" which was his "by nature" (Phil 2:6) but who "emptied himself" (v 7) and took on the "slave" condition of human beings, even to the extent of dying the most shameful death of the cross (v 8)—in terms of Gal 2:20, "the Son of God, who loved me and delivered himself up for me" (cf. 2 Cor 5:14). For believers it is not simply a matter of imitating Christ but of allowing his self-emptying "mind-set" to well up within them because of their own existence "in Christ" (cf. Phil 2:5; Rom 6:10-11).

Curiously, Paul does not here, as in Phil 2:5-11, point directly to something in the "career" of Christ that would illustrate "not pleasing himself." Instead, he quotes (v 3b) Ps 69:9 (LXX 68:10), the immediate relevance of which to the context is far from clear. Admittedly, Psalm 69 is one of the texts most frequently cited in the early Christian tradition in regard to the passion of Jesus. In this sense, citing it is tantamount to pointing to the sufferings of the Lord. But Paul probably intends a more immediate reference. In the original setting, the psalmist protests that his total identification with God's cause (v 7, 9a) has led to the falling upon himself of insults hurled by the impious at God. The present context seems to envisage bearing insults, not only for God's sake but also, and primarily, for the benefit of "others," for "the neighbor" (v 2). The sense, then, is that Christ speaks in the psalm as one who, for love of others and in obedience to God, exposed himself in his passion—and in the whole pattern of his human existence—to the insults and violence of sinful human beings. It was because, like the psalmist, he so identified with "God's cause"—also the "cause of our salvation"—that he was placed in this vulnerable position. The implication is that those who would consider themselves followers of Christ ought be willing to sacrifice their "strength" (v 1)—as he put aside his "likeness to God" (Phil 2:6), his "being rich" (2 Cor 8:9)—for the sake of the "weak."

The role of scripture (v 4). Perhaps realizing that the relevance of the scriptural quotation is not immediately obvious, Paul justifies it (v 4) in terms of a general hermeneutical principle. All scripture is to be read in the light of Christ. Hence everything written (literally "written beforehand") in scripture is written not primarily for its immediate meaning but for the instruction of those who believe in Christ, its primary addressees. Believers, then, can confidently look for instruction *(didaskalia)* to any scriptural passage, including the one just quoted. More specifically (v 4b), the purpose of scripture is to provide those in a situation where "endurance" *(hypomonē)* is required with the kind of "encouragement" *(paraklēsis)* that will help them "to hold fast to hope."

Mention of "hope" seems to presuppose a continuing, if implicit, allusion through the psalm to the suffering of Christ. The psalm foretold the "endurance" of Christ as righteous sufferer in God's cause. It discloses the meaning of his sufferings in the sense that they were enveloped within a divine plan which was to lead him through obedience and death to eventual exaltation and enthronement as Lord (Phil 2:8-11). This scriptural light sheds an aura of hope upon the sufferings and sacrifices which believers endure in union with and for Christ (cf. 8:17). Within the plan of God already seen in Christ, such outwardly negative experience can be richly fruitful (cf. the similar association of "endurance" with "hope" in 5:3-4; 8:25). The allusion is cryptic but Paul seems to want to convey to the "strong" that, in the context of scripture's illumination of the attitude taken by Christ, the sacrifice he is asking them to make in regard to the "weak" is not meaningless. It partakes of the hope attending all suffering in Christ (cf. 8:18).

Final prayer-wish (vv 5-6). Mention of "hope" leads Paul to round off the exhortation in quasi-liturgical mode with a prayer-wish. The "endurance" and "encouragement" just mentioned are both ultimately the gift of God. Therefore it is appropriate to pray that the God who bestows them may also grant the community the grace to be "of one mind according to Christ Jesus." In view of his earlier acceptance of differences in the matter of food (cf. esp. 14:1), Paul is hardly expressing the wish that the community come to a single opinion on every matter. The single "mind-set" (*to auto phronein*; cf. 12:16) he is asking of them has more to do with attitude towards one another, the attitude characteristic of Christ (cf. v 3) which governs their existence "in Christ" (here *kata Christon Iēsoun*). If all are bent upon "pleasing" not themselves but the neighbor, then differences of view on matters such as food will not injure the fundamental unity. The community will be able to fulfill its ultimate goal, expressed in what would appear to be a liturgical formula, that of glorifying "the God and Father of our Lord, Jesus Christ together and with one voice" (v 6).

Notes

1. *We who are strong ought to support the weaknesses of the weak:* For the first time Paul actually uses the description "strong" *(dynatoi)* and, correspondingly, terms the "weak" *adynatoi*, where previously (14:1-2) he had used *asthenēs* (cf., however, the use of *asthenēmata* for "weaknesses"). The Greek verb *bastazein* must be given here its primary literal meaning "support" or "carry," rather than "tolerate," "put up with"; Paul is asking for positive help not mere toleration; cf. also Gal 6:2: "Bear each others' burdens and thus you will fulfill the law of Christ" (that is, the law of love; cf. Gal 6:14; Rom 13:8-10).

2. *and builds up the community:* Lit. "for upbuilding" *(pros oikodomēn)*. As in the similar reference in 14:9, the "building" in question refers primarily to the growth of the entire community, though an individual nuance cannot be excluded.

3. *For Christ did not please himself:* For the links between this expression and the fundamental thrust of the Christ-hymn in Phil 2:6-11, see esp. W. Thüsing, *Per Christum* 40, 50–52.

   as it is written, "The reproaches of those who reproached you fell on me": Paul quotes exactly LXX Ps 68:10b (69:9b). The psalm is quoted with reference to the passion of Christ in Matt 27:34 // Mark 15:23 // Luke 23:36 (cf. also John 2:17; 15:25; 19:29), along with many other citations in other contexts. Paul probably understands the one ("you") addressed by the psalmist to be God but this need not be given undue weight. The stress lies upon Christ's taking on, for the sake of others, "reproaches" which he otherwise need not have borne. The parallel with Phil 2:6-8 and 2 Cor 8:9 suggests that Paul thinks of Christ's "not pleasing himself" as beginning already with a pre-incarnational choice to take on the human condition.

4. *For whatever was written beforehand was written for our instruction:* For similar expressions of the purpose of scripture, see 4:23-24 and 1 Cor 9:9-10; 10:11. This entire verse performs the function of a footnote in modern texts; cf. Ziesler 338.

   in situations where endurance is called for, we might have hope through the encouragement provided by the scriptures: The translation attempts to render the sense of two Greek phrases, which, though similar in form (*dia* + genitive), do not stand in strict parallel. The first *(dia tēs hypomonēs)* indicates "attendant circumstances," the second *(dia tēs paraklēseōs)* qualifies "the scriptures" in an instrumental/causal sense. For Paul's sense of "endurance" *(hypomonē)* as a characteristic virtue of Christian life in the present, see Note on 5:3-4. For the association of *paraklēsis* in the sense of "encouragement" with scripture, 1 Macc 12:9 provides a fine parallel: ". . . we have as encouragement *(paraklēsin)* the holy books . . ."

5. *May the God of endurance and encouragement grant you:* The "prayer-wish" form is a standard mode of concluding exhortatory sections: see 15:13, 33; 1 Thess 3:11-13; 5:23; also 2 Thess 3:5, 16a; Heb 13:20-21. The phrases in the genitive indicate God as the source (genitive *auctoris*) of the qualities named; cf. also 2 Cor 1:3.

6. *that together and with one voice you may glorify the God and Father of our Lord Jesus Christ:* While the phrase has a conventional liturgical ring about it (especially in the closing formula), the double insistence upon unity may imply a sense that differences over food can spill over into worship and prevent the community from truly worshiping God as one body.

For Reference and Further Study

Furnish , V. P. *Love Command* 117–18.
Thompson, M. *Clothed with Christ* 208–30.
Thüsing, W. *Per Christum* 39–41.

d) *Christ's "Acceptance" as Model for Community Acceptance* (15:7-13)

7. Accept one another, therefore, as Christ has accepted you, for the glory of God. 8. For I declare that Christ has become a minister to the circumcised for the sake of God's truthfulness, in order to confirm the promises given to the fathers, 9. and (he has performed a similar function) in the case of the Gentiles that they might glorify God for the receipt of mercy, as it is written, "Therefore I will acknowledge you among the Gentiles, and sing to your name";
10. and again it says, "Rejoice, O Gentiles, with his people";
11. and again, "Praise the Lord, all Gentiles, and let all the peoples praise him";
12. and further Isaiah says, "There shall be the shoot of Jesse, yes, he who rises to rule the Gentiles; in him shall the Gentiles hope."
13. May the God of hope fill you with all joy and peace in believing, so that you may abound in hope by the power of the Holy Spirit.

INTERPRETATION

Introduction. This small section rounds off the entire exhortation concerning tolerance in community life. The opening call, "Accept one another," forms a neat "inclusion" with the appeal to "accept the person weak in faith" with which the whole sequence began (14:1, 3). The section also forms a kind of doublet to the one immediately preceding (15:1-6): both have an opening injunction (15:1-2; cf. 15:7a) supported by reference to the action of Christ (15:3a; cf. 15:8-9a), a reference confirmed by scripture (15:3b; cf. 15:9b-12); both sections conclude with a very similar prayer-wish (15:5-6; 15:13). In particular, the section catches up the idea of the community glorifying God "together and with one voice" (v 6) and develops this into an extended plea for tolerance based upon the truth that Christ "accepted" the Gentiles precisely to bring about this universal glorification of God.

Where the preceding passage spoke in terms of the "strong" and the "weak" within the community, here the focus appears to lie more broadly upon God's (Christ's) action with respect to Jews (literally, the "Circumcision" [v 8a]) and Gentiles. This has led many interpreters either to treat the passage as something quite separate from the preceding exhortation, resuming more general themes of the letter, or else to regard it as evidence that the issue considered in the preceding exhortation revolved around differences dividing Jewish and Gentile believers in the community. But, as the exegesis will show, the implied audience of the passage continues to be Gentile believers; the allusion to Christ's role *vis-à-vis* the "Circumcision" is incidental. The primary focus lies upon what Christ has done for Gentile believers precisely as Gentiles in order that in and through them the "glorification" of God, from which the Gentile world recoiled (1:21-23), might be resumed (cf. 4:20).

"Accept one another" (v 7). At the start of his extended plea for tolerance, Paul had urged "acceptance" of the one weak in faith, on the grounds that "God had accepted that person" (14:3). Here, as a thematic conclusion, he urges precisely the same motivation, save that now it is Christ who is the subject of the "accepting" and those who have been accepted ("you") are the Gentile believers addressed by Paul. Christ "accepted you" for the "glory of God" in the sense that what he did was directed to bringing about the communal "glorification" of God that had been the subject of the prayer-wish uttered in v 6. That glorification "together and with one voice" will only be possible if the acceptance enacted by Christ flows through to mutual community acceptance of one another, in particular those "weak in faith." A familiar biblical pattern of motivation is operative here: what one has oneself received from God one is bound to extend to one's fellow human beings (cf. Deut 24:17-22; Matt 18:32-33).

The example provided by Christ (vv 8-9a). Paul could perhaps have let the sentence in v 7 stand as a conclusion to the entire parenesis. But, in a rather forceful way ("I declare"), he goes on to support it with a more particular indication of the saving role of Christ. The statement is not easy to construe, especially in its final element (v 9a; see Note). Paul is saying something about the purpose of Christ's "ministry" *(diakonon gegenēsthai)*, first in relation to the Jewish people ("the Circumcision")—then in relation to the Gentiles. The statements are not, however, equally balanced. In the following verses bringing scriptural support (9b-12) the stress is entirely upon the Gentiles, showing that they are the chief focus of the argument all through. The allusion to Christ's ministry of the "Circumcision" functions as a foil to what is said about the Gentiles. Paul sets side by side and to some extent contrasts two "economies of salvation."

With respect to the Jews, Christ's "ministry" on behalf of God was impelled by divine faithfulness *(hyper alētheias)*, faithfulness to the "promises" God had made to the patriarchs of Israel (cf. 3:2, 3-5, 7; 9:4; 2 Cor 1:20). Christ discharged God's promises to Israel through his atoning work upon the cross, expiating sin (3:9, 20, 23) and recreating the righteousness that gives access to salvation (cf. esp. 3:21, 25-26).

For the Gentiles (v 9a), however, a different "economy" is operative. They had not received "promises" in the way Israel had (cf. esp. 3:2)—even if Israel guarded on their behalf the promise to Abraham that did concern them (4:16-17; Gal 3:8, 14, 15-22, 29). The benefit that came to them in Christ came as an act of pure "mercy" (*hyper eleous*; cf. 11:30-32) to those who were by definition "Gentile sinners" (cf. Gal 2:15), outside the covenant. The goal of Christ's "service," then, on their behalf is that, where the Jews would praise the divine faithfulness, *they* would glorify God in recognition of the mercy received. With the argument primarily addressed to Gentile believers, Paul's concentration is upon what Christ has done in their regard. But he sharpens the sense of the "debt" they have contracted by pointing out how far back in the race, compared with the Jews, they as Gentiles had started. If they had experienced God's "acceptance" in such measure, how ready *they* ought be to pass it on.

The Gentile praise of God (vv 9b-12). A chain of scriptural quotations supports this view of Christ's role *vis-à-vis* the Gentiles. It is probably no accident that Paul selects texts from all three parts of scripture (the Law [Deut 32:43 in v 10], the Prophets [Isa 11:10 in v 12] and the Writings [Psalm 18 in v 9b; Psalm 118 in v 11]). Scripture gives a broad and unanimous witness to the divine intent, through the ministry of Israel's Messiah, to draw from the nations of the world the praise and glorification that is the true human response to God, reversing the "lapse" recorded in 1:21-23. The final quotation (v 12) in fact presents the Messiah of Israel (literally, "the Branch of David") as the one who will "rise" to "rule the Gentiles" and become the object of their "hope." In terms of his background and historical ministry Jesus is the Jewish Messiah (1:13). As risen Lord (*ho anistamenos*; cf 1:4), however, he has a more universal role, outstripping Jewish messianic categories. He has become the object of "hope" for "all the nations" because the exercise of his "lordship" is destroying the forces of sin and death and preparing the way for the final kingdom (1 Cor 15:24-28; Phil 2:9-11). In recognition of all this the (believing) Gentiles "glorify God for his mercy" (v 9a)—the goal of Christ's "acceptance" of them "for the glory of God" (v 7b).

Prayer-wish (v 13). A second prayer-wish (cf. v 6) forms an appropriate conclusion to the entire parenesis. It was the "faith" of the community—or rather differing levels of it—that had caused the differing judgments about what could be eaten and what ought not. Paul refrained from requiring of all the mature degree of faith that would lead to the "strong" position which is so obviously his own. But now he prays that "in their believing" *(en tǭ pisteuein)*, granted the differences that exist, they may nonetheless have joy and peace with each other. Since faith (believing) shades readily into "hope" (cf. 4:17-22), this will ensure in the community an "overflow" of "hope in the power of the Holy Spirit."

NOTES

7. *as Christ has accepted you:* The clause can be interpreted in either a causal or a comparative sense. The former (cf. 1:28) lends a strong basis to Paul's rea-

soning. The textual variant (B D*) reading "us" *(hēmas)* is almost certainly secondary.

for the glory of God: To take this phrase as qualifying the immediately preceding subordinate clause, rather than the opening command, is more natural in terms of syntax and more consonant with the following reference to Christ as God's empowered agent.

8. *Christ has become a minister to the circumcised:* On the basic sense of *diakonos* as commissioned agent or intermediary, see Note on 12:7. Only here, along with the formulation of the false objection in Gal 2:17 ("Is Christ a *diakonos* of sin?"), does Paul use the word of Christ. But the standard sense can be retained: Christ is God's commissioned agent to perform a role *vis-à-vis* the Jews. There is no need to import "servant" associations stemming from Mark 10:45 (on this, see J. N. Collins, *Diakonia* 227). The use of the perfect tense *gegenēsthai* lends the sense that Christ's ministry, once inaugurated (upon the cross), continues on (in the proclamation of the gospel of the Crucified; cf. 3:21-22). Paul uses the abstract noun "circumcision" *(peritomē)* to denote the community of the circumcised (= "the Jewish people"); cf. 3:30 (where, correspondingly, *akrobystia* denotes the Gentiles; cf. 2:26; Gal 2:7-8).

   for the sake of God's truthfulness: Paul's sense of the virtual equivalence of God's "truth" and God's "faithfulness" is shown in the parallel statements about God found across 3:3, 4 and 7; see Interpretation of 3:1-8.

   in order to confirm the promises given to the fathers: Some interpreters see here a reference specifically to the promise given to Abraham concerning the inclusion of the Gentiles in the "blessing" conferred "in his offspring" (4:13-17; Gal 3:8, 14, 22, 29); see esp. S. K. Williams, "The 'Righteousness of God'" 286. However, Paul does on occasion appear to use the notion of "promise" with respect to Israel apart from the divine intention in regard to the Gentiles (9:4; cf. also 3:2 [*logia*]).

9. *and (he has performed a similar function) in the case of the Gentiles that they might glorify God for the receipt of mercy:* The translation (and Interpretation) takes this statement about the Gentiles (an accusative and infinitive construction in Greek) as dependent upon the opening main verb "I declare" *(legō)* so as to form a parallel to the whole of v 8. On this understanding, Paul makes two parallel assertions concerning the "ministry" of Christ—one describing it as a dispensation of God's "fidelity" in relationship to the Circumcision, the other describing it as a dispensation of God's mercy with respect to the Gentiles. The second statement (v 9a) lacks an explicit reference to the "ministry" Christ performs with respect to the Gentiles but the overall sense requires at least an implicit allusion of this kind. Paul may have felt that there was no need for him to actually formulate such a statement because it was already implicit in the reference to Christ's "acceptance" of "you" (Gentiles) in v 7b. On this understanding, the Greek conjunction *de* at the beginning of v 9a retains something of an adversative sense, placing greater emphasis upon the second statement so as to suggest that the statement about Christ's ministry to the Circumcision is introduced only as a foil to what Paul wants to say

about the Gentiles in support of v 7 (so esp. Lagrange 345–46; Zeller, *Juden und Heiden* 219–20). Alternatively, it is possible to see v 9a as governed by the *eis to . . .* phrase that also governs the immediately preceding infinitive construction concerning the confirmation of the promises (v 8b). This presents Christ's "ministry" to the circumcised as having the function not only of confirming the promises to the fathers but also as causing the Gentiles to glorify God, a connection between the two effects well understandable in the light of Paul's treatment of the promise to Abraham in an inclusive (of the Gentiles) sense in chapter 4 (cf. Galatians 3). The interpretation is, however, harsh in terms of Greek syntax and spoils any sense of parallel between the references, respectively, to God's "faithfulness" and God's "mercy."

"Therefore I will acknowledge you among the Gentiles, and sing to your name": The quotation agrees exactly with LXX Ps 17:50 (18:49), save for the omission of the address "Lord" *(kyrie)*. In the quotation Paul probably intends the audience to hear the voice of the risen Lord, who, through the spread of the gospel, has become among the Gentiles the "choirmaster" leading their praise of God (cf. v 7b); cf. W. Thüsing, *Per Christum* 43.

10. *and again it says, "Rejoice, O Gentiles, with his people":* The quotation agrees exactly with LXX of Deut 32:43. In the original Hebrew the thought is very hostile to the Gentiles. Paul has developed a more benign universalistic meaning already evident in the LXX translation.

11. *and again, "Praise the Lord, all Gentiles, and let all the peoples praise him":* The quotation agrees with LXX Ps 117:1 (118:1), with slight alterations not affecting the sense. Interestingly, in view of vv 8-9a, the second verse of the same brief psalm presents God's "mercy" *(eleos)* and "truth" *(alētheia)* as the grounds for its summons to praise.

12. *and further Isaiah says, "There shall be the shoot of Jesse, yes, he who rises to rule the Gentiles; in him shall the Gentiles hope":* The quotation agrees with the LXX Isa 11:10, save for the omission of a phrase ("on that day") after the initial verb. Based upon its use with reference to the Davidic king in Isa 11:1-5, 10 (cf. also Jer 23:5; 33:15), "Shoot of Jesse" had become an established title for the Davidic Messiah by the time of the rise of Christianity: Sir 47:22; 4QpGen[a] 5:2-4; 4QFlor 1:11-13. While the verb *anistanai* can mean simply "arise," its prevalence in reference to Christ's resurrection in the NT, along with the similarity of the pattern to the credal formula in 1:3-4, strongly suggests that an allusion to Christ as risen Lord is intended here.

13. *May the God of hope:* For Paul's use of similar prayer-wishes, see Note on 15:6.

For Reference and Further Study

Collins J. N. *Diakonia. Re-interpreting the Ancient Sources.* New York and Oxford: Oxford University, 1990, 227–28.

Frid, B. "Jesaja und Paulus in Röm 15:12." *BZ* 27 (1983) 237–41.

Karris, R. J. "Romans 14:1–15:13 and the Occasion of Romans." *Romans Debate* 79–81.
Thompson, M. *Clothed with Christ* 230–34.
Thüsing, W. *Per Christum* 39–46.
Williams, S. K. "The 'Righteousness of God.'" 285–89.
Zeller, D. *Juden und Heiden* 218–23.

CONCLUSION OF THE LETTER (15:14–16:24[27])

i. Paul's Ministry of the Gospel to the Gentiles (15:14-33)

Introduction. Paul has completed the celebratory presentation of the gospel of which he is "not ashamed" (1:16a). He has communicated to the Gentile Christian audience in Rome a sense of the dignity and hope that attends their inclusion within the eschatological people of God (1:18–8:39). At the same time, he has insisted that the God who has acted "inclusively" with respect to their salvation will not fail to include also within the scope of that salvation the bulk of Israel that at present appears "excluded" from it (9:1–11:36). He has summoned the community to allow its way of life to be shaped by this vision of the gospel—specifically, to allow the generosity and mercy they as Gentiles have received from God to flow through and determine the structures of their own relationships, both within the community and with respect to outsiders (12:1–15:13). In this way, reversing the ravages wrought by sin (1:21-23), they, as Gentiles, will fulfill God's original intent that the nations of the world, together with Israel, should glorify the God and Father of Jesus Christ (15:6, 9-12).

Presenting his own vision of the gospel in this "celebratory" way, Paul has, in effect, "preached the gospel" to the Gentile believers in Rome (cf. 1:15). Now it is time to present *himself* more directly to them, not simply as minister of the gospel to the Gentiles (1:1-5, 13-15) but as one intending to pay them a visit. To indicate travel plans, to send greetings to various individuals and to offer prayers for the well-being of the recipients are all standard *topoi* in ancient letter writing. Paul's announcement, however, goes well beyond simple convention. His communication with Rome reaches at this point its most delicate moment. He has to announce his visit without alienating the Roman community or putting them on the defensive; at the same time, he must preserve the sense of himself as apostle charged with responsibility for the Gentile churches and looking to a future field of action in which he hopes the Roman community will play a central role.

Understandably, then, Paul goes about this task according to a careful rhetorical strategy. Diplomatically he acknowledges (vv 14-15) that he has admonished them when in fact they were well capable of admonishing each other. If he has written "rather boldly" in this respect, it has not been as though addressing them as people needing original conversion but "by way of reminder" of the gospel they already know. The justification that he gives for taking this liberty (v 15b) then enables him to provide once more a solemn presentation of his own distinctive role as apostle to the Gentiles (v 16), followed by an outline of the way in which, historically, he has discharged that role in the Eastern Mediterranean up to the present (vv 18-22). The way is then clear to state his plans for the future: to seek new fields of apostolic endeavor in the West, specifically in Spain. So when at last he mentions his plans to visit Rome (v 23), the projected visit sits within the context of this wider apostolic design, as he stands on the threshold of the second stage of his career (vv 22-24).

The most immediate prospect is that of conveying to Jerusalem the "collection for the saints" contributed by the Gentile churches of Macedonia and Achaia. The collection is not only a relief measure for a community in need. It is above all a symbolic acknowledgment, on the part of the Pauline Gentile churches, of the special place of the Jewish-Christian mother church from which the gospel has gone out to the wider world (vv 25-27). Paul enlists his Roman audience into this venture by requesting prayers for its success (vv 30-31). The overall effect is to draw the Gentile community at Rome ever more deeply into his own ambit and mission as minister of the gospel to the Gentiles.

a) *Paul's Apostolic Mission Until Now* (15:14-21)

14. I myself am fully confident, my brothers (and sisters), that you yourselves are full of goodness, filled with all knowledge, and so quite capable of correcting one another. 15. If on some points I have written to you rather boldly, by way of reminder, it is because of the grace given me by God 16. to be a minister of Christ Jesus to the Gentiles, serving the gospel of God as a priest, in order that the offering of the Gentiles may be acceptable (to God), sanctified by the Holy Spirit.

17. This is the boast I have in Christ Jesus in connection with the service of God. 18. For what I am speaking of in such bold terms is nothing else than what Christ has wrought through me to win obedience from the Gentiles, in word and deed, 19. by the power of signs and wonders, by the power of the Holy Spirit. The effect has been that from Jerusalem as far round as Illyricum I have completed the preaching of the gospel of Christ, 20. being eager in this way to avoid preaching where Christ has already been named, lest I build on another person's foundation, 21. but, as it is written, "They shall see who have never been told of him, and they shall understand who have never heard of him." 22. This is why I have so often been hindered from coming to you.

Interpretation

Paul's "boldness" (vv 14-15). Expressions of confidence in one's addressees were a standard ploy of ancient rhetorical technique in situations where the speaker has reason to suspect that the audience feels they are not being regarded with confidence. The aim is to overcome any alienation that may have arisen as a result. In this vein Paul acknowledges (v 14) that the Roman community is "full" of both "goodness" and that "knowledge" (of the gospel and its implications) that would render it capable of performing any self-correction required. The acknowledgment raises the need to explain why, such being the case, Paul has written to them "in some points rather boldly" *(tolmēroteron . . . apo merous).* The reference here is probably to the foregoing plea for tolerance (14:1–15:13), though allusion to earlier material of a parenetic nature (e.g, 8:13-14; 11:17-24; 12:1–13:13) can hardly be ruled out and, in fact, Paul may have in mind the whole enterprise of writing in such authoritative tones to a community he has not founded. Paul explains (v 15) that, if he has written in this way, it is not in any sense as if to provide a first evangelization. Rather, he has done so "by way of reminder" *(hōs epanamimnęskōn)* of the gospel they already know. He has taken this liberty in virtue of the unique and specific grace (*charin*; cf. 1:5) which he, as apostle, has received from God.

Paul as minister of the gospel (v 16). The description of his apostolic calling that Paul now offers (v 16) is one of the most solemn to be found in his writings. It amounts to a forceful claim to unique status in the entire Christian movement. The cultic language ("minister" *[leitourgos]*; "serving . . . as a priest" *[hierogōn]*; "offering" *[prosphora]*) is, of course, metaphorical and reflects the tendency of the early Christian community to apply to itself as eschatological people of God terminology and imagery taken from Israel's worship. Paul is not portraying himself as "priest" in the sense of the distinction between ordained clergy and laity that arose much later in Christian usage. In terms of the original image taken from the ritual of sacrifice, the presence and operation of the priest as God's minister ensures that what is offered is acceptable to the deity. In the present situation, the previously "unclean" Gentiles (cf. 1:24, 26-27, 28-31; Gal 2:15), hitherto denied access to God, have through their conversion made an "offering" of themselves to God. Paul's role as "priest" is to ensure that they come before God no longer as alienated and "unclean" but as an offering truly acceptable because "sanctified through the Holy Spirit." The image suggests not so much the role in which Paul usually depicts himself—that concerned with original preaching and conversion (cf. esp. 1 Cor 1:17)—but rather that of the subsequent "sanctification" of those who were originally unclean.

In this last respect the image bears pointedly upon Paul's relationship with the community of Gentile believers in Rome. He may not have been responsible for their original conversion. But, in virtue of his unique "priestly" role *vis-à-vis* the Gentiles just described, he does have a continuing function in relationship to them as Gentiles—a function of seeing that they are and remain an "offering acceptable" to God. If he has written to them "rather boldly," "reminding" them and "admonishing" them, he has done so in virtue of this God-given responsibility to ensure that their "sanctification" be complete. Paul may express his sense of responsibility for the community subtly and diplomatically. But the claim inherent in the imagery is unmistakable.

Paul's apostolic ministry up to the present (vv 17-19a). From consideration of his apostolic role in itself Paul moves on to state what he has actually achieved in virtue of this role. The description (v 17) of it as his "boast" *(kauchēsis)* is highly charged in view of the exclusion of wrongly based human "boasting" earlier in the letter (3:27). But it is a "boast" that he makes entirely "in Christ Jesus" and concerns solely the "work of God" *(ta pros ton theon)*. It does not rest upon anything he has achieved by himself but solely upon what Christ as risen Lord has worked through him (v 18). What has attested this presence and power of the risen Lord has been not only the success of the preaching in bringing about, through word and deed, the "obedience of the Gentiles" (*eis hypakoēn ethnōn*; cf. 1:5), but also (v 19a) the marvelous phenomena—"signs and wonders" worked through the power of the Spirit—that have attended the proclamation (see Note).

The geographical "sweep" of Paul's mission (v 19b). The upshot (cf. *hōste*) of this impulse of the risen Lord as Spirit has been the completion on Paul's part of a mighty arc (cf. *kyklǭ*) of evangelization taking in the whole of the Eastern Mediterranean seaboard to the borders of what would be the modern state of Albania (Illyricum). Taken at face value, the claim is extraordinary. Paul's preaching, as far as we can judge, was confined to the great cities and even in them probably reached only a small proportion of the population, leaving the vast rural hinterland virtually untouched. But Paul presents himself not so much as an independent agent but as the tool or instrument of the gospel, impelled by the force of the Spirit. In the divine plan the gospel "must" be preached to the "ends of the earth" before the return *(parousia)* of the Lord (cf. Mark 13:10; also Rom 10:18). The "facts" of the matter are completely eclipsed by this overall vision of salvation.

Paul's missionary "policy" (vv 20-21). Paul accounts for the vast sweep of this activity by pointing to the policy that has guided his distinctive apostolic mission. His task has been essentially that of the path-finder, the pioneer, the one ever eager *(philotimoumenon)* to press on outwards to those regions where Christ has "not been named," that is, where missionaries have not yet preached nor communities been founded. In terms of his preferred image of the Christian community as the "building" *(oikodomē)* of the Lord (cf. 14:19-20; 15:2), Paul's role has been that of laying the foundations; he does not build upon foundations already set in place (cf. 1 Cor 3:10). That is why, with an astonishing sense of his role in salvation history, he can arrogate to his own career (v 21) a scriptural text (Isa 52:15b) that originally referred to the way in which the Isaianic "Servant" would become known to those who previously had taken no account of him. Without necessarily identifying himself as the "Servant," Paul presents his own career as the fulfillment of the prophecy inherent in this text. He proclaims knowledge of Jesus to Gentile nations previously untouched by Christian preaching or knowledge of the Jewish Messiah. In this way he communicates to the Roman community a very strong impression, both of his distinctive role within salvation history and the way in which he has fulfilled that role up to the present.

Notes

14. *I myself am fully confident, my brothers (and sisters):* For the background provided by Classical and Hellenistic rhetoric to this expression of confidence in one's addressees, see the studies of S. N. Olson mentioned in Reference.

    filled with all knowledge: The reading *pasēs tēs gnōseōs,* to be preferred over that omitting the article, gives the sense of "all the knowledge (of the gospel) required to handle the situation"; cf. Dunn 2.858.

15. *rather boldly:* Paul uses the comparative adverb to give the sense of somewhat more boldly than the situation might seem to require.

16. *to be a minister of Christ Jesus to the Gentiles, serving the gospel of God as a priest:* From both LXX usage and that of Paul himself (notably Rom 13:6; Phil 2:25) it is clear that the Greek word *leitourgos* does not in itself have a sacral sense but designates one who performs a task under a superior. However, the verb that

follows in the present case, *hierourgein*, is always used in the LXX and related literature (Philo, Josephus) with respect to priestly offering of sacrifice. This, together with the later reference to the "offering of the Gentiles," lends a cultic sense to the entire clause.

the offering of the Gentiles: The genitive following "offering" *(prosphora)* is best taken as epexegetic: "the offering consisting of the Gentiles." If, as some interpreters think, Paul alludes here to the biblical motif of the eschatological pilgrimage of the nations to Zion (cf. esp. Isa 66:20; also 45:14; 60:5-17; 61:6; cf. 1QM 12:13-15), it would be on the basis that the Gentiles were "entering" as full and equal "citizens" into the eschatological Zion; any hint of subordination attaching to the more conventional conception would undermine his case.

acceptable (to God): The Greek adjective *euprosdektos* has, in this context of "sacrifice" (contrast 15:31), the sense "acceptable to God"; cf. 1 Pet 2:5 and *euareston* in Rom 12:2.

17. *This is the boast I have:* The article before "boast" has a demonstrative sense. The flow of Paul's argument is best served if "this boast" is seen as preparing the way for the account of his ministry that is to follow (vv 18-19; cf. *oun*).

in Christ Jesus: The stock phrase "in Christ Jesus" indicates that Paul's "boast" is entirely founded upon and controlled by his existence, as a Christian, within the sphere of power constituted by Christ as risen Lord; see Interpretation of 6:3 and Note on 6:11.

18. *For what I am speaking of in such bold terms is nothing else than:* The translation attempts to bring out the force of what Paul has expressed in a rather roundabout negative fashion so as to place maximum stress upon the fact that *everything* of which he can boast is *solely* the achievement of Christ through him.

19. *signs and wonders:* Paul uses a stereotyped phrase from the biblical tradition (cf. 2 Cor 12:12; Heb 2:4), ultimately going back to a traditional OT way of referring to the miracles accompanying Israel's exodus from Egypt. Paul provides here some personal confirmation (cf. also 1 Cor 2:4-5; 2 Cor 12:12; Gal 3:5; 1 Thess 1:5; 2:13) of the picture drawn from Acts that his ministry was fairly constantly attended by manifestations of the Spirit (14:8-10; 16:16-18, 25-26; 20:9-12; 28:8-9).

from Jerusalem as far round as Illyricum: It is highly unlikely that Paul began his mission to the Gentiles in Jerusalem (cf. esp. Gal 1:22) nor does any source tell of ministry on his part in the Roman province of Illyria (the region centered upon the modern state of Albania). The two geographical references may simply indicate the outer limits *within* which Paul's ministry took place (*mechri* can have the sense of "up to but not including"). More likely, Paul speaks in broadly representative terms, conjuring up a vision of the gospel embracing, through his ministry, a broad sweep around the entire Eastern Mediterranean. Within this perspective, Jerusalem would be mentioned as starting point, not because Paul personally preached to Gentiles there but in accordance with a traditional early Christian view of the gospel as emanating from it, as center, to the "ends of the earth" (Acts 1:8).

I have completed the preaching of the gospel of Christ: The expression seems to contain the eschatological sense of having accomplished one aspect of what was necessary before the *parousia* of Christ; cf. Mark 13:10.

20. *in this way:* The phrase translates the Greek adverb *houtōs*, which can be taken either as looking forward to introduce the apostolic principle stated immediately after (not building upon another person's foundation) or else as referring back to explain the claim made in v 19b, in the sense that Paul has been able to cover so much ground precisely because he has followed this principle of always seeking fresh pastures. Besides serving the overall argument better, the second interpretation makes for a much less harsh transition to v 22.

21. *but as it is written, "They shall see who have never been told of him, and they shall understand who have never heard of him.":* The quotation agrees with the LXX of Isa 52:15b exactly save for a slight alteration of word order. Paul hardly identifies *himself* with the Isaianic Servant (so Dunn 2.866). He preaches where people have not previously heard of Christ—not where they have not previously heard of Paul!

For Reference and Further Study

Byrne, B. "Rather Boldly (Rom 15:15): Paul's Prophetic Bid to Win the Allegiance of the Christians in Rome." *Biblica* 74 (1993) 83–96.

Dahl, N. A. "The Missionary Theology in the Epistle to the Romans." *Studies in Paul* 70–94.

Knox, J. "Rom 15:14-33 and Paul's Conception of His Apostolic Mission." *JBL* 83 (1964) 1–11.

Olson, S. N. "Epistolary Uses of Expressions of Self-Confidence." *JBL* 103 (1984) 585–97.

__________. "Pauline Expressions of Confidence in His Addressees." *CBQ* 47 (1985) 282–95.

Ponthot, J. "L'expression cultuelle du ministère paulinien selon Rom 15:16," *L'Apôtre Paul* (Ed. A. Vanhoye) 254–62.

Wedderburn, A.J.M. *Reasons for Romans* 98–102.

Zeller, D. *Juden und Heiden* 64–69, 224–29.

b) *Paul's Plans for the Future and Concluding "Grace" I* (15:22-33)

22. This is the reason that I have so often been hindered from coming to you. 23. But now, since I no longer have any room for work in these regions, and having had for many years a great desire to come to you, whenever I should be travelling to Spain—24. For I hope to see you as I

pass through and be sped on my journey there by you, once I have enjoyed, at least in some measure, your company.
25. At present, however, I am going to Jerusalem with aid for the saints.
26. For Macedonia and Achaia have been pleased to make some common contribution for the poor among the saints at Jerusalem. 27. They
were pleased to do it, and indeed it was a matter of discharging a debt
to them, for if the Gentiles have come to share in their spiritual blessings,
they are obligated to be of service to them in material benefits.
28. When therefore I have completed and sealed this fruit (of their generosity), I shall go on by way of you to Spain; 29. and I know that when
I come to you I shall come in the fullness of the blessing of Christ.
30. I appeal to you, brothers (and sisters), through the power of our Lord
Jesus Christ and by the love of the Spirit, to strive together with me in
your prayers to God on my behalf, 31. that I may be delivered from the
unbelievers in Judea, and that my service for Jerusalem may be acceptable to the saints, 32. so that by God's will I may come to you with joy
and be refreshed in your company.
33. The God of peace be with you all. Amen.

Interpretation

Paul prevented from visiting Rome (v 22). The foregoing sketch of his wide-ranging apostolic activity allows Paul, not only to present himself as effective apostle to the Gentiles but also to address an issue already touched upon earlier in the letter (1:9-11, 13-15): why, if he is apostle to the Gentiles in this unique sense, has he neglected to visit the significant Gentile community in Rome? The response is that his non-appearance has not been due to indifference or fear, nor does it mean that he considers the Roman Gentile community to be outside his apostolic sphere of responsibility. It is simply that the impulse of the risen Lord (v 18) driving him through the entire span of Asia Minor and Greece at the service of the gospel has "prevented" him (cf. *enekoptomēn*) from effecting the long-desired visit.

Paul's plans to visit Rome (vv 23-24). Now, however, Paul stands at the threshold of a new stage in his apostolic career. There is no longer scope in the East for the pioneering style of preaching and founding churches that is his particular charism (v 23a; cf. vv 20-21). The impulse of the gospel is driving him to look elsewhere. This radical redirection of his ministry presents an opportunity to fulfill at last the long-cherished desire to come to Rome, as he passes through en route to Spain (vv 23b-24a).

The mention of Spain as ultimate destination is almost incidental. Paul appears to assume that the Roman community either knows or will understand from his description of his particular apostolic charism (vv 16-21) that the great "arc" of missionary labor in the Eastern Mediterranean has to be complemented by a similar "arc" in the West. The more pressing issue is to explain the nature of the planned intermediate visit to Rome now that news of it has finally been broached. Hence Paul breaks off the sentence to explain (v 24b) more precisely what he has in mind. He wants to "see them" as he passes through—nothing particularly demanding or threatening in that. But the added phrases suggest rather more. Paul's hope to "be sped on his way there" *(propemphthēnai ekei)* hints at receiving support for his mission from a community well placed—geographically and possibly financially—to do so (see Note). Being "refreshed for a little" *(apo merous emplēsthō)* in their company does not mean simply rest and relaxation but the kind of consolation the apostle to the Gentiles might experience in Rome on finding there a community conformed to the gospel as expounded in the letter.

The collection (vv 25-27). The matter is, however, more complex still. Between Paul and Rome—and ultimately Spain—lies an intermediate task: that of journeying to Jerusalem with relief for "the saints" (v 25). References in other letters (1 Cor 16:1-3; 2 Corinthians 8–9) attest the high premium Paul placed upon this task of collecting and conveying to the Jerusalem church the financial contribution from the Gentile communities. This was no mere relief measure to a community in particular need but the fulfillment of a key "clause" in the agreement made with the "pillars" of the Jerusalem church when they recognized his distinctive ministry (Gal 2:9-10). It is important for Paul to communicate to the Roman community some sense of its central symbolic significance and enlist at least their moral, if not their financial, support for the enterprise.

Hence Paul explains (vv 26-27) the nature of the collection. It is something which the churches of Macedonia and Achaia have contributed as a gesture of solidarity—solidarity (cf. *koinōnian*) with one another and with the recipient community—for the relief of the "poor" among the "saints at Jerusalem." The contribution has been voluntary (cf. the twice stated *eudokēsan*). At the same time—and here the significance of the collection begins to emerge—there are good grounds for the willingness lying behind the generosity. The Gentile communities *(ta ethnē)* are "indebted" *(opheiletai . . . opheilousin)* in this matter because, through the remarkable exercise of God's mercy (11:30-31; 15:8-9), they have shared *(ekoinōnēsan)* in the "spiritual blessings" *(pneumatikois)* of Israel, represented by the Jewish-Christian community in Jerusalem. They are and will always remain the "wild olive" that has been grafted upon and continues to draw its life from the original "root" (the fathers of Israel—11:16-18). The privilege of having shared in these "superior" spiritual blessings (the benefits of salvation) creates for them, on the *a fortiori* logic so beloved of Paul (cf. esp. 5:8-9, 10, 15, 17; 8:32; 11:24), an "obligation" to ensure that a similar sharing takes place on the lesser, material (literally, "fleshly") level. Hence the Gentile churches have freely recognized—undoubtedly with much urging from Paul (cf. 2 Cor 8:9; 9:6-10)—their obligation to "minister" *(leitourgēsai)* to the Jerusalem community in this material way.

What Paul subtly communicates here to the Roman community is a sense that the collection symbolizes recognition on the part of the Pauline Gentile communities of the "priority" of the Jewish-Christian Jerusalem church as regards the history of salvation (cf. 1:16: ". . . Jew first, but also the Greek"). The Gentile communities may be more prosperous in numerical and material terms than the mother church is. But they cannot supplant its role as the first hearer and proclaimer of the worldwide gospel. At the same time, the acceptance of the collection on the part of the Jerusalem community will represent *its* recognition of the full citizenship of the Gentile communities in the one eschatological people of God.

Paul's coming to Rome will be a "blessing" (vv 28-29). The business of conveying the collection to Jerusalem will mean a further postponement of Paul's projected visit to Rome. It represents, however, a "fruit" *(karpos)* which must be completed and "sealed" *(sphragisamenos)* before he is free to undertake new work in the West (v 28). Paul speaks in terms of "this fruit" probably to convey the sense that the collection will be a token of how richly the "spiritual seed" of the gospel, originating in Israel, has borne "fruit" among the Gentiles. This means that he is confident that, when he does come to the community, it will be "in the fullness of the blessing of Christ" (v 29). The phrase is ambiguous (see Note)—perhaps intentionally so. But Paul's "confidence" presumably springs from his sense of having a God-given mandate to reap "fruit" among the Gentiles (1:13), something which the collection so amply attests. He is confident that the benefits mentioned at the beginning of the letter as likely to flow from a visit on his part (1:11-13) will be realized when finally he does come.

Request for prayer (vv 30-32) and a prayer-wish (v 33). Very much on Paul's mind is the precarious nature of his mission to Jerusalem. So, following this expression of confidence, he earnestly entreats (see Note) the community, in virtue of their bond in the Lord Jesus Christ and of the love created by the Spirit that binds them together, to "struggle along with" him *(synagōnisasthai moi)* in prayer to God for a double intention. In the first place, his life will be under threat in Jerusalem from those Jews (literally, "the unbelievers") who regard him as a renegade and a serious threat to the ancestral religion. He asks prayers that he be spared destruction *(hina rhysthō)* at their hands. Secondly, and more poignantly, there is the prospect that even fellow believers in Jerusalem will spurn both the collection and what its acceptance would symbolize: the acknowledgment of Gentile believers as full citizens in the eschatological people of God. If, as a result of their common striving in prayer, Paul's mission in Jerusalem meets with the longed-for acceptance, then, as he puts it in a final comment (v 32), he will be able to come to Rome "in joy" *(en charą)*. Both he and they will then experience the "mutual refreshment" *(synanapausomai hymin)* that (on his part at least) is the anticipated outcome of the long desired visit. A prayer-wish (v 33) then forms a characteristically Pauline conclusion to the entire sequence (cf. already 15:5-6, 13).

Doubtless Paul does value the prayers of the Roman community for the two causes he mentions. But accompanying the request for prayer is almost certainly also the tactic of enlisting at least the moral support of the Roman community for the acceptance of his mission to Jerusalem, with which is bound up the success of his entire life-project in the service of the gospel. To win this significant community to his cause will count strongly for him at this moment of high risk. Paul is, in effect, "boldly" seeking to enlist the Roman community into the view of Christianity that is distinctly—and controversially—his own.

Notes

22. *This is the reason that I have so often been hindered from coming to you:* The reason (cf. *dio*) is best seen as consisting in the missionary activity described in vv 18-19 (so most modern interpreters), not in adherence to the principle outlined in vv 20-21.

23. *I no longer have any room for work in these regions:* This startling statement on Paul's part suggests that "the Gentiles" to whom he considered himself divinely appointed apostle may not have included inhabitants of such well-known areas as Mesopotamia, Egypt and the north coast of Africa. It is highly unlikely that he was unaware of nations beyond the confines of the Roman empire.

    to Spain: Whether Paul did ever get to Spain is not certain. The notice to this effect in 1 Clem 5:7, though comparatively early, could represent a tradition that grew out of the aspiration expressed here in Romans rather than a genuine historical memory. On the Roman province of Spain in Paul's time and why it would have presented an attractive field of evangelization for him, see the excellent discussion of Dunn 2.872.

24. *and be sped on my journey there by you:* The Greek verb, *propempein* was used to denote the fulfillment of various services which a person departing on a journey might require (rations, money, letters of introduction, the provision of companions or an escort).

    once I have enjoyed, at least in some measure, your company: Paul's polite expression seems designed to counter any impression of using the Roman community simply as a staging post.

25. *with aid for the saints:* The reference later in the sentence to "the saints in Jerusalem" and, in particular, the absolute use of the phrase "the saints" in v 31 with clear reference to the Jerusalem community argues that "the saints" here are the object rather than the promoters of this particular *diakonia* on Paul's part. On the nature and purpose of the collection, see esp. S. McKnight, *DPL* 143–47.

26. *For Macedonia and Achaia:* Surprisingly, Paul mentions only the churches of Greece and Macedonia in connection with the collection, though 1 Cor 16:1 makes it clear that the churches of Asia Minor (specifically Galatia) were involved as well.

    to make some common contribution: The translation attempts to convey the sense of solidarity communicated by the Greek word *koinōnia*, which expresses the unity between parties created by their common sharing in some other thing; cf. J. Hainz, *EDNT* 2.303–05.

    for the poor among the saints at Jerusalem: It is likely that the phrase "the poor" *(hoi ptōchoi)* was an honorific self-designation of the early community of believers in Jerusalem, identifying it with the "Poor of Yahweh" in the biblical and post-biblical Jewish tradition (Pss 69:32; 72:2; *Pss. Sol.* 5:2, 11; 10:6; 15:1; 18:2; 1QpHab 12:3, 6, 10; 1QM 11:9, 13; 4QpPs37 2:9-10). The stipulation to "remember the poor" in the agreement cited in Gal 2:10 may reflect this usage. In the present context the use of the genitive is more likely partitive rather than epexegetic, the reference being to the poor *among* the community ("saints") at Jerusalem—though even if the relief was destined for the poorer members it would remain a gift to the community as a whole since care for the poor was a common concern.

27. *spiritual blessings . . . material benefits:* The Greek term *pneumatika* designates the blessings of salvation, already present to some degree and attested by the Spirit (cf. 8:23); *sarkika*, used here in a neutral sense (contrast 7:14), indicates "this-worldly" material support.

28. *When therefore I have completed and sealed this fruit (of their generosity):* The language is open to a variety of interpretation. The Greek term translated here "completed" *(epitelesas)* is used at times in a cultic context and, in view of the cultic allusion in v 16, may have such associations here. "Sealed" *(sphragisamenos)* may simply indicate the finalizing of the matter (cf. the English expression: "signed, sealed and delivered"); on the other hand, it may highlight the significance of what is at stake: "when I have in this way (through the delivery of the collection) set the seal upon all my work in the East." Similarly, "fruit" *(karpos)* could simply indicate the amount of money raised from the Gentile communities or, in a deeper sense, it could suggest that the contribution represents the "fruit" and hence evidence of the success of Paul's labors in this field.

30. *I appeal to you, brothers (and sisters):* Paul reinforces his appeal with a formula *(parakalō)* well known in ancient correspondence for the making of urgent entreaty; see Note on 12:1.

to strive together with me: The Greek verb *synagōnizesthai*, otherwise unknown in the Greek Bible, communicates the sense not so much of a struggle with God (allusions to Gen 32:24-32 [Jacob's "wrestling" with God] are not appropriate) but of an invitation to the Roman community to enlist themselves on the side of Paul in the struggle that lies ahead of him.

31. *that I may be delivered:* The passive of the verb *ryesthai* suggests rescue from life-threatening situations (cf. 7:24; 11:26). The fact that Paul clearly recognizes that journeying to Jerusalem will place his life at risk underlines the importance he attaches to the collection.

from the unbelievers in Judea: For the use of the designation "unbelievers/ unbelief" *(apeithein/ -ia)* with reference to Jews who have not come to faith in Jesus as the Christ, cf. 10:16, 21; 11:30-31; 2 Cor 4:4. 1 Thess 2:14-15 also mentions Jewish hostility to believers in Judea (though some suspect the passage to be an interpolation); cf. also Acts 20:23; 21:10-14; 21:27–26:32 *(passim).*

that my service for Jerusalem may be acceptable to the saints: The curious silence in Acts concerning the collection (save for the enigmatic, retrospective allusion in 24:17) provides some evidence that the fears expressed by Paul in Romans were realized and that the collection was not in fact well received in Jerusalem. Of this we cannot be sure. Acts 21:20-22 also hints at Jewish-Christian hostility to Paul in Jerusalem.

32. *so that by God's will I may come to you with joy and be refreshed in your company:* The verse features a great amount of textual variation, none of it particularly affecting the sense; for details, see Cranfield 2.779, n. 1.

33. *The God of peace be with you all. Amen:* The formula comes closer to the "prayer-wish" (for which see Note on 15:5) than to the regular Pauline concluding greeting, which normally includes the term "grace" *(charis).*

For Reference and Further Study

Aus, R. D. "Paul's Travel Plans to Spain and the 'Full Number of the Gentiles' of Rom. XI. 25." *NovT* 21 (1979) 232–62.

Berger, K. "Almosen für Israel: zum historischen Kontext der paulinischen Kollekte." *NTS* 23 (1976–77) 180–204.

Dahl, N. A. "The Missionary Theology in the Epistle to the Romans." *Studies in Paul* 70–94.

Georgi, D. *Remembering the Poor: The History of Paul's Collection for Jerusalem.* Nashville: Abingdon, 1992, 110–21.

Keck, L. E. "'The Poor among the Saints' in Jewish Christianity and Qumran." *ZNW* 57 (1966) 54–78.

__________. "The Poor among the Saints in the New Testament." *ZNW* 56 (1965) 100–29.

Knox, J. "Rom 15:14-33 and Paul's Conception of His Apostolic Mission." *JBL* 83 (1964) 1–11.

McKnight, S. "Collection for the Saints." *DPL* 143–47.

Munck, J. *Paul and the Salvation of Mankind* 49–55, 297–308.
Nickle, K. F. *The Collection. A Study in the Strategy of Paul.* SBT 48; London: SCM; Naperville: Allison, 1966.
Wedderburn, A.J.M. *Reasons for Romans* 37–41, 70–75, 98–102.
Zeller, D. *Juden und Heiden* 70–76, 229–32.

ii. Commendation and Greetings (16:1-27)

Introduction to Romans 16. The sixteenth and final chapter of Paul's letter to Rome stands apart from all the rest. It consists largely of a long series of greetings, interrupted by a warning (vv 17-20) and concluded by a doxology (vv 25-27) not composed by Paul. At first sight the chapter appears devoid of theological interest in comparison with what has gone before. But recent studies—especially those adopting a sociological approach—have pointed to the rich light it sheds upon the composition and structures of the early Christian church.

Interpreters have long wondered how Paul could have known so many persons (no less than twenty-six are greeted in vv 3-16) in a distant community that he had neither founded himself nor visited. This has led to the suggestion that the material contained in chapter 16 represents all or part of a letter written to a church founded by Paul (Ephesus being the usual suggestion), a theory that received considerable impetus from the discovery of the very early papyrus P^{46}; this, while containing chapter 16, places the doxology making up vv 25-27 at the end of chapter 15. Reasons for rejecting this theory and maintaining the integrity of the full sixteen-chapter version of Romans have been given in the Introduction (E. 1.) and need not be repeated here. As has been increasingly recognized, Paul's intention in asking that so many be greeted in his name is largely strategic. He demonstrates the wide basis of support he already enjoys in Rome and, in the case of those he knows only by repute, attaches compliments to their names to win over further significant supporters to his cause. The list of names—and several of the attached epithets—in fact makes better sense appearing in a letter written by Paul to a community not founded himself; greetings sent to his own communities are briefer and far less fulsome (e.g., 1 Cor 16:19-20).

Preceding the long series of greetings (vv 3-16), as a first element in the chapter (vv 1-2), is a recommendation for Phoebe, deacon of the church at Cenchreae and clearly the bearer of Paul's letter to Rome. The series of greetings (vv 3-16, 20-23) is then interrupted by a sharp warning against being deceived by false teachers (vv 17-20a). For reasons to be explained when the passage is considered in detail, Rom 16:17-20a is best regarded as a secondary (inauthentic) addition to the genuine Pauline text—though this is far from being the majority view. No such doubt attaches to the final element, the concluding doxology (vv 25-27), which is universally regarded as secondary. By far the best manuscripts also omit the "grace" appearing in some versions and older English translations as v 24, an almost exact repetition of the "grace" at v 20b. However, as will be argued, the location of this "grace" in v 24 makes better sense and is to be preferred—though, again, this is not the majority opinion.

a) *Commendation of Phoebe* (16:1-2)

1. I commend to you Phoebe, our sister, who is also a deacon of the church at Cenchreae, 2. that you welcome her in the Lord as befits the saints, and give her assistance in whatever she may have need of you, for she has been a patron of many and of myself as well.

INTERPRETATION

Phoebe, the person Paul commends here is almost certainly the bearer of his letter to Rome. That she be well received by the community and make a favorable impression upon them is clearly central to Paul's whole enterprise in dealing with Rome. Hence the care with which he introduces and commends her.

Besides being a fellow Christian ("our sister") and simply as such entitled to be received with the hospitality customary across the communities of believers, she is a "deacon" *(diakonos)* of the church at Cenchreae, the eastern seaport of Corinth, the city from which the letter is being sent. While it is probably anachronistic to read into the term "deacon" all the features attaching to the office of the "diaconate" in the later church, the description implies that Phoebe exercised the ministry of "service" (*diakonia*; cf. 12:7) in a continuing and officially recognized capacity. The title (the translation "deaconess" is totally misleading) signals to the Roman community that the bearer of the letter is a personage of stature within the churches of the East.

Paul goes on (v 2) to request that Phoebe be welcomed and assisted in whatever business *(pragma)* she may have need. The "business" could be church matters on behalf of the community at Cenchreae. More likely Phoebe comes on business of her own and Paul has taken advantage of her travels to convey his all-important letter. That Phoebe should be a person of some means, able to undertake business journeys with an entourage of some size, accords well with the subsequent description of her as "patron *(prostatis)* of many and myself as well." The term designates wealthy women (or goddesses) who acted as patrons for others. One can only speculate but it may be that in a port city (Cenchreae) where travellers were constantly seeking lodging and other assistance, Phoebe exercised a ministry of hospitality in a way that earned recognition not only amongst her own community but amongst many fellow believers passing through. She would then deserve a welcome, not only on account of her status as fellow Christian and deacon, but also because of the notable hospitality she has provided to the wider community of believers.

Brief though it is, Paul's commendation of Phoebe is an important indication of the leadership roles exercised by women in the early communities. It is also not without significance that the document many have judged to be the most influential in Christian history (Paul's letter to Rome) was entrusted to this woman on the long and risky journey to its destination, its ultimate reception very much dependent upon the impression she herself was to make on the recipient community.

Notes

1. *a deacon of the church at Cenchreae:* On *diakonos/diakonia*, see Note above on 12:7. Though the notion of being an emissary or go-between is prominent in *diakonos*, the title is probably used with reference to Phoebe's service within the Cenchreae community rather than to designate her as an emissary of this church to Rome. Were the latter the case, she would surely bear letters of recommendation from her own church.

2. *a patron:* There is now sufficient evidence from ancient literature, papyri and inscriptions to find in the Greek word *prostatis*, used here of Phoebe, the specific, technical sense of "patron(ess)," rather than simply that of "helper" in a general kind of way; see esp. the review given in *NDIEC* 4 (1987) 242–44 (in the context of discussing a 4th century Greek epitaph of one Sophia, a "deacon" *[diakonos]*). The figure of Lydia as depicted in Acts 16:14-15 (cf. 17:12) provides a similar example.

For Reference and Further Study

On Romans 16 in General:

Donfried, K. P. "A Short Note on Romans 16." *Romans Debate* 44–52.

Fiorenza, E. Schüssler. "Missionaries, Apostles, Coworkers: Romans 16 and the Reconstruction of Women's Early Christian History." *Word and World* 6 (1986) 420–33.

Gamble, H., Jr. *The Textual History of the Letter to the Romans*. Studies and Documents 42; Grand Rapids: Eerdmans, 1977, 84–95.
Lampe, P. *Stadtrömischen Christen* 124–53; an abridged English version appears as, "The Roman Christians of Romans 16." *Romans Debate* 216–30.
Meeks, W. *The First Urban Christians* 55–61.
Ollrog, W.-H. "Die Abfassungsverhältnisse von Röm 16." *Kirche* (FS G. Bornkamm). Eds. D. Lührmann & G. Strecker. Tübingen: Mohr, 1980, 221–44.
Wedderburn, A.J.M. *Reasons for Romans* 12–18.

On Rom 16:1-2
Arichea, D. C. "Who was Phoebe? Translating *diakonos* in Romans 16.1." *Bible Translator* 39 (1988) 401–09.
Fiorenza, E. Schüssler. *In Memory of Her: A Feminist Theological Reconstruction of Christian Origins*. New York: Crossroad; London: SCM, 1983, 170–72.
Jewett, R. "Paul, Phoebe and the Spanish Mission." *The Social World of Formative Christianity and Judaism* (FS H. C. Kee). Ed. J. Neusner et al. Philadelphia: Fortress, 1988, 142–61.
Romaniuk, K. "Was Phoebe in Romans 16,1 a Deaconess?" *ZNW* 81 (1990) 132–34.

b) *Greetings I* (16:3-16)

3. Greet Prisca and Aquila, my fellow workers in Christ Jesus, 4. who risked their necks for my life, to whom not only I but also all the churches of the Gentiles owe thanks; 5. greet also the church in their house. Greet my beloved Epaenetus, who was the firstfruits of Asia for Christ. 6. Greet Mary, who has worked hard for you.

7. Greet Andronicus and Junia, my compatriots and my fellow prisoners; they are outstanding among the apostles, and they were in Christ before me.

8. Greet Ampliatus, my beloved in the Lord. 9. Greet Urbanus, our fellow worker in Christ, and my beloved Stachys. 10. Greet Apelles, so esteemed in Christ. Greet those who belong to the household of Aristobulus. 11. Greet my compatriot Herodion. Greet those in the Lord who belong to the household of Narcissus. 12. Greet Tryphaena and Tryphosa, who have worked hard in the Lord. Greet the beloved Persis, who has worked so hard in the Lord. 13. Greet Rufus, the chosen one in the Lord, also his mother and mine. 14. Greet Asyncritus, Phlegon, Hermes, Patrobas, Hermas, and the brothers (and sisters) who are with them. 15. Greet Philologus, Julia, Nereus and his sister, and Olympas, and all the saints who are with them.

16. Greet one another with a holy kiss. All the churches of Christ greet you.

Interpretation

Greetings to individuals and house churches (vv 3-15). Paul here sends greetings to twenty-four individuals mentioned by name, plus two others indicated simply by their relationship to persons named (the mother of Rufus [v 13]; the sister of Nereus [v 15]), along with vaguer greetings to remaining members of four household churches (v 5a, v 11, v 15, v 16). He frames the greeting in such a way that it does not go directly to the individuals concerned but takes the form of a command *(aspasasthe)* given to the entire church to greet that person in his name. In this way he subtly transforms what could be a series of more or less private communications into a public testimony to the fact that he already has a considerable base of support within the Roman community of believers. The greetings are addressed to the church as a whole, which can feel itself included, in a representative sense, in the greetings and praise bestowed upon individuals.

For most of the list (that is, for the first sixteen individuals mentioned down to and including v 13), Paul adds some epithet to the name. The additions either indicate some special relationship to himself—as fellow workers in Christ (Prisca and Aquila, v 3; Urbanus, v 9) or as "compatriots" (fellow Jews: Andronicus and Junia [also "fellow prisoners"]; Herodion, v 11) or as particularly "beloved" (Epaenetus, v 5; Ampliatus, v 8; Stachys, v 9; Persis, v 12; cf. also the mother of Rufus, v 13)—or else they recall outstanding recognition enjoyed (Epaenetus, v 5; Andronicus and Junia, v 7; Apelles, v 10; Rufus, v 13) or labors undertaken in the service of the Lord (Mary, v 6; Tryphaena and Tryphosa, v 12; Persis, v 12). Though doubtless meant in all sincerity, the epithets fall into a rather stereotyped pattern and eventually give way to the simple lists featured in vv 14-15. In some cases they are based on intimate knowledge and friendship (Prisca and Aquila; Epaenetus; Andronicus and Junia; Rufus and his mother; probably also Ampliatus, Urbanus, Stachys and Persis), in others they probably represent individuals about whom and whose service Paul has heard from afar. In the case of the two final groups mentioned (v 14, v 15) Paul knows the names of several leading members but others are simply included generically in the larger group. Nonetheless, the list as a whole communicates Paul's distinct claim to be—despite failure to visit Rome until now (1:10-11, 13; 15:22)—a familiar and loved figure for a large section of the community. The list of those to be greeted is very much a preliminary foot in the door preparatory to his intended visit.

Of the twenty-six individuals named in this "strategic" list, nine are women. While noteworthy in itself, the proportion is less significant than the fact that these women bear more than half the epithets denoting service and "labor" on behalf of the community and the gospel (Prisca [named before her husband]; Mary; Junia [see Note for the probability that this name denotes a woman]; Tryphaena and Tryphosa; Persis; cf. also the mother of Rufus). Since the "labors" involved obviously ranged over a wide area and since the verb Paul uses to describe them *(kopiān)* is the same as that used to describe his own apostolic labor in the service of the gospel (cf. esp. 1 Cor 15:10; Gal 4:11; Phil 2:16), this is weighty testimony to the apostolic activity of women in the early communities.

Particularly significant in this respect is the first-named on the list, Prisca (vv 3-4), who together with her husband Aquila, worked very closely with Paul, hosting house churches in several of his communities (certainly Corinth and Ephesus at least) before returning to Rome, from where, as Jews, they had originally been expelled by the edict of Claudius (cf. Acts 18:2-3, 18, 26; 1 Cor 16:19; cf. 2 Tim 4:19). Paul's praise of this couple is unstinting. Their "risking of their lives for him" probably alludes to some period of extreme danger during his long sojourn in Ephesus (Acts 19:8-10), where, presumably, he lived in their house. Through the service rendered personally to the "apostle to the Gentiles" in this respect and, it would seem, through participation in his wider mission, they have earned the gratitude of all the Gentile churches. The clear implication is that, if it is not already the case, these best supporters of Paul should enjoy the same prestige in the Roman community as well. Epaenetus (v 5b), Asia's first convert to Christ, is probably a close associate and fellow-worker of this couple, having left his homeland to accompany them to Rome.

Andronicus and Junia (v 7) likely represent another husband-and-wife apostolic team. Paul hails them not only as "compatriots" (fellow Jews) but as believers who, like himself, have suffered imprisonment for Christ. The fulsomeness of the subsequent remark about their being "outstanding among the apostles" and the acknowledgment of their seniority as believers (". . . in Christ before me") has the ring of a studied attempt to be gracious, suggesting a more distant relationship with Paul. They may well have been members of the Greek-speaking Christian community in Jerusalem (Acts 6:1), who at an early stage ended up in Rome to become foundational members of the community of believers in the capital. Their venerable status in this respect would make them important persons for Paul to win to his cause.

Along with Prisca and Aquila, Paul greets "the church *(ekklēsia)* that meets in their house" (v 5a). Though the same wider greeting is not included in the case of Andronicus and Junia, it is likely that they too were the focus of a house church. Similar house churches probably underlie later groupings occurring on the list—those of the household of Aristobulus (v 10b), of Narcissus (v 11b) and those comprising the two long series of names in v 14 and v 15. Paul is aware that the community consists of a number of house churches but this does not prevent him from quite consciously directing his letter to the community as a whole.

The kiss (v 16). The series of greetings concludes with the command to greet one another with "a holy kiss" (*philēma hagion*, v 16a). Through this gesture believers communicated to one another a sense of the *agapē* distinctive of Christian life (12:9; 13:8-10; 1 Cor 13:1-13; Gal 5:6, 14). While doubtless exchanged on less formal occasions, the kiss probably had its chief setting in more public gatherings of the community, where it gave expression to corporate cohesion prior to worship (eucharist?), deliberations and other forms of communal life. By having himself included in the exchange of peace Paul forges an entry right into the heart of the community in Rome formally gathered to hear his letter. He ensures that each and every member, including those he has not greeted by name, will feel themselves greeted by him personally. Nor does Paul speak for himself alone. As apostle with responsibility for the Gentile churches, he formally brings all those communities into the exchange of peace (v 16b). In this way he communicates to the community in Rome a sense of participation in the wider *ekklēsia* of God made up of all the local Gentile churches.

Notes

3–4. *Greet Prisca and Aquila:* For further information on this couple, see the articles of P. Lampe in *ABD* 1.319–20 ("Aquila"); 5.467–68 ("Prisca"); for greater detail, see the same author's *Stadtrömischen Christen* 156–64. It is quite likely that these Christians of Jewish origin (cf. Acts 18:2) formed the vanguard of Paul's approach to Rome.

5. *the church in their house:* For this formula, see also 1 Cor 16:19; Phlm 2; also Col 4:15. "House" *(oikon)* could refer either to a "household" (collection of persons gathered around one significant family) or to the physical building in which members of the household and associates met. In these references we meet the basic cell of Christian community life. In the larger cities the community of believers probably consisted of a collection of such house *ekklēsiai*, no one dwelling, presumably, being large enough to accommodate the entire group on a regular basis. But Paul could also speak of "the whole church" in a city or region (1 Cor 14:23; Rom 16:23; cf. 1 Cor 11:18) and even use the word of the entire world-wide Christian movement (1 Cor 15:9; Gal 1:13; Phil 3:6)—a usage which becomes standard in the deutero-Pauline literature (Colossians and Ephesians).

Epaenetus, who was the firstfruits of Asia for Christ: "Asia" designates the Roman province covering the western half of Asia Minor, with Ephesus as capital. Epaenetus, who is not otherwise known, is likely to have been Paul's first convert in Ephesus, not only a beginning but also a pledge of the wider "harvest" to follow—hence Paul's use of *aparchē*, which means literally "firstfruits" (see Interpretation of 8:23); cf. also 1 Cor 16:15, where the "house(hold) of Stephanas" is described as the "firstfruits of Achaia."

6. *Mary, who has worked hard for you:* This Mary is not otherwise known. Her early ranking on the list, among the names of people Paul obviously knows personally, may indicate that he knows her as well, even though the statement that she has "worked hard for *you*" points to Rome as the field of her labors.

7. *Andronicus and Junia:* Whereas many early interpreters had no difficulty in taking the second of these names (Greek *Iounian*) to be that of a woman, later tradition, hesitant to find a woman named as "outstanding among the apostles," almost universally took the Greek word to be the accusative singular of a masculine name "Junias." Such a name, however, is nowhere attested, whereas the feminine form "Junia," of which we would have here the accusative singular, is a common Roman name. It is now widely accepted that the second name is that of a woman disciple, probably the spouse of Andronicus; cf. Lagrange 366. For a thorough review of the history of interpretation, see Fitzmyer 737–38.

   my compatriots: The Greek word *syngeneis*, though it could mean "relatives," almost certainly, as clearly in 9:3, means "fellow Jews."

   my fellow prisoners: Paul holds being or having once been a "prisoner" for Christ to be a title of honor (Phlm 1 *[desmios Christou]*; Phil 1:13-14; cf. Eph 4:1; Col 4:18) and bestows it upon this couple. It is not clear whether they actually shared a period of imprisonment along with Paul or whether his phrase (cf. also Phlm 23) simply recognizes them as fellow Christians who have at some stage undergone, as he has himself, a period of imprisonment for Christ.

   they are outstanding among the apostles, and they were in Christ before me: On the concept of "apostle" in early Christian and Pauline understanding, see Note on 1:1. The sense here is not that Andronicus and Junia were highly esteemed *by* the apostles (against this, see esp. Cranfield 2.789). Nor, when Paul locates the pair among the "apostles," are we to think in their case of apostleship in a "wider (= weaker) sense" ("itinerant missionaries recognized by the churches as constituting a distinct group" [Cranfield]). Paul has one (technical) understanding of "apostle" and he is happy to apply it here to this couple, just as he is happy to acknowledge their "seniority" to himself as regards initial coming to faith in Christ; cf. the reference in Gal 1:17 to those (in Jerusalem) who were "apostles before me." Thus Andronicus and Junia probably belonged to "the closed group of apostles appointed directly by the risen Christ in a limited period following his resurrection" (Dunn 2.895)—a group which Paul saw himself as just scraping into "as one untimely born" (1 Cor 15:8).

8. *Ampliatus, my beloved in the Lord:* This person bears a common slave name. The epithet suggests he had met Paul during travels in the East, which may point to his being a freedman. It is possible that he is the Ampliatus mentioned in an inscription on a tomb in an early Christian catacomb in the cemetery of Domitilla, Rome—though the identification is highly speculative; see further Cranfield 2.790.

9–10. *Urbanus . . . Stachys . . . Apelles, so esteemed in Christ:* Evidence from inscriptions associates all three names with the imperial household.

Those who belong to the household of Aristobulus: The fact that Aristobulus is referred to but not personally greeted suggests that he himself was not a Christian. The reference may well be to a prominent member of the Herodian dynasty, Aristobulus, grandson of Herod the Great, brother of Agrippa I, who lived in Rome, as a friend of the emperor Claudius. Though he had died in the previous decade, it is possible that his household lingered on. Paul would then be greeting Christian members of this household.

11. *my compatriot Herodion:* The name suggests a further connection with the Herodian family.

those in the Lord who belong to the family of Narcissus: As in the case of the greeting in v 10b, it is likely that "Narcissus" denotes the name, not of a Christian, but the (pagan) head of a household.

12. *Tryphaena and Tryphosa:* These two are likely to be sisters, possibly twins. Both names are connected with the Greek word for "softness" *(tryphē)*; Paul may be consciously drawing out the ironical contrast between this meaning of their names and the fact of their "labors" for the Lord.

13. *Greet Rufus, the chosen one in the Lord, also his mother and mine:* On the supposition that Mark's gospel was written in Rome, this Rufus is very plausibly identified with the Rufus mentioned in Mark 15:21, whose father, Simon of Cyrene, carried the cross of Jesus. Paul also graciously acknowledges that his mother has performed some notable service (hospitality?) in his own regard.

14. *Asyncritus, Phlegon, Hermes, Patrobas, Hermas, and the brothers (and sisters) who are with them:* Paul knows the names of five persons belonging to this household but is aware that there are further members.

15. *Philologus, Julia, Nereus and his sister, and Olympas, and all the saints who are with them:* Julia is possibly the wife of Philologus, Nereus "and his sister" being their children. Again, Paul does not know the names of other members.

16. *Greet one another with a holy kiss:* Paul presumes that the ritual of the "holy kiss" customary in the communities of his own foundation (cf. 1 Cor 16:20; 2 Cor 13:12; 1 Thess 5:26) is also practiced in Rome (cf. also 1 Pet 5:14; Justin, *Apology* 1.65.2); see further W. Klassen, *ABD* 4.89–92.

All the churches: The phrase refers to all the churches for which Paul is responsible, that is, the Gentile communities of Galatia, Asia, Macedonia and Achaia (cf. 15:19b).

For Reference and Further Study

Brooten, B. "'Junia . . . Outstanding among the Apostles' (Romans 16:7)." *Women Priests: A Catholic Commentary on the Vatican Declaration.* Eds. L. Swidler & A. Swidler; New York: Paulist, 1977, 141–44.

_________. *Women Leaders in Ancient Synagogues.* Brown Judaic Studies 36; Chico, CA: Scholars, 1982, 38–39, 149–51.
Donfried, K. P. "A Short Note on Romans 16." *Romans Debate* 44–52.
Fàbrega, V. "War Junia(s), der hervorragende Apostel (Röm. 16,7), eine Frau?" *JAC* 27–28 (1984–85) 47–64.
Fiorenza, E. Schüssler. *In Memory of Her.* New York: Crossroad, 1983; London: SCM, 168–72, 178–83.
Gielen, M. "Zur Interpretation der Formel *hē kat' oikon ekklēsia.*" *ZNW* 77 (1986) 109–25.
Klassen, W. Art. "Kiss (NT)." *ABD* 4.89–92.
Lampe, P. *Stadtrömischen Christen* 124–53; abridged English version appears as "The Roman Christians of Romans 16." *Romans Debate* 216–30.
Meeks, W. *First Urban Christians* 55–61.
Schulz, R. R. "Romans 16:7: Junia or Junias?" *ExpTim* 98 (1986–87) 108–110.
Wedderburn, A.J.M. *Reasons for Romans* 12–18.

c) *A Warning* (16:17-20)

17. I beseech you, brothers (and sisters), to take note of those who create dissensions and difficulties, in opposition to the doctrine which you have been taught; avoid them. 18. For such persons do not serve our Lord Christ but their own appetites, and by fair speech and flattering words they deceive the hearts of the simple-minded.
19. For, while your obedience is known to all, so that I rejoice over you, I want you to be wise as to what is good and guileless as to what is evil;
20. then the God of peace will swiftly crush Satan under your feet.
The grace of our Lord Jesus Christ be with you.

Interpretation

Introduction. The admonition contained in these verses breaks abruptly into the sequence of greetings. In conveying the greeting from all the churches in v 16b Paul has shifted the focus from naming the recipients of the greetings to naming those who send them, a focus which continues in vv 21-23 in the greetings sent by Paul's co-workers. The admonition cuts right across this shift of focus.

Still more striking is the change of tone. The Roman community is "besought" (cf. *parakalō*) and commanded to avoid troublemakers, whose behavior and influence is described in the darkest tones. It is by no means unusual to encounter severe warnings towards the end of Pauline letters (cf. Gal 6:12-13; Phil 3:2 [unless one sees an originally separate letter beginning at this point]; 3:17-19). In 1 Cor 16:22 the brief *anathema* follows directly upon the greetings and, as in the case of Rom 16:20b, immediately precedes the "grace." The present warning could be seen as an expansion of the *anathema* occurring in 1 Cor 16:22. But, all this granted, the admonition in 16:17-20 remains an oddity in Paul's letter to Rome. Up till now, when rejecting contrary positions, he has offered arguments against the substance of those positions, rather than, as here, simply attacking the bad faith of those who defend them. The sentiments expressed would undermine rather than reinforce the careful argument for tolerance in 14:1–15:13. It is not easy to suggest a context, either in Rome or in the situation from which Paul is writing in Corinth, that would account for such a warning. Despite some affinity in content with the warning in Phil 3:17-19, much of the language is untypical of Paul and the tone in general is redolent of the post-Pauline tradition, especially as seen in the Pastoral Letters (1–2 Timothy; Titus). A later writer, feeling authorized to issue a warning in the name of the Apostle, may have seen fit to interpolate this passage at the point (v 20) where Paul's own greetings give way to those of his fellow-workers.

Judgments in such matters are necessarily intuitive and uncertain. Nonetheless, the case for regarding this warning as deutero-Pauline, while not the majority view, remains strong. In view of this, the following commentary will speak of "Paul" rather than Paul.

The first half of the passage (vv 17-18) consists of the warning and characterization of the troublemakers in negative terms. Then (v 19-20a), in positive vein, the focus turns upon the recipients and the hope of victory that may be entertained on the basis of God's action. The sequence concludes (v 20b) with the traditional "grace"—though its original position is more likely to have been at v 24.

Warning (vv 17-18). The warning seems to have in view troublemakers who threaten the peace and faith of the community from outside. Their assault undermines the basic "teaching" *(didachē)* in which the community has been instructed, though no further information is given about the precise nature of the threat. The only tactic to employ in regard to the troublemakers is blunt avoidance *(ekklinete)*. To engage in argument will expose oneself to being taken in by their wiles.

In support (cf. *gar*) of this absolute command, "Paul" proceeds (v 18) polemically to impugn the motives and unmask the deceit of the false teachers. Whereas the true minister of the gospel will always be enlisted in the "service" of Christ (cf. Rom 1:1; Gal 1:10; Phil 1:1), these people essentially serve their own interests. Even if the appearance may be otherwise, this is in reality the case since deceit is the key item in their armory (v 18b). Through fair speech and flattering words they render the "innocent" *(akakoi)* particularly susceptible to their wiles. Hence the need for caution (*skopein*, v 17) and separation.

The attitude to be adopted (vv 19-20a). "Paul" reinforces community compliance with this warning by himself employing a measure, if not of flattery, at least of praise. The community's faithful adherence to the basic gospel (*hypakoē*; cf. 1:5) is renowned throughout the Christian world (cf. 1:8: "your faith") and a cause of rejoicing for "Paul" himself. None too subtly implicit in the compliment is a strong prodding to retain this enviable reputation by remaining steadfast in the face of the present threat.

In view of the danger of deception, "Paul" renews the earlier warning (v 19c) in still more authoritative tone ("I want you" *[thelō]*). The language—"wise with respect to good, guileless with respect to evil"—has the ring of a proverb about it. The argument would seem to run along the following lines. In a context of "good," that is, when surrounded by people of good will, it is appropriate to engage in the kind of discussion that reasonably educated people (the "wise") carry on. But in a context of "evil," when the self-serving and deceitful are about, with smooth talk and fine-sounding phrases, it is better to adopt the guise of being "simple," of being like unlettered people who cannot engage in discussion and so can only break off communication (cf. v 17c).

The warning concludes (v 20a) on a note of confidence in God's power expressed in strikingly apocalyptic terms. The deceptive talk of the troublemakers, threatening to bring discord and scandal into the community (v 17a), is part of the eschatological onslaught of Satan, "Father of lies," whose instruments, willy-nilly, they have become (cf. 2 Cor 11:13-15). By resisting the divisive intrusion, the community will be part of the final victory of the God who makes peace (cf. 15:33). Such are the stakes which "Paul" sees involved in the threat which his warning addresses.

The Grace (v 20b). There follows the "grace" *(charis)* that customarily concludes all Pauline letters (1 Cor 16:23; 2 Cor 13:13; Gal 6:18; Phil 4:23; 1 Thess 5:28; Phlm 25; cf. Eph 6:23-24; Col 4:18b; 2 Thess 3:18). Its present location is odd seeing that a fresh series of greetings (vv 21-23) is still to follow. Several manuscripts of the Western tradition do indeed locate the "grace" (in slightly expanded form) after these greetings (v 24). If, as mentioned above, the warning just considered (vv 17-20) is a very early addition to the original Pauline text, it is possible that the present "grace" (v 20b) represents the "grace" that came with this addition and which caused, either by the hand of the interpolator or soon after, the omission of the original "grace" that now appears in those manuscripts as v 24.

Notes

17. *I beseech you:* On this formula of entreaty, see Note on 12:1.

in opposition to the doctrine which you have been taught: This statement creates some difficulty for those who maintain the Pauline authorship of vv 17-20. How does Paul know what the Roman community—or at least many of them—have been taught (since only a minority were connected with his own foundations)? The warning to adhere to the basic teaching smacks of the "anti-heresy" tone of the post-Pauline literature, esp. as reflected in 1 Tim 1:3-11; 4:1-16; 6:3-5; 2 Tim 3:1–4:5; Titus 1:9-14.

18. *but their own appetites:* Literally, "their own belly" *(koilia)*—a concrete formula apparently denoting a general tendency to selfishness and self-indulgence.

by fair speech and flattering words they deceive the hearts of the simple-minded: "Fair speech" translates *chrēstologia*, used only here in biblical Greek; "flattering words" translates the much more common *eulogia*, normally used in the sense of "blessing," here occurring uniquely in the NT in the bad sense of "flattery." "Simple-minded" translates *akakos;* the sense is that of innocence but with overtones of guilenessness and naivety.

19. *your obedience is known to all:* "Obedience" *(hypakoē)* here seems to have the sense of original and continuing adherence to the gospel (cf. 1:5; 15:18; echoed in 16:26), as the reminiscence of 1:8 ("your faith . . .") also suggests.

wise as to what is good and guileless as to what is evil: There is a certain verbal resemblance between this phrase and the admonition of Jesus in Matt 10:16b to the disciples sent on mission, "Be wise as serpents, innocent *(akeraioi)* as doves." But there is no true correspondence between the pairs "'serpents'—'doves,'" on the one hand, and "'good'—'evil,'" on the other.

20. *crush Satan under your feet:* The phrase gives expression to the common apocalyptic belief that the binding or suppression of the great adversary, Satan, will be the necessary prelude to the final, cosmic victory of God. Paul does sometimes (though not elsewhere in Romans) refer to the activity of Satan, normally in the context of explaining some hindrance or temporary setback (2 Cor 2:11; 11:14; 12:7; 1 Thess 2:18; cf. 2 Cor 4:4). The note of more active Christian aggression against Satan here is reminiscent of the "warfare" against spiritual forces described at length in Eph 6:10-17.

For Reference and Further Study

Donfried, K. P. "A Short Note on Romans 16." *Romans Debate* 44–52.

Jewett, R. *Christian Tolerance: Paul's Message to the Modern Church.* Philadelphia: Westminster, 1982, 17–23.

Ollrog, W.-H. "Die Abfassungsverhältnisse von Röm 16." *Kirche* (FS G. Bornkamm). Eds. D. Lührmann & G. Strecker. Tübingen: Mohr, 1980, 221–44.

Schmithals, W. "The False Teachers of Romans 16:17-20." *Paul and the Gnostics.* Nashville: Abingdon, 1972, 219–38.

d) *Greetings II and Concluding "Grace" II* (16:21-24)

21. Timothy, my fellow worker, greets you; so do Lucius and Jason and Sosipater, my compatriots. 22. I Tertius, the writer of this letter, greet you in the Lord. 23. Gaius, who is host to me and to the whole church, greets you. Erastus, the city treasurer, and our brother Quartus, greet you. 24. The grace of our Lord Jesus Christ be with you all. Amen.

INTERPRETATION

Paul had concluded (v 16b) the long series of greetings to persons in Rome by sending greetings in the name of "all the churches." This reflected the more customary Pauline practice of naming senders rather than the recipients of greetings (1 Cor 16:19-20a; 2 Cor 13:13; Phil 4:21-22; Phlm 23-24; cf. Col 4:10-15). Now, after the intrusive warning (vv 17-20), this more normal pattern resumes.

Timothy and Paul's other companions (v 21). No other co-worker is mentioned so frequently in Paul's letters as is Timothy. His name appears regularly with that of Paul in the opening address of the letters (2 Cor 1:1; Phil 1:1; 1 Thess 1:1; Phlm 1; cf. Col 1:1; 2 Thess 1:1)—though this was not the case at the beginning of Romans, Paul presumably judging it necessary to focus simply upon his own self-introduction. Now at last he signals the unique status of Timothy by making his greeting stand ahead and independently of the rest. There follow greetings from three persons, Lucius, Jason and Sosipater (for possible identifications see Notes), all of whom (or at least the last two) Paul simply names as fellow Jews. All three may be delegates from churches contributing to the collection (see 15:25-27, 31b) who are accompanying Paul to Jerusalem.

Tertius the scribe (v 22). Next Tertius, the letter's scribe, emerges from the customary scribal anonymity to send his own greeting "in the Lord." The last phrase shows his awareness of performing a Christian as well as a purely professional service. He may also have been known personally to several members of the community in Rome.

Greetings from believers in Corinth (v 23). Finally come greetings from important persons in the Corinthian community. The first of these, Gaius, is presumably to be identified with the "Gaius" whom Paul nominates in 1 Cor 1:14 as one of the few persons in Corinth he had himself baptized. It is in his house that Paul is now lodging. The added comment about his being the "host," not only of Paul, but of "the whole church" suggests that he is a person of some means, with a dwelling large enough to accommodate gatherings of the entire community at Corinth. The second individual sending greetings, Erastus, is described as the "treasurer of the city," a significant civic office, even if it could also be held by a slave or freedman. Greetings sent from persons of such status would signal to the audience that the Gentile communities founded by Paul contain members of reasonably high social standing in the wider civic community (the "not many . . ." of 1 Cor 1:26 does not mean "none"). The third person, Quartus, otherwise unknown, is simply described as a "fellow Christian" (literally, "our brother").

The Grace (v 24). As noted above, several manuscripts of the Western tradition feature at this point (as v 24) the "grace" which customarily concludes Pauline letters. A case for regarding it as original is made in commentary on v 20b above (see also Note).

Notes

21. *Timothy:* Timothy receives unparalleled praise and commendation in Paul's letters: see esp. 1 Cor 4:17 ("my beloved and faithful child in the Lord"); 16:10-11; 2 Cor 1:19; Phil 2:19-24; 1 Thess 3:2. According to Acts 16:1-3, his mother was Jewish, his father Greek; Paul had him circumcised to make him more acceptable in Jewish circles; see further Acts 17:14-15; 18:5; 19:22; 20:4-5. For an overview of his career, see J. Gillman, *ABD* 6.558–60.

    Lucius and Jason and Sosipater, my compatriots: Lucius is possibly to be identified with the "Lucius of Cyrene" mentioned among the prophets and teachers at Antioch in Acts 13:1. On the grounds that *"Loukas"* is the Greek form of the Latin name *"Lucius"* some have been prepared to identify this person with the "Luke" of Phlm 24 ("fellow worker"), Col 4:14 ("the beloved physician") and 2 Tim 4:11 (cf. Wilckens 3.146), whom a long-standing tradition has also identified as the author of Luke-Acts. But all this remains speculative. Jason is very likely to be identified with the person of this name mentioned as Paul's host in Thessalonica (Acts 17:5-9), while Sosipater is likely to be the same person as "Sopater" (a more familiar form of the name) mentioned in Acts 20:4.

22. *I Tertius, the writer of this letter, greet you in the Lord:* The phrase "in the Lord" is best taken with the verb of greeting. It is unlikely that Tertius contributed to the actual content of the letter.

23. *Gaius:* According to Acts 18:7, Paul's host in Corinth was a certain Titius Justus. It is quite likely that this is the same person as the Gaius of 1 Cor 1:14 and Rom 16:23, his full name being "Gaius Titius Justus."

    Erastus, the city treasurer: Erastus could be the same person as the Erastus sent by Paul into Macedonia in Acts 19:22 (cf. 2 Tim 4:20). He is possibly to be identified with an Erastus, a civic official ("aedile") mentioned in a first-century C.E. Latin inscription from Corinth as having paved a square in the city. On the identity of Erastus and the nature of his office, see esp. F. M. Gillman, *ABD* 2.571; also Fitzmyer 750.

24. *grace . . .*: H. Gamble, *Textual History* 129–32, reconstructs the textual history of Romans in such a way as to see the "grace" as original in both v 20b and 24. For a critique, see L. W. Hurtado "The Doxology at the End of Romans" (see Reference attached to the following section) 190, 194–96. But Hurtado does not consider the possibly dubious status of the admonition (vv 17-20a) to which the "grace" in v 20b is attached.

For Reference and Further Study

Ellis, E. E. "Paul and His Co-Workers." *NTS* 17 (1970–71) 437–52.
Gamble, H. Jr. *Textual History* 129–32.
Gill, D.W.J. "Erastus the Aedile." *TynBul* 40 (1989) 293–301.
Meeks, W. *First Urban Christians* 57–59
Theissen, G. *Social Setting* 75–83.

e) *(Inauthentic) Concluding Doxology* (16:25-27)

25. Now to the One who is able to strengthen you according to my gospel and the preaching of Jesus Christ, according to the revelation of the mystery, which has been wrapped in silence for long ages 26. but has now been revealed and made known through the prophetic writings, in accordance with the command of the eternal God that an obedience of faith be brought about with respect to all nations—27. to the only wise God be glory for evermore through Jesus Christ! Amen.

Interpretation

Introduction. The doxology comprising these verses appears in this place in most manuscripts (including P[61], ℵ B, D). Some, however, omit it (G); others have it at the end of chapter 14 (some Vulgate mss.) or the end of chapter 15 (P[46]) or in both places (e.g., A). Its textual credentials are, therefore, uncertain. Nowhere else does such a long doxology appear in Paul's letters nor is it his usual practice to conclude a letter in this way. While the content of the doxology echoes some important themes and phrases of Romans (notably the summons of the Gentiles to an "obedience of faith"), the style and phraseology are reminiscent of post-Pauline developments as seen in Colossians, Ephesians and the Pastoral Letters (1–2 Timothy, Titus). These considerations have led to a virtually unanimous judgment that the doxology was not a part of Paul's original letter to Rome but something added to this most significant of his letters at the time when they were being gathered in a single collection.

The doxology features the piling up of phrases and epithets typical of liturgical usage. Not much in the way of a formal structure can be discerned, though the opening address to God and the concluding response in v 27 "frame" the sequence inclusively. In between there is an expansion of the motif of "gospel," subsequently developed in the sense of the once hidden, now revealed "mystery." Syntactically, the final relative clause creates an anacolouthon. This probably reflects its likely origin as a response made by the congregation in a liturgical setting.

The mystery contained in the gospel (v 25). The doxology addresses (and already implicitly praises) God as the One who is able to "strengthen *(stērixai)* you." The strong parallels with Ephesians (esp. 3:14-21) suggest that the "strengthening" in question is necessary in view of the trials expected to intensify as the eschatological battle comes to its climax (cf. Eph 6:10-17). The grounds for the confidence that God is capable of imparting this strength are declared in the gospel as Paul has preached it *(kata to euangelion mou)*, the content of which is the proclamation of Jesus Christ—or Jesus as the Christ *(kata to kērygma Iēsou Christou)*. Behind these phrases lie key Pauline principles such as that of the thematic statement in 1:16 about the gospel's being the "power" *(dynamis)* of God leading to salvation for every believer" (cf. 3:21-26).

The doxology develops (v 25c) the notion of gospel in terms of "mystery" *(mystērion)*. This key term of Jewish apocalypticism proceeds from the sense of the elect community's being granted privileged access, through revelation, to God's currently hidden plans for the working out of the eschatological events. Paul had used the term in 11:25 in connection with the future destiny of Israel (cf. also 1 Cor 2:7; 15:51). The sense here is closer to that of Colossians and Ephesians (Col 1:26-27; 2:2; Eph 3:3-6, 9) where there is similar contrast between past hiddenness and present revelation and where likewise the mystery concerns the Gentiles' sharing in the riches of salvation previously understood as pertaining to Israel alone. The gospel preached by Paul is appropriately denoted "mystery" in the sense that it makes known this plan of God that had "for long ages" been "wrapped in silence" *(sesigēmenou)*, wrapped up, that is, in the eternal design of the Creator, inaccessible to human hearing or knowledge.

The present revelation of the mystery (v 26). The pivot of the entire sequence comes with the proclamation of the present revelation (*phanerōthentos de nyn*; cf. 3:21) of the once-hidden mystery. The "revelation" presumably refers in the first instance to the Christ event, which is the content of the gospel (v 25; cf. 1 Tim 3:16; 2 Tim 1:10). But the doxology immediately adds a further note of "revelation" *(gnōristhentos)* achieved through "prophetic writings" *(graphōn prophētikōn)*; this represents the final stage of fulfillment of God's decree to summon all the Gentiles to an "obedience of faith" (1:5; cf. 15:18). "Prophetic writings" is an unusual phrase to denote the Old Testament scriptures. Taking into account the time when the doxology is likely to have been written, the more likely reference is to later writings, considered "prophetic" in the sense of being filled with revelatory power. These could include New Testament texts such as the letters of Paul (cf. 2 Pet 3:15b-16) and, specifically, Romans itself. In this sense, the doxology would be subtly including Paul's letter to Rome as itself one of the instruments whereby God's design to summon the entire world to an obedience of faith is achieved. The letter would be helping to bring about the accomplishment of what it states as its central message. By not only resuming key themes of the letter but also drawing it into the very scheme of salvation which it proclaims, the doxology provides a very fitting tribute and conclusion to the crowning epistolary work of Paul.

Glory to God (v 27). Perhaps alluding to Paul's own sustained exclamation of praise in 11:33-36, the doxology then resumes the summons to praise God as "only wise." As set forth in Paul's letter to Rome, God has worked out in Christ a plan of salvation for humankind that no merely human mind or imagination could have anticipated or framed (cf. 1 Cor 2:6-10a; Eph 3:14-21). The God who acted inclusively to bring formerly excluded Gentiles within the salvation promised to the human race through Israel will likewise act inclusively to bring that bulk of Israel presently excluded from salvation within the same inclusive scope of salvation. Gentile hearers, knowing themselves to be caught up irrevocably within the grasp of this unfolding plan, can only respond, "Amen!"

Notes

25. *according to my gospel:* A specifically Pauline gospel is not meant but the common gospel as proclaimed by Paul; cf. 2:16.

the preaching of Jesus Christ: This phrase explains the content of the gospel just mentioned: it is the "proclamation about (objective genitive) Jesus Christ."

according to the revelation of the mystery: In the liturgical pattern of the Greek original, this phrase stands in parallel with the preceding one concerning the "gospel," thus defining the latter in terms of "mystery." On "mystery," see Note on 11:25.

wrapped in silence for long ages: This passive use of the Greek verb "to be silent" is unique in the NT. The sense is that of "being kept secret," corresponding to the sense of "concealment" found in passages such as 1 Cor 2:7; Eph 3:5, 9; Col 1:26.

26. *through the prophetic writings:* The Greek particle *te* (which is to be read; cf. Cranfield 2.811–12) conveys the sense of a sequence of two distinct moments of "revelation." The phrase "prophetic writings" is unique in the NT; in particular, Paul never speaks in this way, though he often quotes texts from the OT prophets. The Greek word *prophētikos* can have the general sense of "proceeding from inspired utterance" and so be open to a reference beyond that of the OT prophetic writings, mention of which in the present context is awkward since the stress is upon *present* (cf. *nyn*) revelation.

    in accordance with the command of the eternal God that an obedience of faith be brought about with respect to all nations: The translation takes the final prepositional phrase (*eis panta ta ethnē*) as indicating not the recipients of what is "made known" but the context of the "obedience of faith" required by God. It seems preferable here to translate *ethnē* more generally as "nations" (cf. Dunn 2.912) rather than in the stricter sense of "Gentiles" which it bears throughout the letter proper.

27. *to the only wise God be glory for evermore through Jesus Christ! Amen:* The translation takes the Greek relative pronoun *hǭ*, which in strict syntactical terms ought refer to Christ, in a demonstrative sense (= *ekeinǭ*) referring back to God mentioned as "only wise" at the beginning of the verse.

For Reference and Further Study

Brown, R. E. *The Semitic Background of the Term "Mystery" in the New Testament.* Facet Books; Philadelphia: Fortress, 1968, 50–52.

Elliott, J. K. "The Language and Style of the Concluding Doxology to the Epistle to the Romans." *ZNW* 72 (1981) 124–30.

Hurtado, L. W. "The Doxology at the End of Romans." *New Testament and Textual Criticism* (FS B. M. Metzger). Eds. E. J. Epp & G. D. Fee. Oxford: Clarendon, 1981, 185–97.

INDEXES

SCRIPTURAL INDEX

Old Testament

New Testament

Matthew

Mark

INDEX OF ANCIENT WRITINGS

Jewish Writings

Josephus

Philo of Alexandria

Rabbinic Literature

Greco-Roman Writings

Christian Writings

AUTHOR INDEX

SUBJECT INDEX

[*Note:* **Bold** type indicates principal areas of discussion and definition]